# THE INTERNATIONAL LAW OF THE OCEAN DEVELOPMENT

*Basic documents*

# THE INTERNATIONAL LAW
# OF THE
# OCEAN
# DEVELOPMENT

*Basic documents*

by
## SHIGERU ODA

*Professor of International Law,*
*Tôhoku University, Japan*
*Associé de l'Institut de Droit International*

## VOLUME II

SIJTHOFF | LEIDEN | 1975

ISBN 90 286 0224 0

Library of Congress Catalog Card Number: 72-76418
© A. W. Sijthoff International Publishing Company N.V., 1975

## PREFACE

The first volume which contains documents up to 1971 was published more than two years ago. In 1971, the United Nations Seabed Committee was enlarged in terms both of its size and its mandates, but the preparation of the list of subjects and issues to be discussed at the forthcoming conference on the law of the sea was not completed in that year. The list was finalized in the summer of 1972, and a number of concrete proposals on the law of the sea were presented to the Committee only in 1973, except that those proposals relating to the regime of the international seabed were introduced chiefly in 1972. The years 1972 and 1973 represent the period in which the Third United Nations Conference on the Law of the Sea was being prepared in the real sense.

In 1958, the First United Nations Conference on the Law of the Sea involved mainly the task of the codification of international law. The International Law Commission, consisting of eminent scholars of international law, made a six year preparation of the draft articles as a basis for the forthcoming plenipotentiary conference. The Conference in Geneva, dealing with traditional international law, attempted to transfer the customary rules into written form, although certain new aspects of the law of the sea, such as the regime of the continental shelf, were on the agenda. On the other hand, few doctrines of international law were ever discussed at the Caracas Conference. Not a theory of international law, but a new international regime of the ocean is now being sought for. In addition, as many as 138 nations, compared with 86 nations at Geneva sixteen years ago, participated in the Caracas Conference, and most of new nations were from the developing world of Asia and Africa. Different images and philosophies, held by the various nations towards the future of the international community, laid the foundation of the Caracas Conference.

The increasing demand of all nations for the resources of the sea—fish, oil and manganese nodules—during recent years, has given the Caracas Conference a quite different character from that of the Geneva Conference in 1958. The developing world, which has rapidly become interested in the resources of the sea, challenged the traditional freedom of the sea on the ground that it is nothing but an expression of an ideology used to promote the interests of the industrial nations alone. The developing nations, which find it impossible to compete with the industrial nations economically and technically, tried to secure their interests by expanding their own jurisdictions, thus monopolizing as much of the resources of the sea as possible, and by advocating the concept of the common heritage of mankind, thus gaining a larger share in the profits derived from the exploitation of the seabed. Thus, the concept of the 200 mile economic zone and the appeal for stronger control of the international seabed by an international machinery, represents the demand of the developing world. In promoting their own national interests, the industrial nations are not different from the developing ones. It may be fair to say that some industrial nations continue to maintain the traditional concept of free competition, not because this concept conforms to the established principles of international law, but because it is more suitable for their own national interests. The tradition is always in favour of the industrial nations.

Thus, the confrontation between the developed and the developing nations with respect to the share in the resources of the sea will play an important role in the international order of the ocean in the future. On the other hand, land-locked and geographically disadvantaged nations, either developed or developing, are growing as a strong power block opposed to the monopoly of the maritime interests by those nations facing the ocean. With reference to the exploitation of the deep seabed, the position of some developing nations, which produce mineral resources on land, and thus may well be adversely affected by such exploitation, is not quite the same as that of the other developing nations, which simply tend to favour further exploitation of the seabed. Even in the industrial world, some nations heavily depend upon far-distant water fishing, while others are inclined to favour the 200 mile economic zone. Those exceedingly few nations which are endowed with enormous capital and advanced technology may naturally have different attitudes towards the exploitation of the mineral resources of the deep ocean floor. Thus, the interests of the nations towards the resources of the sea are complex.

Maritime trade, one of the most traditional uses of the sea, causes a different problem. Maritime trade itself is in the interests of all nations, either developed or developing, land-locked or coastal ones. This has, however, resulted in the very serious problem of marine pollution. In order to preserve the ocean from pollution, the regime of the sea should be uniform. In fact, however, the claim of some developing nations to control over off-shore areas casts a dark shadow on the free flow of maritime traffic. In addition, the political concept of national prestige, seen in the claim of certain States to regulate the passage of ships, especially warships, through their straits, and also in the archipelagic concept, has further complicated the problem.

The Conference, convened at Caracas in the summer of 1974, did not produce any tangible results. A showdown itself was avoided at Caracas, and any final solution postponed. Whatever conclusions the Caracas Conference was to draw, would have required each nation to make some very significant decisions. In fact, the Caracas delegates, after lengthy deliberations for ten weeks, seemed to feel relieved. Nevertheless, the law of the sea today is no longer the same as what it was yesterday. It may not be an easy task to formulate an international order of the ocean by placing complicated interests in their proper place. The final solution may not be forthcoming at Geneva in the spring of 1975. But, the time for negotiation among the nations is approaching. The success of the Conference may not be expected without an agreement on the 200 mile economic zone, and international control will eventually extend from the ocean floor to the surface of the sea, thus placing ocean fisheries under a certain type of international control. Whether they like it or not, all nations are bound to realize this trend which is pressing upon them. On the other hand, the failure of the Conference does not revert us to the good old days of the freedom of the sea.

This volume mainly contains documents from 1972 to 1973 in preparation for the Caracas Conference. United Nations resolutions, official declarations, international or national, and drafts and recommendations of non-governmental organizations are printed in Parts I, II and V, respectively. Part IV contains international instruments relating to the marine environment. In Part III which deals with the delimitation of maritime jurisdiction, not only the international treaties on the delimitation of the seabed, but also a number of fishery treaties are reproduced. With respect to these treaties, chiefly the bilateral ones, which recognize the regime of the fishery zones or jurisdictions, the original text is reproduced, because the original text was significant in that the new regime for coastal jurisdiction was thus recognized. The fishery treaties, which are of a completely different nature and chiefly multilateral, and which are concerned with the conservation of fish resources, are printed in Part VII, with their up-to-date versions, because the existing regulations of these treaties are l..re important. The proposals presented to the United Nations Seabed Committee are enormous. Although access to these proposals is not difficult, the editor thought that the reproduction of all the proposals, according to the different issues and subjects, may be of some use to the public. Thus, Part VI contains all the proposals submitted to the Committee from 1972 to 1973.

The editor wishes to express his gratitude to the following for permission to reproduce the papers which were prepared by themselves or under their auspices:

Mrs. Elisabeth Mann Borgese, Senior Fellow at the Center for the Study of Democratic Institution, California; Secretary-General of the Pacem in Maribus

Mr. Northcutt Ely, Attorney at Law in Washington, D.C.; Chairman, Committee on Deep Sea Mineral Resources of the American Branch of the International Law Association

Professor D. H. N. Johnson, Professor of the University of London; Chairman, Deep-Sea Mining Committee of the International Law Association

Mr. Maxwell S. McKnight, Director, Marine Resources of the National Petroleum Council of the United States of America

Professor Louis B. Sohn, Professor of Harvard University; Chairman of the Commission to Study the Organization of Peace, New York

Mr. C. Maxwell Stanley, President of the Stanley Foundation, Iowa

Mr. Orlando R. Rebagliati of the Ministry of Foreign Affairs of Argentina was kind enough to afford the editor the text of the Treaty of Rio de la Plata of 1973 between Argentina and Uruguay.

The editor also is indebted to his colleagues on the United Nations Seabed Committee and at the Caracas Conference, Mr. Shiro Ebisawa of the Fishery Agency who made available to the editor various texts of the international fishery treaties, and to Mr. Tetsuto Akutagawa of the Defence Agency for his assistance in reading the galley-proof. Finally, the editor wishes to express his sincere gratitude to Dr. Jean-Pierre Lévy, who, as his good friend since the meeting of the United Nations Group of Experts on Marine Science and Technology in 1967, has given him valuable suggestions for the editing of this book.

September 1974                                              Shigeru Oda

# TABLE OF CONTENTS

## Part II
### Official Declarations, Reports and Documents, International and National

#### I. *Africa*

#### II. *Latin America*

#### III. *Non-Aligned Countries*

#### IV. *Socialist Countries*

## IV. *Conventions relating to Fishery Zone*

### 1. Northeast Atlantic

### 2. United States of America

### 3. Canada

## Part VI
### Proposals or Draft Articles presented to the United Nations Sea-bed Committee

## Part VII
### Fishery Conventions

#### I. Marine Mammal Conventions

# PART I

# UNITED NATIONS RESOLUTIONS RELATING TO OCEAN DEVELOPMENT

# I. RESOLUTIONS OF THE GENERAL ASSEMBLY, ADOPTED UPON THE REPORTS OF THE FIRST COMMITTEE

## RESOLUTION 3029 (XXVII): 18 DECEMBER 1972:

— Reservation exclusively for peaceful purposes of the sea-bed and the ocean floor, and the subsoil thereof, underlying the high seas beyond the limits of present national jurisdiction and use of their resources in the interests of mankind, and convening of a conference on the law of the sea

### RESOLUTION 3029 A (XXVII)

Adopted unanimously.

*The General Assembly,*

*Recalling* its resolutions 2467 (XXIII) of 21 December 1968, 2750 (XXV) of 17 December 1970 and 2881 (XXVI) of 21 December 1971,

*Having considered* the report of the Committee on the Peaceful Uses of the Sea-Bed and the Ocean Floor beyond the Limits of National Jurisdiction on the work of its sessions in 1972,

*Noting with satisfaction* the further progress made towards the preparations for a comprehensive international conference of plenipotentiaries on the law of the sea, including in particular acceptance of a list of subjects and issues relating to the law of the sea,

*Reaffirming* that the problems of ocean space are closely interrelated and need to be considered as a whole,

*Recalling* its decision, in resolution 2750 C (XXV), to convene a conference on the law of the sea in 1973,

*Expressing the expectation* that the conference may be concluded in 1974 and, if necessary, as may be decided by the conference with the approval of the General Assembly, at a subsequent session or subsequent sessions no later than 1975,

1. *Reaffirms* the mandate of the Committee on the Peaceful Uses of the Sea-Bed and the Ocean Floor beyond the Limits of National Jurisdiction set forth in General Assembly resolutions 2467 (XXIII) and 2750 (XXV), as supplemented by the present resolution;

2. *Requests* the Committee, in the discharge of its mandate in accordance with resolution 2750 C (XXV), to hold two further sessions in 1973, one of five weeks in New York, beginning in early March, and the other of eight weeks at Geneva, beginning in early July, with a view to completing its preparatory work, and to submit a report with recommendations to the General Assembly at its twenty-eighth session and, in the light of the

decision taken under paragraph 5 below, to the conference;

3. *Requests* the Secretary-General to convene the first session of the Third United Nations Conference on the Law of the Sea in New York for a period of approximately two weeks in November and December 1973, for the purpose of dealing with organizational matters, including the election of officers, the adoption of the agenda and the rules of procedure of the Conference, the establishment of subsidiary organs and the allocation of work to these organs;

4. *Decides* to convene the second session of the Conference, for the purpose of dealing with substantive work, at Santiago, Chile, for a period of eight weeks in April and May 1974 and such subsequent sessions, if necessary, as may be decided by the Conference and approved by the General Assembly, bearing in mind that the Government of Austria has offered Vienna as site for the Conference for the succeeding year;

5. *Further decides* to review at its twenty-eighth session the progress of the preparatory work of the Committee and, if necessary, to take measures to facilitate completion of the substantive work for the Conference and any other action it may deem appropriate;

6. *Authorizes* the Secretary-General, in consultation with the Chairman of the Committee, to make such arrangements as may be necessary for the efficient organization and administration of the Conference and the Committee, utilizing to the fullest extent possible the resources of staff at his disposal, to render to the Conference and the Committee all the assistance they may require in legal, economic, technical and scientific matters and to provide them with all relevant documentation of the United Nations, the specialized agencies and the International Atomic Energy Agency;

7. *Decides* to consider as a matter of priority at its twenty-eighth session any further matters requiring decision in connexion with the Conference, including the participation of States in the Conference, and to include in the provisional agenda of that session the item entitled "Reservation exclusively for peaceful purposes of the sea-bed and the ocean floor, and the subsoil thereof, underlying the high seas beyond the limits of present national jurisdiction and use of their resources in the interests of mankind, and convening of a conference on the law of the sea";

8. *Invites* the specialized agencies, the International Atomic Energy Agency and other intergovernmental organizations to co-operate fully with the Secretary-General in the preparations for the Conference and to send observers to the Conference;

9. *Requests* the Secretary-General, subject to approval by the Conference, to invite interested non-governmental organizations having consultative status with the Economic and Social Council to send observers to the Conference;

4

10. *Decides* that the Conference and its main committees shall have summary records of their proceedings.

## RESOLUTION 3029 B (XXVII)

Adopted by a vote of 69 to 15, with 41 abstentions.

*In favour:* Afghanistan, Austria, Bahrain, Barbados, Belgium, Bhutan, Bolivia, Botswana, Bulgaria, Burundi, Byelorussia, Chad, Congo, Costa Rica, Cyprus, Czechoslovakia, Egypt, Ethiopia, Finland, Guyana, Hungary, Iceland, Iraq, Jamaica, Japan, Kenya, Khmer Republic, Kuwait, Laos, Lebanon, Lesotho, Liberia, Libya, Luxembourg, Malawi, Mali, Malta, Mauritius, Mongolia, Morocco, Nepal, Netherlands, Nicaragua, Niger, Nigeria, Oman, Paraguay, Poland, Qatar, Rwanda, Singapore, Somalia, Sudan, Swaziland, Sweden, Syria, Togo, Trinidad and Tobago, Turkey, Uganda, Ukraine, USSR, United Arab Emirates, United Republic of Tanzania, United States, Upper Volta, Yemen, Zaire, Zambia. (Kenya later advised the Secretariat that it had intended to vote against. Morocco and Trinidad and Tobago later advised the Secretariat that they had intended to abstain.)

*Against:* Algeria, Argentina, Brazil, Chile, Democratic Yemen, Dominican Republic, Ecuador, El Salvador, Guatemala, Honduras, Mauritiania, Panama, Peru, Uruguay, Venezuela.

*Abstaining:* Australia, Burma, Cameroon, Canada, Central African Republic, China, Cuba, Dahomey, Denmark, Fiji, France, Gabon, Ghana, Greece, Guinea, India, Indonesia, Iran, Ireland, Israel, Italy, Ivory Coast, Madagascar, Malaysia, Mexico, New Zealand, Norway, Pakistan, Philippines, Portugal, Romania, Saudi Arabia, Senegal, Sierra Leone, South Africa, Spain, Sri Lanka, Thailand, Tunisia, United Kingdom, Yugoslavia. (Guinea, Italy and Sierra Leone later advised the Secretariat that they had intended to vote in favour.)

*Absent:* Albania, Colombia, Equatorial Guinea, Gambia, Haiti, Jordan, Maldives.

*The General Assembly,*

*Recalling* its resolution 2749 (XXV) of 17 December 1970, containing the Declaration of Principles Governing the Sea-Bed and the Ocean Floor, and the Subsoil Thereof, beyond the Limits of National Jurisdiction,

*Noting* that, in the said Declaration, the General Assembly, *inter alia,*

5

declared that the exploration of the area of the sea-bed and the ocean floor, and the subsoil thereof, beyond the limits of national jurisdiction (hereinafter referred to as the area) and the exploitation of its resources should be carried out for the benefit of mankind as a whole, and that an international régime applying to the area and its resources and including appropriate international machinery should be established,

*Realizing* that the economic significance of the area would depend on its final delimitation, as stated in the reports of the Secretary-General [A/AC. 138/36; 73],

*Considering* that there is a close relationship between any decision concerning the activities and functions of the international machinery and any decision concerning limits,

*Convinced* that information and data on the economic implications and significance for the area of the various proposals for limits would be helpful to the participants at the forthcoming United Nations Conference on the Law of the Sea, particularly to developing States, many of which are not members of the Committee on the Peaceful Uses of the Sea-Bed and the Ocean Floor beyond the Limits of National Jurisdiction,

1. *Requests* the Secretary-General to prepare, on the basis of data and information at his disposal, a comparative study of the extent and the economic significance, in terms of resources, of the international area that would result from each of the various proposals on limits of national jurisdiction submitted so far to the Committee on the Peaceful Uses of the Sea-Bed and the Ocean Floor beyond the Limits of National Jurisdiction;

2. *Further requests* the Secretary-General to submit his study as soon as possible, but no later than the opening date of the summer session of the Committee on the Peaceful Uses of the Sea-Bed and the Ocean Floor beyond the Limits of National Jurisdiction in 1973;

3. *Invites* States, the United Nations Conference on Trade and Development, the specialized agencies and other competent organizations of the United Nations system to co-operate with the Secretary-General in the preparation of such a study;

4. *Declares* that nothing in the present resolution or in the study shall prejudice the position of any State concerning limits, the nature of the régime and machinery or any other matter to be discussed at the forthcoming United Nations Conference on the Law of the Sea.

## RESOLUTION 3029 C (XXVII)

Adopted by a vote of 100 to none, with 28 abstentions. Abstaining countries were, as follows: Afghanistan, Austria, Belgium, Bolivia, Bulgaria, Burma, Byelorussia, Cameroon, Dahomey, Finland, Greece, Guinea, Hungary, Israel, Italy, Ivory Coast, Japan, Luxembourg, Mongolia, Nepal, Netherlands, Poland, Trinidad and Tobago, Ukraine, USSR, United Arab Emirates, United Kingdom, Venezuela. (Trinidad and Tobago later advised the Secretariat that it had intended to vote in favour.)

*The General Assembly,*

*Convinced* of the importance to coastal States, for purposes of economic development and social progress, of the ocean resources adjacent to their coasts,

1. *Requests* the Secretary-General to prepare, on the basis of the information at his disposal and in connexion with the study to be submitted pursuant to resolution B above, a comparative study of the potential economic significance for riparian States, in terms of resources, of each of the various proposals on limits of national jurisdiction presented so far to the Committee on the Peaceful Uses of the Sea-Bed and the Ocean Floor beyond the Limits of National Jurisdiction;

2. *Further requests* the Secretary-General to submit his study as soon as possible, but no later than the opening date of the summer session of the Committee on the Peaceful Uses of the Sea-Bed and the Ocean Floor beyond the Limits of National Jurisdiction in 1973, simultaneously with the study to be prepared under resolution B above;

3. *Declares* that nothing in the present resolution or in the study shall prejudice the position of any State concerning limits, the nature of the régime and machinery or any other matter to be discussed at the forthcoming United Nations Conference on the Law of the Sea.

## RESOLUTION 3067 (XXVIII): 16 NOVEMBER 1973:

— **Reservation exclusively for peaceful purposes of the sea-bed and the ocean floor, and the subsoil thereof, underlying the high seas beyond the limits of present national jurisdiction and use of their resources in the interests of mankind, and convening of the Third United Nations Conference on the Law of the Sea**

Adopted by a vote of 117 to none, with 10 abstentions. Abstaining countries were: Bulgaria, Byelorussian SSR, Czechoslovakia, German Democratic Republic, Hungary, Mongoria, Poland, Portugal, Ukrainian SSR, USSR.

*The General Assembly,*

*Recalling* its resolutions 2467 (XXIII) of 21 December 1968, 2750 (XXV) of 17 December 1970, 2881 (XXVI) of 21 December 1971 and 3029 (XXVII) of 18 December 1972,

*Having considered* the report of the Committee on the Peaceful Uses of the Sea-Bed and the Ocean Floor beyond the Limits of National Jurisdiction on the work of its session in 1973,

*Recalling* in particular paragraph 2 of resolution 2750 C (XXV),

*Considering* that the Committee has accomplished, as far as possible, within the limits of its mandate, the work which the General Assembly entrusted to it for the preparation of the Third United Nations Conference on the Law of the Sea, and that it is necessary to proceed to the immediate inauguration of the Conference in 1973 and the convening of a substantive session in 1974, in order to carry out the negotiations and other work required to complete the drafting and adoption of articles for a comprehensive convention on the law of the sea,

*Recalling further* its resolutions 2480 (XXIII) of 21 December 1968, 2539 (XXIV) of 11 December 1969, 2736 (XXV) of 17 December 1970 and 3009 (XXVII) of 18 December 1972 concerning the composition of the Secretariat, as well as the general dispositions on the same matter recommended by the Fifth Committee and adopted by the General Assembly at its twenty-sixth and twenty-seventh sessions,

1. *Expresses its appreciation* to the Committee on the Peaceful Uses of the Sea-Bed and the Ocean Floor beyond the Limits of National Jurisdiction on the work it has done in preparing for the Third United Nations Conference on the Law of the Sea;

2. *Confirms* its decision in paragraph 3 of resolution 3029 A (XXVII) and decides to convene the first session of the Third United Nations Conference on the Law of the Sea in New York from 3 to 14 December 1973 inclusive for the purpose of dealing with matters relating to the organization of the Conference, including the election of officers, the adoption of the agenda and the rules of procedure of the Conference, the establishment of subsidiary organs and the allocation of work to these organs and any other purpose within the scope of paragraph 3 below;

3. *Decides* that the mandate of the Conference shall be to adopt a convention dealing with all matters relating to the law of the sea, taking into account the subject-matter listed in paragraph 2 of General Assembly resolutions 2750 C (XXV) and the list of subjects and issues relating to the law of the sea formally approved on 18 August 1972 by the Committee on the Peaceful Uses of the Sea-Bed and the Ocean Floor beyond the

Limits of National Jurisdiction and bearing in mind that the problems of ocean space are closely interrelated and need to be considered as a whole;

4. *Decides* to convene the second session of the Conference, for the purpose of dealing with the substantive work of the Conference, for a period of ten weeks from 20 June to 29 August 1974 at Caracas and, if necessary, to convene not later than 1975 any subsequent session or sessions as may be decided upon by the Conference and approved by the General Assembly, bearing in mind that the Government of Austria has offered Vienna as the site for the Conference in 1975;

5. *Invites* the Conference to make such arrangements as it may deem necessary to facilitate its work;

6. *Refers* to the Conference the reports of the Committee on the Peaceful Uses of the Sea-Bed and the Ocean Floor beyond the Limits of National Jurisdiction on its work and all other relevant documentation of the General Assembly and the Committee;

7. *Decides*, having regard to the desirability of achieving universality of participation in the Conference, to request the Secretary-General to invite, in full compliance with General Assembly resolution 2758 (XXVI) of 25 October 1971, States Members of the United Nations or members of specialized agencies or the International Atomic Energy Agency and States parties to the Statute of the International Court of Justice, as well as the following States, to participate in the Conference: Republic of Guinea-Bissau and Democratic Republic of Viet-Nam;

8. *Requests* the Secretary-General:

(*a*) To invite to the Conference intergovernmental and non-governmental organizations in accordance with paragraphs 8 and 9 of resolution 3029 A (XXVII);

(*b*) To invite the United Nations Council for Namibia to participate in the Conference;

(*c*) To provide summary records in accordance with paragraph 10 of resolution 3029 A (XXVII);

9. *Decides* that the Secretary-General of the United Nations shall be the Secretary-General of the Conference and authorizes him to appoint a special representative to act on his behalf and to make such arrangements, including recruitment of necessary staff, taking into account the principle of equitable geographical representation, and to provide such facilities as may be necessary for the efficient and continuous servicing of the Conference, utilizing to the fullest extent possible the resources at his disposal;

10. *Requests* the Secretary-General to prepare appropriate draft rules of procedure for the Conference, taking into account the views expressed in the Committee on the Peaceful Uses of the Sea-Bed and the Ocean Floor beyond the Limits of National Jurisdiction and in the General

Assembly, and to circulate the draft rules of procedure in time for consideration and approval at the organizational session of the Conference;

11. *Invites* States participating in the Conference to submit their proposals, including draft articles, on the substantive subject-matter of the Conference to the Secretary-General by 1 February 1974 and requests the Secretary-General to circulate the replies received by him before the second session with a view to expediting the work of the Conference;

12. *Decides* that the provisions of paragraph 11 above shall not preclude any State participating in the Conference from submitting proposals, including draft articles, at any stage of the Conference in accordance with the procedure adopted by the Conference, provided that States which have already submitted any proposals and draft articles need not resubmit them;

13. *Dissolves* the Committee on the Peaceful Uses of the Sea-Bed and the Ocean Floor beyond the Limits of National Jurisdiction as from the inauguration of the Conference.


## RESOLUTION 2992 (XXVII): 15 DECEMBER 1972:
— Declaration of the Indian Ocean as a zone of peace

Adopted by a vote of 96 to none, with 32 abstentions.

*The General Assembly,*

*Recalling* its resolution 2832 (XXVI) of 16 December 1971 entitled "Declaration of the Indian Ocean as a zone of peace",

*Noting* the report of the Secretary-General [A/8809] submitted in accordance with paragraph 4 of that resolution, in which he was requested to report to the General Assembly at its twenty-seventh session on the progress made with regard to implementation of the Declaration,

*Noting further* that the consultations envisaged in paragraphs 2 and 3 of that resolution have not taken place,

*Convinced* that action in furtherance of the objectives of the Declaration would be a substantial contribution to the strengthening of international peace and security,

*Noting* that, in the Georgetown Declaration of 12 August 1972, the Conference of Foreign Ministers of Non-Aligned Countries took note with satisfaction of the adoption by the General Assembly at its twenty-sixth session of the Declaration of the Indian Ocean as a zone of peace and agreed that further steps should be taken at the Assembly's twenty-seventh session towards implementation of the Declaration,

1. *Calls upon* the littoral and hinterland States of the Indian Ocean,

the permanent members of the Security Council and other major maritime users of the Indian Ocean to support the concept that the Indian Ocean should be a zone of peace;

2. *Decides* to establish an *Ad Hoc* Committee on the Indian Ocean, consisting of no more than fifteen members, to study the implications of the proposal, with special reference to the practical measures that may be taken in furtherance of the objectives of General Assembly resolution 2832 (XXVI), having due regard to the security interests of the littoral and hinterland States of the Indian Ocean and the interests of any other State consistent with the purposes and principles of the Charter of the United Nations, and to report to the General Assembly at its twenty-eighth session;

3. *Decides further* that the *Ad Hoc* Committee shall consist of the following States: Australia, China, India, Indonesia, Iran, Iraq, Japan, Madagascar, Malaysia, Mauritius, Pakistan, Sri Lanka, United Republic of Tanzania, Yemen and Zambia;

4. *Urges* all the States concerned to extend their co-operation to the *Ad Hoc* Committee in the discharge of its functions;

5. *Requests* the Secretary-General to render all necessary assistance to the *Ad Hoc* Committee;

6. *Decides* to include in the provisional agenda of its twenty-eighth session the item entitled "Declaration of the Indian Ocean as a zone of peace".


## RESOLUTION 3080 (XXVIII): 6 DECEMBER 1973:
— **Declaration of the Indian Ocean as a zone of peace**

Adopted by a vote of 95 to none, with 35 abstentions.

*The General Assembly,*

*Recalling* its resolution 2832 (XXVI) of 16 December 1971, entitled "Declaration of the Indian Ocean as a Zone of Peace",

*Reaffirming* its conviction that action in furtherance of the objectives of the Declaration would be a substantial contribution to the strengthening of international peace and security,

*Noting* the report of the *Ad Hoc* Committee on the Indian Ocean established by resolution 2992 (XXVII) to study the implications of the proposal, with special reference to the practical measures that may be taken in furtherance of General Assembly resolution 2832 (XXVI) having due regard to the security interests of the littoral and hinterland States of the Indian Ocean and the interests of any other State consistent with the purposes and principles of the Charter of the United Nations,

*Noting* also with satisfaction the progress made by the *Ad Hoc* Committee in fulfilling its mandate,

1. *Urges* all States to accept the principles and objectives contained in the Declaration of the Indian Ocean as a Zone of Peace (resolution 2832 (XXVI)) as a constructive contribution to the strengthening of regional and international security;

2. *Requests* the *Ad Hoc* Committee to continue its work, to carry out consultations in accordance with its mandate and to report with recommendations to the General Assembly at its twenty-ninth session;

3. *Urges* all States and especially the major Powers to extend their co-operation to the *Ad Hoc* Committee in the discharge of its functions;

4. *Requests* the Secretary-General to continue to render all necessary assistance to the *Ad Hoc* Committee;

5. *Decides* that the *Ad Hoc* Committee on the Indian Ocean be provided with summary records of its proceedings;

6. *Requests* the Secretary-General to prepare a factual statement of the great Powers' military presence in all its aspects, in the Indian Ocean, and with special reference to their naval deployments, conceived in the context of great Power rivalry;

7. *Recommends* that the statement should be based on available material and prepared with the assistance of qualified experts and competent bodies selected by the Secretary-General;

8. *Requests* that the statement be transmitted to the *Ad Hoc* Committee at an early date, and, if possible, by 31 March 1974;

9. *Decides* to include in the provisional agenda of its twenty-ninth session the item entitled "Implementation of the Declaration of the Indian Ocean as a Zone of Peace".

## II. RESOLUTION OF THE GENERAL ASSEMBLY, ADOPTED UPON THE REPORTS OF THE SECOND COMMITTEE

### RESOLUTION 3016 (XXVII): 18 DECEMBER 1972:
— Permanent sovereignty over natural resources of the developing countries

> Adopted by a vote of 102 to none, with 22 abstentions. Abstaining countries were: Afghanistan, Austria, Bahrain, Belgium, Bolivia, Denmark, Finland, Italy, Japan, Liberia, Luxembourg, Netherlands, Norway, Paraguay, Portugal, Singapore, South Africa, Spain, Sweden, Thailand, U.K., U.S. France was among the eight countries absent.

*The General Assembly,*

*Recalling* its resolutions 626 (VII) of 21 December 1952, 1803 (XVII) of 14 December 1962, 2158 (XXI) of 25 November 1966, 2386 (XXIII) of 19 November 1968 and 2692 (XXV) of 11 December 1970 concerning permanent sovereignty over natural resources,

*Reaffirming* the need of further examination of these vital issues by the General Assembly,

*Emphasizing* the great importance for the economic progress of all countries, especially the developing countries, of their fully exercising their rights so as to secure the maximum yield from their natural resources, both on land and in their coastal waters,

Taking into account principles II and XI of resolution 46 (III) of 18 May 1972 adopted by the United Nations Conference on Trade and Development at its third session,

*Also taking into account* resolution 45 (III) of 18 May 1972, adopted by the United Nations Conference on Trade and Development at its third session, entitled "Charter of the economic rights and duties of States", and having regard to the relevant principles of the Declaration of the United Nations Conference on the Human Environment,

1. *Reaffirms* the right of States to permanent sovereignty over all their natural resources, on land within their international boundaries, as well as those found in the sea-bed and the subsoil thereof within their national jurisdiction and in the superjacent waters;

2. *Further reaffirms* its resolution 2625 (XXV) of 24 October 1970, containing the Declaration on Principles of International Law concerning Friendly Relations and Co-operation among States in accordance with the Charter of the United Nations, which proclaims that no State may use or encourage the use of economic, political or any other type of measures to

coerce another State in order to obtain from it the subordination of the exercise of its sovereign rights and to secure from it advantages of any kind;

3. *Declares* that actions, measures or legislative regulations by States aimed at coercing, directly or indirectly, other States engaged in the change of their internal structure or in the exercise of their sovereign rights over their natural resources, both on land and in their coastal waters, are in violation of the Charter and of the Declaration contained in resolution 2625 (XXV) and contradict the targets, objectives and policy measures of the International Development Strategy for the Second United Nations Development Decade [A/RES/2626];

4. *Calls upon* Governments to continue their efforts aimed at the implementation of the principles and recommendations contained in the aforementioned resolutions of the General Assembly and, in particular, of the principles enunciated in paragraphs 1 to 3 above;

5. *Takes note* of the report of the Secretary-General on permanent sovereignty over natural resources [E/5170] and requests him to supplement it with a further detailed study on recent developments, taking into account the right of States to exercise permanent sovereignty over their natural resources, as well as the factors impeding States from exercising this right;

6. *Requests* the Economic and Social Council to accord high priority, at its fifty-fourth session, to the item entitled "Permanent sovereignty over natural resources of developing countries", together with the report of the Secretary-General and the present resolution, and to report to the General Assembly at its twenty-eighth session.

# III. RESOLUTIONS OF THE ECONOMIC AND SOCIAL COUNCIL

## RESOLUTION 1737 (LIV): 4 MAY 1973:
— Permanent sovereignty over natural resources

Adopted by a vote of 20 to 2, with 4 abstentions.

*The Economic and Social Council,*

*Recalling* that the inalienable right of each State to exercise sovereignty over its natural resources has been repeatedly recognized by the international community in numerous resolutions of various organs of the United Nations,

*Reiterating* that an intrinsic condition of the exercise of the sovereignty of every State is that it be exercised fully and effectively over all its natural resources,

*Recalling* in particular General Assembly resolutions 1803 (XVII) of 14 December 1962, 2158 (XXI) of 25 November 1966, 2386 (XXIII) of 19 November 1968, 2625 (XXV) of 24 October 1970, 2692 (XXV) of 11 December 1970 and 3016 (XXVII) of 18 December 1972, and Security Council resolution 330 (1973) of 21 March 1973,

*Recalling also* principle II of resolution 46 (III) of 18 May 1972 of the United Nations Conference on Trade and Development, Economic and Social Council resolution 1673 (LII) of 2 June 1972 and the recommendations contained in paragraph 88 of the report of the Committee on Natural Resources on its third session,

*Considering* that the full exercise by each State of sovereignty over its natural resources is an essential condition for achieving the objectives and targets of the Second United Nations Development Decade,

*Bearing in mind* that the adequate utilization of all natural resources, in particular the non-renewable ones, determines the conditions of economic development of developing countries,

*Taking into account* that the exercise of sovereignty over natural resources requires that action by States aimed at achieving a better utilization and use of those resources must cover all stages, from exploration to marketing,

1. *Reaffirms* the right of States to permanent sovereignty over all their natural resources, on land within their international boundaries, as well as those of the sea-bed and the subsoil thereof within their national jurisdiction and in the superjacent waters;

2. *Emphasizes* that both the exploration and the exploitation of such natural resources shall be subject in each country to national laws and regulations;

15

3. *Declares* that any act, measure or legislative provision which one State may apply against another for the purpose of suppressing its inalienable right to the exercise of its full sovereignty over its natural resources, both on land and in coastal waters, or of using coercion to obtain advantages of any other kind, is a flagrant violation of the Charter of the United Nations, contradicts the principles adopted by the General Assembly in its resolutions 2625 (XXV) and 3016 (XXVII) and obstructs the attainment of the goals and objectives of the International Development Strategy for the Second United Nations Development Decade, and that to persist therein could constitute a threat to international peace and security;

4. *Recognizes* that one of the most effective ways in which the developing countries can protect their natural resources is to promote or strengthen machinery for co-operation among them having as its main purpose to concert pricing policies, to improve conditions of access to markets, to co-ordinate production policies and, thus, to guarantee the full exercise of sovereignty by developing countries over their natural resources;

5. *Urges* the international financial organizations and the United Nations Development Programme to provide, in accordance with the priorities established in national development plans, all possible financial and technical assistance to developing countries at their request or for the purpose of establishing, strengthening and supporting, as appropriate, national institutions to ensure the full utilization and control of their natural resources;

6. *Requests* the Secretary-General to complete the study of the political, economic, social and legal aspects of the principle of permanent sovereignty over natural resources referred to in Council resolution 1673 D (LII), and to include therein the aspects of the permanent sovereignty of States over their natural resources of the sea-bed and the subsoil thereof within the limits of national jurisdiction and in the superjacent waters;

7. *Further requests* the Secretary-General to submit to the General Assembly at its twenty-eighth session, through the Economic and Social Council, the study referred to in paragraph 6 above.

## RESOLUTION 1802 (LV): 7 AUGUST 1973:
— Marine co-operation

*The Economic and Social Council,*
*Recalling* its resolution 1537 (XLIX) of 27 July 1970 on marine co-operation, in which it requested the Secretary-General to prepare a study

on the uses of the sea and to invite the Governments of Member States to make proposals for strengthening international co-operation in the marine environment,

*Noting with satisfaction* the study prepared by the Secretary-General entitled "Uses of the sea" [E/5120] which gives a clear and concise picture of the present and foreseeable uses of ocean space and of potential conflicts in the use of marine resources,

*Further noting* the summary of the replies of Governments of Member States to the *note verbale* of the Secretary-General of 12 June 1972 and the proposals for the strengthening of international co-operation in the marine environment, as contained in the report of the Secretary-General on marine co-operation [E/5332],

*Recognizing* that the present approach to the development of ocean space is conducted almost exclusively along sectoral lines,

*Aware* of the need for an integrated approach in the consideration of the problems involved in the various uses of the sea, in order to achieve the proper management of ocean resources and uses, and of the fact that this approach requires an integrated information base,

*Conscious* of the fact that the coastal areas in many countries, particularly the developing countries, represent one of their most valuable possessions and that the proper management and development of these areas constitutes an important factor in their national development planning,

*Noting* the observation of the Administrative Committee on Co-ordination in its annual report for 1972/73 [E/5287] that there is a need for simplifying and rationalizing co-ordination arrangements within the United Nations system in the field of marine co-operation,

*Bearing in mind* the need to avoid prejudicing the work of the United Nations Conference on the Law of the Sea,

## I

1. *Requests* the Secretary-General, in co-operation with the appropriate specialized agencies and the competent bodies at present concerned with marine affairs:

(*a*) To strengthen his capability of collecting economic and technical information relating to the development of the resources and uses of the sea and to arrange for the regular dissemination of relevant information in the most appropriate way;

(*b*) To prepare on a regular basis an updated version of his study on the uses of the sea, based on the latest information available in the economic, technical and scientific fields and drawing upon the expertise of the various competent bodies concerned within the United Nations system, which version should also include a summary of existing arrangements in the United Nations system for making available to interested countries, particularly the developing countries, information on advances in technology and the transfer of such technology to them and a compendium of relevant statistics;

(*c*) To make this study available to Member States and the governing bodies of the various specialized agencies and the International Atomic Energy Agency and other United Nations institutions engaged in activities relating to marine affairs, and, on request, to other interested bodies;

(*d*) To report, at least biennially, to the Council on the implementation of sub-paragraphs (*a*), (*b*) and (*c*) above, transmitting also the comments of the governing bodies of the various specialized agencies and the International Atomic Energy Agency and other United Nations institutions concerned with marine affairs;

## II

2. *Further requests* the Secretary-General, in co-operation with the competent organizations of the United Nations system, and in particular the regional economic commissions and other regional technical bodies:

(*a*) To undertake a comprehensive interdisciplinary study to identify and review the problems of coastal area development, using for this purpose the expertise of the entire United Nations system, in technical and scientific matters, and also in development planning;

(*b*) To submit to the Council at its fifty-ninth session proposals, based on the above-mentioned interdisciplinary study, for coastal area development, particularly in developing countries, including proposals for possible appropriate action at the regional and sub-regional levels;

3. *Requests* the organizations of the United Nations system concerned, and also the regional economic commissions, to give full support to the Secretary-General in this task;

## III

4. *Invites* the Administrative Committee on Co-ordination to prepare a concise report covering the work programmes and the spheres of competence of the components of the United Nations system in the field of marine science and its applications, in order to avoid overlapping and duplication of activities in this field, and to present this report to the Economic and Social Council at its fifty-ninth session.

# IV. RESOLUTIONS OF THE UNITED NATIONS CONFERENCE ON TRADE AND DEVELOPMENT

## RESOLUTION 51 (III): 19 MAY 1972:
— **The exploitation, for commercial purposes, of the resources of the sea-bed and the ocean floor, and the subsoil thereof, beyond the limits of national jurisdiction**

Adopted by a vote of 64 to one, with 24 abstentions.

*The United Nations Conference on Trade and Development,*

*Recalling* General Assembly resolution 2750 A (XXV) of 17 December 1970, in which the Assembly requests the Secretary-General to co-operate with the United Nations Conference on Trade and Development in putting forward recommendations on the measures necessary to avoid the adverse economic effects which the exploitation of the sea-bed and the ocean floor, and the subsoil thereof, beyond the limits of national jurisdiction, may have on the prices of minerals primarily exported by the developing countries,

*Considering* that the exploitation of the sea-bed and the ocean floor beyond the limits of national jurisdiction may have an adverse impact on the ecological balance of the marine environment and of fisheries resources,

*Noting with satisfaction* the report by the UNCTAD secretariat "Mineral production from the area of the sea-bed beyond national jurisdiction: issues of international commodity policy" [TD/113/Supp. 4 : E.73. II. D.5],

1. *Decides* that the question of the economic consequences and implications for the economies of the developing countries resulting from the exploitation of mineral resources shall be kept constantly under review by the Conference and its subsidiary organs, in particular the Trade and Development Board;

2. *Requests* the Secretary-General of UNCTAD, in co-operation with the specialized agencies and in particular the Food and Agriculture Organization of the United Nations, to study the adverse impact which the exploitation of the sea-bed may have on the fisheries resources of the seas and oceans;

3. *Invites* the Secretary-General of UNCTAD to continue to study the measures necessary to avoid the adverse economic effects which the exploitation of the sea-bed and the ocean floor, and the subsoil thereof, beyond the limits of national jurisdiction may have on the prices of minerals exported primarily by developing countries, and to propose specific and detailed measures in that connexion.

## RESOLUTION 52 (III): 19 MAY 1972:
— **The exploitation, for commercial purposes, of the resources of the sea-bed and the ocean floor, and the subsoil thereof, beyond the limits of national jurisdiction**

Adopted by a vote of 57 to 14, with 17 abstentions.

*The United Nations Conference on Trade and Development,*

*Recalling* General Assembly resolution 2574 D (XXIV) of 15 December 1969, in which the Assembly declares that pending the establishment of an international régime for the sea-bed and the ocean floor, States and persons, physical or juridical, are bound to refrain from all activities of exploitation of the resources of the area,

*Bearing in mind* the provisions of the Declaration of Principles Governing the Sea-Bed and the Ocean Floor, and the Subsoil Thereof, beyond the Limits of National Jurisdiction, contained in General Assembly resolution 2749 (XXIV) of 17 December 1970 which declares that the area shall not be subject to appropriation by any means by States or persons, natural or juridical, and that no State shall claim or exercise sovereignty or sovereign rights over any part thereof: and that no State or person, natural or juridical, shall claim, exercise or acquire rights with respect to the area or its resources incompatible with the international régime to be established and the principles of the Declaration,

*Gravely concerned* over the evidence that a number of States, organizations and consortia are already engaged in operational activities in the area,

1. *Calls upon* all States engaged in activities in the sea-bed area, beyond the limits of national jurisdiction, in conformity with the provisions of the two resolutions cited above, to cease and desist from all activities aiming at commercial exploitation in the sea-bed area and to refrain from engaging directly or through their nationals in any operations aimed at the exploitation of the area before the establishment of the international régime;

2. *Reaffirms* that prior to the establishment of the international régime, no legal claims on any part of the area or its resources, based on past, present or future activities will be recognized.

20

# PART II

## OFFICIAL DECLARATIONS, REPORTS AND DOCUMENTS, INTERNATIONAL AND NATIONAL

# I. AFRICA

## AFRICAN STATES REGIONAL SEMINAR ON THE LAW OF THE SEA:
### — General Report of 1972

The African States Regional Seminar on the Law of the Sea was held at Yaoundé, Cameroon, 20-30 June 1972. This seminar came to the following conclusions.

After examining the reports, conclusions and recommendations of the various working groups, which were discussed and amended, the seminar adopted the following recommendations:

I. (*a*) On the territorial sea, the contiguous zone and the high seas:

(1) The African States have the right to determine the limits of their jurisdiction over the Seas adjacent to their coasts in accordance with reasonable criteria which particularly take into account their own geographical, geological, biological and national security factors.

(2) The Territorial Sea should not extend beyond a limit of 12 nautical miles.

(3) The African States have equally the right to establish beyond the Territorial Sea an Economic Zone over which they will have an exclusive jurisdiction for the purpose of control, regulation and national exploitation of the living resources of the Sea and their reservation for the primary benefit of their peoples and their respective economies, and for the purpose of the prevention and control of pollution.

The establishment of such a zone shall be without prejudice to the following freedoms: Freedom of navigation, freedom of overflight, freedom to lay submarine cables and pipelines.

(4) The exploitation of the living resources within the economic zone should be open to all African States both land-locked and near land-locked, provided that the enterprises of these States desiring to exploit these resources are effectively controlled by African capital and personnel. To be effective, the rights of land-locked States shall be complemented by the right of transit.

These rights shall be embodied in multilateral or regional or bilateral agreements.

(5) The limit of the economic zone shall be fixed in nautical miles in accordance with regional considerations taking duly into account the resources of the region and the rights and interests of the land-locked and near land-locked States, without prejudice to limits already adopted by some States within the region.

23

(6) The limits between two or more States shall be fixed in conformity with the United Nations Charter and that of the Organization of African Unity.

(7) The African States shall mutually recognize their existing historic rights.

However certain participants expressed reservations as to a 12 mile limit for the territorial sea and as to fixing a precise limit.

On recommendation No. 5 others thought that the general principles of International Law should be referred to in order to fix maritime limits.

(b) On "Historic Rights" and "Historic Bays":

(1) That the "historic rights" acquired by certain neighbouring African States in a part of the Sea which may fall within the exclusive jurisdiction of another State would be recognized and safeguarded.

(2) The impossibility for an African State to provide evidence of an uninterrupted claim over a historic bay should not constitute an obstacle to the recognition of the rights of that State over such a bay.

*Adopted without reservation.*

II. On the biological resources of the sea, fishing and maritime pollution:
*Recommendations*

The Participants:

Recommend to African States to extend their sovereignty over all the resources of the high sea adjacent to their Territorial Sea within an economic zone to be established and which will include at least the continental shelf;

Call upon all African States to uphold the principle of this extension at the next International Conference on the Law of the Sea;

Suggest that African States should promote a new policy of co-operation for the development of fisheries so as to increase their participation in the exploitation of marine resources;

Recommend to African States to take all measures to fight pollution and in particular;

— by establishing national laws to protect their countries from pollution;

— by advocating in international organizations the conclusion of appropriate agreements on control measures against pollution.

*Adopted without reservation.*

III. On the continental shelf and the sea-bed:
*Recommendations*

(1) The Economic Zone embodies all economic resources comprising both living and non-living resources such as oil, natural gas and other mineral resources.

(2) Political and strategic aspects of the sea-bed were considered. The need to use the sea-bed exclusively for peaceful purposes presupposes the definition of a legal régime to ensure greater security of the sea while guaranteeing the respect of the rights of coastal States.

(3) The participants considered that natural resources outside the Economic Zone should be managed by the international authority.

(4) The participants stressed the necessity for the Agency to function democratically and the need for adequate continental representation therein. Representation should not be based on the sole criterion of maritime strength and account should be taken of the existing imbalance between developed and developing countries.

(5) The Seminar categorically rejected the veto system and considered the system of weighted voting undemocratic.

IV. Concerning settlement to the conflicts which may arise between coastal States and the international community;

*Recommendations*

In the light of their discussions the Seminar approves the principle of setting up an international governing body to manage the common heritage outside the limits of national jurisdiction. It considers that this body must conform with the spirit of the resolution which provided for its creation, and for this reason must be structured and operate in such a way that the developing countries should be the primary controllers and beneficiaries.

The Seminar recommends that the international body should carry out its wishes on the Sea-bed and subsoil for the benefit of the international community.

Therefore, it considers that its action will depend on the desire of States to extend their limits of jurisdiction. The Seminar noted that it was important for this body to avoid being a simple administrative apparatus issuing licences and distributing royalties.

It considers that to be efficient the International body must seek the best ways and means to involve the business concerns of developing countries in exploiting the resources available in its zone of using these resources to promote the progress of mankind in the developing countries so as to correct the grave imbalance between the nations.

The Seminar considers that all these objectives can be achieved if the participation of developing countries in the planning, setting up, and operation of this body is assured without restriction.

*Adopted unanimously:*

The participants expressed the unanimous wish that these recommendations should be notified to all African States and to the OAU.

## ORGANIZATION OF AFRICAN UNITY:
## — Declaration of 1973 on the Issues of the Law of the Sea

> The Council of Ministers of the Organization of African Unity, which met in Addis Ababa, Ethiopia, 17-24 May 1973, adopted the following declaration. CM/Res. 289 (XIX).

*The Council of Ministers of the Organization of African Unity*, meeting in its Twenty-first Ordinary Session in Addis Ababa, Ethiopia, from 17 to 24 May 1973,

1. *Considering* that, in accordance with the Charter of the Organization of African Unity, it is "our responsibility to harness the natural and human resources of our continent for the total advancement of our peoples in all spheres of human endeavour";

2. *Recalling* resolutions CM/Res.245 (XVII) and CM/Res.250 (XVII) of the seventeenth session of the Council of Ministers of OAU on the permanent sovereignty of African countries over their natural resources;

3. *Recalling* the OAU Council of Ministers' resolution CM/Res.289 (XIX); and decision No. CM/Dec.236 (XX);

4. *Recalling* also resolution 2750 (XXV) and 3029 A (XXVII) of the United Nations General Assembly;

5. *Aware* that many African countries did not participate in the 1958 and 1960 Law of the Sea Conferences;

6. *Aware* that Africa, on the basis of solidarity, needs to harmonize her position on various issues before the forthcoming United Nations Conference on the Law of the Sea due to be held in Santiago, Chile in 1974, and to benefit therefrom;

7. *Recognizing* that the marine environment and the living and mineral resources therein are of vital importance to humanity and are not unlimited;

8. *Noting* that these marine resources are currently being exploited by only a few States for the economic benefit of their people;

9. *Convinced* that African countries have a right to exploit the marine resources around the African continent for the economic benefit of African peoples;

10. *Recognizing* that the capacity of the sea to assimilate wastes and render them harmless and its ability to regenerate natural resources are not unlimited;

11. *Noting* the potential of the sea for use for non-peaceful purposes, and convinced that the submarine environment should be used exclusively for peaceful purposes;

12. *Recognizing* the position of archipelagic States;

13. *Recognizing* that Africa has many disadvantaged States, including those that are land-locked or shelf-locked and those whose access to ocean space depends exclusively on passage through straits;

14. *Noting* the recent trends in the extension of coastal States jurisdictions over the area adjacent to their coasts;

15. *Having noted* the positions and the views of other States and regions;

*DECLARES:*

A. *Territorial Sea and Straits*

1. Pending the successful negotiation and general adoption of a new régime to be established in these areas by the forthcoming United Nations Conference on the Law of the Sea, this position prejudices neither the present limits of the territorial sea of any State nor the existing rights of States;

2. That the African States endorse the principle of the right of access to and from the sea by the land-locked African countries, and the inclusion of such a provision in the universal treaty to be negotiated at the Law of the Sea Conference;

3. That the African States in view of the importance of international navigation through straits used as such endorse the régime of innocent passage in principle but recognize the need for further precision of the régime;

4. That the African States endorse the principle that the baselines of any archipelagic State may be drawn by connecting the outermost points of the outermost islands of the archipelago for the purposes of determining the territorial sea of the archipelagic State.

B. *Régime of Islands*

5. That the African States recognize the need for a proper determination of the nature of maritime spaces of islands and recommend that such determination should be made according to equitable principles taking account of all relevant factors and special circumstances including:

   (*a*) The size of islands
   (*b*) Their population or the absence thereof
   (*c*) Their contiguity to the principal territory
   (*d*) Their geological configuration
   (*e*) The special interest of island States and archipelagic States.

C. *Exclusive Economic Zone Concept including Exclusive Fishery Zone*

6. That the African States recognize the right of each coastal State to

establish an exclusive economic zone beyond their territorial seas whose limits shall not *exceed* 200 nautical miles, measured from the baseline establishing their territorial seas;

7. That in such zones the coastal States shall exercise permanent sovereignty over all the living and mineral resources and shall manage the zone without undue interference with the other legitimate uses of the sea: namely, freedom of navigation, overflight and laying of cables and pipelines;

8. That the African countries consider that scientific research and the control of marine pollution in the economic zone shall be subject to the jurisdiction of the coastal States;

9. That the African countries recognize, in order that the resources of the region may benefit all peoples therein, that the land-locked and other disadvantaged countries are entitled to share in the exploitation of living resources of neighbouring economic zones on equal basis as nationals of coastal States on bases of African solidarity and under such regional or bilateral agreements as may be worked out;

10. That nothing in the propositions set herein should be construed as recognizing rights of territories under colonial, foreign or racist domination to the foregoing.

### D. *Regional Arrangements*

11. That the African States in order to develop and manage the resources of the region take all possible measures including co-operation in the conservation and management of the living resources and the prevention and control of pollution to conserve the marine environment, establish such regional institutions as may be necessary and settle disputes between them in accordance with regional arrangements.

### E. *Fishing Activities in the High Seas*

12. That the African States recognize that fishing activities in the high seas have a direct effect on the fisheries within the territorial sea and in the economic zone. Consequently, such activities must be regulated, especially having regard to the highly migratory and anadromous fish species. The African States therefore favour the setting up of an international sea fisheries régime or authority with sufficient powers to make States comply to widely accepted fisheries management principles or, alternatively, the strengthening of the existing FAO Fisheries Commissions or other fisheries regulatory bodies to enable them to formulate appropriate regulations applicable in all the areas of the high seas.

## F. *Training and Transfer of Technology*

13. That the African States in order to benefit in exploration and exploitation of the resources of the sea-bed and subsoil thereof shall intensify national and regional efforts, in the training and assistance of their personnel in all aspects of marine science and technology. Furthermore they shall urge the appropriate United Nations agencies and the technologically advanced countries to accelerate the process of transfer of marine science and technology, including the training of personnel.

## G. *Scientific Research*

14. All States regardless of their geographical situation have the right to carry out scientific research in the marine environment. The research must be for peaceful purposes and should not cause any harm to the marine environment.

Scientific research in the territorial sea or in the exclusive economic zone shall only be carried out with the consent of the coastal State concerned.

States agree to promote international co-operation in marine scientific research in areas beyond limits of national jurisdiction. Such scientific research shall be carried out in accordance with rules and procedures laid down by the international machinery.

## H. *Preservation of the Marine Environment*

15. That African States recognize that every State has a right to manage its resources pursuant to its environmental policies and has an obligation in the prevention and control of pollution of the marine environment.

16. Consequently, African States shall take all possible measures, individually or jointly, so that activities carried out under their jurisdiction or control do not cause pollution damage to other States and to the marine environment as a whole.

17. In formulating such measures, States shall take maximum account of the provisions of existing international or regional pollution control conventions and of relevant principles and recommendations proposed by competent international or regional organizations.

## I. *International Regime and International Machinery for the Sea-Bed and Ocean Floor and Subsoil thereof beyond the Limits of National Jurisdiction*

18. That African States reaffirm their belief in the Declaration of Principles, embodied in resolution 2749 (XXV) of the United Nations General Assembly and that in order to realize its objectives these principles shall

be translated into treaty articles to govern the area.

19. In particular the African States reaffirm their belief in the principles of Common Heritage of Mankind, which principle should in no way be limited in its scope by restrictive interpretations.

20. That with regard to the international sea-bed area, African States affirm that until the establishment of the international régime and international machinery the applicable régime in the area is the Declaration of Principles (resolution 2749 (XXV)) and the moratorium resolutions; and that in accordance with the provisions of the Declaration and the resolutions no State or person, natural or juridical, shall engage in any activities aimed at commercial exploitation of the area.

21. Without prejudice to paragraphs 1 and 6 above, the African States support a limit of the international area determined by distance from appropriate baselines.

22. That the African States affirm that:

(a) The competence of the international machinery shall extend over the sea-bed and ocean floor and the subsoil thereof, beyond the limits of national jurisdiction.

(b) The machinery shall possess full legal personality with functional privileges and immunities. It may have some working relationship with the United Nations system but it shall maintain considerable political and financial independence.

(c) The machinery shall be invested with strong and comprehensive powers. Among others it shall have right to explore and exploit the area, to handle equitable distribution of benefits and to minimize any adverse economic effects by the fluctuation of prices of raw materials resulting from activities carried out in the area; to distribute equitably among all developing countries the proceeds from any tax (fiscal imposition) levied in connexion with activities relating to the exploitation of the area; to protect the marine environment; to regulate and conduct scientific research and in this way give full meaning to the concept of the common heritage of mankind.

(d) There shall be an assembly of all members which shall be the repository of all powers and a council of limited membership whose composition shall reflect the principle of equitable geographical distribution and shall exercise, in a democratic manner, most of the functions of the machinery. There shall also be a secretariat to service all the organs and a tribunal for the settlement of disputes. The Assembly and the Council would be competent to establish as appropriate subsidiary organs for specialized purposes.

# II. LATIN AMERICA

## 1954 SECOND CONFERENCE ON THE EXPLOITATION AND CONSERVATION OF THE MARITIME RESOURCES OF THE SOUTH PACIFIC:
— Agreements between Chile, Ecuador and Peru, 1954

An Agreement Supplementary to the 1952 Declaration of Sovereignty over the Maritime Zone of 200 Miles was signed at the Second Conference on the Exploitation and Conservation of the Maritime Resources of the South Pacific, Lima on 4 December 1954.

The Governments of the Republics of Chile, Ecuador and Peru, in conformity with the provisions of resolution X of 8 October 1954, signed at Santiago de Chile by the Standing Committee of the Conference on the Exploitation and Conservation of the Maritime Resources of the South Pacific,

Having noted the proposals and recommendations approved in October of this year by the said Standing Committee,

Have appointed the following plenipotentiaries:

. . .

*And whereas*

Chile, Ecuador and Peru have proclaimed their sovereignty over the sea adjacent to the coasts of their respective countries to a distance of not less than two hundred nautical miles from the said coasts, the sea-bed and the subsoil of this maritime zone being included:

The Governments of Chile, Ecuador and Peru, at the First Conference on the Exploitation and Conservation of the Maritime Resources of the South Pacific, held at Santiago de Chile in 1952, expressed their intention of entering into agreements or conventions relating to the application of the principles governing that sovereignty, for the purpose in particular of regulating and protecting hunting and fisheries within their several maritime zones:

*Now therefore the said plenipotentiaries hereby agree as follows:*

1. Chile, Ecuador and Peru shall consult with one another for the purpose of upholding, in law, the principle of their sovereignty over the maritime zone to a distance of not less than two hundred nautical miles, including the sea-bed and the subsoil corresponding thereto. The term "nautical mile" means the equivalent of one minute of the arc measured

31

on the Equator, or a distance of 1,852.8 metres.

2. If any complaints or protests should be addressed to any of the Parties, or if proceedings should be instituted against a Party in a court of law or in an arbitral tribunal, whether possessing general or special jurisdiction, the contracting countries undertake to consult with one another concerning the case to be presented for the defence and furthermore bind themselves to co-operate fully with another in the joint defence.

3. In the event of a violation of the said maritime zone by force, the State affected shall report the event immediately to the other Contracting Parties, for the purpose of determining what action should be taken to safeguard the sovereignty which has been violated.

4. Each of the Contracting Parties undertakes not to enter into any agreements, arrangements or conventions which imply a diminution of the sovereignty over the said zone, though this provision shall not prejudice their rights to enter into agreements or to conclude contracts which do not conflict with the common rules laid down by the contracting countries.

5. All the provisions of this Agreement shall be deemed to be an integral and supplementary part of, and not in any way to abrogate, the resolutions and decisions adopted at the Conference on the Exploitation and Conservation of the Maritime Resources of the South Pacific, held at Santiago de Chile in August 1952.


## SPECIALIZED CONFERENCE OF THE CARIBBEAN COUNTRIES ON PROBLEMS OF THE SEA:
## — Santo Domingo Declaration of 1972

The Specialized Conference of the Caribbean Countries on Problems of the Sea was held at Santo Domingo, the Dominican Republic on 7 June 1972. The meeting of Ministers approved the following declaration.

*The specialized conference of the Caribbean countries on problems of the sea*
*Recalling:*

That the International American Conferences held in Bogotá in 1948, and in Caracas in 1954, recognized that the peoples of the Americas depend on the natural resources as a means of subsistence, and proclaimed the right to protect, conserve and develop those resources, as well as the right to ensure their use and utilization;

That the "Principles of Mexico on the Legal Régime of the Sea" which were adopted in 1956 and which were recognized "as the expression of

32

the juridical conscience of the Continent and as applicable, by the American States", established the basis for the evolution of the Law of the Sea which culminated, that year, with the enunciation by the Specialized Conference in the Capital of the Dominican Republic of concepts which deserved endorsement by the United Nations Conference on the Law of the Sea, Geneva, 1958;

*Considering:*

That the General Assembly of the United Nations, in its resolution 2750 (XXV) decided to convoke in 1973 a Conference on the Law of the Sea, and recognized "the need for early and progressive development of the law of the sea";

That it is desirable to define, through universal norms, the nature and scope of the rights of States, as well as their obligations and responsibilities relating to the various oceanic zones, without prejudice to regional or sub-regional agreements, based on the said norms;

That the Caribbean countries, on account of their peculiar conditions, require special criteria for the application of the Law of the Sea, while at the same time the co-ordination of Latin America is necessary for the purpose of joint action in the future;

That the economic and social development of all the peoples and the assurance of equal opportunities for all human beings are essential conditions for peace;

That the renewable and non-renewable resources of the sea contribute to improve the standard of living of the developing countries and to stimulate and accelerate their progress;

That such resources are not inexhaustible since even the living species may be depleted or extinguished as a consequence of irrational exploitation or pollution;

That the law of the sea should harmonize the needs and interests of States and those of the International Community;

That international co-operation is indispensable to ensure the protection of the marine environment and its better utilization;

That as Santo Domingo is the point of departure of the American civilization as well as the site of the First Conference of the Law of the Sea in Latin America in 1956, it is historically significant that the new principles to advance the progressive development of the Law of the Sea be proclaimed in this city;

Formulate the following Declaration of Principles:

*Territorial Sea*

1. The sovereignty of a State extends, beyond its land territory and its internal waters, to an area of the sea adjacent to its coast, designated as the

territorial sea, including the superjacent air space as well as the subjacent sea-bed and subsoil.

2. The breadth of the territorial sea and the manner of its delimitation should be the subject of an international agreement, preferably of a world-wide scope. In the meantime, each State has the right to establish the breadth of its territorial sea up to a limit of 12 nautical miles to be measured from the applicable baseline.

3. Ships of all States, whether coastal or not, should enjoy the right of innocent passage through the territorial sea, in accordance with International Law.

### Patrimonial Sea

1. The coastal State has sovereign rights over the renewable and non-renewable natural resources, which are found in the waters, in the sea-bed and in the subsoil of an area adjacent to the territorial sea called the patrimonial sea.

2. The coastal State has the duty to promote and the right to regulate the conduct of scientific research within the patrimonial sea, as well as the right to adopt the necessary measures to prevent marine pollution and to ensure its sovereignty over the resources of the area.

3. The breadth of this zone should be the subject of an international agreement, preferably of a world-wide scope. The whole of the area of both the territorial sea and the patrimonial sea, taking into account geographic circumstances, should not exceed a maximum of 200 nautical miles.

4. The delimitation of this zone between two or more States should be carried out in accordance with the peaceful procedures stipulated in the Charter of the United Nations.

5. In this zone ships and aircraft of all States, whether coastal or not, should enjoy the right of freedom of navigation and overflight with no restrictions other than those resulting from the exercise by the coastal State of its rights within the area. Subject only to these limitations, there will also be freedom for the laying of submarine cables and pipelines.

### Continental Shelf

1. The coastal State exercises over the continental shelf sovereign rights for the purpose of exploring it and exploiting its natural resources.

2. The continental shelf includes the sea-bed and subsoil of the submarine areas adjacent to the coast, but outside the area of the territorial sea, to a depth of 200 metres or, beyond that limit, to where the depth of the superjacent waters admits the exploitation of the natural resources of the said areas.

3. In addition, the States participating in this Conference consider that the Latin American Delegations in the Committee on the Sea-bed and Ocean Floor of the United Nations should promote a study concerning the advisability and timing for the establishment of precise outer limits of the continental shelf taking into account the outer limits of the continental rise.

4. In that part of the continental shelf covered by the patrimonial sea the legal régime provided for this area shall apply. With respect to the part beyond the patrimonial sea, the régime established for the continental shelf by International Law shall apply.

## International Sea-bed

1. The sea-bed and its resources, beyond the patrimonial sea and beyond the continental shelf not covered by the former, are the common heritage of mankind, in accordance with the Declaration adopted by the General Assembly of the United Nations in resolution 2749 (XXV) of 17 December 1970.

2. This area shall be subject to the régime to be established by international agreement, which should create an international authority empowered to undertake all activities in the area, particularly the exploration, exploitation, protection of the marine environment and scientific research, either on its own, or through third parties, in the manner and under the conditions that may be established by common agreement.

## High Seas

That waters situated beyond the outer limits of the patrimonial sea constitute an international area designated as high seas, in which there exists freedom of navigation, of overflight and of laying submarine cables and pipelines. Fishing in this zone should be neither unrestricted nor indiscriminate and should be the subject of adequate international regulation, preferably of world-wide scope and general acceptance.

## Marine Pollution

1. Is the duty of every State to refrain from performing acts which may pollute the sea and its sea-bed, either inside or outside its respective jurisdiction?

2. The international responsibility of physical or juridical persons damaging the marine environment is recognized. With regard to this matter the drawing up of an international agreement, preferably of a world-wide scope, is desirable.

1. Recognizing the need for the countries in the area to unite their efforts and adopt a common policy vis-à-vis the problems peculiar to the Caribbean Sea relating mainly to scientific research, pollution of the marine environment, conservation, exploration, safeguarding and exploitation of the resources of the sea;

2. Decides to hold periodic meetings, if possible once a year, of senior governmental officials, for the purpose of co-ordinating and harmonizing national efforts and policies in all aspects of oceanic space with a view to ensuring maximum utilization of resources by all the peoples of the region.

The first meeting may be convoked by any of the States participating in this Conference.

Finally, the feelings of peace and respect for international law which have always inspired the Latin American countries are hereby reaffirmed. It is within this spirit of harmony and solidarity, and for the strengthening of the norms of the inter-American system, that the principles of this document shall be realized.

The present Declaration shall be called: *"Declaration of Santo Domingo"*.

## INTER-AMERICAN JURIDICAL COMMITTEE OF ORGANIZATION OF AMERICAN STATES:
## — Resolution of 1971 on the Law of the Sea

Adopted on 10 September 1971 at Rio de Janeiro.

I. Decides to continue its study of the topic "Law of the Sea", with a view to preparing a declaration that expresses the principles supported in common by most of the American states on the most relevant aspects of international maritime law and that can serve as guidance to the international community in its work of codifying the material on this topic.

II. The declaration to be prepared by the Committee must be as comprehensive and complete as possible, taking into account the topics currently being discussed within the United Nations and the fact that these are closely related to each other, which means that they must be considered as a whole and not as isolated entities.

III. The Committee therefore requests the rapporteurs, as well as any of its other members who wish to do so, to present studies to the next meeting and, especially, specific draft resolutions on the following matters in particular, so that they may be included in the declaration:

I. *Territorial sea*

a. Nature and characteristics. Question of more than one system governing the territorial sea.

b. Delimitation and breadth. Applicable criteria. Regional criteria. Open oceans and seas, semiclosed seas, and closed seas.

II. *Zones of special jurisdiction*

a. Rights of coastal states in relation to national security, tax and customs control, health regulations, and immigration.

b. Rights of coastal states in relation to conservation, maintenance, reservation, and exclusive or preferential exploitation of resources; establishment of economic zones and fishing zones, or both; administration of resources; protection of the marine environment; and scientific research. Applicable criteria including the need for economic and social development.

c. Rights of the coastal states with regard to preventing contamination and other dangerous and harmful effects resulting from use of the seas.

d. Delimitation and breadth of these zones of special jurisdiction. Applicable criteria. Regional criteria. Open oceans and seas, semiclosed seas, and closed seas.

III. *Guarantees for international communication*

a. Freedom of navigation. Innocent passage.

b. Flight in air space over the territorial sea in open oceans and seas and zones of special jurisdiction.

IV. *Continental shelf*

a. Nature and scope of the rights of coastal states.

b. Outer limit; applicable criteria.

V. *International zone of sea bed and ocean floor*

a. International system, including an authority for sea bed and ocean floor and their subsoil beyond the limits of national jurisdiction.

b. Delimitation of the international zone submitted to national jurisdiction.

VI. *Regional agreements*

Regional agreements on the administration of live resources and other resources in the zones located beyond national jurisdictions.

VII. *Straits*

Navigation through international straits.

VIII. *Peaceful uses of oceans*

a. Principles and purposes of peaceful uses of oceans.

b. Nuclear explosions in oceans.

c. Denuclearization of ocean space.

d. Possibilities of demilitarization of ocean space beyond national jurisdictions.

*e*. Inspection and verification by international agencies.

IV. Without prejudice to the foregoing provisions, the Committee considers, of course, that the principles on the law of the sea contained in the declarations of Montevideo and Lima of May and August 1970, respectively, and particularly the ones mentioned below, should be included in the aforementioned declaration:

a. By virtue of their sovereignty over the natural resources of contiguous marine space, the right of coastal states to avail themselves of these resources, in order to make full use of them for the economic, social, and cultural development of their peoples.

b. Without affecting the principle of freedom of international communication, the right of coastal states, for the purpose of protecting the interest of their peoples and in accordance with international law, to establish the zones over which they shall exercise their maritime sovereignty or jurisdiction, in keeping with reasonable criteria and their geographic and ecological characteristics, and also with the need to make use of their resources.

## INTER-AMERICAN JURIDICAL COMMITTEE OF ORGANIZATION OF AMERICAN STATES:
— Resolution of 1973 on the Law of the Sea

Adopted on 9 February 1973 at Rio de Janeiro. OAS/SER.G, CP/Doc.262/73/Rev.1.

Having studied the topic of its work program entitled "Law of the Sea" since its meeting in March and April 1971, and having devoted numerous sessions to studying the problems of a new legal system governing the seas, for which it received valuable papers written by its members, agrees that the following principles and standards represent the common elements of the positions of the American States and, consequently, it recommends to the American States that they take them into consideration in order to present them at the regional or worldwide conferences on a new legal system governing the seas:

1. The sovereignty or jurisdiction of a coastal state extends beyond its territory and its internal waters to an area of the sea adjacent to its coasts up to a maximum distance of 200 nautical miles, as well as to the air space above and the bed and subsoil of that sea. Consequently, the setting of limits of up to 200 miles that has been done or may be done by any American State is valid, provided that the provisions of paragraph 4 are respected.

38

2. Within that area of the sea two zones are distinguished; one that extends to a distance of 12 nautical miles, and another that extends from the outer limit of the first zone up to a distance of 200 nautical miles, measured in accordance with the applicable rules of international law. The distinction between the two zones is made for the purposes set forth in paragraphs 3, 4, 7, and 8.

3. Within the limits of the zone of up to 12 miles, the ships of any state, whether coastal or not, shall enjoy the right of innocent passage, in accordance with international law.

4. Within the limits of the zone adjacent to the zone of up to 12 miles, the ships and aircraft of any state, whether coastal or not, shall enjoy the right of free navigation and overflight, subject to the pertinent regulations of the coastal state with regard to the preservation of the marine environment, the activities of exploration, exploitation, and scientific research conducted therein, and the safety of maritime navigation and transportation, all in accordance with international law.

5. Ships and aircraft that transit through or over international straits that are customarily used for international navigation and that join two free seas enjoy the freedom of navigation and overflight regulated in paragraph four. The present provision shall be understood to be without prejudice to the legal status of certain straits, transit through or over which is regulated by international agreements in force that deal specifically with those straits.

6. In the utilization of the resources that exist in the area that extends from the 12-mile limit to the limit of 200 miles, beyond which the high seas extend, the coastal states shall have as objectives the maximum development of their economics and the raising of the standards of living of their peoples.

7. With respect to the zone that extends from the 12-mile limit to that of 200 nautical miles, a coastal state has the following powers:

*a.* to regulate and conduct exploration of the sea, its bed, and its subsoil, and exploitation of the living and nonliving resources that are found there; and it may reserve those activities for itself or its nationals or allow them also to third parties in accordance with the provisions of its domestic legislation or of any international agreements it concludes in this regard;

*b.* to regulate and adopt the measures necessary for the purpose of preventing, reducing, or eliminating the damage and risks of pollution and other effects harmful or dangerous to the ecological system of the marine environment, the quality and use of the waters, the living resources, human health, and other interests of its population, in accordance with the criteria established by its authorities and taking into account the recommendations and guidelines of international technical organizations, as well as cooperation with other states;

*c.* to promote scientific research activities, to participate in carrying them out, and to receive the results obtained, taking into account the advisability of facilitating such activities without unjustified discrimination or restriction;

*d.* to exchange information on the plans and activities of the coastal state in the zone of the sea referred to in paragraph 4, in order to ensure the most effective international cooperation;

*e.* to establish specific regulations for the purposes of exploration and economic exploitation, with respect to the various zones of the sea that it may believe it advisable to establish in the area up to the limit of 200 nautical miles.

8. Within the zone that extends from the 12-mile limit to the limit of 200 nautical miles, the coastal state shall authorize the laying of underwater cables and conduits recognized under international law, subject to the domestic regulations of that state for the regulation of navigation, scientific research, and preservation of the marine environment.

9. The coastal state shall authorize the non-coastal states in the region to exploit living resources within the zone that extends from the 12-mile limit to the limit of 200 nautical miles, granting them preferential rights in relation to third states and in accordance with criteria that shall be set forth in multilateral, regional, or bilateral agreements.

10. The sovereignty or jurisdiction of any territory subject to colonial domination, in the second zone mentioned in paragraph 2 of this declaration, shall not be recognized so long as that domination lasts.

11. The sovereignty of the coastal state extends beyond the zone mentioned in paragraph 1 throughout its sector of the continental shelf, for the purposes of exploration and exploitation of the natural resources existing in the bed and subsoil of the sea.

12. The continental shelf comprises the seabed and the subsoil of the undersea areas adjacent to the coasts up to the outer border of the continental rise, that is, the boundary with the ocean basin or abyssal depths.

13. The seabeds and ocean floors located beyond the zone of 200 nautical miles and beyond the continental shelf, as well as the resources that may be extracted from them, are the common heritage of mankind.

14. The future legal system governing the high seas and the exploitation of their resources should be organized on regional and not on worldwide bases.

15. The rational and peaceful use of the sea demands commitment by all states to avoid every form of pollution and of depredation of living resources, and it requires putting a stop to all testing of nuclear weapons in the sea, in its bed or subsoil, or in the atmosphere.

## III. NON-ALIGNED COUNTRIES

## FOURTH SUMMIT CONFERENCE OF THE NON-ALIGNED COUNTRIES:
— Resolution of 1973 concerning the Law of the Sea and Political Declaration relating to the Question of the Sea-bed

Adopted at the fourth conference of Heads of State or Government of Non-Aligned Countries held in Algiers, 5-9 September 1973.

### A. Resolution concerning the Law of the Sea

The Fourth Conference of Heads of State or Government of Non-Aligned Countries, meeting in Algiers from 5 to 9 September 1973,

*Considering* that the Non-Aligned Countries, at the Lusaka and Georgetown Conferences, formulated important principles concerning the law of the sea which have influenced the position of the United Nations General Assembly as well as the preparations for the next Conference on the Law of the Sea,

*Recalling* General Assembly resolution 2749 (XXV) which contains a statement of the principles relating to the sea-bed and ocean floor based on the declaration adopted in September 1970 at Lusaka,

*Recalling also* General Assembly resolution 3016 (XXVII) which re-affirms the right of States to permanent sovereignty over all their natural resources, both in territories included within their international frontiers and in the sea-bed and ocean floor and the subsoil thereof within the limits of their national jurisdiction and in the superjacent waters,

*Recalling further* the principles, recommendations and declarations adopted at the meetings of the Asian-African Legal Advisory Committee (Colombo 1971, Lagos 1972 and New Delhi 1973), at the second Ministerial Meeting of the Group of 77 (Lima 1971), at the Conference of Foreign Ministers of the Caribbean Countries (Santo Domingo 1972), at the regional seminar of African States on the law of the sea (Yaounde 1972), at UNCTAD III (Santiago de Chile 1972) and at the Conference of the Organization of African Unity (Addis Ababa 1973),

*Reaffirming* the vital importance of the rational exploitation of marine and ocean resources for the economic development and promotion of the well-being of peoples,

*Considering,* finally, the need for further co-ordination between the Non-Aligned Countries to ensure international recognition of these principles at the Conference on the Law of the Sea to be held in Santiago de Chile in 1974 and which, according to resolution 2750 C (XXV), is to

41

globally consider the various subjects and questions of the juridical régime governing oceanic space, having regard to the political and economic realities as well as to scientific and technological progress in the last decade,

1. *Welcomes* the adoption by the United Nations General Assembly of resolutions 2740 (XXV) and 3016 (XXVII);

2. *Supports* the recognition of the rights of coastal States in seas adjacent to their coasts and in the soil and subsoil thereof, within zones of national jurisdiction not exceeding 200 miles measured from the baselines, for the purposes of exploiting natural resources and protecting the other connected interests of their peoples, without prejudice either to the freedom of navigation and overflight, where applicable, or to the régime relating to the continental shelf;

3. *Stresses* the need to establish a preferential system for geographically handicapped developing countries, including land-locked countries, in respect both of access to the sea and of the exploitation of living resources in zones of national jurisdiction;

4. *Recommends* that the new law of the sea take into account the particular conditions in each region;

5. *Reaffirms* the principles that the zone and resources of the sea-bed and ocean floor and the subsoil thereof beyond the limits of national jurisdiction are the common heritage of mankind;

— the need to set up an international authority to undertake, under its effective control either directly or by any other means on which it might decide, all activities related to exploration of the zone and exploitation of its resources, having due regard to the economic and ecological repercussions of such activities on the special needs and interests of developing countries whether coastal or land-locked and distributing equitably the benefits and other advantages resulting from such activities;

6. *Recommends* also that the new rules governing the use and exploitation of ocean space should take into consideration the conservation of the marine environment;

7. *Considers* that the new rules should effectively help to remove threats to the security of States and ensure respect for their sovereignty and territorial integrity;

8. *Stresses* the urgency of the Conference on the Law of the Sea to be held in Santiago de Chile in 1974, and the need to ensure its success through adequate preparation and the adoption of rules of procedure permitting the rapid achievement of positive results and ensuring the maximum possible degree of agreement;

9. *Reiterates* that, in accordance with the Declaration of Principles

Governing the Sea-Bed and the Ocean Floor and the Subsoil thereof Outside the Limits of National Jurisdiction, as adopted under resolution 2749 (XXV), and with the provisions of resolution 2574 (XXIV), no State or persons, physical or juridical, may exploit the resources of the area pending the establishment of the international régime agreed on;

10. *Recommends* that the representatives of the non-aligned countries at the next session of the General Assembly of the United Nations and at the Conference on the Law of the Sea, should hold prior meetings to co-ordinate their positions and actions on matters of organization and substance relating to that Conference with a view to ensuring the establishment of a new régime governing ocean space which is based on the principles of justice, security, peaceful coexistence, development and well-being for all peoples.

### B. Extract from the Political Declaration relating to the Question of the Sea-bed

The Heads of State or Government of Non-Aligned Countries recalled the Statement on the Sea-Bed and the Declaration on Non-Alignment and Economic Progress adopted at Lusaka, and reviewed the progress made since then. They noted with satisfaction that the Declaration of Principles adopted by the United Nations General Assembly in 1970 was in harmony with the principles set forth in the Lusaka Statement on the Sea-Bed, and that those principles had continued to guide the work of the United Nations Committee on the Peaceful Uses of the Sea-Bed. They also noted with satisfaction that the suggestion made at Lusaka for the convening of a conference on the law of the sea to deal with all the questions relating to the marine environment in a comprehensive manner had been accepted by the international community.

The Heads of State or Government agree to support the adoption of zones of national jurisdiction not exceeding 200 miles, measured from base lines, within which the riparian State would exercise its rights to exploit natural resources and to protect the other related interests of its peoples, bearing in mind the special rights and interests of developing countries, whether coastal, land-locked or geographically handicapped, without prejudice either to freedom of navigation and overflight, where applicable, or to the régime concerning the continental shelf.

The Heads of State or Government reaffirm the vital importance of a rational exploitation of the resources of the seas and oceans, in the interests of economic development and the promotion of the well-being of peoples.

The participants reaffirm their adherence to the basic principle that the area and resources of the sea-bed beyond the limits of national jurisdiction are the common heritage of mankind and recommend the setting up of an international authority, possessing wide powers which would be responsible for administering this area for the benefit of the international community as a whole, and especially the developing countries.

The participants urge all interested parties to abide by the moratorium banning the exploitation of the resources of the international zone until such time as a régime is established.

They stress that the new rules of the law of the sea must effectively contribute to the elimination of threats to the security of States and ensure respect for their sovereignty and territorial integrity.

The participants recommend that the legislation on utilization and exploitation of ocean space include appropriate measures for ensuring the preservation of the sea environment.

The Heads of State or Government proclaim the urgency of holding the Conference on the Law of the Sea at Santiago, Chile, in 1974, as well as the need to ensure its success by proper preparation, and consider that prior consultation among non-aligned countries is essential in order to co-ordinate their positions and actions concerning problems of substance and procedure with a view to arriving rapidly at satisfactory results.

# IV. SOCIALIST COUNTRIES

## MINISTERIAL CONFERENCE OF THE SOCIALIST COUNTRIES:
— Declaration of 1972 on Principles of Rational Exploitation of the Living Resources of the Seas and Oceans in the Common Interests of All Peoples of the World

> The Ministers of Bulgaria, Czechoslovakia, the German Democratic Republic, Hungary, Poland and the Union of Soviet Socialist Republics adopted the Declaration on Principles of Rational Exploitation of the Living Resources of the Seas and Oceans in the Common Interests of All Peoples of the World at their conference held at Moscow on 6-7 July 1972.

The Ministers responsible for fisheries in the People's Republic of Bulgaria, the Hungarian People's Republic, the German Democratic Republic, the Polish People's Republic, the Union of Soviet Socialist Republics and the Czechoslovak Socialist Republic, having considered, at a meeting held in Moscow on 6-7 July 1972, problems relating to the exploration and rational exploitation of the living resources of the seas and oceans;

Noting that the seas and oceans are one of the most important sources of food for mankind and of raw materials for various branches of modern industry;

Considering that the findings of fishery science demonstrate the possibility of further increasing the catch of fish and of many other marine animals without harm to the reproduction of stocks;

Being convinced that the fishing régime on the high seas should be based on the principle of the equal right of all States to engage in fishing and on strict observance of scientific measures for maintaining the living resources of the sea at the maximum sustainable level;

Considering that one of the prospective ways of solving the problem of increasing the yield of food resources from the seas and oceans is to combine the efforts of all interested States in research on, and the reproduction of, marine organisms;

Have resolved to set forth their views on principles of rational utilization of the living resources of the seas and oceans.

1. The co-operation of all interested States in studying and regulating activity relating to the living resources of the sea is an essential condition for their rational use and for increasing the yield of fish from the seas and oceans. However, the partitioning among States of a substantial part of biologically interrelated areas of the high seas through the establishment

by coastal States of special zones of great width (for example, more than 12 miles) and the proclamation of exclusive rights of coastal States over constantly migrating shoals of fish would make this task impossible to fulfil.

2. The socialist States signatories of this declaration advocate rational and scientifically-based fishing and support proposals for more effective scientific research and regulation of fishing on the high seas by international fishery organizations.

Existing systems of international regulation of fishing must be continuously improved. The role of regional international fishing organizations should be increased, and their functions broadened; the exchange of scientific, technical and fishery information should be improved with a view to the objective assessment of stocks of fish, and all interested States, without exception, should be given the opportunity to participate in such organizations, on the principle of sovereign equality. It is necessary to give international organizations functions of international verification of compliance with fishing regulations, in view of the fact that such a measure will promote the more effective protection of fishery resources and their maintenance at the maximum sustainable level.

3. Marine fishing among the countries of the world today is characterized by unequal development.

This is not entirely due to differences in the natural factors which affect the biological productivity of marine areas frequented by shoals of fish. Planned exploitation of fishery resources in the common interest is hampered by the grave consequences of the colonial domination and oppression of many countries of Asia, Africa and Latin America, for which the colonial powers bear responsibility.

4. The socialist States jointly making this declaration support the struggle of developing countries to establish independent national economies, including fishing. They deeply sympathize with the aspirations of those countries to create a fishing industry based on the modern achievements of fishery science and marine technology, and they are assisting them in the establishment and technical equipment of their fishing industries. They will continue to co-operate with the developing countries in the sphere of marine fishing and, to the extent of their own and their partners' capacities, to assist them in the establishment of a modern marine fishing industry with the necessary shore installations, and will broaden their aid in the training of national cadres for fish industries and fishing fleets.

5. In view of the different economic and technological capacities of coastal and other developing States and of countries which engage in long-distance fishing in the same areas as those States, developing countries should be given certain preferential rights enabling them to develop their

46

national fishing industry and overcome their technological backwardness.

6. Firmly convinced of the need for a speedy solution of the problem of full utilization of the living resources of the seas and oceans on a rational basis and in the common interests of all peoples of the world, the socialist countries signing this declaration consider that such a solution can be found on the basis of a reasonable combination, through the international regulation of fishing, of the interests of coastal States and of countries which engage in long-distance fishing operations, and not by the adoption of unilateral measures by individual countries.

7. The living resources of the seas and oceans must become a constant source for improving the well-being and raising the standards of living of the peoples of our planet and be of benefit to all mankind.

# V. UNITED STATES OF AMERICA

**UNITED STATES SENATE:**
— **Metcalf Bill (S. 2801, 92d Congres—1st Session) of 2 November 1971**

> Mr. Metcalf, US Senator, introduced a bill to provide the Secretary of the Interior with authority to promote the conservation and orderly development of the hard mineral resources of the deep seabed, pending adopting of an international regime therefor. S. 1134, 93d Congress - 1st Session of 8 March 1973 is identical to this bill.

Be it enacted by the Senate and House of Representatives of the United States of America in Congress assembled. That this Act may be cited as the "Deep Seabed Hard Mineral Resources Act".

*Definitions*

Sec. 2. When used in this Act—

(*a*) "Secretary" means the Secretary of the Interior;

(*b*) "deep seabed" means the seabed and subsoil vertically below lying seaward and outside the Continental Shelf of the United States and the continental shelves of foreign states, as defined in the 1958 Convention on the Continental Shelf;

(*c*) "block" means an area of the deep seabed having four boundary lines which are lines of longitude and latitude, the width of which may not be less than one-sixth the length and shall include either of two types of blocks: (i) "surface blocks" comprising not more than forty thousand square kilometers and extending downward from the seabed surface to a depth of ten meters; (ii) "subsurface blocks" comprising not more than five hundred square kilometers and extending from ten meters below the seabed surface downward without limitation;

(*d*) "hard mineral" means any mineral, metalliferous mud, or other nonliving substance other than oil, gas, hydrocarbons, and any other substance which both naturally occurs and is normally recovered in liquid or gaseous form;

(*e*) "development" means any operation of exploration and exploitation, other than prospecting, having the purpose of discovery, recovery, or delivery of hard minerals from the deep seabed;

(*f*) "prospecting" means any operation conducted for the purpose of making geophysical or geochemical measurements, bottom sampling, or comparable activities so long as such operation is carried on in a manner that does not significantly alter the surface or subsurface of the deep seabed;

(g) "commercial recovery" means recovery of hard minerals at a substantial rate of production (without regard to profit or loss) for the primary purpose of marketing or commercial use and does not include recovery for any other purpose such as sampling, experimenting in recovery methods, or testing equipment or plant for recovery or treatment of hard minerals;

(h) "person" means any government or unit thereof and any juridical or natural person;

(i) "reciprocating state" means any foreign state designated by the President as a state having legislation or state practice or agreements with the United States which establish an interim policy and practice comparable to that of the United States under this Act;

(j) "international registry clearinghouse" shall mean a recording agency or organization designated by the President in cooperation with reciprocating states.

## Secretary's Powers; Requirement of License

Sec. 3. The Secretary shall administer the provisions of this Act and may prescribe such regulations as are necessary to its execution. No person subject to the jurisdiction of the United States shall directly or indirectly develop any portion of the deep seabed except as authorized by license issued pursuant to this Act or by a reciprocating state. Nothing in this Act or any regulation prescribed thereunder shall preclude, or impose any restriction upon, scientific research or prospecting by any person of any portion of the deep seabed not subject to an outstanding license issued under this Act or by any reciprocating state, or shall require any applicant for a license or any licensee to divulge any information which could prejudice its commercial position.

## Exclusive Licenses; Limitations and Conditions

Sec. 4. (a) The Secretary shall issue licenses pursuant to section 5, recognizing rights, which shall be exclusive as against all persons subject to the jurisdiction of the United States or of any reciprocating state, to develop the block designated in such license, as follows: (i) as to each surface block, the rights shall extend to manganese-oxide nodules and all other hard minerals at the surface of the deep seabed or located vertically below to a depth not exceeding ten meters; (ii) as to each subsurface block, the rights shall extend to all hard minerals located more than ten meters beneath the surface of the deep seabed.

(*b*) Where a subsurface block leased to one person is subjacent to a surface block leased to a different person, the licensee of the subsurface block shall have the right to penetrate the surface block and the Secretary shall prescribe regulations to prevent undue interference by one with the other, giving reasonable priority to the first licensee. No license shall preclude scientific research by any person in licensed areas where such activities do not interfere with development by the licensees.

(*c*) Every license issued under this Act shall remain in force for fifteen years and, where commercial recovery of hard minerals has been achieved from a licensed block within fifteen years, such license shall remain in force so long as commercial recovery from the block continues. The Secretary shall prescribe, as conditions for every license issued pursuant to this Act, minimum annual expenditures as specified in section 7, and requirements to protect the environment, prevent unreasonable interference with other ocean uses, and promote arbitral settlement of disputes. Where circumstances beyond the control of a licensee impair its ability to develop any portion of the deep seabed held under such license, the term of the license and the dates for complying with any other license condition shall be extended for an equal length of time.

*Licensing Procedures; Clearinghouse*

Sec. 5. (*a*) A license as specified in section 4 shall be issued by the Secretary to the first qualified person who makes written application and tenders a fee of $5,000 for the block specified in the application, except for portions of the deep seabed excluded from licensing pursuant to section 6. A person shall be deemed qualified for a license under this Act if and only if that person is a citizen of the United States, or a corporation or other juridical entity organized under the laws of the United States, its States, territories, or possessions, and meets such technical and financial requirements as the Secretary may prescribe in order to assure effective and orderly development of the licensed portion.

(*b*) The Secretary shall act upon each license application within sixty days of its filing, and if the license is not issued or is issued for less than the entire portion of the deep seabed sought in the application, the Secretary shall in announcing his action to the applicant state reasons in writing for declining to issue the license for the entire portion sought. The Secretary shall, and the applicant or licensee may, notify within fourteen days the international registry clearinghouse of the filing or withdrawal of an application for a license under this Act, the issuance, denial, expiration, surrender, transfer, or revocation of such license, or the relinquishment of any licensed portion of the deep seabed.

(*c*) The function of the international registry clearinghouse shall consist solely of keeping records of notices of applications for licenses, the issuance, denial, transfer, or termination of licenses, and the relinquishment of licensed portions of the deep seabed. Its records shall be available for public inspection during the business hours of every working day. Pending designation of such clearinghouse, notice to the Secretary shall constitute notice to the international registry clearinghouse within the meaning of this Act.

## Areas withdrawn from Licensing: Density Limitations

Sec. 6. (*a*) No license shall be issued under this Act for any portion of the deep seabed (i) which has been relinquished by the applicant under license issued by any State within the prior three years: (ii) which is subject either to a prior application for a license or an outstanding license under this Act or from a reciprocating State: *Provided*, That notice thereof has been received by the international registry clearinghouse within fourteen days of such application or license; (iii) which if licensed would result in the applicant holding under licenses issued by any State or States more than 30 per centum of that area of the deep seabed which is within any circle with a diameter of one thousand two hundred and fifty kilometers where the licensed area consists of surface blocks and one hundred and twenty-five kilometers where the licensed area consists of subsurface blocks; or (iv) which if licensed would result in the United States licensing more than 30 per centum of such area.

(*b*) No license shall be issued or transferred under this Act, and no person subject to the jurisdiction of the United States shall have any substantial interest in any license issued by any State, which would result in any person directly or indirectly holding, controlling, or having any substantial interest in licenses for any portion of the deep seabed licensed by any State which that person could not hold directly under this Act because of the limitations of items (i) and (iii).

## Minimum Annual Expenditures

Sec. 7. It shall be a condition of each license issued under this Act that the licensee make or cause to be made minimum expenditures for development of each licensed block in the following amounts per block until commercial recovery from such block is first achieved:

| Year: | Amount per year |
|---|---|
| 1 | $100,000 |
| 2 to 5 | 200,000 |
| 6 to 10 | 350,000 |
| 11 to 15 | 700,000 |

51

Expenditures for off-site operations, facilities, or equipment shall be included in computing required minimum expenditures where such off-site expenditures are directly related to development of the licensed block or blocks. Expenditures in any year in excess of the required minimum may be credited to later years by the licensee.

## Relinquishment; Transfer or Loss of License

Sec. 8. (*a*) Within ten years of the date any block is licensed under this Act and not later than the start of commercial recovery from such block, the licenses shall by written notice to the Secretary relinquish 75 per centum of such block measured laterally. The relinquishment shall be such that the unrelinquished area conforms to the shape of a block as defined under section 2 (*c*). The licensee shall select the area of the block to be relinquished and as many as four contiguous blocks of the same type held by the licensee may be treated as a single unit for purposes of selecting the 75 per centum to be relinquished.

(*b*) Any license issued under this Act may be surrendered at will and, on written consent of the Secretary, transferred to any person who qualifies under section 5 (*a*) and is not precluded from holding such license by section 6 (*b*). Such license may be revoked for willful, substantial failure to comply with this Act, any regulation prescribed thereunder, or any license condition, in a proceeding in an appropriate United States district court: *Provided*, That the Secretary has first given the licensee written notice of such violation and the licensee has failed to remedy the violation within a reasonable period of time.

## Escrow Fund

Sec. 9. A fund shall be established for assistance, as Congress may hereafter direct, to developing reciprocating States. The United States shall deposit in this fund each year an amount equivalent to ———— * per centum of all license fees collected during that year by the United States pursuant to section 5 (*a*) and an amount equivalent to ———— * per centum of all income tax revenues derived by the United States which are directly attributable to recovery of hard minerals from the deep seabed pursuant to licenses issued under this Act: *Provided*, That the amount deposited by the United States per license issued and per unrelinquished square kilometer under license shall not exceed the amount contributed for assistance to developing reciprocating States by other licensing reciprocating States (except developing States) per license issued by them and per unrelinquished square kilometer licensed by them. For the

* An appropriate amount to be determined by the Congress.

purposes of this section, "developing reciprocating State" means a reciprocating State designated by the President, taking into consideration per capita gross national product and other appropriate criteria.

## Investment Protection

Sec. 10. (*a*) Licenses issued under this Act may be made subject to any international regime for development of the deep seabed hereafter agreed to by the United States: *Provided*, That such regime fully recognizes and protects the exclusive rights of each licensee to develop the licensed block for the term of the license: *And provided further*, That the United States fully reimburses the licensee for any loss of investment or increased costs of the licensee incurred within forty years after issuance of the license due to requirements or limitations imposed by the regime more burdensome than those of this Act. The United States shall bear any payment of whatever kind required of the licensee under the international regime. The Secretary shall determine in the first instance the amount owing on all claims for reimbursement under this subsection.

(*b*) On annual payment by any licensee of a premium of $———— * per $1,000 of insured risk of loss, the United States shall guarantee to reimburse the licensee for any loss caused through any interference by any other person (whether or not violative of international law) with development by the licensee pursuant to the license and from any loss caused by recovery by any person not authorized by the licensee of hard minerals from any block subject to such a license. The Secretary shall determine in the first instance the amount owing on all claims for reimbursement under this subsection.

## Nondiscriminatory Treatment

Sec. 11. All hard minerals recovered from the deep seabed under a license issued pursuant to this Act shall be deemed to have been recovered within the United States for purposes of the import and tax laws and regulations of the United States and such laws and regulations shall be administered so that there shall be no discrimination between hard minerals recovered from the deep seabed and comparable hard minerals recovered within the United States.

## Penalties; Rights of Action

Sec. 12. (*a*) Any person subject to the jurisdiction of the United States may be enjoined from directly or indirectly violating this Act or any regulations prescribed thereunder, interfering with development pursuant

* A suitable premium to be determined by the Congress.

to any license issued under this Act or by any reciprocating state, or removing without authority of the licensee any hard minerals from any block subject to such a license. Any such person who directly or indirectly commits such violation, interference, or removal shall be liable to any person injured thereby for actual damages. Any such willful violation, interference, or removal by such person shall be a misdemeanor punishable by up to six months' imprisonment, a fine of $2,000, or both.

(b) The United States district courts shall have original jurisdiction to enforce subsection (a) and to revoke licenses under section 8 (b), and such actions may be initiated in any judicial district where the defendant resides or may be found. Any regulation prescribed by the Secretary under this Act, any issuance, denial, or condition of a license under this Act by the Secretary, any consent or refusal of consent by the Secretary to the transfer of such license, and any determination of the Secretary allowing or disallowing reimbursement under section 10, shall be subject to judicial review on petition of any interested person in accordance with chapter 158 of title 28 of the United States Code.

*Enactment Date; Separability*

Sec. 13. This Act shall take effect on the date of its enactment. If any provision of this Act or any application thereof is held invalid, the validity of the remainder of the Act or of any other application shall not be affected thereby.

# PART III

# DELIMITATION OF MARITIME JURISDICTION

# I. TERRITORIAL SEAS AND FISHERY ZONES

## EXTENT OF THE TERRITORIAL SEA AND THE FISHERY ZONES

As of 1 November 1973. Some data are based upon unconfirmed sources.

| Territorial Sea | | Fishery Zone | |
| --- | --- | --- | --- |
| | | None | |
| Unknown | 2 | | |
| 3 miles | 21 | Bahrein, Barbados, Belgium, Cuba, Fiji, German Dem. Rep., Guyana, Japan, Jordan, Netherlands, Qatar, Singapore, United Arab Emirates | 13 |
| 4 miles | 4 | Finland | 1 |
| 6 miles | 10 | Greece, Israel, Italy | 3 |
| 10 miles | 1 | Yugoslavia | 1 |
| 12 miles | 56 | Albania, Algeria, Bangladesh, Bulgaria, Burma, Canada, China, Colombia, Cyprus, Dahomey, Egypt, Ethiopia, France, Guatemala, Honduras, Equatorial Guinea, India, Indonesia, Iraq, Jamaica, Kenya, Khmer, Korea (Dem. People's Rep. of), Kuwait, Liberia, Libya, Malaysia, Mauritius, Mexico, Monaco, Nauru, Romania, Saudi Arabia, Somalia, Sri Lanka, Sudan, Syria, Thailand, Togo, Tonga, Trinidad and Tobago, Tunisia, Ukrainian SSR, USSR, Venezuela, Viet-Nam (Dem. Rep. of), Viet-Nam (Rep. of), Yemen, South Yemen, Zaire | 50 |
| 18 miles | 1 | Cameroon | |
| 30 miles | 4 | Congo (People's Rep. of), Ghana, Mauritania, Nigeria | 4 |

56

| | | Fishery Zone | | |
|---|---|---|---|---|
| *s* | | *12 miles* | *more than 12 miles* | *area specifically set up* |
| on | 1 | | Nicaragua (200) | 1 |
| | | Australia, Denmark, Germany (Fed. Rep. of), Ireland, New Zealand, Poland, UK, US | 8 | |
| | | Norway, Sweden | 2 | Iceland (50) | 1 |
| | | Ivory Coast, Dominica, Malta, Portugal, South Africa, Spain, Turkey | 7 | |
| | | | Haiti (15), Iran (50), Morocco (70), Oman (50), Pakistan (50), Senegal (112) | 6 |

| Territorial Sea | | Fishery Zone | |
| --- | --- | --- | --- |
| | | *None* | |
| 50 miles | 3 | Gambia, Tanzania | 2 |
| 100 miles | 1 | Gabon | 1 |
| 130 miles | 1 | Guinea | 1 |
| 200 miles | 10 | Argentina, Brazil, Chile, Costa Rica, Ecuador, El Salvador, Panama, Peru, Sierra Leone, Uruguay | 10 |
| area specifically set up | 2 | Philippines | 1 |
| | 116 | | 88 |

| | Fishery Zone | | |
| --- | --- | --- | --- |
| 12 miles | | more than 12 miles | area specifically set up |
| | | Madagascar (100) | 1 |
| | | | Maldives 1 |
| 1 | | 17 | 9 | 1 |

# EXTENT OF THE TERRITORIAL SEA

As of 1 November 1973. Some data are based upon unconfirmed sources. Asterisk indicates States claiming additional fishery zones.

| | | Asia | Oceania | Africa |
|---|---|---|---|---|
| 3 miles | 21 | Bahrein, Japan, Jordan, Qatar, Singapore, United Arab Emirates | Australia *, Fiji, New Zealand * | |
| 4 miles | 4 | | | |
| 6 miles | 10 | Israel, Turkey * | | Ivory Coast *, South A |
| 10 miles | 1 | | | |
| 12 miles | 56 | Bangladesh, Burma, China, Cyprus, India, Indonesia, Iran *, Iraq, Khmer, Korea (Dem. People's Rep. of), Kuwait, Malaysia, Oman *, Pakistan *, Saudi Arabia, Sri Lanka, Syria, Thailand, Viet-Nam (Dem. Rep. of), Viet-Nam (Rep. of), Yemen, South Yemen | Nauru, Tonga | Algeria, Dahomey, Egy Equatorial Guinea, Eth Kenya, Liberia, Libya, Mauritius, Morocco *, Senegal *, Somalia, Sud Togo, Tunisia, Zaire |
| 18 miles | 1 | | | Cameroon |
| 30 miles | 4 | | | Congo (People's Rep. o Ghana, Mauritania, Ni |
| 50 miles | 3 | | | Gambia, Madagascar *, Tanzania |
| 100 miles | 1 | | | Gabon |
| 130 miles | 1 | | | Guinea |
| 200 miles | 10 | | | Sierra Leone |
| area specifically set up | 2 | Maldives *, Philippines | | |
| | 114 | 32 | 5 | 29 |

| America | North America | Western Europe | Eastern Europe |
|---|---|---|---|
| ados, Cuba, na | US * | Belgium, Denmark *, Germany (Fed. Rep. of) *, Ireland *, Netherlands, UK * | German Dem. Rep., Poland * |
| | | Finland, Iceland *, Norway *, Sweden * | |
| inica * | | Greece, Italy, Malta *, Portugal *, Spain * | |
| | | | Yugoslavia |
| mbia, Guatemala, *, Honduras, ica, Mexico, dad and Tobago, zuela | Canada | France, Monaco | Albania, Bulgaria, Romania, Ukrainian SSR, USSR |

ntina, Brazil,
, Costa Rica,
dor, El Salvador,
ma, Peru,
uay

| 2 | 17 | 8 |
|---|---|---|

As of 1 November 1973. Some data are based upon unconfirmed sources. Under and lower lines in an entry indicate the claims to fishery jurisdiction in terms of territorial sea and of fishery zones respectively.

| | Total | | Asia | Oceania | Africa | Latin America | North America | Western Europe | Eastern Europe |
|---|---|---|---|---|---|---|---|---|---|
| 3 miles | 13 | 13 | 6 | 1 | 0 | 3 | 0 | 2 | 1 |
| | | 0 | 0 | 0 | 0 | 0 | 0 | 0 | 0 |
| 4 miles | 1 | 1 | 0 | 0 | 0 | 0 | 0 | 1 | 0 |
| | | 0 | 0 | 0 | 0 | 0 | 0 | 0 | 0 |
| 6 miles | 4 | 3 | 1 | 0 | 0 | 0 | 0 | 2 | 0 |
| | | 1 | 1 | 0 | 0 | 0 | 0 | 0 | 0 |
| 10 miles | 1 | 1 | 0 | 0 | 0 | 0 | 0 | 0 | 1 |
| | | 0 | 0 | 0 | 0 | 0 | 0 | 0 | 0 |
| 12 miles | 67 | 50 | 19 | 2 | 14 | 7 | 1 | 2 | 5 |
| | | 17 | 1 | 2 | 2 | 1 | 1 | 9 | 1 |
| 15 miles | 1 | 0 | 0 | 0 | 0 | 0 | 0 | 0 | 0 |
| | | 1 | 0 | 0 | 0 | 1 | 0 | 0 | 0 |
| 18 miles | 1 | 1 | 0 | 0 | 1 | 0 | 0 | 0 | 0 |
| | | 0 | 0 | 0 | 0 | 0 | 0 | 0 | 0 |
| 30 miles | 4 | 4 | 0 | 0 | 4 | 0 | 0 | 0 | 0 |
| | | 0 | 0 | 0 | 0 | 0 | 0 | 0 | 0 |
| 50 miles | 6 | 2 | 0 | 0 | 2 | 0 | 0 | 0 | 0 |
| | | 4 | 3 | 0 | 0 | 0 | 0 | 1 | 0 |
| 70 miles | 1 | 0 | 0 | 0 | 0 | 0 | 0 | 0 | 0 |
| | | 1 | 0 | 0 | 1 | 0 | 0 | 0 | 0 |
| 100 miles | 2 | 1 | 0 | 0 | 1 | 0 | 0 | 0 | 0 |
| | | 1 | 0 | 0 | 1 | 0 | 0 | 0 | 0 |
| 112 miles | 1 | 0 | 0 | 0 | 0 | 0 | 0 | 0 | 0 |
| | | 1 | 0 | 0 | 1 | 0 | 0 | 0 | 0 |
| 130 miles | 1 | 1 | 0 | 0 | 1 | 0 | 0 | 0 | 0 |
| | | 0 | 0 | 0 | 0 | 0 | 0 | 0 | 0 |
| 200 miles | 11 | 10 | 0 | 0 | 1 | 9 | 0 | 0 | 0 |
| | | 1 | 0 | 0 | 0 | 1 | 0 | 0 | 0 |
| area specifically set up | 2 | 1 | 1 | 0 | 0 | 0 | 0 | 0 | 0 |
| | | 1 | 1 | 0 | 0 | 0 | 0 | 0 | 0 |
| | 116 | 88 | 33 | 5 | 29 | 22 | 2 | 17 | 8 |
| | | 28 | | | | | | | |

## II. BOUNDARY OF THE CONTINENTAL SHELF

### IRAN—BAHRAIN:
— Agreement concerning Delimitation of the Continental Shelf, 1971

Signed at Bahrain on 17 June 1971. Entered into force on 14 May 1972.

The Imperial Government of Iran and The Government of Bahrain,
*Desirous* of establishing in a just equitable and precise manner the boundary line between the respective areas of the continental shelf over which they have sovereign rights in accordance with international law, have agreed as follows:

**Art. 1.** The line dividing the continental shelf lying between the territory of Iran on the one side and the territory of Bahrain on the other side shall consist of geodetic lines between the following points in the sequence hereinafter set out: —

Point (1) is the Eastern-most point on the Eastern-most part of the Northern boundary line of the continental shelf appertaining to Bahrain as formed by the intersection of a line starting from the point having the latitude of 27 degrees, 00 minutes, 35 seconds North and longitude 51 degrees, 23 minutes, 00 seconds East, and having a geodetic azimuth of 278 degrees, 14 minutes, 27 seconds, with a boundary line dividing the continental shelf appertaining to Bahrain and Qatar, thence:

|           | *Lat. North*  | *Long. East*  |
|-----------|---------------|---------------|
| Point (2) | 27° 02' 46"   | 51° 05' 54"   |
| Point (3) | 27° 06' 30"   | 50° 57' 00"   |
| Point (4) | 27° 10' 00"   | 50° 54' 00"   |

**Art. 2.** If any single geological petroleum structure or petroleum field, or any single geological structure or field of any other mineral extends across the boundary line set out in Article 1 of this Agreement and the part of such structure or field which is situated on one side of that boundary line could be exploited wholly or in part by directional drilling from the other side of the boundary line then:

(*a*) No well shall be drilled on either side of the boundary line as set out in Article 1 so that any producing section thereof is less than 125 metres from the said boundary line except by mutual agreement between the Imperial Government of Iran and the Government of Bahrain.

(*b*) If the circumstances considered in this Article shall arise both

63

Parties hereto shall use their best endeavours to reach agreement as to the manner in which the operations on both sides of the boundary line could be co-ordinated or unitized.

**Art. 3.** The boundary line referred to in Article 1 hereof has been illustrated on the British Admiralty chart. No. 2847 which is annexed hereto and has been thereon marked in red.

**Art. 4.** Nothing in this Agreement shall affect the status of the superjacent waters or air-space above any part of the continental shelf.

**Art. 5.** (*a*) This Agreement shall be ratified and the instruments of ratification shall be exchanged at Teheran.

(*b*) This Agreement shall enter into force on the date of the exchange of instruments of ratification.


### FEDERAL REPUBLIC OF GERMANY—UNITED KINGDOM:
### — Agreement on the Delimitation of the Continental Shelf, 1971

Signed at London on 25 November 1971.

The United Kingdom of Great Britain and Northern Ireland and the Federal Republic of Germany;

Desiring to establish the common boundary between their respective parts of the Continental Shelf under the North Sea;

Have agreed as follows:

**Art. 1.** (1) The dividing line between that part of the Continental Shelf which appertains to the United Kingdom of Great Britain and Northern Ireland and that part which appertains to the Federal Republic of Germany shall be arcs of Great Circles between the following points in the sequence given below:

1. 55° 45′ 54 · 0″ N    03° 22′ 13 · 0″ E
2. 55° 50′ 06 · 0″ N    03° 24′ 00 · 0″ E
3. 55° 55′ 09 · 4″ N    03° 21′ 00 · 0″ E

The positions of the points in this article are defined by latitude and longitude on European Datum (1st Adjustment 1950).

(2) In the south the termination point of the dividing line shall be point No. 1, which is the point of intersection of the dividing lines between the Continental Shelves of the United Kingdom of Great Britain and Northern Ireland, the Federal Republic of Germany, and the Kingdom of the Netherlands.

(3) In the north the termination point of the dividing line shall be point No. 3, which is the point of intersection of the dividing lines between the Continental Shelves of the United Kingdom of Great Britain and Northern Ireland, the Federal Republic of Germany, and the Kingdom of Denmark.

(4) The dividing line has been drawn on the chart annexed to this Agreement.

**Art. 2.** Should any dispute arise concerning the position of any installation or other device or a well's intake in relation to the dividing line, the Contracting Parties shall in consultation determine on which side of the dividing line the installation or other device or the well's intake is situated.

**Art. 3.** (1) If any single geological mineral oil or natural gas structure or field, or any single geological structure or field of any other mineral deposit extends across the dividing line and the part of such structure or field which is situated on one side of the dividing line is exploitable, wholly or in part, from the other side of the dividing line, the Contracting Parties shall seek to reach agreement as to the exploitation of such structure or field.

(2) In this Article the term "mineral" is used in its most general, extensive and comprehensive sense and includes all non-living substances occurring on, in or under the ground, irrespective of chemical or physical state.

**Art. 4.** Where a structure or field referred to in Article 3 of this Agreement is such that failure to reach agreement between the Contracting Parties would prevent maximum ultimate recovery of the deposit or lead to unnecessary competitive drilling, then any question upon which the Contracting Parties are unable to agree concerning the manner in which the structure or field shall be exploited or concerning the manner in which the costs and proceeds relating thereto shall be apportioned, shall, at the request of either Contracting Party, be referred to a single Arbitrator to be jointly appointed by the Contracting Parties. The decision of the Arbitrator shall be binding upon the Contracting Parties.

**Art. 5.** This Agreement shall also apply to Land Berlin, provided that the Government of the Federal Republic of Germany has not made a contrary declaration to the Government of the United Kingdom within three months from the date of entry into force of this Agreement.

**Art. 6.** (1) This Agreement shall be ratified. Instruments of ratification shall be exchanged at London as soon as possible.

(2) This Agreement shall enter into force on the 30th day after the exchange of instruments of ratification.

# DENMARK—UNITED KINGDOM:
## — Agreement on the Delimitation of the Continental Shelf, 1971

Signed at London on 25 November 1971. This Agreement replaces the Agreement of 3 March 1966 relating to the Delimitation of the Continental Shelf between Denmark and the United Kingdom (printed on p. 388 of Vol. I).

The Government of the United Kingdom of Great Britain and Northern Ireland and the Government of the Kingdom of Denmark;

Having regard to the Agreement concluded between them on 3 March 1966 relating to the Delimitation of the Continental Shelf between their two countries;

Having decided to establish their common boundary between the parts of the Continental Shelf over which the Kingdom of Denmark and the United Kingdom of Great Britain and Northern Ireland respectively exercise sovereign rights for the purpose of exploration and exploitation of the natural resources of the Continental Shelf;

Have agreed as follows:

**Art. 1.** The dividing line between that part of the Continental Shelf which appertains to the United Kingdom of Great Britain and Northern Ireland and that part which appertains to the Kingdom of Denmark is in principle a line which at every point is equidistant from the nearest points of the baselines from which the territorial sea of each country is measured.

**Art. 2.** (1) In implementation of the principle set forth in Article 1, the dividing line shall be an arc of a Great Circle between the following points:

1. 56° 05′ 12 · 0″ N    03° 15′ 00 · 0″ E
2. 55° 55′ 09 · 4″ N    03° 21′ 00 · 0″ E

The positions of the two above-mentioned points are defined by latitude and longitude on European Datum (1st Adjustment 1950).

(2) The dividing line has been drawn on the chart annexed to this Agreement.

**Art. 3.** (1) In the north the termination point of the dividing line is the point of intersection of the dividing lines between the Continental Shelves of the United Kingdom of Great Britain and Northern Ireland, the Kingdom of Denmark and the Kingdom of Norway.

(2) In the south the termination point of the dividing line is the point of intersection of the dividing lines between the Continental Shelves of the United Kingdom of Great Britain and Northern Ireland, the Kingdom of Denmark and the Federal Republic of Germany.

**Art. 4.** If any single geological petroleum structure or petroleum field, or any single geological structure or field of any other mineral deposit, including sand or gravel, extends across the dividing line and the part of such structure or field which is situated on one side of the dividing line is exploitable, wholly or in part, from the other side of the dividing line, the Contracting Parties shall seek to reach agreement as to the exploitation of such structure or field.

**Art. 5.** With the entry into force of this Agreement the Agreement relating to the Delimitation of the Continental Shelf between the two countries signed at London on 3 March 1966 shall cease to have effect.

**Art. 6.** (1) This Agreement shall be ratified. Instruments of ratification shall be exchanged at London.

(2) The Agreement shall enter into force on the thirtieth day after the exchange of instruments of ratification.


## NETHERLANDS—UNITED KINGDOM:
— **Protocol amending Agreement on the Delimitation of the Continental Shelf, 1971**

>Signed at London on 25 November 1971. This Protocol amends the Agreement of 6 October 1965 between the Netherlands and the United Kingdom relating to the Delimitation of the Continental Shelf (printed on p. 384 of Vol. I).

The Government of the United Kingdom of Great Britain and Northern Ireland and the Government of the Kingdom of the Netherlands;

Having regard to the Agreement concluded between them on 6 October 1965 relating to the Delimitation of the Continental Shelf under the North Sea between their countries (hereinafter referred to as "the Agreement"); and

In view of the dividing line which, by the Agreement of 28 January 1971 between the Kingdom of the Netherlands and the Federal Republic of Germany, was established between the Netherlands part and the German part of the Continental Shelf under the North Sea;

Have agreed as follows:

**Art. 1.** Point No. 19 mentioned in Article 1, paragraph 1, of the Agreement shall be cancelled and be superseded by a new point No. 19, the co-ordinates of which shall be: 55° 45′ 54″ N    03° 22′ 13″ E.

67

**Art. 2.** Article 2, paragraph 2, of the Agreement shall be amended and shall read as follows:

"In the north the termination point of the dividing line shall be point No. 19, which is the point of intersection of the dividing lines between the continental shelves of the United Kingdom of Great Britain and Northern Ireland, the Kingdom of the Netherlands and the Federal Republic of Germany."

**Art. 3.** (1) This Protocol shall be ratified. The instruments of ratification shall be exchanged at London.

(2) This Protocol shall enter into force on the thirtieth day after the exchange of instruments of ratification.

## AUSTRALIA—INDONESIA:
— **Agreement establishing certain Seabed Boundaries in the Area of the Timor and Arafura Seas, Supplementary to the Agreement of 18 May, 1971**

Signed at Jakarta on 9 October 1972.

The Government of the Commonwealth of Australia, and the Government of the Republic of Indonesia,

*Recalling* the Agreement between the two Governments, signed on the eighteenth day of May One thousand nine hundred and seventy-one, establishing seabed boundaries in the Arafura Sea and in certain areas off the coasts of the island of New Guinea (Irian),

*Recalling* further that in the aforesaid Agreement the two Governments left for later discussion the question of the delimitation of the respective areas of adjacent seabed in the Arafura and Timor Seas westward of longitude 133 degrees 23′ east,

*Resolving*, as good neighbours and in a spirit of co-operation and friendship, to settle permanently the limits of the areas referred to in the preceding paragraph within which the respective Governments shall exercise sovereign rights with respect to the exploration of the seabed and the exploitation of its natural resources,

*Have agreed* as follows:

**Art. 1.** In the area to the south of the Tanimbar Islands, the boundary between the area of seabed that is adjacent to and appertains to the Commonwealth of Australia and the area of seabed that is adjacent to and appertains to the Republic of Indonesia shall be the straight lines shown on the chart annexed to this Agreement commencing at the point of latitude 8 degrees 53' south, longitude 133 degrees 23' east (point A12, specified in the Agreement between the two countries dated the eighteenth day of May One thousand nine hundred and seventy-one), thence connecting in a westerly direction the points specified hereunder in the sequence so specified:

A13  the point of latitude 8 degrees 54' south,
                   longitude 133 degrees 14' east
A14  the point of latitude 9 degrees 25' south,
                   longitude 130 degrees 10' east
A15  the point of latitude 9 degrees 25' south,
                   longitude 128 degrees 00' east
A16  the point of latitude 9 degrees 28' south,
                   longitude 127 degrees 56' east

**Art. 2.** In the area south of Roti and Timor Islands, the boundary between the area of seabed that is adjacent to and appertains to the Commonwealth of Australia and the area of seabed that is adjacent to and appertains to the Republic of Indonesia shall be the straight lines, shown on the chart annexed to this Agreement commencing at the point of latitude 10 degrees 28' south, longitude 126 degrees 00' east (point A17), and thence connecting in a westerly direction the points specified hereunder in the sequence so specified:

A18  the point of latitude 10 degrees 37' south,
                   longitude 125 degrees 41' east
A19  the point of latitude 11 degrees 01' south,
                   longitude 125 degrees 19' east
A20  the point of latitude 11 degrees 07' south,
                   longitude 124 degrees 34' east
A21  the point of latitude 11 degrees 25' south,
                   longitude 124 degrees 10' east
A22  the point of latitude 11 degrees 26' south,
                   longitude 124 degrees 00' east
A23  the point of latitude 11 degrees 28' south,
                   longitude 123 degrees 40' east
A24  the point of latitude 11 degrees 23' south,
                   longitude 123 degrees 26' east
A25  the point of latitude 11 degrees 35' south,
                   longitude 123 degrees 14' east

**Art. 3.** The lines between points A15 and A16 and between points A17 and A18 referred to in Article 1 and Article 2 respectively, indicate the direction of those portions of the boundary. In the event of any further delimitation agreement or agreements being concluded between governments exercising sovereign rights with respect to the exploration of the seabed and the exploitation of its natural resources in the area of the Timor Sea, the Government of the Commonwealth of Australia and the Government of the Republic of Indonesia shall consult each other with a view to agreeing on such adjustment or adjustments, if any, as may be necessary in those portions of the boundary lines between points A15 and A16 and between points A17 and A18.

**Art. 4.** The Government of the Commonwealth of Australia and the Government of the Republic of Indonesia mutually acknowledge the sovereign rights of the respective Governments in and over the seabed areas within the limits established by this Agreement and that they will cease to claim or to exercise sovereign rights with respect to the exploration of the seabed and the exploitation of its natural resources beyond the boundaries so established.

**Art. 5.** For the purpose of this Agreement, "seabed" includes the subsoil thereof, except where the context otherwise requires.

**Art. 6.** 1. The co-ordinates of the points specified in Articles 1 and 2 of this Agreement are geographical co-ordinates, and the actual location of these points and of the lines joining them shall be determined by a method to be agreed upon by the competent authorities of the two Governments.

2. For the purpose of paragraph 1 of this Article, the competent authorities in relation to the Commonwealth of Australia shall be the Director of National Mapping and any person acting with his authority, and in relation to the Republic of Indonesia shall be the Chief of the Co-ordinating Body for National Survey and Mapping (Ketua Badan Koordinasi Survey dan Pemetaan Nasional) and any person acting with his authority.

**Art. 7.** If any single accumulation of liquid hydrocarbons or natural gas, or if any other mineral deposit beneath the seabed, extends across any of the lines that are specified or described in Articles 1 and 2 of this Agreement, and the part of such accumulation or deposit that is situated on one side of the line is recoverable in fluid form wholly or in part from the other side on the line, the two Governments will seek to reach agreement on the manner in which the accumulation or deposit shall be most effectively exploited and on the equitable sharing of the benefits arising from such exploitation.

**Art. 8.** 1. Where the Government of the Commonwealth of Australia has granted an exploration permit for petroleum or a production licence for petroleum under the Petroleum (Submerged Lands) Acts of the Commonwealth of Australia over a part of the seabed over which that Govern-

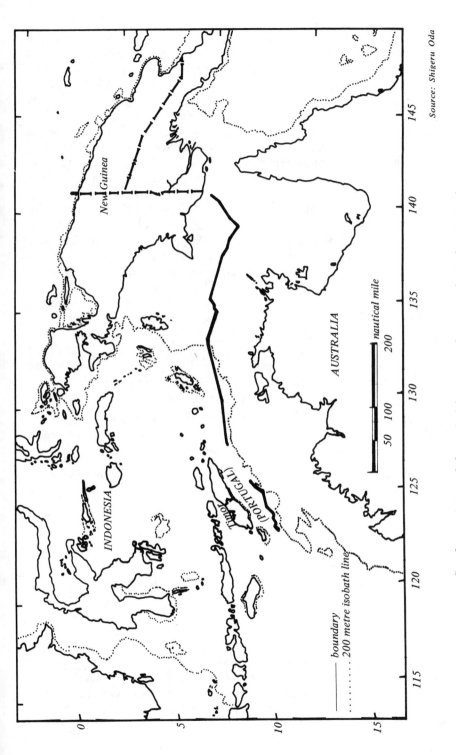

*Southeast Asia and Oceania (Agreement between Australia and Indonesia)*

ment ceases to exercise sovereign rights by virtue of this Agreement, and that permit or licence is in force immediately prior to the entry into force of this Agreement, the Government of the Republic of Indonesia or its authorised agent shall, upon application by the registered holder of the permit or licence, or where there is more than one registered holder, by the registered holders acting jointly, be willing to offer and to negotiate a production sharing contract under Indonesian law to explore for and to produce oil and natural gas in respect of the same part of the seabed on terms that are not less favourable than those provided under Indonesian law in existing production sharing contracts in other parts of the seabed under Indonesian jurisdiction.

2. An application for negotiation in accordance with paragraph 1 of this Article must be made by the registered holder or holders within nine months after the entry into force of this Agreement. If no application is made within this period, or if an offer made in accordance with paragraph 1 of this Article is, after negotiation not accepted by the permittee or licensee, the Government of the Republic of Indonesia shall have no further obligation to the registered holder or holders of a permit or licence to which paragraph 1 of this Article applies.

3. For the purpose of this Article, "registered holder" means a company that was a registered holder of an exploration permit for petroleum or a production licence for petroleum, as the case may be under the Petroleum (Submerged Lands) Acts of the Commonwealth of Australia immediately prior to the entry into force of this Agreement.

**Art. 9.** Any dispute between the two Governments arising out of the interpretation or implementation of this Agreement shall be settled peacefully by consultation or negotiation.

**Art. 10.** This Agreement is subject to ratification in accordance with the constitutional requirements of each country, and shall enter into force on the day on which the Instruments of Ratification are exchanged.

## ARGENTINA—URUGUAY:
## — Treaty of the Rio de la Plata and its Maritime Front, 1973

Signed at Montevideo on 19 November 1973. Came into force on 12 February 1974.

Los Gobiernos de la República Oriental del Uruguay y de la República Argentina, inspirados en el mismo espíritu de cordialidad y buena armonía que señaló el Protocolo Ramírez-Sáenz Peña de 1910 y reafirmaron la

Declaración Conjunta sobre Límite Exterior del Río de la Plata de 1961 y el Protocolo del Río de la Plata de 1964, animados del propósito común de eliminar las dificultades que puedan derivarse de toda situación de indefinición jurídica con relación al ejercicio de sus iguales derechos en el Río de la Plata y de la falta de determinación del limite entre sus respectivas jurisdicciones marítimas, y decididos a sentar las bases de una más amplia cooperación entre los dos Países y estrechar los arraigados vínculos de tradicional amistad y hondo afecto que unen a sus Pueblos, han resuelto celebrar un Tratado que dé solución definitiva a aquellos problema, de acuerdo con las características especiales de los territorios fluviales y marítimos involucrados y las exigencias técnicas de su utilización y aprovechamiento integrales, en el marco del respeto a la soberanía y a los derechos e intereses respectivos de los dos Estados. . . .

## PARTE PRIMERA — RIO DE LA PLATA

### Chapitulo I — *Jurisdiccion*

**Art. 1.** El Río de la Plata se extiende desde el paralelo de Punta Gorda hasta la línea recta imaginaria que une Punta del Este (República Oriental del Uruguay) con Punta Rasa del Cabo San Antonio (República Argentina), de conformidad a lo dispuesto en el Tratado de Límites del Río Uruguay del 7 de abril de 1961 y en la Declaración Conjunta sobre el Límite Exterior del Río de la Plata del 30 de enero de 1961.

**Art. 2.** Se establece una franja de jurisdicción exclusiva adyacente a las costas de cada Parte en el Río.

Esta franja costera tiene una anchura de siete millas marinas entre el límite exterior del Río y la línea recta imaginaria que une Colonia (República Oriental del Uruguay) con Punta Lara (República Argentina) y desde esta última línea hasta el paralelo de Punta Gorda tiene una anchura de dos millas marinas. Sin embargo, sus límites exteriores harán las inflexiones necesarias pura que no sobrepasen los veriles de los canales en las aguas de uso común y para que queden incluídos los canales de acceso a los puertos.

Tales límites no se aproximarán a menos de quinientos metros de los veriles de los canales situados en las aguas de uso común ni se alejarán más de quinientos metros de los veriles y la boca de los canales de acceso a los puertos.

**Art. 3.** Fuera de las franjas costeras, la jurisdicción de cada Parte se aplicará, asimismo, a los buques de su bandera.

La misma jurisdicción se aplicará también a buques de terceras banderas involucrados en siniestros con buques de dicha Parte.

No obstante lo establecido en los parrafos primero y segundo, será apli-

73

cable la jurisdicción de una Parte en todos los casos en que se afecte su seguridad o se cometan ilícitos que tengan efecto en su territorio, cualquiera fuere la bandera del buque involucrado.

En el caso en que se afecte la seguridad de ambas Partes o el ilícito tenga efecto en ambos territorios, privará la jurisdicción de la Parte cuya franja costera esté más próxima que la franja costera de la otra Parte, respecto del lugar de aprehensión del buque.

**Art. 4.** En los casos no previstos en el artículo 3° y sin perjuicio de lo establecido específicamente en otras disposiciones del presente Tratado, será aplicable la jurisdicción de una u otra Parte conforme al criterio de la mayor proximidad a una u otra franja costera del lugar en que se produzcan los hechos considerados.

**Art. 5.** La autoridad interviniente que verificara un ilícito podrá realizar la persecución del buque infractor hasta el limite de la franja constera de la otra Parte.

Si el buque infractor penetrara en dicha franja costera, se solicitará la colaboración de la otra Parte, la que en todos los casos hará entrega del infractor para su sometimiento a la autoridad que inició la represión.

**Art. 6.** Las autoridades de una Parte podrán apresar a un buque de bandera de la otra cuando sea sorprendido en flagrante violación de las disposiciones sobre pesca y conservación y preservación de recursos vivos y sobre contaminación vigentes en las aguas de uso común, debiendo comunicarlo de inmediato a dicha Parte y poner el buque infractor a disposición de sus autoridades.

Capitulo II — *Navegacion y Obras*

**Art. 7.** Las Partes se reconocen recíprocamente, a perpetuidad y bajo cualquier circunstancia, la libertad de navegación en todo el Río para los buques de sus banderas.

**Art. 8.** Las Partes se garantizan mutuamente el mantenimiento de las facilidades que se han otorgado hasta el presente, para el acceso a sus respectivos puertos.

**Art. 9.** Las Partes se obligan recíprocamente a desarrollar en sus respectivas franjas costeras las ayudas a la navegación y el balizamiento adecuados y a coordinar el desarrollo de los mismos en las aguas de uso común, fuera de los canales, en forma tal de facilitar la navegación y garantizar su seguridad.

**Art. 10.** Las Partes tienen derecho al uso, en igualdad de condiciones y bajo cualquier circunstancia, de todos los canales situados en las aguas de uso común.

**Art. 11.** En las aguas de uso común se permitirá la navegación de buques públicos y privados de los países de la Cuenca del Plata, y de mercantes, públicos y privados, de terceras banderas, sin perjuicio de los derechos ya otorgados por las Partes en virtud de Tratados vigentes. Además, cada Parte permitirá el paso de buques de guerra de terceras banderas autorizados por la otra, siempre que no afecte su orden público o su seguridad.

**Art. 12.** Fuera de las franjas costeras las Partes, conjunta o individualmente, pueden construir canales u otros tipos de obras de acuerdo con las disposiciones establecidas en los artículos 17° a 22°.

La Parte que construya o haya construído una obra tendrá, a su cargo el mantenimiento y la administración de la misma.

La Parte que construya o haya construido un canal dictará, asimismo, la reglamentación respectiva, ejercerá el control de su cumplimiento con los medios adecuados a ese fin y tendrá a su cargo la extracción, remoción y demolición de buques, artefactos navales, aeronaves, restos náufragos o de carga o cualesquiera otros objetos que constituyan un obstáculo o peligro para la navegación y que se hallen hundidos o encallados en dicha vía.

**Art. 13.** En los casos no previstos en el artículo 12°, las Partes coordinarán, a través de la Comisión Administradora, la distribución razonable de responsabilidades en el mantenimiento, administración y reglamentación de los distintos tramos de los canales, teniendo en cuenta los intereses especiales de cada Parte y las obras que cada una de ellas hubiese realizado.

**Art. 14.** Toda reglamentación referida a los canales situados en las aguas de uso común y su modificación sustancial o permanente se efectuará previa consulta con la otra Parte.

En ningún caso y bajo ninguna circunstancia, una reglamentación podrá causar perjuicio sensible a los intereses de la navegación de cualquiera de las Partes.

**Art. 15.** La responsabilidad civil, penal y administrativa derivada de hechos que afecten la navegación de un canal, el uso del mismo o sus instalaciones, estará bajo la competencia de las autoridades de la Parte que mantiene y administra el canal y se regirá por su legislación.

**Art. 16.** La Comisión Administradora distribuirá entre las Partes la obligación de extraer, remover o demoler los buques, artefactos navales, aeronaves, restos náufragos o de carga, o cualesquiera otros objetos que constituyan un obstáculo o peligro para la navegación y que se hallen hundidos o encallados, fuera de los canales, teniendo en cuenta el criterio establecido en el artículo 4° y los intereses de cada Parte.

**Art. 17.** La Parte que proyecte la construcción de nuevos canales, la

75

modificación o alteración significativa de los ya existentes o la realización de cualesquiera otras obras, deberá communcarlo a la Comisión Administradora, la cual determinará sumariamente y en un plazo máximo de treinta días, si el proyecto puede producir perjuicio sensible al interés de la navegación de la otra Parte o al régimen del Río.

Si así se resolviere o no se llegase a un acuerdo al respecto, la Parte interesada deberá notificar el proyecto a la otra Parte a través de la misma Comisión.

En la notificación deberán figurar los aspectos esenciales de la obra y, si fuere el caso, el modo de su operación y los demás datos técnicos que permitan a la Parte notificada hacer una evaluación del efecto probable que la obra ocacionará a la navegación o al régimen del Río.

**Art. 18.** La Parte notificada dispondrá de un plazo de ciento ochenta días para expedirse sobre el proyecto, a partir del día en que su Delegación ante la Comisión Administradora haya recibido la notificación.

En el caso de que la documentación mancionada en el artículo 17° fuera incompleta, la Parte notificada dispondrá de treinta días para hacérselo saber a la Parte que proyecta realizar la obra, por intermedio de la Comisión Administradora.

El plazo de ciento ochenta días precedentemente señalado sólo comenzará a correr a partir del día en que la Delegación de la Parte notificada haya recibido la documentación completa.

Este plazo podrá ser prorrogado prudencialmente por la Comisión Administradora si la complejidad del proyecto así lo requiriese.

**Art. 19.** Si la Parte notificada no opusiera objeciones o no contestara dentro del plazo establecido en el artículo 18°, la otra Parte podrá realizar o autorizar la realización de la obra proyectada.

La Parte notificada tendrá, asimismo, derecho a optar por participar en igualdad de condiciones en la realización de la obra, en cuyo caso deberá comunicarlo a la otra Parte, por intermedio de la Comisión Administradora, dentro del mismo plazo a que se alude en el párrafo primero.

**Art. 20.** La Parte notificada tendrá derecho a inspeccionar las obras que se estén ejecutando para comprobar si se ajustan al proyecto presentado.

**Art. 21.** Si la Parte notificada llegare a la conclusión de que la ejecución de la obra o el programa de operación puede producir perjuicio sensible a la navegación o al régimen del Río; lo comunicará a la otra Parte por intermedio de la Comisión Administradora, dentro del plazo de ciento ochenta días fijado en el artículo 18°.

La comunicación deberá precisar cuáles aspectos de la obra o del programa de operación podrán causar un perjuicio sensible a la navegación o al régimen del Río, las razones técnicas que permitan llegar a esa conclusión y las modificaciones que sugiera al proyecto o al programa de operación.

**Art. 22.** Si las Partes no llegaran a un acuerdo dentro de los ciento ochenta días contados a partir de la comunicación a que se refiere el artículo 21°, se observará el procedimiento indicado en la Parte Cuarta (Solución de Controversias).

## Capitulo III — *Practicaje*

**Art. 23.** La profesión de práctico en el Río sólo será ejercida por los profesionales habilitados por las autoridades de una u otra Parte.

**Art. 24.** Todo buque que zarpe de puerto argentino o uruguayo tomará práctico de la nacionalidad del puerto de zarpada.

El buque que provenga del exterior del Río tomará práctico de la nacionalidad del puerto de destino.

El contacto que el buque tenga, fuera de puerto, con la autoridad de cualquiera de las Partes, no modificará el criterio inicialmente seguido para determinar la nacionalidad del práctico.

En los demás casos no previstos anteriormente el práctico prodrá ser indistintamente argentino o uruguayo.

**Art. 25.** Terminadas sus tareas de pilotaje, los prácticos argentinos y uruguayos podrán desembarcar libremente en los puertos de una u otra Parte a los que arriben los buques en los que cumplieron su cometido.

Las Partes brindarán a los mencionados prácticos las máximas facilidades para el mejor cumplimiento de su función.

**Art. 26.** Las Partes establecerán, en sus respectivas reglamentaciones, normas coincidentes sobre practicaje en el Río y el régimen de exenciones.

## Capitulo IV — *Facilidades Portuarias; Alijos y Complementos de Carga*

**Art. 27.** Las Partes se comprometen a realizar los estudios y adoptar las medidas necesarias con vistas a dar la mayor eficacia posible a sus servicios portuarios, de modo de brindar las mejores condiciones de rendimiento y seguridad, y ampliar las facilidades que mutuamente se otorgan en sus respectivos puertos.

**Art. 28.** Sin perjuicio de lo establecido en el artículo 27° las tareas de alijo y complemento de carga se realizarán, exclusivamente, en las zonas que fije la Comisión Administradora de acuerdo con las necesidades técnicas y de seguridad en materia de cargas contaminantes o peligrosas.

Habrá siempre un número igual de zonas situadas en la proximidad de las costas de cada Parte, pero fuera de las respectivas franjas costeras.

77

**Art. 29.** Las zonas a que se refiere el artículo 28° podrán ser utilizadas indistintamente por cualquiera de las Partes.

**Art. 30.** En las operaciones de alijo intervendrán las autoridades de la Parte a cuyo puerto tenga destino la carga alijada.

**Art. 31.** En las operaciones de complemento de carga intervendrán las autoridades de la Parte de cuyo puerto provenga la carga complementaria.

**Art. 32.** En los casos en que los puertos de destino y de procedencia de la carga pertenezcan a terceros Estados, las operaciones de alijo y de complemento de carga serán fiscalizadas por las autoridades argentinas o uruguayas según se realicen respectivamente en las zonas situadas más próximas a una u otra franja costera, de conformidad con lo que establece el artículo 28°.

## Capitulo V — *Salvaguarda de la Vida Humana*

**Art. 33.** Fuera de las franjas costeras, la autoridad de la Parte que inicie la operación de búsqueda y rescate tendrá la dirección de la misma.

**Art. 34.** La autoridad que inicie una operación de búsqueda y rescate, lo comunicará inmediatamente a la autoridad competente de la otra Parte.

**Art. 35.** Cuando la magnitud de la operación lo aconseje, la autoridad de la Parte que la dirige podrá solicitar a la de la otra el concurso de medios, reteniendo el control de la operación y obligándose a su vez, a suministrar información sobre su desarrollo.

**Art. 36.** Cuando por cualquier causa la autoridad de una de las Partes no pueda iniciar o continuar una operación de búsqueda y rescate, solicitará a la de la otra que asuma la responsabilidad de la dirección y ejecución, facilitándole toda la colaboración posible.

**Art. 37.** Las unidades de superficie o aéreas de ambas Partes que se hallen efectuando operaciones de búsqueda y rescate, podrán entrar o salir de cualquiera de los respectivos territorios, sin cumplir las formalidades exigidas normalmente.

## Capitulo VI — *Salvamento*

**Art. 38.** El salvamento de un buque de la bandera de unasdes las Partes, fuera de las franjas costeras, podrá ser efectuado por la autoridad o las empresas de cualquiera de ellas a opción del capitán o armador del buque siniestrado, sin perjuicio de lo que respecto de esa opción dispongan las reglamentaciones internas de cada Parte.

Sin embargo, la tarea de salvamento de un buque de bandera de cualquiera de las Partes, siniestrado en un canal situado en las aguas de uso común, se efectuará por la autoridad o las empresas de la Parte que lo administra cuando el buque siniestrado constituya un obstáculo o peligro para la navegación en dicho canal.

**Art. 39.** El salvamento de un buque de tercera bandera se efectuará por la autoridad o las empresas de la Parte cuya franja costera esté más próxima al lugar en que se encuentre el buque que solicita asistencia.

No obstante, la tarea de salvamento de un buque de tercera bandera siniestrado en un canal situado en las aguas de uso común se efectuara por la autoridad o las empresas de la Parte que administra dicho canal.

**Art. 40.** Sin perjuicio de lo establecido en los artículos 38° y 39°, cuando la autoridad o las empresas de la Parte a la que corresponda la tarea de salvamento desistan de realizarla, dicha tarea podrá ser efectuada por la autoridad o las empresas de la otra Parte.

El desistimiento a que se refiere el párrafo primero será notificado de inmediato a la otra Parte.

## Capitulo VII — *Lecho y Subsuelo*

**Art. 41.** Cada Parte podrá explorar y explotar los recursos del lecho y del subsuelo del Río en Las zonas adyacentes a sus respectivas costas, hasta la línea determinada por las siguientes puntos geográficos fijados en las cartas confeccionadas por la Comisión Mixta Uruguayo-Argentina de Levantamiento Integral del Río de la Plata, publicadas por el Servicio de Hidrografía Naval de la República Argentina, que forman parte del presente Tratado:

[23 points: omitted] (see the map on p. 87).

**Art. 42.** Las instalaciones u otras obras necesarias para la exploración o explotación de los recursos del lecho y del subsuelo, no podrán interferir la navegación en el Río en los pasajes o canales utilizados normalmente.

**Art. 43.** El yacimiento o depósito que se extienda a uno y otro lado de la línea establecida en el artículo 41°, será explotado de froma tal que la distribución de los volumenes del recurso que se extraiga de dicho yacimiento o depósito sea proporcional al volumen del mismo que se encuentre respectivamente a cada lado de dicha línea.

Cada Parte realizará la explotación de los yacimientos o depósitos que se hallen en esas condiciones, sin causar perjuicio sensible a la otra Parte y de acuerdo con las exigencias de un aprovechamiento integral y racional del recurso, ajustado al criterio establecido en el párrafo primero.

## Capitulo VIII — *Islas*

**Art. 44.** Las islas existentes o las que en el futuro emerjan en el Río, pertenecen a una u otra Parte según se hallen a uno u otro lado de la línea indicada en el artículo 41°, con excepción de lo que se establece para la Isla Martín García en el artículo 45°.

**Art. 45.** La Isla Martín García será destinada exclusivamente a reserva natural para la conservación y preservación de la fauna y flora autóctonas, bajo jurisdicción de la República Argentina, sin perjuicio de lo establecido en el artículo 63°.

**Art. 46.** Si la Isla Martín Garciá se uniera en el futuro a otra isla, el límite correspondiente se trazará siguiendo el perfil de la Isla Martín García que resulta de la carta H-118 a la que se refiere el artículo 41°. Sin embargo, los aumentos por aluvión de Martín García, que afecten sus actuales accesos naturales a les canales de Martín García (Buenos Aires) y del Infierno, pertenecerán a esta Isla.

Capitulo IX — *Contaminacion*

**Art. 47.** A los efectos del presente Tratado se entiende por contaminación la introducción directa o indirecta, por el hombre, en el medio acuático, de sustancias o energía de las que resulten efectos nocivos.

**Art. 48.** Cada Parte se obliga a proteger y preservar el medio acuático y, en particular, a prevenir su contaminación, dictando las normas y adoptando las medidas apropiadas, de conformidad a los convenios internacionales aplicables y con adecuación, en lo pertinente, a las pautas y recomendaciones de los organismos tècnicos internacionales.

**Art. 49.** Las Partes se obligan a no disminuir en sus respectivos ordenamientos jurídicos:

(*a*) las exigencias técnicas en vigor para provenir la contaminación de las aguas, y

(*b*) la severidad de las sanciones establecidas para los easos de infracción.

**Art. 50.** Las Partes se obligan a informarse recíprocamente sobre toda norma que prevean dictar con relación a la contaminación de las aguas.

**Art. 51.** Cada Parte será responsable frente a la otra por los daños inferidos como consecuencia de la contaminación causada por sus propias actividades o por las de personas físicas o jurídicas domiciliadas en su territorio.

**Art. 52.** La jurisdicción de cada Parte respecto de toda infracción cometida en materia de contaminación se ejercerá sin perjuicio de los derechos de la otra Parte a resarcirse de los daños que haya sufrido, a su vez, como consecuencia de la misma infracción.

A esos efectos, las Partes se prestarán mutua cooperación.

Capitulo X — *Pesca*

**Art. 53.** Cada Parte tiene derecho exclusivo de pesca en la respectiva franja costera indicada en el artículo 2°.

Fuera de las franjas costeras, las Partes se reconocen mutuamente la libertad de pesca en el Río para los buques de sus banderas.

**Art. 54.** Las Partes acordarán las normas que regularán las actividades de pesca en el Río en relación con la conservación y preservación de los recursos vivos.

**Art. 55.** Cuando la intensidad de la pesca lo haga necesario, las Partes acordarán los volúmenes máximos de captura por especies como asimismo los ajustes periódicos correspondientes. Dichos volúmenes de captura serán distribuídos por igual entre las Partes.

**Art. 56.** Las Partes intercambiarán, regularmente, la información pertinente sobre esfuerzo de pesca y captura por especie así como sobre la nómina de buques habilitados para pescar en las aguas de uso común.

Capitulo XI — *Investigacion*

**Art. 57.** Cada Parte tiene derecho a realizar estudios e investigaciones de carácter científico en todo el Río, bajo condición de dar aviso previo a la otra Parte, indicando las características de los mismos, y de hacer conocer a ésta los resultados obtenidos.

Cada Parte tiene, además, derecho a participar en todas las obras de cualquier estudio o investigación que emprenda la otra Parte.

**Art. 58.** Las Partes promoverán la realización de estudios conjuntos de carácter científico de interés común y, en especial, los relativos al levantamiento integral del Río.

Capitulo XII — *Comision Administradora*

**Art. 59.** Las Partes constituyen una comisión mixta que se denominará Comisión Administradora del Río de la Plata, compuesta de igual número de delegados por cada una de ellas.

**Art. 60.** La Comisión Administradora gozará de personalidad jurídica para el cumplimiento de su cometido. Las Partes le asignarán los recursos necesarios y todos los elementos y facilidades indispensables para su funcionamiento.

**Art. 61.** La Comisión Administradora podrá constituir los órganos técnicos que estime necesarios.

Funcionará en forma permanente y tendrá su correspondiente Secretaría.

**Art. 62.** Las Partes acordarán, por medio de notas reversales, el Estatuto de la Comisión Administradora. Esta dictará se reglamento interno.

**Art. 63.** Las Partes acuerdan asignar como sede de la Comisión Administradora la Isla Martín García.

La Comisión Administradora dispondrá de los locales y terrenos adecuados para su funcionamiento y construirá y administrará un parque dedicado a la memoria de los héroes comunes a ambos pueblos, respetando la jurisdicción y el destino convenidos en el artículo 45°. La República Argentina dispondrá de los locales, instalaciones y terrenos para el ejercicio de su jurisdicción.

En el acuerdo de sede correspondiente se incluirán las disposiciones que regulen las relaciones entre la República Argentina y la Comisión, sobre la base de que la sede asignada de conformidad con el párrafo primero está amparada por la inviolabilidad y demás privilegios establecidos por el Derecho Internacional.

**Art. 64.** La Comisión Administradora celebrará, oportunamente, con ambas Partes, los acuerdos conducentes a precisar los privilegios e inmunidades reconocidos por la práctica internacional a los miembros y personal de la misma.

**Art. 65.** Para la adopción de las decisiones de la Comisión Administradora cada Delegación tendrá un voto.

**Art. 66.** La Comisión Administradora desempeñará las siguientes funciones:

*(a)* promover la realización conjunta de estudios e investigaciones de carácter científico, con especial referencia a la evaluación, conservación y preservación de los recursos vivos y su racional explotación y la prevención eliminación de la contaminación y otros efectos nocivos que puedan derivar del uso, exploración y explotación de las aguas del Río;

*(b)* dictar las normas reguladoras de la actividad de pesca en el Río en relación con la conservación y preservación de los recursos vivos;

*(c)* coordinar las normas reglamentarias sobre practicaje;

*(d)* coordinar la adopción de planes, manuales, terminología y medios de comunicación comunes en materia de búsqueda y rescate;

*(e)* establecer el procedimiento a seguir y la información a suministrar en los casos en que las unidades de una Parte que participen en operaciones de búsqueda y rescate ingresen al territorio de la otra o salgan de él;

*(f)* determinar las formalidades a cumplir en los casos en que deba ser introducido transitoriamente, en territorio de la otra Parte, material para la ejecución de operaciones de búsqueda y rescate;

*(g)* coordinar las ayudas a la navegación y el balizamiento;

*(h)* fijar las zonas de alijo y complemento de carga conforme a lo esta-

blecido en el artículo 28°;

(*i*) trasmitir en forma expedita, a las Partes, las comunicaciones, consultas, informaciones y notificaciones que las mismas se efectúen de conformidad a la Parte Primera del presente Tratado;

(*j*) cumplir las otras funciones que la han sido asignadas por el presente Tratado y aquéllas que las Partes convengan otorgarle en su Estatuto o por medio de notas reversales u otras formas de acuerdo.

**Art. 67.** La Comisión Administradora informará periódicamente a los Gobiernos de cada una de las Partes sobre el desarrollo de sus actividades.

Capitulo XIII — *Procedimiento Conciliatorio*

**Art. 68.** Cualquier controversia que se suscitare entre las Partes con relación al Río de la Plata será considerada por la Comisión Administradora, a propuesta de cualquiera de ellas.

**Art. 69.** Si en el término de ciento veinte días la Comisión no lograra llegar a un acuerdo, lo notificará a ambas Partes, las que procurarán solucionar la cuestión por negociaciones directas.

## PARTE SEGUNDA — FRENTE MARITIMO

Capitulo XIV — *Limite Lateral Maritimo*

**Art. 70.** El límite lateral marítimo y el de la plataforma continental, entre la República Oriental del Uruguay y la República Argentina, está definido por la línea de equidistancia determinada por el método de costas adyacentes, que parte del punto medio de la línea de base constituída por la recta imaginaria que une Punta del Este (República Oriental del Uruguay) con Punta Rasa del Cabo San Antonio (República Argentina).

**Art. 71.** El yacimiento o depósito que se extienda a uno y otro lado del límite establecido en el artículo 70°, será explotado en forma tal que la distribución de los volúmenes del recurso que se extraiga de dicho yacimiento o depósito sea proporcional al volumen del mismo que se encuentre respectivamente a cada lado de dicho límite.

Cada Parte realizará la explotación de los yacimientos o depósitos que se hallen en esas condiciones sin causar perjuicio sensible a la otra Parte y de acuerdo con las exigencias de un aprovechamiento integral y racional del recurso, ajustado al criterio establecido en el párrafo primero.

Capitulo XV — *Navegacion*

**Art. 72.** Ambas Partes garantizan la libertad de navegación y sobrevuelo en los mares bajo sus respectivas jurisdicciones más allá de las doce millas marinas medidas desde las correspondientes líneas de base y en la desembocadura del Río de la Plata a partir de su límite exterior, sin otras restricciones que las derivadas del ejercicio, por cada Parte, de sus potestades en materia de exploración, conservación y explotación de recursos; protección y preservación del medio; investigación cientiífica y construcción y emplazamiento de instalaciones y las referidas en el artículo 86°.

Capitulo XVI — *Pesca*

**Art. 73.** Las Partes acuerdan establecer una zona común de pesca, más allá de las doce millas marinas medidas desde las correspondientes líneas de base costeras, para los buques de su bandera debidamente matriculados. Dicha zona es la determinada por dos arcos de circunferencias de doscientas millas marinas de radio, cuyos centros de trazado están ubicados respectivamente en Punta del Este (República Oriental del Uruguay) y en Punta Rasa del Cabo San Antonio (República Argentina).

**Art. 74.** Las volúmenes de captura por especies se distribuirán en forma equitativa, proporcional a la riqueza ictícola que aporta cada una de las Partes, evaluada en base a criterios científicos y económicos.

El volumen de captura que una de las Partes autorice a buques de terceras banderas se imputará al cupo que corresponda a dicha Parte.

**Art. 75.** Las áreas establecidas en los permisos de pesca que la República Argentina y la República Oriental del Uruguay expidan a buques de terceras banderas en sus respectivas jurisdicciones marítimas, no podrán exceder la línea fijada en el artículo 70°.

**Art. 76.** Las Partes ejercerán las correspondientes funciones de control y vigilancia a ambos lados, respectivamente, de la línea a que se refiere el artículo 75° y las coordinarán adecuadamento.

Las Partes intercambiarán la nómina de los buques de sus respectivas banderas que operen en la zona común.

**Art. 77.** En ningún caso las disposiciones de este capítulo son aplicables a la captura de mamíferos acuáticos.

Capitulo XVII — *Contaminacion*

**Art. 78.** Se prohibe el vertimiento de hidrocarburos provenientes del lavado de tanques, achique de sentinas y de lastre y, en general, cualquier otra acción capaz de tener efectos contaminantes, en la zona comprendida entre las siguientes líneas imaginarias:

(*a*) partiendo de Punta del Este (República Oriental del Uruguay) hasta
(*b*) un punto de latitud 36°14' Sur, longitud 53°32' Oeste; de aquí hasta
(*c*) un punto de latitud 37°32' Sur, longitud 55°23' Oeste; de aquí hasta

84

(*d*) Punta Rasa del Cabo San Antonio (República Argentina) y finalmente desde este punto hasta el inicial en Punta del Este.

## Capitulo XVIII — *Investigacion*

**Art. 79.** Cada Parte autorizará a la otra a efectuar estudios e investigaciones de carácter exclusivamente científico en su respectiva jurisdicción marítima dentro de la zona de interés común determinada en el artículo 73°, siempre que le haya dado aviso previo con la adecuada antelación e indicado las características de los estudios o investigaciones a realizarse, y las áreas y plazas en que se efectuarán.

Esta autorización sólo podrá ser denegada en circumstancias excepcionales y por períodos limitados.

La Parte autorizante tiene derecho a participar en todas las fases de esos estudios e investigaciones y a conocer y disponer de sus resultados.

## Capitulo XIX — *Comisión Técnica Mixta*

**Art. 80.** Las Partes constituyen una Comisión Técnica Mixta compuesta de igual número de delegados por cada Parte, que tendrá por cometido la realización de estudios y la adopción y coordinación de planes y medidas relativas a la conservación, preservación y racional explotación de los recursos vivos y a la protección del medio marino en la zona de interés común que se determina en el artículo 73°.

**Art. 81.** La Comisión Técnica Mixta gozará de personalidad para el cumplimiento de su cometido y dispondrá de los fondos necesarios a esos efectos.

**Art. 82.** La Comisión Técnica Mixta desempeñará las siguientes funciones:

(*a*) fijar los volúmenes de captura por especie y distribuirlos entre las Partes, de conformidad a lo establecido en el artículo 74°, así como ajustarlos periódicamente;

(*b*) promover la realización conjunta de estudios e investigaciones de carácter científico, particularmente dentro de la zona de interés común, con especial referencia a la evaluación, conservación y preservación de los recursos vivos y su racional explotación y a la prevención y eliminación de la contaminación y otros efectos nocivos que puedan derivar del uso, exploración y explotación del medio marino;

(*c*) formular recomendaciones y presentar proyectos tendientes a asegurar el mantenimiento del valor y equilibrio en los sistemas bioecológicos;

(*d*) establecer normas y medidas relativas a la explotación racional de las especies en la zona de interés común y a la prevención y eliminación de la contaminación;

(*e*) estructurar planes de preservación, conservación y desarrollo de los recursos vivos en la zona de interés común, que serán sometidos a la consideración de los respectivos Gobiernos;

(*f*) promover estudios y presentar proyectos sobre armonización de las legislaciones de las Partes repectivas a las materias que son objeto del cometido de la Comisión;

(*g*) trasmitir, en forma expedita, a las Partes las comunicaciones, consultas e informaciones que las mismas intercam — bien de acuerdo con lo dispuesto en la Parte Segunda del presente Tratado;

(*h*) cumplir las demás funciones que las Partes le asignen en su Estatuto, o por medio de notas reversales u otras formas de acuerdo.

**Art. 83.** La Comisión Técnica Mixta tendrá su sede en la Ciudad de Montevideo, pero podrá reunirse en los territorios de ambas Partes.

**Art. 84.** Las Partes acordarán, por medio de notas reversales, el Estatuto de la Comisión Técnica Mixta. Esta dictará su reglamento interno.

## PARTE TERCERA — DEFENSA

Capitulo XX

**Art. 85.** Las cuestiones relativas a la defensa de toda el área focal del Río de la Plata son de competencia exclusiva de las Partes.

**Art. 86.** En ejercicio de su propia defensa ante amenaza de agresión, cada Parte podrá adoptar las medidas necesarias y transitorias para ello en dicha área focal, fuera de las respectivas franjas costeras de jurisdicción exclusiva en el Río de la Plata y de una franja de doce millas marinas a partir de las respectivas líneas de base costeras del mar territorial, sin causar perjuicios sensibles a la otra Parte.

## PARTE CUARTA — SOLUCION DE CONTROVERSIAS

Capitulo XXI

**Art. 87.** Toda controversia acerca de la interpretación o aplicación del presente Tratado, que no pudiere solucionarse por negociaciones directas, podrá ser sometida, por cualquiera de las Partes, a la Corte Internacional de Justicia.

En los casos a que se refieren los artículos 68° y 69°, cualquiera de las Partes podrá someter toda controversia sobre la interpretación o aplicación del presente Tratado a la Corte Internacional de Justicia cuando dicha controversia no hubiese podido solucionarse dentro de los ciento ochenta días siguientes a la notificación aludida en el artículo 69°.

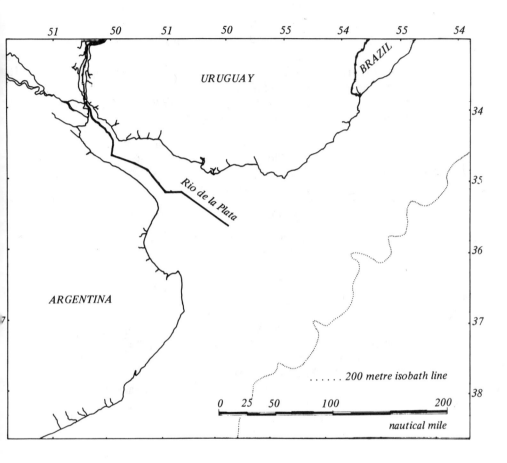

51   50   51   50   55   54   55   54

URUGUAY

BRAZIL

34

Rio de la Plata

35

36

ARGENTINA

37

...... 200 metre isobath line

0   25   50   100   200

nautical mile

38

Source: Shigeru Oda

*Off the coasts of Argentina and Uruguay (Article 41 of the*
*Agreement between Argentina and Uruguay, p. 79)*

PARTE QUINTA — DISPOSICIONES TRANSITORIAS Y FINALES

Capitulo XXII — *Disposiciones Transitorias*

**Art. 88.** Hasta tanto la Comisión Administradora fije las zonas de alijos y complementos de carga referidas en el artículo 28°, se establecen, a esos efectos, las siguientes zonas:

Zona A: entre los parelelos de latitud Sur 35°04′ y 35°08′; y entre los meridianos de longitud Oeste 56°00′ y 56°02′;

Zona B: entre los paralelos de latitud Sur 35°30′ y 35°33′; y entre los meridianos de longitud Oeste 56°30′ y 56°36′.

**Art. 89.** La Comisión Administradora se constituirá dentrode los setenta días siguientes al canje de los instrumentos de ratificación del presente Tratado.

**Art. 90.** Las Partes publicarán oportunamente, en las cartas marinas correspondientes, el trazado del límite lateral marítimo.

**Art. 91.** La Comisión Técnica Mixta se constituirá dentro de los sesenta días siguientes al canje de los instrumentos de ratificación del presente Tratado.

Capitulo XXIII — *Ratificación y Entrada en Vigor*

**Art. 92.** El presente Tratado será ratificado de acuerdo con los procedimientos previstos en los respectivos ordenamientos jurídicos de las Partes y entrará en vigor por el canje de los instrumentos de ratificación que se realizará en la Ciudad de Buenos Aires.

En fe de lo cual, los Plenipotenciarios arriba mencionados firman y sellan dos ejemplares del mismo tenor en la Ciudad de Montevideo a los diecinueve días del mes de noviembre de mil novecientos setenta y tres.

**CANADA—DENMARK:**
— **Agreement relating to the Delimitation of the Continental Shelf between Greenland and Canada, 1973**

Signed at Ottawa on 17 December 1973.

The Government of Canada and the Government of the Kingdom of Denmark,

Having decided to establish in the area between Greenland and the

Canadian Arctic Islands a dividing line beyond which neither Party in exercising its rights under the Convention on the Continental Shelf of April 29, 1958 will extend its sovereign rights for the purpose of exploration and exploitation of the natural resources of the continental shelf,

Have agreed as follows:

**Art. I.** The dividing line in the area between Greenland and the Canadian Arctic Islands, established for the purpose of each Party's exploration and exploitation of the natural resources of that part of the continental shelf which in accordance with international law appertains to Denmark and to Canada respectively, is a median line which has been determined and adjusted by mutual agreement.

**Art. II.** 1. In implementation of the principle set forth in Article I, the dividing line in the area between latitude 61°00′ N and latitude 75°00′ N (Davis Strait and Baffin Bay) shall be a series of geodesic lines joining the following points:

| Point No. | Latitude | Longitude |
|---|---|---|
| 1 | 61°00′0 | 57°13′1 |
| . | [omitted: See map on p. 91] | |
| . | | |
| . | | |
| 113 | 75°00′0 | 73°16′3 |

The positions of the above mentioned points have been computed from straight baselines along the coast of the Canadian Arctic Islands and of Greenland. . . .

2. In *Nares Strait* the dividing line shall be two series of geodesic lines joining the following points:

| Point No. | Latitude | Longitude |
|---|---|---|
| Series A: | | |
| 114 | 76°41′4 | 75°00′0 |
| | [omitted: See map on p. 91] | |
| 122 | 80°49′2 | 66°29′0 |
| Series B: | | |
| 123 | 80°49′8 | 66°26′3 |
| | [omitted: See map on p. 91] | |
| 127 | 82°13′0 | 60°00′0 |

The positions of the above mentioned points are defined by latitude and longitude on Canadian Hydrographic Service Charts 7071 of July 31, 1964 and 7072 of April 30, 1971. . . .

3. That portion of the dividing line joining point 113 to point 114 is a geodesic line.

4. For the time being the Parties have not deemed it necessary to draw the dividing line further north than point No. 127 or further south than point No. 1. . . .

**Art. III.** In view of the inadequacies of existing hydrographic charts for certain areas and failing a precise determination of the low-water line in all sectors along the coast of Greenland and the eastern coasts of the Canadian Arctic Islands, neither Party shall issue licences for exploitation of mineral resources in areas bordering the dividing line without the prior agreement of the other Party as to the exact determination of the geographic co-ordinates of points of that part of the dividing line bordering upon the areas in question.

**Art. IV.** 1. The Parties undertake to co-operate and to exchange all relevant data and measurements with a view to obtaining and improving the hydrographic and geodetic knowledge necessary for more precise charting and mapping of the region covered by this Agreement. When knowledge is obtained enabling the Parties to estimate the datum shift between the 1927 North American Datum and the Qornoq Datum, the geographic coordinates of points listed in Article II shall be adjusted and re-listed in relation to both the 1927 North American Datum and the Qornoq Datum.

2. If new surveys or resulting charts or maps should indicate that the dividing line requires adjustment, the Parties agree that an adjustment will be carried out on the basis of the same principles as those used in determining the dividing line, and such adjustment shall be provided for in a Protocol to this Agreement.

**Art. V.** If any single geological petroleum structure or field, or any single geological structure or field of any other mineral deposit, including sand and gravel, extends across the dividing line and the part of such structure or field which is situated on one side of the dividing line is exploitable, wholly or in part, from the other side of the dividing line, the Parties shall seek to reach an agreement as to the exploitation of such structure or field.

**Art. VI.** Should international law concerning the delimitation of national jurisdiction over the continental shelf be altered in a manner acceptable to both Parties which could have an effect upon the dividing line in the area between 67° and 69° North latitude, each of the Parties shall waive jurisdiction over any part of the continental shelf which appertains to the other Party on the basis of the new agreed rules of international law concerning the delimitation of national jurisdiction over the continental shelf.

**Art. VII.** 1. This Agreement is subject to ratification. Instruments of

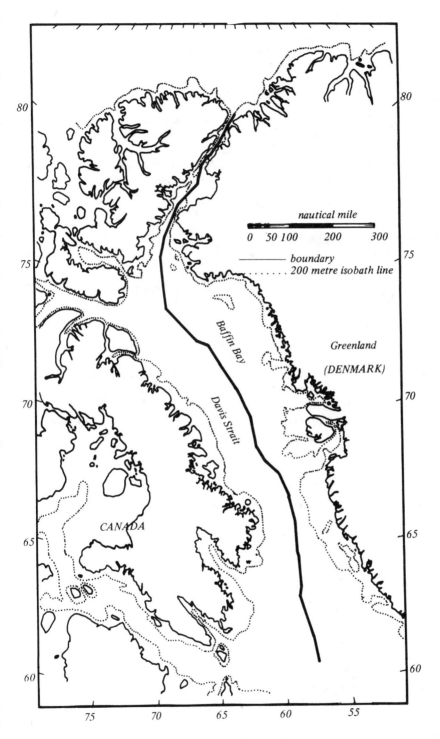

*Baffin Bay and Davis Strait*
*(Agreement between Canada and Denmark)*

ratification shall be exchanged at Copenhagen as soon as possible.

2. This Agreement shall enter into force on the date of the exchange of instruments of ratification.

*Annex* 1-4: [omitted: see the map on p. 94].

## JAPAN—REPUBLIC OF KOREA:
## — Agreement concerning the Establishment of Boundary in the Northern Part of the Continental Shelf adjacent to the two Countries

Signed at Seoul on 30 January 1974.

Japan and the Republic of Korea,

Desiring to promote the friendly relations existing between the two countries,

Desiring to establish the boundary in the northern part of the continental shelf adjacent to the two countries over which Japan and the Republic of Korea respectively exercise sovereign rights for the purpose of exploration and exploitation of mineral resources,

Have agreed as follows:

**Art. I.** 1. The boundary line between that part of the continental shelf appertaining to Japan and that part of the continental shelf appertaining to the Republic of Korea in the northern part of the continental shelf adjacent to the two countries shall be straight lines connecting the following points in the sequence given below:

| Point | 1  | 32°57.0′ N | 127°41.1′ E |
|-------|----|-----------|------------|
| Point | 2  | 32°57.5′ N | 127°41.9′ E |
| Point | 3  | 33°01.3′ N | 127°44.0′ E |
| Point | 4  | 33°08.7′ N | 127°48.3′ E |
| Point | 5  | 33°13.7′ N | 127°51.6′ E |
| Point | 6  | 33°16.2′ N | 127°52.3′ E |
| Point | 7  | 33°45.1′ N | 128°21.7′ E |
| Point | 8  | 33°47.4′ N | 128°25.5′ E |
| Point | 9  | 33°50.4′ N | 128°26.1′ E |
| Point | 10 | 34°08.2′ N | 128°41.3′ E |
| Point | 11 | 34°13.0′ N | 128°47.6′ E |
| Point | 12 | 34°18.0′ N | 128°52.8′ E |
| Point | 13 | 34°18.5′ N | 128°53.3′ E |
| Point | 14 | 34°24.5′ N | 128°57.3′ E |
| Point | 15 | 34°27.6′ N | 128°59.4′ E |

| Point 16 | 34°29.2′ N | 129°00.2′ E |
| Point 17 | 34°32.1′ N | 129°00.8′ E |
| Point 18 | 34°32.6′ N | 129°00.8′ E |
| Point 19 | 34°40.3′ N | 129°03.1′ E |
| Point 20 | 34°49.7′ N | 129°12.1′ E |
| Point 21 | 34°50.6′ N | 129°13.0′ E |
| Point 22 | 34°52.4′ N | 129°15.8′ E |
| Point 23 | 34°54.3′ N | 129°18.4′ E |
| Point 24 | 34°57.0′ N | 129°21.7′ E |
| Point 25 | 34°57.6′ N | 129°22.6′ E |
| Point 26 | 34°58.6′ N | 129°25.3′ E |
| Point 27 | 35°01.2′ N | 129°32.9′ E |
| Point 28 | 35°04.1′ N | 129°40.7′ E |
| Point 29 | 35°06.8′ N | 130°07.5′ E |
| Point 30 | 35°07.0′ N | 130°16.4′ E |
| Point 31 | 35°18.2′ N | 130°23.3′ E |
| Point 32 | 35°33.7′ N | 130°34.1′ E |
| Point 33 | 35°42.3′ N | 130°42.7′ E |
| Point 34 | 36°03.8′ N | 131°08.3′ E |
| Point 35 | 36°10.0′ N | 131°15.9′ E |

2. The boundary line is shown on the map annexed to this Agreement.

**Art. II.** If any single geological structure or field of mineral deposit beneath the seabed extends across the boundary line and the part of such structure or field which is situated on one side of the boundary line is exploitable, wholly or in part, from the other side of the boundary line, the Parties shall seek to reach agreement on the manner in which such structure or field shall be most effectively exploited. Any question upon which the Parties are unable to agree concerning the manner in which such structure or field shall be most effectively exploited shall, at the request of either Party, be referred to third-party arbitration. The decision of the arbitration shall be binding upon the Parties.

**Art. III.** This Agreement shall not affect the legal status of the superjacent waters or air space above.

**Art. IV.** This Agreement shall be ratified. The instruments of ratification shall be exchanged at Tokyo as soon as possible. This Agreement shall enter into force as from the date on which such instruments of ratification are exchanged.

*Map:* [omitted: see the map on p. 94].

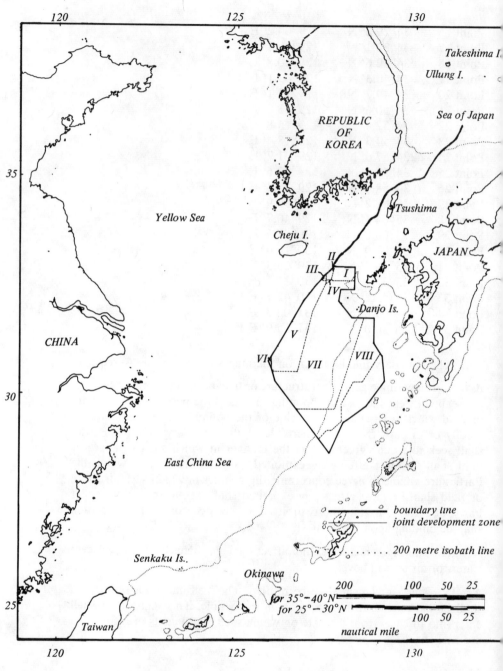

Sea of Japan and East China Sea (Agreement between Japan and Republic of Korea)

*Agreed Minutes*

1. The geographical coordinates as specified in paragraph 1 of Article I are based on Japan Maritime Safety Agency charts No. 302 of November 1958, 5th print and No. 1200 of July 1958, 2nd print.

2. Upon the request of either Government, the two Governments shall hold consultations regarding questions which may arise in connection with exploration and exploitation of mineral resources in the area which is the subject of the Agreement, including questions relating to fisheries.

### JAPAN—REPUBLIC OF KOREA:
— Agreement concerning Joint Development of the Southern Part of the Continental Shelf adjacent to the two Countries

Signed at Seoul on 30 January 1974.

Japan and the Republic of Korea,

Desiring to promote the friendly relations existing between the two countries,

Considering their mutual interest in carrying out jointly exploration and exploitation of petroleum resources in the southern part of the continental shelf adjacent to the two countries,

Resolving to reach a final practical solution to the question of the development of such resources,

Have agreed as follows:

**Art. I.** For the purposes of the Agreement:

(1) The term "natural resources" means petroleum (including natural gas) resources and other underground minerals which are produced in association with such resources;

(2) The term "concessionaire" means a person authorized by either Party under the laws and regulations of that Party to explore and/or exploit natural resources in the Joint Development Zone;

(3) The term "concessionaires of both Parties" means a concessionaire of one Party and a concessionaire of the other Party respectively authorized with respect to the same subzone of the Joint Development Zone;

(4) The term "operating agreement" means a contract concluded between concessionaires of both Parties for the purpose of exploring and exploiting natural resources in the Joint Development Zone;

(5) The term "operator" means a concessionaire designated and acting as such under the operating agreement with respect to a subzone of the Joint Development Zone.

95

**Art. II.** 1. The Joint Development Zone shall be the area of the continental shelf bounded by straight lines connecting the following points in the sequence given below:

|  | | |
|---|---|---|
| Point 1 | 32°57.0' N | 127°41.1' E |
| Point 2 | 32°53.4' N | 127°36.3' E |
| Point 3 | 32°46.2' N | 127°27.8' E |
| Point 4 | 32°33.6' N | 127°13.1' E |
| Point 5 | 32°10.5' N | 126°51.5' E |
| Point 6 | 30°46.2' N | 125°55.5' E |
| Point 7 | 30°33.3' N | 126°00.8' E |
| Point 8 | 30°18.2' N | 126°05.5' E |
| Point 9 | 28°36.0' N | 127°38.0' E |
| Point 10 | 29°19.0' N | 128°00.0' E |
| Point 11 | 29°43.0' N | 128°38.0' E |
| Point 12 | 30°19.0' N | 129°09.0' E |
| Point 13 | 30°54.0' N | 129°04.0' E |
| Point 14 | 31°13.0' N | 128°50.0' E |
| Point 15 | 31°47.0' N | 128°50.0' E |
| Point 16 | 31°47.0' N | 128°14.0' E |
| Point 17 | 32°12.0' N | 127°50.0' E |
| Point 18 | 32°27.0' N | 127°56.0' E |
| Point 19 | 32°27.0' N | 128°18.0' E |
| Point 20 | 32°57.0' N | 128°18.0' E |
| Point 1 | 32°57.0' N | 127°41.1' E |

2. The straight lines bounding the Joint Development Zone are shown on the map annexed to this Agreement.

**Art. III.** 1. The Joint Development Zone may be divided into subzones, each of which shall be explored and exploited by concessionaires of both Parties.

2. Each subzone shall be numbered and defined by reference to geographical coordinates in the Appendix to this Agreement. The Appendix may be amended by mutual consent of the Parties without modification of this Agreement.

**Art. IV.** 1. Each Party shall authorize one or more concessionaires with respect to each subzone within three months after the date of entry into force of this Agreement. When one Party authorizes more than one concessionaire with respect to one subzone, all such concessionaires shall have an undivided interest and shall be represented, for the purposes of this Agreement, by one concessionaire. In case of any change in concessionaire or in subzone, the Party concerned shall authorize one or more new concessionaires as soon as possible.

2. Each Party shall notify the other Party of its concessionaire or concessionaires without delay.

**Art. V.** 1. Concessionaires of both Parties shall enter into an operating agreement to carry out jointly exploration and exploitation of natural resources in the Joint Development Zone. Such operating agreement shall provide, inter alia, for the following:

(*a*) details relating to the sharing of natural resources and expenses in accordance with Article IX;

(*b*) designation of operator;

(*c*) treatment of sole risk operations;

(*d*) adjustment of fisheries interests;

(*e*) settlement of disputes.

2. The operating agreement and modifications thereof shall enter into force upon approval by the Parties. Approval of the Parties shall be deemed to have been given unless either Party explicitly disapproves the operating agreement or modifications thereof within two months after such operating agreement or modifications thereof have been submitted to the Parties for approval.

3. The Parties shall endeavour to ensure that the operating agreement enter into force within six months after concessionaires of both Parties have been authorized under paragraph 1 of Article IV.

**Art. VI.** 1. The operator shall be designated by agreement between concessionaires of both Parties. If concessionaires of both Parties fail to reach agreement between themselves as to the designation of the operator within three months after such concessionaires have been authorized, the Parties shall hold consultations concerning the designation of the operator. If the operator is not designated within two months after such consultations have started, concessionaires of both Parties shall determine the operator by lot-drawing.

2. The operator shall have exclusive control of all operations under the operating agreement and employ all personnel required for such operations, pay and discharge all expenses incurred in connection with such operations, and obtain all assets, including equipment, materials and supplies, necessary for carrying out such operations.

**Art. VII.** A concessionaire of one Party may acquire, construct, maintain, use and dispose of, in the territory of the other Party, buildings, platforms, tanks, pipelines, terminals and other facilities necessary for exploration or exploitation of natural resources in the Joint Development Zone in accordance with the laws and regulations of that other Party.

**Art. VIII.** A concessionaire of one Party shall not interfere with the discharging by a concessionaire of the other Party of its obligations under the laws and regulations of that other Party, insofar as such obligations are consistent with the provisions of this Agreement.

**Art. IX.** 1. Concessionaires of both Parties shall be respectively entitled to an equal share of natural resources extracted in the Joint Development Zone.

2. Expenses reasonably attributable to exploration and exploitation of such natural resources shall be shared in equal proportions between concessionaires of both Parties.

**Art. X.** 1. The right of concessionaires under this Agreement shall be exploration right and exploitation right.

2. The duration of exploration right shall be eight years from the date of entry into force of the operating agreement, subject to the provisions of paragraph 4 (3) of this Article.

3. The duration of exploitation right shall be thirty years from the aate of the establishment of such right. Concessionaires of both Parties may apply to the respective Parties for an extension of an additional period of five years. Such application may be made as many times as necessary. The Parties shall, upon receipt of such application, consult with each other to decide whether to approve such application.

4. (1) When commercial discovery of natural resources is made during the period of exploration right, concessionaires of both Parties may apply to the respective Parties for the establishment of exploitation right. When the Parties receive such application, they shall promptly hold consultations and shall without delay approve such application.

(2) When the Parties recognize that commercial discovery is made, each Party may request its concessionaire concerned to present an application for the establishment of exploitation right. Such concessionaire shall present such application within three months after receiving the request.

(3) If exploitation right is established during the period of exploration right, the period of exploration right shall expire on the date of the establishment of exploitation right.

5. In case of any change in concessionaire of one Party, the period of exploration right or exploitation right of a new concessionaire shall expire on the date of expiration of the period of exploration right or exploitation right of the original concessionaire.

6. Exploration right or exploitation right of a concessionaire may be transferred in its entirety subject to the approval of the Party that has authorized it and to the consent of the other concessionaire authorized with respect to the same subzone, provided that the rights and obligations of that concessionaire under this Agreement and the operating agreement are transferred in whole.

**Art. XI.** 1. Concessionaires of both Parties shall be required to drill a certain number of wells during the period of exploration right in accordance with a separate arrangement to be made between the Parties. However, the minimum number of wells to be drilled in each subzone shall not exceed two respectively for the first three-year period, the following three-year period and the remaining two-year period, from the date of entry into force of the operating agreement. The Parties shall, when agreeing upon the minimum number of wells to be drilled in each subzone, take into account the depths of the superjacent waters and the size of each subzone.

2. If concessionaires of both Parties have drilled wells in excess of the requirements during any of the periods referred to in paragraph 1 of this Article, such excess wells shall be regarded as having been drilled in the succeeding period or periods.

**Art. XII.** Concessionaires of both Parties shall start operations within six months from the date of the establishment of exploration right or exploitation right and shall not suspend operations for more than six consecutive months.

**Art. XIII.** 1. Subject to the provisions of paragraph 2 of this Article, concessionaires of both Parties shall release twenty-five per cent of the original subzone concerned within three years, fifty per cent of such subzone within six years, and seventy-five per cent of such subzone within eight years, from the date of entry into force of the operating agreement.

2. The size, shape and location of the area to be released and the time of release shall be determined by agreement between concessionaires of both Parties. However, no single area smaller than seventy-five square kilometres shall be released except under paragraph 3 of this Article.

3. (1) If concessionaires of both Parties are unable to agree on the area to be released under paragraph 1 of this Article, concessionaires of both Parties shall release, on the date of the expiration of the release period concerned, the area mutually proposed for release and fifty per cent of the areas respectively proposed for release in such a way that the total area to be released will be a single area whenever possible.

(2) If there is no area mutually proposed for release, concessionaires of both Parties shall release fifty per cent of the areas respectively proposed for release.

4. Concessionaires of both Parties may release voluntarily any area subject to the provisions of paragraph 2 of this Article.

5. Notwithstanding the provisions of paragraph 2 of this Article, a concessionaire may unilaterally release the total subzone concerned after two years have elapsed from the date of entry into force of the operating agreement.

**Art. XIV.** 1. Either Party may, by pertinent procedures laid down in its laws and regulations concerning the protection of concessionaires, cancel exploration right or exploitation right of its concessionaire after consultations with the other Party if such concessionaire fails to discharge any of its obligations under this Agreement or the operating agreement.

2. When either Party intends to cancel in accordance with its laws and regulations exploration right or exploitation right of its concessionaire, that Party shall notify the other Party of its intention at least fifteen days prior to such cancellation, except under paragraph 1 of this Article.

3. The cancellation of exploration right or exploitation right by one Party shall be notified to the other Party without delay.

**Art. XV.** 1. When a concessionaire of one Party has unilaterally released a subzone under paragraph 5 of Article XIII, when exploration right or exploitation right of a concessionaire of one Party has been cancelled under Article XIV or when a concessionaire of one Party has ceased to exist (any such concessionaire hereinafter referred to as "the former concessionaire"), the remaining concessionaire in the subzone concerned may, until such time as the Party that has authorized the former concessionaire authorizes a new concessionaire, carry out exploration or exploitation of natural resources under the terms of the sole risk operation clauses and under other relevant provisions of the operating agreement to which such remaining concessionaire and the former concessionaire were parties, subject to the approval of the Party that has authorized the former concessionaire.

2. For the purposes of paragraph 1 of this Article, the remaining concessionaire shall be regarded as a concessionaire of the Party that has authorized the former concessionaire in respect of rights and obligations of a concessionaire, while retaining its own concessionaireship. The provisions of the above sentence shall not apply to taxation upon the remaining concessionaire with respect to its income derived from exploration or exploitation of natural resources under paragraph 1 of this Article.

3. When a new concessionaire is authorized by one Party, the new concessionaire and the remaining concessionaire shall be bound by the operating agreement to which the remaining concessionaire and the former concessionaire were parties until such time as a new operating agreement enters into force. The remaining concessionaire who has started exploration or exploitation of natural resources under paragraph 1 of this Article may continue such exploration or exploitation under the terms of the sole risk operation clauses of the operating agreement to which such remaining concessionaire and the former concessionaire were parties until such time as the new operating agreement referred to above enters into force.

**Art. XVI.** In the application of the laws and regulations of each Party to natural resources extracted in the Joint Development Zone, the share of such natural resources to which concessionaires of one Party are entitled under Article IX shall be regarded as natural resources extracted in the continental shelf over which that Party has sovereign rights.

**Art. XVII.** 1. Neither Party (including local authorities) shall impose taxes or other charges upon concessionaires of the other Party with respect to:

(a) exploration or exploitation activities in the Joint Development Zone;

(b) income derived from such activities;

(c) the possession of fixed assets in the Joint Development Zone necessary for carrying out such activities; or

(d) the subzones with respect to which such concessionaires are authorized.

2. Each Party (including local authorities) may impose taxes and other charges upon its concessionaires with respect to:

(a) exploration or exploitation activities in the Joint Development Zone;

(b) the possession of fixed assets in the Joint Development Zone necessary for carrying out such activities; and

(c) the subzones with respect to which such concessionaires are authorized.

**Art. XVIII.** In the application of the laws and regulations of each Party on customs duties, imports and exports:

(1) the introduction of equipment, materials and other goods necessary for exploration or exploitation of natural resources in the Joint Development Zone (hereinafter referred to as "equipment") into the Joint Development Zone, the subsequent use of equipment therein or the shipment of equipment therefrom shall not be regarded as imports or exports;

(2) the shipment of equipment from areas under the jurisdiction of one Party to the Joint Development Zone shall not be regarded as imports or exports by that Party;

(3) the users of equipment in the Joint Development Zone which has been introduced into the Joint Development Zone from areas under the jurisdiction of either Party may be required to submit reports to that Party on the use of such equipment;

(4) notwithstanding the provisions of (1) of this Article, the shipment of the equipment referred to in (3) of this Article from the Joint Development Zone to areas other than those under the jurisdiction of that Party shall be regarded as exports by that Party.

**Art. XIX.** Except where otherwise provided in this Agreement, the laws and regulations of one Party shall apply with respect to matters relating to exploration or exploitation of natural resources in the subzones with respect to which that Party has authorized concessionaires designated and acting as operators.

**Art. XX.** The Parties shall agree on measures to be taken to prevent collisions at sea and to prevent and remove pollution of the sea resulting from activities relating to exploration or exploitation of natural resources in the Joint Development Zone.

**Art. XXI.** 1. When damage resulting from exploration or exploitation of natural resources in the Joint Development Zone has been sustained by nationals of either Party or other persons who are resident in the territory of either Party, actions for compensation for such damage may be brought by such nationals or persons in the court of one Party (*a*) in the territory of which such damage has occured, (*b*) in the territory of which such nationals or persons are resident or (*c*) which has authorized the concessionaire designated and acting as the operator in the subzone where the incident causing such damage has occured.

2. The court of one Party in which actions for compensation for such damage have been brought under paragraph 1 of this Article shall apply the laws and regulations of that Party.

3. (1) When damage referred to in paragraph 1 of this Article has been caused by digging operations of seabed and subsoil, or discharging of mine water or used water:

(*a*) concessionaires of both Parties who have exploration right or exploitation right with respect to the subzone concerned at the time of occurrence of such damage,

(*b*) in case no concessionaire has exploration right or exploitation right with respect to the subzone concerned at the time of occurrence of such damage, the concessionaires who had exploration right or exploitation right most recently with respect to the subzone concerned or

(*c*) in case only one concessionaire has exploration right or exploitation right with respect to the subzone concerned at the time of occurrence of such damage, such concessionaire and the former concessionaire as defined in paragraph 1 of Article XV,

shall be jointly and severally liable for the compensation for such damage in accordance with the laws and regulations applicable under paragraph 2 of this Article.

(2) For the purposes of (1) of this paragraph, when exploration right or exploitation right has been transferred after the occurrence of the damage referred to in (1) of this paragraph, the concessionaire who has transferred exploration right or exploitation right and the concessionaire who has obtained exploration right or exploitation right by such transfer shall be jointly and severally liable for the compensation.

102

**Art. XXII.** 1. Each Party shall, when assigning a frequency or frequencies to a radio station on a fixed installation for exploration or exploitation of natural resources in the Joint Development Zone, inform as soon as possible prior to such assignment the other Party of such frequency or frequencies, class of emission, antenna power, location of the station and other particulars deemed necessary. Each Party shall likewise inform the other Party of any subsequent changes in the above particulars.

2. The Parties shall hold consultations at the request of either Party for necessary coordination concerning the above particulars.

**Art. XXIII.** 1. If any single geological structure or field of natural resources extends across any of the lines specified in paragraph 1 of Article II and the part of such structure or field which is situated on one side of such lines is exploitable, wholly or in part, from the other side of such lines, concessionaires and other persons authorized by either Party to exploit such structure or field (hereinafter referred to as "concessionaires and other persons') shall, through consultations, seek to reach agreement as to the most effective method of exploiting such structure or field.

2. (1) If concessionaires and other persons fail to reach agreement as to the method referred to in paragraph 1 of this Article within six months after such consultations have started, the Parties shall, through consultations, endeavour to make a joint proposal concerning such method to concessionaires and other persons within a reasonable period of time.

(2) When agreement concerning such method is reached among all or some of concessionaires and other persons, the agreement (including modifications thereof) shall enter into force upon approval by the Parties. Such agreement shall provide for details relating to the sharing, in accordance with paragraph 3 of this Article, of natural resources and expenses.

3. In cases of exploitation under the agreement referred to in paragraph 2 (2) of this Article, natural resources extracted from such structure or field and expenses reasonably attributable to exploitation of such natural resources shall be shared among concessionaires and other persons in proportion to the quantities of producible reserves in the respective parts of such structure or field which are situated in the area with respect to which they have been authorized by either Party.

4. The provisions of the foregoing paragraphs of this Article shall apply mutatis mutandis with respect to exploitation of a single geological structure or field of natural resources extending across lines bounding the subzones of the Joint Development Zone.

5. (1) For the purposes of Article XVI, the share of natural resources extracted in the Joint Development Zone to which persons (other than concessionaires) authorized by one Party are entitled under paragraph 3

of this Article and the agreement referred to in paragraph 2 (2) of this Article shall be regarded as the share of natural resources to which concessionaires of that Party are entitled.

(2) For the purposes of Article XVII, persons (other than concessionaires) authorized by one Party who are parties to the agreement referred to in paragraph 2 (2) of this Article shall be regarded as concessionaires of that Party.

(3) Neither Party (including local authorities) shall impose taxes or other charges upon concessionaires of the other Party with respect to:

(*a*) exploitation activities carried out outside the Joint Development Zone in accordance with the agreement referred to in paragraph 2 (2) of this Article;

(*b*) income derived from such activities; or

(*c*) the possession of fixed assets necessary for carrying out such activities.

**Art. XXIV.** 1. The Parties shall establish and maintain the Japan-Republic of Korea Joint Commission (hereinafter referred to as "the Commission") as a means for consultations on matters concerning the implementation of this Agreement.

2. The Commission shall be composed of two national sections, each consisting of two members appointed by the respective Parties.

3. All resolutions, recommendations and other decisions of the Commission shall be made only by agreement between the national sections.

4. The Commission may adopt and amend, when necessary, rules of procedure for its meetings.

5. The Commission shall meet at least once each year and whenever requested by either national section.

6. At its first meeting, the Commission shall select its Chairman and Vice-Chairman from different national sections. The Chairman and the Vice-Chairman shall hold office for a period of one year. Selection of the Chairman and the Vice-Chairman from the national sections shall be made in such a manner as will provide in turn each Party with representation in these offices.

7. A permanent secretariat may be established under the Commission to carry out the clerical work of the Commission.

8. The official languages of the Commission shall be Japanese, Korean and English. Proposals and data may be submitted in any official language.

9. In case the Commission decides that joint expenses are necessary, such expenses shall be paid by the Commission through contributions made by the Parties as recommended by the Commission and approved by the Parties.

**Art. XXV.** 1. The Commission shall perform the following functions:

(*a*) to review the operation of this Agreement and, when necessary, deliberate on and recommend to the Parties measures to be taken to improve the operation of this Agreement;

(*b*) to receive technical and financial reports of concessionaires, which shall be submitted annually by the Parties;

(*c*) to recommend to the Parties measures to be taken to settle disputes incapable of solution by concessionaires;

(*d*) to observe operations of operators and installations and other facilities for exploration or exploitation of natural resources in the Joint Development Zone;

(*e*) to study problems, including those relating to the application of laws and regulations of the Parties, unexpected at the time of entry into force of this Agreement, and, when necessary, recommend to the Parties appropriate measures to solve such problems;

(*f*) to receive notices concerning the laws and regulations promulgated by the Parties relating to exploration or exploitation of natural resources in the Joint Development Zone, which shall be submitted by the Parties;

(*g*) to discuss any other matter relating to the implementation of this Agreement.

2. The Parties shall respect to the extent possible recommendations made by the Commission under paragraph 1 of this Article.

**Art. XXVI.** 1. Any dispute between the Parties concerning the interpretation and implementation of this Agreement shall be settled, first of all, through diplomatic channels.

2. Any dispute which fails to be settled under paragraph 1 of this Article shall be referred for decision to an arbitration board composed of three arbitrators, with each Party appointing one arbitrator within a period of thirty days from the date of receipt by either Party from the other Party of a note requesting arbitration of the dispute, and the third arbitrator to be agreed upon by the two arbitrators so chosen within a further period of thirty days or the third arbitrator to be appointed by the government of a third country agreed upon within such further period by the two arbitrators, provided that the third arbitrator shall not be a national of either Party.

3. If the third arbitrator or the third country is not agreed upon between the arbitrators appointed by each Party within a period referred to in paragraph 2 of this Article, the Parties shall request the President of the International Court of Justice to appoint the third arbitrator who shall not be a national of either Party.

4. At the request of either Party, the arbitration board may in urgent cases issue a provisional order, which shall be respected by the Parties, before an award is made.

105

5. The Parties shall abide by any award made by the arbitration board under this Article.

**Art. XXVII.** Exploration and exploitation of natural resources in the Joint Development Zone shall be carried out in such a manner that other legitimate activities in the Joint Development Zone and its superjacent waters such as navigation and fisheries will not be unduly affected.

**Art. XXVIII.** Nothing in this Agreement shall be regarded as determining the question of sovereign rights over all or any portion of the Joint Development Zone or as prejudicing the positions of the respective Parties with respect to the delimitation of the continental shelf.

**Art. XXIX.** Upon the request of either Party, the Parties shall hold consultations regarding the implementation of this Agreement.

**Art. XXX.** The Parties shall take all necessary internal measures to implement this Agreement.

**Art. XXXI.** 1. This Agreement shall be ratified. The instruments of ratification shall be exchanged at Tokyo as soon as possible. This Agreement shall enter into force as from the date on which such instruments of ratification are exchanged.

2. This Agreement shall remain in force for a period of fifty years and shall continue in force thereafter until terminated in accordance with paragraph 3 of this Article.

3. Either Party may, by giving three years' written notice to the other Party, terminate this Agreement at the end of the initial fifty-year period or at any time thereafter.

4. Notwithstanding the provisions of paragraph 2 of this Article, when either Party recognizes that natural resources are no longer economically exploitable in the Joint Development Zone, the Parties shall consult with each other whether to revise or terminate this Agreement. If no agreement is reached as to the revision or termination of this Agreement, this Agreement shall remain in force during the period as provided for in paragraph 2 of this Article.

*Appendix*

The Subzones shall be those areas of the Joint Development Zone bounded respectively by straight lines connecting the following points in the sequence given below: [omitted: see the map on p. 94].

*Agreed Minutes to the Agreement*

1. "The laws and regulations" referred to in the Agreement shall be construed, unless the context otherwise requires, to include concession

106

agreements between the Government of the Republic of Korea and its concessionaires.

2. The geographical coordinates as specified in paragraph 1 of Article II and the Appendix to the Agreement are based on Japan Maritime Safety Agency Chart No. 210 of December 1955, New Edition.

3. (1) Regardless of whether the sole risk party is the operator, sole risk operations referred to in paragraph 1 of Article V shall be carried out by the operator of the subzone concerned.

(2) Natural resources extracted through sole risk operations shall be equally shared between the concessionaires concerned in accordance with Article IX.

(3) The non-sole risk party shall pay in money to the sole risk party the reasonable price for the portion of natural resources equal to the half of the sole risk bonus, less expenses incurred in connection with the sale of such portion and tax or other charges paid in connection with such portion.

4. As regards "adjustment of fisheries interests" referred to in paragraph 1 of Article V, the Government of each Party shall give administrative guidance to its concessionaires so that they will, before operations for exploration or exploitation of natural resources begin in the subzones with respect to which they have been authorized, endeavour to adjust fisheries interests of nationals concerned of that Party.

5. As regards paragraph 2 of Article V, the two Governments shall notify each other of the date on which the operating agreement was submitted to them and the date on which they intend to approve or disapprove the operating agreement.

6. As regards Article VI, the two Governments shall endeavour to ensure that the designation of operators be made in such a way as to be equitable to the greatest possible extent.

7. "Expenses reasonably attributable to exploration and exploitation" referred to in paragraph 2 of Article IX shall include expenses incurred for the purposes of survey in the Joint Development Zone prior to the date of entry into force of the Agreement.

8. The provisions of paragraph 2 of Article IX shall not apply to expenses incurred by sole risk operations.

9. As regards paragraph 3 of Article X, application for an extension of the period of exploitation right shall be made at least six months prior to the expiration of each of such periods.

10. As regards paragraph 4 of Article X, the two Governments shall, after consultations, grant exploitation right respectively to concessionaires of both Parties on the same date.

11. As regards paragraph 5 of Article X, the new concessionaire may apply for an extension of the period of exploitation right under paragraph 3

of Article X.

12. For the purposes of Article XII, sole risk operations shall be regarded as having been carried out by concessionaires of both Parties.

13. When concessionaires of both Parties are unable to comply with the provisions of Article XII for unavoidable reasons, they shall submit for approval a statement setting forth reasons for, and the period of, such delay or suspension to the respective Governments authorizing them. The two Governments shall consult with each other before giving such approval.

14. The approval of the Party referred to in paragraph 1 of Article XV shall not be withheld without justifiable reasons.

15. As regards paragraph 2 of Article XV, when the remaining concessionaire of one Party who was not the operator under the operating agreement to which such concessionaire and the former concessionaire were parties carries out exploration or exploitation of natural resources under paragraph 1 of Article XV, such concessionaire shall be regarded as the concessionaire of the other Party designated and acting as the operator, while retaining its own concessionaireship.

16. As regards paragraph 2 of Article XV, taxes on income shall not include royalty.

17. Taxes and other charges to be imposed under paragraph 2 of Article XVII include
  (1) for Japan
      (a) mineral product tax,
      (b) fixed assets tax and
      (c) mine lot tax;
  (2) for the Republic of Korea
      (a) royalty,
      (b) property tax and
      (c) rental.

18. (1) "Damage caused by digging operations of seabed and subsoil" referred to in paragraph 3 of Article XXI include damage caused by blow-out of oil or natural gas.

   (2) "Mine water" referred to in paragraph 3 of Article XXI means water flowing out in the course of drilling wells for exploration or exploitation of natural resources, and oil and other substances flowing out together with such water.

19. The provisions of paragraph 3 (1) (a) of Article XXI shall apply when a concessionaire of one Party carries out exploration or exploitation of natural resources under paragraph 1 of Article XV. In such a case, the provisions of paragraph 3 (1) (c) of Article XXI shall not apply.

20. As regards paragraph 2 (1) of Article XXIII, each Government shall take, within its powers, necessary measures so that its concessionaires and other persons will not exploit independently the structure or field

108

referred to in paragraph 1 of Article XXIII during the six-month period referred to in paragraph 2 (1) of Article XXIII or during the period in which the two Governments hold consultations for the purpose of making a joint proposal.

21. A concessionaire shall not enter into the agreement referred to in paragraph 2 (2) of Article XXIII unless the other concessionaire authorized with respect to the same subzone also enters into such agreement.

*Arrangements concerning drilling obligations of concessionaires*
(Exchange of Notes)

1. (1) Concessionaires of both Parties authorized with respect to each subzone as specified in the Appendix to the Agreement shall drill one well during the first three-year period, the following three-year period and the remaining two-year period respectively.

(2) For the purposes of (1), sole risk operations shall be regarded as having been performed by concessionaires of both Parties.

(3) Subzones I and IX shall be deemed to constitute a single subzone for the purposes of (1).

(4) Notwithstanding the provisions of (1), concessionaires authorized with respect to Subzone VIII shall be exempted from the obligations under (1) during the first three-year period and concessionaires authorized with respect to Subzones II, III, IV and VI shall be exempted from the obligations under (1).

2. The present arrangements shall become applicable as from the date of entry into force of the Agreement.

*Arrangements concerning the prevention of collisions at sea*
(Exchange of Notes)

1. The Government of either Party shall take the following measures in the subzones of the Joint Development Zone with respect to which that Party has authorized concessionaires designated and acting as operators:

(1) (*a*) When the exploration under the Agreement is carried out in such subzones by surface vessels, that Government shall promptly inform the other Government and mariners of the areas covered by, and the durations of, such exploration activities.

(*b*) When a fixed installation hazardous to navigation (hereinafter referred to as "fixed installation") is erected, that Government shall promptly inform the other Government and mariners of the exact location of the fixed installation and other particulars necessary for the safety of navigation, such as markings to be fixed to such installation while being erected. That Government shall take similar measures when a fixed installation is dismantled or removed.

(2) When a fixed installation has been erected which rises above the water, that Government shall ensure that:

(*a*) The fixed installation is marked at night by one or more white lights so constructed that at least one light is visible from any direction. Such lights shall be placed not less than 15 metres above Mean High Water and shall flash Morse letter U (. . —) every 15 seconds or less. The intensity of such lights shall be not less than 6,000 candelas.

(*b*) The horizontal and vertical extremities of the fixed installation are marked at night by red lights having intensity of not less than 300 candelas.

(*c*) The fixed installation is equipped with one or more sound signals so constructed and fixed as to be audible from any direction. The sound signals shall have a rated range of not less than 2 nautical miles and shall emit blasts corresponding to Morse letter U (. . —) every 30 seconds. The signals shall be operated when the meteorological visibility is less than 2 nautical miles.

(*d*) A radar reflector is so fixed as to enable vessels approaching the fixed installation from any direction to clearly detect the presence of the fixed installation on their radar from a distance of not less than 10 nautical miles.

(*e*) The fixed installation is equipped with appropriate markings to prevent collisions with aircraft.

(3) When an underwater fixed installation such as submerged well or pipe-line has been erected, that Government shall ensure that it is adequately marked.

(4) (*a*) When a number of fixed installations are situated in close proximity to one another and when safety of navigation can be secured without each of fixed installations being individually equipped with signals referred to in (2) (*a*), (*b*), (*c*) and (*d*), such fixed installations may be regarded as constituting a single fixed installation for the purposes of (2) (*a*), (*b*), (*c*) and (*d*).

(*b*) When a fixed installation itself possesses radar reflectory capability which meets the requirements of (2) (*d*), the fixing of a radar reflector may be omitted.

2. The present arrangements shall become applicable as from the date of entry into force of the Agreement.

3. The present arrangements may be terminated by either Government by giving one year's written notice to the other Government.

4. The two Governments shall meet before the present arrangements are terminated in accordance with 3 to decide on future arrangements.

*Arrangements concerning the prevention and removal of pollution of the sea*
(Exchange of Notes)

## I

The Government of either Party shall ensure that the following measures are taken with respect to (*a*) a well or a marine facility relating to exploration or exploitation of natural resources in the subzones of the Joint Development Zone with respect to which that Party has authorized concessionaires designated and acting as operators or (*b*) a vessel under the flag of that Party engaged in activities relating to exploration or exploitation of natural resources in the Joint Development Zone (hereinafter referred to as "ship"):

1. Blow-out Preventor etc.

(1) (*a*) A well which is being drilled shall be equipped with blow-out preventor in case blow-out of oil or natural gas is likely to occur.

(*b*) The provisions of (*a*) shall not apply when oil testing or repair works are performed and automatic oil- or gas-collecting devices for blow-out have been installed.

(2) The blow-out preventor referred to in (1) shall meet the following requirements:

(*a*) The blow-out preventor installed at the entrance of a well shall be of an open-and-close type, and of a remote control type which can be promptly operated, with an independent power source;

(*b*) The operating gear or warning devices for emergency use of such blow-out preventor shall be located close to the person who operates the draw-works;

(*c*) Flow-bean or other devices shall be installed to control the quantity of oil or natural gas flowing from the outlet of such blow-out preventor;

(*d*) Devices capable of prevention of blow-out of oil or natural gas from inside drilling pipes, tubing pipes or casing pipes shall be installed.

(3) (*a*) When drilling of a well or oil testing is performed, muddy water or its materials for emergency use and such materials as are necessary for making heavy muddy water or for controlling the quality of muddy water shall be stocked at the drilling site.

(*b*) The provisions of (*a*) shall not apply when automatic oil- or gas-collecting devices for blow-out have been installed.

(4) The blow-out preventor, automatic oil- or gas-collecting devices for blow-out and other devices installed at the entrance of a well shall be such that they can withstand at least the pressures prescribed in the schedule attached to this Note.

(5) In the course of drilling operations, the following requiremen... shall be met:

(*a*) When a well has been drilled to an appropriate depth, the insertion of casing pipes and cementing shall be performed promptly;

(*b*) When cementing has been performed, its effectiveness shall be confirmed by applying pressure or by other means;

(*c*) Devices capable of immediate detection of any unusual increases or decreases in the quantity of muddy water in the tank for circulating muddy water shall be installed.

(6) Pressure proof tests of the blow-out preventor shall be conducted at least once a month by applying appropriate pressures.

(7) The blow-out preventor shall be closed when drilling operations are suspended because of difficulties arising from meteorological conditions in maintaining the position of a drilling facility or because of the occurrence, or the danger, of an accident.

2. Discharge of Oil

(1) (*a*) Crude oil, fuel oil, heavy diesel oil, lubricating oil or a mixture containing such oils (hereinafter referred to as "oil") shall not be discharged from a ship or a marine facility.

(*b*) The provisions of (*a*) shall not apply to:

(i) the discharge of oil from a ship other than a tanker or the discharge of bilge from a tanker, when the following conditions are all satisfied:

i) the ship or tanker is proceeding en route;

ii) the instantaneous rate of discharge of oil content does not exceed 60 litres per nautical mile;

iii) the oil content of the discharge is less than 100/1,000,000 of the discharge;

(ii) the discharge of oil from a tanker, when the following conditions are all satisfied:

i) the tanker is proceeding en route;

ii) the instantaneous rate of discharge of oil content does not exceed 60 litres per nautical mile;

iii) the total quantity of oil discharged on a ballast voyage does not exceed 1/15,000 of the total cargo-carrying capacity;

iv) the tanker is more than 50 nautical miles from the nearest land;

(iii) the discharge of water ballast from a cargo tank which has been so cleaned that any effluent therefrom would produce no visible traces of oil on the surface of the water, if it were discharged from a stationary tanker into clean calm water on a clear day.

(2) The provisions of (1) shall not apply to:

(*a*) the discharge of oil for the purpose of securing the safety of a ship or a marine facility, preventing damage to a ship or a marine facility

112

or cargo of a ship or saving life at sea;

(*b*) the escape of oil resulting from damage to a ship or a marine facility or unavoidable leakage, if all reasonable precautions have been taken after the occurrence of the damage or discovery of the leakage for the purpose of preventing or minimizing the escape;

(*c*) the discharge of oil from a marine facility if the oil content of such discharge is less than 10/1,000,000 of the discharge;

(*d*) the discharge of oil from tankers of under 150 tons gross tonnage and other ships of under 500 tons gross tonnage.

3. Discharge of Waste

(1) Waste shall not be discharged from a ship or a marine facility.

(2) The provisions of (1) shall not apply to:

(*a*) the discharge of refuse, excretion, sewage or similar waste resulting from daily life or the personnel aboard a ship or a marine facility;

(*b*) the discharge of cuttings or dirty water in a manner in which pollution of the sea is not likely to occur;

(*c*) the discharge of waste other than cuttings or dirty water from a ship in a manner in which pollution of the sea is not likely to occur, and at a location where such discharge is not likely to hinder the maintenance of the sea-environment;

(*d*) the discharge of waste for the purpose of securing the safety of a ship or a marine facility, preventing damage to a ship or a marine facility or cargo of a ship or saving life at sea;

(*e*) the discharge of waste resulting from damage to a ship or a marine facility or unavoidable discharge, if all reasonable precautions have been taken after the occurrence of the damage or discovery of the discharge for the purpose of preventing or minimizing the discharge.

4. Prevention and Removal of Pollution

When large quantities of oil have been discharged from a ship or a marine facility, measures shall be taken promptly to prevent the spread of such pollution, to prevent the continued discharge of oil and to remove the discharged oil.

5. Abandonment of a Well

When a well is abandoned, measures such as sealing of the well shall be taken to prevent leakage of mine water or other substances from such well.

## II

1. One Government shall promptly provide the other Government with all available information when any of the following occurs:

(*a*) Discharge of large quantities of oil from a ship or a marine facility;

113

(*b*) Collisions between a marine facility and a ship or other objects;

(*c*) Evacuation of personnel from a marine facility due to dangerous meteorological conditions or other emergencies.

2. When information concerning 1. (*a*) is provided, the Government concerned shall also inform the other Government of the measures taken in accordance with I. 4.

### III

1. Under special circumstances, each Gorvenment may authorize exceptions to the provisions of I. 1. (2) (*a*), (*b*), (*c*) or (*d*).

2. With respect to a well exceeding 1500 metres in depth, each Government may authorize exceptions to the provisions of I. 1. (4).

### IV

Either Government may take necessary measures to prevent and remove pollution of the sea when measures are not taken in accordance with I. 4 or when that Government considers that such measures are not sufficient to prevent or remove pollution of the sea.

### V

The two Governments shall cooperate closely for the effective implementation of the present arrangements.

### VI

1. The present arrangements shall become applicable six months after the date of entry into force of the Agreement or on an earlier date as may be mutually agreed upon between the two Governments.

2. The present arrangements may be terminated by either Government by giving one year's written notice to the other Government.

3. The two Governments shall meet before the present arrangements are terminated in accordance with 2 to decide on future arrangements.

*Schedule:* [omitted].

# III. FISHERIES JURISDICTION CASE (INTERNATIONAL COURT OF JUSTICE)

## INTERNATIONAL COURT OF JUSTICE:
— Fisheries Jurisdiction Cases (U.K. v. Iceland; Federal Republic of Germany v. Iceland)

On 15 February 1972, the Althing of Iceland adopted a draft of resolution, which resolved that "the fishery limits will be extended 50 miles from base-lines round the country, to become effective not later than 1 September 1972" and that "the Governments of the United Kingdom and the Federal Republic of Germany be again informed that because of the vital interests of the nation and owing to changed circumstances, the Notes concerning fishery limits exchanged in 1961 are no longer applicable and that their provisions do not constitute an obligation for Iceland." The Exchange of Notes between Iceland and the U.K. of 11 March 1961 and between Iceland and the Federal Republic of Germany of 19 July 1961 read that in case of a dispute in relation to the extension of fisheries jurisdiction around Iceland, the matter should, at the request of either party, be referred to the International Court of Justice. The U.K. and the Federal Republic of Germany filed applications on 14 April 1972 and 5 June 1972, respectively, instituting proceedings against Iceland in respect of a dispute concerning the proposed extension by Iceland of its fisheries jurisdiction.

The Court was asked by the U.K. to adjudge and declare:
(a) That there is no foundation in international law for the claim by Iceland to be entitled to extend its fisheries jurisdiction by establishing a zone of exclusive fisheries jurisdiction extending to 50 nautical miles from the baselines hereinbefore referred to; and that its claim is therefore invalid; and
(b) that questions concerning the conservation of fish stocks in the waters around Iceland are not susceptible in international law to regulation by the unilateral extension by Iceland of its exclusive fisheries jurisdiction to 50 nautical miles from the aforesaid baselines but are matters that may be regulated, as between Iceland and the United Kingdom, by arrangements agreed between those two countries, whether or not together with other interested countries and whether in the form of arrangements reached in accordance with the North-East Atlantic Fisheries Convention of 24 January 1959, or in the

form of arrangements for collaboration in accordance with the Resolution on Special Situations relating to Coastal Fisheries of 26 April 1958, or otherwise in the form of arrangements agreed between them that give effect to the continuing rights and interests of both of them in the fisheries of the waters in question.

The Court was similarily asked by the Federal Republic of Germany to adjudge and declare:

(a) That the unilateral extension by Iceland of its zone of exclusive fisheries jurisdiction to 50 nautical miles from the present baselines, to be effective from 1 September 1972, which has been decided upon by the Parliament (Althing) and the Government of Iceland and communicated by the Minister for Foreign Affairs of Iceland to the Federal Republic of Germany by aide-mémoire handed to its Ambassador in Reykjavik on 24 February 1972, would have no basis in international law and could therefore not be opposed to the Federal Republic of Germany and to its fishing vessels.

(b) That if Iceland, as a coastal State specially dependent on coastal fisheries, establishes a need for special fisheries conservation measures in the waters adjacent to its coast but beyond the exclusive fisheries zone provided for by the Exchange of Notes of 1961, such conservation measures, as far as they would affect fisheries of the Federal Republic of Germany, may not be taken, under international law, on the basis of a unilateral extension by Iceland of its fisheries jurisdiction, but only on the basis of an agreement between the Federal Republic of Germany and Iceland concluded either bilaterally or within a multilateral framework.

## 1. JUDGMENT ON JURISDICTION OF THE COURT, 2 FEBRUARY 1973

### U.K. v. Iceland

. . .

23. This history reinforces the view that the Court has jurisdiction in this case, and adds emphasis to the point that the real intention of the parties was to give the United Kingdom Government an effective assurance which constituted a *sine qua non* and not merely a severable condition of the whole agreement: namely, the right to challenge before the Court the validity of any further extension of Icelandic fisheries jurisdiction in the waters above its continental shelf beyond the 12-mile limit.

116

In consequence, the exercise of jurisdiction by the Court to entertain the present Application would fall within the terms of the compromissory clause and correspond exactly to the intentions and expectations of both Parties when they discussed and consented to that clause. It thus appears from the text of the compromissory clause, read in the context of the 1961 Exchange of Notes and in the light of the history of the negotiations, that the Court has jurisdiction. It has however been contended that the agreement either was initially void or has since ceased to operate. The Court will now consider these contentions.

\* \* \*

24. . . . The history of the negotiations which led up to the 1961 Exchange of Notes reveals that these instruments were freely negotiated by the interested parties on the basis of perfect equality and freedom of decision on both sides. No fact has been brought to the attention of the Court from any quarter suggesting the slightest doubt on this matter.

\* \*

. . .
29. . . . [The 1961 Exchange of Notes] contains a definite compromissory clause establishing the jurisdiction of the Court to deal with a concrete kind of dispute which was foreseen and specifically anticipated by the parties. In consequence, when a dispute arises of precisely the sort contemplated, and is referred to the Court, the contention that the compromissory clause has lapsed, or is terminable, cannot be accepted.

\* \*

. . .
34. It is possible that today Iceland may find that some of the motives which induced it to enter into the 1961 Exchange of Notes have become less compelling or have disappeared altogether. But this is not a ground justifying the repudiation of those parts of the agreement the object and purpose of which have remained unchanged. Iceland has derived benefits from the executed provisions of the agreement, such as the recognition by the United Kingdom since 1961 of a 12-mile exclusive fisheries jurisdiction, the acceptance by the United Kingdom of the baselines established by Iceland and the relinquishment in a period of three years of the pre-existing traditional fishing by vessels registered in the United Kingdom. Clearly it then becomes incumbent on Iceland to comply with its side of the bargain, which is to accept the testing before the Court of the validity of its further claims to extended jurisdiction. Moreover, in the case of a treaty which is in part executed and in part executory, in which

117

one of the parties has already benefited from the executed provisions of the treaty, it would be particularly inadmissible to allow that party to put an end to obligations which were accepted under the treaty by way of *quid pro quo* for the provisions which the other party had already executed.

\* \* \*

...

42. .... The exceptional dependence of Iceland on its fisheries and the principle of conservation of fish stocks having been recognized, the question remains as to whether Iceland is or is not competent unilaterally to assert an exclusive fisheries jurisdiction extending beyond the 12-mile limit. The issue before the Court in the present phase of the proceedings concerns solely its jurisdiction to determine the latter point.

\* \* \*

43. Moreover, in order that a change of circumstances may give rise to a ground for invoking the termination of a treaty it is also necessary that it should have resulted in a radical transformation of the extent of the obligations still to be performed. The change must have increased the burden of the obligations to be executed to the extent of rendering the performance something essentially different from that originally undertaken. .... The compromissory clause enabled either of the parties to submit to the Court any dispute between them relating to an extension of Icelandic fisheries jurisdiction in the waters above its continental shelf beyond the 12-mile limit. The present dispute is exactly of the character anticipated in the compromissory clause of the Exchange of Notes. Not only has the jurisdictional obligation not been radically transformed in its extent; it has remained precisely what it was in 1961.

\* \*

...

45. In the present case, the procedural complement to the doctrine of changed circumstances is already provided for in the 1961 Exchange of Notes, which specifically calls upon the parties to have recourse to the Court in the event of a dispute relating to Iceland's extension of fisheries jurisdiction. Furthermore, any question as to the jurisdiction of the Court, deriving from an alleged lapse through changed circumstances, is resolvable through the accepted judicial principle enshrined in Article 36, paragraph 6, of the Court's Statute, which provides that "in the event of a dispute as to whether the Court has jurisdiction, the matter shall be settled by the decision of the Court". In this case such a dispute obviously exists, as can be seen from Iceland's communications to the Court, and to the other Party, even if Iceland has chosen not to appoint an Agent, file a Counter-Memorial or submit preliminary objections to the Court's juris-

diction; and Article 53 of the Statute both entitles the Court and, in the present proceedings, requires it to pronounce upon the question of its jurisdiction. This it has now done with binding force.

* * * * *

46. For these reasons,

*The Court,*
by fourteen votes to one,
finds that it has jurisdiction to entertain the Application filed by the Government of the United Kingdom of Great Britain and Northern Ireland on 14 April 1972 and to deal with the merits of the dispute.

[Judge Padilla Nervo appends a dissenting opinion.]

**Federal Republic of Germany v. Iceland**

Identical in substance to the Judgment as quoted above.


## 2. ORDER ON INTERIM MEASURES OF PROTECTION, 17 AUGUST 1972

On 14 July 1972, the Government of Iceland issued Regulations to implement the draft of resolution of 15 February 1972 (p. 115). On 19 July 1972 and 21 July 1972 respectively, the U.K. and the Federal Republic of Germany asked to the Court to indicate interim measures of protection, pending the final decision in the cases. On 17 August 1972, the Court indicated the following interim measures of protection.

**U.K. v. Iceland**

. . .

11. Whereas according to the jurisprudence of the Court and of the Permanent Court of International Justice the non-appearance of one of the parties cannot by itself constitute an obstacle to the indication of provisional measures, provided the parties have been given an opportunity of presenting their observations on the subject;

*

. . .

15. Whereas on a request for provisional measures the Court need not, before indicating them, finally satisfy itself that it has jurisdiction on the merits of the case, yet it ought not to act under Article 41 of the Statute if the absence of jurisdiction on the merits is manifest;

. . .

17. Whereas the above-cited provision in an instrument emanating from both Parties to the dispute appears, prima facie, to afford a possible basis on which the jurisdiction of the Court might be founded;

. . .

19. Whereas the contention of the Government of Iceland, in its letter of 29 May 1972, that the above-quoted clause contained in the Exchange of Notes of 11 March 1961 has been terminated, will fall to be examined by the Court in due course;

. . .

21. Whereas the right of the Court to indicate provisional measures as provided for in Article 41 of the Statute has as its object to preserve the respective rights of the Parties pending the decision of the Court, and presupposes that irreparable prejudice should not be caused to rights which are the subject of dispute in judicial proceedings and that the Court's judgment should not be anticipated by reason of any initiative regarding the measures which are in issue;

22. Whereas the immediate implementation by Iceland of its Regulations would, by anticipating the Court's judgment, prejudice the rights claimed by the United Kingdom and affect the possibility of their full restoration in the event of a judgment in its favour;

23. Whereas it is also necessary to bear in mind the exceptional dependence of the Icelandic nation upon coastal fisheries for its livelihood and economic development as expressly recognized by the United Kingdom in its Note addressed to the Foreign Minister of Iceland dated 11 March 1961;

24. Whereas from this point of view account must be taken of the need for the conservation of fish stocks in the Iceland area;

25. Whereas the total catch by United Kingdom vessels in that area in the year 1970 was 164,000 metric tons and in the year 1971 was 207,000 metric tons; and whereas the figure of 185,000 metric tons mentioned in the United Kingdom request from interim measures was based on the average annual catch for the period 1960-1969;

26. Whereas in the Court's opinion the average of the catch should, for purposes of interim measures, and so as to reflect the present situation concerning fisheries of different species in the Iceland area, be based on the available statistical information before the Court for the five years 1967-1971, which produces an approximate figure of 170,000 metric tons,

Accordingly,

*The Court,*

by fourteen votes to one,

(1) Indicates, pending its final decision in the proceedings instituted on 14 April 1972 by the Government of the United Kingdom against the Government of Iceland, the following provisional measures:

(*a*) the United Kingdom and the Republic of Iceland should each of them ensure that no action of any kind is taken which might aggravate or extend the dispute submitted to the Court;

(*b*) the United Kingdom and the Republic of Iceland should each of them ensure that no action is taken which might prejudice the rights of the other Party in respect of the carrying out of whatever decision on the merits the Court may render;

(*c*) the Republic of Iceland should refrain from taking any measures to enforce the Regulations of 14 July 1972 against vessels registered in the United Kingdom and engaged in fishing activities in the waters around Iceland outside the 12-mile fishery zone;

(*d*) the Republic of Iceland should refrain from applying administrative, judicial or other measures against ships registered in the United Kingdom, their crews or other related persons, because of their having engaged in fishing activities in the waters around Iceland outside the 12-mile fishery zone;

(*e*) the United Kingdom should ensure that vessels registered in the United Kingdom do not take an annual catch of more than 170,000 metric tons of fish from the "Sea Area of Iceland" as defined by the International Council for the Exploration of the Sea as area Va;

(*f*) the United Kingdom Government should furnish the Government of Iceland and the Registry of the Court with all relevant information, orders issued and arrangements made concerning the control and regulation of fish catches in the area.

(2) Unless the Court has meanwhile delivered its final judgment in the case, it shall, at an appropriate time before 15 August 1973, review the matter at the request of either Party in order to decide whether the foregoing measures shall continue or need to be modified or revoked.

[Judge Padilla Nervo appends a dissenting opinion.]

**Federal Republic of Germany v. Iceland**

Identical in substance to the Order as quoted above, except that (1) - (e) of the Order reads, as follows:

(*e*) the Federal Republic should ensure that vessels registered in the Federal Republic do not take an annual catch of more than 119,000 metric tons of fish from the "Sea Area of Iceland" as defined by the International Council for the Exploration of the Sea as area Va;

## 3. ORDER ON CONTINUANCE OF INTERIM MEASURES OF PROTECTION, 12 JULY 1973

### U.K. v. Iceland

*The Court,*
by 11 votes to 3,

Confirms that the provisional measures indicated in operative paragraph (1) of the Order of 17 August 1972 should, subject to the power of revocation or modification conferred on the Court by paragraph 7 of Article 61 of the 1946 Rules, remain operative until the Court has given final judgment in the case.

[Judge Ignacio-Pinto makes a declaration; Judges Gros and Petrén append dissenting opinions to the Order of the Court; Judge Padilla Nervo does not participate.]

### Federal Republic of Germany v. Iceland

Identical in substance to the Order above.

# IV. CONVENTIONS RELATING TO FISHERY ZONE

## 1. NORTHEAST ATLANTIC

## THE 1959 AGREEMENT RELATING TO THE TEMPORARY REGULATION OF FISHING AROUND THE FAROE ISLANDS PENDING THE ENTRY INTO FORCE OF A GENERAL CONVENTION REGULATING THE BREADTH OF THE TERRITORIAL SEA AND FISHERY LIMITS (Denmark and United Kingdom of Great Britain and Northern Ireland)

Exchange of Notes at Copenhagen on 27 April 1959. U.N. Treaty Series, vol. 337, p. 416. Terminated on 28 April 1964.

I. The Government of the United Kingdom shall raise no objection to the exclusion by the competent Danish of Faroese authorities of vessels registered in the United Kingdom from fishing in the area between the coast of the Faroe Islands and the blue line shown on the map annexed hereto.

II. Having regard to the fisheries traditionally exercised in waters around the Faroe Islands by vessels registered in the United Kingdom, the Government of Denmark shall raise no objection to such vessels continuing to fish in the area between the blue line mentioned in paragraph I and a line twelve sea miles from low water mark along the coast of the Faroe Islands drawn as shown by the red dotted line on the map annexed thereto.

III. In view of the exceptional dependence of the Faroese economy on fisheries in the three areas hatched red on the map annexed hereto, lying within the area mentioned in paragraph II, fishing by vessels registered in the Faroe Islands or Denmark and vessels registered in the United Kingdom shall be limited to fishing with long line and hand line between the dates specified in sub-paragraph (*a*), (*b*) and (*c*) of this paragraph. The areas and dates referred to are: . . .

IV. The Danish Government shall accord to fishing vessels registered in the United Kingdom treatment no less favourable than that accorded to the fishing vessels of any other foreign country.

V. . . .

VI. The Governments of Denmark and the United Kingdom shall arrange for experts to report each year what, if any, measures additional to those currently in force may be necessary for the conservation of the stocks of fish around the Faroe Islands and the two Governments shall consider together any recommendations for such measures that may be

123

made by the experts.

VII. Nothing in the present Agreement shall be deemed to prejudice the views held by either Government as to the delimitation and limits in international law of territorial waters or of exclusive jurisdiction in fishery matters.

VIII. (a) The present Agreement shall enter into force on this day's date and shall, subject to the provisions of sub-paragraph (b) of this paragraph, remain in force until the entry into force of a general Convention regulating the breadth of the territorial sea and fishery limits.

(b) If by the 27th of October, 1961, a Convention as mentioned in sub-paragraph (a) of this paragraph has not entered into force, the Governments of Denmark and the United Kingdom shall consider whether any modifications should be made to the present Agreement and, subject to such modifications as may be agreed, the present Agreement shall continue in force provided that at any time after the 27th of April, 1962, either Government may give to the other Government notice in writing terminating the Agreement which notice shall take effect one year after the date on which such notice is given.

*Map:* [omitted].


## THE 1960 FISHERY AGREEMENT (Norway and United Kingdom of Great Britain and Northern Ireland)

Signed at Oslo on 17 November 1960. Entered into force on 3 March 1961. U.N. Treaty Series, vol. 398, p. 190.

**Art. I.** . . .

**Art. II.** As from a date of which the Norwegian Government shall give due notice to the United Kingdom Government, the latter Government shall not object to the exclusion, by the competent authorities of the Norwegian Government, of vessels registered in the territory of the United Kingdom from fishing in an area contiguous to the territorial sea of Norway extending to a limit of 6 miles from the base line from which that territorial sea is measured.

**Art. III.** During the period between the date referred to in Article II of this Agreement and the thirty-first day of October, 1970, the Norwegian Government shall not object to vessels registered in the territory of the United Kingdom continuing to fish in the zone between the limits of 6 and

124

12 miles from the base line from which the territorial sea of Norway is measured.

**Art. IV.** After the thirty-first day of October, 1970, the United Kingdom Government shall not object to the exclusion by the competent authorities of the Norwegian Government, of vessels registered in the territory of the United Kingdom from fishing within the limit of 12 miles from the base line from which the territorial sea of Norway is measured.

**Art. V.** If at any time before the thirty-first day of October, 1970, the Norwegian Government considers that there has been a fundamental change in the character of the fishing carried on in the zone referred to in Article III of this Agreement by vessels registered in the territory of the United Kingdom, the Norwegian Government may raise the matter with the United Kingdom Government, and the two Governments shall together review the position.

**Art. VI.** Except in the case of arrangements between the Norwegian Government and the Government of any other Scandinavian country in respect of the Skagerrak, the Norwegian Government shall accord to vessels registered in the territory of the United Kingdom treatment no less favourable than that accorded to the vessels of other foreign countries.

**Art. VII.** As from the date referred to in Article II of this Agreement, the Contracting Parties shall apply to vessels registered in their respective territories the provisions of the Annexes to this Agreement which shall be an integral part of the Agreement.

**Art. VIII.** Nothing in this Agreement shall be deemed to prejudice the views held by either Contracting Party as to the delimitation and limitation in international law of territorial waters or of exclusive jurisdiction in fishery matters.

**Art. IX.** . . .

*Annexes:* [omitted].

## THE 1961 AGREEMENT SETTLING THE FISHERIES DISPUTE
### (Iceland and United Kingdom of Great Britain and Northern Ireland)

Exchange of Notes at Reykjavik on 11 March 1961. U.N. Treaty Series, vol. 397, p. 275.

1. The United Kingdom Government will no longer object to a twelve-

mile fishery zone around Iceland measured from the base lines specified in paragraph 2 below which relate solely to the delimitation of that zone.

2. The base lines, which will be used for the purpose referred in paragraph 1 above, will be those set out in the Icelandic Regulation No. 70 of June 30, 1958, as modified by the use of the base lines drawn between the following points: ...

These modifications will enter into force immediately.

3. For a period of three years ..., the Icelandic Government will not object to vessels registered in the United Kingdom fishing within the outer six miles of the fishery zone referred to in paragraphs 1 and 2 above within the following areas during the periods specified: ...

4. There will, however, be no fishing by vessels registered in the United Kingdom in the outer six miles of the fishery zone referred to in paragraphs 1 and 2 during the aforesaid period of three years in the following areas: ...

The Icelandic Government will continue to work for the implementation of the Althing Resolution of May 5, 1959, regarding the extension of fisheries jurisdiction around Iceland, but shall give to the United Kingdom Government six months' notice of such extension and, in case of a dispute in relation to such extension, the matter shall, at the request of either party, be referred to the International Court of Justice.


## THE 1961 AGREEMENT CONCERNING THE FISHERY ZONE AROUND ICELAND (Iceland and Federal Republic of Germany)

Exchange of Notes at Reykjavik on 19 July 1961. U.N. Treaty Series, vol. 409, p. 47.

(1) The Government of the Federal Republic of Germany shall not object in future to a twelve-mile fishery zone around Iceland, measured from the base lines specified in paragraph (2) below which relate solely to the delimitation of that zone.

(2) The base lines which shall be used for the purpose referred to in paragraph (1) shall be those set out in Icelandic Regulations No. 70 of 30 June 1958, as modified by the use of the base lines drawn between the following points: ...

These modifications shall enter into force immediately.

(3) Until 10 March 1964 the Republic of Iceland shall not object to fishing by vessels registered in the Federal Republic of Germany within the outer six miles of the fishery zone referred to in paragraphs (1) and (2) within the following areas during the periods specified: ...

(4) Until the date referred to in paragraph (3) there shall, however,

be no fishing by vessels registered in the Federal Republic of Germany within the outer six miles of the fishery zone referred to in paragraph (1) and (2) in the following areas: . . .

(5) The Government of the Republic of Iceland shall continue to work for the implementation of the Althing Resolution of 5 May 1959 regarding the extension of the fishery jurisdiction of Iceland. However, it shall give the Government of the Federal Republic of Germany six months' notice of any such extension; in case of a dispute relating to such an extension, the matter shall, at the request of either party, be referred to the International Court of Justice.

(6)-(7): [omitted].

## THE 1962 AGREEMENT ON FISHING (Norway and Union of Soviet Socialist Republics)

Signed at Moscow on 16 April 1962. Entered into force on 1 August 1962. U.N. Treaty Series, vol. 437, p. 175.

**Art. 1.** . . .

**Art. II.** From the moment of the entry into force of this Agreement until 31 October 1970, the Government of the Kingdom of Norway shall permit fishing vessels registered in the Union of Soviet Socialist Republics and manned by Soviet nationals to fish in a Norwegian fishing zone between the limits of six and twelve miles from the base line from which the territorial waters of the Kingdom of Norway are measured.

However, in the areas indicated below, vessels of the Contracting Parties shall be limited to fishing with fixed nets and hand tackle: . . .

**Art. III.** During the period indicated in article II of this Agreement the Government of the Union of Soviet Socialist Republics shall permit fishing vessels registered in the Kingdom of Norway and manned by Norwegian nationals to engage in fishing in Soviet territorial waters in Varangerfjord between the limits of six and twelve miles from the shore in a zone bounded to the south by a line drawn along the Soviet coast six miles from the shore, to the south-east by a line drawn six miles from the base line from which Soviet territorial waters are measured, running from the promontory at the entrance to the bay of Dolgaya Shchel through the north-western extremity of the island of Bolshoy Ainov to Cape Nemetsky on Rybachy Peninsula, and to the north-east by a line joining Cape Nemetsky to Cape Kibergnes, as indicated on the map annexed to this Agreement.

127

**Art. IV.** Fishing in the zones indicated in articles II and III of this Agreement shall be carried on in accordance with the annexed Protocol,[2] which is an integral part of the Agreement.

For purposes other than fishing, Norwegian nationals and vessels present in Soviet territorial waters shall be subject to the laws and regulations of the Union of Soviet Socialist Republics relating to the presence in these waters of foreign nationals and vessels, without prejudice to the provisions of this Agreement.

Particulars of such laws and regulations and of amendments and additions thereto shall be notified to the Government of the Kingdom of Norway through the diplomatic channel.

**Art. V.** If at any time before 31 October 1970 either Contracting Party finds that there has been a radical change in the character of the fishing carried on by vessel of the other Party in the zones indicated in articles II and III of this Agreement, the Government concerned may raise the matter with the Govermennt of the other country and they shall together review the position.

**Art. VI.** If in the zones indicated in articles II and III of this Agreement fishing gear belonging to fishermen of one Party should be damaged by the fault of fishermen of the other Party, claims for compensation shall be examined in accordance with the Agreement between the Government of the Union of Soviet Socialist Republics and the Norwegian Government of 9 December 1959 concerning the handling of claims in connection with damage to fishing gear.

**Art. VII.** The Contracting Parties shall take the appropriate steps to ensure compliance with the provisions of this Agreement by their nationals and by vessels registered in their territories.

**Art. VIII.** . . .

*Protocol:* [omitted].
*Map:* [omitted].


## THE 1964 AGREEMENT REGARDING THE RIGHTS TO BE ACCORDED TO POLISH VESSELS WITHIN THE BRITISH FISHERY LIMITS TO BE ESTABLISHED ON 30 SEPTEMBER 1964 (Poland and United Kingdom of Great Britain and Northern Ireland)

Exchange of Notes at Warsaw on 26 September 1964. U.N. Treaty Series, vol. 539, p. 153.

(1) Polish fishing vessels shall have the right to continue to fish for herring until the 31st of December, 1967, in the zone between six and twelve miles from the baselines of the territorial sea of the United Kingdom, subject to the general fishery regulations in force in that zone, in the area extending from a line due East of the Longstone Lighthouse to a line due East of the river Tyne North Pier Lighthouse.

(2) Polish mother ships shall be permitted to enter the British fishery limits outside the territorial sea for purposes ancillary to fishing provided that these ships comply with the regulations applicable within the fishery limits. The Government of the United Kingdom may terminate this permission by giving one year's notice in writing to the Polish Government starting from the 31st of December of any year. However, at least one month before giving such notice the Government of the United Kingdom shall inform the Polish Government of their readiness to enter into consultations on this matter.

(3) These arrangements shall be without prejudice to the rights of either Government under any multilateral agreement regarding fisheries in coastal waters which may hereafter take effect as between the two Governments.

## THE 1964 AGREEMENT FOR THE CONTINUANCE OF FISHING BY NORWEGIAN VESSELS WITHIN THE FISHERY LIMITS OF THE UNITED KINGDOM OF GREAT BRITAIN AND NORTHERN IRELAND (Norway and United Kingdom of Great Britain and Northern Ireland)

Signed at London on 28 September 1964. Entered into force on 11 March 1965. U.N. Treaty Series, vol. 548, p. 63.

**Art. 1.** The United Kingdom Government, in fulfilment of the obligations in the Note addressed by Her Majesty's Chargé d'Affaires at Oslo to the Norwegian Minister for Foreign Affairs on the occasion of the signing on 17th November, 1960, of the Fishery Agreement between the United Kingdom Government and the Norwegian Government, and in consideration of the particular nature of the fisheries involved, agree that fishing vessels registered in the Kingdom of Norway (hereinafter referred to as "Norwegian vessels") may continue to fish within the fishery limits of the United Kingdom of Great Britain and Northern Ireland as provided in Articles 2 to 6 of this Agreement.

**Art. 2.** Norwegian vessels may continue to fish until 31th December, 1984, in the zone between 6 and 12 miles from the baselines of the territorial sea of the United Kingdom:

(a) for dogfish: . . .

(b) for basking sharks: . . .

**Art. 3.** Norwegian vessels may also continue to fish for dogfish and basking sharks off those parts of the coast described in Article 2 (a) and (b) of this Agreement up to a limit of three miles from the baselines of the territorial sea of the United Kingdom until 31st December, 1965, or where straight baselines or bay closing lines in excess of 10 miles are drawn, until 31st December, 1966.

**Art. 4.** If the United Kingdom Government should extend to any third country any right to fish for dogfish or basking sharks in the areas described in Article 2 (a) and (b) of this Agreement the same right shall extend automatically to the Kingdom of Norway.

**Art. 5.** If at any time there has been a fundamental change in the character of the fishing carried on by Norwegian vessels in the areas described in Article 2 (a) and (b) of this Agreement, the United Kingdom Government may raise the matter with the Norwegian Government and the two Governments shall together review the position.

**Art. 6.** Unless and until the two Governments otherwise agree, the rules of conduct to be enforced by the United Kingdom Government on Norwegian vessels fishing in the areas described in Article 2 (a) and (b) of this Agreement shall be those set out in the Convention for Regulating the Police of the North Sea Fisheries, signed at The Hague on 6th May, 1882.

**Art. 7.** The United Kingdom Government shall not require Norwegian vessels to observe any conservation measures which have the effect of abridging the right to fish for dogfish or basking sharks in the areas described in Article 2 (a) and (b) of this Agreement, unless the Norwegian Government has agreed to such measures.

**Art. 8.** . . .

## THE 1964 AGREEMENT ON MATTERS ARISING FROM THE ESTABLISHMENT BY THE UNITED KINGDOM OF THE FISHERY REGIME PROVIDED FOR BY THE FISHERY LIMITS ACT, 1964 (Union of Soviet Socialist Republics and United Kingdom of Great Britain and Northern Ireland)

Exchange of Notes at Moscow on 30 September 1964. U.N. Treaty Series, vol. 539, p. 159.

1. Fishing vessels and depot ships of the Soviet Union shall be permitted to anchor, navigate, tranship fish and perform other activities ancillary to fishing operations within the belt between 3 and 12 miles from the baseline from which the territorial sea of the United Kingdom is measured around the Shetland Islands north of a line drawn due west from Esha Ness lighthouse and a line drawn due east from the southernmost point of Bressay. They shall comply with the fishery regulations there in force which shall not discriminate as between vessels of the Soviet Union and those of other countries.

2. These arrangements shall ... remain in force until they are replaced by a more formal agreement or until the Government of the Soviet Union inform the Government of the United Kingdom that they no longer desire to make use of these arrangements subject, however, to the right of the Government of the United Kingdom at any time to give notice to the Government of the Soviet Union to terminate these arrangements, which shall then remain in force until the expiration of one year from the date on which such notice is given.

## THE 1964 FISHERIES CONVENTION

Signed at London on 9 March 1964. Entered into force on 15 March 1966 among Belgium, Denmark, France, Ireland, Spain, Sweden and U.K. Italy, Poland and Portugal thereafter acceded to the Convention. U.N. Treaty Series, vol. 581, p. 58.

**Art. 1.** (1) Each Contracting Party recognizes the right of any other Contracting Party to establish the fishery régime described in Articles 2 to 6 of the present Convention.

(2) Each Contracting Party retains however the right to maintain the fishery régime which it applies at the date on which the present Convention is opened for signature, if this régime is more favourable to the fishing of other countries than the régime described in Articles 2 to 6.

**Art. 2.** The coastal State has the exclusive right to fish and exclusive jurisdiction in matters of fisheries within the belt of six miles measured from the baseline of its territorial sea.

**Art. 3.** Within the belt between six and twelve miles measured from the baseline of the territorial sea, the right to fish shall be exercised only by the coastal State and by such other Contracting Parties, the fishing vessels of which have habitually fished in that belt between 1st January, 1953 and 31st December 1962.

**Art. 4.** Fishing vessels of the Contracting Parties, other than the coastal State, permitted to fish under Article 3, shall not direct their fishing effort towards stocks or fish or fishing grounds substantially different from those which they have habitually exploited. The coastal State may enforce this rule.

**Art. 5.** (1) Within the belt mentioned in Article 3 the coastal State has the power to regulate the fisheries and to enforce such regulations, including regulations to give effect to internationally agreed measures of conservation, provided that there shall be no discrimination in form or in fact against fishing vessels of other Contracting Parties fishing in conformity with Articles 3 and 4.

(2) Before issuing regulations, the coastal State shall inform the other Contracting Parties concerned and consult those Contracting Parties, if they so wish.

**Art. 6.** Any straight baseline or bay closing line which a Contracting Party may draw shall be in accordance with the rules of general international law and in particular with the provisions of the Convention on the Territorial Sea and the Contiguous Zone opened for signature at Geneva on 29th April, 1958.

**Art. 7.** Where the coasts of two Contracting Parties are opposite or adjacent to each other, neither of these Contracting Parties is entitled, failing agreement between them to the contrary, to establish a fisheries régime beyond the median line, every point of which is equidistant from the nearest points on the low water lines of the coasts of the Contracting Parties concerned.

**Art. 8.** (1) Once a Contracting Party applies the régime described in Articles 2 to 6, any right to fish which it may thereafter grant to a State not a Contracting Party shall extend automatically to the other Contracting Parties, whether or not they could claim this right by virtue of habitual fishing, to the extent that the State not a Contracting Party avails itself effectively and habitually of that right.

(2) If a Contracting Party which has established the régime described in Articles 2 to 6 should grant to another Contracting Party any right to fish which the latter cannot claim under Articles 3 and 4, the same right shall extend automatically to all other Contracting Parties.

**Art. 9.** (1) In order to allow fishermen of other Contracting Parties, who have habitually fished in the belt provided for in Article 2 to adapt themselves to their exclusion from that belt, a Contracting Party which establishes the régime provided for in Articles 2 to 6, shall grant to such fishermen the right to fish in that belt for a transitional period, to be determined by agreement between the Contracting Parties concerned.

132

(2) If a Contracting Party establishes the régime described in Articles 2 to 6, it may, notwithstanding the provisions of Article 2, continue to accord the right to fish in the whole or part of the belt provided for in Article 2 to other Contracting Parties of which the fishermen have habitually fished in the area by reason of voisinage arrangements.

**Art. 10.** Nothing in the present Convention shall prevent the maintenance or establishment of a special régime in matters of fisheries:
(a) as between States Members and Associated States of the European Economic Community,
(b) as between States Members of the Benelux Economic Union,
(c) as between Denmark, Norway and Sweden,
(d) as between France and the United Kingdom of Great Britain and Northern Ireland in respect of Granville Bay and the Minquiers and the Ecrehos,
(e) as between Spain, Portugal and their respective neighbouring countries in Africa,
(f) in the Skagerrak and the Kattegat.

**Art. 11.** Subject to the approval of the other Contracting Parties, a coastal State may exclude particular areas from the full application of Articles 3 and 4 in order to give preference to the local population if it is overwhelmingly dependent upon coastal fisheries.

**Art. 12.** The present Convention applies to the waters adjacent to the coasts of the Contracting Parties listed in Annex I. This Annex may be amended with the consent of the Governments of the Contracting Parties. Any proposal for amendment shall be sent to the Government of the United Kingdom of Great Britain and Northern Ireland which shall notify it to all Contracting Parties, and inform them of the date on which it enters into force.

**Art. 13.** Unless the parties agree to seek a solution by another method of peaceful settlement, any dispute which may arise between Contracting Parties concerning the interpretation or application of the present Convention shall at the request of any of the parties be submitted to arbitration in accordance with the provisions of Annex II to the present Convention.

**Art. 14.** ...

**Art. 15.** The present Convention shall be of unlimited duration. However at any time after the expiration of a period of twenty years from the initial entry into force of the present Convention, any Contracting Party may denounce the Convention by giving two years' notice in writing to the Government of the United Kingdom of Great Britain and Northern Ireland. The latter shall notify the denunciation to the Contracting Parties.

*Annex 1 (areas):* [omitted].
*Annex 2 - Arbitration:* [omitted].


## 2. UNITED STATES OF AMERICA


### THE 1967 AGREEMENT ON CERTAIN FISHERY PROBLEMS IN THE NORTHEASTERN PART OF THE PACIFIC OCEAN OFF THE COAST OF THE UNITED STATES OF AMERICA (Union of Soviet Socialist Republics and United States of America)

Exchange of Notes at Washington on 13 February 1967. U.N. Treaty Series, vol. 688, p. 157. Extended on 18 December 1967 (U.N. Treaty Series vol. 697, p. 362), amended and extended by the Agreements of 31 January 1969 (U.N. Treaty Series, vol. 714, p. 352) and of 12 February 1971, the latter being extended by an exchange of notes of 31 December 1972, and replaced by the Agreement of 21 February 1973. The text of the 1973 Agreement is printed on International Legal Materials, vol. 12, p. 553.

1. Fishing vessels of the Soviet Union may fish and conduct loading operations in the nine-mile zone contiguous to the territorial sea of the United States in the following areas: . . .
Fishing effort in these areas will not exceed the present level.
2. In addition, fishing vessels of the Soviet Union may conduct loading operations in the following areas in the nine-mile zone contiguous to the territorial sea of the United States: . . .
3. The Government of the Soviet Union will adopt the measures necessary to ensure that citizens and vessels of the Soviet Union:
*a.* Refrain from fishing in the waters off the Pacific coast of the United States between 46°14′ north latitude and 46°56′ north latitude landward of the isobath of 110 metres and in the waters bounded by an arc with a radius of 15 nautical miles with its center at the mouth of Alsea Bay in the State of Oregon;
*b.* Refrain from concentrating fishing vessels during the period from June 15th through September 15th between 47°54′ north latitude and 48°28′ north latitude east of 125°10′ west longitude;
*c.* During the period May 9th to May 23rd, refrain from fishing in

the following areas:

(1) The area enclosed by straight lines connecting the following co-ordinates in the order listed: . . .

(2) The area enclosed by straight lines connecting the following co-ordinates in the order listed: . . .

4. It is agreed that nationals and vessels of the respective countries shall not engage in trawl fishing in the following areas of high concentrations of ocean perch for the period of this agreement: . . .

This paragraph shall not apply to vessels under 110 feet in length.

5. The Government of the United States will adopt the measures necessary to ensure that nationals and vessels under its control engaged in the ocean perch fishery in waters off the coasts of the States of Oregon and Washington will use trawl gear having a mesh size of no less than three inches (76 mm.) in the cod end.

6. Each Government will take appropriate measures with regard to areas of heavy concentration of fishing operations of both countries directed at prevention of damage to fishing gear, including:

*a.* Measures leading to improvement of the means for marking fixed fishing gear and for reciprocal notification of areas in which fixed gear is concentrated;

b. Measures to ensure that fixed gear is set with due regard for the operation of mobile gear;

*c.* Measures to ensure that vessels operating with mobile gear will pass clearly marked fixed gear at a distance of not less than 400 metres from the nearest marker.

7. Both Governments will take appropriate measures to ensure that, to the extent practicable, waste materials are discharged at sea only in waters deeper than 1000 meters.

8. Both Governments consider it useful to arrange, when appropriate, for visits of representatives of fishermen's organization of the two countries to each other's fishing fleets operating in the northeastern part of the Pacific Ocean. Such visits may be arranged on mutually agreeable terms determined in each particular case by the Chief of the Joint Expedition in the Soviet fleet, Dalryba, and the Regional Director of the United States Bureau of Commercial Fisheries in Seattle, Washington or Juneau, Alaska, as may be appropriate.

9. Both Governments consider it desirable to expand fishery research in the northeastern part of the Pacific Ocean on species of common interest, both on a national basis and in the form of joint investigations. The competent agencies of the two Governments will arrange for the exchange of scientific data and results of research on the fisheries, for meetings of scientists and, when appropriate, for participation by scientists of each Government in investigations carried out on board research vessels of the

other Government. Each Government will, within the scope of its domestic laws and regulations, facilitate entry into appropriate port for research vessels of the other Government engaged in such joint research.

10. Nothing in this agreement shall be interpreted as prejudicing the views of either Government with regard to freedom of fishing on the high seas or to traditional fisheries.

11. This agreement shall remain in force for the period of one year. Representatives of the two Governments will meet at a mutually convenient time prior to the expiration of the period of validity of this agreement to review the operation of this agreement and to decide on future arrangements.

## THE 1967 AGREEMENT CONCERNING FISHERIES OFF THE COAST OF THE UNITED STATES OF AMERICA (Japan and United States of America)

> Signed at Tokyo on 9 May 1967. U.N. Treaty Series, vol. 685, p. 285. Extended and amended on 23 December 1968 (U.N. Treaty Series, vol. 714, p. 330); replaced by the Agreement of 11 December 1970 and further replaced by the Agreement of 20 December 1972.

1. The Government of Japan will take necessary measures to ensure that nationals and vessels of Japan will not engage in fishing except such fishing as listed below in the waters which are contiguous to the territorial sea of the United States of America and extend to a limit of twelve nautical miles from the baseline from which the United States territorial sea is measured.

   (1)   (i)  Crab fishing in the waters off the Pribilof Islands.

          (ii)  Dragnet and longline fishing in the waters:

                (A)  off the Bering Sea coast of the Aleutian Islands: . . .

                (B)  off the Pacific coast of the Aleutian Islands: . . .

                (C)  off the Pribilof Islands.

         (iii)  Tuna fishing in all waters except off the mainland of the United States of America (including Alaska), Puerto Rico, Virgin Islands, Panama Canal Zone and Hawaii, Maui, Molokai, Oahu, Kauai, Lanai and Niihau of the Hawaiian Islands.

        (iv)  Whaling in all waters off the coast of the State of Alaska except off the Pacific coast between 150° and 163° West Longitude.

   (2)  Loading operations:

         (i)  On the east side of Kayak Island in the State of Alaska between 59°52′ and 59°56′ North Latitude west of 143°53′ West

136

Longitude and on the west side of Kayak Island between 59°56' and 60° North Latitude.

(ii) On the west side of Sanak Island in the State of Alaska in the waters bounded on the north by 54°36' North Latitude, on the south by 54°26' North Latitude, on the west by 163°05' West Longitude and on the east by 162°40' West Longitude.

2. Nothing in the present arrangements shall be deemed to prejudice the claims of either Government in regard to the jurisdiction of a coastal state over fisheries.

3. The present arrangements shall be effective as of May 9, 1967 and shall continue in effect until December 31, 1968, provided that, in regard to the fishing as specified in paragraph 1. (1) (ii) (A) (c), the present arrangements shall continue in effect until May 31, 1969. The two Governments shall meet before December 31, 1968 to review the operation of the present arrangements and to decide on future arrangements.

## THE 1967 AGREEMENT ON CERTAIN FISHERY PROBLEMS ON THE HIGH SEAS IN THE WESTERN AREAS OF THE MIDDLE ATLANTIC OCEAN (Union of Soviet Socialist Republics and United States of America)

Signed at Moscow on 25 November 1967. Entered into force on the same date. U.N. Treaty Series, vol. 701, p. 161. Extended by the exchange of notes of 9 October and 3 December 1968 (U.N. Treaty Series, vol. 720, p. 342). Replaced by the Agreement of 13 December 1968 (TIAS 6603; International Legal Materials, vol. 8, p. 502), the Agreement of 11 December 1970 and the Agreement of 21 June 1973.

The Government of the United States of America and the Government of the Union of Soviet Socialist Republics, considering it desirable that the fisheries in the Western areas of the high seas in the Middle Atlantic Ocean be conducted on a rational basis with due attention to their mutual interests, proceeding from generally recognized principles of international law,

Considering it necessary to conduct the fisheries in the said area with due regard for the state of fish stocks, based on the results of scientific investigation, for the purpose of ensuring the maintenance of maximum sustainable yields and the maintenance of the said fisheries,

Taking into account the need for expanding and coordinating scientific research in the field of fisheries and the exchange of scientific data,

137

Have agreed on the following:

1. The Government of the United States of America and the Government of the Union of Soviet Socialist Republics consider it desirable to expand research pertaining to the species of fish of interest to both parties, on a national basis as well as in the form of coordinated research according to agreed programs. The competent agencies of both Governments shall ensure the following:

*a.* An exchange of scientific and statistical data, published works and the results of fishery research;

*b.* Meetings of scientists and, in appropriate cases, the participation of the scientists of each Government in fishery research conducted on the research vessels of the other Government.

Each Government will take the necessary steps to ensure that its competent agencies conduct the corresponding fishery research as well as develop the most rational fishing technology in accordance with a co-ordinated program, which has been developed by the scientists of both countries.

2. The Government of the United States of America and the Government of the Union of Soviet Socialist Republics, for the purpose of reproduction and maintenance of fish stocks, will take appropriate measures to ensure that their citizens and vessels will:

*a.* Refrain from fishing during the period from January 1 to April 1, to ensure access of red hake and silver hake to the spawning grounds; said abstention will apply to an area of the Mid-Atlantic bounded by straight lines with the following coordinates: on the east, along the meridian 71°40′ W. Long.; on the west, along the meridian 72°40′ W. Long; on the south, by a line connecting points with coordinates 39°00′ N. Lat., 71°40′ W. Long. and 39°00′ N. Lat., 72°40′ W. Long., and on the north by the outer limit of the nine-mile fishery zone contiguous to the territorial sea of the United States of America;

*b.* Refrain from increasing fish catch above the 1967 level in the waters situated west and south of Sub-area 5 of the Convention area of the 1949 International Convention for Fisheries in the Northwest Atlantic and north of Cape Hatteras;

*c.* Refrain from conducting specialized fisheries for scup and fluke and not increase their incidental catch in the waters specified in sub-paragraph *b.* of this paragraph.

The above provisions shall not apply to vessels under 110 feet in length, nor to vessels fishing for crustacea or molluscs.

3. *a.* Fishing vessels of the Union of Soviet Socialist Republics may, during the period from November 15 to May 15, conduct loading operations in the waters of the nine-mile fishery zone contiguous to the territorial sea of the United States of America enclosed by straight lines

connecting the following coordinates in the order listed:

| North Latitude | West Longitude |
|----------------|----------------|
| 40°40′55″      | 72°40′00″      |
| 40°34′31″      | 72°40′00″      |
| 40°33′28″      | 72°43′44″      |
| 40°39′48″      | 72°43′44″      |

*b.* Fishing vessels of the Union of Soviet Socialist Republics may conduct loading operations during the period from September 15 to May 15 within the nine-mile fishery zone contiguous to the territorial sea of the United States of America, in the area between 39°20′ N. Lat. and 39°45′ N. Lat. The Government of the United States of America will communicate to the Government of the Union of Soviet Socialist Republics, prior to January 1, 1968, the coordinates of the area most suitable for this purpose, which shall be three nautical miles long, and six nautical miles wide measured landward from the outer limits of the nine-mile fishery zone contiguous to the territorial sea of the United States of America.

4. Fishing vessels of the Union of Soviet Socialist Republics may fish during the period from January 1 to April 1, within the nine-mile fishery zone contiguous to the territorial sea of the United States of America, in the waters bounded by straight lines connecting the following coordinates in the order listed:

| North Latitude | West Longitude |
|----------------|----------------|
| 40°40′55″      | 72°40′00″      |
| 40°34′31″      | 72°40′00″      |
| 40°32′41″      | 72°46′26″      |
| 40°32′32″      | 72°53′26″      |
| 40°36′54″      | 72°53′26″      |

5. Each Government will, within the scope of its domestic laws and regulations, facilitate entry into appropriate ports for fishing and fishery research vessels of the other Government. This shall apply with respect to the procedure for presenting crew lists for the above-mentioned vessels and to the providing of fresh water, fuel and provisions.

6. Under conditions of force majeure, each Government will, within the scope of its domestic laws and regulations, facilitate entry of fishing and fishery research vessels into its respective open ports after appropriate notification has been given.

7. Nothing in this agreement shall be interpreted as prejudicing the views of either Government with regard to freedom of fishing on the high seas or to traditional fisheries.

8. This agreement shall remain in force for the period of one year. Representatives of the two Governments will meet at a mutually con-

venient time prior to the expiration of the period of validity of this agreement to review the operation of this agreement and to decide on future arrangements.


## 3. CANADA


## THE 1972 ARRANGEMENTS WITH RESPECT TO DANISH FISHING PRACTICES OFF THE ATLANTIC COAST OF CANADA (Canada and Denmark)

Exchange of Notes at Ottawa on 25 March 1972.

1. Faroese fishing vessels may continue to fish for cod by trawl and by longline until January 1, 1972, in that part of the outer nine miles of the territorial sea of Canada where such vessels have fished during the period of five years immediately preceding December 31, 1970. The territorial sea on the Atlantic coast of Canada is measured from baselines as determined by the provisions of Annex A to this Note.

2. Faroese fishing vessels may continue to fish for cod until January 1, 1975, as follows:

    (*a*)  (i)  by trawl, . . .

           (ii)  by longline, . . . in Zone 1 (Gulf of St. Lawrence) of the fishing zones of Canada, . . . outside a distance of 12 miles from the low water line of the coast and 12 miles from a line joining Cape St. George with Cape Anguille;

    (*b*)  by trawl, up to a distance of three miles from the low water line of the coast of St. Paul Island northeastward of . . .

3. Faroese fishing vessels may further continue to fish for cod by trawl until May 15, 1976, and by longline until December 31, 1976, in the areas described in sub-paragraph 2, on the same conditions as before January 1, 1975, save only that such continued fishing thereafter shall be on the basis of a licence or licences to be issued by the Canadian authorities.

4. Faroese fishing vessels may continue to fish for porbeagle shark by longline until January 1, 1975, in that part of Zone 1 (Gulf of St. Lawrence) of the fishing zones of Canada . . . and thereafter for successive periods of two years, on the same conditions as before January 1, 1975, save only that such continued fishing shall be on the basis of a licence or licences to be issued by the Canadian authorities and may be terminated by the Canadian authorities upon not less than one year's notice in writing prior to the conclusion of any two-year period.

140

5. Faroese fishing vessels may retain other species caught incidentally while fishing for cod in accordance with the foregoing provisions of this Note.

6. Faroese fishing vessels shall be subject, without discrimination, to the same laws and regulations as Canadian fishing vessels while operating within the areas in which they may continue to fish pursuant to this Note. The Canadian authorities shall inform the Danish authorities of the fisheries regulations applicable to such areas. On transmission from the Canadian authorities, the Danish Government shall make known to the Faroese authorities these laws and regulations with a view to ensuring their strict observance. The Canadian Government shall not, without the agreement of the Danish Government, change the existing fishing laws and regulations previously made known to the Danish Government in a manner which would have the effect of curtailing the areas in which Faroese fishing vessels could, in practice, fish pursuant to this agreement.

7. If at any time before December 31, 1976, the Canadian Government considers that there has been a fundamental change in the intensity, character and pattern of the fishing carried on by Faroese fishing vessels in any of the areas referred to herein, the Canadian Government may raise the matter with the Danish Government and the two Governments shall review the situation.

## THE 1972 ARRANGEMENTS WITH RESPECT TO BRITISH FISHING PRACTICES OFF THE ATLANTIC COAST OF CANADA
### (Canada and United Kingdom of Great Britain and Northern Ireland)

Exchange of Notes at Ottawa on 27 March 1972.

(1) British fishing vessels may continue, until January 1, 1978, to fish in that part of the outer nine miles of the territorial sea of Canada which is specified in Annex A to this Note, subject to the provisions of sub-paragraphs (3), (4), (5) and (6) of this paragraph. The territorial sea on the Atlantic coast of Canada shall be measured from baselines as determined by the provisions of Annex B to this Note.

(2) British fishing vessels may continue, until January 1, 1973, to fish in that part of Zone 1 (Gulf of St. Lawrence) of the fishing zones of Canada . . . , subject to the provisions of sub-paragraphs (3), (4) and (5) of this paragraph . . .

(3) British fishing vessels may fish for cod and haddock (but may retain other species caught incidentally such as flounder and halibut) in the areas and for the periods as set out in sub-paragraphs (1) and (2) of this paragraph.

(4) If at any time before the 1st day of January, 1978, the Canadian Government considers that there has been a fundamental change in the intensity, character and pattern of the fishing carried on by British fishing vessels in the territorial sea and fishing zones on the Atlantic coast of Canada, as set out in sub-paragraphs (1) and (2) of this paragraph, the Canadian Government may raise the matter with the British Government and the two Governments shall together review the situation.

(5) British fishing vessels shall be subject, without discrimination, to the same laws and regulations as Canadian fishing vessels while operating within the outer nine miles of Canada's territorial sea or within that part of Zone 1 of the fishing zones of Canada as set out in sub-paragraph (2) of this paragraph. The Canadian authorities shall inform the British authorities of the fisheries regulations applicable to such areas. On transmission from the Canadian authorities, the British Government shall make known to its nationals these laws and regulations with a view to ensuring their strict observation. Before the expiration of the periods of time referred to in sub-paragraphs (1) and (2) above respectively, the Canadian Government shall not, after the 27th day of March, 1972, without the agreement of the British Government, change the existing laws and regulations previously made known to the British Government in a manner which would have the effect of curtailing the areas in which British fishing vessels could, in practice, fish pursuant to these arrangements.

(6) The Canadian authorities will give the British authorities advance notice of particular areas and periods during which concentrations of gear are probable within the outer nine miles of the territorial sea of Canada:

(a) from Cape Gabarus northward to Cape North (Cape Breton Island, Nova Scotia); and

(b) from Lamaline Shag Rock passing east and north to Gull Island, Newfoundland.

The British authorities will transmit any such information to British vessels likely to fish in the area and will request such vessels, before actually fishing, to establish communication, as appropriate, with the regional fisheries office of the Canadian Government in Halifax, Nova Scotia, or St. John's, Newfoundland, to obtain current information about the local situation for the purpose of enabling vessels the better to avoid damage to gear. The British Government will not object to action by the Canadian authorities in cases of emergency to direct British fishing vessels clear of gear concentrations, provided that Canadian and other fishing vessels of similar class are subject to the same directions, and subject to the rights of the British Government under sub-paragraph (5) of this paragraph if such directions should seriously interfere with the pattern of fishing by British vessels.

(7) Nothing in this agreement shall affect the right of British fishing

vessels to innocent passage through Zone 1 of the fishing zones of Canada during the period of this agreement or after its expiry.


## THE 1972 ARRANGEMENTS WITH RESPECT TO PORTUGUESE FISHING PRACTICES OFF THE ATLANTIC COAST OF CANADA
### (Canada and Portugal)

Exchange of Notes at Ottawa on 27 March 1972.

1. Portuguese fishing vessels may continue to fish for cod by trawl and line until July 1, 1978, in those areas of the outer nine miles of the territorial sea af Canada where such vessels have fished during the period of five years immediately preceding December 31, 1970, subject to the provisions of sub-paragraphs 3, 4 and 5. The territorial sea on the Atlantic coast of Canada is measured from the baselines as determined by the provisions of Annex A to this Note.

2. Portuguese fishing vessels may continue to fish for cod by trawl in the months of January, February and March each year until April 1, 1976, east of the meridian of longitude 61°30′ west in Zone 1 (Gulf of St. Lawrence) of the fishing zones of Canada, . . . and outside a distance of 12 miles from the low-water line of the coast and 12 miles from a line joining Cape St. George with Cape Anguille, subject to the provisions of sub-paragraphs 3 and 5.

3. Portuguese fishing vessels shall be subject, without discrimination in form or fact to the same laws and regulations as Canadian fishing vessels while operating within the outer nine miles of Canada's territorial sea or within Zone 1 (Gulf of St. Lawrence) of the fishing zones of Canada. The Canadian authorities shall inform the Portuguese authorities of the fishing regulations applicable to these areas.

4. The Canadian authorities will give the Portuguese authorities advance notice of particular areas and periods during which concentrations of gear of inshore fishermen may occur in those areas of the outer nine miles of the territorial sea of Canada where Portuguese trawlers have fished during the period of five years immediately preceding December 31, 1970. The Portuguese authorities will transmit any such information to Portuguese trawlers likely to fish in such areas and will request such vessels, before actually fishing, to establish communication, as appropriate, with the Regional Fisheries Office of the Canadian Government in Halifax, Nova Scotia, or St. John's, Newfoundland, to obtain current information about the local situation for the purpose of enabling vessels the better to avoid damage to gear. The Portuguese Government will not object to action

by the Canadian authorities in cases of emergency to direct Portuguese fishing vessels clear of gear concentrations, provided that Canadian and other fishing vessels of a similar size and class are subject to the same directions.

5. If at any time before January 1, 1978, the Canadian Government considers that there has been a fundamental change in the intensity, character and pattern of the fishing carried on by Portuguese fishing vessels in any of the areas referred to herein, the Canadian Government may raise the matter with the Portuguese Government and the two Governments shall review the situation.

6. The Government of Canada undertakes to review in good faith at the request of the Government of Portugal the provisions of this exchange of Notes prior to the expiration of the periods referred to in sub-paragraphs 1 and 2 above, including the consideration of a continuance of the Portuguese fishing effort in the areas covered by this agreement on the basis of a licence or licences on such terms as may be determined by the Canadian Government taking into account the nature, extent and socio-economic aspects of the Portuguese fishing effort in the areas concerned, and conservation requirements.

## THE 1972 AGREEMENT ON MUTUAL FISHING PRACTICES
(Canada and France)

Signed at Ottawa on 27 March 1972. Entered into force on the same day.

**Art. 1.** The Government of France renounces the privileges established to its advantage in fishery matters by the Convention signed at London, on April 8, 1904, between the United Kingdom and France. The present agreement supersedes all previous treaty provisions relating to fishing by French nationals off the Atlantic coast of Canada.

**Art. 2.** In return, the Canadian Government undertakes in the event of a modification to the juridicial regime relating to the waters situated beyond the present limits of the territorial sea and fishing zones of Canada on the Atlantic coast, to recognize the right of French nationals to fish in these waters subject to possible measures for the conservation of resources, including the establishment of quotas. The French Government undertakes for its part to grant reciprocity to Canadian nationals off the coast of Saint-Pierre and Miquelon.

**Art. 3.** Fishing vessels registered in metropolitan France may continue

144

to fish from January 15 to May 15 each year, up to May 15, 1986, on an equal footing with Canadian vessels, in the Canadian fishing zone within the Gulf of St. Lawrence, east of the meridian of longitude 61 degrees 30 mins west, subject to the provisions of Articles 5 and 6.

**Art. 4.** In view of the special situation of Saint-Pierre and Miquelon and as an arrangement between neighbours:

(*a*) French coastal fishing boats registered in Saint-Pierre and Miquelon may continue to fish in the areas where they have traditionally fished along the coasts of Newfoundland, and Newfoundland coastal fishing boats shall enjoy the same right along the coasts of Saint-Pierre and Miquelon;

(*b*) A maximum of ten French trawlers registered in Saint-Pierre and Miquelon, of a maximum length of 50 metres, may continue to fish along the coasts of Newfoundland, of Nova Scotia (with the exception of the Bay of Fundy), and in the Canadian fishing zone within the Gulf of St. Lawrence, on an equal footing with Canadian trawlers; Canadian trawlers registered in the ports on the Atlantic coast of Canada may continue to fish along the coasts of Saint-Pierre and Miquelon on an equal footing with French trawlers.

**Art. 5.** French fishing vessels covered by the provision of Article 3 must not direct their fishing effort to the taking of species other than those which they have traditionally exploited in the five-year period immediately preceding this agreement, nor shall they substantially increase the level of such effort.

**Art. 6.** 1. Canadian fishery regulations shall be applied without discrimination in fact or in law to the French fishing vessels covered by Articles 3 and 4, including regulations concerning the dimensions of vessels authorized to fish less than 12 miles from the Atlantic coast of Canada.

2. French fishery regulations shall be applied under the same conditions to the Canadian fishing vessels covered by Article 4.

3. Before promulgating new regulations applicable to these vessels, the authorities of each of the parties shall give three months prior notice to the authorities of the other party.

**Art. 7.** The French patrol vessel which usually accompanies the French fishing fleet may continue to exercise its functions of assistance in‧ the Gulf of St. Lawrence.

**Art. 8.** The line defined in the annex to the present agreement determines, in the area between Newfoundland and the islands of Saint-Pierre and Miquelon, the limit of the territorial waters of Canada and of the zones submitted to the fishery jurisdiction of France.

**Art. 9.** No provision of the present agreement shall be interpreted as

145

prejudicing the views and future claims of either party concerning internal waters, territorial waters or jurisdiction with respect to fisheries or the resources of the continental shelf, or the bilateral or multilateral agreements to which either government is a party.

**Art. 10.** 1. The contracting parties shall establish a Commission to consider all disputes concerning the application of this agreement.

2. The Commission shall consist of one national expert nominated by each of the parties for ten years. In addition, the two Governments shall designate by mutual agreement a third expert who shall not be a national of either party.

3. If, in connection with any dispute referred to the Commission by either of the contracting parties, the Commission has not within one month reached a decision acceptable to the contracting parties, reference shall be made to the third expert. The Commission shall then sit as an arbitral tribunal under the chairmanship of the third expert.

4. Decisions of the Commission sitting as an arbitral tribunal shall be taken by a majority, and shall be binding on the contracting parties.

## 4. LATIN AMERICA

### THE 1967 AGREEMENT ON TRADITIONAL FISHING IN THE EXCLUSIVE FISHERY ZONES CONTIGUOUS TO THE TERRITORIAL SEAS OF BOTH COUNTRIES (Mexico and United States of America)

> Signed at Washington, D.C. on 27 October 1967. Entered into force on 1 January 1968. TIAS 6359. U.N. Treaty Series, vol. 693, p. 175.

*Considering:*

I. That the Government of the United States of America, pursuant to Public Law 89-658, approved October 14, 1966, established an exclusive fishery zone contiguous to the territorial sea of the United States in which it will exercise the same exclusive rights in respect to fisheries as it has in its territorial sea, subject to the continuation of traditional fishing by the foreign states within this zone as may be recognized by the Government of the United States;

II. That the Government of Mexico, pursuant to the law of December 9, 1966, promulgated by the Mexican Congress, established the exclusive jurisdiction of Mexico, for fishing purposes, in a zone of 12 nautical miles

146

(22,224 meters) in breadth, measured from the base line used to measure the breadth of the territorial sea, and provided that the legal regime for the exploitation of the living resources of the sea within the territorial sea extends to the entire exclusive fishery zone of the nation and that nothing contained in this law modifies in any way the legal provisions which determine the breadth of the territorial sea, and finally that Mexico's Federal Executive will determine the conditions and terms under which nationals of countries which traditionally have exploited the living resources of the sea within the 3 nautical mile zone beyond the territorial sea may be authorized to continue their activities for a period not to exceed five years, beginning on January 1, 1968;

III. That both Governments consider it necessary and convenient to establish the terms and conditions under which, without any modification of and in total accord with the laws cited in previous paragraphs I and II, fishing vessels of the United States and those of Mexico may, beginning January 1, 1968, continue their activities during five years in the waters within the exclusive fishery zone of the other country in which vessels of the same flag fished in a sustained manner during the five years immediately preceding January 1, 1968; and

IV. That both Governments state that the establishment of said terms and conditions does not imply a change of position or an abandonment of the positions maintained by each Government regarding the breadth of the teritorial sea, this matter not being the object of this agreement, nor does it limit their freedom to continue defending them in the international forum or in any of the ways recognized by international law;

*The Government of the United States of America and the Government of the United Mexican States*

Agree to establish the following terms and conditions under which American and Mexican fishermen will continue to operate in the above-mentioned waters during the established period of five years:

1. Fishing vessels of the United States will be permitted to continue their activities in the exclusive fishery zone of the United Mexican States in the Gulf of Mexico:

(*a*) In the waters between 9 and 12 nautical miles off the coast of the mainland and around the islands of Mexico, measured from the baseline from which the breadth of the territorial sea is measured, bounded on the north by a line to be constructed by the International Boundary and Water Commission, United States and Mexico, as the maritime boundary between both countries, extended to the twelve nautical mile limit, and bounded on the south by a straight line connecting the geographic coordinates of 21°20′00″ north latitude, 86°38′00″ west longitude, and 21°20′00″ north latitude, 86°35′00″ west longitude (north-east of Isla Mujeres), where fishing vessels of the United States have traditionally carried on shrimp fishing, they will be permitted to continue to take shrimp and such species of fish as are taken incidentally;

(b) United States fishing vessels will be permitted to continue to fish for snappers, groupers, and other genera that are captured incidentally, such as . . . in waters between 9 and 12 nautical miles around Cayo Arcas, Arrecifes Triangulos, Cayo Arenas, and Arrecifes Alacran;

(c) The fishing referred to in subparagraphs (a) and (b) above will continue during the five years beginning January 1, 1968, at levels such that the total catch by U.S. vessels will not exceed the total in the five years immediately preceding that date.

2. In the maritime waters off the Mexican coast in the Pacific Ocean:

(a) In the waters between 9 and 12 nautical miles measured from the baseline from which the breadth of the territorial sea is measured, off the mainland and around the islands of Mexico, bounded on the north by a line to be constructed by the International Boundary and Water Commission, United States and Mexico, as the maritime boundary between both countries, extended to the 12 nautical mile limit and bounded on the south by a straight line connecting the geographical coordinates of 14°32′42″ north latitude, 92°27′00″ west longitude, and 14°30′36″ north latitude, 92°29′18″ west longitude, where fishing vessels of the United States have traditionally carried on fishing, they will be permitted to fish for albacore, yellowfin tuna, bluefin tuna, skipjack, bonito, thread herring, white sea bass, giant sea bass, rockfishes, California halibut, yellowtail, barracuda, groupers, and such other species are commonly taken incidentally in fishing for the above-mentioned species, and for anchoveta, northern anchovy and Pacific sardine exclusively as tuna bait fish;

(b) The fishing referred to in subparagraph (a) above will continue during five years beginning on January 1, 1968, up to a total volume that will not exceed the total catch taken by U.S. vessels in the five years immediately preceding that date; and

(c) U.S. fishing vessels will be permitted, during the same term of five years, to continue sport or recreational fishing in the waters indicated.

3. Mexican fishermen will be permitted to continue their activities within the exclusive fishery zone of the United States, in regards to the Gulf of Mexico:

(a) In the waters between 9 and 12 nautical miles measured from the base line from which the breadth of the territorial sea is measured, off the mainland and around the islands of the United States, from the maritime boundary indicated in paragraph 1 (a) above to a line on the 26th parallel of north latitude connecting points 9 and 12 miles from the said baseline on the West Coast of Florida where fishing vessels of Mexico have carried on fishing traditionally and in a sustained manner, they will be permitted to fish for shrimp and other genera that are captured incidentally, as well as to fish for snappers; and

(b) The fishing referred to in subparagraph (a) above will continue during five years beginning on January 1, 1968, up to a total volume that will not exceed the total catch taken by Mexican vessels in the five years immediately preceding that date.

4. In the maritime waters off the United States coast on the Pacific Ocean:

(a) In the waters between 9 and 12 nautical miles measured from the baseline from which the breadth of the territorial sea is measured, off the mainland and around the islands of the United States, from the maritime boundary indicated in paragraph 2 (a) above, to a western extension of the California-Oregon border (42° north latitude) where fishing vessels of Mexico have carried on fishing traditionally and in a sustained manner, they will be permitted to fish for Pacific mackerel, yellowfin tuna, bluefin tuna, albacore, yellowtail, hake, giant sea bass, rockfishes, and such other species as are commonly taken incidentally in fishing for tuna, as well as anchoveta, northern anchovy and Pacific sardine, these last ones exclusively as tuna bait fish; and

(b) The fishing referred to in subparagraph (a) above will continue during five years beginning on January 1, 1968, up to a total volume that will not exceed the total catch taken by Mexican vessels in the five years immediately preceding that date.

5. In the event that the International Boundary and Water Commission, United States and Mexico, is unable to complete the lines referred to in paragraphs 1 (a), 2 (a), 3 (a) and 4 (a) prior to January 1, 1968, it will, prior to that date, for the purposes of this agreement, prepare lines to be used as provisional boundaries until the two countries are able to agree on permanent boundaries of their exclusive fishery zones.

6. In view of the fact that the catch by United States vessels within the exclusive fishery zone of Mexico and the catch by Mexican vessels within the exclusive fishery zone of the United States have not substantially increased during recent years, both Governments agree that said catches should not increase, and because of this they do not consider it necessary to establish during the five years beginning January 1, 1968 specific control measures, other than the following:

(a) The Government of the United States of America will submit to the Government of Mexico, and the latter will submit to the former, before January 1, 1968, or, at the latest, 30 days after that date, a report designating the areas now included within the exclusive fishery zone of the other country where its fishermen have operated in a sustained manner during the years 1963 to 1966 inclusive, indicating the species caught and the volume of each species, and the two Governments will submit to each other similar reports for the year 1967 no later than June 30, 1968;

(*b*) The two Governments will report to each other before January 1, 1968, or, at the latest, 30 days after that date, the number of vessels and the types and net tonnage of said vessels as well as the types of fishing gear used during the previous years by their respective nationals;

(*c*) The two Governments will exchange, no later than January 31 of each year, and at such other times as it may become necessary owing to special circumstances, lists of vessels that will operate under the terms of the present agreement;

(*d*) Representatives of the two Governments will meet annually on mutually agreeable dates to review the operation of this agreement and to determine the need for any additional arrangements. To facilitate this review, the Government of the United States will submit to the Government of Mexico, and the latter will submit to the former, as soon as practicable after January 1, but not later than April 1, each year a report on the fishing activities of its nationals in the exclusive fishery zone of the other country, indicating the volume of catch of each species authorized to be taken and the areas in which such catches were made.

7. The United States and Mexican fishermen may continue to use, within the exclusive fishery zone of the other country, only vessels and fishing gear not prohibited by the laws of the respective country and of the same types as those employed during the five years prior to January 1, 1968, except that technological improvements to existing types of vessels and gear are not precluded, provided they are not inconsistent with the legislation of the respective country.

8. Notwithstanding the limitations on fishing indicated in paragraphs 1, 2, 3, 4, and 7 of this agreement, each Government may establish additional limitations when, in its judgment, they become indispensable in order to protect the living resources of the sea in the exclusive fishery zone under its jurisdiction, or when each Government or both Governments must establish extraordinary restrictions pursuant to resolutions or recommendations of international organizations of which they are members. In any of these eventualities, the interested Government will consult with the other Government before establishing the new limitations and will notify the other Government 60 days in advance of their application in order to reasonably allow the fishermen of the other country to adjust their activities accordingly.

9. The United States of America and the United Mexican States, in accordance with their respective laws on the exclusive fishery zone, will exercise within their respective zones the same exclusive rights with respect to fisheries as they exercise in their territorial sea. Nevertheless, without renouncing their sovereign powers and in order to respect the traditional fisheries by their respective nationals in the zone of the other country

150

during the period indicated in this agreement, both Governments state that it is their intention neither to impose duties or taxes nor to impose other fiscal obligations, nor to propose to their respective Congresses the establishment of financial burdens upon the fishermen of the other country, who, within the terms of this agreement, will continue to operate in the waters within their respective exclusive fishery zones during the five years beginning January 1, 1968.

10. Notwithstanding the provisions of the previous paragraph, if either of the two Governments, due to circumstances which may arise during the life of this agreement, should deem it necessary or convenient to establish and collect such taxes, duties or fiscal obligations from the fishermen of the other country, it will first grant the other Government the opportunity to express its point of view. If, finally, such taxes, duties or obligations are established, the other Government, in strict reciprocity, will have the right to impose identical or similar fiscal measures, within its exclusive fishery zone, upon the fishermen of the country that first applied them.

11. For purposes of this agreement, the Government of Mexico will permit only vessels flying the flag of the United States of America to continue to operate within its exclusive fishery zone. For purposes of this agreement, only vessels flying the Mexican flag will be permitted to operate within the exclusive fishery zone of the United States of America.

12. Any fishing vessel of either country operating under the present agreement which acts contrary to the provisions of the agreement will not have the protection of the agreement in the particular case and will be subject exclusively to the legal regime, penal and administrative, of the country having jurisdiction over the exclusive fisheries zone.

13. The Government of the United States understands that neither the enactment of the Mexican law on the exclusive fishery zone of the nation nor the provisions of the present agreement imply *ipso facto* and of themselves any change regarding the legal regime on the exploitation of the living resources of the Mexican territorial sea, including the provisions of Mexico's law relating to the imposition of fees and taxes on foreign fishermen who fish within Mexico's territorial sea, since the law on the fishery zone of the nation, in accordance with its Article 2 (transitory), only repeals previous provisions contrary to it, and this agreement, as was expressed in the points of initial consideration, is based on said law.

14. The Government of the United States of America will cooperate with the Government of Mexico in the formulation and execution of a program of scientific research and conservation of the stocks of shrimp and fish of common concern off the coast of Mexico, consistent with the Convention on Fishing and Conservation of Living Resources of the High Seas, opened for signature at Geneva on April 29, 1968, to which both

151

Governments are parties. The two Governments at an appropriate time will meet to make the special arrangements necessary to formulate and execute such a program.

15. The provisions of this agreement will be enforced by the Government of the United States of America and by the Government of Mexico in their respective exclusive fishing zones.

16. This agreement shall be in effect for a period of five years beginning on January 1, 1968, provided that either Party may denounce the agreement at any time after one year from that date if in its judgment the agreement is not operating satisfactorily. Such denunciation shall have the effect of terminating the agreement six months from the date of the formal notice of denunciation.

## THE 1968 AGREEMENT ON FISHING BY JAPANESE VESSELS IN THE WATERS CONTIGUOUS TO THE MEXICAN TERRITORIAL SEA (Japan and Mexico)

Signed at Tlateloco on 7 March 1968. Entered into force on 10 June 1968. U.N. Treaty Series, vol. 683, p. 257. Terminated on 31 December 1972.

**Art. 1.** Japanese vessels shall not fish in the zones contiguous to the Mexican territorial sea which extend up to twelve nautical miles from the baseline from which the breadth of the said territorial sea is measured, except in those areas of the Pacific Ocean indicated below (hereinafter referred to as "areas of operation"), in which Japanese vessels duly authorized by the Government of Japan may fish:

(1) Between nine and twelve nautical miles from the baseline from which the breadth of the territorial sea is measured around the Mexican islands, with the exception of the Islas Marias, the islands lying off the west coast of the Baja California peninsula north of the parallel 30° north latitude and the islands lying to the west of the meridian 109°05′ west longitude in the Gulf of California.

(2) Between nine and twelve nautical miles from the baseline from which the breadth of the territorial sea is measured off the coast of the Mexican mainland:

(*a*) From a line connecting the geographical co-ordinates 14°32′42″ north latitude—92°27′ west longitude and 14°30′36″ north latitude—92°29′18″ west longitude, up to the meridian 94°40′ west longitude;

(*b*) From the meridian 95°40′ west longitude to the meridian 99°25′ west longitude;

(c) From the meridian 102° west longitude to the meridian 106°10′ west longitude;

(d) From the meridian 106°55′ west longitude to the meridian 109°05′ west longitude, and

(e) Off the west coast of the Baja California peninsula, from the parallel 23°10′ north latitude to the parallel 30° north latitude.

**Art. 2.** In the areas of operation Japanese vessels shall use the longline system which they have been using hitherto.

**Art. 3.** Japanese vessels shall fish in the areas of operation for the following species: bigeye tuna (*Thunnus obesus*, Thunnidae family), yellowfin tuna (*Thunnus albacares*, Thunnidae family), sailfish (*Istiophorus orientalis*, Istiophoridae family), striped marlin (*Tetrapturus audax*, Istiophoridae family), swordfish (*Xiphias gladius*, Xiphiidae family) and any other species caught incidentally in the course of fishing for the above-mentioned species.

**Art. 4.** The total fish catch by Japanese vessels in the areas of operation during the five-year period ending 31 December 1972 shall not exceed 15,500 metric tons, excluding species caught incidentally. Every possible effort shall be made to ensure that the total fish catch is distributed evenly over the five years of the above-mentioned period.

**Art. 5.** The authorities of Japan shall notify to the authorities of the United Mexican States:

1. Not later than 31 January each year, the types and approximate number of Japanese vessels expected to be engaged in fishing in the areas of operation in the course of that year, and

2. Not later than 1 June each year, the results of the fishing activities of Japanese vessels in the areas of operation in the course of the immediately preceding year, including the fish catch and the approximate areas in which fishing operations were conducted.

**Art. 6.** Representatives of the two Governments shall hold annual meetings to review the implementation of this Agreement. When it is deemed necessary in pursuance of international agreements to which either Government is a party or in compliance with resolutions or recommendations adopted by international organizations of which either Government is a member, and when it appears advisable in the interests of the conservation of the living resources of the sea, the Governments may, at the said meetings, establish regulatory measures applicable to Japanese vessels in the areas of operation, for the purpose of supplementing the execution of this Agreement.

**Art. 7.** Japanese vessels operating in violation of any of the provisions of this Agreement shall be excluded from the benefits deriving from it.

**Art. 8.** When it is deemed necessary, the two Governments shall hold consultations on the planning and execution of co-ordinated scientific research on the species mentioned in article 3 of this Agreement for the purpose of ensuring the rational utilization of those species.

**Art. 9.** None of the provisions of this Agreement may be interpreted in such a way as to prejudice the respective positions of the two Governments with regard to the breadth of the territorial sea or the jurisdiction of States in matters of fisheries.

**Art. 10.** This Agreement . . . shall remain in force until 31 December 1972.

**Art. 11.** Without prejudice to the provisions of article 10, either Government may give notice to the other of its intention to denounce this Agreement, at any time after one year has elapsed since its entry into force. The denunciation shall take effect six months after the date on which the notice is received by the other Government.

*Memorandum*

. . .

4. The representatives of the United Mexican States stated that their Government does not intend to impose duties, taxes or other fiscal charges on Japanese vessels fishing under the terms of the Agreement. It was understood that the two Governments would consult each other on the question, if the Government of the United Mexican States should wish to impose duties, taxes or other fiscal charges on the above-mentioned Japanese vessels.

## THE 1972 SHRIMP CONSERVATION AGREEMENT (Brazil and United States of America)

> Signed at Brazilia on 9 May 1972. It is reported that the United States of America failed in completing its internal procedures and that the provisions of this Agreement have in fact applied. See International Legal Materials, vol. 11, p. 453.

*The Parties to this Agreement,*

*Note* the position of the Government of the Federative Republic of Brazil,

that it considers its territorial sea to extend to a distance of 200 nautical miles from Brazil's coast,

154

that the exploitation of crustaceans and other living resources, which are closely dependent on the seabed under the Brazilian territorial sea, is reserved to Brazilian fishing vessels, and

that exceptions to this provision can only be granted through international agreements,

*Note also* the position of the Government of the United States of America that it does not consider itself obligated under international law to recognize territorial sea claims of more than 3 nautical miles nor fisheries jurisdiction of more than 12 nautical miles, beyond which zone of jurisdiction all nations have the right to fish freely, and that it does not consider that all crustaceans are living organisms belonging to sedentary species as defined in the 1958 Geneva Convention on the Continental Shelf, and further

*Recognizing* that the difference in the respective juridical positions of the Parties has given rise to certain problems relating to the conduct of shrimp fisheries,

*Considering* the tradition of both Parties for resolving international differences by having recourse to negotiation,

*Believing* it is desirable to arrive at an interim solution for the conduct of shrimp fisheries without prejudice to either Party's juridical position concerning the extent of territorial seas or fisheries jurisdiction under international law,

*Concluding* that, while general international solutions to issues of maritime jurisdiction are being sought and until more adequate information regarding the shrimp fisheries is available, it is desirable to conclude an interim agreement which takes into account their mutual interest in the conservation of the shrimp resources of the area of this Agreement,

*Have Agreed as Follows:*

**Art. I.** This Agreement shall apply to the fishery for shrimp (...) in an area of the broader region in which the shrimp fisheries of the Parties are conducted, hereinafter referred to as the "area of agreement" and defined as follows: the waters off the coast of Brazil having the isobath of thirty (30) meters as the south-west limit and the latitude 1° north as the southern limit and 47°30′ west longitude as the eastern limit.

**Art. II.** 1. Taking into account their common concern with preventing the depletion of the shrimp stocks in the area of agreement and the substantial difference in the stages of development of their respective fishing fleets, which results correspondingly in different kinds of impact on the resources, the two Parties agree that, during the term of this Agreement, the Government of the Federative Republic of Brazil is to apply the measures set forth in Annex I to this Agreement and the Government of the United States of America is to apply the measures set forth in Annex II to this Agreement.

155

2. The measures set forth in Annexes may be changed by agreement of the Parties through consultation pursuant to Article X.

**Art. III.** 1. Information on catch and effort and biological data relating to shrimp fisheries in the area of agreement shall be collected and exchanged, as appropriate, by the Parties. Unless the Parties decide otherwise, such exchange of information shall be made in accordance with the procedure described in this Article.

2. Each vessel fishing under this Agreement shall maintain a fishing log, according to a commonly agreed model. Such fishing logs shall be delivered quarterly to the appropriate Party which shall use the data therein contained, and other information it obtains about the area of agreement, to prepare reports on the fishing conditions in that area, which shall be transmitted periodically to the other Party as appropriate.

3. Duly appointed organizations from both Parties shall meet in due time to exchange scientific data, publications and knowledge acquired on the shrimp fisheries in the area of agreement.

**Art. IV.** 1. The Party which under Article V has the responsibility for enforcing observance of the terms of the Agreement by vessels of the other Party's flag shall receive from the latter Party the information necessary for identification and other enforcement functions, including name, port of registry, port where operations are usually based, general description with photograph in profile, radiofrequencies by which communications may be established, main engine horsepower and speed, length, and fishing method and gear employed.

2. Such information shall be assembled and organized by the flag Government and communications relating to such information shall be carried out each year between the appropriate authorities of the Parties.

3. The Party which receives such information shall verify whether it is complete and in good order, and shall inform the other Party about the vessels found to comply with the requirements of paragraph 1 of this Article, as well as about those which would, for some reason, require further consultation among the Parties.

4. Each of those vessels found in order shall receive and display an identification sign, agreed between the Parties.

**Art. V.** 1. In view of the fact that Brazilian authorities can carry out an effective enforcement presence in the area of Agreement, it shall be incumbent on the Government of Brazil to ensure that the conduct of shrimp fisheries conforms with the provisions of this Agreement.

2. A duly authorized official of Brazil, in exercising the responsibility described in paragraph 1 of this Article may, if he has reasonable cause to believe that any provision of this Agreement has been violated, board

and search a shrimp fishing vessel. Such action shall not unduly hinder fishing operations. When, after boarding or boarding and searching a vessel, the official continues to have reasonable cause to believe that any provision of this Agreement has been violated, he may seize and detain such vessel. In the case of a boarding or seizure and detention of a United States vessel, the Government of Brazil shall promptly inform the Government of the United States of its action.

3. After satisfaction of the terms of Article VI as referred to in paragraph 4 of this Article, a United States vessel seized and detained under the terms of this Agreement shall, as soon as practicable, be delivered to an authorized official of the United States at the nearest port to the place of seizure, or any other place which is mutually acceptable to the competent authorities of both Parties. The Government of Brazil shall, after delivering such vessel to an authorized official of the United States, provide a certified copy of the full report of the violation and the circumstances of the seizure and detention.

4. If the reason for seizure and detention falls within the terms of Article II or Article IV, paragraph 4 of this Agreement, a United States vessel seized and detained shall be delivered to an authorized official of the United States, after satisfaction of the terms of Article VI relating to unusual expenses.

5. If the nature of the violation warrants it, and after carrying out the provision of Article X, vessels may also suffer forfeiture of that part of the catch determined to be taken illegally and forfeiture of the fishing gear.

6. In the case of vessels delivered to an authorized official of the United States under paragraphs 3 or 4 of this Article, the Government of Brazil will be informed of the institution and disposition of any case by the United States.

**Art. VI.** In connection with the enforcement arrangements specified in Article V, including in particular any unusual expenses incurred in carrying out the seizure and detention of a United States vessel under the terms of paragraph 4 of Article V, and taking into account Brazil's regulation of its flag vessels in the area of agreement, the Government of Brazil will be compensated in an amount determined and confirmed in an exchange of notes between the Parties. The amount of compensation shall be related to the level of fishing by United States nationals in the area of agreement and to the total enforcement activities to be undertaken by the Government of Brazil pursuant to the terms of this Agreement.

**Art. VII.** The implementation of this Agreement may be reviewed at the request of either Party six months after the date on which this Agreement becomes effective, in order to deal with administrative issues arising in connection with this Agreement.

**Art. VIII.** The Parties shall examine the possibilities of cooperating in the development of their fishing industries; the expansion of the international trade of fishery products; the improvement of storage, transportation and marketing of fishery products; and the encouragement of joint ventures between the fishing industries of the two Parties.

**Art. IX.** Nothing contained in this Agreement shall be interpreted as prejudicing the position of either Party regarding the matter of territorial seas or fisheries jurisdiction under international law.

**Art. X.** Problems concerning the interpretation and implementation of this Agreement shall be resolved through diplomatic channels.

**Art. XI.** This Agreement shall enter into force on a date to be mutually agreed by exchange of notes, upon completion of the internal procedures of both parties and shall remain in force until January 1, 1974, unless the Parties agree to extend it.

## ANNEX I

*a.* Prohibition of shrimp fishing activities, for conservation purposes, in spawning and breeding areas;

*b.* Prohibition of the use of chemical, toxic or explosive substances in or near fishing areas;

*c.* Registry of all fishing vessels with the Maritime Port Authority (Capitania dos Portos) and with SUDEPE;

*d.* Payment of fees and taxes for periodical inspections;

*e.* Use of the SUDEPE fishing logs to be returned after each trip or weekly;

*f.* Prohibition of the use of fishing gear and of other equipment considered by SUDEPE to have destructive effects on the stocks;

*g.* Prohibition of discharging oil and organic waste.

## ANNEX II

*a.* Not more than 325 vessels flying the United States flag shall fish for shrimp in the area of agreement and the United States Government undertakes to maintain a presence of no more than 160 of those vessels in the area at any one time. Such vessels shall be of the same type and have the same gear as those commonly employed in this fishery in the past, noting that electric equipment for fishing purposes has not been commonly employed by boats in this fishery in the past.

*b.* Shrimp fishing in the area of agreement shall be limited to the period from March 1 to November 30.

*c.* Shrimp fishing in that part of the area of agreement southeast of a bearing of 240° from Ponta do Ceu radio-beacon shall be limited to the period March 1 to July 1.

*d.* Transshipment of catch may be made only between vessels authorized under this Agreement to fish in the area of agreement.

*Agreed Minute:* [omitted].

*Exchange of Notes*

*a.* The Government of the United States of America shall, after the appropriation of funds by Congress, compensate the Government of Brazil in an annual amount of U.S. $200,000 (two hundred thousand dollars) pursuant to the terms of Article VI;

*b.* The Government of the United States of America shall, after the appropriation of funds by Congress, further compensate the Government of Brazil in the amount of U.S. $100.00 (one hundred dollars) for each day a United States flag shrimp fishing vessel is under the control of Brazilian enforcement authorities pursuant to the terms of paragraph 2 of Article V.

*Note of the U.S. Embassy and the Reply of the Brazilian Ministry of External Relations*

Pending the entering into force of the agreement as provided for in article eleven, the Government of the United States of America is prepared to make every effort to encourage the voluntary compliance by its industry of the provisions of the Agreement so as to ensure that events in the interim period do not prejudice the successful implementation of those provisions. It is the understanding of the Government of the United States of America that the Government of the Federative Republic of Brazil intends also to abide by the spirit of the proposed interim Agreement.

Following the exchange of instruments of ratification, but prior to the passage of enabling legislation, the Government of the United States of America proposes to continue its efforts to encourage voluntary compliance.

In the period between the completion of internal procedures as noted in article eleven and the entering into force of the Agreement, the Government of the United States of America will seek, *inter alia*, with the voluntary cooperation of U.S. flag vessel owners,

1. To achieve the objectives of Article II
2. To institute appropriate Article III procedures
3. To achieve the intent of Articles IV and V.

In stating its willingness to encourage the voluntary compliance with appropriate provisions of the Agreement so that the intent of the accord may be achieved while awaiting its entering into force, it is the understanding of the Government of the United States of America that the Government of the Federative Republic of Brazil agrees that in this same interim period both Parties should have as their objective the achievement of the intent of the Agreement.

With specific reference to Article III, paragraph 2, the Government of the United States of America shall treat the information obtained from individual fishing logs as confidential.

- - -

3. ... the Ministry of External Relations wishes to state that, pending the entry into force of the Agreement, it is the intent of the Brazilian Government to apply its provisions in sofar as possible from today and in a manner which will ensure that events in the interim will not prejudice the successful implementation of those provisions.

4. With specific reference to Article III, paragraph 2, the Government of the Federative Republic of Brazil shall treat the information obtained from individual fishing logs as confidential.


## 5. OCEANIA


### THE 1967 AGREEMENT ON FISHERIES (Japan and New Zealand)

Signed at Wellington on 12 July 1967. Entered into force on 26 July 1968. U.N. Treaty Series, vol. 683, p. 54.

The Government of Japan and the Government of New Zealand,
Desiring to conclude an agreement concerning fishing by Japanese vessels in waters adjacent to New Zealand,
Have agreed as follows:

**Art. I.** For the purpose of this Agreement, "the Area" means the waters which are contiguous to the territorial sea of New Zealand and extend to a limit of twelve nautical miles from the base line from which the territorial sea of New Zealand is measured.

**Art. II.** Japanese vessels and persons on board those vessels will not engage in fishing in the Area, except that, until 31 December 1970, Japanese vessels duly licensed by the Government of Japan may engage in bottom fish longline fishing on a scale to be agreed upon between the two Governments in terms of the number of mother ships and their tonnage, within the waters between six and twelve nautical miles from the base line from which the territorial sea of New Zealand is measured, in that part of the Area:

(*a*) Off the coast of the North Island of New Zealand and adjacent islands; and

(*b*) Off the northern coast of the South Island of New Zealand and adjacent islands, north of 41°30′ South Latitude and east of 172°30′ East Longitude.

**Art. III.** Any infringement of the provisions of this Agreement by a Japanese vessel will be dealt with either by the Japanese or by the New Zealand authorities, and the two Governments may make arrangements in accordance with which their respective jurisdictions will be exercised.

**Art. IV.** The New Zealand authorities may visit Japanese vessels within the Area to inspect their licences and to ascertain that the provisions of this Agreement are being observed.

**Art. V.** Upon the request of either Government, the two Governments shall hold consultations regarding the implementation of this Agreement.

**Art. VI.** This Agreement shall be subject to ratification. The instruments of ratification shall be exchanged at Tokyo as soon as possible. The Agreement shall enter into force on the thirtieth day after the date of exchange of the instruments of ratification.

*Exchange of Notes regarding Article II:* [omitted]

*Exchange of Notes regarding Article III*

1. Without prejudice to New Zealand Jurisdiction, it will be primarily the responsibility of the Government of Japan to deal with any infringement of the provisions of the Agreement by a Japanese vessel.

(1) Accordingly, if any Japanese vessel is found by the New Zealand authorities to be infringing the provisions of the Agreement, they will notify the Japanese authorities of the infringement. In appropriate cases they may furnish evidence of the infringement.

(2) When they receive any such approach, the Japanese authorities will take the necessary action and will keep the New Zealand authorities informed of all measures taken.

2. These arrangements may be terminated at any time by either Government on giving three months' notice to that effect.

*Agreed Minutes:* [omitted]

*Exchange of Notes regarding Provisional Effect of the Agreement pending its entry into force:* [omitted]

## THE 1968 AGREEMENT ON FISHERIES (Australia and Japan)

Signed at Canberra on 27 November 1968. Entered into force on 24 August 1969. U.N. Treaty Series, vol. 708, p. 20.

The Government of Japan and the Government of the Commonwealth of Australia,

Desiring to conclude an agreement concerning fishing by Japanese vessels in waters contiguous to the territorial seas of Australia, the Territory of Papua and the Trust Territory of New Guinea,

Have agreed as follows:

**Art. I.** 1. Except as provided in paragraph 2 of this Article, Japanese vessels will not engage in fishing in the waters which are contiguous to the territorial seas of Australia, the Territory of Papua and the Trust Territory of New Guinea and extend to a limit of twelve nautical miles from the baselines from which those territorial seas are measured.

2. For the periods described hereunder Japanese vessels may engage in tuna long-line fishing in accordance with the provisions of this Agreement in those parts of the waters described in paragraph 1 of this Article that are within the areas designated hereunder:

A. Until the twenty-seventh day of November, 1975—

(i) in the Tasman Sea. . . .

(ii) in the Coral Sea: . . .

(iii) in the Indian Ocean: . . .

B. Until the twenty-seventh day of November, 1971 [1975—so understood as the result of the exchange of notes on 25 December 1970] or such later date as may be agreed in consultation between the two Governments—

the area off the coasts of the Territory of Papua and the Trust Territory of New Guinea, with the exception of

(*a*) the area off the south coast of the Territory of Papua bounded on the east by 145° East Longitude; and

(*b*) the area off the south coast of the Territory of Papua that is bounded on the west by 145° East Longitude and on the east by 151° East Longitude, is contiguous to the territorial sea of the Territory of Papua and extends to a limit of six nautical miles from the baseline from which that territorial sea is measured.

The parts of the waters described in paragraph 1 of this Article that are within the areas designated in sub-paragraphs A and B of this paragraph are hereinafter referred to as "the Designated Waters".

**Art. II.** 1. The Japanese authorities will provide the Australian authorities with the names, the registration numbers, the names of the managers

162

and the numbers of the fishing crews of any Japanese vessels that are likely to engage in tuna long-line fishing in the Designated Waters.

2. The information referred to in paragraph 1 of this Article will be provided at least fourteen days before the day on which it is anticipated that any vessel in relation to which the information is provided will first commence fishing in the Designated Waters in any calendar year, and the information thus provided will relate to that calendar year, except that information provided during December in any year will also relate to the following calendar year.

**Art. III.** 1. On receipt of the information referred to in paragraph 1 of Article II of this Agreement in respect of any Japanese vessels, the Government of the Commonwealth of Australia will make necessary administrative arrangements to facilitate the operation of those vessels in the Designated Waters in accordance with the provisions of this Agreement.

2. The vessels referred to in paragraph 1 of this Article will make reasonable payments in relation to the administrative arrangements mentioned in that paragraph.

**Art. IV.** 1. The annual level of Japanese tuna long-line operations under this Agreement will not be increased beyond the average annual level of the calendar years 1963 to 1967.

2. The Japanese authorities will provide the Australian authorities not later than the thirtieth day of June in each year with information relating to the total weight of fish taken during each quarter of the preceding calendar year, and with information relating to the weight of each species of tuna taken during the preceding calendar year, by the Japanese vessels from the Designated Waters.

**Art. V.** 1. The Japanese authorities will take appropriate measures to ensure that the provisions of this Agreement are observed.

2. The Australian authorities may board Japanese vessels in the waters described in paragraph 1 of Article 1 of this Agreement, to ascertain that the provisions of the Agreement are being observed.

**Art. VI.** 1. Japanese vessels equipped for tuna longline fishing may, until the twenty-seventh day of November, 1975, enter the Australian ports of Brisbane, Fremantle, Hobart and Sydney for the purpose of securing supplies.

2. Not later than the twenty-seventh day of May, 1975, the two Governments will consult with respect to the continued access after the twenty-seventh day of November, 1975, to Australian ports of Japanese vessels equipped for tuna long-line fishing.

**Art. VII.** Upon the request of either Government, the two Governments will hold consultations regarding the operation of this Agreement.

**Art. VIII.** Nothing in this Agreement shall be deemed to prejudice the position of either Government in regard to the jurisdiction of a coastal state over fisheries.

**Art. IX.** . . .

*Agreed Minutes:* [omitted].

# PART IV

# INTERNATIONAL INSTRUMENTS RELATING TO THE MARINE ENVIRONMENT

## UNITED NATIONS CONFERENCE ON THE HUMAN ENVIRON-MENT:
## — Declaration of 1972

The United Nations Conference on the Human Environment held at Stockholm from 5 to 16 June 1972, having considered the need for a common outlook and for common principles to inspire and guide the peoples of the world in the preservation and enhancement of the human environment, adopted a declaration, in which 26 principles were agreed upon, of which the following three are relevant to the problem of marine pollution.

. . .

*Principle 7* States shall take all possible steps to prevent pollution of the seas by substances that are liable to create hazards to human health, to harm living resources and marine life, to damage amenities or to interfere with other legitimate uses of the sea

. . .

*Principle 21* States have, in accordance with the Charter of the United Nations and the principles of international law, the sovereign right to exploit their own resources pursuant to their own environmental policies, and the responsibility to ensure that activities within their jurisdiction or control do not cause damage to the environment of other States or of areas beyond the limits of national jurisdiction.

*Principle 22* States shall co-operate to develop further the international law regarding liability and compensation for the victims of pollution and other environmental damage caused by activities within the jurisdiction or control of such States to areas beyond their jurisdiction.

## UNITED NATIONS CONFERENCE ON THE HUMAN ENVIRON-MENT:
## — Action Plan for the Human Environment

The United Nations Conference on the Human Environment held at Stockholm from 5 to 16 June 1972 adopted 109 recommendations, some of which are relevant to the problem of marine pollution.

86. *It is recommended* that Governments, with the assistance and guidance of appropriate UN bodies, in particular the Joint Group of Experts on the Scientific Aspects of Marine Pollution:

(*a*) Accept and implement available instruments on the control of the maritime sources of marine pollution;

(*b*) Ensure that the provisions of such instruments are complied with by ships flying their flags and by ships operating in areas under their jurisdiction and that adequate provisions are made for reviewing the effectiveness of, and revising, existing and proposed international measures for control of marine pollution;

(*c*) Ensure that ocean dumping by their nationals anywhere, or by any person in areas under their jurisdiction, is controlled and that Governments shall continue to work towards the completion of, and bringing into force as soon as possible of, an over-all instrument for the control of ocean dumping as well as needed regional agreements within the framework of this instrument, in particular for enclosed and semi-enclosed seas, which are more at risk from pollution;

(*d*) Refer the draft articles and annexes contained in the reports of the intergovernmental meetings at Reykjavik, Iceland, in April 1972 and in London in May 1972 to the UN Committee on the Peaceful Uses of the Seabed and the Ocean Floor beyond the Limits of National Jurisdiction at its session in July/August 1972 for information and comments and to a conference of Governments to be convened by the Government of the United Kingdom of Great Britain and Northern Ireland in consultation with the Secretary-General before November 1972 for further consideration, with a view to opening the proposed convention for signature at a place to be decided by that Conference, preferably before the end of 1972;

(*e*) Participate fully in the 1973 (IMCO) Conference on Marine Pollution and the UN Conference on the Law of the Sea scheduled to begin in 1973, as well as in regional efforts, with a view to bringing all significant sources of pollution within the marine environment, including radioactive pollution from nuclear surface ships and submarines, and in particular in enclosed and semi-enclosed seas, under appropriate controls and particularly to complete elimination of deliberate pollution by oil from ships, with the goal of achieving this by the middle of the present decade;

(*f*) Strengthen national controls over land-based sources of marine pollution, in particular in enclosed and semi-enclosed seas, and recognize that, in some circumstances, the discharge of residual heat from nuclear and other power-stations may constitute a potential hazard to marine ecosystems.

87. *It is recommended* that Governments:

(*a*) Support national research and monitoring efforts that contribute to agreed international programmes for research and monitoring in the marine environment, in particular the Global Investigation of Pollution in the Marine Environment and the Integrated Global Ocean Station System;

(*b*) Provide to the UN, FAO and UNCTAD, as appropriate to the data-gathering activities of each, statistics on the production and use of toxic or dangerous substances that are potential marine pollutants, especially if they are persistent;

(*c*) Expand their support to components of the UN system concerned with research and monitoring in the marine environment and adopt the measures required to improve the constitutional, financial and operational basis under which the IOC is at present operating so as to make it an effective joint mechanism for the Governments and UN organizations concerned (UNESCO, FAO, WMO, IMCO, ESA) and in order that it may be able to take on additional responsibilities and co-ordination of scientific programmes and services.

88. *It is recommended* that the Secretary-General, together with the sponsoring agencies, make it possible for the Joint Group of Experts on the Scientific Aspects of Marine Pollution:

(*a*) To re-examine annually, and revise as required, its "Review of Harmful Chemical Substances", with a view to elaborating further its assessment of sources, pathways and resulting risks of marine pollutants;

(*b*) To assemble, having regard to other work in progress, scientific data and to provide advice on scientific aspects of marine pollution, especially those of an interdisciplinary nature.

89. *It is recommended* that the Secretary-General ensure:

(*a*) That mechanisms for combining world statistics on mining, production, processing, transport and use of potential marine pollutants shall be developed along with methods for identifying high-priority marine pollutants based in part on such data;

(*b*) That the Joint Group of Experts on the Scientific Aspects of Marine Pollution, in consultation with other expert groups, propose guidelines for test programmes to evaluate toxicity of potential marine pollutants;

(*c*) That FAO, WHO, IOC and IAEA encourage studies of the effects of high-priority marine pollutants on man and other organisms, with appropriate emphasis on chronic, low-level exposures;

(*d*) That IOC, with FAO and WHO explore the possibility of establishing an international institute for tropical marine studies, which would undertake training as well as research.

90. *It is recommended* that IOC, jointly with WMO and, as appropriate, in co-operation with other interested intergovernmental bodies, promote the monitoring of marine pollution, preferably within the framework of the Integrated Global Ocean Station System, as well as the development

169

of methods for monitoring high-priority marine pollutants in the water, sediments and organisms, with advice from the Joint Group of Experts on the Scientific Aspects of Marine Pollution on intercomparability of methodologies.

91. *It is recommended* that the IOC:

(*a*) Ensure that provisions shall be made in international marine research, monitoring and related activities for the exchange, dissemination, and referral to sources of data and information on baselines and on marine pollution and that attention shall be paid to the special needs of developing countries;

(*b*) Give full consideration, with the FAO, WMO, the IMCO, WHO, IAEA, IHO and ICES and other interested and relevant organizations, to the strengthening of on-going marine and related data and information exchange and dissemination activities;

(*c*) Support the concept of development of an interdisciplinary and interorganizational system primarily involving centres already in existence;

(*d*) Initiate an interdisciplinary marine pollution data and scientific information referral capability.

92. *It is recommended:*

(*a*) That Governments collectively endorse the principles set forth in paragraph 197 of Conference document A/CONF.48/8 as guiding concepts for the UN Conference on the Law of the Sea and the Marine Pollution Conference scheduled to be held in 1973 and also the statement of objectives agreed on at the second session of the Intergovernmental Working Group on Marine Pollution, which reads as follows:

"The marine environment and all the living organisms which it supports are of vital importance to humanity, and all people have an interest in assuring that this environment is so managed that its quality and resources are not impaired. This applies especially to coastal nations, which have a particular interest in management of coastal area resources. The capacity of the sea to assimilate wastes and render them harmless and its ability to regenerate natural resources are not unlimited. Proper management is required and measures to prevent and control marine pollution must be regarded as an essential element in this management of the oceans and seas and their natural resources.",

and that, in respect of the particular interest of coastal States in the marine environment and recognizing that the resolution of this question is a matter for consideration at the Conference on the Law of the Sea, they take note of the principles on the rights of coastal States discussed but neither endorsed nor rejected at the second session of the Intergovernmental Working Group on Marine Pollution and refer those principles to the 1973 IMCO Conference for information and to the 1973 Conference on the Law

170

of the Sea for such action as may be appropriate;

(*b*) That Governments take early action to adopt effective national measures for the control of all significant sources of marine pollution, including land-based sources, and concert and co-ordinate their actions regionally and where appropriate on a wider international basis;

(*c*) That the Secretary-General, in co-operation with appropriate international organizations, endeavour to provide guidelines which Governments might wish to take into account when developing such measures.

93. *It is recommended* that any mechanism for co-ordinating and stimulating the actions of the different UN organs in connexion with environmental problems include among its functions over-all responsibility for ensuring that needed advice on marine pollution problems shall be provided to Governments.

94. *It is recommended* that the Secretary-General, with the co-operation of UN bodies, take steps to secure additional financial support to those training and other programmes of assistance that contribute to increasing the capacity of developing countries to participate in international research, monitoring and pollution-control programmes.


## CONVENTION ON THE PREVENTION OF MARINE POLLUTION BY DUMPING OF WASTES AND OTHER MATTERS, 1972

Drawn up at the Inter-Governmental Conference on the Dumping of Wastes at Sea, held in London from 30 October to 10 November 1972.

*The Contracting Parties to this Convention,*

*Recognizing* that the marine environment and the living organisms which it supports are of vital importance to humanity, and all people have an interest in assuring that it is so managed that its quality and resources are not impaired;

*Recognizing* that the capacity of the sea to assimilate wastes and render them harmless, and its ability to regenerate natural resources, is not unlimited;

*Recognizing* that States have, in accordance with the Charter of the United Nations and the principles of international law, the sovereign right to exploit their own resources pursuant to their own environmental policies, and the responsibility to ensure that activities within their jurisdiction or control do not cause damage to the environment of other States or of areas beyond the limits of national jurisdiction;

*Recalling* Resolution 2749 (XXV) of the General Assembly of the

United Nations on the principles governing the sea-bed and the ocean floor and the subsoil thereof, beyond the limits of national jurisdiction;

*Noting* that marine pollution originates in many sources, such as dumping and discharges through the atmosphere, rivers, estuaries, outfalls and pipelines, and that it is important that States use the best practicable means to prevent such pollution and develop products and processes which will reduce the amount of harmful wastes to be disposed of;

*Being convinced* that international action to control the pollution of the sea by dumping can and must be taken without delay but that this action should not preclude discussion of measures to control other sources of marine pollution as soon as possible; and

*Wishing* to improve protection of the marine environment by encouraging States with a common interest in particular geographical areas to enter into appropriate agreements supplementary to this Convention;

*Have agreed* as follows:

**Art. 1.** Contracting Parties shall individually and collectively promote the effective control of all sources of pollution of the marine environment, and pledge themselves especially to take all practicable steps to prevent the pollution of the sea by the dumping of waste and other matter that is liable to create hazards to human health, to harm living resources and marine life, to damage amenities or to interfere with other legitimate uses of the sea.

**Art. 2.** Contracting Parties shall, as provided for in the following Articles, take effective measures individually, according to their scientific, technical and economic capabilities, and collectively, to prevent marine pollution caused by dumping and shall harmonize their policies in this regard.

**Art. 3.** For the purposes of this Convention:
1. (*a*) "Dumping" means:
    (i) any deliberate disposal at sea of wastes or other matter from vessels, aircraft, platforms or other man-made structures at sea;
    (ii) any deliberate disposal at sea of vessels, aircraft, platforms or other man-made structures at sea.
  (*b*) "Dumping" does not include:
    (i) the disposal at sea of wastes or other matter incidental to, or derived from the normal operations of vessels, aircraft, platforms or other man-made structures at sea and their equipment, other than wastes or other matter transported by or to vessels, aircraft, platforms or other man-made structures at sea, operating for the purpose of disposal of such matter or derived from the treatment of such wastes or other matter on such vessels, aircraft, platforms or structures;
    (ii) placement of matter for a purpose other than the mere disposal

172

thereof, provided that such placement is not contrary to the aims of this Convention.

(c) The disposal of wastes or other matter directly arising from, or related to the exploration, exploitation and associated off-shore processing of sea-bed mineral resources will not be covered by the provisions of this Convention.

2. "Vessels and aircraft" means waterborne or airborne craft of any type whatsoever. This expression includes air cushioned craft and floating craft, whether self-propelled or not.

3. "Sea" means all marine waters other than the internal waters of States.

4. "Wastes or other matter" means material and substance of any kind, form or description.

5. "Special permit" means permission granted specifically on application in advance and in accordance with Annex II and Annex III.

6. "General permit" means permission granted in advance and in accordance with Annex III.

7. "The Organisation" means the Organisation designated by the Contracting Parties in accordance with Article XIV (2).

**Art. 4.** 1. In accordance with the provisions of this Convention Contracting Parties shall prohibit the dumping of any wastes or other matter in whatever form or condition except as otherwise specified below:

(a) the dumping of wastes or other matter listed in Annex I is prohibited;

(b) the dumping of wastes or other matter listed in Annex II requires a prior special permit;

(c) the dumping of all other wastes or matter requires a prior general permit.

2. Any permit shall be issued only after careful consideration of all the factors set forth in Annex III, including prior studies of the characteristics of the dumping site, as set forth in Sections B and C of that Annex.

3. No provision of this Convention is to be interpreted as preventing a Contracting Party from prohibiting, insofar as that Party is concerned, the dumping of wastes or other matter not mentioned in Annex I. That Party shall notify such measures to the Organisation.

**Art. 5.** 1. The provisions of Article IV shall not apply when it is necessary to secure the safety of human life or of vessels, aircraft, platforms or other man-made structures at sea in cases of *force majeure* caused by stress of weather, or in any case which constitutes a danger to human life or a real threat to vessels, aircraft, platforms or other man-made structures at sea, if dumping appears to be the only way of averting the threat and if there is every probability that the damage consequent upon such dumping will be less than would otherwise occur. Such dumping shall be so conducted as to minimise the likelihood of damage to human or marine life and shall be reported forthwith to the Organisation.

2. A Contracting Party may issue a special permit as an exception to Article IV (1) (*a*), in emergencies, posing unacceptable risk relating to human health and admitting no other feasible solution. Before doing so the Party shall consult any other country or countries that are likely to be affected and the Organisation which, after consulting other Parties, and international organisations as appropriate, shall in accordance with Article XIV promptly recommend to the Party the most appropriate procedures to adopt. The Party shall follow these recommendations to the maximum extent feasible consistent with the time within which action must be taken and with the general obligation to avoid damage to the marine environment and shall inform the Organisation of the action it takes. The Parties pledge themselves to assist one another in such situations.

3. Any Contracting Party may waive its rights under paragraph (2) at the time of, or subsequent to ratification of, or accession to this Convention.

**Art. 6.** 1. Each Contracting Party shall designate an appropriate authority or authorities to:

(*a*) issue special permits which shall be required prior to, and for, the dumping of matter listed in Annex II and in the circumstances provided for in Article V (2);

(*b*) issue general permits which shall be required prior to, and for, the dumping of all other matter;

(*c*) keep records of the nature and quantities of all matter permitted to be dumped and the location, time and method of dumping;

(*d*) monitor individually, or in collaboration with other Parties and competent International Organisations, the condition of the seas for the purposes of this Convention.

2. The appropriate authority or authorities of a Contracting Party shall issue prior special or general permits in accordance with paragraph (1) in respect of matter intended for dumping:

(a) loaded in its territory;

(*b*) loaded by a vessel or aircraft registered in its territory or flying its flag, when the loading occurs in the territory of a State not party to this Convention.

3. In issuing permits under sub-paragraphs (1) (*a*) and (*b*) above, the appropriate authority or authorities shall comply with Annex III, together with such additional criteria, measures and requirements as they may consider relevant.

4. Each Contracting Party, directly or through a Secretariat established under a regional agreement, shall report to the Organisation, and where appropriate to other Parties, the information specified in sub-paragraphs

174

(c) and (d) of paragraph (1) above, and the criteria, measures and requirements it adopts in accordance with paragraph (3) above. The procedure to be followed and the nature of such reports shall be agreed by the Parties in consultation.

**Art. 7.** 1. Each Contracting Party shall apply the measures required to implement the present Convention to all:

(a) vessels and aircraft registered in its territory or flying its flag;

(b) vessels and aircraft loading in its territory or territorial seas matter which is to be dumped;

(c) vessels and aircraft and fixed or floating platforms under its jurisdiction believed to be engaged in dumping.

2. Each Party shall take in its territory appropriate measures to prevent and punish conduct in contravention of the provisions of this Convention.

3. The Parties agree to co-operate in the development of procedures for the effective application of this Convention particularly on the high seas, including procedures for the reporting of vessels and aircraft observed dumping in contravention of the Convention.

4. This Convention shall not apply to those vessels and aircraft entitled to sovereign immunity under international law. However each Party shall ensure by the adoption of appropriate measures that such vessels and aircraft owned or operated by it act in a manner consistent with the object and purpose of this Convention, and shall inform the Organisation accordingly.

5. Nothing in this Convention shall affect the right of each Party to adopt other measures, in accordance with the principles of international law, to prevent dumping at sea.

**Art. 8.** In order to further the objectives of this Convention, the Contracting Parties with common interests to protect in the marine environment in a given geographical area shall endeavour, taking into account characteristic regional features, to enter into regional agreements consistent with this Convention for the prevention of pollution, especially by dumping. The Contracting Parties to the present Convention shall endeavour to act consistently with the objectives and provisions of such regional agreements, which shall be notified to them by the Organisation. Contracting Parties shall seek to co-operate with the Parties to regional agreements in order to develop harmonized procedures to be followed by Contracting Parties to the different conventions concerned. Special attention shall be given to co-operation in the field of monitoring and scientific research.

**Art. 9.** The Contracting Parties shall promote, through collaboration within the Organisation and other international bodies, support for those Parties which request it for:

175

(*a*) the training of scientific and technical personnel;

(*b*) the supply of necessary equipment and facilities for research and monitoring;

(*c*) the disposal and treatment of waste and other measures to prevent or mitigate pollution caused by dumping;

preferably within the countries concerned, so furthering the aims and purposes of this Convention.

**Art. 10.** In accordance with the principles of international law regarding State responsibility for damage to the environment of other States or to any other area of the environment, caused by dumping of wastes and other matter of all kinds, the Contracting Parties undertake to develop procedures for the assessment of liability and the settlement of disputes regarding dumping.

**Art. 11.** The Contracting Parties shall at their first consultative meeting consider procedures for the settlement of disputes concerning the interpretation and application of this Convention.

**Art. 12.** The Contracting Parties pledge themselves to promote, within the competent specialised agencies and other international bodies, measures to protect the marine environment against pollution caused by:

(*a*) hydrocarbons, including oil, and their wastes;

(*b*) other noxious or hazardous matter transported by vessels for purposes other than dumping;

(*c*) wastes generated in the course of operation of vessels, aircraft, platforms and other man-made structures at sea;

(*d*) radio-active pollutants from all sources, including vessels;

(*e*) agents of chemical and biological warfare;

(*f*) wastes or other matter directly arising from, or related to the exploration, exploitation and associated off-shore processing of sea-bed mineral resources.

The Parties will also promote, within the appropriate international organisation, the codification of signals to be used by vessels engaged in dumping.

**Art. 13.** Nothing in this Convention shall prejudice the codification and development of the law of the sea by the United Nations Conference on the Law of the Sea convened pursuant to Resolution 2750 C (XXV) of the General Assembly of the United Nations nor the present or future claims and legal views of any State concerning the law of the sea and the nature and extent of coastal and flag State jurisdiction. The Contracting Parties agree to consult at a meeting to be convened by the Organisation after the Law of the Sea Conference, and in any case not later than 1976, with a view to defining the nature and extent of the right and the responsibility of a coastal State to apply the Convention in a zone adjacent to its coast.

176

**Art. 14.** 1. The Government of the United Kingdom of Great Britain and Northern Ireland as a depositary shall call a meeting of the Contracting Parties not later than three months after the entry into force of this Convention to decide on organisational matters.

2. The Contracting Parties shall designate a competent Organisation existing at the time of that meeting to be responsible for Secretariat duties in relation to this Convention. Any Party to this Convention not being a member of this Organisation shall make an appropriate contribution to the expenses incurred by the Organisation in performing these duties.

3. The Secretariat duties of the Organisation shall include:

(a) the convening of consultative meetings of the Contracting Parties not less frequently than once every two years and of special meetings of the Parties at any time on the request of two-thirds of the Parties;

(b) preparing and assisting, in consultation with the Contracting Parties and appropriate International Organisations, in the development and implementation of procedures referred to in sub-paragraph (4) (e) of this Article;

(c) considering enquiries by, and information from the Contracting Parties, consulting with them and with the appropriate International Organisations, and providing recommendations to the Parties on questions related to, but not specifically covered by the Convention;

(d) conveying to the Parties concerned all notifications received by the Organisation in accordance with Articles IV (3), V (1) and (2), VI (4), XV, XX and XXI.

Prior to the designation of the Organisation these functions shall, as necessary, be performed by the depositary, who for this purpose shall be the Government of the United Kingdom of Great Britain and Northern Ireland.

4. Consultative or special meetings of the Contracting Parties shall keep under continuing review the implementation of this Convention and may, *inter alia*:

(a) review and adopt amendments to this Convention and its Annexes in accordance with Article XV;

(b) invite the appropriate scientific body or bodies to collaborate with and to advise the Parties or the Organisation on any scientific or technical aspect relevant to this Convention, including particularly the content of the Annexes;

(c) receive and consider reports made pursuant to Article VI (4);

(d) promote co-operation with and between regional organisations concerned with the prevention of marine pollution;

(e) develop or adopt, in consultation with appropriate International Organisations procedures referred to in Article V (2), including basic criteria for determining exceptional and emergency situations, and procedures for consultative advice and the safe disposal of matter in such circumstances, including the designation of appropriate dumping areas, and recommend accordingly;

(*f*) consider any additional action that may be required.

5. The Contracting Parties at their first consultative meeting shall establish rules of procedure as necessary.

**Art. 15.** 1. (*a*) At meetings of the Contracting Parties called in accordance with Article XIV amendments to this Convention may be adopted by a two-thirds majority of those present. An amendment shall enter into force for the Parties which have accepted it on the sixtieth day after two-thirds of the Parties shall have deposited an instrument of acceptance of the amendment with the Organization. Thereafter the amendment shall enter into force for any other Party 30 days after that Party deposits its instrument of acceptance of the amendment.

(*b*) The Organisation shall inform all Contracting Parties of any request made for a special meeting under Article XIV and of any amendments adopted at meetings of the Parties and of the date on which each such amendment enters into force for each Party.

2. Amendments to the Annexes will be based on scientific or technical considerations. Amendments to the Annexes approved by a two-thirds majority of those present at a meeting called in accordance with Article XIV shall enter into force for each Contracting Party immediately on notification of its acceptance to the Organisation and 100 days after approval by the meeting for all other Parties except for those which before the end of the 100 days make a declaration that they are not able to accept the amendment at that time. Parties should endeavour to signify their acceptance of an amendment to the Organisation as soon as possible after approval at a meeting. A Party may at any time substitute an acceptance for a previous declaration of objection and the amendment previously objected to shall thereupon enter into force for that Party.

3. An acceptance or declaration of objection under this Article shall be made by the deposit of an instrument with the Organisation. The Organisation shall notify all Contracting Parties of the receipt of such instruments.

4. Prior to the designation of the Organisation, the Secretarial functions herein attributed to it, shall be performed temporarily by the Government of the United Kingdom of Great Britain and Northern Ireland, as one of the depositaries of this Convention.

**Art. 16.** This Convention shall be open for signature by any State at London, Mexico City, Moscow and Washington from 29 December 1972 until 31 December 1973.

**Art. 17.** This Convention shall be subject to ratification. The instruments of ratification shall be deposited with the Governments of Mexico, the Union of Soviet Socialist Republics, the United Kingdom of Great Britain and Northern Ireland, and the United States of America.

**Art. 18.** After 31 December 1973, this Convention shall be open for accession by any State. The instruments of accession shall be deposited with the Governments of Mexico, the Union of Soviet Socialist Republics, the United Kingdom of Great Britain and Northern Ireland, and the United States of America.

**Art. 19.** 1. This Convention shall enter into force on the thirtieth day following the date of deposit of the fifteenth instrument of ratification or accession.

2. For each Contracting Party ratifying or acceding to the Convention after the deposit of the fifteenth instrument of ratification or accession, the Convention shall enter into force on the thirtieth day after deposit by such Party of its instrument of ratification or accession.

**Art. 20.** The depositaries shall inform Contracting Parties:

(*a*) of signatures to this Convention and of the deposit of instruments of ratification, accession or withdrawal, in accordance with Articles XVI, XVII, XVIII and XXI, and

(*b*) of the date on which this Convention will enter into force, in accordance with Article XIX.

**Art. 21.** Any Contracting Party may withdraw from this Convention by giving six months' notice in writing to a depositary, which shall promptly inform all Parties of such notice.

**Art. 22.** The original of this Convention of which the English, French, Russian and Spanish texts are equally authentic, shall be deposited with the Governments of Mexico, the Union of Soviet Socialist Republics, the United Kingdom of Great Britain and Northern Ireland and the United States of America who shall send certified copies thereof to all States.

## ANNEX I

1. Organohalogen compounds.
2. Mercury and mercury compounds.
3. Cadmium and cadmium compounds.
4. Persistent plastics and other persistent synthetic materials, for example, netting and ropes, which may float or may remain in suspension in the sea in such a manner as to interfere materially with fishing, navigation or other legitimate uses of the sea.
5. Crude oil, fuel oil, heavy diesel oil, and lubricating oils, hydraulic fluids,

and any mixtures containing any of these, taken on board for the purpose of dumping.

6. High-level radio-active wastes or other high-level radio-active matter, defined on public health, biological or other grounds, by the competent international body in this field, at present the International Atomic Energy Agency, as unsuitable for dumping at sea.

7. Materials in whatever form (*e.g.* solids, liquids, semi-liquids, gases or in a living state) produced for biological and chemical warfare.

8. The preceding paragraphs of this Annex do not apply to substances which are rapidly rendered harmless by physical, chemical or biological processes in the sea provided they do not:

    (i) make edible marine organisms unpalatable, or

    (ii) endanger human health or that of domestic animals.

The consultative procedure provided for under Article XIV should be followed by a Party if there is doubt about the harmlessness of the substance.

9. This Annex does not apply to wastes or other materials (*e.g.* sewage sludges and dredged spoils) containing the matters referred to in paragraphs 1-5 above as trace contaminants. Such wastes shall be subject to the provisions of Annexes II and III as appropriate.

## ANNEX II

The following substances and materials requiring special care are listed for the purposes of Article VI (1) (*a*).

    A. Wastes containing significant amounts of the matters listed below:

      arsenic

      lead

      copper     and their compounds

      zinc

      organosilicon compounds

      cyanides

      fluorides

      pesticides and their by-products not covered in Annex I.

    B. In the issue of permits for the dumping of large quantities of acids and alkalis, consideration shall be given to the possible presence in such wastes of the substances listed in paragraph A and to the following additional substances:

      beryllium

      chromium

      nickel     and their compounds

      vanadium

    C. Containers, scrap metal and other bulky wastes liable to sink to the sea bottom which may present a serious obstacle to fishing or navigation.

D. Radio-active wastes or other radio-active matter not included in Annex I. In the issue of permits for the dumping of this matter, the Contracting Parties should take full account of the recommendations of the competent international body in this field, at present the International Atomic Energy Agency.

## ANNEX III

Provisions to be considered in establishing criteria governing the issue of permits for the dumping of matter at sea, taking into account Article IV (2), include:

A. *Characteristics and composition of the matter*

1. Total amount and average composition of matter dumped (*e.g.* per year).
2. Form, *e.g.* solid, sludge, liquid, or gaseous.
3. Properties: physical (*e.g.* solubility and density), chemical and biochemical (*e.g.* oxygen demand, nutrients) and biological (*e.g.* presence of viruses, bacteria, yeasts, parasites).
4. Toxicity.
5. Persistence: physical, chemical and biological.
6. Accumulation and biotransformation in biological materials or sediments.
7. Susceptibility to physical, chemical and biochemical changes and interaction in the aquatic environment with other dissolved organic and inorganic materials.
8. Probability of production of taints or other changes reducing marketability of resources (fish, shellfish, *etc.*).

B. *Characteristics of dumping site and method of deposit*

1. Location (*e.g.* co-ordinates of the dumping area, depth and distance from the coast), location in relation to other areas (*e.g.* amenity areas, spawning, nursery and fishing areas and exploitable resources).
2. Rate of disposal per specific period (e.g. quantity per day, per week, per month).
3. Methods of packaging and containment, if any.
4. Initial dilution achieved by proposed method of release.
5. Dispersal characteristics (*e.g.* effects of currents, tides and wind on horizontal transport and vertical mixing).
6. Water characteristics (*e.g.* temperature, pH, salinity, stratification, oxygen indices of pollution-dissolved oxygen (DO), chemical oxygen demand (COD), biochemical oxygen demand (BOD)-nitrogen present in organic and mineral form including ammonia, suspended matter, other nutrients and productivity).
7. Bottom characteristics (*e.g.* topography, geochemical and geological characteristics and biological productivity).

8. Existence and effects of other dumpings which have been made in the dumping area (*e.g.* heavy metal background reading and organic carbon content).

9. In issuing a permit for dumping, Contracting Parties should consider whether an adequate scientific basis exists for assessing the consequences of such dumping, as outlined in this Annex, taking into account seasonal variations.

C. *General considerations and conditions*

1. Possible effects on amenities (*e.g.* presence of floating or stranded material, turbidity, objectionable odour, discolouration and foaming).

2. Possible effects on marine life, fish and shellfish culture, fish stocks and fisheries, seaweed harvesting and culture.

3. Possible effects on other uses of the sea (*e.g.* impairment of water quality for industrial use, underwater corrosion of structures, interference with ship operations from floating materials, interference with fishing or navigation through deposit of waste or solid objects on the sea floor and protection of areas of special importance for scientific or conservation purposes).

4. The practical availability of alternative land-based methods of treatment, disposal or elimination, or of treatment to render the matter less harmful for dumping at sea.


# INTERNATIONAL CONVENTION FOR THE PREVENTION OF POLLUTION FROM SHIPS, 1973

Adopted by 58 votes to none, with 3 abstentions at the International Conference on Marine Pollution held at London, 8 October-2 November 1973.

*The Parties to the Convention,*

*Being conscious* of the need to preserve the human environment in general and the marine environment in particular,

*Recognizing* that deliberate, negligent or accidental release of oil and other harmful substances from ships constitutes a serious source of pollution,

*Recognizing also* the importance of the International Convention for the Prevention of Pollution of the Sea by Oil, 1954, as being the first multilateral instrument to be concluded with the prime objective of protecting the environment, and appreciating the significant contribution which that Convention has made in preserving the seas and coastal environment from pollution,

*Desiring* to achieve the complete elimination of intentional pollution of the marine environment by oil and other harmful substances and the minimization of accidental discharge of such substances,

*Considering* that this object may best be achieved by establishing rules not limited to oil pollution having a universal purport,

*Have agreed* as follows:

**Art. 1.** *General Obligations under the Convention*

(1) The Parties to the Convention undertake to give effect to the provisions of the present Convention and those Annexes thereto by which they are bound, in order to prevent the pollution of the marine environment by the discharge of harmful substances or effluents containing such substances in contravention of the Convention.

(2) Unless expressly provided otherwise, a reference to the present Convention constitutes at the same time a reference to its Protocols and to the Annexes.

**Art. 2.** *Definitions*

For the purposes of the present Convention, unless expressly provided otherwise:

(1) "Regulations" means the Regulations contained in the Annexes to the present Convention.

(2) "Harmful substance" means any substance which, if introduced into the sea, is liable to create hazards to human health, to harm living resources and marine life, to damage amenities or to interfere with other legitimate uses of the sea, and includes any substance subject to control by the present Convention.

(3) (*a*) "Discharge", in relation to harmful substances or effluents containing such substances, means any release howsoever caused from a ship and includes any escape, disposal, spilling, leaking, pumping, emitting or emptying.

(*b*) "Discharge" does not include:

(i) dumping within the meaning of the Convention on the Prevention of Marine Pollution by Dumping of Wastes and Other Matter done at London on 13 November 1972; or

(ii) release of harmful substances directly arising from the exploration, exploitation and associated off-shore processing of sea-bed mineral resources; or

(iii) release of harmful substances for purposes of legitimate scientific research into pollution abatement or control.

(4) "Ship" means a vessel of any type whatsoever operating in the marine environment and includes hydrofoil boats, air-cushion vehicles, submersibles, floating craft and fixed or floating platforms.

(5) "Administration" means the Government of the State under whose

183

authority the ship is operating. With respect to a ship entitled to fly a flag of any State, the Administration is the Government of that State. With respect to fixed or floating platforms engaged in exploration and exploitation of the sea-bed and subsoil thereof adjacent to the coast over which the coastal State exercises sovereign rights for the purposes of exploration and exploitation of their natural resources, the Administration is the Government of the coastal State concerned.

(6) "Incident" means an event involving the actual or probable discharge into the sea of a harmful substance, or effluents containing such a substance.

(7) "Organization" means the Inter-Governmental Maritime Consultative Organization.

**Art. 3.** *Application*

(1) The present Convention shall apply to:

(*a*) ships entitled to fly the flag of a Party to the Convention; and

(*b*) ships not entitled to fly the flag of a Party but which operate under the authority of a Party.

(2) Nothing in the present Article shall be construed as derogating from or extending the sovereign rights of the Parties under international law over the sea-bed and subsoil thereof adjacent to their coasts for the purposes of exploration and exploitation of their natural resources.

(3) The present Convention shall not apply to any warship, naval auxiliary or other ship owned or operated by a State and used, for the time being, only on government non-commercial service. However, each Party shall ensure by the adoption of appropriate measures not impairing the operations or operational capabilities of such ships owned or operated by it, that such ships act in a manner consistent, so far as is reasonable and practicable, with the present Convention.

**Art. 4.** *Violation*

(1) Any violation of the requirements of the present Convention shall be prohibited and sanctions shall be established therefor under the law of the Administration of the ship concerned wherever the violation occurs. If the Administration is informed of such a violation and is satisfied that sufficient evidence is available to enable proceedings to be brought in respect of the alleged violation, it shall cause such proceedings to be taken as soon as possible, in accordance with its law.

(2) Any violation of the requirements of the present Convention within the jurisdiction of any Party to the Convention shall be prohibited and sanctions shall be established therefor under the law of that Party. Whenever such a violation occurs, that Party shall either:

(*a*) cause proceedings to be taken in accordance with its law; or

(*b*) furnish to the Administration of the ship such information and

184

evidence as may be in its possession that a violation has occurred.

(3) Where information or evidence with respect to any violation of the present Convention by a ship is furnished to the Administration of that ship, the Administration shall promptly inform the Party which has furnished the information or evidence, and the Organization, of the action taken.

(4) The penalties specified under the law of a Party pursuant to the present Article shall be adequate in severity to discourage violations of the present Convention and shall be equally severe irrespective of where the violations occur.

**Art. 5.** *Certificates and Special Rules on Inspection of Ships*

(1) Subject to the provisions of paragraph (2) of the present Article a certificate issued under the authority of a Party to the Convention in accordance with the provisions of the Regulations shall be accepted by the other Parties and regarded for all purposes covered by the present Convention as having the same validity as a certificate issued by them.

(2) A ship required to hold a certificate in accordance with the provisions of the Regulations is subject while in the ports or off-shore terminals under the jurisdiction of a Party to inspection by officers duly authorized by that Party. Any such inspection shall be limited to verifying that there is on board a valid certificate, unless there are clear grounds for believing that the condition of the ship or its equipment does not correspond substantially with the particulars of that certificate. In that case, or if the ship does not carry a valid certificate, the Party carrying out the inspection shall take such steps as will ensure that the ship shall not sail until it can proceed to sea without presenting an unreasonable threat of harm to the marine environment. That Party may, however, grant such a ship permission to leave the port or off-shore terminal for the purpose of proceeding to the nearest appropriate repair yard available.

(3) If a Party denies a foreign ship entry to the ports or off-shore terminals under its jurisdiction or takes any action against such a ship for the reason that the ship does not comply with the provisions of the present Convention, the Party shall immediately inform the consul or diplomatic representative of the Party whose flag the ship is entitled to fly, or if this is not possible, the Administration of the ship concerned. Before denying entry or taking such action the Party may request consultation with the Administration of the ship concerned. Information shall also be given to the Administration when a ship does not carry a valid certificate in accordance with the provisions of the Regulations.

(4) With respect to the ships of non-Parties to the Convention, Parties shall apply the requirements of the present Convention as may be necessary to ensure that no more favourable treatment is given to such ships.

**Art. 6.** *Detection of Violations and Enforcement of the Convention*

(1) Parties to the Convention shall co-operate in the detection of violations and the enforcement of the provisions of the present Convention, using all appropriate and practicable measures of detection and environmental monitoring, adequate procedures for reporting and accumulation of evidence.

(2) A ship to which the present Convention applies may, in any port or off-shore terminal of a Party, be subject to inspection by officers appointed or authorized by that Party for the purpose of verifying whether the ship has discharged any harmful substances in violation of the provisions of the Regulations. If an inspection indicates a violation of the Convention, a report shall be forwarded to the Administration for any appropriate action.

(3) Any Party shall furnish to the Administration evidence, if any, that the ship has discharged harmful substances or effluents containing such substances in violation of the provisions of the Regulations. If it is practicable to do so, the competent authority of the former Party shall notify the master of the ship of the alleged violation.

(4) Upon receiving such evidence, the Administration so informed shall investigate the matter, and may request the other Party to furnish further or better evidence of the alleged contravention. If the Administration is satisfied that sufficient evidence is available to enable proceedings to be brought in respect of the alleged violation, it shall cause such proceedings to be taken in accordance with its law as soon as possible. The Administration shall promptly inform the Party which has reported the alleged violation, as well as the Organization, of the action taken.

(5) A Party may also inspect a ship to which the present Convention applies when it enters the ports or off-shore terminals under its jurisdiction, if a request for an investigation is received from any Party together with sufficient evidence that the ship has discharged harmful substances or effluents containing such substances in any place. The report of such investigation shall be sent to the Party requesting it and to the Administration so that the appropriate action may be taken under the present Convention.

**Art. 7.** *Undue Delay to Ships*

(1) All possible efforts shall be made to avoid a ship being urduly detained or delayed under Articles 4, 5 and 6 of the present Convention.

(2) When a ship is unduly detained or delayed under Articles 4, 5 and 6 of the present Convention, it shall be entitled to compensation for any loss or damage suffered.

**Art. 8.** *Reports on Incidents Involving Harmful Substances*

(1) A report of an incident shall be made without delay to the fullest extent possible in accordance with the provisions of Protocol I to the pre-

sent Convention.

(2) Each Party to the Convention shall:

(a) make all arrangements necessary for an appropriate officer or agency to receive and process all reports on incidents; and

(b) notify the Organization with complete details of such arrangements for circulation to other Parties and Member States of the Organization.

(3) Whenever a Party receives a report under the provisions of the present Article, that Party shall relay the report without delay to:

(a) the Administration of the ship involved; and

(b) any other State which may be affected.

(4) Each Party to the Convention undertakes to issue instructions to its maritime inspection vessels and aircraft and to other appropriate services, to report to its authorities any incident referred to in Protocol I to the present Convention. That Party shall, if it considers it appropriate, report accordingly to the Organization and to any other party concerned.

**Art. 9.** *Other Treaties and Interpretation*

(1) Upon its entry into force, the present Convention supersedes the International Convention for the Prevention of Pollution of the Sea by Oil, 1954, as amended, as between Parties to that Convention.

(2) Nothing in the present Convention shall prejudice the codification and development of the law of the sea by the United Nations Conference on the Law of the Sea convened pursuant to Resolution 2750 C (XXV) of the General Assembly of the United Nations nor the present or future claims and legal views of any State concerning the law of the sea and the nature and extent of coastal and flag State jurisdiction.

(3) The term "jurisdiction" in the present Convention shall be construed in the light of international law in force at the time of application or interpretation of the present Convention.

**Art. 10.** *Settlement of Disputes*

Any dispute between two or more Parties to the Convention concerning the interpretation or application of the present Convention shall, if settlement by negotiation between the Parties involved has not been possible, and if these Parties do not otherwise agree, be submitted upon request of any of them to arbitration as set out in Protocol II to the present Convention.

**Art. 11.** *Communication of Information*

(1) The Parties to the Convention undertake to communicate to the Organization:

(a) the text of laws, orders, decrees and regulations and other instruments which have been promulgated on the various matters within the scope of the present Convention;

(*b*) a list of non-governmental agencies which are authorized to act on their behalf in matters relating to the design, construction and equipment of ships carrying harmful substances in accordance with the provisions of the Regulations;

(*c*) a sufficient number of specimens of their certificates issued under the provisions of the Regulations;

(*d*) a list of reception facilities including their location, capacity and available facilities and other characteristics;

(*e*) official reports or summaries of official reports in so far as they show the results of the application of the present Convention; and

(*f*) an annual statistical report, in a form standardised by the Organization, of penalties actually imposed for infringement of the present Convention.

(2) The Organization shall notify Parties of the receipt of any communications under the present Article and circulate to all Parties any information communicated to it under sub-paragraphs (1) (*b*) to (*f*) of the present Article.

**Art. 12.** *Casualties to Ships*

(1) Each Administration undertakes to conduct an investigation of any casualty occurring to any of its ships subject to the provisions of the Regulations if such casualty has produced a major deleterious effect upon the marine environment.

(2) Each Party to the Convention undertakes to supply the Organization with information concerning the findings of such investigation, when it judges that such information may assist in determining what changes in the present Convention might be desirable.

**Art. 13.** *Signature, Ratification, Acceptance, Approval and Accession*

(1) The present Convention shall remain open for signature at the Headquarters of the Organization from 15 January 1974 until 31 December 1974 and shall thereafter remain open for accession. States may become Parties to the present Convention by:

(*a*) signature without reservation as to ratification, acceptance or approval; or

(*b*) signature subject to ratification, acceptance or approval, followed by ratification, acceptance or approval; or

(*c*) accession.

(2) Ratification, acceptance, approval or accession shall be effected by the deposit of an instrument to that effect with the Secretary-General of the Organization.

(3) The Secretary-General of the Organization shall inform all States which have signed the present Convention or acceded to it of any signature

or of the deposit of any new instrument of ratification, acceptance, approval or accession and the date of its deposit.

**Art. 14.** *Optional Annexes*

(1) A State may at the time of signing, ratifying, accepting, approving or acceding to the present Convention declare that it does not accept any one or all of Annexes III, IV and V (hereinafter referred to as "Optional Annexes") of the present Convention. Subject to the above, Parties to the Convention shall be bound by any Annex in its entirety.

(2) A State which has declared that it is not bound by an Optional Annex may at any time accept such Annex by depositing with the Organization an instrument of the kind referred to in Article 13 (2).

(3) A State which makes a declaration under paragraph (1) of the present Article in respect of an Optional Annex and which has not subsequently accepted that Annex in accordance with paragraph (2) of the present Article shall not be under any obligation nor entitled to claim any privileges under the present Convention in respect of matters related to such Annex and all references to Parties in the present Convention shall not include that State in so far as matters related to such Annex are concerned.

(4) The Organization shall inform the States which have signed or acceded to the present Convention of any declaration under the present Article as well as the receipt of any instrument deposited in accordance with the provisions of paragraph (2) of the present Article.

**Art. 15.** *Entry into Force*

(1) The present Convention shall enter into force twelve months after the date on which not less than 15 States, the combined merchant fleets of which constitute not less than fifty per cent of the gross tonnage of the world's merchant shipping, have become parties to it in accordance with Article 13.

(2) An Optional Annex shall enter into force twelve months after the date on which the conditions stipulated in paragraph (1) of the present Article have been satisfied in relation to that Annex.

(3) The Organization shall inform the States which have signed the present Convention or acceded to it of the date on which it enters into force and of the date on which an Optional Annex enters into force in accordance with paragraph (2) of the present Article.

(4) For States which have deposited an instrument of ratification, acceptance, approval or accession in respect of the present Convention or any Optional Annex after the requirements for entry into force thereof have been met but prior to the date of entry into force, the ratification, acceptance, approval of accession shall take effect on the date of entry into force of the Convention or such Annex or three months after the date

of deposit of the instrument whichever is the later date.

(5) For States which have deposited an instrument of ratification, acceptance, approval or accession after the date on which the Convention or an Optional Annex entered into force, the Convention or the Optional Annex shall become effective three months after the date of deposit of the instrument.

(6) After the date on which all the conditions required under Article 16 to bring an amendment to the present Convention or an Optional Annex into force have been fulfilled, any instrument of ratification, acceptance, approval or accession deposited shall apply to the Convention or Annex as amended.

**Art. 16.** *Amendments*

(1) The present Convention may be amended by any of the procedures specified in the following paragraphs.

(2) Amendments after consideration by the Organization:

(*a*) any amendment proposed by a Party to the Convention shall be submitted to the Organization and circulated by its Secretary-General to all Members of the Organization and all Parties at least six months prior to its consideration;

(*b*) any amendment proposed and circulated as above shall be submitted to an appropriate body by the Organization for consideration;

(*c*) Parties to the Convention, whether or not Members of the Organization, shall be entitled to participate in the proceedings of the appropriate body;

(*d*) amendments shall be adopted by a two-thirds majority of only the Parties to the Convention present and voting;

(*e*) if adopted in accordance with sub-paragraph (*d*) above, amendments shall be communicated by the Secretary-General of the Organization to all the Parties to the Convention for acceptance;

(*f*) an amendment shall be deemed to have been accepted in the following circumstances:

(i) an amendment to an Article of the Convention shall be deemed to have been accepted on the date on which it is accepted by two-thirds of the Parties, the combined merchant fleets of which constitute not less than fifty per cent of the gross tonnage of the world's merchant fleet;

(ii) an amendment to an Annex to the Convention shall be deemed to have been accepted in accordance with the procedure specified in sub-paragraph (*f*) (iii) unless the appropriate body, at the time of its adoption, determines that the amendment shall be deemed to have been accepted on the date on which it is accepted by two-thirds of the Parties, the combined merchant fleets of which constitute not less than fifty per cent of the gross tonnage of the world's merchant fleet. Nevertheless, at any time

190

before the entry into force of an amendment to an Annex to the Convention, a Party may notify the Secretary-General of the Organization that its express approval will be necessary before the amendment enters into force for it. The latter shall bring such notification and the date of its receipt to the notice of Parties;

(iii) an amendment to an Appendix to an Annex to the Convention shall be deemed to have been accepted at the end of a period to be determined by the appropriate body at the time of its adoption, which period shall be not less than ten months, unless within that period an objection is communicated to the Organization by not less than one-third of the Parties or by the Parties the combined merchant fleets of which constitute not less than fifty per cent of the gross tonnage of the world's merchant fleet whichever condition is fulfilled;

(iv) an amendment to Protocol I to the Convention shall be subject to the same procedures as for the amendments to the Annexes to the Convention, as provided for in sub-paragraphs (f) (ii) or (f) (iii) above;

(v) an amendment to Protocol II to the Convention shall be subject to the same procedures as for the amendments to an Article of the Convention, as provided for in sub-paragraphs (f) (i) above;

(g) the amendment shall enter into force under the following conditions:

(i) in the case of an amendment to an Article of the Convention, to Protocol II, or to Protocol I or to an Annex to the Convention not under the procedure specified in sub-paragraph (f) (iii), the amendment accepted in conformity with the foregoing provisions shall enter into force six months after the date of its acceptance with respect to the Parties which have declared that they have accepted it;

(ii) in the case of an amendment to Protocol I, to an Appendix to an Annex or to an Annex to the Convention under the procedure specified in sub-paragraph (f) (iii), the amendment deemed to have been accepted in accordance with the foregoing conditions shall enter into force six months after its acceptance for all the Parties with the exception of those which, before that date, have made a declaration that they do not accept it or a declaration under sub-paragraph (f) (ii), that their express approval is necessary.

(3) Amendment by a Conference:

(a) Upon the request of a Party, concurred in by at least one-third of the Parties, the Organization shall convene a Conference of Parties to the Convention to consider amendments to the present Convention.

(b) Every amendment adopted by such a Conference by a two-thirds majority of those present and voting of the Parties shall be communicated by the Secretary-General of the Organization to all Contracting Parties for their acceptance.

(c) Unless the Conference decides otherwise, the amendment shall be

191

deemed to have been accepted and to have entered into force in accordance with the procedures specified for that purpose in paragraph (2) (*f*) and (*g*) above.

(4) (*a*) In the case of an amendment to an Optional Annex, a reference in the present Article to a "Party to the Convention" shall be deemed to mean a reference to a Party bound by that Annex.

(*b*) Any Party which has declined to accept an amendment to an Annex shall be treated as a non-Party only for the purpose of application of that amendment.

(5) The adoption and entry into force of a new Annex shall be subject to the same procedures as for the adoption and entry into force of an amendment to an Article of the Convention.

(6) Unless expressly provided otherwise, any amendment to the present Convention made under this Article which relates to the structure of a ship shall apply only to ships for which the building contract is placed, or in the absence of a building contract, the keel of which is laid, on or after the date on which the amendment comes into force.

(7) Any amendment to a Protocol or to an Annex shall relate to the substance of that Protocol or Annex and shall be consistent with the Articles of the present Convention.

(8) The Secretary-General of the Organization shall inform all Parties of any amendments which enter into force under the present Article, together with the date on which each such amendment enters into force.

(9) Any declaration of acceptance or of objection to an amendment under the present Article shall be notified in writing to the Secretary-General of the Organization. The latter shall bring such notification and the date of its receipt to the notice of the Parties to the Convention.

**Art. 17.** *Promotion of Technical Co-operation*

The Parties to the Convention shall promote, in consultation with the Organization and other international bodies, with assistance and co-ordination by the Executive Director of the United Nations Environment Programme, support for those Parties which request technical assistance for:

(*a*) the training of scientific and technical personnel;

(*b*) the supply of necessary equipment and facilities for reception and monitoring;

(*c*) the facilitation of other measures and arrangements to prevent or mitigate pollution of the marine environment by ships; and

(*d*) the encouragement of research;

preferably within the countries concerned, so furthering the aims and purposes of the present Convention.

192

**Art. 18.** *Denunciation*

(1) The present Convention or any Optional Annex may be denounced by any Parties to the Convention at any time after the expiry of five years from the date on which the Convention or such Annex enters into force for that Party.

(2) Denunciation shall be effected by notification in writing to the Secretary-General of the Organization who shall inform all the other Parties of any such notification received and of the date of its receipt as well as the date on which such denunciation takes effect.

(3) A denunciation shall take effect, twelve months after receipt of the notification of denunciation by the Secretary-General of the Organization or after the expiry of any other longer period which may be indicated in the notification.

**Art. 19.** *Deposit and Registration*

(1) The present Convention shall be deposited with the Secretary-General of the Organization who shall transmit certified true copies thereof to all States which have signed the present Convention or acceded to it.

(2) As soon as the present Convention enters into force, the text shall be transmitted by the Secretary-General of the Organization to the Secretary-General of the United Nations for registration and publication, in accordance with Article 102 of the Charter of the United Nations.

**Art. 20.** *Languages*

The present Convention is established in a single copy in the English, French, Russian and Spanish languages, each text being equally authentic. Official translations in the Arabic, German, Italian and Japanese languages shall be prepared and deposited with the signed original.

*Annex I-V; Protocol I-II* (see p. 580)

## PROTOCOL RELATING TO INTERVENTION ON THE HIGH SEAS IN CASES OF MARINE POLLUTION BY SUBSTANCES OTHER THAN OIL, 1973

Adopted by 36 votes to 10, with 6 abstentions at the International Conference on Marine Pollution held at London, 8 October-2 November 1973.

*The States Parties to the present Protocol,*

*Being Parties* to the International Convention relating to Intervention on the High Seas in Cases of Oil Pollution Casualties done at Brussels on

29 November 1969,

*Taking into account* the resolution on International Co-operation concerning Pollutants other than Oil adopted by the International Legal Conference on Marine Pollution Damage, 1969,

*Further taking into account* that pursuant to the resolution, the Inter-Governmental Maritime Consultative Organization has intensified its work, in collaboration with all interested international organizations, on all aspects of pollution by substances other than oil,

*Have agreed* as follows:

**Art. 1.** 1. Parties to the present Protocol may take such measures on the high seas as may be necessary to prevent, mitigate or eliminate grave and imminent danger to their coastline or related interests from pollution or threat of pollution by substances other than oil following upon a maritime casualty or acts related to such a casualty, which may reasonably be expected to result in major harmful consequences.

2. "Substances other than oil" as referred to in paragraph 1 shall be:

(*a*) those substances enumerated in a list which shall be established by an appropriate body designated by the Organization and which shall be annexed to the present Protocol, and

(*b*) those other substances which are liable to create hazards to human health, to harm living resources and marine life, to damage amenities or to interfere with other legitimate uses of the sea.

3. Whenever an intervening Party takes action with regard to a substance referred to in paragraph 2 (*a*) that Party shall have the burden of establishing that the substance under the circumstances present at the time of the intervention could reasonably pose a grave and imminent danger analogous to that posed by any of the substances enumerated in the list referred to in paragraph 2 (*a*).

**Art. 2.** 1. The provisions of paragraph 2 of Article I and Articles II to VIII of the Convention Relating to Intervention on the High Seas in Cases of Oil Pollution Casualties, 1969 and the Annex thereto as they relate to oil shall be applicable with regard to the substances referred to in Article I of the present Protocol.

2. For the purpose of the present Protocol the list of experts referred to in Articles III (*c*) and IV of the Convention shall be extended to include experts qualified to give advice in relation to substances other than oil. Nominations to the list may be made by Member States of the Organization and by Parties to the present Protocol.

**Art. 3.** 1. The list referred to in paragraph 2 (*a*) of Article I shall be maintained by the appropriate body designated by the Organization.

2. Any amendment to the list proposed by a Party to the present Pro-

194

tocol shall be submitted to the Organization and circulated by it to all Members of the Organization and all Parties to the present Protocol at least three months prior to its consideration by the appropriate body.

3. Parties to the present Protocol whether or not Members of the Organization shall be entitled to participate in the proceedings of the appropriate body.

4. Amendments shall be adopted by a two-thirds majority of only the Parties to the present Protocol present and voting.

5. If adopted in accordance with paragraph 4 above, the amendment shall be communicated by the Organization to all Parties to the present Protocol for acceptance.

6. The amendment shall be deemed to have been accepted at the end of a period of six months after it has been communicated, unless within that period an objection to the amendment has been communicated to the Organization by not less than one-third of the Parties to the present Protocol.

7. An amendment deemed to have been accepted in accordance with paragraph 6 above shall enter into force three months after its acceptance for all Parties to the present Protocol, with the exception of those which before that date have made a declaration of non-acceptance of the said amendment.

**Art. 4.** 1. The present Protocol shall be open for signature by the States which have signed the Convention referred to in Article II or acceded thereto, and by any State invited to be represented at the International Conference on Marine Pollution 1973. The Protocol shall remain open for signature until 31 December 1974 at the Headquarters of the Organization.

2. Subject to paragraph 4, the present Protocol shall be subject to ratification, acceptance or approval by the States which have signed it.

3. Subject to paragraph 4, this Protocol shall be open for accession by States which did not sign it.

4. The present Protocol may be ratified, accepted, approved or acceded to only by States which have ratified, accepted, approved or acceded to the Convention referred to in Article II.

**Art. 5.** 1. Ratification, acceptance, approval or accession shall be effected by the deposit of a formal instrument to that effect with the Secretary-General of the Organization.

2. Any instrument of ratification, acceptance, approval or accession deposited after the entry into force of an amendment to the present Protocol with respect to all existing Parties or after the completion of all measures required for the entry into force of the amendment with respect to all existing Parties shall be deemed to apply to the Protocol as modified by the amendment.

**Art. 6.** 1. The present Protocol shall enter into force on the ninetieth day following the date on which fifteen States have deposited instruments of ratification, acceptance, approval or accession with the Secretary-General of the Organization, provided however that the present Protocol shall not enter into force before the Convention referred to in Article II has entered into force.

2. For each State which subsequently ratifies, accepts, approves or accedes to it, the present Protocol shall enter into force on the ninetieth day after the deposit by such State of the appropriate instrument.

**Art. 7.** 1. The present Protocol may be denounced by any Party at any time after the date on which the Protocol enters into force for that Party.

2. Denunciation shall be effected by the deposit of an instrument to that effect with the Secretary-General of the Organization.

3. Denunciation shall take effect one year, or such longer period as may be specified in the instrument of denunciation, after its deposit with the Secretary-General of the Organization.

4. Denunciation of the Convention referred to in Article II by a Party shall be deemed to be a denunciation of the present Protocol by that Party. Such denunciation shall take effect on the same day as the denunciation of the Convention takes effect in accordance with paragraph 3 of Article XII of that Convention.

**Art. 8.** 1. A conference for the purpose of revising or amending the present Protocol may be convened by the Organization.

2. The Organization shall convene a conference of Parties to the present Protocol for the purpose of revising or amending it at the request of not less than one-third of the Parties.

**Art. 9.** 1. The present Protocol shall be deposited with the Secretary-General of the Organization.

2. The Secretary-General of the Organization shall:

(*a*) inform all States which have signed the present Protocol or acceded thereto of:

  (i) each new signature or deposit of an instrument together with the date thereof;

  (ii) the date of entry into force of the present Protocol;

  (iii) the deposit of any instrument of denunciation of the present Protocol together with the date on which the denunciation takes effect;

  (iv) any amendments to the present Protocol or its Annex and any objection or declaration of non-acceptance of the said amendment;

(*b*) transmit certified true copies of the present Protocol to all States which have signed the present Protocol or acceded thereto.

**Art. 10.** As soon as the present Protocol enters into force, a certified true copy thereof shall be transmitted by the Secretary-General of the Organization to the Secretariat of the United Nations for registration and publication in accordance with Article 102 of the Charter of the United Nations.

**Art. 11.** The present Protocol is established in a single original in the English, French and Spanish languages, all three texts being equally authentic. An official translation in the Russian language shall be prepared by the Secretariat of the Organization and deposited with the signed original.

# PART V

# DRAFTS AND RECOMMENDATIONS OF NON-GOVERNMENTAL ORGANIZATIONS

# COMMISSION TO STUDY THE ORGANIZATION OF PEACE:
— **Twenty-third Report (The United Nations and the Oceans: Current Issues in the Law of the Sea), 1973**

The Commission, presided over by Professor Louis S. Sohn, Chairman of the Commission, prepared in June 1973 a report, the second part of which contains the following recommendations.

## A. General Principles

1. The new Law of the Sea, to be embodied in the 1974 (or 1975) Convention or Conventions, should be based on the concept that the sea, the sea-bed and their resources are the common heritage of mankind. That concept should apply not only to the sea-bed and its resources but also to the sea itself and to all resources of the sea, including its living resources, and should be taken into account in the conduct of all activities relating to the sea and the sea-bed and all uses of the sea and the sea-bed.

2. No part of the sea or the sea-bed or of their resources should be subject to appropriation by any means by States or persons, natural or juridical. No State should claim or exercise any sovereign rights beyond the territorial sea, except to the extent recognized by international law and the new Law of the Sea Conventions. No State or person, natural or juridical, should be allowed to claim, acquire or exercise any rights with respect to the resources of the sea or the sea-bed, except in cases specified in the new Law of the Sea Conventions.

3. The sea, the sea-bed and their resources should be open to use by all States and persons, natural or juridical, without discrimination, subject only to such conditions as the new Law of the Sea Conventions may establish.

4. The high seas and the sea-bed of the high seas should be reserved exclusively for peaceful purposes. Special agreements should be promptly concluded to curtail the arms race in the oceans by establishing peace zones or by other generally acceptable measures. All uses of the sea and all activities relating to the sea-bed and the resources of the sea and the sea-bed should conform to the Charter of the United Nations, the Law of the Sea Conventions, other applicable principles and rules of international law, and the Declaration of Principles of International Law concerning Friendly Relations and Co-operation among States.

5. All activities on, in and above the sea or with respect to the sea-bed or the resources of the sea or the sea-bed should be carried out with due regard for the benefit of mankind as a whole and taking into particular consideration the interests and needs of the developing countries and geographically disadvantaged States.

6. The new Law of the Sea Conventions should be based on a functional

201

rather than territorial division of powers. While some functions would be exercised directly by the institutions of the international community, others would be delegated to States, which in all matters relating to the common heritage would be acting merely as agents of the international community.

7. The powers of the international community needed to preserve the common heritage of mankind for the present and future generations should be exercised by an International Ocean Authority which should be closely related to the United Nations. For this purpose, the Authority should be granted specifically the following powers: to adopt policy guidelines and general regulations, and to supervise their observance by States and persons, natural and juridical.

8. The new Law of the Sea Conventions should delegate some important functions with respect to the administration of the resources of the sea and the sea-bed or the enforcement of international regulations enacted under the new Law of the Sea Conventions to coastal States in specified areas or, with respect to certain marine activities, to the States under whose flag, authority, or jurisdiction these activities are conducted. The overall responsibility for protecting the common heritage of mankind should remain, however, in the hands of the International Ocean Authority acting in the name and for the benefit of mankind as a whole, and all delegated activities should conform to the overriding principle of the common heritage of mankind.

9. A State acting as an administrator of certain areas or resources on the basis of authority delegated to it by the international community, should remain subject to such measures of supervision for the benefit of mankind as a whole and to such procedures for the peaceful settlement of disputes as would be provided for in the new Law of the Sea Conventions.

## B. Limits of National and International Jurisdiction

1. The new Law of the Sea Conventions should provide for an equitable sharing of the resources of the sea and the sea-bed. While allowing coastal States to extend their jurisdiction, on a functional basis, to adjacent areas of the sea and the sea-bed, they should at the same time ensure that the need of the international community to protect the common heritage of mankind in areas thus placed under the jurisdiction of coastal States would be properly recognized.

2. The territorial sea of a State should not extend beyond twelve miles from the baseline established in accordance with the 1958 Convention on the Territorial Sea and the Contiguous Zone, and the rights of coastal States in the portion of the high seas newly incorporated in the territorial sea should be subject to the conditions specified in Section C below.

3. The new Law of the Sea Conventions should allow a coastal State to establish an economic resource zone adjacent to its territorial sea. This

202

zone should not extend beyond two hundred miles from the baseline specified in para. 2 above, and the rights of coastal States in the zone should be subject to the conditions specified in Section D below.

4. The area beyond any such economic resource zone should be under direct international control and should be called the international zone.

5. The respective powers of the coastal State and the International Ocean Authority in the territorial sea and the economic resource zone, and the respective powers of States and the International Ocean Authority in the international zone, should be specified in the Law of the Sea Conventions, keeping in mind that all those areas and their resources form a part of the common heritage of mankind.

### C. Territorial Sea and International Straits

1. The provisions of the 1958 Convention on the Territorial Sea and the Contiguous Zone should apply to that part of the territorial sea which a coastal State might acquire in accordance with the new Law of the Sea Conventions (para. B.2 above), except when otherwise specified in this section.

2. International regulations for the protection of the marine environment should be applied to the territorial sea. Any stricter regulations by the coastal State which might interfere with international navigation should require the approval of the International Ocean Authority.

3. Enlarging the width of the territorial sea to twelve miles should not affect the special status of international shipping lanes passing through international straits. The use of these lanes for navigation purposes should be governed by international regulations, to be enacted in accordance with para. 4 below.

4. In cooperation with other competent international agencies, the International Ocean Authority should issue regulations governing the use of international shipping lanes passing through international straits by foreign vessels, both private and governmental. These regulations might require: (*a*) the observance of any internationally agreed upon traffic separation schemes as well as other rules for the avoidance of collisions between ships or other accidents and for the preservation and protection of the marine environment; (*b*) a prior certification by the flag State that the vessel has been built in accordance with international construction and safety standards and that all precautions have been taken, in accordance with applicable international provisions, to prevent contamination of the territorial sea; and (*c*) the acceptance by the flag State of the obligation either to ensure prompt payment of adequate compensation in case of any damage caused by a vessel under its flag to the marine environment or to the shore, or to contribute its appropriate share to an international com-

pensation fund designed to provide compensation in such cases to anyone who has suffered damage. The International Ocean Authority should adopt special rules with respect to the use of international shipping lanes passing through international straits by super-tankers, ships carrying toxic materials, nuclear-powered ships and other ships of a similar kind. Subject to the regulations adopted under this paragraph, warships should be allowed to use international shipping lanes passing through international straits without the need for a special authorization, and there should be no special restrictions on submerged traverse by submarines. The regulations should, on the one hand, protect the coastal State against any abuse of the right to use the international shipping lane passing through an international strait and should ensure, on the other hand, that no undue restrictions are imposed on such use. Pending the adoption of such regulations, the existing right to use international shipping lanes passing through international straits should remain unaffected.

5. The International Ocean Authority should determine from time to time which straits should be considered as international straits, taking into account the amount of traffic through such straits by ships of States other than the coastal State.

6. Foreign vessels using an international shipping lane passing through an international strait should not engage in fishing or trading in the international strait without special permission of the coastal State. Such vessels should be required to take all necessary steps to avoid any threat to the security of the coastal State, and a warship using such shipping lanes should not engage in any military exercise or in any other activity unrelated to such use.

7. In cooperation with the International Civil Aviation Organization, the International Ocean Authority should adopt appropriate regulations governing the overflight by foreign airplanes, private or governmental, over international straits. These regulations should parallel, to the greatest extent possible, the regulations for vessels using an international shipping lane passing through an international strait, including those relating to compensation for any damage, and their object should be, on the one hand, to protect the coastal State against any abuse of the right of overflight and, on the other hand, to ensure that no undue restrictions are imposed on such right.

## D. Economic Resource Zone

1. The coastal State should have jurisdiction over the exploration and exploitation of all the resources of the economic resource zone, but such exploration and exploitation should conform to any international regulations enacted under this section.

2. The establishment of an economic resource zone should not affect

204

either the status of the waters of the zone as high seas or the freedom of overflight in the air above them, but they should be subject to the international regulations adopted under this section.

3. The International Ocean Authority should adopt regulations: to protect the freedoms of navigation, overflight, and laying of submarine cables and pipelines; to prevent unjustifiable interference, on the one hand, with the exploitation of resources and, on the other hand, with other uses of the sea and the sea-bed, including scientific research; to protect the marine environment; and to protect human life and safety. While the regulations should be as uniform as possible, they should take into account the special characteristics of certain areas or regions, some of which might require either stricter or more lenient controls. To the greatest extent possible, the day-to-day application and enforcement of the regulations should be delegated to the coastal State, subject to the general supervision of the International Ocean Authority, which should require submission of periodic and special reports on measures taken. Should a dispute arise in any particular case about the applicability of the regulations or the measures of enforcement, any party concerned should be entitled to submit the dispute to the Ocean Tribunal.

4. The coastal State should have full control in the economic resource zone over the exploration and exploitation of the resources of the sea-bed, subject to any international regulations enacted under this section.

5. Subject to any regulations adopted by the International Ocean Authority, either directly or through the appropriate regional fishery organizations, to ensure adequate conservation of the living resources, and to determine reasonable conditions for the licensing of foreign fishermen in cases in which the local State does not have the capacity or the desire to appropriate the whole permissible catch, the coastal State should have full control over the exploitation of the coastal and anadromous species in the economic resource zone. The regulations of the International Ocean Authority with respect to the catch of migratory oceanic species, enacted under Section E below, should apply also to the fishing for this species in the economic resource zone, but the Authority should delegate the necessary administrative and enforcement powers to the coastal State, subject to a reporting requirement analogous to that specified in para. 3 above.

6. The coastal State should also have full control over the exploitation of resources of the economic resource zone other than those mentioned in paras. 4 and 5 above, subject to any international regulations enacted under paras. 3 and 5 above.

7. The Authority should receive half of all payments to be made by those engaged in the exploration or exploitation of the resources of the sea-bed to the coastal State, in accordance with a schedule to be established

by the Authority and subject to any maximum and minimum established in the Law of the Sea Conventions. Should a coastal State grant certain tax concessions or rebates to those investing in the zone under its administration, it should nevertheless make payments to the Authority based on full amounts specified in the schedule.

8. The coastal State should retain all revenues from the exploitation of coastal species in the economic resource zone, but it should divide equally with the International Ocean Authority the revenues from the anadromous and the migratory oceanic species, calculated in accordance with a schedule to be adopted by the International Ocean Authority, subject to conditions similar to those specified in para. 7 above.

### E. International Zone

Subject to the basic principles to be specified in the Law of the Sea Conventions:

1. The International Ocean Authority should have full control over the exploitation of the resources of the sea-bed in the international zone.

2. The International Ocean Authority should have the authority to adopt the necessary regulations for the conservation of the migratory oceanic species and such other living resources of the zone as are deemed by it to be in need of special protection.

3. The International Ocean Authority should also have full control over the exploitation of resources of the zone other than those mentioned in paras. 1 and 2 above, and should adopt such regulations for that purpose as it may deem necessary.

4. The International Ocean Authority should adopt for the international zone regulations of the kind specified in para. D. 3 above, and such other regulations as may be necessary to protect the sea, the sea-bed and their resources as the common heritage of mankind.

5. The International Ocean Authority should be entitled to require reasonable payments from those authorized by it to explore or exploit the resources of the international zone, to be calculated in accordance with regulations adopted by the Authority, subject to any minimum or maximum specified in the new Law of the Sea Conventions. No State should be allowed, without special authorization of that Authority, to impose any taxes or other imposts on such exploration or exploitation. The Authority might divide its revenue from certain activities in the international zone with any State to which it has delegated administrative or enforcement functions with respect to these activities.

6. The International Ocean Authority should take part in the preparation of international commodity agreements designed to minimize fluctuations in prices of those minerals which are produced from both land and sea-bed sources, and to ensure that the exports of these minerals

206

by the developing countries are not unduly affected.

### F. The International Ocean Authority

1. An International Ocean Authority should be established to protect the oceans and the sea-bed and their resources, and to ensure that this common heritage of mankind will be used for the benefit of mankind as a whole.

2. The principal organs of the Authority should be the Ocean Assembly, the various Councils and Commissions, an Ocean Tribunal and the Secretariat.

3. The Assembly should be composed of all States which ratify, or accede to, the new Law of the Sea Conventions. It should meet annually during the first five years, and thereafter biennially.

4. Subject to any conditions specified in the Law of the Sea Conventions, the Assembly should establish, as soon as it deems it necessary, separate Councils for the major fields of the Authority's activity, and should determine their composition and functions as well as their relationship to existing organizations. In particular, the Assembly should establish separate Councils for: the exploration and exploitation of the resources of the sea-bed, the conservation of the living resources of the sea, the protection of the freedoms of navigation and overflight, the preservation and enhancement of the marine environment, the promotion of ocean research, and the control of the Ocean Fund.

5. The Sea-Bed Council should be composed of thirty-six States. The seats on the Council should be divided equally between the developed and the developing States. In accordance with United Nations practice, the dividing line between developed and developing States should be a per capita gross national product of $1,000 per year. Within each group, half of the members should be selected on the basis of specified objective criteria and a permanent member should hold his seat only as long as he fulfills these criteria. The permanent members in the group of the developed States should be the nine States with the highest gross national product. The permanent members in the group of the developing States should be the three most populous States in Asia, the three most populous States in Africa and the three most populous States in Latin America. At least eight of the members of the Council should come from among the land-locked and shelf-locked States, and at least one of these should come from each of the five major regions (Africa, Asia, the Americas, Eastern Europe and Western Europe). All decisions of the Council should require a three-fourths vote of all the members of the Council.

6. Similar arrangements should be made for the other Councils, although the number and distribution of members should vary so as to ensure the protection of the major interests involved. For instance, two-thirds of

the seats on the Council controlling the Ocean Fund might be reserved to the developing States.

7. Each Council should be assisted by special Commissions. In particular, as far as the sea-bed is concerned, there should be a Rules and Recommended Practices Commission and an Operations Commission.

8. The Ocean Tribunal should decide all disputes, and advise on all legal questions, relating to the interpretation and application of the new Law of the Sea Conventions. The Statute of the Tribunal should provide for direct access to the Trubunal of any person affected by a decision made under these Conventions, and should provide for appropriate national and international measures to enforce the decisions of the Tribunal against any person. The Tribunal should be competent also to decide any jurisdictional disputes between the various organs of the Authority and between the Authority and any specialized or regional agency. Subject to proper authorization under Article 96 of the Charter of the United Nations, the Tribunal should be empowered to request the International Court of Justice to give an advisory opinion on any question of general international law, and should be bound by such opinion.

9. The Secretariat should be under the direction of a Director-General, and subject to approval of the Council concerned he should appoint separate Deputy Directors-General for each Council. An inspection service should be formed within the Secretariat, and should watch over the compliance by States and persons with the Law of the Sea Conventions and the regulations enacted thereunder.

10. Special arrangements, including joint working parties and even common subsidiary organs, should be made with the various organs and specialized agencies of the United Nations the functions of which overlap those of the International Ocean Authority.


**STANLEY FOUNDATION—SEVENTH CONFERENCE ON THE UNITED NATIONS OF THE NEXT DECADE:**
**— Conference Statement on Ocean Management and World Order, 1972**

> The Seventh Conference on the United Nations of the Next Decade under the sponsorship of the Stanley Foundation assembled at South Egremont, Massachusetts, 9-16 July 1972. The participants were as follows: C. M. Stanley (Chairman), O. Adeniji (Nigeria), G. Aldrich (U.S.), M. Bacescu (Romania), P. B. Engo (Cameroon), R. G. Fairweather (Canada), V. N. Fedorov (USSR), R. Galindo Pohl (El Salvador), P. Jankowitsch (Austria), J. J. Logue (U.S.), P. Lusaka (Zambia), L.

Mates (Yugoslavia), S. Oda (Japan), A. Pardo (Malta), R. K. Ramphul (Mauritius), N. G. Reyes (Philippines), S. Sen (India), S. N. Smirnov (USSR), J. Stevenson (U.S.), A. van der Essen (Belgium) and F. Zegers (Chile). The conference statements were prepared by the rapporteurs simply to reflect the gist of the conclusions.

*Common heritage*

We welcome and endorse the concept that ocean space beyond the limits of national jurisdiction is the common heritage of mankind. The oceans' resources must be utilized prudently, efficiently, and equitably and its fragile ecological system must be conserved and restored for the benefit of all.

The ocean situation is changing rapidly. The oceans and their resources are becoming increasingly important. Developing technology allows greater penetration of the oceans and the world's rapidly growing demands are placing greater pressures on their use. These pressures are causing gradual undermining of existing international law. Individual nations are unilaterally appropriating the resources of areas beyond national jurisdiction and unilaterally extending their claimed areas of jurisdiction further and further into ocean space, thus reducing the common heritage.

Preservation of the common heritage requires stabilization of national jurisdiction and an effective global ocean regime. Without these, the benefits of the common heritage will be lost and the oceans will become an increasing source of problems and tensions. We must avoid chaos in the oceans. We must bring about a new type of international cooperation within an equitable and orderly legal framework.

It is therefore with a sense of urgency that we call upon all peoples and nations to carry forward the concept of common heritage of mankind and to establish the necessary agreements, understandings, and mechanisms to make this principle a reality. Unless this is done promptly, the brief opportunity to confirm this principle will be lost and the consequences will be severe and irreversible.

To this end, we welcome the "Declaration of Principles" governing the seabed and the ocean floor and the subsoil thereof, beyond the limits of national jurisdiction, passed by the Twenty-Fifth General Assembly and the proposal for a United Nations Conference on the Law of the Sea to be held in 1973. We urge universal participation in this conference. We support and encourage the work of the United Nations Seabed Committee and other preparatory activities. We call upon all nations, international agencies, interested public and private organizations, and concerned individuals to make all possible effort to assist in preparations for this conference and to assure that it will lead to positive action commensurate with the opportunities and challenges afforded by ocean space. We also welcome the results of the 1972 Stockholm Conference on the Human Environment and call particular attention to its recommendations on the ocean environment.

In the interim, we urge all involved in development and use of ocean space to exercise restraint and conduct their activities in a manner consistent with the principle of common heritage.

*Objectives of ocean space development*

The nations of the international community must cooperate together to build an agreed system of law and regulation and to manage the development and utilization of ocean space. In this effort, conflicting demands must be harmonized and the following objectives fulfilled:

1. Full and efficient development of the resources of ocean space for the benefit of all mankind.

2. Participation of all interested nations, including landlocked and shelf-locked nations.

3. International cooperation in scientific research and exploration of ocean space and wide dissemination of the results.

4. Equitable sharing of the benefits derived from ocean space to promote economic development and enhance economic and social justice.

5. Coordination of various uses of the oceans.

6. Preservation of freedom of navigation in the oceans.

7. Exploitation of ocean resources in a manner consistent with wise conservation practices.

8. Preservation and protection of the ocean ecological system, with appropriate restoration measures in areas where damage has occurred.

9. Strengthening of international cooperation and the principles of peace and security fostered by the United Nations.

*Complexity of ocean space*

Ocean space is an intricate and delicate ecological system which is not fully understood. Various uses of the seas, and exploitation activities in particular, affect the ecological balance in ways which are both predictable and unpredictable. As a result, great care must be exercised and available scientific understanding utilized fully. We must avoid the hazards of irreparable and possibly disastrous damage to this vital resource.

The resources of ocean space are limited. Living resources are replaceable only to the extent that overutilization and damage to the biological balance is avoided. Non-living resources are extensive, yet exhaustible. They must be exploited prudently and efficiently and in such

210

a way that their availability is extended to the maximum reasonable degree and allocated to the most desirable uses.

While we differ as to the mechanics and procedures which should be utilized to manage the use and development of ocean space, we are unanimous that ocean space must be recognized as an ecological unity and that its management requires full consideration to the many factors involved.

*Ocean space management*

We agree that ocean space must be managed even though the problems of such management are immense.

Ocean space falls partly within and partly beyond national sovereign control. Jurisdictional boundaries pose difficulties. The degree of jurisdiction or competence exercised by national and international bodies in any location may also vary.

Further, ocean space activities are numerous and include those relating to: seabed and mineral resources, military uses, living resources, navigation, environmental conservation and restoration, cables and pipelines, and scientific research.

Any system of ocean space management or ocean regime must be established by means of international agreement, requiring the consideration and consent of participating nations. New ocean regime elements should build upon existing agreements, understandings, and practices; improving, strengthening, and replacing them as may be appropriate and possible.

There are many possible approaches to an ocean regime. At the present time, several international agencies are involved in various facets of ocean space management, working on the basis of voluntary cooperation and action by individual nations. These agencies include FAO-fisheries, IMCO-technical and navigational activities, WMO-atmospheric effects of interaction of sea and air, UNESCO's IOC-ocean exploration and research, and other UN agencies and regional groups. This segmented pattern might be continued with gradual development of single purpose conventions and organizations to handle specific areas. Alternatively, ocean management could be handled by a single comprehensive convention and ocean management organization.

Consideration of ocean management elements raises many interrelated questions regarding the scope, authority, functions, jurisdiction, organization, benefits and financing. Agreement on any new convention and organization is best achieved if all of these matters are considered together. For example, the question of voting power will be of considerably greater concern in an organization with broad powers and jurisdiction than in one of lesser scope. Similarly, agreement on geographic areas of jurisdiction depends on the ocean space activity or activities involved.

We have differences regarding the extent, timing, and type of ocean space management system which should be developed and the appropriate characteristics of any new conventions and related organizations. These areas were explored in some detail to search for common ground to form a basis of understanding.

### Scope

We agree that improvements are needed in the present system of ocean management and that, utilizing international cooperation, we should move toward an effective and comprehensive legal order. We differ on timing and priorities.

A majority of participants support early establishment, by means of an appropriate convention, of a new and comprehensive ocean management organization dealing with all aspects of ocean space.

Other participants believe that efforts at this time should be devoted to establishing a convention and ocean management organization dealing only with the seabed and perhaps another dealing with environmental control. Participants holding this view support the gradual strengthening of existing law and mechanisms dealing with ocean problems, the development of other conventions as required to deal with other facets of ocean management, and perhaps eventual consolidation of ocean management activities into a single ocean management organization, when this becomes appropriate and practical.

### Authority

The amount of authority which should be granted to an ocean management organization is controversial. Those participants favoring a new and comprehensive convention and ocean management organization also tend to favor an organization with substantial powers over matters within its competence. In contrast, those participants favoring a more limited convention and ocean management organization also tend to favor more limited powers.

The authority which nations will agree to delegate to an ocean management organization is strongly affected by the voting system used in the decision-making body. Nations will more easily delegate power to an international decision-making body having representation which they perceive to be equitable.

Some participants suggest that the question of authority is best handled by distinguishing between general and executive policy. In the absence of a voting system considered equitable by all nations, general policy could be stated in the convention establishing the ocean management organization

212

and amended from time to time by subsequent agreements. The ocean management executive body could be given authority to develop executive policy within the limits of the general policy. This approach has substantial precedent.

*Functions*

The functions assigned to an ocean management organization depend on the scope of its activities and the extent of its authority. Inasmuch as participants do not agree on scope and authority, there is also difference of opinion on functions.

Those participants favoring a comprehensive ocean management organization with substantial authority would assign it most, if not all, of the functions listed below. Those participants favoring a less comprehensive organization would reduce the assigned functions appropriately.

1. Provide a forum for debate, development of initiatives, establishment of general policies on ocean space within the jurisdiction of the organization, and development of international law and harmonization of national law regarding the oceans.

2. Within such general policies establish regulations and norms for use and development of ocean space in areas of the organization's jurisdiction and competence.

3. Administer established regulations and norms for use and development of ocean space, including necessary registration, licensing, taxing, and inspection.

4. Take measures to preserve and enhance the ocean ecological system.

5. Plan rational use and development of ocean space and harmonize uses of ocean space.

6. Assist nations in the planning and development of ocean space falling within national jurisdiction.

7. Carry out exploration and exploitation operations either directly, through joint ventures, or through license of activities.

8. Take measures to protect and harmonize the legitimate special interests of landlocked nations, archipelago and island states, shelf-locked nations, and less developed countries with economies that depend heavily on mineral and raw materials derived from landbased sources.

9. Allocate revenues derived in accordance with objectives established for the organization.

10. Promote, coordinate, and disseminate scientific research and encourage and provide means for the transfer of technology.

11. Maintain juridical and territorial integrity of international area of ocean space.

12. Provide procedures for the settlement of disputes.

13. Provide appropriate services to the international community, such as an international system of marine parks, regulation of dumping of wastes into oceans, and similar services which are best handled by an international ocean space agency.

14. Coordinate ocean space matters with U.N. specialized agencies and appropriate nongovernmental organizations.

15. Coordinate regional organizations or arrangements which may be created to help manage ocean space.

## Jurisdiction

Participants differ on specific jurisdiction limits.

Most participants accept the concept that different lines of demarcation between national and international jurisdiction could be used for different ocean space activities. For example, some participants urge that international jurisdiction over environmental protection and restoration, at least to the extent of minimum standards, must extend to the shoreline in order to be effective. Assuming suitable agreement regarding straits and passages, national jurisdiction over navigation might extend some distance, perhaps twelve miles from the shoreline. Other lines of demarcation between national and international jurisdiction could be appropriately established for other ocean space activities.

Some participants favor a less complex system of uniform boundaries and graduated jurisdiction. For example, nations might have full sovereignty over all activities out to an agreed distance, depth, or combination thereof. Beyond that to another agreed distance, depth, or combination thereof, activity within national jurisdiction might be subject to appropriate international regulations. The intermediate zone may be described as a zone of economic jurisdiction, trusteeship zone, or patrimonial sea. Ocean space beyond this intermediate zone would be under international regulation.

## Organizational structure

While participants differ regarding organizational structure and voting, there is general, though not unanimous, agreement with an organizational structure consisting of four major elements.

The first element would be a general policy-making body with all participating nations represented. The participants differed on voting representation and means of decision making, whether by consensus or lesser majority. In spite of these differences most participants hold the view that it would be very difficult to achieve agreement at this time to any system of voting other than one nation-one vote.

The second element would be an executive body of moderate size,

214

perhaps in the range of 25 to 35 members. Representation could be determined on a regional basis or in some manner so as to reflect such factors as population, economic strength and others. Various representation and voting proposals were discussed.

The third element would be an administrative unit or secretariat which would work under the jurisdiction of the executive body to carry out the various functions assigned to the ocean management organization. Structure and organization of the secretariat are not major problems except that participation from all nations should be encouraged. Inclusion of technical and scientific panels in the secretariat is appropriate.

The fourth organizational element would be for the purpose of adjudicating disputes. There is general agreement that arbitration should be encouraged and that the ocean management organization should include mechanics for consultation and arbitration. Most participants suggest a tribunal for cases which cannot be resolved by consultation or arbitration. Others urge use of the International Court of Justice for determination of the treaty rights of the parties.

Some participants suggest that the ocean management organization include provision for regional management or administration related to specific ocean basins. This could be handled within the four element organizational structure described.

Any new ocean management organization should be closely coordinated with the United Nations system and some participants favor its establishment within the framework of the United Nations system.

It was also suggested that, as a minimum, consolidation of existing United Nations ocean space activities into a single specialized agency would enhance efficiency and effectiveness.

*Benefits*

Perhaps the most significant gain from effective ocean management is the opportunity to halt unilateral national extension of jurisdiction and to protect and enhance the ocean environment, thus preserving the common heritage for the benefit of all mankind.

Additional benefits to be derived from ocean space management would be both tangible and intangible. Intangible benefits include the existence of an agreed system of laws and regulations, the possibility of planned and orderly development of 70 percent of the earth's surface, and dissemination of scientific knowledge on ocean space. Tangible benefits would result from more prudent and efficient management of the resources and harmonization of the uses of ocean space. Specifically, they include those derived from the effective conservation, management, and exploitation of the living resources of the seas, including fisheries and future mariculture enterprises, and the non-living resources of the seas including hydrocarbons and manganese nodules. A portion of these tangible benefits may accrue directly to the ocean space management organization through taxes, fees, and participation in exploitation activities. The extent of such accrual depends on the nature of the ocean management organization. The benefits to an organization having limited jurisdiction will be less than those to a more comprehensive one.

Some participants caution that expectation of vast revenues from the oceans is unrealistic. Even optimistic estimates of such benefits yield total annual revenues to a comprehensive ocean management organization which are small in comparison with the general problems of economic and social development.

Differences of opinion exist regarding use of revenues. There is general agreement that a portion of the revenues should be used to finance the operations of the ocean management organization or organizations, including development of ocean space and enhancement of the common heritage. This would provide the ocean management organization with an assured source of revenue independent of voluntary contributions. Most participants favor use of any additional revenues to encourage economic and social development. Some urge that a portion of the revenues be used as a source of additional revenue for the general purposes of the United Nations.

*The next decade*

The next decade is crucial for the preservation of the common heritage. Changing technology and growing world resource demands are undermining the possibility of making this concept a reality.

The nations of the world must seize the opportunities afforded by this unique challenge. We must grasp for all mankind the benefits of effective ocean management, including resource development consistent with economic and social justice and preservation and enhancement of the ocean environment. We must, in ocean space, develop a normative pattern of international cooperation within an agreed legal order. This example will raise the confidence of men and nations in international institutions. It will contribute to the effectiveness of the United Nations in its vital role of maintaining peace and security, freeing it from its present crisis of confidence.

While preparing for the 1973 United Nations Conference on the Law of the Sea, the international community should look into the future with a strong sense of purpose. Ocean management systems and functions which seem adequate today may be seriously inadequate within a decade and must be made flexible enough to respond to changing needs. We urge the Conference on the Law of the Sea to take positive action to assure an

216

effective ocean regime. We call upon all nations to exercise the determination, will, and cooperation to make this assurance possible.

We dare not lose this fleeting opportunity to provide for man's common heritage.


**PACEM IN MARIBUS IV:**
**— Recommendations to the United Nations Committee on the Peaceful Uses of the Sea-bed, 1973**

Pacem in Maribus, which held its fourth annual meeting at Malta, 23-26 June 1973, made the following recommendations.

... the United Nations Committee on the Peaceful Uses of the Sea-Bed might consider the following points as a possible basis for the United Nations Conference on the Law of the Sea.

*Ocean space as a whole*

1. Ocean space and the air column above it are an ecological unity. Increasing world industrialization, multiplying populations, coastal congestion, increased world use of chemicals, and many other factors are subjecting the marine environment to unprecedented pressures particularly in the vicinity of highly industrialized countries. No one State can cope alone with the developing situation. Minimum world-wide standards are thus required with regard to the avoidance of pollution in the marine environment.

2. Rapidly advancing technology is enabling man significantly to change the state of the marine environment through diversion of important rivers and marine currents, weather modification and other means. Use of technology which can seriously affect the natural state of the marine environment over large areas must be subjected to international control.

3. The development of super-tankers, liquified natural gas carriers, submarine navigation, ships with nuclear propulsion and other developments are creating new hazards to the marine environment and to the safety of navigation. Minimum international standards must be elaborated through global marine institutions with comprehensive functions which can take into due account the interaction between major peaceful uses of the sea.

4. Ocean space is becoming an economic unity in that the uses of the surface of the sea, of the water column and of the seabed are becoming increasingly interlinked. International law must recognize this fundamental

217

fact by consolidating existing legal regimes for different activities.

5. The rapid increase of man's multiple activities requires the management of the seas and its resources to a much larger extent than has been the case in the past. Present realities make it mandatory that control and management of the oceans must be shared between coastal states and the international community in accordance with the principle of the common heritage of mankind.

*Ocean space within national jurisdiction*

6. Precise over-all limits to national jurisdiction are required.

7. Navigation, overflight, scientific research, the laying of submarine cables and perhaps some other activities are vital public international interests and as such must be internationally protected within the limits of national jurisdiction.

8. Due to technological advance and increasing fishing effort, intolerable pressures are developing on desirable fish stocks in some parts of the world. Global minimum standards of biological and economic management must be elaborated to be implemented through regional bodies and marine institutions for ocean space with comprehensive functions.

9. Special international protection must be accorded to slowly reproducing marine species, such as sea mammals.

10. Coastal states have obligations as well as rights in the area of ocean space within their jurisdiction; these obligations extend not only to the protection within the jurisdiction of such activities as may be considered public international interests, but also to management of the environment and of living resources in a manner conforming at least to minimum international standards.

11. States which do not possess the financial or technical capability to attain minimum international standards must receive the assistance needed through comprehensive institutions for ocean space.

*Ocean space beyond national jurisdiction*

12. It is strongly recommended that not only the seabed, but also ocean space and its resources beyond national jurisdiction be considered a common heritage of mankind and that appropriate treaty articles embodying this concept be included in any draft treaty.

13. It is believed that only through the adoption and subsequent implementation by the international community of the basic concept of common heritage of ocean space beyond national jurisdiction, can the future beneficial use of ocean space and its resources by all states be assured, and indeed expanded, in contemporary conditions of intensive exploitation accompanied by increasingly powerful technology.

218

14. *The concept of common heritage of mankind of ocean space and its resources beyond national jurisdiction must form the basis of future international law of the sea* and be given expression in an international treaty or treaties generally agreed upon by the international community which harmonize the rights of states with the emerging world interest.

15. The treaty or treaties to which reference has been made must include provision for a machinery balanced in such a manner as to insure that the decisions of the machinery reasonably reflect the wishes of the majority of the population of the world giving due weight to the needs of the developing nations and to the economic dependence of states on ocean space.

16. Land-locked and shelf-locked countries must be assured access to ocean space, must be given the opportunity, on an equal basis with coastal states, to take part in the exploitation of resources beyond national jurisdiction and must participate in the sharing of benefits derived from the exploitation of ocean resources beyond national jurisdiction.

*The international machinery*

17. The international machinery must perform, *inter alia*, the following functions:

*a.* Providing a general forum for the discussion, negotiation and accommodation of national interests in ocean space;

*b.* General and non-discriminatory standard setting and regulation in respect to major peaceful uses of ocean space;

*c.* Biological and economic management and conservation of the living resources of the sea beyond national jurisdiction and conservation and management, in cooperation with the coastal state, of living resources which migrate between ocean space under national jurisdiction and ocean space beyond national jurisdiction;

*d.* Exploration and exploitation of non-living resources of ocean space beyond national jurisdiction either directly or in participation with states or through a system of licenses;

*e.* Equitable sharing of benefits derived from the exploitation of the living and non-living resources of ocean space beyond national jurisdiction, which also makes provision for a contribution from coastal states in respect to benefits derived from the exploitation of resources in areas of ocean space under their jurisdiction. Such a contribution appears justified in view of the benefits that would be derived by the coastal state from the management of resources outside its jurisdiction;

*f.* Protection and general regulation in ocean space of such activities exclusively for peaceful purposes as may be considered to be of vital international public interest;

*g.* Providing a mechanism for the effective access of technologically less developed countries to advanced marine technology relevant to their needs and for the transfer of such technology.

*h.* Promotion of scientific research in ocean space and establishment of an effective mechanism for associating scientifically less advanced countries in such research.

*i.* Providing to the international community such services in ocean space as may be considered necessary or desirable; *inter alia*, to sail vessels for rescue, scientific or other international community purposes.

18. Many of the proposed functions of the international institutions could, it is believed, be appropriately undertaken through regional bodies.

19. It is believed that it is of great importance either to consolidate existing U.N. bodies primarily dealing with questions concerning ocean space into the future international institutions for ocean space, or at least to coordinate their activities through the institutions in order to avoid bureaucratic proliferation, duplication of activities, inadequate or excessively complex coordination machineries at the international level.

20. The international regime should provide machinery for interdisciplinary discussion and decision-making involving, as far as possible, all users of ocean space and resources and including, in particular, science, industry and the service sector.

21. It is considered very important to stress that international law and practice concerning the legal responsibility of states and of the persons under their jurisdiction with regard to culpable activities which cause damage to other states in the marine environment must be considerably expanded and made more precise: in particular a course of action must be given to the international community through the international institutions with regard to deleterious activities in ocean space beyond national jurisdiction.

22. It is scarcely necessary to stress that no institutional system for ocean space would be complete without appropriate machinery for the compulsory settlement of disputes.


**INTERNATIONAL LAW ASSOCIATION:**
— **Draft Declaration of Principles which should Govern the Activities of States in the Exploration and Exploitation of the Mineral Resources of the Sea-Bed and Subsoil beyond the Limits of National Jurisdiction, 1972**

The text was prepared by I.L.A.'s Deep-Sea Mining Committee in February 1972 and introduced at the session held in New

York in August 1972. The chairman of the Committee was Professor D. H. N. Johnson of the United Kingdom and the rapporteur, Dr. L. J. Bouchez of the Netherlands.

**Art. 1.** For the purposes of this Draft Declaration the area referred to in Article II shall be known as the "continental shelf" and the area referred to in Article III shall be known as the "international area".

**Art. 2.** (1) The coastal State exercises over the sea-bed and subsoil of the submarine areas adjacent to its coast sovereign rights for the purpose of exploring it and exploiting its natural resources.

(2) No State should object if a coastal State exercises the sovereign rights referred to in paragraph 1 of this Article over submarine areas adjacent to its coast to a depth of 200 metres or 50 nautical miles from the baseline from which the breadth of the territorial sea is measured, whichever alternatives gives the coastal State a larger area.

**Art. 3.** (1) The sea-bed and subsoil beyond the area referred to in Article II shall not be subject to appropriation by any means by States or persons, natural or juridical, and no State shall claim or exercise sovereignty or sovereign rights over any part thereof.

(2) No State or person, natural or juridical, shall claim, exercise or acquire rights with respect to the international area or its resources incompatible with the international régime laid down in this Draft Declaration.

**Art. 4.** The mineral resources of the international area shall be developed for the benefit of all mankind.

**Art. 5.** (1) There shall be established an International Sea-bed Organization and a Sea-bed Tribunal.

(2) The main functions of the International Sea-bed Organization are:
- (i) registration of claims;
- (ii) supervision of exploration and exploitation activities in accordance with the provisions laid down in the Sea-bed Treaty and the International Mining Regulations;
- (iii) enforcement of the Sea-bed Treaty and the International Mining Regulations;
- (iv) advising States on the adaptation of their mining legislation to the international standards laid down in the Sea-bed Treaty and the International Mining Regulations or on drafting such legislation;
- (v) co-ordination of production of mineral resources if joint production in two or more adjacent areas of special rights is required from the economic point of view;

221

(vi) collection of surface rentals and royalty payments and transfer of a proportion of the royalty payments and the surface rentals to a special fund to be known as the International Sea-bed Fund;

(vii) consideration of the effect that the production of minerals produced from the international area has or may have on the world market;

(viii) co-ordination of scientific research of the sea-bed and dissemination of scientific information in close co-operation with the Intergovernmental Oceanographic Commission and other international organizations involved;

(ix) development of training programmes, particularly on behalf of the developing countries.

(3) There shall be established as the principal organs of the International Sea-bed Organization: an Assembly, a Council and a Secretariat.

(4) There shall be established three Commissions which operate under the supervision of the Council, *viz.*: a Mining Supervisory Commission, an Economic and Financial Commission, and a Scientific Research and Training Promotion Commission.

(5) There shall be established an International Sea-bed Fund.

**Art. 6.** (1) States are entitled to areas of special rights for the purpose of exploring and exploiting the mineral resources of the international area by means of registration of their claims with the International Sea-bed Organization.

(2) The total area of special rights accruing to a State shall not exceed ...... square kilometres.

(3) Entitlement to an area of special rights shall endure for a period of ...... years as from the date the International Sea-bed Organization publishes the claim and the area in question accrues to that State.

**Art. 7.** (1) The international area shall be divided as far as possible into rectangular blocks of ...... square kilometres.

(2) All States have the right to register claims for blocks within a period of three months after the date on which the international area or part of it becomes open for registration. The claims registered should be kept secret by the International Sea-bed Organization until the date of the official publication of the claims by that Organization. Within three months after the period for registration has been closed, the International Sea-bed Organization shall publish the list of claims registered and the blocks accruing to the several States.

(3) States shall list their claims in order of preference. Registration of a claim confers a right to an area of special rights if no other State has registered a claim for the same block, provided the total number of blocks

accruing to that particular State does not exceed the maximum area determined in Article VI. In case of overlapping claims the block concerned accrues to the State which has given it the highest preference on its claims list provided that the total number of blocks accruing to the State which has attributed to the block concerned the higher preference does not exceed the maximum area for that State as determined in Article VI. If the blocks claimed are equal in rank on the list of preferences of more than one State, the State having so far acquired fewer blocks than the other State(s) involved acquires the block in question. If the blocks claimed are equal in rank on the list of preferences of more than one State and these States have so far acquired an equal number of blocks, the block in question shall accrue to the State which makes the highest bid.

**Art. 8.** The rights of States in areas of special rights do not affect the legal status of the superjacent waters as high seas, or that of the air space above these waters.

**Art. 9.** (1) The exploration of an area of special rights and the exploitation of its mineral resources must not result in any unjustifiable interference with navigation, fishing or the conservation of the living resources of the sea nor in any interference with scientific research undertaken with the intention of open publication. Subject to the right to take reasonable measures for the exploration of the international area and the exploitation of its mineral resources, a State may not impede the laying or maintenance of submarine cables or pipelines within its area of special rights.

(2) All States which acquire areas of special rights under Article VI shall be subject to the International Mining Regulations and liable for any and all damage resulting from a violation of those Regulations or of any relevant rules of conventional or customary international law.

(3) If a State violates the International Mining Regulations and substantial damage has been caused to the interests of other States, the Mining Supervisory Commission is entitled to demand a suspension of all activities within the area(s) of special rights of that State until this State guarantees the strict implementation of these Regulations and compensation for the damage caused has been paid.

(4) The International Mining Regulations shall *inter alia* contain provisions concerning the preservation of the marine environment.

(5) Strict rules relating to the prevention of pollution of the marine environment shall be laid down in the International Mining Regulations.

(6) The operator of mining activities shall be absolutely liable for any and all damage caused by his activities to the marine environment. This liability shall be limited to the amount of ...... francs for damage caused by a pollution incident. The operator shall be required to have and maintain insurance or other financial security for the maximum

amount of his liability. In addition to the operator's liability, the State under whose jurisdiction the operator is conducting his operations shall be absolutely liable to the same fixed limit.

(7) The operator shall not be liable for pollution damage if he proves that the damage resulted from an act of war, hostilities, civil war, insurrection or a natural phenomenon of an exceptional, inevitable and irresistible character, or was wholly caused by an act or omission done with the intent to cause damage by a third party, or was wholly caused by the negligence or other wrongful act of any Government.

(8) Apart from the State's residual liability referred to in paragraph 6 of this Article, the State is absolutely liable for any and all damage without any limitation which has been caused by pollution incidents which are the result of non-execution or violation of the International Mining Regulations on the part of the State.

(9) A Pollution Fund shall be established for those cases (i) where it appears to be impossible to identify the cause of the pollution; (ii) where damage results from a natural phenomenon of an exceptional, inevitable and irresistible character; (iii) where the damage exceeds the fixed limit imposed on the operator and/or the State concerned; and (iv) when there has been caused general damage to the marine environment as opposed to damage directly affecting the specific interests of States and/or natural or juridical persons. Contributions to the Pollution Fund shall be made by means of a pollution tax to be paid by all operators and States involved in the exploration and exploitation of the natural resources of the international area. The liability of the Pollution Fund shall be limited to the amount of . . . . . . francs for damage caused by a pollution incident.

**Art. 10.** (1) Subject to the provisions of Article IX, paragraphs 1 and 2, and paragraph 5 of this Article, States are entitled to construct and maintain or operate in their area(s) of special rights installations and other devices necessary for the exploration and the exploitation of their mineral resources, to establish safety zones around such installations and devices and to take in these zones measures necessary for their protection.

(2) The safety zones referred to in paragraph 1 of this Article may extend to a distance of 500 metres around the installations and other devices which have been erected, measured from each point of their outer edge. Ships of all nationalities must respect these safety zones.

(3) Such installations and devices come under the jurisdiction of the State in whose area of special rights they have been erected.

(4) The installations and devices do not possess the status of islands and have no territorial sea of their own.

(5) Due notice must be given of the construction of any such installations, and permanent means for giving warning of their presence must be

maintained.

(6) Any installations which are abandoned or disused must be entirely removed.

(7) Neither the installations or devices, nor the safety zones around them, may be established where interference may be caused to the use of recognized sea lanes essential to international navigation.

(8) The State which exercises jurisdiction over the safety zones is obliged to undertake therein all appropriate measures for the protection of the living resources of the sea from harmful agents.

**Art. 11.** (1) States shall pay annually surface rentals of . . . . . . francs per square kilometre of their area(s) of special rights to the International Sea-Bed Organization.

(2) States, under whose jurisdiction the production of minerals from the international area is carried out, shall pay an annual contribution on a royalty basis per quantity of product recovered from the international area during the preceding year to the International Sea-bed Organization. The contribution shall be a fixed percentage of the market value of the product recovered less the costs of recovery.

**Art. 12.** (1) Each State is entitled to surrender at any time an area of special rights or part of it, provided that according to the Mining Supervisory Commission all obligations as defined in the International Mining Regulations have been fulfilled.

(2) Each State is entitled to transfer at any time an area of special rights or part of it to another State, provided that (a) the latter is a party to the Sea-bed Treaty and agrees to take over all international obligations connected with the area; (b) according to the Mining Supervisory Commission all obligations as defined in the International Mining Regulations have been fulfilled; and (c) no transfer shall be permitted if it would result in the total area of special rights accruing to a State exceeding the maximum provided for in Article VI, paragraph 2.

(3) The surrender or transfer of a certain area is subject to approval of the Mining Supervisory Commission which, in accordance with the powers conferred on it in its Statute, shall state its terms and conditions for its approval within 90 days after the notification of the intention to surrender or to transfer.

**Art. 13.** If any single geological structure extends across the dividing lines of two or more adjacent blocks coming within the jurisdiction of different States and the part of such structure which is situated on one side of the dividing line is exploitable, wholly or in part, from the other side of the dividing line, the States involved will seek to reach agreement as to: (1) the manner in which the structure shall be most effectively exploited, and

(2) the manner in which the costs and proceeds relating thereto shall be apportioned. If the States concerned fail to reach agreement, each State involved is entitled to submit any question in dispute to the Sea-bed Tribunal.

**Art. 14.** (1) Scientific research of, or physically carried out on, any part of the international area undertaken with the intention of open publication shall be free.

(2) If scientific research is planned to be undertaken in an area of special rights, consultation with the State involved is required as to the manner in which and the location where such research will be carried out.

(3) Disputes arising out of the conduct of such research may, in the case of parties to the Statutes of all the institutions referred to in Article V, be submitted to the Sea-bed Tribunal.

(4) A State is always entitled to participate in research which is planned to be carried out in its area of special rights.

**Art. 15.** (1) Any dispute whatever relating to the interpretation and application of the Sea-bed Treaty and the International Mining Regulations may be brought before the Sea-bed Tribunal by an application made by any party to the dispute qualified to appear before the Sea-bed Tribunal.

(2) The following may appear before the Sea-bed Tribunal:
  (i) States parties to the Sea-bed Treaty;
  (ii) Natural and juridical persons having the nationality of States parties to the Sea-bed Treaty;
  (iii) The International Sea-bed Organization;
  (iv) The International Sea-bed Fund;
  (v) The Pollution Fund;
  (vi) An agency for the preservation of the marine environment.

(3) Disputes between States may, at the option of the States concerned, be submitted to the International Court of Justice rather than to the Sea-bed Tribunal.

## AMERICAN BRANCH OF THE INTERNATIONAL LAW ASSOCIATION:
## — Report of the Committee on Deep-Sea Mineral

The American Branch of the International Law Association prepared in 1972 a report, some parts of which are herein reproduced.

## IV. Striking a Balance

A. *Limits of National Jurisdiction*

1. With respect to the *territorial sea*, we propose a uniform limit of 12 miles, subject to concurrent acceptance of our proposal 2 below. Within this belt, measured in accordance with the rules laid down in the Territorial Sea Convention, the rights and duties of the coastal State would be those established by the Convention and by customary law.

2. With respect to *straits*, we propose the affirmation of a universal right of free transit by sea and air through straits used for international navigation which are more than six miles wide.

3. With respect to *ocean archipelago States*, we make no specific proposal, except to point out the obvious need of preserving rights of free passage along existing international air and sea routes. We note with interest, however, the concept recently suggested of "insular waters". Such waters would comprise those lying within an archipelago but beyond a 12-mile limit as normally constructed around each island. In these waters the archipelago State would have all the rights associated with the territorial sea except that a right of free transit by sea and air, rather than a mere right of innocent passage, would exist. A possible variant would be to limit this right of free transit to air and sea routes that have been customarily used for international navigation.

4. With respect to right over the *continental shelf*, as those rights are defined in existing law, we propose that by an appropriate protocol to the Continental Shelf Convention or by some similar device the limits of such rights be defined as coinciding with the outer edge of the continental margin or with a line drawn 200 miles seaward of the baseline from which the width of the territorial sea is measured, whichever lies further offshore. Though perhaps the point is more political than legal, we also propose that by the same arrangement the coastal State be obligated to pay to the international seabed regime, or into a fund to be administered by the World Bank, for the benefit of less developed countries, a stated portion of the value of the minerals produced each year from the area lying between the 200-meter depth line (or the 12-mile limit, whichever is further seaward), and the limits proposed above. We would, of course, preserve the principle of Article 3 of the Convention on the Continental Shelf, that "The rights of the coastal State over the continental shelf do not affect the legal status of the superjacent waters as high seas, or that of the airspace above these waters". In our opinion this twofold solution reconciles fairly, without violating rights acquired or acquirable under existing law, the legitimate interests of both the coastal State and the international community. It also satisfies, we think, the admirable objectives set forth in

227

President Nixon's ocean policy statement of May 1970.

5. With respect to *pollution*, we propose that, by the arrangement mentioned above, the coastal State be obligated to enforce internationally agreed standards for the protection of the marine environment from pollution arising from operations within the limits suggested in proposal 4 above. We assume, in so proposing, that pollution originating from passing vessels will be dealt with in international arrangements now being framed by the Intergovernmental Maritime Consultative Organization. We would also note that much pollution in coastal waters arises from sources other than these, *e.g.*, outflow from activities on land.

6. With respect to *scientific research*, not including penetration of the seabed, we propose the affirmation of a right for all States to conduct such research in the ocean beyond the 12-mile limit or in the seabed beyond the 200-meter line. Within the further limit suggested in proposal 4 above, the coastal State should be informed of any research undertaken and supplied with the scientific data resulting therefrom, but its consent should not be prerequisite to such research.

7. With respect to *fisheries*, we make no specific proposal since the subject is not part of this Committee's assignment. We note, however, the proposal advanced by the United States delegation at the Seabeds Committee meeting in March 1972. This urged, in general, a species approach to fisheries management, rather than the establishment of geographical limits of national fisheries jurisdiction. Coastal and anadromous species would be subjected to appropriate coastal State controls as far offshore as the particular stock ranges. (Later developments, *e.g.*, an agreement with Brazil, appear to indicate that shrimp are deemed to be in this category.) Tuna and other highly migratory species, however, would be managed under international arrangements in which all interested States could participate. We find this general approach not incompatible in principle with our approach to mineral resource problems.

### B. *International Seabed Regime*

With respect to an *international regime* for the seabed and subsoil beyond the limits of national jurisdiction, we reaffirm the views in our 1970 Report favoring a claims registration system, an international supervisory authority with adequate but clearly defined powers, and appropriate arrangements for the expeditious settlement of disputes. We also reaffirm our views on the need to assure security of investments, and on the many subsidiary problems considered in that report. We recognize, however, that on many aspects of the regime there is room for negotiation. For this reason we could support in general, for example, the pattern of regime for this area, beyond the limits of national jurisdiction, proposed in the United

228

States working paper of 1970 or the United Kingdom proposals of the same year, even though in our view the organizational arrangements in the United States paper are unnecessarily complicated.

On the other hand, we are strongly opposed to the creation of an international regime which would place in the hands of a single agency exclusive operating rights, control over production and distribution, allocation of profits, authority over scientific research, or any combination of these powers. Not only is such a monopoly unacceptable in principle, but it would be wholly unworkable in practice. Even if investment capital were available, the conditions for its employment would be such as to halt all progress for the foreseeable future in the development of the resources of the ocean floor. This would be particularly injurious, we would note, to the economic development plans of the developing States.

It may seem that a design so obviously counter-productive need not be a matter for alarm. We are concerned, however, lest it might come about as a consequence of negotiations to reach desired solutions on other issues in the law of the sea. We believe that a viable regime for deep sea resources must be founded on technological and economic realities, not on unrelated political bargains or abstract dogmas. Resources in the deep sea, like natural resources everywhere, are of no benefit to anyone until they are recovered for use by consumers. If the goal is to make such resources widely available for the common advantage, the applicable regime must encourage the necessary development. If the 1973 Conference is to have any success in this field, it must deal honestly and fairly with these realities.

## V. Interim Arrangements

Even if a Law of the Sea Conference is successful in 1973 or later in producing appropriate instruments on the subjects before it, it will be almost inevitably five to ten years before these can be brought into force. (The 1958 Conventions took from four to eight years to come into force, with an average of six years.) In relation to deep sea mineral resources in particular, this time-lag appears to be especially acute since technological progress is already at the point where it is possible to begin work on some such resources.

At the same time, the world's need to seek out these resources, in order to meet the demands of more and more peoples for better living standards, indicates the desirability of proceeding at a steady pace toward such development. "Crash" programs to meet shortages when they arise should be avoided: we should plan instead for orderly development with all deliberate speed. This view suggests to us a need for interim arrangements which will encourage development, prevent a lawless free-for-all at sea,

229

and yet will merge without disruption into the permanent international regime when the latter becomes effective.

One approach to this question which we believe to have merit is embodied in the concept of reciprocal legislation. This would call for a municipal statute which would operate only upon persons subject to the jurisdiction of the enacting State, to whom the enacting State would issue licenses covering stated sections of the deep seabed.

The statute would not make any territorial or proprietary claims, but it would confer an exclusive right as against any other national of the enacting State. Nationals of other States would be free to mine in that same area (subject, of course, to the regulation of their own governments).

The proposed legislation, however, would contemplate reciprocity in the following sense. Nationals of the enacting States would be prohibited from mining in areas under licenses issued by other countries with comparable legislation which impose parallel restraints on their nationals. This type of legislation, it should be noted would be no less available to landlocked States than to coastal States, and would be equally available to the less developed nations and the industrialized nations. Suitable safeguards, of course, against the speculative licensing of excessively large areas by any one State, or to any one licensee, should be included. In recognition of the interest of all mankind, not only in the orderly development of the resources of the deep seabed but in sharing the benefits, the proposed legislation could provide for payment into a fund which would be available for lending or giving to less developed nations.

In our opinion, despite reservations on matters of detail, the proposed system would appear to have two advantages: it would provide for orderly development, and yet, because it founds jurisdiction on the principle of nationality, it would rest on a sound basis in existing law.


## NATIONAL PETROLEUM COUNCIL (U.S.):
## — Law of the Sea, 1973

> The Council's Committee on Petroleum Resources under the Ocean Floor prepared in May 1973 a report, Law of the Sea (particular aspects affecting the petroleum industry), upon the request by the Department of the Interior. The following is an extract of the Council's findings and recommendations.

### CHAPTER 1. INTERNATIONAL COMMUNITY INTEREST IN NAVIGATION
1. The first of these recommendations is fundamental: Merchant vessels

230

engaging in mere transit through straits used for international navigation enjoy a right of unimpeded navigation provided such vessels in transit are in compliance with internationally agreed safety standards, including ship design and construction and pollution prevention provisions, and internationally agreed standards designed to accommodate other uses in the area.

2. The right of merchant vessels engaging in mere transit should be generally applicable in territorial waters subject of course to the same standards as those applicable in straits used for international navigation.

3. In waters seaward of the territorial sea including those of the area in which the Coastal State exercises limited resource jurisdiction, the present character of the waters as high seas must be preserved with continued freedom of navigation.

4. Coastal States should be authorized by the Convention to determine compliance with internationally agreed navigation standards, including adherence to internationally prescribed safety lanes, in limited areas in the waters adjacent to their coasts to be internationally determined which under all of the circumstances necessitate the applicability of such standards. The interests of all States in freedom of navigation, however, require that prompt procedures be agreed upon so as to permit the immediate release of a vessel upon provision of appropriate guarantees to comply with a properly adjudicated order enforcing such internationally agreed standards. In the view of the National Petroleum Council, such disputes should be settled in accordance with the dispute settlement procedures to be provided for in the Law of the Sea Convention. And in a case in which it is found under those procedures that a Coastal State, in exercising this limited enforcement jurisdiction against a vessel, acted arbitrarily or without reasonable cause, the vessel owner or cargo owner would be entitled to damages for any injury resulting from such exercise.

5. Whatever general provisions of a Law of the Sea Convention might be adopted regarding the status of archipelagic waters, the right of navigation as described herein should be applicable to merchant shipping transiting archipelagos. Such transit would only involve movement through the archipelago for the purpose of reaching points beyond.

The U.S. position should take account of the particular interests of Coastal States in the safety of navigation and the problem of pollution in unusually congested coastal waters. Certain straits heavily used by merchant shipping are illustrative of such interests of the adjacent Coastal States. In such situations, the Law of the Sea Convention could provide for the establishment of regional commissions comprised of Coastal States flanking the area and other nations having and interest in navigation of those waters. These commissions could develop, in conjunction and consultation with the Inter-Governmental Maritime Consultative Organization (IMCO), international regulations relating to navigational safety, pollution prevention and the nature and funding of needed facilities.

## CHAPTER 2. INTERNATIONAL COMMUNITY INTEREST IN STABLE INVESTMENT CONDITIONS

. . ., the National Petroleum Council strongly recommends that a Law of the Sea Convention dealing with the exploitation of the mineral resources of the continental margin under Coastal State resource jurisdiction and the deep ocean area beyond include provisions along the following lines:

### 1. *Integrity of Agreement between a State and a Foreign Investor*

An agreement between a State and a foreign investor or operator for exploration and development of mineral resources in seabed areas subject to the economic jurisdiction of such State or with respect to which it is entitled to grant rights, whether in the form of a license, permit, concession or any other form, shall be binding, according to its terms, upon both parties.

### 2. *Integrity of Agreement between an International Organization and an Operator*

An agreement between an international organization and an operator for exploration and development of mineral resources seaward of the offshore areas subject to the economic jurisdiction of Coastal States, whether in the form of a license, permit, concession or any other form, shall be binding, according to its terms, upon both parties.

### 3. *Taking of an Investment*

Should a State expropriate or otherwise take or impair the investment of a foreign investor or operator in mineral resource development in a seabed area subject to its jurisdiction or with respect to which it is entitled to grant rights, such State shall promptly provide such investor or operator with compensation in an effectively realizable form representing the full value of the property and rights taken or impaired. Should there be any circumstances in which under the Convention an international organization might legitimately impair the rights of an investor or operator, such compensation shall be promptly provided as aforesaid.

Disputes arising with respect to a particular investment or operation governed by this Convention including those involving private parties should be resolved under the dispute settlement procedures included in the Convention.

# CHAPTER 3. PROTECTION OF THE MARINE ENVIRONMENT

It is recommended that a Law of the Sea Convention embody the following principles and standards regarding pollution control:

## 1. *Standards for Vessel Pollution Control and Their Enforcement*

(*a*) Jurisdiction to prescribe standards, including standards of liability relating to pollution from vessels, should be vested exclusively in appropriate international organizations, existing or newly established, particularly those with specialized knowledge and experience in ocean pollution control. It is anticipated that Coastal States will participate in the work of such organizations. Such broadly agreed standards should be applicable upon all oceans and not limited to any particular area or zone of the oceans, but should reflect, where appropriate, special circumstances or unique environmental conditions.

(*b*) Jurisdiction to enforce standards relating to pollution from vessels should be vested in the States of registry and confirmed as regards a Coastal State when a discharge occurs within its territorial sea. In addition, a Coastal State should have limited jurisdiction to enforce internationally prescribed pollution control standards in an agreed breadth of waters adjacent to its coast and seaward of its territorial sea. Such enforcement jurisdiction of a Coastal State should include the power to detain a vessel only in circumstances where it is either engaged in an act of pollution prohibited by the applicable standards or where there is a clear and present danger that such an incident of pollution will occur if the vessel is permitted to continue on its course. This detention should terminate in a particular case where the vessel has furnished a guarantee that compensation will be made available to cover damage that in fact is found to have resulted from such an act. The type and limits for such a guarantee should be fixed by international agreement.

In the event of an arbitrary exercise of the limited jurisdiction by a Coastal State or an exercise without reasonable cause, the vessel owner, cargo owner, State of registry of the vessel, or State of nationality of the cargo owner, should have a right to appeal the dispute to the international disputes settlement procedures with a claim for damages for any injury as a result of such exercise of jurisdiction.

The treaty should affirm the principle of Flag State enforcement with respect to areas beyond those in which the treaty grants enforcement jurisdiction to the Coastal State. However, when in the view of the appropriate international organization, circumstances warrant, it should be empowered to delegate supplementary jurisdiction to enforce the internationally agreed standards, to any appropriate Coastal State. This delegation of supplementary enforcement jurisdiction should be on an ad hoc basis and should also be subject to compulsory dispute settlement. In special circumstances, when regional organizations are created for pollution control and are given delegated enforcement rights, such organizations should assure adequate representation for user States as well as Coastal States in the region.

## 2. *Seabed Pollution Control Standards and Their Enforcement*

(*a*) Jurisdiction to prescribe standards of conduct relating to pollution from seabed resource exploitation on the continental margin, including necessary pipeline and terminal operations, should be vested in the adjacent Coastal State, but the appropriate international organization should have authority to prescribe standards which the Coastal State may raise but not lower in order to protect the interests of all States in the marine environment.

(*b*) Jurisdiction to enforce such standards should be vested in the adjacent Coastal State having jurisdiction to prescribe them.

## 3. *Settlement of Pollution Control Disputes*

In the event of a dispute involving the application of pollution control standards or regulations established by or under the Convention, it should provide appropriate procedures and institutions, as set forth in Chapter Five, to:

(*a*) Review compliance by a State with its Convention obligations upon the complaint of any other party State;

(*b*) Hear and decide disputes as provided for in Chapter Five with respect to pollution under the Convention involving any party State or international organization; and

(*c*) Issue, in connection with the preceding paragraph, such interim orders as may be necessary to prevent injustices pending consideration and resolution of such disputes.

## CHAPTER 4. ACCOMMODATION OF USES

The National Petroleum Council recommends that:

1. The international authority or a commission established under the Convention have responsibility for developing standards and criteria for utilization in resolving conflicts among uses and that close consultation with Coastal States be maintained in this process;

2. In the event of conflict among uses in the marine area involving rights and obligations under the Convention or under general rules of international law, the procedures and institutions provided for in the Convention be resorted to in order to reach accommodation.

# CHAPTER 5. SETTLEMENT OF DISPUTES

It is recommended that the United States urge the following:

1. All disputes arising under the Convention or its application should be subject to compulsory dispute settlement.

2. Whatever international authority is established by the Convention should contain an expert commission or commissions with powers to review and make recommendations for the settlement of disputes of a technical nature, such recommendations as to technical issues which are not accepted by the parties to be submitted to the adjudicating authority under 3 or 4 below.

3. Subject to adoption of the proposals in the U.S. draft Convention relating to the composition of the Council and the appointment of members of the tribunal, or proposals substantially similar, a separate tribunal should be provided in the Convention with competence to decide on a legal basis disputes of a State nature arising under the treaty between States or between a State and an international organization, and to which private parties will have a right to apply for emergency measures and for the settlement of disputes between them and an international organization or between them and States.

4. In cases involving disputes between a State and a private party or between an international organization and a private party, and also in cases of disputes between States or between a State and an international organization where the U.S. proposals referred to in 3 above, or substantially similar proposals, are not adopted, provision should be made for resort to adjudication by a tribunal established under the Rules of the Permanent Court of Arbitration.

5. In matters requiring emergency action, including that of an interim nature, there should be procedures and institutions available to private parties for immediate relief pending final resolution of the dispute. Such institutions could include expert commissions for various uses or the Secretariat itself or its designee for the purpose involved.

# PART VI

# PROPOSALS OR DRAFT ARTICLES PRESENTED TO THE UNITED NATIONS SEA-BED COMMITTEE

## LIST OF SUBJECTS AND ISSUES RELATING TO THE LAW OF THE SEA

The list, which should serve as a framework for discussion and drafting necessary articles, had been prepared in accordance with the General Assembly Resolution 2750 C (XXV) and was approved by the UN Seabed Committee on 18 August 1972. It was agreed that the list was not necessarily complete nor did it establish the order of priority for consideration of the various subjects and issues.

1. International régime for the sea-bed and the ocean floor beyond national jurisdiction
   1.1   Nature and characteristics
   1.2   International machinery: structure, functions, powers
   1.3   Economic implications
   1.4   Equitable sharing of benefits bearing in mind the special interests and needs of the developing countries, whether coastal or landlocked
   1.5   Definition and limits of the area
   1.6   Use exclusively for peaceful purposes
2. Territorial sea
   2.1   Nature and characteristics, including the question of the unity or plurality of régimes in the territorial sea
   2.2   Historic waters
   2.3   Limits ·
   2.3.1  Question of the delimitation of the territorial sea; various aspects involved
   2.3.2  Breadth of the territorial sea, Global or regional criteria. Open seas and oceans, semi-closed seas and enclosed seas
   2.4   Innocent passage in the territorial sea
   2.5   Freedom of navigation and overflight resulting from the question of plurality of régimes in the territorial sea
3. Contiguous zone
   3.1   Nature and characteristics
   3.2   Limits
   3.3   Rights of coastal States with regard to national security, customs and fiscal control, sanitation and immigration regulations
4. Straits used for international navigation
   4.1   Innocent passage
   4.2   Other related matters including the question of the right of transit

5. Continental shelf
    5.1    Nature and scope of the sovereign rights of coastal States over the continental shelf. Duties of States
    5.2    Outer limit of the continental shelf: applicable criteria
    5.3    Question of the delimitation between States; various aspects involved
    5.4    Natural resources of the continental shelf
    5.5    Régime for waters superjacent to the continental shelf
    5.6    Scientific research
6. Exclusive economic zone beyond the territorial sea
    6.1    Nature and characteristics, including rights and jurisdiction of coastal States in relation to resources, pollution control and scientific research in the zone. Duties of States
    6.2    Resources of the zone
    6.3    Freedom of navigation and overflight
    6.4    Regional arrangements
    6.5    Limits: applicable criteria
    6.6    Fisheries
    6.6.1    Exclusive fishery zone
    6.6.2    Preferential rights of coastal States
    6.6.3    Management and conservation
    6.6.4    Protection of coastal States' fisheries in enclosed and semi-enclosed seas
    6.6.5    Régime of islands under foreign domination and control in relation to zones of exclusive fishing jurisdiction
    6.7    Sea-bed within national jurisdiction
    6.7.1    Nature and characteristics
    6.7.2    Delineation between adjacent and opposite States
    6.7.3    Sovereign rights over natural resources
    6.7.4    Limits: applicable criteria
    6.8    Prevention and control of pollution and other hazards to the marine environment
    6.8.1    Rights and responsibilities of coastal States
    6.9    Scientific research
7. Coastal State preferential rights or other non-exclusive jurisdiction over resources beyond the territorial sea
    7.1    Nature, scope and characteristics
    7.2    Sea-bed resources
    7.3    Fisheries
    7.4    Prevention and control of pollution and other hazards to the marine environment
    7.5    International co-operation in the study and rational exploitation of marine resources

7.6     Settlement of disputes
7.7     Other rights and obligations
8.  High seas
    8.1     Nature and characteristics
    8.2     Rights and duties of States
    8.3     Question of the freedoms of the high seas and their regulation
    8.4     Management and conservation of living resources
    8.5     Slavery, piracy, drugs
    8.6     Hot pursuit
9.  Land-locked countries
    9.1     General Principles of the Law of the Sea concerning the land-locked countries
    9.2     Rights and interests of land-locked countries
    9.2.1   Free access to and from the sea: freedom of transit, means and facilities for transport and communications
    9.2.2   Equality of treatment in the ports of transit States
    9.2.3   Free access to the international sea-bed area beyond national jurisdiction
    9.2.4   Participation in the international régime, including the machinery and the equitable sharing in the benefits of the area
    9.3     Particular interests and needs of developing land-locked countries in the international régime
    9.4     Rights and interests of land-locked countries in regard to living resources of the sea
10. Rights and interests of shelf-locked States and States with narrow shelves or short coastlines
    10.1    International régime
    10.2    Fisheries
    10.3    Special interests and needs of developing shelf-locked States and States with narrow shelves or short coastlines
    10.4    Free access to and from the high seas
11. Rights and interests of States with broad shelves
12. Preservation of the marine environment
    12.1    Sources of pollution and other hazards and measures to combat them
    12.2    Measures to preserve the ecological balance of the marine environment
    12.3    Responsibility and liability for damage to the marine environment and to the coastal State
    12.4    Rights and duties of coastal States
    12.5    International co-operation
13. Scientific research

## I. BREADTH AND BOUNDARY OF THE TERRITORIAL SEA AND NATIONAL JURISDICTION

In addition to the proposals herein referred to, see the proposals in II. Territorial Sea and Resources Jurisdiction.

## UNION OF SOVIET SOCIALIST REPUBLICS:
— Draft Article on the Breadth of the Territorial Sea

> Submitted to the United Nations Seabed Committee on 13 March 1973, as UN Doc. A/AC.138/SC.II/L.7/Add.1. See A/AC.138/SC.II/L.7 (p. 299)

Subject to the provisions of articles 2 and 3, each State shall have the right to establish the breadth of its territorial sea at no more than 12 nautical miles measured in accordance with the provisions of the 1958 Geneva Convention on the Territorial Sea and the Contiguous Zone.

## TURKEY:
— Breadth of the Territorial Sea; Global or Regional Criteria; Open Seas and Oceans, Semi-enclosed Seas and Enclosed Seas

> Submitted to the United Nations Seabed Committee on 12 July 1973, as UN Doc. A/AC.138/SC.II/L.16/Rev.1.

1. Each State shall have the right to determine the breadth of its territorial sea within limits of no more than (. . .) miles, subject to the provisions of paragraph 2.
2. In areas with special characteristics, such as the semi-closed and enclosed seas, where the exercise of this right by one State for the purpose of extending the breadth of its territorial sea may prejudice the rights and interests of other States of the area, the determination of the breadth of the territorial sea, within the limits specified in paragraph 1 above, shall be effected by the agreement of the States of that area.

**GREECE:**
**— Amendment to the Turkey Proposal (SC.II/L.16/Rev.1)**

> Submitted to the United Nations Seabed Committee on 12 July 1973, as UN Doc. A/AC.138/SC.II/L.17.

3. Failing such agreement, no State is entitled to extend its territorial sea beyond the median line every point of which is equidistant from the nearest points on the baselines, continental or insular, from which the breadth of the territorial seas of each of the two States is measured.

**TUNISIA AND TURKEY:**
**— Sub-amendment to the Greece Proposal (SC.II/L.17)**

> Submitted to the United Nations Seabed Committee on 16 July 1973, as UN Doc. A/AC.138/SC.II/L.32.

Delete "or insular".

**CYPRUS:**
**— Breadth of the Territorial Sea**

> Submitted to the United Nations Seabed Committee on 28 March 1973, as UN Doc. A/AC.138/SC.II/L.19.

Where the coasts of two States are opposite or adjacent to each other, neither of the two States is entitled, failing agreement between them to the contrary, to extend its territorial sea beyond the median line, every point of which is equidistant from the nearest points on the baselines, continental or insular, from which the breadth of the territorial seas of each of the two States is measured.

**TUNISIA AND TURKEY:**
**— Amendment to the Cyprus Proposal (SC.II/L.19)**

> Submitted to the United Nations Seabed Committee on 16 July 1973, as UN Doc. A/AC.138/SC.II/L.31.

Delete the words "or insular".

## TURKEY:
## — Delimitation

Submitted to the United Nations Seabed Committee on 13 July 1973, as UN Doc. A/AC.138/SC.II/L.22/Rev.1.

1. Where the coasts of two or more States are adjacent or opposite to each other, the delimitation of the respective maritime boundaries shall be determined by agreement among them in accordance with equitable principles, taking into account all the relevant circumstances.

2. In the course of the negotiations which will be held with a view to arriving at an agreement, the States shall take into account, *inter alia*, special circumstances such as the general configuration of the respective coasts, the existence of islands or islets of another State and the physical and geological structure of the marine area involved, including the sea-bed and subsoil thereof.

3. The States shall make use of the methods envisaged in Article 33 of the United Nations Charter or other peaceful means and methods open to them, in order to resolve differences which may arise in the course of negotiations.

4. In the absence of special circumstances, due regard should be given to the principles of median line or equidistance in delimitation of respective boundaries.


## ICELAND:
## — Working Paper on Jurisdiction of Coastal States over Natural Resources of the Area adjacent to their Territorial Sea

Submitted to the United Nations Seabed Committee on 5 April 1973, as UN Doc. A/AC.138/SC.II/L.23.

A coastal State may determine the extent of its exclusive jurisdiction and control over the natural resources of the maritime area adjacent to its territorial sea.

The outer limits of this area shall be reasonable, keeping in view the geographical, geological, ecological, economic and other relevant local considerations, and shall not exceed 200 nautical miles.

**BRAZIL:**

— **Draft Articles containing Basic Provisions on the Question of the Maximum Breadth of the Territorial Sea and other Modalities or Combinations of Legal Regimes of Coastal State Sovereignty, Jurisdiction or Specialized Competences**

Submitted to the United Nations Seabed Committee on 13 July 1973, as UN Doc. A/AC.138/SC.II/L.25.

**Art. A.** 1. Each State has the right to establish the breadth of its territorial sea within reasonable limits, taking into account geographical, social, economic, ecological and national security factors.

2. The breadth of the territorial sea shall in no case exceed two hundred nautical miles measured from the baselines determined in accordance with article . . . of the present Convention.

3. States whose coasts do not face the open ocean shall enter into consultations with other States of the region with a view to determining a mutually agreed maximum breadth of the territorial sea appropriate to the particular characteristics of the region.

**Art. B.** Within the limitations determined by article A, each State has the right to establish other modalities or combinations of legal regimes of sovereignty, jurisdiction or specialized competences in the marine area adjacent to its coasts.


**U.S.S.R.:**

— **Rough Draft of Basic Provisions on the Question of the Outer Limit of the Continental Shelf**

Submitted to the United Nations Seabed Committee on 13 July 1973, as UN Doc. A/AC.138/SC.II/L.26.

(1) The outer limit of the continental shelf may be established by the coastal State within the 500-metre isobath.

(2) In areas where the 500-metre isobath referred to in paragraph (1) hereof is situated at a distance less than 100 nautical miles measured from the baselines from which the territorial sea is measured, the outer limit of the continental shelf may be established by the coastal State by a line every point of which is at a distance from the nearest point of the said baselines not exceeding 100 nautical miles.

(3) In areas where there is no continental shelf, the coastal State may have the same rights in respect of the sea-bed as in respect of the continental shelf, within the limits provided for in paragraph (2) hereof.

**GREECE:**
**— Regime of Islands**

Submitted to the United Nations Seabed Committee on 16 July 1973, as UN Doc. A/AC.138/SC.II/L.29.

1. An island is a naturally formed area of land, surrounded by water which is above water at high-tide.

2. An island forms an integral part of the territory of the State to which it belongs. The territorial sovereignty over the island extends to its territorial waters, to the air space over the island and its territorial sea to its bed and subsoil and to its continental shelf for the purpose of exploring it and exploiting its natural resources.

3. The territorial sea of the island is determined in accordance with the same provisions applicable for the measurements of the territorial sea of the continental part of the territory of the State.

4. The provisions applicable for the determination of the continental shelf and the zones of national jurisdiction of the continental part of the State are as a general rule applicable to islands.

5. The above provisions do not prejudice the regime of archipelagic islands.

**AUSTRALIA AND NORWAY:**
**— Certain Basic Principles on an Economic Zone and on Delimitation**

Submitted to the United Nations Seabed Committee on 16 July 1973, as UN Doc. A/AC.138/SC.II/L.36.

1. *Economic zone*

A. The coastal state has the right to establish, beyond its territorial sea, in accordance with these principles, an (economic zone - patrimonial sea) in which it shall have sovereign rights over the natural resources for the primary benefit of its people and its economy.

B. The natural resources of the (economic zone - patrimonial sea) comprise the renewable and non-renewable natural resources of the waters, the seabed and the subsoil thereof.

C. The coastal state has the right to determine the outer limit of the (economic zone - patrimonial sea) up to a maximum distance of 200 nautical miles from the applicable baselines for measuring the territorial sea. However the coastal state has the right to retain, where the natural prolongation of its land mass extends beyond the (economic zone - patrimonial sea), the sovereign rights with respect to that area of the seabed and the subsoil thereof which it had under international law before the entry into force of this convention: such rights do not extend beyond the outer edge of the continental margin.

D. In the (economic zone - patrimonial sea) ships and aircraft of all states, whether coastal or not, shall enjoy the right of freedom of navigation and overflight.

## 2. Delimitation

A. Adjacent and opposite states shall use their best endeavours to reach agreement on the delimitation between them of their (economic zones - patrimonial seas) and their seabed areas in accordance with equitable principles.

B. Where there is an agreement between the states concerned, questions relating to the delimitation of their (economic zones - patrimonial seas) and their seabed areas shall be determined in accordance with the provisions of that agreement.

C. No state shall by reason of this Convention claim or exercise rights over the natural resources of any area of the seabed and subsoil over which another state had under international law immediately before the coming into force of this convention sovereign rights for the purposes of exploring it or exploiting its natural resources.

D. Subject to principles A, B and C above, and unless the drawing up of another boundary is justified by special circumstances, the boundary shall be an equidistant line in the case of adjacent coasts and a median line in the case of opposite coasts.

## CAMEROON, KENYA, MADAGASCAR, TUNISIA AND TURKEY:
— Regime of Islands

Submitted to the United Nations Seabed Committee on 19 July 1973, as UN Doc. A/AC.138/SC.II/L.43.

1. Maritime spaces of islands shall be determined according to equitable principles taking into account all relevant factors and circumstances including, *inter alia*:

(a) The size of islands;

(b) The population or the absence thereof;

(c) Their contiguity to the principal territory;

(d) Whether or not they are situated on the continental shelf of another territory;

248

(*e*) Their geological and geomorphological structure and configuration.

2. Island States and the régime of archipelagic States as set out under the present Convention shall not be affected by this article.

## PHILIPPINES:
### — Draft Article on Historic Waters

Submitted to the United Nations Seabed Committee on
6 August 1973, as UN Doc. A/AC.138/SC.II/L.46.

**Art. . . .** Historic rights or title acquired by a State in a part of the sea adjacent to its coasts shall be recognized and safeguarded.

## PHILIPPINES:
### — Draft Article on Breadth of Territorial Sea

Submitted to the United Nations Seabed Committee on
10 August 1973, as UN Doc. A/AC.138/SC.II/L.47/Rev.1.

**Art. 1.** Each State shall have the right to establish the breadth of its territorial sea up to a limit not exceeding . . . . . . nautical miles, measured from the applicable baseline.

The maximum limit provided in this Article shall not apply to historic waters held by any State as its territorial sea.

Any State which, prior to the approval of this Convention, shall have already established a territorial sea with a breadth more than the maximum provided in this Article shall not be subject to the limit provided herein.

## BULGARIA:
### — Draft Articles on the Nature and Characteristics of the Territorial Sea and its Breadth

Submitted to the United Nations Seabed Committee on
9 August 1973, as UN Doc. A/AC.138/SC.II/L.51.

**Art. . . .** 1. The sovereignty of a coastal State extends beyond its land territory and its internal waters to a belt of sea adjacent to its coast described as the territorial sea.

2. The sovereignty of a coastal State extends also to the air space over

the territorial sea as well as to its bed and the subsoil thereof.

3. The coastal State exercise this sovereignty subject to the provisions of these articles and to other rules of international law.

**Art. . . .** Each State shall have the right to establish the breadth of its territorial sea up to a limit not exceeding twelve nautical miles, measured from baselines drawn in accordance with Articles . . . of this Convention and subject to the provisions of Articles . . . concerning straits used for international navigation.

## PAKISTAN:
— Breadth of the Territorial Sea and Boundaries of the Exclusive Economic Zone

Submitted to the United Nations Seabed Committee on 9 August 1973, as UN Doc. A/AC.138/SC.II/L.52.

Each coastal State shall have the right to establish the breadth of its territorial sea within limits not exceeding 12 nautical miles, measured from applicable baselines determined in accordance with article . . . of this Convention.

Each coastal State shall also have the right to establish its exclusive economic zone not exceeding 200 nautical miles, calculated from the baseline used for the determination of the limits of the territorial sea.

## ROMANIA:
— Certain Specific Aspects of the Regime of Islands in the Context of Delimitation of the Marine Spaces between Neighbouring States

Submitted to the United Nations Seabed Committee on 10 August 1973, as UN Doc. A/AC.138/SC.II/L.53.

1. Islets and small islands, uninhabited and without economic life, which are situated on the continental shelf of the coast do not possess any of the shelf or other marine space of the same nature.

2. Such islands may have waters—of their own or forming part of the territorial sea of the coast—the extent of which shall be determined by agreement, taking into account all the circumstances affecting the maritime area concerned and all relevant geographical, geological and other features. The waters thus determined shall not, in any event, affect marine spaces which belong to the State or to neighbouring States.

250

**JAPAN:**

**— Principles on the Delimitation of the Coastal Seabed Area**

Submitted to the United Nations Seabed Committee on
15 August 1973, as UN Doc. A/AC.138/SC.II/L.56.

1. The coastal State shall have the right to establish, beyond its territorial sea, a coastal seabed area up to a maximum distance of . . . . . . nautical miles from the applicable baseline for measuring the breadth of the territorial sea. The coastal State exercises sovereign rights for the purpose of exploring the coastal seabed area and exploiting its mineral resources.

2. In cases where the coasts of two or more coastal States are adjacent or opposite to each other, the boundary of the coastal seabed areas appertaining to such States shall be determined by agreement in accordance with the principle of equidistance.

3. Nothing herein shall prejudice the existing agreements between the coastal States concerned relating to the delimitation of their respective coastal seabed areas.


## II. TERRITORIAL SEA AND RESOURCES JURISDICTION

**KENYA:**
**— Draft Articles on Exclusive Economic Zone Concept**

Submitted to the United Nations Seabed Committee on 7 August 1972, as UN Doc. A/AC.138/SC.II/L.10.

**Art. 1.** All States have a right to determine the limits of their jurisdiction over the seas adjacent to their coasts beyond a territorial sea of 12 miles in accordance with the criteria which take into account their own geographical, geological, biological, ecological, economic and national security factors.

**Art. 2.** In accordance with the foregoing Article, all States have the right to establish an Economic Zone beyond the territorial sea for the primary benefit of their peoples and their respective economies in which they shall exercise sovereign rights over natural resources for the purpose of exploration and exploitation. Within the zone they shall have exclusive jurisdiction for the purpose of control, regulation and exploitation of both living and non-living resources of the Zone and their preservation, and for the purpose of prevention and control of pollution.

The coastal State shall exercise jurisdiction over its Economic Zone and third States or their nationals shall bear responsibility for damage resulting from their activities within the Zone.

**Art. 3.** The establishment of such a Zone shall be without prejudice to the exercise of freedom of navigation, freedom of overflight and freedom to lay submarine cables and pipelines as recognized in international law.

**Art. 4.** The exercise of jurisdiction over the Zone shall encompass all the economic resources of the area, living and non-living, either on the water surface or within the water column, or on the soil or sub-soil of the seabed and ocean floor below.

**Art. 5.** Without prejudice to the general jurisdictional competence conferred upon the coastal State by Article II above, the State may establish special regulations within its Economic Zone for:

(*a*) Exclusive exploration and exploitation of non-renewable marine resources;

(*b*) Exclusive or preferential exploitation of renewable resources;

(*c*) Protection and conservation of the renewable resources;

(*d*) Control, prevention and elimination of pollution of the marine environment;

(*e*) Scientific research.

Any State may obtain permission from the coastal State to exploit the resources of the Zone where permitted on such terms as may be laid down

252

and in conformity with laws and regulations of the coastal State.

**Art. 6.** The coastal State shall permit the exploitation of the living resources within its zone to the neighbouring developing land-locked, near land-locked and countries with a small shelf provided the enterprises of those States desiring to exploit these resources are effectively controlled by their national capital and personnel.

To be effective the rights of land-locked or near land-locked States shall be complemented by the right of access to the sea and the right of transit. These rights shall be embodied in multilateral or regional or bilateral agreements.

**Art. 7.** The limits of the Economic Zone shall be fixed in nautical miles in accordance with criteria in each region, which take into consideration the resources of the region and the rights and interests of developing land-locked, near land-locked, shelf-locked States and States with narrow shelves and without prejudice to limits adopted by any State within the region. The Economic Zone shall not in any case exceed 200 nautical miles, measured from the baselines for determining territorial sea.

**Art. 8.** The delineation of the Economic Zone between adjacent and opposite States shall be carried out in accordance with international law. Disputes arising therefrom shall be settled in conformity with the Charter of the United Nations and any other relevant regional arrangements.

**Art. 9.** Neighbouring developing States shall mutually recognize their existing historic rights. They shall also give reciprocal preferential treatment to one another in the exploitation of the living resources of their respective Economic Zones.

**Art. 10.** Each State shall ensure that any exploration or exploitation activity within its Economic Zone is carried out exclusively for peaceful purposes and in such a manner as not to interfere unduly with the legitimate interests of other States in the region or those of the International Community.

**Art. 11.** No territory under foreign domination and control shall be entitled to establish an Economic Zone.


**AUSTRALIA AND NEW ZEALAND:**
**— Working Paper on Principles for a Fisheries Regime**

> Submitted to the United Nations Seabed Committee on 11 August 1972, as UN Doc. A/AC.138/SC.II/L.11.

I. The coastal State shall have exclusive jurisdiction, in accordance with the Principles elaborated herein, over the living resources of the sea in an adequately wide zone of the high seas adjacent to its territorial sea.

II. It shall be the responsibility of the coastal State to provide proper management and utilization of the living resources within its zone of exclusive jurisdiction, including:—

(a) maintenance of the level of stocks which will provide the maximum sustainable yield;

(b) rational utilization of the resources and the promotion of economic stability coupled with the highest possible food production; and

(c) where the resource is required for direct human consumption in the coastal state, the highest possible priority to be given to the production of fish for direct human consumption.

III. Measures that the coastal State may take include:—

(a) requiring licensing by it of fishing vessels and equipment to operate in the zone;

(b) limiting the number of vessels and the number of units of gear that may be used;

(c) specifying the gear permitted to be used;

(d) fixing the period during which fish or fish of a species or class may be taken;

(e) fixing the size of fish that may be taken;

(f) specifying the method of fishing that may be used in a specified area or for taking a specified species or class of fish and prohibiting any other methods.

IV. Pursuant to its exclusive jurisdiction, it would be for the coastal State to determine the allowable catch of any particular species, and to allocate to itself that portion of the allowable catch, up to 100 per cent, that it can harvest.

V. Where the coastal State is unable to take 100 per cent of the allowable catch of a species as determined under the Principles, it shall allow the entry of foreign fishing vessels with a view to maintaining the maximum possible food supply.

Such access shall be granted up to the level of allowable catch on an equitable basis without the imposition of unreasonable conditions and without discrimination between nationals of other States, except as may be provided for under phasing-out arrangements made in accordance with these Principles.

VI. Measures adopted by the coastal State shall take account of traditional subsistence fishing carried out in any part of the fisheries zone.

VII. When the coastal State intends to allocate to itself the whole of the allowable catch of a species, in accordance with these Principles, it shall enter into consultations with any other State which requests such consultations and which is able to demonstrate that its vessels have carried on fishing in the fishery resources zone on a substantial scale for a period of not less then [ten] years with a view to:—

(a) analysing the catch and effort statistics of the other state in order to establish the level of fishing operations carried out in the zone by the other state;

(b) negotiating special arrangements with the other state under which the latter's vessels would be "phased out" of the fishery having regard to the developing fishing capacity of the coastal State; and

(c) in the event of agreement not being reached through consultation there shall be a "phasing out" period of [five] years.

VIII. The coastal State, as an exercise of its jurisdiction over the resources of the zone, shall have powers of boarding, arrest and detention of fishing vessels. Breaches of a condition of a licence or of a law or regulation applying in the zone in accordance with these Principle shall be triable in the Courts of the coastal State concerned.

IX. In respect of "wide-ranging" species of fish that are exploited within the zone, the coastal State shall participate in the formulation and implementation of international arrangements for the management of the species.

X. The coastal State has responsibility to conduct research on the resources within the zone to enable it to fulfil its responsibility to provide proper management and rational utilization of those resources. It shall publish the results of that research within a reasonable period. Other States operating within the zone shall assist in the research programmes and shall provide comprehensive catch, effort and biological data at reasonable intervals as required.

XI. It is recognized that the anadromous species is a species in respect of which the coastal State concerned exercises onerous and unique responsibilities. On this basis that coastal State should have the sole right to manage the stocks of anadromous species bred in its home waters.

XII. Where a State alleges that:—

(a) the living resources of the zone are being substantially under-exploited; or

(b) generally agreed conservation principles are being substantially departed from by the coastal State concerned,

it may request the coastal State to review the measures taken by it. The State making the allegation may require it to be referred to an advisory expert body that would be empowered to convey its findings to the States concerned and, if that body considers it desirable, to make recommendations with a view to resolving the issue.

XIII. International arrangements, including where appropriate international fisheries commissions, shall be established for the management

255

of the "wide-ranging" species and as appropriate the "bathypelagic" species and other species that inhabit the waters beyond the limits of national fisheries resource jurisdiction. All States shall have an equal right to participate in such organizations.

XIV. [The role of international bodies.]

XV. It shall be the responsibility of the coastal State to ensure that fishing operations in the fishery zone shall be conducted with reasonable regard for other activities in the marine environment.

Other activities shall be conducted with reasonable regard for fishing operations carried out within the zone.


## COLOMBIA, MEXICO AND VENEZUELA:
— Draft Articles of Treaty - Territorial Sea

Submitted to the United Nations Seabed Committee on 2 April 1973, as UN Doc. A/AC.138/SC.II/L.21.

*Section 1. General Provisions*

**Art. 1.** 1. The coastal State has sovereignty over an area of the sea immediately contiguous to its territory and inland waters designated as the territorial sea.

2. The sovereignty of a coastal State extends to the sea-bed and subsoil and the superjacent air space of the territorial sea.

3. The sovereignty of the coastal State is exercised in accordance with the provisions of these articles and other rules of international law.

**Art. 2.** The breadth of the territorial sea shall not exceed 12 nautical miles to be measured from the applicable baselines.

**Art. 3.** Without prejudice to the provisions of these articles, ships of all States, whether coastal or not, shall enjoy the right of innocent passage through the territorial sea.

*Section 2. Limits (Applicable baselines and delimitation between States)*
. . .

*Section 3. Right of Innocent Passage*
. . .

*Patrimonial sea*

**Art. 4.** The coastal State has sovereign rights over the renewable and non-renewable natural resources which are found in the waters, in the sea-bed

256

and in the subsoil of an area adjacent to the territorial sea called the patrimonial sea.

**Art. 5.** The coastal State has the right to adopt the necessary measures to ensure its sovereignty over the resources and prevent marine pollution of its patrimonial sea.

**Art. 6.** The coastal State has the duty to promote and the right to regulate the conduct of scientific research within the patrimonial sea.

**Art. 7.** The coastal State shall authorize and regulate the emplacement and use of artificial islands and any kind of facilities on the surface of the sea, in the water column and on the sea-bed and subsoil of the patrimonial sea.

**Art. 8.** The outer limit of the patrimonial sea shall not exceed 200 nautical miles from the applicable baselines for measuring the territorial sea.

**Art. 9.** In the patrimonial sea, ships and aircraft of all States, whether coastal or not, shall enjoy the right of freedom of navigation and overflight with no restrictions other than those resulting from the exercise by the coastal State of its rights within the area.

**Art. 10.** Subject only to the limitations established in the preceding article, the coastal State shall respect the freedom to lay submarine cables and pipelines.

**Art. 11.** 1. The coastal State shall exercise jurisdiction and supervision over the exploration and exploitation of the renewable and non-renewable resources of the patrimonial sea and over allied activities.

2. In exercising such powers, the coastal State shall take appropriate measures to ensure that such activities are carried out with due consideration for other legitimate uses of the sea by other States.

**Art. 12.** In exercising the freedoms and rights this Convention confers on other States, the latter shall not interfere in the activities referred to in the preceding article.

*Continental shelf*

**Art. 13.** The term "continental shelf" means:
(*a*) The sea-bed and subsoil of the submarine areas adjacent to the coast, but outside the area of the territorial sea, to the outer limits of the continental rise bordering on the ocean basin or abyssal floor;
(*b*) The sea-bed and subsoil of analogous submarine regions adjacent to the coasts of islands.

**Art. 14.** The coastal State exercises sovereign rights over the continental shelf for the purpose of exploring it and exploiting its natural resources.

**Art. 15.** In that part of the continental shelf covered by the patrimonial sea, the legal régime provided for the latter shall apply.

With respect to the part beyond the patrimonial sea, the régime established by international law for the continental shelf shall apply.

*High seas*

**Art. 16.** Freedom of navigation, overflight and the laying of submarine cables and pipelines shall exist in the high seas. Fishing in this zone shall be neither unrestricted nor indiscriminate.

**Art. 17.** The coastal State has a special interest in maintaining the productivity of the living resources of the sea in an area adjacent to the patrimonial sea.

*Regional agreements*

**Art. 18.** No provision of this Treaty shall be interpreted as preventing or restricting the right of any State to conclude regional or subregional agreements to regulate exploitation or distribution of the living resources of the sea, preservation of the marine environment or scientific research, or as affecting the legal validity of existing agreements.


**TUNISIA AND TURKEY:**
**— Amendment to the Colombia, Mexico and Venezuela Proposal (SC.II/L.21)**

> Submitted to the United Nations Seabed Committee on 16 July 1973, as UN Doc. A/AC.138/SC.II/L.33.

Delete subparagraph (b) in article 13.


**URUGUAY:**
**— Draft Treaty Articles on the Territorial Sea**

> Submitted to the United Nations Seabed Committee on 3 July 1973, as UN Doc. A/AC.138/SC.II/L.24.

*Section 1. General*

**Art. 1.** 1. A coastal State exercises sovereignty over a belt of sea adjacent to its coast and to its internal waters, described as the territorial sea.

2. The sovereignty of a coastal State extends to the air space over the territorial sea as well as to its bed and subsoil.

*Section 2. Limits of the territorial sea*

**Art. 2.** 1. Every State is entitled to determine the breadth of its territorial sea within limits not exceeding a distance of 200 nautical miles measured from the applicable baselines, subject to the provisions of the succeeding paragraphs.

2. In regions with special characteristics, such as semi-enclosed or inland seas, where it is impossible for coastal States to fix the maximum breadth of their territorial seas, the breadth of the said seas shall be determined by agreement between the coastal States of the same region.

**Art. 3.** 1. Where the coasts of two States are opposite or adjacent to each other, neither of them is entitled, failing agreement between them, to extend its territorial sea beyond a median line determined exclusively for that purpose, every point of which is equidistant from the nearest points on the continental or insular baselines from which the breadth of the territorial sea of each of the two States is measured.

2. The line of delimitation between the territorial seas of two States lying opposite to each other or adjacent to each other shall be marked on large-scale charts officially recognized by the coastal States.

**Art. 4.** [Identical with article 3 of the Geneva Convention (baseline).]

**Art. 5.** [Identical with article 4 of the Geneva Convention (baseline).]

**Art. 6.** [Identical with article 5 of the Geneva Convention (internal waters).]

**Art. 7.** [Identical with article 6 of the Geneva Convention (outer limit).]

**Art. 8.** [Identical with article 7 of the Geneva Convention (bays) (under study).]

**Art. 9.** [Identical with article 8 of the Geneva Convention (permanent harbour works).]

**Art. 10.** [Identical with article 9 of the Geneva Convention (roadsteads).]

**Art. 11.** [Identical with article 10 of the Geneva Convention (islands).]

**Art. 12.** 1. The territorial sea of an archipelagic State whose constituent islands and other natural characteristics form an intrinsic geographical, economic and political entity that has been or may have been historically regarded as such may be measured from the straight baselines joining the furthest points of the islands and the outermost low-tide reefs of the archipelago.

2. Waters enclosed by the baselines drawn in accordance with paragraph 1, irrespective of their depth or distance from the coast, shall be regarded as internal waters without prejudice to the innocent passage of ships flying any flag.

259

**Art. 13.** [Identical with article 11 of the Geneva Convention.]

**Art. 14.** [Identical with article 13 of the Geneva Convention.]

*Section 3. Regimes applicable to international communication*

**Art. 15.** On territorial seas whose breadth does not exceed 12 nautical miles measured from the applicable baselines, ships of all States, whether coastal or not, shall enjoy the right of innocent passage subject to the provisions of articles . . . . .

**Art. 16.** On territorial seas whose breadth exceeds 12 nautical miles measured from the applicable baselines, ships of all States, whether coastal or not, shall enjoy the right of innocent passage in the form prescribed in article 15, within the belt of the first 12 nautical miles.

Beyond the said 12 nautical miles, ships and aircraft of all States, whether coastal or not, shall enjoy the right of free navigation on and over-flight over the territorial sea without restrictions other than those which may derive from the regulations enacted by the coastal State with regard to its security, the preservation of the environment, the exploration, conservation and exploitation of resources, scientific research and the safety of navigation and aviation and from the corresponding measures adopted by it in conformity with international law.

**Art. 17 et seq.** [Definition of innocent passage. Rules applicable to the various types of ships.]

*Section 4. Laying of submarine pipelines and cables*

**Art. . . . .** Subject to the regulations and measures referred to in article 16, the coastal State may not impede the laying or maintenance of submarine pipelines and cables on the bed of the area of its territorial sea situated beyond 12 nautical miles measured from the applicable baselines.

In such cases the coastal State shall be given advance notice and due account shall be taken of cables and pipelines already in position and, in particular, of the possibility of repairing them.

**Art. . . . .** Any break in or damage to a submarine cable in the area referred to in the preceding article, caused deliberately or by culpable negligence, which interrupts or obstructs telegraphic or telephonic communications, and any break or damage caused, under the same conditions, in or to a high-voltage cable or submarine pipeline shall be punishable and shall give rise to the consequent liabilities under the laws of the coastal State and the jurisdiction of its courts.

Nothing in the laws enacted on the subject by the coastal State shall affect the lawful exercise of the right of other States to lay submarine pipelines and cables under the conditions laid down in theses articles, or shall penalize the perpetrator of any break or damage if he acted solely for the legitimate purpose of protecting his life or the safety of his vessel after taking all necessary precautions to prevent such break or damage.

## Section 5. *Protection of the marine environment*

**Art. . . .** A coastal State is under a duty to adopt on its territorial sea appropriate measures to shield the marine environment from the damage and risks of pollution and other effects harmful or dangerous to its eco-system and to protect the quality and use of the waters, living resources, human health and other interests of its population, taking into consider-ation the recommendations and standards of international technical or-ganizations and co-operation with other States.

## Section 6. *Scientific research*

**Art. . . .** In making regulations on scientific research in its territorial sea, a coastal State shall take special account of the general interest in pro-moting and facilitating such activities, provided that they do not affect its security and without prejudice to its right to participate in them and to receive the results obtained.

## Section 7. *Regime for countries having no sea-coast*
(See p. 369).


## ECUADOR, PANAMA AND PERU:
## — Draft Articles for Inclusion in a Convention on the Law of the Sea

Submitted to the United Nations Seabed Committee on 13 July 1973, as UN Doc. A/AC.138/SC.II/L.27. Supplemented by A/AC.138/SC.II/L.54.

## PART I [ADJACENT SEA]

## Section 1. *General provisions*

**Art. 1.** 1. The sovereignty of the coastal State and, consequently, the exercise of its jurisdiction, shall extend to the sea adjacent to its coast up to a limit not exceeding a distance of 200 nautical miles measured from the appropriate baselines.

2. The aforesaid sovereignty and jurisdiction shall also extend to the air space over the adjacent sea, as well as to its bed and subsoil.

**Art. 2.** It shall be the responsibility of every coastal State to fix the limits of the adjacent sea under its sovereignty and jurisdiction, within the maximum distance referred to in article 1, with due regard to reasonable criteria taking account of the relevant geographical, geological, ecological, economic and social factors, as well as of considerations of the preservation of the marine environment and of national security.

*Section 2. Baselines*

[Provisions on delimitation between States whose coasts are opposite or contiguous].

**Art. 3.** 1. The area of sovereignty and jurisdiction of an archipelagian State may be measured from straight baselines joining the outermost points of the outer islands and reefs of the archipelago.

2. In such cases, the waters enclosed by the baselines shall be considered internal waters, though vessels of any flag may sail in them, in accordance with the provisions laid down by the archipelagian State.

... (Complementary provisions) ...............

*Section 3. Navigation régime*

**Art. 4.** 1. In the sea under the sovereignty and jurisdiction of the coastal State, vessels of any flag may sail freely, without restrictions other than those imposed by the duties of peaceful co-existence and compliance with the provisions laid down by the coastal State as regards the prospecting, exploration, conservation and exploitation of resources, the preservation of the marine environment, scientific research, the emplacement of installations and safeguards for navigation and shipping.

2. In so far as they are relevant, the provisions of the preceding paragraph shall also apply to aircraft.

**Art. 5.** Notwithstanding the provisions of article 4, the coastal State may lay down additional provisions for the passage of foreign vessels and aircraft within a limit close to its coast, for the purpose of safeguarding national peace, order and security.

[Complementary provisions, including passage through straits used for international navigation].

*Section 4. Natural resources régime*

**Art. 6.** The renewable and non-renewable resources of the sea, and of its bed and subsoil, within the limits referred to in article 1 shall be subject to the sovereignty and jurisdiction of the coastal State.

**Art. 7.** The prospecting and exploration of the adjacent sea, as well as the

262

exploitation of its non-renewable resources, shall be subject to the regulations of the coastal State, which may reserve the aforesaid activities for itself or its nationals, or permit them to be carried out by third parties in accordance with the provisions of its internal legislation and of any relevant international agreements it may conclude.

**Art. 8.** The prospecting, protection, conservation and exploitation of the renewable resources of the adjacent sea shall also be subject to the regulations of the coastal State and to any relevant agreements which it may conclude, with due regard, so far as may be appropriate, to co-operation with other States and the recommendations of international technical organizations.
[Complementary provisions on natural resources].

### Section 5. *Pollution control régime*

**Art. 9.** It shall be the responsibility of the coastal State to establish measures to prevent, reduce or eliminate in its adjacent sea any damage or risks arising from pollution or other effects detrimental or dangerous to the ecological system of the marine environment, water quality and use, living resources, human health and the recreation of its population, with due regard to co-operation with other States and the recommendations of international technical organizations.
[Complementary provisions on pollution].

### Section 6. *Scientific research régime*

**Art. 10.** 1. It shall be for the coastal State to authorize any scientific research activities that may be conducted in its adjacent sea; the coastal State shall also have the right to participate in such activities and to receive the results obtained.

2. In the regulations which it establishes for this purpose, the coastal State shall bear particularly in mind the desirability of promoting and facilitating such activities and of co-operating with other States and international organizations in disseminating the results of the research.
[Complementary provisions on scientific research].

### Section 7. *Régime governing installations*

**Art. 11.** The coastal State shall permit the laying of submarine cables and pipelines in its adjacent sea, without restrictions other than those that may result from the provisions referred to in article 4, paragraph 1.

**Art. 12.** The emplacement and use of artificial islands and other installations and devices on the surface of the sea, in the water column and

on the bed or in the subsoil of the adjacent sea shall be subject to authorization and regulation by the coastal State.
[Complementary provisions on installations].

*Section 8. Regional and subregional régimes*

**Art. 13.** 1. In regions or subregions in which certain coastal States, owing to geographical or ecological factors, are unable, before all their coastlines, to extend the limits of their sovereignty and jurisdiction up to distances equal to those adopted by other coastal States in the same region or subregion, the former States shall enjoy, in the seas of the latter States, a preferential régime vis-à-vis third States in matters relating to the exploitation of renewable resources, the said régime to be determined by regional, subregional or bilateral agreements taking into account the interests of the respective States.

2. Enjoyment of the preferential régime referred to in the preceding paragraph shall be reserved to nationals of the usufructuary States for internal use.

**Art. 14.** The coastal States of a single region or subregion shall promote such forms of co-operation and consultation as they consider most appropriate in the legal, economic, scientific and technical spheres relating to maritime questions.
[Complementary provisions on regional and subregional agreements].

*Section 9. Land-locked countries régime*
(See p. 369).

## PART II CONTINENTAL SHELF

[Provisions to be considered for cases in which the continental shelf extends beyond the limits referred to in article 1].

## PART III INTERNATIONAL SEAS

(See p. 353).

**ECUADOR, PANAMA AND PERU:**
— **Draft Articles on Fisheries in National and International Zones in Ocean Space**

> Submitted at the United Nations Seabed Committee on 10 August 1973, as UN Doc. A/AC.138/SC.II/L.54. Supplementing A/AC.138/SC.II/L.27.

264

## I. Fisheries in zones of national sovereignty and jurisdiction

**Art. A.** It shall be the responsibility of the coastal State to prescribe legal provisions relating to the management and exploitation of living resources in the maritime zone under its sovereignty and jurisdiction, primarily for the purposes of ensuring the conservation and rational utilization of such resources, the development of its fishing and related industries and the improvement of the nutritional levels of peoples.

**Art. B.** The coastal State may reserve the exploitation of living resources in the maritime zone under its sovereignty and jurisdiction to itself or its nationals, having regard to the need to promote the efficient utilization of such resources, economic stability and maximum social benefits.

**Art. C.** Where the coastal State permits nationals of other States to exploit living resources in the maritime zone under its sovereignty and jurisdiction, it shall establish conditions for such exploitation, including, *inter alia*:

(*a*) obtaining fishing and marine hunting licences and permits through payment of the corresponding fees;

(*b*) specifying the species that may be caught;

(*c*) fixing the age and size of the fish or other resources that may be caught;

(*d*) establishing prohibited areas for fishing and hunting;

(*e*) fixing the periods during which the indicated species may be caught;

(*f*) fixing the maximum size of catches;

(*g*) limiting the number and tonnage of the vessels and the gear that may be used;

(*h*) specifying the gear permitted to be used;

(*i*) procedures and penalties applicable in cases of violation.

**Art. D.** 1. In adopting measures to conserve living resources in the maritime zone subject to its sovereignty and jurisdiction, the coastal State shall endeavour to maintain the productivity of species and avoid harmful effects for the survival of living resources outside the said zone.

2. The coastal State shall, for the foregoing purposes, promote any necessary co-operation with other States and with competent international organizations.

**Art. E.** The coastal State may, within the limits of the maritime zone under its sovereignty and jurisdiction, board and inspect foreign-flag fishing or hunting vessels; if it finds evidence or indications of a breach of the legal provisions of the coastal State, it shall proceed to apprehend the vessel in question and take it to port for the corresponding proceedings.

265

**Art. F.** Any dispute concerning fishing or hunting activities by foreign-flag vessels within the zone under the sovereignty and jurisdiction of the coastal State shall be settled by the competent authorities of the coastal State.

II. *Fisheries in international seas*
(See p. 354).

**MALTA:**
— **Preliminary Draft Articles on the Delimitation of Coastal State Jurisdiction in Ocean Space and on the Rights and Obligations of Coastal States in the Area under their Jurisdiction**

> Submitted to the United Nations Seabed Committee on 16 July 1973, as UN Doc. A/AC.138/SC.II/L.28. This is intended to replace and to amplify Parts II and III of A/AC.138/53 (p. 148 of Volume I).

## PART I COASTAL STATE JURISDICTION IN OCEAN SPACE

Chapter 1. *Definitions*

**Art. 1.** National jurisdiction means the legal power of a coastal State to control and regulate a defined area of ocean space adjacent to its coast, subject to limitations of international law designed to protect the interests of the international community.

Ocean space comprises the surface of the sea, the water column and the sea-bed beyond internal waters.

National ocean space means that part of ocean space which is under the jurisdiction of a State.

Sea-bed means (*a*) the floor of the sea or of the ocean and (*b*) the sub-soil or rock underlying the sea floor or the ocean floor.

An island is a naturally formed area of land, more than one square kilometre in area, surrounded by water, which is above water at high tide.

An islet is a naturally formed area of land, less than one square kilometre in area, surrounded by water, which is above water at high tide.

A low-tide elevation is a naturally formed area of land which is surrounded by and above water at low tide but submerged at high tide.

A bay is a well-marked indentation whose penetration is in such proportion to the width of its mouth as to contain land-locked waters and constitute more than a mere curvature of the coast. An indentation shall not be regarded as a bay unless its area is a large as, or larger than, that

266

of the semi-circle whose diameter is a line drawn across the mouth of that indentation.

The term vessel includes boats, ships, submersibles, man-made installations or systems which, whether self-propelled or by some other means moves or can be moved from one part of ocean space to another. Man-made installations do not possess the legal status of vessels when they are joined to the sea-bed in a manner that denotes a degree of permanency.

## Chapter 2. *General*

**Art. 2.** 1. The jurisdiction of a State extends to a belt of ocean space adjacent to its coast, described as national ocean space.

2. This jurisdiction is exercised subject to the provisions of these articles and to other rules of international law.

3. The jurisdiction of a coastal State extends to the air space above national ocean space.

## Chapter 3. *Baselines*

**Art. 3.** 1. The normal baseline for measuring the breadth of national ocean space is the low-water line along the coast as marked on large-scale charts officially recognized by the coastal State and deposited with the international ocean space institutions.

2. The international ocean space institutions shall give wide publicity to the charts deposited with them.

**Art. 4.** 1. In localities where the coastline is deeply indented or if there are islands or islets in the immediate vicinity of the coast the method of straight baselines joining appropriate land points not more than 24 nautical miles apart may be employed in drawing the baselines from which the breadth of national ocean space is measured.

2. The drawing of such baselines must not depart to any appreciable extent from the general direction of the coast and the areas lying within the lines must be sufficiently closely linked to the land domain to be subject to the régime of internal waters.

3. Baselines shall not be drawn to and from low-tide elevations, unless lighthouses or similar installations which are permanent above sea level have been built on them.

4. Baselines shall not be drawn from man-made islands, or from off-shore fixed or floating installations of whatever nature, whether or not joined to the sea-bed.

5. The system of straight baselines may not be applied by a State in such a manner as to cut off from international ocean space the national ocean space of another State.

6. The coastal State must clearly indicate straight baselines on large-scale charts which shall be deposited with the international ocean space institutions.

7. The international ocean space institutions shall give due publicity to the charts deposited. The competent organs of the institutions may object within two years of the deposit of the charts to baselines drawn by the coastal State which do not appear to be consistent with the provisions of these articles: in the event of continued disagreement between the international ocean space institutions and the coastal State the matter shall be submitted for binding adjudication to the International Maritime Court.

**Art. 5.** 1. Waters on the landward side of the baseline of national ocean space form part of the internal waters of a State.

2. Where the establishment of a straight baseline in accordance with article 4 or in accordance with the 1958 Geneva Convention on the Territorial Sea and the Contiguous Zone has, or has had, the effect of enclosing as internal waters areas which previously had been considered as part of the territorial sea or of the high seas, a right of passage as defined in the present Convention shall exist in those waters.

**Art. 6.** 1. If the distance between the low-water marks of the natural entrance points of a bay does not exceed 24 miles, a closing line may be drawn between these two low-water marks and the waters enclosed thereby shall be considered as internal waters.

2. Where the distance between the low-water marks of the natural entrance points of a bay exceeds 24 nautical miles, a straight baseline of 24 nautical miles may be drawn within the bay in such a manner as to enclose the maximum area of water that is possible with a line of that length.

3. The foregoing provisions shall not apply to so-called historic bays or in any case where the straight baseline system provided for in article 4 is applied.

4. Within one year of the entry into force of the present Convention, Contracting Parties shall deposit with the international ocean space institutions a list of historic bays under their jurisdiction. Within two years of the deposit of the lists, the competent organs of the institutions may object to the contents of lists, deposited with them. In the event of continued disagreement between the institutions and the States concerned, the matter shall be submitted to the International Maritime Court for binding adjudication.

**Art. 7.** 1. For the purpose of delimiting national ocean space, the outermost permanent harbour works which form an integral part of a coastal harbour system and which are above water at high tide shall be regarded as forming part of the coast.

2. Floating harbour installations which move or can be moved shall not be regarded as forming an integral part of a coastal harbour system.

**Art. 8.** If a river flows directly into the sea, the baseline shall be a straight line across the mouth of the river between points on the low-tide line of its banks.

Chapter 4. *Limits of national ocean space*

**Art. 9.** Jurisdiction over ocean space may not be claimed by a State by virtue of sovereignty or control over (*a*) reefs and low-tide elevations, whether or not lighthouses or other installations have been built on them; (*b*) islets; (*c*) man-made islands of whatever size; (*d*) fixed or floating installations of whatever nature, whether joined to the sea-bed or not; (*e*) underwater installations or works of whatever nature.

**Art. 10.** 1. When reefs, low-tide elevations and islets are not situated within national ocean space, as defined in article 11, safety zones not exceeding 12 nautical miles in breadth may be established around such reefs, low-tide elevations and islets.

2. When reefs, low-tide elevations and islets are situated within the national ocean space of a State other than the State exercising sovereignty or control over them, the breadth of the safety zones and the regulations to be observed within such zones shall be established by agreement between the States concerned. In the case of disagreement between the States concerned the matter shall be submitted to arbitration or to the International Maritime Court for binding adjudication.

3. When the reefs, low-tide elevations and islets are not situated within the national ocean space of any State, the breadth of the safety zones and the regulations to be observed within such zones shall be established by agreement between the State exercising sovereignty or control and the international ocean space institutions. In the case of disagreement between the institutions and the State exercising sovereignty or control, the matter shall be submitted to arbitration or to the International Maritime Court for binding adjudication.

4. The international ocean space institutions shall pay special regard to the interests of the State exercising sovereignty or control over reefs, islets and low-tide elevations in all matters relating to the uses of ocean space, including exploitation of natural resources, within the safety zones referred to in the foregoing paragraph.

5. The State exercising sovereignty or control over reefs, low-tide elevations and islets has the obligation to erect and maintain on them lighthouses or other facilities designed to reduce dangers to navigation.

**Art. 11.** 1. The jurisdiction of a State may extend to a belt of ocean space adjacent to its coast, the breadth of which is 200 nautical miles measured from baselines drawn in accordance with the provisions of chapter III of this Convention.

2. The jurisdiction of an island State or of an archipelago State may extend to a belt of ocean space adjacent to the coast of the principal island or islands, the breadth of which is 200 nautical miles measured from baselines drawn in accordance with the provisions of chapter III of this Convention. The principal island or islands of an archipelago State shall be designated by the State concerned and notified to the international ocean space institutions. In the event of disagreement with the designations made by the archipelago State any Contracting Party may submit the matter to the International Maritime Court for binding adjudication.

3. When islands are less than 10 square kilometres in area, the jurisdiction of the State exercising sovereignty or control may extend only to a belt of ocean space, adjacent to the coasts of such an island, the breadth of which does not exceed 12 nautical miles measured from the applicable baseline.

*Special rules concerning atolls*

**Art. 12.** Atolls are a chain of islands or islets crowning a circular or oval reef which encloses a lagoon.

**Art. 13.** 1. In the case of atolls, the baseline for measuring the breadth of national ocean space is the seaward edge of the reef whether or not the reef is submerged at high tide.

2. If the distance between the low-water marks of the natural entrance points of the reef does not exceed 24 nautical miles, a closing line may be drawn between these low-water marks and the waters enclosed thereby shall be considered as internal waters.

3. Where the distance between the low-water marks of the natural entrance points of the reef exceeds 24 nautical miles, straight baselines of 24 nautical miles may be drawn within the reef in such a manner as to enclose the maximum area of water that is possible with lines of that length.

**Art. 14.** 1. Jurisdiction over ocean space outside the area enclosed by the reef may not be claimed by a State by virtue of sovereignty or control over an atoll when the total land area of the islets crowning the reef does not exceed one square kilometre.

2. When the islands or islets crowning the reef of an atoll have a total land area exceeding one square kilometre but less than 10 square kilometres, the jurisdiction of the State exercising sovereignty or control may extend to a belt of ocean space adjacent to the outer edge of the reef the

breadth of which does not exceed 12 nautical miles.

**Art. 15.** The extent of jurisdiction over ocean space which may be claimed by a State by virtue of sovereignty or control over islands and atolls other than those referred to in the foregoing articles of this chapter shall be determined in a special convention or conventions to be negotiated within the framework of the international ocean space institutions, taking into account all relevant circumstances.

**Art. 16.** The outer limit of national ocean space is the line every point of which is at a distance from the nearest point of the baseline equal to the breadth of national ocean space.

**Art. 17.** 1. Contracting Parties agree to surrender against equitable and appropriate compensation their claims to jurisdiction over the sea-bed or waters beyond the limits indicated in these articles.

2. The compensation referred to in the foregoing paragraph shall be determined by the international ocean space institutions in the light of all relevant factors, including the known resources of the areas of ocean space surrendered and the practical possibilities of exploration. In the event that the compensation proffered by the international ocean space institutions is considered inadequate by the Contracting Party concerned, the matter shall be submitted for binding adjudication to the International Maritime Court.

3. No compensation may be proffered by the international ocean space institutions in the case of surrender of claims to jurisdiction over areas of ocean space adjacent to (*a*) reefs and low-tide elevations; (*b*) man-made islands; (*c*) fixed or floating installations of whatever nature; (*d*) underwater installations or works of whatever nature; (*e*) islets situated within the national ocean space of a State other than the State exercising sovereignty or control over them.

**Art. 18.** Ocean space not comprised within the limits indicated in the foregoing articles forms part of international ocean space, not part of which is subject to national jurisdiction for any purpose.

Chapter 5. *Delimitation of national ocean space*

**Art. 19.** 1. Where two or more States, whose coasts are opposite each other, are separated by an area of ocean space less than 400 nautical miles in breadth, the boundary of national ocean space appertaining to such States shall be the median line every point of which is equidistant from the nearest points of the baselines from which the breadth of national ocean space of each State is measured.

2. Where two States are adjacent to each other the boundary of ocean space appertaining to such States shall be determined by the application

of the principle of equidistance from the nearest points of the baselines from which the breadth of national ocean space is measured.

3. The provisions of the foregoing paragraphs shall not apply where it is necessary by reason of historic title or other exceptional circumstance to delimit the national ocean space of the States opposite or adjacent to each other in a manner which is at variance with those provisions.

4. In the event of disagreement between States opposite or adjacent to each other with regard to the manner of delimitation of their respective national ocean space, the matter shall be submitted to arbitration or to the International Maritime Court for binding adjudication at the request of any of the States concerned.

5. In the event of disagreement between a coastal State or States and the international ocean space institutions with regard to the manner of delimitation of international ocean space and national ocean space respectively, the matter shall be submitted to arbitration or to the International Maritime Court for binding adjudication at the request of any Parties concerned.

6. The lines of delimitation between the national ocean space of two States lying opposite or adjacent to each other shall be marked on large-scale charts officially recognized by the States concerned and deposited with the international ocean space institutions.

## PART II RIGHTS AND OBLIGATIONS OF THE COASTAL STATE WITHIN NATIONAL OCEAN SPACE

Chapter 6. *Navigation* - Chapter 7. *Overflight*
(See p. 307).

Chapter 8. *Submarine cables*

**Art. 53.** Subject to the provisions of these articles, all States, whether coastal or not, shall enjoy the right to lay and to maintain submarine cables on the sea-bed of national ocean space.

**Art. 54.** The coastal State must not hamper the exercise of the right to lay or to maintain submarine cables on the sea-bed of national ocean space beyond 12 nautical miles from the coast when cables are laid in accordance with such general and non-discriminatory regulations as may be adopted by the international ocean space institutions or as are contained in widely ratified multilateral conventions.

**Art. 55.** In the absence of relevant regulations adopted by the international ocean space institutions or contained in widely ratified multilateral conventions, the coastal State may enact reasonable and non-discriminatory

272

regulations relating to the laying of submarine cables in national ocean space.

**Art. 56.** 1. Coastal State regulations mentioned in the foregoing article may be brought to the attention of the international ocean space institutions by any Contracting Party when these regulations are considered discriminatory or unreasonable or inconsistent with regulations adopted by the institutions or contained in widely ratified multilateral conventions.

2. The international ocean space institutions may recommend that the coastal State rescind or modify regulations which are found to be discriminatory or to constitute an unreasonable impediment to the exercise of the right to lay submarine cables or to be inconsistent with regulations adopted by the institutions.

3. In the event of continued disagreement between the international ocean space institutions and the coastal State, the matter shall be submitted to the International Maritime Court for binding adjudication.

**Art. 57.** 1. When laying submarine cables due regard shall be paid to cables already in position on the sea-bed: in particular the possibility of repairing existing cables shall not be prejudiced.

2. Failure to comply with the provisions of the foregoing paragraph entails legal responsibility.

**Art. 58.** 1. States and persons under their jurisdiction which own submarine cables in the national ocean space of another State shall transmit to that State and to the international ocean space institutions a chart showing the position of the cables owned.

2. The coastal State has the obligation to protect submarine cables shown on charts transmitted to it.

**Art. 59.** Every State shall take the necessary legislative measures to provide that the breaking or injury by a vessel flying its flag or by a person subject to its jurisdiction of a submarine cable in the national ocean space of another State done wilfully or through culpable negligence shall be a punishable offence. This provision shall not apply to any break or injury caused by persons who acted merely with the legitimate object of saving their lives or vessels, after having taken all necessary precautions to avoid such break or injury.

**Art. 60.** 1. Every State shall take the necessary legislative measures to provide that any persons who cause a break in, or injury to, a submarine cable shall bear the cost of repairs.

2. Every State shall take the necessary legislative measures to ensure that owners of vessels who can prove that they sacrificed an anchor, a net or any fishing or other gear to avoid injuring a submarine cable in national ocean space shall be indemnified by the owner of the cable, provided that

the owner of the vessel has taken all reasonable precautionary measures beforehand.

**Art. 61.** Failure to take the measures mentioned in articles 58, 59 and 60 may be brought to the attention of the international ocean space institutions by any Contracting Party when interruption or obstruction has been caused to telegraphic or telephonic communications or to the supply of electric energy.

**Art. 62.** 1. The laying of submarine cables in a belt of ocean space adjacent to the coast not exceeding 12 nautical miles in breadth measured from the applicable baseline is subject to authorization of the coastal State.

2. The coastal State shall not normally withhold its authorization if the application is submitted by a responsible entity which gives assurance of abiding by the laws and regulations of the coastal State.

Chapter 9. *Scientific Research*
(See p. 428).

Chapter 10. *Peaceful uses*

**Art. 76.** No State may utilize the sea-bed of national ocean space of another State for military purposes without the latter's consent.

**Art. 77.** 1. Nuclear or thermonuclear weapon test explosions and the emplacement of nuclear weapons or other weapons of mass destruction on the sea-bed are prohibited in national ocean space.

2. The foregoing provision shall not affect the rights of the coastal State under the 1971 Treaty on the Prohibition of the Emplacement of Nuclear Weapons and Other Weapons of Mass Destruction on the Sea-Bed and the Ocean Floor and in the Subsoil Thereof.

**Art. 78.** Nuclear and thermonuclear explosions for peaceful purposes in national ocean spare are permitted only with the authorization of the international ocean space institutions.

**Art. 79.** Non-compliance with the provisions of the foregoing articles may be brought to the attention of the international ocean space institutions by any Contracting Party.

Chapter 11. *Exploitation of natural resources*

**Art. 80.** 1. The exploration and exploitation of the natural resources of national ocean space shall be conducted with reasonable regard to other uses of national ocean space, in particular navigation, scientific research and the laying and repair of submarine cables and pipelines.

2. The coastal State shall have the obligation to transfer to the inter-

national ocean space institutions a portion of the financial benefits received from the exploitation of the natural resources of national ocean space. The institutions shall prepare a special draft convention on this matter for consideration by Contracting Parties.

Chapter 12. *Living resources of national ocean space*

**Art. 81.** 1. The term "conservation of living resources" means the aggregate of measures rendering possible the optimum sustainable yield from such resources.

2. Conservation programmes shall be formulated with a view to securing in the first place a supply of food for human consumption.

**Art. 82.** 1. It shall be the responsibility in the first instance of the coastal State to formulate and implement appropriate and effective programmes of conservation of the living resources of national ocean space. Such conservation programmes shall not discriminate between national and foreign fishermen and shall be based on appropriate and reliable scientific findings.

2. Conservation programmes shall include:

(*a*) measures of biological management which may be necessary or desirable to maintain or increase the stock of living resources of national ocean space;

(*b*) measures of economic management which may be necessary or desirable to maintain fishing effort in national ocean space at levels providing maximum net returns in relation to potential sustained catch;

(*c*) measures of regulation—including, *inter alia*, licensing, closed areas, closed seasons, limitations on size and condition of specific living resources which may be caught and limitations on type of gear—designed to render possible the successful implementation of measures of biological and economic management.

3. Programmes of conservation of the living resources of national ocean space shall be given due publicity by the coastal State and shall be communicated to the international ocean space institutions.

**Art. 83.** 1. In view of the vital interest of the international community in the maintenance of the productivity of fisheries, the coastal State has the obligation:

(*a*) to consult with other States in the region and with the international ocean space institutions before undertaking or permitting activities in national ocean space which could substantially reduce the living resources of ocean space outside its jurisdiction;

(*b*) to maintain the quality of the marine environment in national ocean space in a state which (i) does not adversely affect fish-spawning areas within its jurisdiction; (ii) does not produce significant deleterious

275

effects on the living resources of ocean space outside its jurisdiction;

(c) to co-operate with the international ocean space institutions in the formulation and implementation of programmes of conservation of living resources of its national ocean space when the recommendations of the institutions are based on reliable and appropriate scientific findings;

(d) to co-operate with coastal States in the region in the formulation and implementation of programmes of conservation of the living resources of national ocean space when there is need for the application of regional conservation measures in the light of the existing knowledge of the fishery.

**Art. 84.** 1. The international ocean space institutions, and persons or entities under their sponsorship, may conduct in national ocean space beyond 12 nautical miles from the coast, giving prior notice thereof to the coastal State, investigations for the purpose of obtaining such biological samples and scientific information relating to the living resources of ocean space as may be necessary to formulate rational and effective programmes of conservation.

2. The coastal State shall be offered reasonable opportunity to appoint its nationals to participate in the investigations mentioned in the foregoing paragraph and, in any case, shall be provided with the full data obtained and an interpretation thereof by the international ocean space institutions.

3. The international ocean space institutions have the obligation to assist at its request any State to formulate and to implement appropriate and effective programmes of conservation of the living resources of its national ocean space.

**Art. 85.** The international ocean space institutions and the coastal State or States concerned shall elaborate in close consultation and shall implement through appropriate regional bodies programmes for the conservation of such living resources of national ocean space the migratory range of which extends into international ocean space. The living resources to which reference is made include, *inter alia*, anadromous resources and sea mammals.

**Art. 86.** Disagreements between coastal States or between the international ocean space institutions and a coastal State relating to matters contained in articles 83 and 85 shall be submitted to the International Maritime Court for binding adjudication.

**Art. 87.** Every State shall take the necessary legislative measures to provide that violations of programmes of conservation of living resources adopted by the coastal State, or jointly by the coastal State and the international ocean space institutions, by vessels flying its flag or persons subject to its jurisdiction shall be a punishable offence.

**Art. 88.** 1. The coastal State may reserve to its nationals the exploitation of some or of all the living resources of its national ocean space.

2. The international ocean space institutions and the coastal State or States concerned shall elaborate and implement in close consultation, if necessary through appropriate regional bodies, non-discriminatory programmes for the exploitation of such living resources of national ocean space the migratory range of which extends into international ocean space.

3. Nothing in the foregoing paragraphs shall affect traditional subsistence fishing or the catching of fish for immediate human consumption by foreign fishermen in national ocean space: such activities shall be defined and regulated in special conventions negotiated between States in the region.

4. Notwithstanding the provisions of subparagraph 1, the coastal State has an obligation to provide adjacent land-locked countries with access to the living resources of its national ocean space on conditions similar to those applicable to its own nationals.

**Art. 89.** 1. The coastal State has the obligation to exploit, or permit the exploitation of, the living resources of its national ocean space in accordance with appropriate and effective programmes of conservation.

2. Failure to comply with the provisions of the foregoing paragraph entails legal liability for damages and may be brought to the attention of the international ocean space institutions, when such failure causes a significant reduction of fish stocks or produces significant deleterious effects on the living resources of ocean space outside the jurisdiction of the coastal State.

**Art. 90.** 1. The coastal State may inspect with due consideration in its national ocean space foreign flag fishing and fish processing vessels.

2. The coastal State may seize a foreign flag fishing or fish processing vessel and its cargo and arrest the persons on board when upon inspection it is found that the vessel has gravely and intentionally violated programmes of conservation of living resources, or when it is found that the vessel had engaged in fishing in national ocean space in contravention of the laws of the coastal State.

3. The coastal State shall promptly inform the consular authorities of the flag State of the offending vessel and, if the captain so requests, the international ocean space institutions, of the measures taken with respect to the vessel, its cargo and crew.

4. The courts of the coastal State shall in the first instance be competent to adjudicate the offences to which reference is made in paragraph 2. The captain and crew of the offending vessel shall have access to legal assistance of their choice and, before trial, shall be subject only to such personal restraint as may be necessary to prevent their departure from the jurisdiction of the competent court of the coastal State. The flag State of

the offending vessel shall be promptly informed of the disposition of the case.

5. Appeal from the courts of the coastal State shall lie to the International Maritime Court.

**Art. 91.** Activities of foreign fishing and fish processing vessels within national ocean space as defined in article 11 shall be brought into conformity with the provisions of article 88 within five years of the entry into force of this convention.

### Chapter 13. *Mineral and other non-living resources of national ocean space*

**Art. 92.** It shall be the responsibility of the coastal State to formulate and implement such programmes of conservation of the mineral and other non-living resources of national ocean space as may appear to be necessary or desirable.

**Art. 93.** 1. The coastal State may reserve to its nationals the exploitation of the mineral and other non-living resources of national ocean space.

2. Notwithstanding the provisions of the foregoing paragraph, the coastal State has an obligation to provide adjacent land-locked countries with access to the mineral and other non-living resources of its national ocean space on conditions similar to those applicable to its own nationals.

**Art. 94.** 1. The exploitation of the mineral resources of national ocean space by a coastal State must not cause significant change in the natural state of the marine environment of ocean space beyond its jurisdiction or significant interference with navigation, scientific research or the laying and repair of submarine cables and pipelines.

2. The coastal State has the obligation to take special precautions before undertaking or authorizing the exploitation of petroleum and natural gas in areas of national ocean space subject to frequent natural disasters.

3. Non-compliance with the provisions contained in the foregoing paragraph entails legal responsibility and may be brought to the attention of the international ocean space institutions by any Contracting Party.

**Art. 95.** 1. If any single geological petroleum or natural gas structure or field or any single geological structure or field of any other mineral deposit extends across the line dividing the national ocean space of two or more coastal States, they shall seek to reach agreement as to the manner in which the structure or field can be most efficiently exploited and the manner in which the costs and proceeds relating thereto shall be apportioned.

2. In the event of disagreement between the coastal States concerned, the matter shall be submitted to arbitration or to the International Ma-

ritime Court for an advisory opinion at the request of any of the States concerned.

3. The provisions of the foregoing paragraphs shall apply also to the international ocean space institutions in the event that a petroleum or natural gas structure or field or any single geological field or structure of any other mineral deposit extends across the line dividing national ocean space from international ocean space.

Chapter 14. *Waste Disposal and Storage*
(See p. 389).

Chapter 15. *Submarine pipelines*

**Art. 100.** 1. No State may utilize the national ocean space of another State for the purpose of laying submarine pipelines without the consent of that State.

2. Notwithstanding the provisions of the foregoing paragraph, the coastal State may not impede the maintenance of submarine pipelines already in position on the sea-bed of its national ocean space.

**Art. 101.** 1. Every coastal State may utilize its national ocean space for the purpose of laying submarine pipelines, provided that:

(*a*)  due regard is paid to pipelines already in position on the sea-bed;

(*b*)  the possibility of repairing existing pipelines is not prejudiced;

(*c*)  the pipelines conform to such international standards of construction as may be adopted by the international ocean space institutions;

(*d*)  the pipelines cause no significant interference with other uses of ocean space and in particular with navigation, the exploitation of living resources and the laying and maintenance of submarine cables.

2. Every coastal State has the obligation to take and enforce in its national ocean space strict precautions in the construction, siting and maintenance of submarine pipelines containing petroleum or substances which may cause serious deleterious effects to human health, to the living resources or to the quality of the marine environment. No such pipelines shall be laid in areas subject to frequent natural disasters.

3. Failure on the part of the coastal State to comply with the provisions contained in the foregoing paragraphs of this article entails legal responsibility and the payment of damages in the event of significant deleterious effects on ocean space or its resources outside the jurisdiction of that State.

**Art. 102.** 1. States and persons under their jurisdiction which own or administer submarine pipelines in the national ocean space of another State shall transmit to that State and to the international ocean space institutions a chart showing the position of the submarine pipelines owned or administered by them.

2. The coastal State has the obligation to protect submarine pipelines shown on the charts transmitted to it.

**Art. 103.** Every State shall take the necessary legislative measures to provide that the breaking or injury by a vessel flying its flag or by a person subject to its jurisdiction of a submarine pipeline in the national ocean space of another State done wilfully or through culpable negligence shall be a serious punishable offence. This provision shall not apply to any break or injury caused by persons who acted merely with the legitimate object of saving their lives or vessels after having taken all necessary precautions to avoid such break or injury.

**Art. 104.** 1. Every State shall take the necessary legislative measures to provide that any persons who cause a break in, or injury to, a submarine pipeline shall bear the cost of repairs and shall be responsible for the payment of damages in the event that deleterious effects have been caused to the quality of the marine environment or to the living resources therein.

2. Every State shall take the necessary legislative measures to ensure that owners of vessels who can prove that they sacrificed an anchor, a net or any fishing or other gear to avoid injuring a submarine pipeline in national ocean space shall be indemnified by the owner of the pipeline provided that the owner of the vessel has taken all reasonable precautionary measures beforehand.

**Art. 105.** Failure to take the precautions and measures mentioned in articles 101 and 102 may be brought to the attention of the international ocean space institutions by any Contracting Party when interruption has been caused to the flow of petroleum, water, gas or other substance contained in the pipeline.

## Chapter 16. *Other non-extractive uses*

Other uses of national ocean space may conveniently be classified as:
    (*a*) uses of the subsoil of the sea-bed;
    (*b*) uses of the surface of the sea-bed;
    (*c*) uses of the water column;
    (*d*) uses of the surface of the sea.

These latter in turn may involve man-made islands—that is, islands created by man from natural materials, dredged or otherwise transported, to form an area of land surrounded by water which is above water at high tide—surface installations, systems and devices permanently joined to the sea-bed created from man-made materials, floating installations, systems and devices joined to the sea-bed but which can be moved, floating installations and systems which are dynamically positioned and floating systems and devices which are neither joined to the sea-bed nor dynamically positioned.

From the point of view of jurisdictional areas, man-made islands, off-shore installations, systems and devices may be located in national ocean space (including a belt of ocean space adjacent to the coast not more than 12 nautical miles in breadth) or in international ocean space.

From the point of view or activities, man-made islands, offshore installations, systems and devices (whether installed on the surface of the sea, in the water column or on or under the sea-bed) may be used for some or all of the following purposes:

(a) military purposes;

(b) scientific purposes;

(c) industrial purposes;

(d) mineral extractive purposes, including extraction of minerals from sea water;

(e) international communications purposes (off-shore harbours, air-ports, telecommunications, etc.);

(f) international community purposes (monitoring marine environment for pollution; aids to navigation, etc.);

(g) energy production purposes, including nuclear energy production;

(h) other purposes.

In view of the multiplicity of purposes for which man-made islands, offshore installations, systems and devices can be used, it would appear desirable to clarify the present state of technology, the practical purposes for which such islands, installations and devices may be used, and the implications of such uses for international order in ocean space, for navigation, fisheries and other activities before suggesting detailed regulations with regard to safety zones, jurisdictional questions, standards, harmonization with other activities of vital international interest, etc.

## CHINA:
## — Working Paper on Sea Area within the Limits of National Jurisdiction

Submitted to the United Nations Seabed Committee on 16 July 1973, as UN Doc. A/AC.138/SC.II/L.34.

### I. Territorial Sea

(1) The territorial sea, as delimited by a coastal State by virtue of sovereignty, is a specified area of sea adjacent to its coast or internal waters, including the airspace over the territorial sea and its bed and sub-soil thereof, over which it exercises sovereignty.

(2) A coastal State is entitled to reasonably define the breadth and limits of its territorial sea according to its geographical features and its needs of economic development and national security and having due

regard to the legitimate interests of its neighbouring countries and the convenience of international navigation, and shall give publicity thereto.

(3) Coastal States in the same region may, through consultations on an equal footing, define a unified breadth or a limit for the territorial sea in the region.

(4) Coastal States adjacent or opposite to each other shall define the boundaries between their territorial seas on the principles of mutual respect for sovereignty and territorial integrity, equality and reciprocity.

(5) The breadth and limits of the territorial sea as defined by a coastal State are, in principle, applicable to the islands belonging to that State.

(6) An archipelago or an island chain consisting of islands close to each other may be taken as an integral whole in defining the limits of the territorial sea around it.

(7) A strait lying within the territorial sea, whether or not it is frequently used for international navigation, forms an inseparable part of the territorial sea of the coastal State.

(8) A coastal State may, for the purpose of regulation of its territorial sea, enact necessary laws and regulations and give publicity thereto. Ships and aircraft of a foreign State, passing through the territorial sea and the airspace thereabove of another State, shall comply with the laws and regulations of the latter State.

Foreign non-military ships enjoy innocent passage through territorial seas.

Passage is innocent when it is not prejudicial to the peace, security and good order of a coastal State.

A coastal State may, in accordance with its laws and regulations, require military ships of foreign States to tender prior notification to, or seek prior approval from, its competent authorities before passing through its territorial sea.

## II. *Exclusive Economic Zone or Exclusive Fishery Zone*

(1) A coastal State may reasonably define an exclusive economic zone (hereinafter referred to as the economic zone) beyond and adjacent to its territorial sea in accordance with its geographical and geological conditions, the state of its natural resources and its needs of national economic development.

The outer limit of the economic zone may not, in maximum, exceed 200 nautical miles measured from the baseline of the territorial sea.

(2) All natural resources within the economic zone of a coastal State, including living and non-living resources of the whole water column, seabed and its subsoil, are owned by the coastal State.

A coastal State exercises exclusive jurisdiction over its economic zone for the purpose of protecting, using, exploring and exploiting the resources as described in the preceding paragraph.

(3) A coastal State shall, in principle, grant to the landlocked and shelf-locked States adjacent to its territory common enjoyment of a certain proportion of the rights of ownership in its economic zone. The coastal State and its adjacent landlocked and shelf-locked States shall, through consultations on the basis of equality and mutual respect for sovereignty, conclude bilateral or regional agreements on the relevant matters.

(4) The normal navigation and overflight on the water surface of and in the airspace above the economic zone by ships and aircraft of all States shall not be prejudiced. The delineation of the course for laying cables and pipelines in the sea-bed of the economic zone is subject to the consent of the coastal State.

(5) Other States may engage in fishery, mining or other activities in the economic zone of a coastal State pursuant to agreement reached with the coastal State.

(6) A coastal State may enact necessary laws and regulations for the effective regulation of its economic zone.

Other States, in carrying out any activities in the economic zone of a coastal State, are required to observe the relevant laws and regulations of the coastal State.

(7) A coastal State is entitled, when necessary, to deal with unauthorized fishery, mining or other activities in its economic zone and with violations of its relevant laws and regulations even though permission for such activities has been given.

(8) The delimitation of boundaries between the economic zones of coastal States adjacent or opposite to each other shall be jointly determined through consultations on a equal footing.

Coastal States adjacent or opposite to each other shall, on the basis of safeguarding and respecting the sovereignty of each other, conduct necessary consultations to work out reasonable solutions for the exploitation, regulation and other matters relating to the natural resources in the contiguous parts of their economic zones.

(9) The above provisions relating to the economic zone shall also apply to the exclusive fishery zone as reasonably defined by a coastal State beyond its territorial sea, except that the resources in the exclusive fishery zone are confined to the living resources of the water column in the said fishery zone.

### III. Continental Shelf

(1) By virtue of the principle that the continental shelf is the natural prolongation of the continental territory, a coastal State may reasonably define, according to its specific geographical conditions, the limits of the continental shelf under its exclusive jurisdiction beyond its territorial sea

or economic zone. The maximum limits of such continental shelf may be determined among States through consultations.

(2) The natural resources of the continental shelf, including the mineral resources of the sea-bed and subsoil and the living resources of sedentary species, appertain to the coastal State.

(3) The superjacent waters of the continental shelf beyond the territorial sea, the economic zone or the fishery zone are not subject to the jurisdiction of the coastal State.

The normal navigation and overflight on the superjacent wa s of the continental shelf and in the airspace thereabove by ships and aircraft of all States shall not be prejudiced.

(4) A coastal State may enact all necessary laws and regulations for the effective management of its continental shelf.

The delineation of the course for laying submarine cables and pipelines on the continental shelf by a foreign State is subject to the consent of the coastal State.

(5) States adjacent or opposite to each other, the continental shelves of which connect together, shall jointly determine the delimitation of the limits of jurisdiction of the continental shelves through consultations on an equal footing.

(6) States adjacent or opposite to each other, the continental shelves of which connect together, shall, on the basis of safeguarding and respecting the sovereignty of each other, conduct necessary consultations to work out reasonable solutions for the exploitation, regulation and other matters relating to the natural resources in their contiguous parts of the continental shelves.

## UNITED STATES OF AMERICA:
### — Draft Articles for a Chapter on the Rights and Duties of States in the Coastal Seabed Economic Area

Submitted to the United Nations Seabed Committee on 16 July 1973, as UN Doc. A/AC.138/SC.II/L.35.

**Art. 1.** 1. The coastal State shall have the exclusive right to explore and exploit and authorize the exploration and exploitation of the natural resources of the seabed and subsoil in accordance with its own laws and regulations in the Coastal Seabed Economic Area.

2. The Coastal Seabed Economic Area is the area of the seabed which is

(a) seaward of ———; and
(b) landward of an outer boundary of ———

284

3. The coastal State shall in addition have the exclusive right to authorize and regulate in the Coastal Seabed Economic Area or the superjacent waters:

(*a*) the construction, operation and use of offshore installations affecting its economic interests, and

(*b*) drilling for purposes other than exploration and exploitation of resources.

4. The coastal State may, where necessary, establish reasonable safety zones around such offshore installations in which it may take appropriate measures to protect persons, property, and the marine environment. Such safety zones shall be designed to ensure that they are reasonably related to the nature and function of the installation. The breadth of the safety zones shall be determined by the coastal State and shall conform to international standards in existence or to be established pursuant to Article 3.

5. (*a*) For the purposes of this Chapter, the term "installations" refers to all offshore facilities, installations, or devices other than those which are mobile in their normal mode of operation at sea.

(*b*) Installations do not possess the status of islands. They have no territorial sea or Coastal Seabed Economic Area of their own, and their presence does not affect the delimitation of the territorial sea of the coastal State.

6. The coastal State may, with respect to the activities set forth in this Article, apply standards for the protection of the marine environment higher than those required by applicable international standards pursuant to Article 2.

7. The coastal State may, with respect to the activities set forth in this Article, take all necessary measures to ensure compliance with its laws and regulations subject to the provisions of this Chapter.

**Art. 2.** The coastal State, in exercising the rights referred to in Article 1, shall ensure that its laws and regulations, and any other actions it takes pursuant thereto in the Coastal Seabed Economic Area, are in strict conformity with the provisions of this Chapter and other applicable provisions of this Convention, and in particular:

(*a*) the coastal State shall ensure that there is no unjustifiable interference with other activities in the marine environment, and shall ensure compliance with international standards in existence or promulgated by the Authority or the Inter-Governmental Maritime Consultative Organization, as appropriate, to prevent such interference;

(*b*) the coastal State shall take appropriate measures to prevent pollution of the marine environment from the activities set forth in Article 1 and shall ensure compliance with international standards in existence or promulgated by the Authority or the Inter-Governmental Maritime

Consultative Organization, as appropriate, to prevent such pollution;

(c) the coastal State shall not impede, and shall co-operate with the Authority in the exercise of its inspection functions in connection with subparagraph (b) above;

(d) the coastal State shall ensure that licenses, leases, or other contractual arrangements which it enters into with the agencies or instrumentalities of other States, or with natural or juridical persons which are not nationals of the coastal State, for the purpose of exploring for or exploiting seabed resources are strictly observed according to their terms. Property of such agencies, instrumentalities or persons shall not be taken except for a public purpose, on a non-discriminatory basis, nor shall it be taken without the prompt payment of just compensation. Such compensation shall be in an effectively realizable form and shall represent the full equivalent of the property taken and adequate provision shall have been made at or prior to the time of the taking to ensure compliance with the provisions of this paragraph;

(e) the coastal State shall make available in accordance with the provisions of Article ———, such share of revenues in respect of mineral resource exploitation from such part of the Coastal Seabed Economic Area as is specified in that Article.

**Art. 3.** 1. All activities in the marine environment shall be conducted with reasonable regard to the rights of the coastal State referred to in Article 1.

2. States shall ensure compliance with international standards in existence or to be promulgated by Inter-Governmental Maritime Consultative Organization in consultation with the Authority:

(a) regarding the breadth, if any, of safety zones around offshore installations;

(b) regarding navigation outside the safety zones, but in the vicinity of offshore installations.

**Art. 4.** Nothing in this Chapter shall affect the rights of freedom of navigation and overflight and other rights to carry on activities unrelated to seabed resource, exploration and exploitation in accordance with general principles of international law, except as otherwise specifically provided in this Convention.

**Art. 5.** 1. Any dispute between two or more Contracting Parties with respect to the interpretation or application of this Chapter shall, if requested by any party to the dispute, be resolved by the compulsory dispute settlement procedure contained in Article ———, of Chapter ———.

2. In the case of a dispute involving a violation of Article 2 (d) of this Chapter, if the Contracting Party of which a natural or juridical person is

a national has not brought a complaint under paragraph 1 of this Article, such person may submit the dispute for settlement in accordance with the 1962 Rules of Arbitration and Conciliation for Settlement of International Disputes Between Two Parties of Which Only One Is a State, adopted by the Permanent Court of Arbitration.

## ARGENTINA:
— **Draft Articles**

Submitted to the United Nations Seabed Committee on 16 July 1973, as UN Doc. A/AC.138/SC.II/L.37.

1. The sovereignty of a coastal State extends to a belt of sea adjacent to its coast, described as the territorial sea, and to the air space, bed and subsoil of that sea.

2. It is for each State to fix the breadth of its territorial sea up to a maximum distance of 12 nautical miles measured from the applicable baselines.

3. Ships of all States, whether coastal or not, shall enjoy the right of innocent passage through the territorial sea in accordance with the following provisions:

3.1 ... (definition of "innocent passage").

3.2 ... (precise determination of the regulatory powers of the coastal State).

4. A coastal State has sovereign rights over an area of sea adjacent to its territorial sea up to a distance of 200 nautical miles measured from the baseline from which the breadth of the territorial sea is measured or up to a greater distance coincident with the epicontinental sea.

For the purposes of this and the succeeding articles, the term "epicontinental sea" means the column of water covering the seabed and subsoil which are situated at an average depth of 200 metres.

The scope of the above-mentioned rights is laid down in the succeeding articles.

5. It is for each coastal State to fix the breadth of the area adjacent to its territorial sea up to the maximum distance prescribed in artcle 4, in accordance with criteria which take into account the regional geographical, geological, ecological, economic and social factors involved and interests relating to the preservation of the marine environment.

6. The delimitation of that area between two or more States shall be effected in accordance with the principles of international law.

7. A coastal State has sovereign rights over the renewable and non-renewable natural resources, living and non-living, which are to be found

in the said area.

8. States in a particular region or subregion which for geographical or economic reasons do not see fit to extend their sovereign rights to an exclusive maritime area adjacent to their territorial sea shall enjoy a preferential régime for purposes of fishing in the exclusive maritime areas of other States belonging to the region or subregion, such régime to be determined by bilateral agreements providing for a fair adjustment of their mutual interests.

The said régime shall be granted provided that the enterprises of the State which wishes to exploit the resources in question are effectively controlled by capital and nationals of that State and that the ships which operate in the area fly the flag of that State.

9. The prospecting and exploration of the maritime area adjacent to the territorial sea and the exploitation of the natural resources existing therein are subject to the regulations of the coastal States concerned, which may reserve those activities to themselves or to their nationals or may allow third parties to engage in them in accordance with the provisions of their internal laws and of such international agreements as they may conclude on the matter.

10. The protection and conservation of renewable resources existing in the area are likewise subject to the regulations of the coastal States concerned and to such agreements as they may conclude on the matter, taking into account, where relevant, co-operation with other States and the recommendations of international technical bodies.

11. A coastal State shall also have jurisdiction to enforce in the maritime area adjacent to its territorial sea such measures as it may enact in order to prevent, mitigate or eliminate pollution damage and risks and other effects harmful or dangerous to the ecosystem of the marine environment, the quality and use of water, living resources, human health and the recreation of its people, taking into account co-operation with other States and in accordance with internationally agreed principles and standards.

12. It is also for the coastal State to authorize such scientific research activities as are carried on in the area; it is entitled to participate in them and to receive the results obtained. In such regulations as the coastal State may issue on the matter, the desirability of promoting and facilitating such activities shall be taken especially into account.

13. In the maritime area adjacent to the territorial sea, ships and aircraft of all States, whether coastal or not, have the right to free navigation and overflight without restrictions other than those which may result from the exercise by the coastal State of its rights in the matters of exploration, conservation and exploitation of resources, pollution and scientific research. Subject solely to these limitations, there shall also be freedom to lay submarine cables and pipelines.

288

14. Through bilateral and, where appropriate, subregional agreements, a coastal State shall facilitate for neighbouring States having no sea-coast the right of access to the sea and of transit. In the same way agreement shall be reached with States having no sea-coast on an equitable régime for the exercise in the maritime area of fishing rights which shall be preferential in relation to third States. The said preferential rights shall be granted provided that the enterprises of the State which wishes to exploit the resources in question are effectively controlled by capital and nationals of that State and that the ships which operate in the area fly the flag of that State.

15. The sovereignty of a coastal State extends to its continental shelf. The continental shelf comprises the bed and subsoil of the submarine areas adjacent to the territory of the State but outside the area of the territorial sea, up to the outer lower edge of the continental margin which adjoins the abyssal plains or, when that edge is at a distance of less than 200 miles from the coast, up to that distance.

16. The rights of the coastal State over the continental shelf do not affect the legal régime of the superjacent waters or air space.

17. The rights of the coastal State over the continental shelf do not depend on occupation, effective or national, or on any proclamation.

18. A coastal State has sovereignty over the renewable and non-renewable natural resources of its continental shelf. The said resources include the mineral and other non-living resources of the seabed and subsoil together with living vegetable organisms and animals belonging to sedentary species, that is to say, animals which, at the harvestable stage, either are immobile on or under the seabed or are unable to move except in constant physical contact with the seabed or the subsoil.

19. The prospecting and exploration of the continental shelf and the exploitation of its natural resources are subject to the regulations of the coastal States concerned, which may reserve those activities to themselves or to their nationals or may allow third parties also to engage in them in accordance with the provisions of their internal laws and of such international agreements as they may conclude on the matter.

20. The protection and conservation of renewable resources existing on the continental shelf are likewise subject to the regulations of the coastal States concerned and to such agreements as they may conclude on the matter, taking into account, where relevant, co-operation with other States and the recommendations of technical international bodies.

21. It is also for the coastal State to enact measures designed to prevent, mitigate or eliminate pollution of or from the continental shelf and of its natural resources, taking into account co-operation with other States and the recommendations of international technical bodies.

22. It is likewise for the coastal State to authorize scientific research

activities on the continental shelf; it is entitled to participate in them and to receive the results thereof. In such regulations as the coastal State may issue on the matter, the desirability of promoting and facilitating such activities shall be taken especially into account.

23. A coastal State shall authorize the laying of submarine cables and pipelines on the continental shelf, without restrictions other than those which may result from its rights over the same.

24. The establishment of any other type of installation by third States or their nationals is subject to the permission of the coastal State.

25. The coastal State is entitled to construct, maintain or operate on or over the continental shelf installations and other devices necessary for the exercise of its rights over the same, to establish safety zones around such devices and installations, and to take in those zones measures necessary for their protection. Ships of all nationalities shall respect these safety zones, which may extend up to 500 metres around the installations or devices.

26. The construction of any installation or device shall be officially made public and permanent means for giving warning of its presence shall be maintained. Any installation which is disused shall be removed by the coastal State.

27. The exercise of the coastal State's rights over the continental shelf shall not result in any unjustifiable interference with the freedom of navigation in the superjacent waters and of overflight in the superjacent air space, nor shall it impede the use of recognized lanes essential to international navigation.

28. Delimitation.

29. Safeguard of existing international, bilateral or regional agreements on delimitation of the continental shelf.


## CANADA, INDIA, KENYA AND SRI LANKA:
### — Draft Articles on Fisheries

> Submitted to the United Nations Seabed Committee on 16 July 1973, as UN Doc. A/AC.138/SC.II/L.38. The substance of this proposal is complementary to the concept of the exclusive economic zone and should be considered as a part thereof. Cf. A/AC.138/SC.II/L.8: Canada—Working Paper on Management of the Living Resources of the Sea (27 July 1972).

**Art. 1.** A coastal State has a right to establish an exclusive fishery zone beyond its territorial sea. The coastal State shall exercise sovereign rights for the purpose of exploration, exploitation, conservation and management of the living resources, including fisheries, in this zone, and shall adopt from time to time such measures as it may deem necessary and appropriate. The living resources may be plant or animal, and may be located on the water surface, within the water column, on the sea bed or in the subsoil thereof.

**Art. 2.** The exclusive fishery zone may not extend beyond ... nautical miles* from the baseline from which the breadth of the territorial sea is measured.

**Art. 3.** Each coastal State shall notify to the Authority designated for the purpose by the Conference on the Law of the Sea the limits of the exclusive fishery zone defined by co-ordinates of latitude and longitude or by any other internationally recognized method and marked on large scale charts officially recognized by that State.

**Art. 4.** The coastal State may allow nationals of other States to fish in its exclusive fishery zone, subject to such terms, conditions and regulations as it may from time to time prescribe. These may, *inter alia*, relate to the following:

(*a*) Licensing of fishing vessels and equipment, including payment of fees and other forms of remuneration;

(*b*) Limiting the number of vessels and the number of gear that may be used;

(*c*) Specifying the gear permitted to be used;

(*d*) Fixing the periods during which the prescribed species may be caught;

(*e*) Fixing the age and size of fish that may be caught;

(*f*) Fixing the quota of catch, whether in relation to particular species of fish or to catch per vessel over a period of time or to the total catch of nationals of one State during a prescribed period.

**Art. 5.** Neighbouring developing coastal States shall allow each other's nationals the right to fish in a specified area of their respective fishery zones on the basis of long and mutually recognized usage and economic dependence on exploitation of the resources of that area. The modalities of the exercise of this right shall be settled by agreement between the States concerned. This right will be available to the nationals of the State concerned and cannot be transferred to third parties by lease or license, by establishing joint collaboration ventures, or by any other arrangement. Jurisdiction and control over the conservation, development and management of the resources of the specified area shall lie with the coastal State in whose zone that area is located.

*The figure for the nautical miles in this Article will correspond to the figure mentioned for the concept of the exclusive economic zone.

**Art. 6.** Nationals of a developing landlocked State shall enjoy the privilege to fish in the neighbouring area of the exclusive fishery zone of the adjoining coastal State on the basis of equality with the nationals of that State. The modalities of the enjoyment of this privilege and the area to which they relate shall be settled by agreement between the coastal State and the landlocked State concerned. This privilege will be available to the nationals of the landlocked State concerned and cannot be transferred to third parties by lease or license, by establishing joint collaboration ventures, or by any other arrangement. Jurisdiction and control over the conservation, development and management of the resources of the specified area shall lie with the coastal State in whose zone that area is located.

**Art. 7.** No State exercising foreign domination or control over a territory shall be entitled to establish an exclusive fishery zone or to enjoy any other right or privilege referred to in these Articles with respect to such territory.

**Art. 8.** A coastal State has a special interest in the maintenance of the poductivity of the living resources of the area of the sea adjacent to the exclusive fishery zone, and may take appropriate measures to protect this interest. A coastal State shall enjoy preferential rights to the resources of this area and may reserve for its nationals a portion of the allowable catch of these resources corresponding to its harvesting capacity.

**Art. 9.** Regulations may be made on a regional basis for the exploration, exploitation, conservation and development of the living resources of the area of the sea outside the limits of the exclusive fishery zone, where these resources are of limited migratory habits and breed, feed and survive on the resources of the region. The States of the region may establish these regulations by entering into an agreement or convention between themselves, or request the Authority, designated for the purpose by the Conference on the Law of the Sea, to formulate these regulations for the region subject to ratification by them.

**Art. 10.** In respect of fisheries of highly migratory habits outside the limits of the exclusive fishery zone, regulations for their exploration, exploitation, conservation and development shall be made by the Authority designated for the purpose by the Conference on the Law of the Sea.

**Art. 11.** (On Anadromous Species).

**Art. 12.** All fishing activities in the exclusive fishery zone and the rest of the sea shall be conducted with due regard to the interests of the other States in the legitimate uses of the sea. In the exercise of their rights, the other States shall not interfere with fishing activities in the exclusive fishery zone.

292

**Art. 13.** The jurisdiction and control over all fishing activities within the exclusive fishery zone shall lie with the coastal State concerned. Any difference or dispute concerning the limits of the zone or the interpretation or validity of the terms, conditions or regulations referred to in Article 5, or the interpretation and application of these Articles shall be settled by the competent institutions of the coastal State concerned.

Any difference or dispute concerning fishing activities outside the exclusive fishery zone shall be referred to the Authority designated for the purpose by the Conference on the Law of the Sea.

**Art. 14.** (Final clauses, *etc.*).

## AFGHANISTAN, AUSTRIA, BELGIUM, BOLIVIA, NEPAL AND SINGAPORE:
— **Draft Articles on Resource Jurisdiction of Coastal States beyond the Territorial Sea**

Submitted to the United Nations Seabed Committee on 16 July 1973, as UN Doc. A/AC.138/SC.II/L.39.

**Art. 1.** (1) Coastal States shall have the right to establish, adjacent to the territorial sea, a . . . . Zone which may not extend beyond . . . . nautical miles from the baselines from which the breadth of the territorial sea is measured.

(2) Coastal States shall have, subject to the provisions of Articles II and III, jurisdiction over the . . . . Zone and the right to explore and exploit all living and non-living resources therein.

**Art. 2.** (1) Landlocked and coastal States which cannot or do not declare a . . . . Zone pursuant to Article I (hereinafter referred to as the Disadvantaged States), as well as natural or juridical persons under their control, shall have the right to participate in the exploration and exploitation of the living resources of the . . . . Zone of neighbouring coastal States on an equal and non-discriminatory basis. For the purpose of facilitating the orderly development and the rational management and exploitation of the living resources of particular . . . . Zones, the States concerned may decide upon appropriate arrangements to regulate the exploitation of the resources in that Zone.

(2) In the . . . . Zone the coastal State may annually reserve for itself and such other Disadvantaged States as may be exercising the right under the preceding paragraph, that part of the maximum allowable yield, as determined by the relevant international fisheries organization, which corresponds to the harvesting capacity and needs of these States.

(3) States other than those referred to in paragraph 1 shall have the right to exploit that part of the remaining allowable yield subject to payments, to be determined under equitable conditions, and regulations laid down by the coastal States for the exploitation of the living resources of the .... Zone.

(4) Disadvantaged States shall not transfer the right conferred upon them in paragraph 1 to third parties. However, this provision shall not preclude the Disadvantaged States from entering into arrangements with third parties for the purpose of enabling them to develop viable fishing industries of their own.

(5) A developed coastal State, which establishes a .... Zone pursuant to Article I, paragraph 1, shall contribute .... per cent of its revenues derived from the exploitation of the living resources in that Zone to the International Authority. Such contributions shall be distributed by the International Authority on the basis of equitable sharing criteria.

(6) In exploiting the living resources the States referred to in paragraphs 1 and 3 of this Article shall observe the regulations and measures pertaining to management and conservation in the respective .... Zones.

**Art. 3.** (1) A coastal State shall make contributions to the International Authority out of the revenues* derived from exploitation of the non-living resources of its .... Zone in accordance with the following paragraph.

(2) The rate of contribution shall be .... per cent** of the revenues from exploitation carried out within forty miles or 200 metres isobath of the .... Zone, whichever limit the coastal State may choose to adopt, and .... per cent*** of the revenues from exploitation carried out beyond forty miles or 200 metres isobath within the .... Zone.

(3) The International Authority shall distribute these contributions on the basis of equitable sharing criteria.

**Art. 4.** Any dispute arising from the interpretation and application of the provisions of the foregoing Articles shall be subject to the procedures for the compulsory settlement of disputes provided for in the Convention.

*The word "revenues" shall have to be defined.

**It is understood that different rates should apply to developed and developing countries.

***It is understood that different rates should apply to developed and developing countries.

## ALGERIA, CAMEROON, GHANA, IVORY COAST, KENYA, LIBERIA, MADAGASCAR, MAURITIUS, SENEGAL, SIERRA LEONE, SOMALIA, SUDAN, TUNISIA AND UNITED REPUBLIC OF TANZANIA:
### — Draft Articles on Exclusive Economic Zone

Submitted to the United Nations Seabed Committee on 16 July 1973, as UN Doc. A/AC.138/SC.II/L.40.

**Art. 1.** All States have a right to determine the limits of their jurisdiction over the seas adjacent to their coasts beyond a territorial sea of .... miles in accordance with the criteria which take into account their own geographical, geological, biological, ecological, economic and national security factors.

**Art. 2.** In accordance with the foregoing Article, all States have the right to establish an Economic Zone beyond the territorial sea for the benefit of their peoples and their respective economies in which they shall have sovereignty over the renewable and non-renewable natural resources for the purpose of exploration and exploitation. Within the zone they shall have exclusive jurisdiction for the purpose of control, regulation and exploitation of both living and non-living resources of the Zone and their preservation, and for the purpose of prevention and control of pollution.

The rights exercised over the Economic Zone shall be exclusive and no other State shall explore and exploit the resources therein without obtaining permission from the Coastal State on such terms as may be laid down in conformity with the laws and regulations of the Coastal State.

The Coastal State shall exercise jurisdiction over its Economic Zone and third States or their nationals shall bear responsibility for damage resulting from their activities within the Zone.

**Art. 3.** The limits of the Economic Zone shall be fixed in nautical miles in accordance with criteria in each region, which take into consideration the resources of the region and the rights and interests of developing land-locked, near land-locked, shelf-locked States and States with narrow shelves and without prejudice to limits adopted by any State within the region. The Economic Zone shall not in any case exceed 200 nautical miles, measured from the baselines for determining territorial sea.

**Art. 4.** In the Economic Zone, ships and aircrafts of all States, whether coastal or not, shall enjoy the right of freedom of navigation and overflight and to lay submarine cables and pipelines with no restrictions other than those resulting from the exercise by the coastal state within the area.

**Art. 5.** Each State shall ensure that any exploration or exploitation activity within its Economic Zone is carried out exclusively for peaceful purposes and in such a manner as not to interfere unduly with the legitimate interests of other States in the region or those of the International Community.

**Art. 6.** The exercise of sovereignty over the resources and jurisdiction over the zone shall encompass all the economic resources of the area, living and non-living, either on the water surface or within the water column, or on the soil or sub-soil of the sea-bed and ocean floor below.

**Art. 7.** Without prejudice to the general jurisdictional competence conferred upon the coastal State by Article II above, the State may establish special regulations within its Economic Zone for:

(*a*) Exclusive exploration and exploitation of renewable resources;

(*b*) Protection and conservation of the renewable resources;

(*c*) Control, prevention and elimination of pollution of the marine environment;

(*d*) Scientific research.

**Art. 8.** Nationals of a developing land-locked State and other geographically disadvantaged States shall enjoy the privilege to fish in the exclusive economic Zones of the adjoining neighbouring coastal States. The modalities of the enjoyment of this privilege and the area to which they relate shall be settled by agreement between the coastal State and the land-locked State concerned. The right to prescribe and enforce management measures in the area shall be with the Coastal State.

The African States endorse the principle of the right of access to and from the sea by the land-locked countries, and the inclusion of such a provision in the universal treaty to be negotiated at the Law of the Sea Conference.

**Art. 9.** The delineation of the Economic Zone between adjacent and opposite States shall be carried out in accordance with international law. Disputes arising therefrom shall be settled in conformity with the Charter of the United Nations and any other relevant regional arrangements.

**Art. 10.** Neighbouring developing States shall give reciprocal preferential treatment to one another in the exploitation of the living resources of their respective Economic Zones.

**Art. 11.** No State exercising foreign domination and control over a territory shall be entitled to establish an Economic Zone or to enjoy any other right or privilege referred to in these articles with respect to such territory.

**Art. 12.** (*Draft Article Under Article 19, Regime of Islands*)

1. Maritime spaces of islands shall be determined according to equitable principles taking into account all relevant factors and circumstances including, *inter alia*:

(a) The size of islands;

(b) The population or the absence thereof;

(c) Their contiguity to the principal territory;

(d) Whether or not they are situated on the continental shelf of another territory;

(e) Their geological and geomorphological structure and configuration.

2. Island States and the regime of archipelagic States as set out under the present Convention shall not be affected by this article.

## UGANDA AND ZAMBIA:
— Draft Articles on the Proposed Economic Zone

Submitted to the United Nations Seabed Committee on 16 July 1973, as UN Doc. A/AC.138/SC.II/L.41.

*Section 1. Territorial Sea*

**Art. 1.** 1. The sovereignty of a State extends, beyond its land territory and its internal waters, to a belt of sea adjacent to its coast, described as the territorial sea.

2. This sovereignty is exercised subject to the provisions of these articles and other rules of international law.

**Art. 2.** The sovereignty of a coastal State extends to the air space over the territorial sea as well as to its bed and sub-soil.

**Art. 3.** 1. The uniform outer limit of the territorial sea is the line every point of which is at a distance from the nearest point of the baseline equal to ———— nautical miles.

2. Where the coasts of two States are opposite or adjacent to each other and the distance between them is less than double the uniform breadth provided in this article, the limits of the territorial sea shall, failing agreement between them to the contrary, be the median line every point of which is equidistant from the nearest points or baselines from which the breadth of the territorial sea of each of the two States is measured. The provision of this paragraph shall not apply, however, where it is necessary by reason of historic title or other special circumstances to delimit the territorial seas of the two States in a way which is at variance with this provision.

*Section 2. Economic Zone*

**Art. 4.** 1. Beyond the uniform limits of the territorial seas of coastal States, there shall be established economic zones, the outer limit of which shall be a line every point of which shall not exceed ———— nautical miles measured from the baselines, known as Regional or Sub-regional economic zones.

2. Fisheries within the Regional or Sub-regional economic zones shall be reserved for the exclusive use, exploration and exploitation by all the States within the relevant Region or Sub-region.

3. Relevant Regional or Sub-regional authorities shall have the exclusive right to explore, exploit and manage the non-living resources of the Regional or Sub-regional economic zones on behalf of all States in the Region or Sub-region.

4. The regulation and supervision of activities within such Regional or Sub-regional Economic Zones shall be the responsibility of the relevant Regional or Sub-regional commissions.

5. The provisions of the preceding paragraphs of this Article shall not affect the freedoms of navigation, overflight, and the laying of submarine cables and pipelines referred to in Article ——— which shall be applicable in the Regional or Sub-regional zones.

*International Area*

The area beyond Regional or Sub-regional economic zones shall be known as the International Area.
*etc.*

## III. NAVIGATION WITHIN NATIONAL JURISDICTION

# UNION OF SOVIET SOCIALIST REPUBLICS:
## — Draft Articles on Straits used for International Navigation

Submitted to the United Nations Seabed Committee on 25 July 1972, as UN Doc. A/AC.138/SC.II/L.7.

**Art. . . .** 1. In straits used for international navigation between one part of the high seas and another part of the high seas, all ships in transit shall enjoy the same freedom of navigation, for the purpose of transit through such straits, as they have on the high seas. Coastal States may, in the case of narrow straits, designate corridors suitable for transit by all ships through such straits. In the case of straits where particular channels of navigation are customarily employed by ships in transit, the corridors shall include such channels.

2. The freedom of navigation provided for in this article, for the purpose of transit through the straits, shall be exercised in accordance with the following rules:

(*a*) Ships in transit through the straits shall take all necessary steps to avoid causing any threat to the security of the coastal States of the straits, and in particular warships in transit through such straits shall not in the area of the straits engage in any exercises or gunfire, use weapons of any kind, launch their aircraft, undertake hydrographical work or engage in other acts of a nature unrelated to the transit;

(*b*) Ships in transit through the straits shall strictly comply with the international rules concerning the prevention of collisions between ships or other accidents and, in straits where separate lanes are designated for the passage of ships in each direction, shall not cross the dividing line between the lanes. They shall also avoid making unnecessary manoeuvres;

(*c*) Ships in transit through the straits shall take precautionary measures to avoid causing pollution of the waters and coasts of the straits, or any other kind of damage to the coastal States of the straits;

(*d*) Liability for any damage which may be caused to the coastal States of the straits as a result of the transit of ships shall rest with the flag-State of the ship which has caused the damage or with juridical persons under its jurisdiction or acting on its behalf;

(*e*) No State shall be entitled to interrupt or stop the transit of ships through the straits, or engage therein in any acts which interfere with the transit of ships, or require ships in transit to stop or communicate information of any kind.

3. The provisions of this article:

(*a*) shall apply to straits lying within the territorial waters of one or more coastal States;

(*b*) shall not affect the sovereign rights of the coastal States with respect to the surface, the sea-bed and the living and mineral resources of the straits;

(c) shall not affect the legal régime of straits through which transit is regulated by international agreements specifically relating to such straits.

**Art.** .... 1. In the case of straits over which the airspace is used for flights by foreign aircraft between one part of the high seas and another part of the high seas, all aircraft shall enjoy the same freedom of overflight over such straits as they have in the airspace over the high seas. Coastal States may designate special air corridors suitable for overflight by aircraft, and special altitudes for aircraft flying in different directions, and may establish particulars for radio-communication with them.

2. The freedom of overflight by aircraft over the straits, as provided for in this article, shall be exercised in accordance with the following rules:

(a) Overflying aircraft shall take the necessary steps to keep within the boundaries of the corridors and at the altitude designated by the coastal States for flights over the straits, and to avoid overflying the territory of a coastal State, unless such overflight is provided for by the delimitation of the corridor designated by the coastal State;

(b) Overflying aircraft shall take all necessary steps to avoid causing any threat to the security of the coastal States, and in particular military aircraft shall not in the area of the straits engage in any exercises or gunfire, use weapons of any kind, take aerial photographs, circle or dive down towards ships, take on fuel or engage in other acts of a nature unrelated to the overflight;

(c) Liability for any damage which may be caused to the coastal States as a result of the overflight of aircraft over the straits shall rest with the State to which the aircraft that has caused the damage belongs, or with juridical persons under its jurisdiction or acting on its behalf;

(d) No State shall be entitled to interrupt or stop the overflight of foreign aircraft, in accordance with this article, in the airspace over the straits.

3. The provisions of this article:

(a) shall apply to flights by aircraft over straits lying within the territorial waters of one or more coastal States;

(b) shall not affect the legal régime of straits over which overflight is regulated by international agreements specifically relating to such straits.

# CYPRUS, GREECE, INDONESIA, MALAYSIA, MOROCCO, PHILIPPINES, SPAIN AND YEMEN:
## — Draft Articles on Navigation through the Territorial Sea including Straits used for International Navigation

Submitted to the United Nations Seabed Committee on 2 April 1973, as UN Doc. A/AC.138/SC.II/L.18.

The question of navigation through the territorial sea including straits used for international navigation is one of the problems facing the Committee in its task to comply with the terms of General Assembly resolutions 2750 C (XXV) and 3029 A (XXVII).

The delegations co-sponsoring the present document wish to contribute to the progress of the Committee's work at this new and important stage of its proceedings and they consider that an appropriate means to achieve this aim is to submit draft articles on items 2.4 and 4.1 of the list of subjects and issues concerning navigation through the territorial sea and through straits used for international navigation, independently of the solutions that item 2.5 may receive in due course.

Although presented as separate articles, this draft is not intended to prejudge its eventual location within the convention or conventions which may be adopted by the future conference.

In drafting this document the following basic considerations have been taken into account:

(1) Navigation through the territorial sea and through straits used for international navigation should be dealt with as an entity since the straits in question are or form part of territorial seas.

(2) Regulation of navigation should establish a satisfactory balance between the particular interests of coastal States and the general interests of international maritime navigation. This is best achieved through the principle of innocent passage which is the basis of the traditional régime for navigation through the territorial sea.

(3) The regulation should contribute both to the security of coastal States and to the safety of international maritime navigation. This can be achieved by the reasonable and adequate exercise by the coastal State of its right to regulate navigation through its territorial sea, since the purpose of the regulation is not to prevent or hamper passage but to facilitate it without causing any adverse effects to the coastal State.

(4) The regulation should take due account of the economic realities and scientific and technological developments which have occurred in recent years; this requires the adoption of appropriate rules to regulate navigation of certain ships with "special characteristics".

(5) The regulation should, finally, meet the deficiencies of the 1958

301

Geneva Convention, especially those concerning the passage of warships through the territorial sea, including straits.

## Section I. Rules applicable to all ships

*Subsection A. Right of innocent passage*

**Art. 1.** Subject to the provisions of these articles, ships of all States, whether coastal or not, shall enjoy the right of innocent passage through the territorial sea.

**Art. 2.** 1. Passage means navigation through the territorial sea for the purpose either of traversing that sea without entering internal waters, or of proceeding to internal waters, or of making for the high seas from internal waters.

2. Passage includes stopping and anchoring, but only so far as the same are incidental to ordinary navigation or are rendered necessary by "force majeure" or by distress.

**Art. 3.** 1. Passage is innocent so long as it is not prejudicial to the peace, good order or security of the coastal State. Such passage shall take place in conformity with these articles and with other rules of international law.

2. Passage shall be continuous and expeditious. Passing ships shall refrain from manoeuvring unnecessarily; hovering, or engaging in any activity other than mere passage.

3. Foreign ships exercising the right of innocent passage shall comply with the laws and regulations enacted by the coastal State in conformity with these articles and other rules of international law.

4. Passage of foreign fishing vessels shall not be considered innocent if they do not observe such laws and regulations as the coastal State may make and publish in order to prevent these vessels from fishing in the territorial sea.

5. Submarines and other underwater vehicles are required to navigate on the surface and to show their flag.

**Art. 4.** The coastal State must not hamper innocent passage through the territorial sea. In particular, it shall not impede the innocent passage of a foreign ship flying the flag of a particular State or carrying goods owned by a particular State, proceeding from the territory of or consigned to such a State.

**Art. 5.** 1. The coastal State may take the necessary steps in its territorial sea to prevent passage which is not innocent.

2. In the case of ships proceeding to internal waters, the coastal State shall also have the right to take the necessary steps to prevent any breach of the conditions to which admission of those ships to those waters is subject.

302

3. Subject to the provisions of paragraph 4, the coastal State may, without discrimination amongst foreign ships, suspend temporarily and in specified areas of its territorial sea the innocent passage of foreign ships, if such suspension is essential for the protection of its security. Such suspension shall take effect only after having been duly published.

4. Subject to the provisions of articles 8, 22, paragraph 3 and 23, there shall be no suspension of the innocent passage of foreign ships through straits used for international navigation which form part of the territorial sea.

*Subsection B. Regulation of passage*

**Art. 6.** The coastal State may enact regulations relating to navigation in its territorial sea. Such regulations may relate, *inter alia*, to the following:

(*a*) Maritime safety and traffic and, in particular, the establishment of sea lanes and traffic separation schemes;

(*b*) Installation and utilization of facilities and systems of aids to navigation and the protection thereof;

(*c*) Installation and utilization of facilities to explore and exploit marine resources and the protection thereof;

(*d*) Maritime transport;

(*e*) Passage of ships with special characteristics;

(*f*) Preservation of marine and coastal environment and prevention of all forms of pollution;

(*g*) Research of the marine environment.

**Art. 7.** In exercising the right of innocent passage through the territorial sea, foreign ships will not be allowed to perform activities such as

(*a*) Engaging in any act of espionage or collecting of information affecting the security of the coastal State;

(*b*) Engaging in any act of propaganda against the coastal State or of interference with its systems of communications;

(*c*) Embarking or disembarking troops, crew members, frogmen or any other person or device without the authorization of the coastal State;

(*d*) Engaging in illicit trade;

(*e*) Destroying or damaging submarine or aerial cables, tubes, pipelines or all forms of installations and constructions;

(*f*) Exploring or exploiting marine and subsoil resources without the authorization of the coastal State.

**Art. 8.** The coastal State may designate in its territorial sea sea lanes and traffic separation schemes, taking into account those recommended by competent international organizations, and prescribe the use of such sea lanes and traffic separation schemes as compulsory for passing ships.

**Art. 9.** 1. The coastal State is required to give appropriate publicity to any dangers of navigation, of which it has knowledge, within its territorial sea.

2. The coastal State is required to give appropriate publicity to the existence in its territorial sea of any facilities or systems of aid to navigation and of any facilities to explore and exploit marine resources which could be an obstacle to navigation, and to install in a permanent way the necessary marks to warn navigation of the existence of such facilities and systems.

**Art. 10.** The coastal State may require any foreign ship that does not comply with the provisions concerning regulation of passage to leave its territorial sea.

## Section II. Rules applicable to certain types of ships

*Subsection A. Merchant ships*

**Art. 11.** 1. No charge may be levied upon foreign ships by reason only of their passage through the territorial sea.

2. Charges may be levied upon a foreign ship passing through the territorial sea as payment only for specific services. These charges shall be levied without discrimination.

3. The coastal State shall have the right to be compensated for works undertaken to facilitate passage.

**Art. 12.** 1. The criminal jurisdiction of the coastal State should not be exercised on board a foreign ship passing through the territorial sea to arrest any person or to conduct any investigation in connexion with any crime committed on board the ship during its passage, save only in the following cases:

(*a*) If the consequences of the crime extend to the coastal State; or

(*b*) If the crime is of a kind to disturb the peace of the country or the good order of the territorial sea; or

(*c*) If the assistance of the local authorities has been requested by the captain of the ship or by the consul of the country whose flag the ship flies; or

(*d*) If it is necessary for the suppression of illicit traffic in narcotic drugs.

2. The above provisions do not affect the right of the coastal State to take any steps authorized by its laws for the purpose of an arrest or investigation on board a foreign ship passing through the territorial sea after leaving internal waters.

3. In the cases provided for in paragraphs 1 and 2 of this article, the coastal State shall, if the captain so requests, advise the consular authority

of the country whose flag the ship flies, before taking any steps, and shall facilitate contact between such authority and the ship's crew. In cases of emergency this notification may be communicated while the measures are being taken.

4. In considering whether or how an arrest should be made, the local authorities shall pay due regard to the interests of navigation.

5. The coastal State may not take steps on board a foreign ship passing through the territorial sea to arrest any person or to conduct any investigation in connexion with any crime committed before the ship entered the territorial sea, if the ship, proceeding from a foreign port, is only passing through the territorial sea without entering internal waters.

**Art. 13.** 1. The coastal State should not stop or divert a foreign ship passing through the territorial sea for the purpose of exercising civil jurisdiction in relation to a person on board the ship.

2. The coastal State may not levy execution against or arrest the ship for the purpose of any civil proceedings, save only in respect of obligations or liabilities assumed or incurred by the ship itself in the course or for the purpose of its voyage through the waters of the coastal State.

3. The provisions of the previous paragraph are without prejudice to the right of the coastal State, in accordance with its laws, to levy execution against or to arrest, for the purpose of any civil proceeding, a foreign ship lying in the territorial sea, or passing through the territorial sea after leaving internal waters.

*Subsection B. Ships with special characteristics*

**Art. 14.** The coastal State may regulate the passage through its territorial sea of the following:

(*a*) Nuclear-powered ships or ships carrying nuclear weapons;

(*b*) Ships carrying nuclear substances or any other material which may endanger the coastal State or pollute seriously the marine environment;

(*c*) Ships engaged in research of the marine environment.

**Art. 15.** 1. The coastal State may require prior notification to or authorization by its competent authorities for the passage through its territorial sea of foreign nuclear-powered ships or ships carrying nuclear weapons, in conformity with regulations in force in such a State.

2. The provisions of paragraph 1 shall not prejudice any agreement to which the coastal State may be a party.

**Art. 16.** The coastal State may require that the passage through its territorial sea of foreign ships carrying nuclear substances or any other material which may endanger the coastal State or pollute seriously the marine environment be conditional upon any or all of the following:

(*a*) Prior notification to its competent authorities;

(*b*) Coverage by an international insurance or guarantee certificate for damages that might be caused by such carriage;

(*c*) Use of designated sea lanes.

**Art. 17.** 1. The coastal State may require prior notification to its competent authorities for the passage through its territorial sea of foreign ships engaged in research of the marine environment, in conformity with regulations in force in such a State.

2. During their passage through the territorial sea, foreign ships engaged in research of the marine environment will not be entitled to carry out any scientific research or hydrographic survey without the explicit authorization of the coastal State.

**Art. 18.** In order to expedite passage the coastal State shall ensure that the procedure of notification referred to in different articles of this section shall not cause undue delay.

*Subsection C. Government ships other than warships*

**Art. 19.** The rules contained in subsections A and B of this section shall also apply to government ships operated for commercial purposes.

**Art. 20.** 1. The rules contained in articles 11, 15, 16 (a) and (c), 17 and 18 of this convention shall apply to government ships operated for noncommercial purposes.

2. With such exceptions as are contained in any of the provisions referred to in the preceding paragraphs, nothing in these articles affects the immunities which such ships enjoy under these articles or other rules of international law.

*Subsection D. Warships*

**Art. 21.** The coastal State may require prior notification to or authorization by its competent authorities for the passage of foreign warships through its territorial sea, in conformity with regulations in force in such a State.

**Art. 22.** 1. Foreign warships exercising the right of innocent passage shall comply with the laws and regulations enacted by the coastal State in conformity with these articles and other rules of international law.

2. Foreign warships exercising the right of innocent passage shall not perform any activity which does not have a direct bearing with the passage, such as:

(*a*) Carrying out any exercise or practice with weapons of any kind;

(*b*) Assuming combat position by the crew;

(*c*) Flying their aircraft;

(*d*) Intimidation or displaying of force;

(*e*) Carrying out research operations of any kind.

3. Foreign warships exercising the right of innocent passage may be required to pass through certain sea lanes as may be designated for this purpose by the coastal State.

**Art. 23.** If any warship does not comply with the regulations of the coastal State concerning passage through the territorial sea and disregards any request for compliance which is made to it, the coastal State may require the warship to leave the territorial sea.

**MALTA:**

**— Preliminary Draft Articles on the Delimitation of Coastal State Jurisdiction in Ocean Space and on the Rights and Obligations of Coastal States in the Area under their Jurisdiction**

> Submitted to the United Nations Seabed Committee on 16 July 1973, as UN Doc. A/AC.138/SC.II/L.28. This is intended to replace and to amplify Parts II and III of A/AC.138/53 (p. 148 of Volume I).

PART I. COASTAL STATE JURISDICTION IN OCEAN SPACE
(See p. 266)

PART II. RIGHTS AND OBLIGATIONS OF THE COASTAL STATE WITHIN NATIONAL OCEAN SPACE

Chapter 6. *Navigation*

**Art. 20.** 1. Subject to the provisions of these articles, vessels of all States, whether coastal or not, shall enjoy the right of passage through national ocean space.

2. Passage means navigation through national ocean space for the purpose either of traversing it without entering internal waters or of proceeding to internal waters, or of making for international ocean space from internal waters.

3. Passage includes stopping and anchoring in so far as the same are incidental to ordinary navigation or are rendered necessary by *force majeure* or by distress.

**Art. 21.** The coastal State must not hamper in any way the exercise of the right of passage through its national ocean space when such passage conforms with such general and non-discriminatory standards and rules for the regulation of navigation as may be adopted by the international ocean space institutions or as are contained in widely ratified multilateral conventions.

**Art. 22.** In the absence of relevant standards and rules adopted by the international ocean space institutions or contained in widely ratified multilateral conventions, the coastal State may enact reasonable non-discriminatory regulations with regard to navigation in national ocean space and in particular with regard to maritime safety and traffic, maritime transport and the prevention of pollution.

**Art. 23.** 1. Foreign vessels exercising the right of passage shall comply (*a*) with the rules and regulations concerning navigation adopted by the international ocean space institutions or enacted by the coastal State or contained in widely ratified multilateral conventions; (*b*) with the customs, fiscal, immigration or sanitary regulations of the coastal State to which due publicity has been given through the international ocean space institutions.

2. Foreign fishing and fish-processing vessels exercising the right of passage shall observe such laws and regulations as the coastal State may make and publish through the international ocean space institutions in order to prevent these vessels from fishing or processing fish in national ocean space.

**Art. 24.** The coastal State may require any foreign vessel which does not comply with the provisions concerning the exercise of the right of passage contained in the foregoing articles to leave national ocean space.

**Art. 25.** 1. Coastal State regulations mentioned in the foregoing articles may be brought to the attention of the international ocean space institutions by any Contracting Party when these regulations are considered discriminatory, or an unreasonable impediment to navigation, or contrary to general international practice, or inconsistent with standards and rules adopted by the institutions or contained in widely ratified multilateral conventions.

2. The international ocean space institutions may recommend that the coastal State rescind or modify such regulations as are found to be discriminatory, or an unreasonable impediment to navigation, or contrary to general international practice, or inconsistent with standards and rules adopted by the institutions or contained in widely ratified multilateral conventions.

3. In the event of continued disagreement between the international ocean space institutions and the coastal State the matter shall be submitted to the International Maritime Court for binding adjudication.

**Art. 26.** 1. The coastal State is required to give appropriate and immediate publicity through the international ocean space institutions to any dangers or obstacles to navigation of which it has knowledge within its national ocean space.

2. The coastal State is required within its national ocean space to take effective measures, conforming to international standards and practice, for the safety of navigation, including the installation of appropriate aids to navigation, for assistance to vessels in distress and for the rescue of human life. Such measures and the facilities available shall be notified to the international ocean space institutions.

3. Failure to comply with the provisions of the foregoing paragraphs of this article entails legal responsibility. In the event of loss of life or of property caused by non-compliance, claims for compensation shall be adjudicated by the International Maritime Court.

**Art. 27.** 1. No charge may be levied upon foreign vessels by reason only of their passage through national ocean space.

2. The coastal State may levy charges upon a foreign vessel passing through national ocean space as payment only for specific services rendered to the vessel. These charges shall be reasonable and shall be levied without discrimination.

3. Disputes on the reasonableness or otherwise of the charges mentioned in the foregoing paragraph shall be adjudicated by the International Maritime Court.

**Art. 28.** 1. The criminal jurisdiction of the coastal State shall not be exercised on board a foreign vessel passing through national ocean space in connexion with any crime committed on board the vessel during its passage save only in the following cases:

(a) If the consequences of the crime extend to the coastal State; or

(b) If the crime is of a nature gravely to disturb the peace of the country or the good order of ocean space under its jurisdiction; or

(c) If the assistance of the local authorities has been requested by the captain of the vessel or by the consul of the country whose flag the vessel flies; or

(d) If it is essential for the suppression of the slave trade, piracy or the illicit traffic in narcotic drugs.

2. The above provisions do not affect the right of the coastal State to take any steps authorized by its laws for the purpose of an arrest or investigation on board a foreign vessel traversing national ocean space after leaving internal waters.

3. In considering whether or how an arrest should be made, the local authorities shall pay due regard to the interests of navigation.

4. In the cases provided for in paragraphs 1 and 2 of this article, the

coastal State shall act on probable cause only and shall advise also the consular authority of the flag State and, if the captain so requests, shall advise also the international ocean space institutions before taking any steps. The authorities of the coastal State shall facilitate contact between the consular authority of the flag State or the international ocean space institutions and the vessel's crew. In cases of emergency the notification may be communicated while the measures are being taken.

5. In the event that action taken under the provisions of paragraphs 1 and 2 proves to have been unfounded, the vessel, the crew and passengers and the State whose flag the vessel flies shall be compensated for any loss or damage that may have been sustained.

6. Non-compliance with the obligations under paragraph 4 of this article may be brought to the attention of the international ocean space institutions by the State whose flag the vessel flies.

7. Disputes with regard to the compliance or otherwise with the provisions of the foregoing paragraphs may be submitted to the International Maritime Court for binding adjudication on the initiative either of the flag State or of the coastal State.

**Art. 29.** 1. The coastal State may not take any steps on board a foreign vessel passing through national ocean space to arrest any person or to conduct any investigation in connexion with any crime committed before the vessel entered ocean space subject to its jurisdiction, if the vessel, proceeding from a foreign port, is only passing through national ocean space without entering internal waters.

2. Non-compliance with the obligations under paragraph 1 of this article may be brought to the attention of the appropriate organs of the international ocean space institutions and shall entail legal responsibility, unless the action was taken at the request of the captain of the vessel or of the State whose flag the vessel was flying.

**Art. 30.** 1. The coastal State may not stop or divert a foreign vessel passing through national ocean space for the purpose of exercising civil jurisdiction in relation to a person on board the vessel.

2. The coastal State may not levy execution against or arrest the vessel for the purpose of any civil proceedings save only in respect of obligations or liabilities assumed or incurred by the vessel itself in the course or for the purpose of its voyage through the waters of the coastal State.

3. The provisions of the previous paragraph are without prejudice to the right of the coastal State, in accordance with its laws, to levy execution against or to arrest for the purpose of any civil proceedings, a foreign vessel lying in waters under its jurisdiction or passing through these waters after leaving internal waters.

**Art. 31.** 1. The rules contained in the foregoing articles shall also apply

310

to government vessels operated for commercial purposes.

2. The rules contained in the foregoing articles shall also apply to government vessels operated for non-commercial purposes with the exception of articles 28, 29 and 30.

3. With such exceptions as are contained in the provisions referred to in the preceding paragraph, nothing in these articles affects the immunities which government vessels operated for non-commercial purposes enjoy under these articles or other rules of international law.

**Art. 32.** In a belt of ocean space adjacent to its coast, not exceeding 12 nautical miles in breadth measured from the applicable baseline, the coastal State, in addition to the measures contemplated in the foregoing articles, may:

(*a*) establish compulsory traffic separation schemes, designate safe sea lanes and establish draft limits for navigation in certain areas;

(*b*) require that passage be continuous and expeditious;

(*c*) take such measures as may be necessary to bring to the surface of the sea an unknown submersible found lurking in the sea or resting on the sea-bed;

(*d*) prevent passage which it deems to be seriously prejudicial to its peace, good order or security;

(*e*) subject to the provisions of articles 36 and 37, suspend temporarily in specified areas the passage of foreign vessels if such suspension is essential for the protection of its security;

(*f*) subject to the provisions of articles 36 and 37, establish precisely delimited zones closed to foreign warships for reasons of national security;

(*g*) in the case of vessels proceeding to internal waters, the necessary steps to prevent any breach of the conditions to which admission of those vessels to those waters is subject.

**Art. 33.** 1. Measures taken by the coastal State under subparagraphs (*a*), (*b*), (*d*), (*e*) and (*f*) of the foregoing article shall be non-discriminatory and shall not take effect unless notified to the international ocean space institutions and duly published.

2. The international ocean space institutions may recommend that the coastal State rescind or modify measures found to be discriminatory or to constitute an unreasonable impediment to navigation. In the event of continued disagreement between the international ocean space institutions and the coastal State the matter shall be submitted to the International Maritime Court for binding adjudication.

**Art. 34.** Foreign warships exercising the right of passage within a belt of ocean space adjacent to the coast of a State not exceeding 12 nautical miles in the breadth measured from the applicable baseline shall not fly their aircraft, practise their weapons, engage in research or intelligence-gathering operations or in activities deemed unfriendly by the coastal State nor shall they exercise the right of passage in such a manner as to impede the navigation of other vessels.

**Art. 35.** 1. The coastal State may require a foreign warship which does not comply with the provisions of the foregoing article and disregards any request for compliance to leave national ocean space.

2. Grave or repeated violations of the provisions of these articles and of article 42 relating to the exercise of the right of passage by warships may be brought to the attention of the international ocean space institutions by the coastal State.

*Special rules applicable to straits used for international navigation*

**Art. 36.** 1. There shall be no suspension of passage through straits more than 24 nautical miles wide which are, or can be, used for international navigation.

2. Subject to the provisions of articles 21, 22 and 23, the coastal State must not hamper passage through straits more than 24 miles wide which are, or can be, used for international navigation.

**Art. 37.** 1. The coastal State must not hamper passage through straits less than 24 miles wide which are, or can be, used for international navigation subject only to the provisions of the following paragraph and of article 38.

2. In the case of straits less than 24 nautical miles wide which are, or can be, used for international navigation, the coastal State or States may as a condition of passage:

(*a*) require compliance with compulsory traffic separation schemes, with designated safe sea lanes and, when necessary, with safe draft limits;

(*b*) require that passage be continuous and expeditious;

(*c*) require, when passage is hazardous, the use by transiting vessels of pilots designated by the coastal State;

(*d*) require three days prior notification of the passage of foreign submersibles or of foreign warships. In addition the coastal State may:

    (i) take such measures as may be necessary to bring to the surface an unknown submersible found lurking in the strait;

    (ii) in the case of vessels proceeding to internal waters, take the necessary steps to prevent any breach of the conditions to which admission of those vessels to those waters is subject.

3. Measures taken by the coastal State under subparagraphs (*a*), (*b*), (*c*) and (*d*) of the foregoing paragraph shall be non-discriminatory and shall not take effect unless notified to the international ocean space

institutions and duly published.

4. The international ocean space institutions may recommend that the coastal State rescind or modify measures found to be discriminatory or unreasonable or to constitute an unnecessary impediment to navigation. In the event of continued disagreement between the international ocean space institutions and the coastal State the matter shall be submitted to the International Maritime Court for binding adjudication.

**Art. 38.** The coastal State or States may take measures to prevent or suspend passage through straits less than 24 nautical miles wide which are or can be used for international navigation only in case of reasonable fear of grave and imminent threat to its or their security. Such measures shall be notified to the international ocean space institutions, and shall lapse after 30 days unless the consent of the institutions to such measures is obtained.

**Art. 39.** 1. The coastal State or States are required to take effective measures to maintain and facilitate navigation through straits used for international navigation the breadth of which is less than 24 nautical miles.

2. Failure to comply with the provisions of the foregoing paragraph entails legal responsibility. In the event of accidents caused by non-compliance, claims for compensation for injury to persons or for loss or damage to vessel on cargo shall be adjudicated by the International Maritime Court.

**Art. 40.** 1. The coastal State or States may not levy charges or tolls on vessels, their cargo, crew or passengers exercising the right of passage through straits used for international navigation.

2. Nevertheless, when a strait used for international navigation the breadth of which is less than 24 nautical miles (a) requires dredging, the installation and maintenance of aids to navigation or the adoption of other measures to maintain or facilitate safe passage, or (b) when passage of certain types or classes of vessels, in the event of accident, could cause considerable loss of human life or substantial injury to economic activities or to the marine environment in the area, the coastal State or States may request the international ocean space institutions to establish an equitable charge payable without discrimination by all vessels or by all vessels of the relevant class or type, as the case may be, using the strait.

3. The charge mentioned in the foregoing paragraph shall be collected by the coastal State or States and the proceeds shall be paid into a fund administered by the international ocean space institutions, the resources of which shall be employed to maintain and facilitate safe passage of the strait and to compensate the coastal State or States for any injury or

313

damage which they might suffer from the exercise of the right of passage by foreign vessels.

4. The charge payable by vessels exercising the right of passage through straits less than 24 nautical miles in breadth shall be determined in special conventions between the international ocean space institutions and the State or States concerned.

**Art. 41.** 1. Vessels exercising the right of passage through straits shall take strict precautionary measures for the avoidance of accidents of navigation and for the prevention of damage to the marine environment or to offshore installations.

2. Liability for damages negligently caused by a vessel exercising the right of passage shall rest with the State whose flag the vessel flies.

3. The courts of the coastal State shall be competent to adjudicate cases involving accidents of navigation and damages to the marine environment or to installations resulting from negligence in the exercise of the right of passage.

**Art. 42.** 1. Foreign warships passing through straits less than 24 nautical miles wide which are, or can be, used for international navigation shall:

(*a*) comply with the provisions of article 34 of this Convention;

(*b*) comply with such regulations as may be adopted by the coastal State under article 37 of this Convention;

(*c*) take strict precautionary measures for the avoidance of accidents to navigation and for the prevention of damage to the marine environment or to offshore installations.

2. Foreign warships passing through straits less than 24 nautical miles wide shall be exempt from any charges which may be levied under article 40 (2) of this Convention.

*Chapter 7. Overflight*

**Art. 43.** 1. Subject to the provisions of these articles, aircraft of all States, whether coastal or not, shall enjoy the right of overflight over national ocean space.

2. Overflight means the right to fly aircraft over national ocean space for the purpose of traversing it or of landing on vessels passing through national ocean space.

3. Overflight includes landing in national ocean space and low-altitude circling and manoeuvring in so far as the same are incidental to aerial navigation or are rendered necessary by *force majeure* or by distress.

**Art. 44.** The coastal State must not hamper in any way overflight over its national ocean space when such overflight conforms with such regulations of a general and non-discriminatory character as may be adopted by the

314

competent international institutions or as are contained in widely ratified international conventions.

**Art. 45.** In the absence of relevant regulations adopted by the competent international institutions or contained in widely ratified international conventions, the coastal State may enact reasonable and non-discriminatory regulations concerning the conduct of aerial navigation over its national ocean space.

**Art. 46.** Foreign aircraft exercising the right of overflight shall comply with regulations concerning aerial navigation adopted by the competent international institutions or contained in widely ratified multilateral conventions or enacted by the coastal State as the case may be.

**Art. 47.** In exercising the right of overflight, foreign aircraft shall not engage in activities which adversely affect the security of the coastal State or in manoeuvres which might endanger shipping or installations in national ocean space.

**Art. 48.** The coastal State may require any foreign aircraft which does not comply with the provisions of the foregoing articles to leave the air space above national ocean space.

**Art. 49.** 1. The coastal State is required to take effective measures conforming to international standards and practice for the safety of aerial navigation over its national ocean space.

2. Failure to comply with the provisions of the foregoing paragraph entails legal responsibility.

**Art. 50.** 1. In a belt of ocean space adjacent to its coast not exceeding 12 nautical miles in breadth measured from the applicable baseline, the coastal State, in addition to the measures contemplated in the foregoing article, may:

(*a*) require three days advance notice of overflight by foreign military aircraft;

(*b*) require that overflight be continuous and expeditious;

(*c*) prevent overflight which it deems to be seriously prejudicial to its peace, good order or security;

(*d*) without discrimination among foreign aircraft, suspend temporarily the exercise of the right of overflight by foreign aircraft over specified areas if such suspension is essential for the protection of its security.

2. The coastal State or States may take measures to prevent or suspend overflight over straits less than 24 nautical miles wide which are, or can be, used for international navigation only in case of reasonable fear of grave and imminent threat to its or their security. Measures taken by the

coastal State or States shall be notified immediately to the competent international institutions and shall lapse after 30 days unless the consent of the institutions to such measures is obtained.

**Art. 51.** 1. Foreign military aircraft exercising the right of overflight over a belt of national ocean space not exceeding 12 nautical miles in breadth measured from the applicable baseline shall not practise their weapons, engage in intimidating manoeuvres, in research or intelligence-gathering operations or in activities deemed unfriendly by the coastal State, nor shall they exercise the right of overflight in such a manner as to hamper or endanger transit of commercial aircraft.

2. The coastal State may require a foreign military aircraft which does not comply with the provisions of the foregoing paragraph, immediately to leave the air space over which it has jurisdiction.

**Art. 52.** 1. The coastal State may establish over a belt of national ocean space adjacent to its coast not exceeding 100 nautical miles in breadth precisely delimited zones of air space closed to foreign military aircraft for reasons of national security. Such zones shall be established with due regard to the normal exercise of the right of overflight. Measures establishing aerial zones closed to foreign military aircraft shall not take effect unless notified to the competent international institutions and duly published.

2. Subject to the provisions contained in article 50 (2), nothing in the foregoing paragraph shall affect the exercise of the right of overflight over straits which area can be used for international navigation.

Chapter 8 - Chapter 16.
(See p. 272)

**ITALY:**
**— Draft Articles on Straits**

Submitted to the United Nations Seabed Committee on 16 July 1973, as UN Doc. A/AC.138/SC.II/L.30.

(A) Subject to the provisions of paragraph (B), all ships and all aircraft shall enjoy, for purposes of transit through or over straits connecting two parts of the high seas or connecting part of the high seas with the territorial sea of a foreign State, the same freedom of navigation or overflight as exists on the high seas.

The freedom of transit shall be so exercised as to avoid (all unnecessary) obstruction of traffic. The coastal States may designate appropriate channels and corridors to be used by transit traffic passing through and over the straits.

(B) Transit and overflight shall be governed by the provisions concerning innocent passage in straits which:

(1) Are not more than six miles wide;

(2) Lie between coasts of the same State; and

(3) Are near other routes of communication between the parts of the sea connected by the straits.

**FIJI:**
**— Draft Articles relating to Passage through the Territorial Sea**

Submitted to the United Nations Seabed Committee on 19 July 1973, as UN Doc. A/AC.138/SC.II/L.42.

### Section I. Rules Applicable to all Ships

*Subsection A. Right of innocent passage*

**Art. 1.** Subject to the provisions of these articles, ships of all States, whether coastal or not, shall enjoy the right of innocent passage through the territorial sea.

**Art. 2.** 1. Passage means navigation through the territorial sea for the purpose either of traversing that sea without entering any port in the coastal State, or of proceeding to any port in the coastal State from the high seas, or of making for the high seas from any port in the coastal State.

2. Passage includes stopping and anchoring, but only in so far as the same are incidental to ordinary navigation or are rendered necessary by *force majeure* or by distress; otherwise passage shall be continuous and expeditious.

3. For the purposes of these articles the term "port" includes any harbour or roadstead normally used for the loading, unloading or anchoring of ships.

**Art. 3.** 1. Passage is innocent so long as it is not prejudicial to the peace, good order or security of the coastal State. Such passage shall take place in conformity with these articles and with other rules of international law.

2. Passage of a foreign ship shall be considered to be prejudicial to the peace, good order or security of the coastal State, if in the territorial sea it engages in any of the following activities:

(*a*) any warlike act against the coastal or any other State;

(*b*) any exercise or practice with offensive weapons of any kind;

317

(c) the launching or taking on board of any aircraft;

(d) the launching, landing or taking on board of any warlike device;

(e) the embarking or disembarking of any person;

(f) any act of espionage affecting the defence or security of the coastal State;

(g) any act of propaganda affecting the security of the coastal State;

(h) any act of interference with any systems of communication of the coastal State;

(i) any act of interference with any other facility or installation of the coastal State;

(j) any other activity not having a direct bearing on passage.

3. The provisions of paragraph 2 of this article shall not apply to any activities carried out with the prior authorization of the coastal State or as are rendered necessary by *force majeure* or distress or for the purpose of rendering assistance to persons or vessels in danger or distress.

4. The coastal State shall not hamper the innocent passage of foreign ships through the territorial sea and, in particular, it shall not, in the application of these articles or of any laws or regulations made under the provisions of these articles, discriminate against the ships of any particular State or against ships carrying cargoes to, from or on behalf of any particular State.

5. The coastal State is required to give appropriate publicity to any obstacles or dangers to navigation, of which it has knowledge, within the territorial sea.

6. The coastal State may take the necessary steps in its territorial sea to prevent passage which is not innocent.

7. In the case of ships proceeding to any port in the coastal State, the coastal State shall also have the right to take the necessary steps to prevent any breach of the conditions to which admission of those ships to such port is subject.

**Art. 4.** 1. Subject to the provisions of paragraph 2 of this article, the coastal State may, without discrimination amongst foreign ships, suspend temporarily in specified areas of the territorial sea the innocent passage of foreign ships if such suspension is essential for the protection of its security. Such suspension shall take effect only after having been given due publicity.

2. Except to the extent authorized under the provisions of these articles, there shall be no suspension of the innocent passage of foreign ships through straits used for international navigation or through sea lanes designated under the provisions of these articles.

*Subsection B. Regulation of passage*

**Art. 5.** 1. The coastal State may make laws and regulations, in conformity with the provisions of these articles or other rules of international law, relating to passage through the territorial sea, which laws and regulations may be in respect of all or any of the following:

(*a*) the safety of navigation and the regulation of marine traffic;

(*b*) the utilization of, and the prevention of destruction or damage to, facilities and systems of aids to navigation;

(*c*) the prevention of destruction or damage to facilities or installations for the exploration and exploitation of the marine resources, including the resources of the sea-bed and subsoil, of the territorial sea;

(*d*) the prevention of destruction or damage to submarine or aerial cables and pipelines;

(*e*) the preservation of the environment of the coastal State, and the prevention of pollution thereto;

(*f*) research of the marine environment;

(*g*) prevention of infringement of the customs, fiscal, immigration, quarantine or sanitary regulations of the coastal State.

2. The coastal State shall give due publicity to all laws and regulations made under the provisions of this article.

3. Foreign ships exercising the right of innocent pasasge through the territorial sea shall comply with all such laws and regulations of the coastal State.

*Subsection C. Ships having special characteristics*

**Art. 6.** 1. Submarines and other underwater vehicles may be required to navigate on the surface and to show their flag except in cases where they:

(*a*) have given prior notification of their passage to the social State; and

(*b*) if so required by the coastal State, confine their passage to such sea lanes as may be designated for that purpose by the coastal State.

2. Tankers and ships carrying nuclear or other inherently dangerous or noxious substances or materials may be required to give prior notification of their passage to the coastal State and to confine their passage to such sea lanes as may be designated for that purpose by the coastal State.

3. For the purposes of this article, the term "tanker" includes any ship used for the carriage in bulk in a liquid state of petroleum, natural gas or any other highly inflammable, explosive or pollutive substance.

4. Marine research and hydrographic survey ships may be required to give prior notification of their passage to the coastal State and to confine their passage to such sea lanes as may be designated for that purpose by the coastal State.

5. During their passage through the territorial sea foreign marine research and hydrographic survey ships may not carry out any research or survey activities without the prior authorization of the coastal State.

6. A coastal State which designates sea lanes under the provisions of this article may also prescribe traffic separation schemes including depth separation schemes for the regulation of the passage of ships through those sea lanes.

7. A coastal State may from time to time, after giving due publicity thereto, substitute other sea lanes for any sea lanes previously designated by it under the provisions of this article.

8. In the designation of sea lanes and the prescription of traffic separation schemes under the provisions of this article a coastal State shall take into account:

(a) The recommendations of competent international organizations;

(b) Any channels customarily used for international navigation;

(c) The special characteristics of particular channels; and

(d) The special characteristics of particular ships.

9. The coastal State shall clearly demarcate all sea lanes designated by it under the provisions of this article and indicate them on charts to which due publicity shall be given.

10. In order to expedite the passage of ships through the territorial sea the coastal State shall ensure that the procedures for notification under the provisions of this article shall be such as not to cause any undue delay.

### Section II. Rules Applicable to Merchant Ships

**Art. 7.** 1. No charge may be levied upon foreign ships by reason only of their passage through the territorial sea.

2. Charges may be levied upon a foreign ship passing through the territorial sea as payment only for specific services rendered to the ship. These charges shall be levied without discrimination.

**Art. 8.** 1. The criminal jurisdiction of the coastal State shall not be exercised on board a foreign ship passing through the territorial sea to arrest any person or to conduct any investigation in connexion with any crime committed on board the ship during its passage, save only in the following cases:

(a) if the consequences of the crime extend to the coastal State; or

(b) if the crime is of a kind to disturb the peace of the country or the good order of the territorial sea; or

(c) if the assistance of the local authorities has been requested by the captain of the ship or by the consul of the country whose flag the ship flies; or

(d) if it is necessary for the suppression of illicit traffic in narcotic drugs.

2. The provisions of paragraph 1 of this article do not affect the right of the coastal State to take any steps authorized by its laws for the purpose of an arrest or investigation on board a foreign ship passing through the territorial sea after leaving any port in the coastal State.

3. In the cases provided for in paragraphs 1 and 2 of this article, the coastal State shall, if the captain so requests, advise the consular authority of the flag State before taking any steps, and shall facilitate contact between such authority and the ship's crew. In cases of emergency this notification may be communicated while the measures are being taken.

4. In considering whether or how an arrest should be made, the local authorities shall pay due regard to the interests of navigation.

5. The coastal State may not take any steps on board a foreign ship passing through the territorial sea to arrest any person or to conduct any investigation in connexion with any crime committed before the ship entered the territorial sea, if the ship, proceeding from a foreign port, is only passing through the territorial sea without entering any port in the coastal State.

**Art. 9.** 1. The coastal State shall not stop or divert a foreign ship passing through the territorial sea for the purpose of exercising civil jurisdiction in relation to a person on board the ship.

2. The coastal State may not levy execution against or arrest the ship for the purpose of any civil proceedings, save only in respect of obligations or liabilities assumed or incurred by the ship itself in the course or for the purpose of its passage through the waters of the coastal State.

3. The provisions of paragraph 2 of this article are without prejudice to the right of the coastal State, in accordance with its laws, to levy execution against or to arrest, for the purpose of any civil proceedings, a foreign ship lying in the territorial sea, or passing through the territorial sea after leaving any port in the coastal State.

### Section III. Rules Applicable to Government Ships

*Subsection A. Government ships other than warships*

**Art. 10.** The rules contained in sections I and II of these articles shall apply to government ships operated for commercial purposes.

**Art. 11.** 1. The rules contained in section I and in article 7 of these articles shall apply to government ships operated for non-commercial purposes.

2. With such exceptions as are contained in paragraph 1 of this article or in article 14 of these articles nothing in these articles affects the immunities which such ships enjoy under the provisions of these articles or other rules of international law.

321

## Subsection B. Warships

**Art. 12.** 1. For the purposes of this article, the term "warship" means a ship belonging to the naval forces of a State bearing the external marks distinguishing naval vessels of its nationality, under the command of an officer duly commissioned by the Government of that State and whose name appears in the Navy List, and manned by a crew who are under regular naval discipline.

2. The rules contained in section I of these articles shall apply to warships.

3. Foreign warships exercising the right of innocent passage shall not, in the territorial sea:

    (*a*) carry out any manoeuvres other than those having direct bearing on passage; or

    (*b*) undertake any hydrographical survey work or any marine research activities.

4. If any warship does not comply with the laws and regulations of the coastal State relating to passage through the territorial sea or fails to comply with the requirements of paragraph 3 of this article, and disregards any request for compliance which is made to it, the coastal State may suspend the right of passage of such warship and may require it to leave the territorial sea by such route as may be directed by the coastal State. In addition to such suspension of passage, the coastal State may prohibit the passage of that warship through the territorial sea for such period as may be determined by the coastal State.

**Art. 13.** With such exceptions as are contained in articles 12 and 14 of these articles nothing in these articles affects the immunities which warships enjoy under the provisions of these articles or other rules of international law.

## Subsection C. Liability of government ships

**Art. 14.** If, as a result of any non-compliance by any warship or other government ship operated for non-commercial purposes with any of the laws or regulations of the coastal State relating to passage through the territorial sea or with any of the provisions of these articles or other rules of international law, and damage is caused to the coastal State, including its environment and any of its facilities, installations or other property, or to any of its flag vessels, then liability for such damage shall be borne by the flag State of the ship causing such damage.

# IV. ARCHIPELAGO

## FIJI, INDONESIA, MAURITIUS AND THE PHILIPPINES:
## — Archipelagic Principles

> Submitted to the United Nations Seabed Committee on 14
> March 1973, as UN Doc. A/AC.138/SC.II/L.15. See A/AC.
> 138/SC.II/L.48.

1. An archipelagic State, whose component islands and other natural features form an intrinsic geographical, economic and political entity, and historically have or may have been regarded as such, may draw straight baselines connecting the outermost points of the outermost islands and drying reefs of the archipelago from which the extent of the territorial sea of the archipelagic State is or may be determined.

2. The waters within the baselines, regardless of their depth or distance from the coast, the sea-bed and the subsoil thereof, and the superjacent airspace, as well as all their resources, belong to, and are subject to the sovereignty of the archipelagic State.

3. Innocent passage of foreign vessels through the waters of the archipelagic State shall be allowed in accordance with its national legislation, having regard to the existing rules of international law. Such passage shall be through sealanes as may be designated for that purpose by the archipelagic State.

## FIJI, INDONESIA, MAURITIUS AND THE PHILIPPINES:
## — Draft Articles on Archipelago

> Submitted to the United Nations Seabed Committee on
> 6 August 1973, as UN Doc. A/AC.138/SC.II/L.48. See A/
> AC.138/SC.II/L.15.

**Art. 1.** 1. These articles apply only to archipelagic States.

2. An archipelagic State is a State constituted wholly or mainly by one or more archipelagos.

3. For the purposes of these articles an archipelago is a group of islands and other natural features which are so closely interrelated that the component islands and other natural features form an intrinsic geographical, economic and political entity or which historically have been regarded as such.

**Art. 2.** 1. An archipelagic State may employ the method of straight baselines joining the outermost points of the outermost islands and drying reefs of the archipelago in drawing the baselines from which the extent of the territorial sea is to be measured.

2. The drawing of such baselines shall not depart to any appreciable extent from the general configuration of the archipelago.

3. Baselines shall not be drawn to and from low-tide elevations unless lighthouses or similar installations which are permanently above sea level have been built on them or where a low-tide elevation is situated wholly or partly at a distance not exceeding the breadth of the territorial sea from the nearest island.

4. The system of straight baselines shall not be applied by an archipelagic State in such a manner as to cut off the territorial sea of another State.

5. The archipelagic State shall clearly indicate its straight baselines on charts to which due publicity shall be given.

**Art. 3.** 1. The waters enclosed by the baselines, which waters are referred to in these articles as archipelagic waters, regardless of their depth or distance from the coast, belong to and are subject to the sovereignty of the archipelagic State to which they appertain.

2. The sovereignty and rights of the archipelagic State extend to the air space over its archipelagic waters as well as to the water column, the seabed and subsoil thereof, and to all of the resources contained therein.

**Art. 4.** Subject to the provisions of article V, innocent passage of foreign ships shall exist through archipelagic waters.

**Art. 5.** 1. An archipelagic State may designate sealanes suitable for the safe and expeditious passage of ships through its archipelagic waters and may restrict the innocent passage by foreign ships through those waters to those sealanes.

2. An archipelagic State may, from time to time, after giving due publicity thereto, substitute other sealanes for any sealanes previously designated by it under the provisions of this article.

3. An archipelagic State which designates sealanes under the provisions

324

of this article may also prescribe traffic separation schemes for the passage of foreign ships through those sealanes.

4. In the prescription of traffic separation schemes under the provisions of this article, an archipelagic State shall, *inter alia*, take into consideration:

*a.* the recommendation or technical advice of competent international organizations;

*b.* any channels customarily used for international navigation;

*c.* the special characteristics of particular channels, and

*d.* the special characteristics of particular ships or their cargoes.

5. An archipelagic State may make laws and regulations, not inconsistent with the provisions of these articles and having regard to other applicable rules of international law, relating to passage through sealanes and traffic separation schemes as designated by the archipelagic State under the provisions of this article, which laws and regulations may be in respect of, *inter alia*, the following:

*a.* the safety of navigation and the regulation of marine traffic, including ships with special characteristics;

*b.* the utilization of, and the prevention of destruction or damage to, facilities and systems of aids to navigation;

*c.* the prevention of destruction or damage to facilities or installations for the exploration and exploitation of the marine resources, including the resources of the water column, the seabed and subsoil;

*d.* the prevention of destruction or damage to submarine or aerial cables and pipelines;

*e.* the preservation of the environment of the archipelagic State and the prevention of pollution thereto;

*f.* research of marine environment;

*g.* the prevention of infringement of the customs, fiscal, immigration, quarantine or sanitary regulations of the archipelagic State;

*h.* the preservation of the peace, good order and security of the archipelagic State.

6. The archipelagic State shall give due publicity to all laws and regulations made under the provisions of paragraph 5 of this article.

7. Foreign ships exercising innocent passage through those sealanes shall comply with all laws and regulations made under the provisions of this article.

8. If any warship does not comply with the laws and regulations of the archipelagic State concerning passage through any sealane designated by the archipelagic State under the provisions of this article and disregards any request ʿor compliance which is made to it, the archipelagic State may suspend the passage of such warship and require it to leave the archipelagic waters by such route as may be designated by the archipelagic State.

In addition to such suspension of passage the archipelagic State may prohibit the passage of that warship through the archipelagic waters for such period as may be determined by the archipelagic State.

9. Subject to the provisions of paragraph 8 of this article, an archipelagic State may not suspend the innocent passage of foreign ships through sealanes designated by it under the provisions of this article, except when essential for the protection of its security, after giving due publicity thereto, and substituting other sealanes for those through which innocent passage has been suspended.

10. An archipelagic State shall clearly demarcate all sealanes designated by it under the provisions of this article and indicate them on charts to which due publicity shall be given.

## UNITED KINGDOM:
## — Draft Article on the Rights and Duties of Archipelagic States

Submitted to the United Nations Seabed Committee on
2 August 1973, as UN Doc. A/AC.138/SC.II/.44.

1. On ratifying or acceding to this Convention, a state may declare itself to be an archipelagic state where:

(a) the land territory of the state is entirely composed of 3 or more islands; and

(b) it is possible to draw a perimeter, made up of a series of lines or straight baselines, around the outermost points of the outermost islands in such a way that:

(i) no territory belonging to another state lies within the perimeter,

(ii) no baseline is longer than 48 nautical miles, and

(iii) the ratio of the area of the sea to the area of land territory inside the perimeter does not exceed five to one:

Provided that any straight baseline between two points on the same island shall be drawn in conformity with Articles .... of the Convention (on straight baselines).

2. A declaration under paragraph 1 above shall be accompanied by a chart showing the perimeter and a statement certifying the length of each baseline and the ratio of land to sea within the perimeter.

3. Where it is possible to include within a perimeter drawn in conformity with paragraph 1 above only some of the islands belonging to a state, a declaration may be made in respect of those islands. The provisions of this Convention shall apply to the remaining islands in the same way as they apply to the islands of a state which is not an archipelagic

state and references in this Article to an archipelagic state shall be construed accordingly.

4. The territorial sea, [Economic Zone] and any continental shelf of an archipelagic state shall extend from the outside of the perimeter in conformity with Articles .... of this Convention.

5. The sovereignty of an archipelagic state extends to the waters inside the perimeter, described as archipelagic waters: this sovereignty is exercised subject to the provisions of these Articles and to other rules of international law.

6. An archipelagic state may draw baselines in conformity with Articles .... (bays) and .... (river mouths) of this Convention for the purpose of delimiting internal waters.

7. Where parts of archipelagic waters have before the date of ratification of this Convention been used as routes for international navigation between one part of the high seas and another part of the high seas or the territorial sea of another state, the provisions of Articles .... of this Convention apply to those routes (as well as to those parts of the territorial sea of the archipelagic state adjacent thereto) as if they were straits. A declaration made under paragraph 1 of this Article shall be accompanied by a list of such waters which indicates all the routes used for international navigation, as well as any traffic separation schemes in force in such waters in conformity with Articles .... of this Convention. Such routes may be modified or new routes created only in conformity with Articles .... of this Convention.

8. Within archipelagic waters, other than those referred to in paragraph 7 above, the provisions of Articles .... (innocent passage) apply.

9. In this Article, references to an island include a part of an island and reference to the territory of a state includes its territorial sea.

10. The provisions of this Article are without prejudice to any rules of this Convention and international law applying to islands forming an archipelago which is not an archipelagic state.

11. The depositary shall notify all states entitled to become a party to this Convention of any declaration made in conformity with this Article, including copies of the chart and statement supplied pursuant to paragraph 2 above.

12. Any dispute about the interpretation or application of this Article which cannot be settled by negotiations may be submitted by either party to the dispute to the procedures for the compulsory settlement of disputes contained in Articles .... of this Convention.

# V. SEAS BEYOND TERRITORIAL SEA AND NATIONAL JURISDICTION

In addition to the proposals herein referred to, see, also, the following texts:
A/AC.138/SC.II/L.4 (U.S.), Art. 3. (p. 218 of Volume I)
— L.21 (Colombia, Mexico and Venezuela), Art. 16-17 (p. 358)
As to the regime of the seabed beyond national jurisdiction, see A/AC.138/25, 26, 27, 33, 43, 44, 46, 49, 53, 55, 59 and 63 (Proposals submitted in the 1971 session) printed in Volume I.

## GREECE:
— **Archeological and Historical Treasures of the Sea-bed and the Ocean Floor beyond the Limits of National Jurisdiction**

Submitted to the United Nations Seabed Committee on 2 August 1972, as UN Doc. A/AC.138/SC.I/L.16.

*General principles*

1. The International Convention should ensure that the archeological and historical treasures of the sea-bed and the ocean floor, beyond the limits of national jurisdiction should be protected as a common heritage of mankind.

2. The territorial jurisdiction of the International Sea-Bed Authority as far as the protection of the archeological and historical treasures is concerned is confined to the sea-bed and the ocean floor and the subsoil thereof beyond the limits of the continental shelf and to the extent that the international limits of the Sea-Bed Authority are prescribed in the Convention.

3. Exploration and exploitation of the resources of the international sea-bed area shall be carried out in such a manner as to prevent damage to the archeological and historical treasures to be found in the area.

4. If the International Authority will not undertake itself exploitation activities of the resources of the sea-bed area, all persons, natural or juridical, public or private, national or international, exploiting the area by a system of contracts or by the establishment of joint ventures, are to be obliged to report to the Authority the discovery of any item of archeological or historical value.

5. The exploration and utilization of the archeological and historical treasures of the international sea-bed in closed or semi-closed seas could be supervised by appropriate regional organs established or to be established for this purpose, in which the coastal States of the region whose scientific institutions desire to explore the sea-bed area will have an equal right to participate. For this purpose regional committees of experts could exercise advisory functions with the International Sea-Bed Authority. The activities of these regional organs will not interfere with the right of the international Authority to supervise any exploration and archeological activity.

6. As soon as an item of antiquity is spotted in the international sea-bed area operations should be temporarily suspended if necessary until the appropriate international or regional competent organ studies the discovery and takes proper protective measures for safeguarding the item during the recovery operation.

7. The person, natural or juridical, conducting the exploration of the international sea-bed area will be obliged not to sell to an unauthorized person, natural or juridical any discovered archeological or historical object.

8. Such items have to be surrendered to the International Sea-Bed Authority or to the Regional Organ.

9. The International Authority and the competent Regional Organ will notify the State or States of cultural origin of the object or discovery.

10. The Authority should pay due regard to the interests of the State or group of States of origin of the discovered archeological or historical treasures. To this effect the Authority should promote, in co-operation with the regional organ, the universal sharing of the cultural benefits derived from the discovery of such treasures, taking into particular consideration the rightful interests of the State of historical origin of the discovered treasure.

11. The State of historical origin of the archeological or historical discovery possesses preferential rights to acquire this item. If such a right to acquire by compensating the finder is not exercised within a reasonable time, the object will be disposed of at the discretion of the finder.

12. Each State shall make it an offence for its nationals and vessels to violate the relevant regulations adopted pursuant to the International Sea-Bed Convention.

### TURKEY:
— **Archeological and Historical Treasures on the Sea-bed and Ocean Floor beyond the Limits of National Jurisdiction**

Submitted to the United Nations Seabed Committee on exploitation 28 March 1973, as UN Doc. A/AC.138/SC.I/L.21.

1. Archeological and historical treasures to be discovered during the exploration and explicitation of the area constitute a part of the common heritage of mankind and as such shall enjoy the protection of the International Authority.

The Authority shall bring the discovery of such treasures to the notice of member States.

2. The State of the country of origin shall have the right to acquire the treasure from the International Authority against payment.

In case the State of the country of origin opts not to exercise its right to acquire the treasure, the International Authority shall have the right to sell the treasure to authorized third parties or keep it in a museum belonging to the International Authority or to the United Nations.

3. The International Authority, in consultation with concerned specialized agencies of the United Nations, shall draw up rules for regulating the discovery, identification, protection, acquisition and disposal of the archeological and historical treasures discovered in the area.

### GREECE:
— **Draft Article on Protection of Archeological and Historical Treasures**

Submitted to the United Nations Seabed Committee on
14 August 1973, as UN Doc. A/AC.138/SC.I/L.25.

1. The State Parties to this Convention recognize that all objects of archeological or historical value in the area beyond the limits of national jurisdiction are part of the common heritage of mankind.

2. The Authority shall, in co-operation with the appropriate Specialized Agencies of the United Nations, take measures for the identification, protection and conservation of the objects of archeological or historical value found in the area.

3. The State of cultural origin of such objects shall have the preferential right to undertake the salvaging of such objects and to acquire any such object under procedures to be established by the Assembly, including compensation of the Authority.

4. If the State of cultural origin does not avail itself of its preferential right under paragraph 3 above the Authority will see to it that such object is disposed of in accordance with the principle in paragraph 1 above.

## ITALY:
## — Draft Articles (concerning the Council of the Sea-bed Authority)

Submitted to the United Nations Seabed Committee on 24 July 1973, as UN Doc. A/AC.138/SC.I/L.24. See A/AC.138/SC.I/L.15: Italy—Institutional Problems concerning the Sea-bed Authority (1 August 1972).

### I. *Composition of the Council*

The Council shall be composed of thirty-six members, of whom twenty shall be elected by the Assembly and sixteen shall be designated in accordance with the following criteria.

A. Of the sixteen designated members, eight members shall be designated on the basis of the Gross National Product scale.

To the exclusion of the States already designated in pursuance of the foregoing paragraph, seven members shall be designated on the basis of their particular role as coastal States.

One member shall be designated on the basis of its status as a land-locked State.

The seven members having a particular role as coastal States shall be designated as follows. In each of the geographical regions numbered 1 to 7 in the list in paragraph B. below, that State shall be designated which has the highest figure when the length of its coasts in nautical miles is multiplied by the number of its inhabitants.

The State designated as a member on the basis of its status as a land-locked State shall be that land-locked State which has the highest figure when its surface area is multiplied by the number of its inhabitants.

B. The Assembly shall elect twenty members of the Council from among the following groups of countries:

1. Africa
2. North America
3. Latin America
4. Asia

5. Western Europe
6. Eastern Europe
7. Oceania
8. Land-locked States

The above twenty members shall be elected by the Assembly in such a manner that the Council as a whole shall at all times include a specified number (to be determined) of members representing the groups of countries listed in the foregoing paragraph.

II. *System of voting in the Council*

The Council shall take decisions on matters of substance by a three-quarters majority, while decisions on questions of procedure shall be taken by a simple majority.

The Council shall decide by a simple majority whether a question is a matter of substance or procedure.

In all cases, the quorum shall consist of the number of States present and voting.

## ITALY:
— **Preliminary Draft Articles concerning the Basic Principles of the Regime of the International Area of the Sea-bed and the Subsoil thereof, and Regulations for the Granting and Administration of Licences for the Exploration and Exploitation of Minerals**

Submitted to the United Nations Seabed Committee on 14 August 1973, as UN Doc. A/AC.138/SC.I/L.26.

**Section A. Preliminary Draft Articles on the Basic Principles of the Regime of the International Area of the Sea-Bed and the Subsoil Thereof**

**Art. 1.** *International area of the sea-bed and the subsoil thereof*
1. The international area of the sea-bed and the subsoil thereof comprises the sea-bed and the ocean floor, and the subsoil thereof, beyond the limits of national jurisdiction.

2. An International Authority shall be established for the international area of the sea-bed and the subsoil thereof, which constitute the common heritage of mankind.

**Art. 2.** *Protection of other activities*
1. Operations carried out in the international area of the sea-bed and the subsoil thereof shall not in any way impair the preservation of the living resources of the sea or cause any unjustifiable interference with the

other uses of the high seas such as navigation, overflight, fishing, and the laying and utilization of submarine cables and pipelines.

2. Scientific research in the international area shall be free; however, before undertaking any research operation, the party in question shall submit its research plan to the competent organ of the International Authority. "Scientific research" means all operations carried out by qualified persons or institutions for the purpose of obtaining data, which shall be made public and be made available to all.

**Art. 3.** *Regulations concerning licenses for the exploration and exploitation of minerals*

1. The International Authority shall be the exclusive administrator of the mineral resources of the international area's sea-bed and the subsoil thereof.

2. The International Authority shall issue instruments authorizing the exploration and exploitation of minerals to High Contracting Parties or to physical or juridical persons sponsored by a High Contracting Party.

3. A High Contracting Party which acts as patron of a physical or juridical person shall vouch for the technical and financial capabilities of the sponsored person, as well as for the application of the provisions of this Convention and measures adopted by the Authority in conformity with those provisions.

4. The High Contracting Party may require the sponsored person to pay a presentation fee covering the reimbursement of expenses and excluding any other payment by the sponsored person, for whatever purpose, in connexion with activities of prospecting, exploration and exploitation.

5. Licences for the exploration and exploitation of minerals shall be divided into three categories:

    (*a*) non-exclusive prospecting licences;

    (*b*) exclusive exploration licences;

    (*c*) exclusive exploitation licences.

6. Licences shall be issued for the prospecting, exploration and exploitation of one of the following three categories of minerals:

    (*a*) minerals of the sea-bed's subsoil extracted in a fluid state, such as petroleum, natural gas, sulphur, salts which can be extracted by dissolution, *etc.* . . .;

    (*b*) minerals situated on the surface of the sea-bed, such as manganese nodules, metal-bearing muds, *etc.* . . .;

    (*c*) solid minerals of the sea-bed's subsoil, such as coal, metal ores, *etc.* . . . .

7. Licenses issued by the International Authority for the various categories of the minerals referred to in the preceding paragraph may totally or partially superimpose one another and may be issued to different

applicants and to applicants of different nationalities. The various licensees for different categories of minerals in the same sector or in over-lapping sectors shall carry out their respective activities in such a way as not to hinder unnecessarily the activities of the others.

8. Minerals extracted in the international area in conformity with the licences issued shall be so divided between the holder of an exclusive licence for exploitation and the International Authority as to ensure the licensee reimbursement of his operating costs and prior exploration costs, as well as compensation for his mining risk. The International Authority may require the licensee to market the output.*

**Art. 4.** *Provisions to prevent any oligopolistic situations in the international area of the sea-bed and the subsoil thereof*

The International Authority may not issue to any one High Contracting Party and to the physical or juridical persons sponsored by any one High Contracting Party exploration licences for more than . . . . . . km² and exploitation licences for more than . . . . . . km².

### Section B. Preliminary Draft of Articles concerning Regulations for the Granting and Administration of Exploration Licences for Minerals in the International Zone of the Sea-Bed and its Subsoil

**Art. 1.** *Non-exclusive prospecting licences*

1. Application for a non-exclusive prospecting licence shall be made to the International Authority by a High Contracting Party or by a physical or juridical person sponsored by a High Contracting Party.

2. A non-exclusive prospecting licence authorizes the licensee to engage in prospecting by geophysical and geochemical methods, to take samples from the sea-bed and drill into the subsoil to a depth of not more than 300 m.

3. Non-exclusive prospecting licences shall be issued for a specified area.

4. Non-exclusive prospecting licences cannot be used in areas for which exclusive exploration or exploitation licences have been granted.

5. Non-exclusive prospecting licences shall be issued for a period of two years; they may be extended for successive periods of the same duration.

6. Non-exclusive prospecting licences shall be issued against payment —at the time the licence is granted and on each successive renewal, if any—of a fee the amount of which shall be proportionate to the area in question.

---

* Reimbursement of the costs borne by the licensee and compensation for his mining risk may be effected on a lump-sum basis.

7. A non-exclusive prospecting licence shall not give the licensee either an exclusive right of exploration, or any right of priority in applying for an exploitation licence.

**Art. 2.** *Exclusive exploration licences*

1. Application for an exclusive exploration licence shall be made to the International Authority by a High Contracting Party or by a physical or juridical person sponsored by a High Contracting Party.

2. An exclusive exploration licence shall give the licensee the exclusive right to search for minerals of one of the categories mentioned in Section "A", article 3 (6), by geophysical and geochemical prospecting methods, and to drill into the subsoil without any limit as to depth.

3. The area covered by the exclusive search licence may not exceed:
...... km² in the case of minerals of category (*a*);
...... km² in the case of minerals of category (*b*);
...... km² in the case of minerals of category (*c*).

4. The total area covered by the exclusive search licences granted to a High Contracting Party for one of the three categories of minerals, added to the area covered by the exclusive search licences for the same category of minerals granted to physical or juridical persons sponsored by the same High Contracting Party, may in no case exceed a maximum limit. This limit will be determined by the International Authority in accordance with the principles of an equitable distribution among the High Contracting Parties.

5. Exclusive exploration licences for minerals of category (*a*) shall be granted for ... years and may be renewed, in the first instance, for ... years and, in the second instance, for ... years. Exclusive exploration licences for minerals of category (*b*) shall be granted for ... years and may be renewed for ... years. In no case may their validity exceed ... years. Exploration licences for minerals of category (*c*) shall be granted for ... years and may be renewed for ... years. In no case may their validity exceed ... years.

6. Renewals of exploration licences shall be conditional on fulfilment of the work programmes and on actual expenditure of the minimum amount fixed at the time the application was made.

7. On each renewal, the area initially covered by an exclusive exploration licence shall be reduced by ... per cent. This reduction shall not be applicable to licences covering an area of less than ... km².

8. The licensee may at any time give up his licence or make voluntary reductions in the area initially covered. Voluntary reductions of area shall be regarded as anticipated reductions in respect of the reductions which are mandatory at the time of renewal.

9. At the time of application for the licence or of request for its renewal,

the licensee shall submit to the International Authority a programme of work. This programme shall give a breakdown of the exploration operations which the licensee undertakes to carry out, and the length of time he will engage in them.

10. A specific programme of *minimum* expenditure commitments shall be submitted along with the programme of work. In no case may the total amount be less than . . . per km².

11. Non-fulfilment of the obligations contained in the programme of work, as regards either the conditions or the time-limits laid down, shall entail revocation of the licence and the payment of a sum proportionate to the *minimum* amount corresponding to the part of the work programme not carried out.

12. Exclusive exploration licences for minerals of category (*a*) shall be granted against payment of a "registration fee" amounting to . . ., and an annual rental of . . . per km² during the initial period of the licence's validity, and of . . . per km² during the period of renewal. Exclusive exploration licences for minerals of category (*b*) shall be granted on the same terms, against payment of a "registration fee" amounting to . . ., and an annual rental of . . . per km² during the initial period of the licence's validity, and of . . . per km² for the period of renewal. Exclusive exploration licences for minerals of category (*c*) shall be granted against payment of a "registration fee" amounting to . . ., and an annual rental of . . . per km² for the initial period of the licence's validity, and of . . . per km² for the period of renewal.

**Art. 3.** *Application for and granting of exclusive exploration licences*

1. Application for an exclusive exploration licence shall be made to the International Authority by a High Contracting Party or by a physical or juridical person sponsored by a High Contracting Party.

2. The International Authority shall be required to make public the applications submitted to it.

3. During a period of six months from the date of publication of an application for an exclusive exploration licence, subsequent applications with respect to the same area or part of the same area shall be considered on an equal footing.

4. On the expiry of the period indicated in the preceding paragraph, the International Authority shall review the applications and assign the area applied for to the applicant who has submitted the work programme considered most appropriate for the rapid and efficacious development of the mineral resources of the area.

**Art. 4.** *Exclusive exploitation licences*

1. Application for an exclusive exploitation licence shall be made to the International Authority by a High Contracting Party or by a physical

or juridical person sponsored by a High Contracting Party.

2. An exclusive exploitation licence shall give the licensee the exclusive right to exploit the minerals discovered.

3. An exclusive exploitation licence shall be granted where a discovered deposit has been accepted as exploitable in accordance with the criteria established by the International Authority and in the light of the general situation in the area (geological, logistical, economic factors, *etc.*).

4. The area covered by the exclusive exploitation licence may not exceed:

...... km² in the case of minerals of category (*a*);
...... km² in the case of minerals of category (*b*);
...... km² in the case of minerals of category (*c*).

5. The total area covered by exclusive exploitation licences granted to a High Contracting Party for one of the three categories of minerals, added to the area covered by the exclusive exploitation licences for the same category of minerals granted to physical or juridical persons sponsored by the same High Contracting Party may in no case exceed a maximum limit. This limit shall be determined by the International Authority in accordance with the principles of an equitable distribution among the High Contracting Parties.

6. An exclusive exploitation licence granted to a holder of an exploration licence shall not exceed the limits of the pre-existing exploration licence.

7. The extent of the area covered by the exploitation licence shall be fixed in a way that will permit rational exploitation of the deposit discovered.

8. Exploitation licences shall be valid for a period of 30 years and may be renewed only for a period of 10 years.

9. At the time of application for the licence or for any renewal, the licensee shall submit to the International Authority a programme of work giving a breakdown of the operations he undertakes to carry out for the exploitation of the deposit and the length of time he will engage in them.

10. A specific programme of the *minimum* investment, the total of which may in no case be less than ... per km², shall also be submitted along with the programme of work.

11. Non-fulfilment of the programme of work, as regards either the ways in which it is carried out or the time-limits laid down shall entail the revocation of the licence and the payment of an indemnity equal to the amount corresponding to the part of the programme not carried out.

12. Exclusive exploitation licences shall be granted against payment of a "registration fee" amounting to .... and an annual rental of .....
per km².

13. The holder of an exclusive exploitation licence shall be entitled to

make use of any installations necessary for the extraction, storage and transport of the minerals extracted, in keeping with the security standards laid down by the International Authority.

**Art. 5.** *Distribution of output*

1. The holder of an exclusive exploitation licence shall be entitled to receive annually a percentage of the minerals extracted corresponding in value to the annual operating costs of the deposit.

2. In addition to the percentage specified in paragraph (1) above, the holder of an exclusive exploitation licence shall be entitled to an annual percentage—not exceeding ..... per cent—of the minerals extracted. This latter percentage shall be granted by way of reimbursement either for costs incurred as a result of operations carired out in the area covered by the initial exclusive exploration licence or for related interest charges, until such costs have been completely reimbursed.*

3. The holder of an exclusive exploitation licence shall also be entitled, by way of compensation for his "mining risk", to a further indemnity, which shall not exceed . . . . per cent of the minerals extracted.*

4. The share of the output which does not go to the licensee shall be allocated to the International Authority, which may request him to market it.

## UNION OF SOVIET SOCIALIST REPUBLICS:
**— Preamble to a Treaty on the Use of the Sea-bed for Peaceful Purposes**

Submitted to the United Nations Seabed Committee on 16 August 1973, as UN Doc. A/AC.138/SC.I/L.28.

*The States Parties to this Treaty,*

*Attaching* great importance to the rational and orderly use of the sea-bed and the subsoil thereof beyond the limits of the continental shelf exclusively for peaceful purposes and for the benefit of the peoples of all countries,

*Considering* that co-operation in this field between States, on the basis of a treaty, would contribute to the maintenance of international peace and security and to the development of international co-operation, and

*In order to simplify financial calculations, reimbursement of the costs incurred by the licensee and compensation for his "mining risk" may also be determined on a lump-sum basis. In such a case, provision might be made for a minimum and maximum sum so as to take into account the geological, operating and logistical conditions of the particular deposit.

would also promote the utilization of the resources of the sea-bed in the interests of economic progress, including the interests of the economies of the peoples of the developing countries.

*Noting* the great importance of the Treaty on the Prohibition of the Emplacement of Nuclear Weapons and Other Weapons of Mass Destruction on the Sea-bed and the Ocean-Floor and in the Subsoil Thereof, as an important step towards the exclusion of the sea-bed and the ocean floor from the arms race,

*Recalling* General Assembly resolution 2749 (XXV), which provides *inter alia* that an international régime applying to the sea-bed and the subsoil thereof shall be established by "an international treaty of a universal character, generally agreed upon",

*Convinced* that the conclusion of a treaty on the use of the sea-bed for peaceful purposes will contribute to the realization of the Purposes and Principles of the United Nations Charter and to the strengthening of the principles of international law governing the freedom of the high seas, including the freedom of research,

*Have agreed as follows:*

## UNION OF SOVIET SOCIALIST REPUBLICS:
## — Draft Articles on Fishing

Submitted to the United Nations Seabed Committee on 18 July 1972, as UN Doc. A/AC.138/SC.II/L.6.

*Basic provisions*

1. In the areas of the high seas directly adjacent to its territorial sea or fishery zone (not exceeding 12 miles), a developing coastal State may annually reserve to itself such part of the allowable catch of fish as can be taken by vessels navigating under that State's flag.

With the growth of the fishing fleet of the developing coastal State the above-mentioned part of the allowable catch of fish reserved by that State may increase accordingly.

The developing coastal State shall notify the size of the reserved part of the catch to the international fisheries organization whose competence covers the particular area, and also to States engaged in fishing in the above-mentioned areas.

2. In the areas of the high seas directly adjacent to its territorial sea or fishery zone (not exceeding 12 miles), any coastal State may annually reserve to itself such part of the allowable catch of the stock of anadromous fish spawning in its rivers as can be taken by vessels navigating

339

under that State's flag.

3. The part of the allowable catch of fish which is not reserved in accordance with paragraphs 1 and 2 above may be taken by vessels navigating under the flags of other States, including land-locked States, without detriment to the reproduction of the stocks of fish.

4. In those of the areas referred to above where fishing regulatory measures are carried out through international fisheries organizations, such regulatory régime shall remain effective in the future.

Control over the observance of the fishing regulatory measures in such areas shall continue to be exercised on the basis of the provisions adopted within the framework of the respective international fisheries organizations.

5. In the areas referred to in this article which are not covered by the measures specified in paragraph 4, the coastal State may itself establish fishing regulatory measures on the basis of scientific findings. Such measures shall be established by the coastal State in agreement with the States also engaged in fishing in the said areas.

Regulatory measures shall not discriminate in form or in substance against fishermen of any of those States.

6. The coastal State may itself exercise control over the observance of the fishing regulatory measures initiated by it under paragraph 5.

In cases where the competent authorities of the coastal State have sufficient reasons for believing that a foreign vessel engaged in fishing is violating these measures, they may stop the vessel and inspect it, and also draw up a statement of the violations. The consideration of cases which may arise in connexion with violations of the said measures by a foreign vessel, as well as the punishment of members of the crew guilty of such violations, shall be effected by the flag-State of the vessel which has committed the violation. Such State shall notify the coastal State of the results of the investigation and of measures taken by it.

7. Disputes between States on matters connected with the application of the provisions of this article may, at the request of one of the parties to the dispute, be settled by arbitration unless the parties agree to settle it by another means of pacific settlement provided for in Article 33 of the United Nations Charter.


## UNITED STATES OF AMERICA:
## — Revised Draft Fisheries Article

Submitted to the United Nations Seabed Committee on 4 August 1972, as UN Doc. A/AC.138/SC.II/L.9, in order to revise the relevant part of the Draft Articles on the Breadth of the Territorial Sea, Straits, and Fisheries submitted by the United States on 30 July 1971 as UN Doc. A/AC.138/SC.II/L.4 (p. 218 of Volume I).

See A/AC.138/SC.II/L.20: U.S.—Special Considerations regarding the Management of Anadromous Fishes and Highly Migratory Oceanic Fishes (2 April 1973).

## I. Regulatory Authority

Authority to regulate the living resources of the high seas shall be determined by their biological characteristics and such authority shall be exercised so as to assure their conservation, maximum utilization and equitable allocation.

## II. Coastal and Anadromous Living Resources

The coastal State shall regulate and have preferential rights to all coastal living resources off its coast beyond the territorial sea to the limits of their migratory range. The coastal State in whose fresh or estuarine waters anadromous resources (e.g. salmon) spawn shall have authority to regulate and have preferential rights to such resources beyond the territorial sea throughout their migratory range on the high seas (without regard to whether or not they are off the coast of said State).

A. The term "coastal resource" refers to all living resources off the coast of a coastal State except the highly migratory species listed in Annex A, and anadromous resources.

B. The coastal State may annually reserve to its flag vessels, in accordance with this article, that portion of such coastal and anadromous resources as they can harvest.

C. Such coastal and anadromous resources which are located in or migrate through waters adjacent to more than one coastal State shall be regulated by agreement among such States.

## III. Highly Migratory Oceanic Resources

The highly migratory oceanic resources listed in Annex A shall be regulated by appropriate international fishery organizations.

A. Any coastal State party, or other State party whose flag vessels harvest or intend to harvest a regulated resource, shall have an equal right to participate in such organizations.

B. No State party whose flag vessels harvest a regulated resource may refuse to co-operate with such organizations. Regulations of such organizations in accordance with this Article shall apply to all vessels fishing the regulated resources regardless of their nationality.

C. In the event the States concerned are unable or deem it unnecessary to establish an international organization the resources shall be regulated by agreement or consultation among such States.

## IV. *Conservation Principles*

In order to assure the conservation of living marine resources, the coastal State or appropriate international organization shall apply the following principles:

A. Allowable catch and other conservation measures shall be established which are designed, on the basis of the best evidence available, to maintain or restore the maximum sustainable yield, taking into account relevant environmental and economic factors.

B. For this purpose scientific information, catch and effort statistics, and other relevant data shall be contributed and exchanged on a regular basis.

C. Conservation measures and their implementation shall not discriminate in form or fact against any fishermen. Conservation measures shall remain in force pending the settlement, in accordance with the relevant provisions of this Article, of any disagreement as to their validity.

## V. *Utilization and Allocation*

In order to assure the maximum utilization and equitable allocation of coastal and anadromous resources, the coastal State shall apply the following principles:

A. The coastal State may reserve to its flag vessels that portion of the allowable annual catch they can harvest.

B. The coastal State shall provide access by other states, under reasonable conditions, to that portion of the resources not fully utilized by its vessels on the basis of the following priorities:

(1) States that have traditionally fished for a resource, subject to the conditions of sub-paragraph C;

(2) other States in the region, particularly landlocked States and other States with limited access to the resources, with whom joint or reciprocal arrangements have been made; and

(3) all States, without discrimination among them.

C. Whenever necessary to accommodate the allocations to the coastal States traditional fishing may be reduced, without discrimination among those States that have traditionally fished for a resource, in the following manner:

(Formula to be negotiated within Subcommittee II which takes into account the interests of traditional fishing States.)

States whose fishermen harvest a resource under regulation by a coastal

State may be required, without discrimination, to pay reasonable fees to defray their share of the cost of such regulation.

## VI. *Notification Consultation*

The coastal State shall give to all affected states timely notice of any conservation, utilization and allocation regulations, prior to their implementation, and shall consult with other States concerned.

## VII. *Technical Assistance*

An international register of independent fisheries experts shall be established and maintained by the Food and Agriculture Organization of the United Nations. Any developing State party to this convention requiring assistance may select an appropriate number of such experts to serve as a fishery management advisory group to that State.

## VIII. *Enforcement*

Actions under this paragraph shall be taken in such a manner as to minimize interference with fishing and other activities in the marine environment.

A. Coastal State—the coastal State may inspect and arrest vessels for fishing in violation of its regulations. The coastal State may try and punish vessels for fishing in violation of its regulations, provided that where the state of nationality of a vessel has established procedures for the trial and punishment of violations of coastal State fishing regulations adopted in accordance with this article, an arrested vessel shall be delivered promptly to duly authorized officials of the State of nationality for trial and punishment, who shall notify the coastal State of the disposition of the case within six months.

B. International fisheries organization—Each State party to an international organization shall make it an offence for its flag vessels to violate the regulations adopted by such organization in accordance with this article. Officials authorized by the appropriate international organization, or of any State so authorized by the organization, may inspect and arrest vessels for violating the fishery regulations adopted by such organizations. An arrested vessel shall be promptly delivered to the duly authorized officials of the flag State. Only the flag State of the offending vessel shall have jurisdiction to try the case or impose any penalties regarding the violation of fishery regulations adopted by international organizations pursuant to this article. Such State has the responsibility of notifying the enforcing organization within a period of six months of the disposition of the case.

## IX. Disputes Settlement

Any dispute which may arise between States under this article shall, at the request of any of the parties to the dispute, be submitted to a special commission of five members unless the parties agree to seek a solution by another method of peaceful settlement, as provided for in Article 33 of the Charter of the United Nations. The commission shall proceed in accordance with the following provisions.

A. The members of the commission, one of whom shall be designated as chairman, shall be named by agreement between the States in dispute within two months of the request for settlement in accordance with the provisions of this article. Failing agreement they shall, upon request of any State party to the dispute, be named by the Secretary General of the United Nations, within a further two-month period, in consultation with the States involved and with the President of the International Court of Justice and the Director-General of the Food and Agriculture Organization of the United Nations, from amongst well-qualified persons being nationals of States not involved in the dispute and specializing in legal, administrative or scientific questions relating to fisheries, depending upon the nature of the dispute to be settled. Any vacancy arising after the original appointment shall be filled in the same manner as provided for the initial selection.

B. Any State party to proceedings under these articles shall have the right to name one of the nationals to sit with the special commission, with the right to participate fully in the proceedings on the same footing as a member of the commission but without the right to vote or to take part in the writing of the commission's decision.

C. The commission shall determine its own procedure, assuring each party to the proceedings a full opportunity to be heard and to present its case. It shall also determine how the costs and expenses shall be divided between the parties to the dispute failing agreement by the parties on this matter.

D. Pending the final award by the special commission, measures in dispute relating to conservation shall be applied; the commission may decide whether and to what extent other measures shall be applied pending its final award.

E. The special commission shall render its decision, which shall be binding upon the parties, within a period of five months from the time it is appointed unless it decides, in the case of necessity to extend the time limit for a period not exceeding two months.

F. The special commission shall, in reaching its decision, adhere to this article and to any agreements between the disputing parties implementing this article.

344

## X. *Other Uses*

The exploitation of the living resources shall be conducted with reasonable regard for other activities in the marine environment.

## XI. *Existing Conventions*

The provisions of this article may be applied to fishery conventions and other international fishery agreements already in force.

## JAPAN:
## — Proposals for a Regime of Fisheries on the High Seas

> Submitted to the United Nations Seabed Committee on 14 August 1972, as UN Doc. A/AC.138/SC.II/L.12. This is a text revised on the basis of a working paper which the Government of Japan presented at the Asian-African Legal Consultative Committee in January 1972 (p. 222 of Volume I).

*Summary of the proposals*

This paper, which contains, *inter alia*, a set of proposals on preferential rights of coastal States in fishing on the high seas, attempts to formulate a broad and equitable accommodation of interests of States in the exploitation and use of the living resources of the high seas, taking into account the dependence on fishing of both coastal and other States. While according a preferential right of catch to developing coastal States corresponding to their harvesting capacities and a differentiated preferential right to developed coastal States, the proposals also take into consideration the legitimate interests of other States. Thus, they seek to ensure that a gradual accommodation of interests can be brought about in the expanding exploitation and use of fishery resources of the high seas, without causing any abrupt change in the present order in fishing which might result in disturbing the economic and social structures of States. The proposals may be summarized as follows:

   (i) The proposed general rules concerning preferential rights of coastal States are intended to ensure sufficient protection for coastal fisheries of States, particularly of developing coastal States, in relation to the activities of distant water fisheries of other States, in areas of the sea adjacent to their 12-mile limit;

  (ii) Preferential rights shall entitle a developing coastal State annually to an allocation of resources that corresponds to its harvesting capacity; the rate of growth of the fishing capacity of that developing coastal State shall be duly taken into account to the extent that it is able to catch a major portion of the allowable catch. They shall entitle a developed coastal State to an allocation of resources necessary for the maintenance of its locally conducted small-scale coastal fishery; the interests of traditionally established fisheries of other States shall be duly taken into account in determining the part of the allowable catch thus reserved;

(iii) Since situations vary greatly according to areas of the sea, the general rules for protection of coastal States interests shall be flexible enough, as regards the methods to be employed to safeguard such interests, to allow the parties to adopt any measures which are effective and suited to the individual cases. The substance of protection, i.e. concrete applicable measures implementing preferential rights of coastal States, shall be the subject of negotiation between the coastal and other States concerned and shall be finalized in agreement;

(iv) If negotiation fails, the case in dispute shall be referred to a body of experts for a binding decision unless settled by any other means to be agreed upon between the parties concerned. During the period of dispute, distant water fishing States shall assume obligations to restrain their fishing efforts according to specific plans provided for in interim measures (6.1 of the proposal);

(v) In concluding agreement on the preferential right of a developing coastal State, international co-operation shall be carried out in the field of fisheries and other related industries between the developing coastal State and other fishing States concerned with a view to improving the effectiveness of protection of the interests of that developing coastal State;

(vi) No special status in respect of conservation and no preferential rights of catch shall be recognized to coastal States with regard to the harvesting of highly migratory, including anadromous stocks of fish. The conservation and regulation of these stocks shall be made pursuant to international or regional consultations or agreements, or should such be already the case, through the existing regional fishery commissions;

(vii) Enforcement jurisdiction under the rules shall be retained by flag States though the right of coastal States to inspect foreign vessels to identify violation, and to arrest vessels in violation for prompt delivery to the flag States, shall be recognized.

## General Provisions

1.1 The proposed régime applies to fisheries on the high seas in the areas adjacent to the limit of 12 miles from the coast of a State, measured in accordance with the relevant rules of international law (such areas hereinafter shall be referred to as "adjacent waters").

1.2 All States have the right for their nationals to engage in fishing on the high seas, subject to the present régime and to their existing treaty obligations.

1.3 The proposed régime shall not affect the rights and obligations of States under existing international agreements relating to specific fisheries on the high seas.

## Conservation of Fishery Resources

2.1 *Objective of Conservation measures*

The objective of conservation measures is to achieve the maximum sustainable yields of fishery resources and thereby to secure and maintain a maximum supply of food and other marine products.

2.2 *Obligations to adopt conservation measures*

(1) In cases where nationals of one State are exclusively engaged in fishing a particular stock of fish, that State shall adopt, when necessary, appropriate conservation measures.

In cases where nationals of two or more States are engaged in fishing a particular stock of fish, these States shall, at the request of any of them, negotiate and conclude arrangements which will provide for appropriate conservation measures.

These conservation measures shall be consistent with the objective of conservation referred to in para. 2.1 above and shall be adopted having regard to the principles referred to in para. 2.3 below.

(2) In cases where conservation measures have already been adopted by States with respect to a particular stock of fish which is exploited by their nationals, a new-comer State shall adopt its own conservation measures which should be as restrictive as the existing measures until new arrangements are concluded among all the States concerned. If the existing conservation measures include a catch limitation or some other regulations not permitting nationals of the new-comer State to engage in fishing the stock of fish concerned, the States applying the existing conservation measures shall immediately enter into negotiation with the new-comer State for the purpose of concluding new arrangements. Pending such arrangements, nationals of the new-comer State shall not engage in fishing the stock concerned.

(3) States shall make use of the international or regional fishery organizations, as far as possible, to adopt appropriate conservation measures.

2.3 *Basic principles relating to conservation measures*

(1) Conservation measures must be adopted on the basis of the best scientific evidence available. If the States concerned cannot reach agreement on the assessment of the conditions of the stock to which conserva-

347

tion measures are to be applied, they shall request an appropriate international body or other impartial third party to undertake the assessment. In order to obtain the fairest possible assessment of the stock conditions, the States concerned shall co-operate in the establishment of regional institutions for surveying and research into fishery resources.

(2) No conservation measure shall discriminate in form or fact between fishermen of one State from those of other States.

(3) Conservation measures shall be determined, to the extent possible, on the basis of the allowable catch estimated with respect to the individual stocks of fish. The foregoing principle however shall not preclude conservation measures from being determined on some other bases in cases where, due to lack of sufficient data, an estimate of the allowable catch is not possible with any reasonable degree of accuracy.

(4) No State can be exempted from the obligation to adopt conservation measures on the ground that sufficient scientific findings are lacking.

(5) The conservation measures adopted shall be designed so as to minimize interference with fishing activities relating to stocks of fish, if any, which are not the object of such measures.

(6) Conservation measures and the data on the basis of which such measures are adopted shall be subject to review at appropriate intervals.

2.4 *Special status of coastal States in conservation of resources*

A coastal State shall be recognized as having special status with respect to the conservation of fishery resources in its adjacent waters. Thus, the coastal State will have the right of participating, on an equal footing, in any survey on fishery resources conducted in its adjacent waters for conservation purposes, whether or not nationals of that coastal State are actually engaged in fishing the particular stocks concerned. Non-coastal States conducting the survey shall, at the request of the coastal State, make available to the coastal State the findings of their surveys and researches concerning such stocks.

Also, except for interim measures (6.1 below), no conservation measure may be adopted with respect to any stock of fish, without the consent of the coastal State whose nationals are engaged in fishing the particular stock concerned (or the majority of the coastal States in cases where there are three or more such coastal States).

A coastal State shall at the same time have the obligation to take, in co-operation with other States, necessary measures with a view to maintaining the productivity of fishery resources in its adjacent waters at a level that will enable an effective and rational utilization of such resources.

### Preferential Rights of Coastal States

3.1 *Preferential rights*

To the extent consistent with the objective of conservation, a coastal

348

State shall have a preferential right to ensure adequate protection to its coastal fisheries conducted in its adjacent waters.

(i) In the case of a developing coastal State:

The coastal State is entitled annually to reserve for its flag vessels that portion of the allowable catch of a stock of fish it can harvest on the basis of the fishing capacity of its coastal fisheries. In determining the part of the allowable catch to be reserved for the developing coastal State, the rate of growth of the fishing capacity of that State shall be duly taken into account until it has developed that capacity to the extent of being able to fish or major portion of the allowable catch of the stock of fish.

(ii) In the case of a developed coastal State:

The coastal State is entitled annually to reserve for its flag vessels that portion of the allowable catch of a stock of fish which is necessary to maintain its locally conducted small-scale coastal fisheries. The interests of traditionally established fisheries of other States shall be duly taken into account in determining the catch to be reserved for such small-scale coastal fisheries.

3.2 *Implementation of preferential rights*

(1) Measures to implement the preferential rights shall be determined by agreement among the coastal and non-coastal States concerned on the basis of the proposals made by the coastal State. For the purpose of such proposals, the coastal State may seek technical assistance from the Food and Agriculture Organization of the United Nations or such other appropriate organs.

(2) The size of the preferential right of a coastal State shall be fixed within the limit of the allowable catch of the stock of fish subject to allocation, if the allowable catch for that stock is already estimated for conservation purposes. In cases where the estimate of the allowable catch is not available, the coastal and non-coastal States concerned shall agree on necessary measures in a manner which will best enable the coastal State to benefit fully from its preferential right.

(3) The regulatory measures adopted to implement the preferential right of a coastal State may include catch allocation (quota by country) and/or such other supplementary measures that will be made applicable to vessels of non-coastal States engaged in fishing in the adjacent waters of the coastal State, including:

(*a*) the establishment of open and closed seasons during which fish may or may not be harvested,

(*b*) the closing of specific areas to fishing,

(*c*) the regulation of gear or equipment that may be used,

(*d*) the limitation of catch of a particular stock of fish that may be harvested.

(4) The regulatory measures adopted shall be so designed as to minimize interference with the fishing of non-coastal States directed to stocks of fish, if any, which are not covered by such measures.

(5) Non-coastal States shall co-operate with coastal States in the exchange of available scientific information, catch and effort statistics and other relevant data.

(6) In cases where nationals of two or more coastal States which are entitled to preferential rights are engaged in fishing a common stock of fish, no coastal States may invoke their preferential right with respect to such stock without the consent of the other coastal State or States concerned. In such a case, those coastal States shall enter into regional consultations with the other States concerned with a view to implementing their preferential rights.

(7) The measures adopted under this paragraph shall be subject to review at such intervals as may be agreed upon by the States concerned.

3.3 *International Co-operation*

In order to assist in the development of the fishing capacity of a developing coastal State and thereby to facilitate the full enjoyment of its preferential right, international co-operation shall be carried out in the field of fisheries and related industries between the developing coastal State and other fishing States in concluding agreement on the preferential right of that developing coastal State.

### Regulation of Highly Migratory Stocks

4.1 No special status in the conservation of resources (2.4) and no preferential rights (3.1) shall be recognized to a coastal State in respect of highly migratory, including anadromous, stocks of fish. The conservation and regulation of such stocks shall be carried out pursuant to international consultations or agreements in which all interested States shall participate, or through the existing international or regional fishery organizations should such be the case.

### Enforcement

5.1 *Right of control by coastal States*

With respect to regulatory measures adopted pursuant to the present régime, those coastal States which are entitled to preferential rigts, and/or special status with respect to conservation, have the right to control the fishing activities in their respective adjacent waters. In the exercise of such right, the coastal States may inspect vessels of other States and arrest those vessels violating the regulatory measures adopted. The arrested vessels shall however be promptly delivered to the flag States concerned. The coastal States may not refuse the participation of other States in controlling the operation, including boarding officials of the other States

350

on the coastal States patrol vessels at the request of the latter States. Details of control measures shall be agreed upon among the parties concerned.

5.2 *Jurisdiction*

(*a*) Each State shall make it an offence for its nationals to violate any regulatory measures adopted pursuant to the present régime.

(*b*) Nationals on board a vessel violating the regulatory measures in force shall be duly prosecuted by the flag State concerned.

(*c*) Reports prepared by the officials of a coastal State on the offence committed by a vessel of a non-coastal State shall be fully respected by that non-coastal State, which shall notify the coastal State of the disposition of the case as soon as possible.

## Interim Measures and Disputes Settlement

6.1 *Interim measures*

If the States concerned fail to reach agreement within six months of negotiations on measures concerning preferential rights under para. 3.1 and/or on arrangements concerning conservation measures under para. 2.2, any of the States may initiate the procedure for the settlement of disputes. Pending the settlement of disputes, the States concerned shall adopt interim measures. Such interim measures shall in no way prejudice the respective positions of any States concerned with respect to the dispute in question.

(*a*) In cases where the limitation of catch is disputed, each State in dispute shall take necessary measures to ensure that its catch of the stock concerned will not exceed on an annual basis its average annual catch of the preceding [five] year period.

(*b*) In cases where some other factors are in dispute, e.g. fishing grounds, fishing gear or fishing seasons, in connexion with measures to implement the preferential right of a coastal State, or with arrangements concerning conservation measures, the other States concerned shall adopt the latest proposals of the coastal State with respect to the matter in dispute. However, the other States shall be exempted from such obligation if the adoption of the proposal of the coastal State would seriously affect either its catch permitted under sub-para. (*a*) above, or its catch of some other stock not related to the preferential right of a coastal State which it is substantially exploiting. In such a case, those other States shall take all possible measures which they consider appropriate for the protection of the coastal fisheries concerned.

(*c*) Any of the parties to the dispute may request the special Commission to decide on provisional measures regarding the matter in dispute.

(*d*) Each State shall inform the special Commission established in accordance with para. 6.2 as well as all other States concerned of the

351

specific interim measures it has taken in accordance with any of the preceding provisions.

6.2 *Procedure for disputes settlement (special Commission)*

Any dispute which may arise between States under the present régime shall be referred by any of the States concerned to a special Commission of five members in accordance with the following procedure, unless the parties concerned agree to settle the dispute by some other method provided for in Article 33 of the Charter of the United Nations.

(*a*) Not more than two members may be named from among nationals of the parties, one each from among nationals of the coastal and the non-coastal State respectively.

(*b*) Decisions of the special Commission shall be by majority vote and shall be binding upon the parties.

(*c*) The special Commission shall render its decision within a period of six months from the time it is constituted.

(*d*) Notwithstanding the interim measures taken by the parties under para. 6.1, the special Commission may, at the request of any of the parties or at its own initiative, decide on provisional measures to be applied if the Commission deems it necessary. The Commission shall render its final decision within a further period of six months from its decision on such provisional measures.

## Other Provisions

7.1 *Co-operation with developing States*

For the purpose of promoting the development of fishing industries and the domestic consumption and exports of fishery products of developing States, including land-locked States, developed non-coastal States shall co-operate with developing States with every possible means in such fields as survey of fishery resources, expansion of fishing capacity, construction of storage and processing facilities and improvements in marketing systems.

7.2 *Co-operation within regional fishery commissions*

Co-operation between coastal and non-coastal States under the present régime shall be carried out, as far as possible, through regional fishery commissions. For this purpose, the States concerned shall endeavour to strengthen the existing commissions and shall co-operate in establishing new commissions whenever desirable and feasible.

**ECUADOR, PANAMA AND PERU:**
**— Draft Articles for Inclusion in a Convention on the Law of the Sea**

Submitted to the United Nations Seabed Committee on 13 July 1973, as UN Doc. A/AC.138/SC.II/L.27. Supplemented by A/AC.138/SC.II/L.54.

PART I   ADJACENT SEA
PART II   CONTINENTAL SHELF
(See p. 261)

PART III   INTERNATIONAL SEAS

**Art. 17.** The term "international seas" shall denote that part of the sea which is not subject to the sovereignty and jurisdiction of coastal States.

**Art. 18.** The international seas shall be open to all States, whether coastal or land-locked, and their use shall be reserved for peaceful purposes.

**Art. 19.** The following freedoms shall be exercised on the international seas:

(1) freedom of navigation;

(2) freedom of overflight;

(3) freedom to lay submarine cables and pipelines;

(4) freedom to emplace artificial islands and other installations permitted under international law, without prejudice to the provisions of article 24;

(5) freedom of fishing, subject to the conditions laid down in article 20;

(6) freedom of scientific research, subject to the conditions laid down in article 23.

These freedoms shall be exercised by any State, with due consideration for the interests of other States in the exercise of the same freedom.

... (Complementary provisions) .   .   .   .   .   .   .   .   .   .

**Art. 20.** 1. Fishing and hunting in the international seas shall be subject to regulations of a world-wide and regional nature.

2. The aforesaid activities shall be carried out by techniques and methods which do not jeopardize adequate conservation of the renewable resources of the international seas.

**Art. 21.** The coastal State has a special interest in maintaining the productivity of renewable resources in any part of the international seas adjacent to the area subject to its sovereignty and jurisdiction.

**Art. 22.** All States shall be obliged to comply with international regulations designed to prevent, reduce or eliminate any damage or risks arising from pollution or other effects detrimental or dangerous to the ecological system of the international seas, water quality and use, living resources and human health.

... (Complementary provisions on pollution) . . . . . . . .

**Art. 23.** Scientific research in the international seas shall be open to any State and shall be promoted and facilitated under forms of co-operation and assistance which permit the participation of all States, irrespective of their level of development or of whether they are coastal or land-locked.

... (Complementary provisions on scientific research) . . . . . .

**Art. 24.** The emplacement of artificial islands or any other type of installations apart from submarine cables or pipelines shall be subject to international regulations.

... (Complementary provisions on the international seas) . . . . .

PART IV  BED AND SUBSOIL OF THE INTERNATIONAL SEAS


**ECUADOR, PANAMA AND PERU:**
— **Draft Articles on Fisheries in National and International Zones in Ocean Space**

> Submitted to the United Nations Seabed Committee on 10 August 1973, as UN Doc. A/AC.138/SC.II/L.54. Supplementing A/AC.138/SC.II/L.27.

I. *Fisheries in zones of national sovereignty and jurisdiction*
(See p. 265)

II. *Fisheries in international seas*

**Art. G.** Fishing and marine hunting activities in the international seas shall be conducted in conformity with the articles of this Convention and with any agreements that are concluded at the world or regional level.

**Art. H.** 1. Regulations adopted to regulate fishing and hunting in the international seas shall ensure the conservation and rational utilization of living resources and the equitable participation of all States in their exploitation, with due regard to the special needs of the developing countries, including those of the land-locked countries.

2. Such regulations shall establish conditions and methods of fishing and hunting which prevent the indiscriminate exploitation of species and avert the danger of their extinction.

**Art. I.** The coastal State shall enjoy preferential rights to exploit living resources in a sector of the sea adjacent to the zone under its sovereignty and jurisdiction, and may reserve to itself or its nationals a part of the permissible catch of such resources.

**Art. J.** With regard to the living resources of an area of the sea situated beyond the limits of the zones of sovereignty and jurisdiction of two or more States, which breed, feed and live by reason of the resources of that area, the States concerned may agree among themselves on appropriate regulations for the exploration, conservation and exploitation of such resources.

**Art. K.** States shall ensure that the vessels of their flag comply with the fishing and hunting regulations applicable in the international seas; and they shall punish those responsible for any breach that may come to their notice.

**Art. L.** Where a State has good reason to believe that vessels of the flag of another State have violated fishing and hunting regulations applicable to the international seas, the former State may request the flag State to take the necessary steps to punish those responsible.

**Art. M.** Any dispute relating to the interpretation or application of articles G to L of this Convention and of any international or regional regulations that may be adopted, or in respect of fishing and hunting activities in the international sea, shall be submitted to the procedures for peaceful settlement provided for in the Convention.

## CHINA:
### — Working Paper on General Principles for the International Sea Area

Submitted to the United Nations Seabed Committee on 6 August 1973, as UN Doc. A/AC.138/SC.II/L.45.

(1) The international sea area denotes all the sea and ocean space beyond the limits of national jurisdiction. The international sea area and its resources are, in principle, jointly owned by the people of all countries.

(2) In order to have access to and from the international sea area for trade and other peaceful purposes, land-locked States have the right to pass through the territory, territorial sea and other waters of adjacent coastal States. Coastal States and adjacent land-locked States shall, through consultations on the basis of equality and mutual respect for sovereignty, conclude bilateral or regional agreements on the relevant matters.

(3) Uses of the international sea area shall not prejudice the legitimate

355

interests of other States and the common interests of all States.

(4) Subject to the provisions of paragraph (3) above, ships and aircraft of all States have the right of navigation and overflight in the international sea area and in the airspace thereabove, provided that they fly the flag or show the insignia of the State to which they belong.

(5) Subject to the provisions of paragraph (3) above, all States have the right to lay cables and pipelines on the sea-bed of the international sea area.

(6) Fishing in the international sea area shall be properly regulated to prohibit indiscriminate fishing and other violations of rules and regulations for the conservation of fishery resources.

Pending the establishment of a unified international fishery organization, States of a given sea area may set up a regional committee to work out appropriate rules and regulations for the regulation of fishing and the conservation of marine living resources in the international sea area. Fishing vessels of States of other regions may enter the said region for fishing activities provided they comply with the relevant rules and regulations of the region.

(7) The exploration, exploitation and all other activities conducted in the sea-bed, ocean floor and their subsoil of the international sea area shall be governed by the international regime and the international machinery to be established.

## NETHERLANDS:
## — Proposal concerning an Intermediate Zone

Submitted to the United Nations Seabed Committee on 17 August 1973, as UN Doc. A/AC.138/SC.II/L.59. See A/AC. 138/86: Netherlands - Working Paper concerning the Concept of an Intermediate Zone (16 March 1973).

**Art. 1.** *Limits*

The Intermediate zone comprises:

(*a*) Insofar as the living resources, with the exception of "highly migratory oceanic fish species" are concerned, the superjacent waters contiguous to the territorial sea (12 miles) up to an outer limit of ... miles;

(*b*) Insofar as the non-living resources are concerned, the sea-bed and subsoil underlying a belt of sea up to 40 miles seaward of the outer limit of the "continental shelf" * but not exceeding the distance of ... N.M. measured from the baselines of the territorial sea.

**Art. 2.** *Issuing of licenses*

All exploration for, and exploitation of the living or non-living resources of the intermediate zone shall be licensed by the coastal State, subject to the rules and regulations established by the competent international authorities [global, regional and/or sub-regional authorities].

**Art. 3.** *Limitation of licenses*

Coastal States which have been determined to be advantaged, in accordance with the provisions of article 5, may limit the total amount of living or non-living resources which may be extracted from the intermediate zone during a specified period and reserve licenses for the option of such operators as are its own nationals and nationals of disadvantaged States, in proportions to be determined in accordance with the rules and procedures set forth in article 5.

**Art. 4.** *Limitation of disposal of a resource*

The advantaged coastal state may determine that the whole or part of the living or non-living resources extracted by licensed foreign operators from the intermediate zone during a specified period, shall be offered at world market prices for processing or consumption in its territory and in the territories of the disadvantaged states in proportions to be determined in accordance with the rules and procedures set forth in article 5.

**Art. 5.** *Determination of advantaged and disadvantaged states*

1. The proportions mentioned in articles 3 and 4 shall be determined by the competent international authority in such a manner that the sum total of the "advantages" of States advantaged in the intermediate zone, can be shared among the disadvantaged States *pro rata* of the "disadvantage" of each of them.

The rates of (dis)advantage may be determined in two г˙ ases:

*The continental shelf is understood here as the sea-bed and subsoil adjacent to the coast:
— not exceeding the 200 meters isobath or
— underlying a belt of sea the breadth of which is 40 N.M. measured from the baselines of the territorial sea,
according to the choice between the two methods of delimitation to be made by the State concerned at the moment of ratification. Such choice shall be final and the method of delimitation shall apply to the whole of the coastline of the State concerned.

(*a*) The competent International Authority shall determine firstly, in accordance with the provisions of paragraph 2 of this article, rates of "(dis)advantage" in terms of surface;

(*b*) The competent International Authority has the power to revise from time to time the rates determined in accordance with (a), with a view to equalize possible gross disproportions among actual benefits accruing to particular states, if such disproportions result from grossly unequal distribution of resources in the respective areas of intermediate zone.

2. For the determination of the rates mentioned under (a) of the preceding paragraph the "advantage" of a given State is the amount of surface (N.M.$^2$) by which the actual intermediate zone of that state exceeds ....% of a theoretical surface "A" and the "disadvantage" of a given State is the amount of surface by which the actual intermediate zone of that State falls short of ....% of "A".

"A" in relation to any State is the surface, expressed in square nautical miles, of a theoretical sea-area of a width of .... nautical miles around a theoretical circular island area equal in size to the actual total land area of that State.

### Art. 6. *Negotiations between advantaged and disadvantaged states*

1. Any disadvantaged state is entitled to enter into negotiations with any advantaged state, within groups of States to be determined by the competent international authority, in order to determine by agreement its share for the purpose of the application of article 3 or 4.

Notification shall be made to the competent international authority of any such negotiations having been entered into and of any agreement reached. [The competent international authority shall have the power once in 20 years to revise its determination of groups of States].

2. If agreement is not reached within three years after negotiations have commenced, the competent international authority shall be requested to make recommendations to the Contracting Parties concerned.

If agreement is not reached within one year after such recommendations are made, the determination recommended by the authority shall take effect unless either Party, within 90 days thereafter, brings the matter before the Tribunal.

### Art. 7. *Optional transfer of part of the intermediate zone to the competent International Authority*

Any geographically advantaged state may decide to transfer a part of its intermediate zone equal to its "advantage" to the competent international authority to be administered by it in accordance with articles 5 and 6.

### Art. 8. *Revenue sharing*

Any State which derives revenue from exploitation of the intermediate zone shall make available . . . .% of these revenues to the competent international authority.

## VI. ARTIFICIAL ISLANDS

**BELGIUM:**
**— Working Paper on Artificial Islands and Installations**

Submitted to the United Nations Seabed Committee on 11 July 1973, as UN Doc. A/AC.138/91.

A. *The territorial sea*

**Art. (a).** The coastal State is entitled to construct artificial islands or immovable installations in its territorial sea; it must not, through such structures, impede access to the ports of a neighbouring State or cause damage to the marine environment of the territorial seas of neighbouring States.

**Art. (b).** Before commencing the construction of artificial islands or installations as mentioned in the preceding article, the coastal State shall publish the plans thereof and take into consideration any observations submitted to it by other States. In the event of disagreement, an interested State which deems itself injured may appeal to IMCO, which though not empowered to prohibit the construction, may prescribe such changes or adjustments as it considers essential to safeguard the lawful interests of other States.

B. *The continental shelf*

**Art. (c).** The coastal State may, on the conditions specified in the following article, authorize the construction on its continental shelf of artificial islands or immovable installations serving purposes other than the exploration or exploitation of natural resources. Such structures shall be placed under its jurisdiction or under that of the State which undertakes their construction, and, with a view to their protection, may be surrounded by safety zones extending not more than 500 metres. Such artificial islands or immovable installations have no territorial sea of their own.

**Art. (d).** Before commencing the construction of artificial islands or installations as mentioned in article (c), the State shall publish the plans thereof and take into consideration any observations submitted to it by other States. In the event of disagreement, an interested State which deems itself injured may appeal to . . .\*, which shall prescribe, where appropriate, such changes or adjustments as it considers essential to safeguard the lawful interests of other States.

### C. The high seas beyond the limits of the continental shelf

**Art. (e).** Any construction of an artificial island or immovable installation on the high seas beyond the limits of the continental shelf shall be subject to the authority and jurisdiction of the international machinery for the sea bed. The international authority may authorize a State to erect such islands or installations and delegate jurisdiction over such structures to that State.

### POLAND:
#### — Proposal concerning Aspects of Navigation through Straits

> Submitted to the United Nations Seabed Committee on 8 August 1973, as UN Doc. A/AC.138/SC.II/L.49.

The coastal State shall not place, in the straits used for international navigation, structures of any kind which could hamper or obstruct the passage of ships through such straits.

---

\*It would seem advisable not to specify at present the body which would be competent to entertain such an appeal. It could be the tribunal of the international machinery, if that was thought appropriate, or there could be the triple possibility of recourse to IMCO in respect of complaints affecting navigation, to the regional fisheries organization in respect of those concerning fishing, or to the international authority for the marine environment and pollution, if one is established.

# VII. LAND-LOCKED AND GEOGRAPHICALLY DISADVANTAGED COUNTRIES

## BOLIVIA:
### — Draft Articles relating to Land-Locked Countries

Submitted to the United Nations Seabed Committee on 12 July 1973, as UN Doc. A/AC.138/92.

**Art. ...** The right of land-locked States to free access to the sea (what ever the origin and nature of their land-locked conditions) is one of the basic principles of the law of the sea and forms an integral part of the principles of international law.

**Art. ...** States situated between the sea and one or more land-locked States retain full sovereignty over their territory and have the right to adopt such measures as may be necessary to ensure that the right of land-locked States to free access to the sea in no way prejudices their legitimate interests.

361

**Art. ...** For the purpose of enjoying the freedom of the sea and participating in the exploitation of the resources of the sea-bed and the ocean floor, and the sub-soil thereof, beyond the limits of national jurisdiction on an equal footing with coastal States, land-locked States shall exercise the right of free access to the sea in the manner and subject to the conditions established in this Convention.

**Art. ...** (1) The existence and the nature of the right of land-locked States to free access to the sea derive from the application of the principles of the freedom of the sea and the designation of the sea-bed and the ocean floor, and the sub-soil thereof, beyond the limits of national jurisdiction, as well as the resources of that area, as the common heritage of mankind.

(2) Its validity and application do not depend exclusively on the unilateral will (or national laws) of States situated between the sea one or more land-locked States, but concern the community of nations as a whole.

(3) Depending on the nature of each case, its exercise shall be governed by agreement between the land-locked States and the States situated between them and the sea.

**Art. ...** Conventions or other international agreements governing the exercise of this right shall not contain any clauses or provisions which limit the rights recognized by this Convention as an integral part of the right of land-locked States to free access to the sea.

**Art. ...** The lack or inadequacy of conventions or other international agreements to cover particular cases of the right of land-locked States to free access to the sea shall neither nullify that right as recognized in this Convention nor restrict the exercise thereof in the manner set out herein. (articles .... etc.).

**Art. ...** States situated between the sea and one or more land-locked countries shall, without discriminating between the latter and in accordance with the principles (articles) of this Convention, guarantee to the land-locked State or States:

(*a*) Free and unrestricted transit through their territory (for all classes of movable goods, livestock, objects, merchandise and persons);

(*b*) for vessels flying the flag of the land-locked State, the same treatment as that given to their own vessels or vessels of any other State in respect of entry into and departure from seaports;

(*c*) the use of such ports, installations and equipment as may be appropriate for the movement of traffic in transit, under the same conditions as for themselves;

(*d*) alternatively, free zones in the aforesaid ports in which land-locked States may, at their own expense, erect or construct warehouses or stores,

362

facilities for the separation of cargoes, goods-yards and railway sidings, oil or gas tanks and pipes for the loading of tank vessels, office and residential buildings, etc.;

(e) the right to appoint, in the ports of transit or free zones, national customs officials who may, without prior notice and without control or supervision by the local authorities, authorize the docking of vessels whose cargo is destined for, or originates primarily in, the land-locked country, and organize and supervise the loading and unloading of such vessels, as well as such port or free zone services as may be necessary for that purpose, without restrictions other than those relating to security, public health and the police regulations of the coastal transit State;

(f) the use of the means of transport and communication existing in their territory, under the same conditions as for themselves.

**Art.** ... When means of transport and communication in the States situated between the sea and one or more land-locked States are insufficient to give effect to the right of land-locked States to free access to the sea or when the aforesaid means of transport and communication or the port installations and equipment are inadequate or may be improved in any respect, the land-locked States may construct, modify or improve them at their own expense.

**Art.** ... If the port installations and equipment and the means of transport and communication existing in the country of transit are used in a proportion equal to or greater than fifty per cent of their capacity by the land-locked State or States, any tariffs, fees or other charges for services rendered shall be fixed by agreement among the States concerned.

**Art.** ... Goods and passengers in transit traffic to or from the land-locked State shall not be subject to the jurisdiction or competence of the judicial authorities of the coastal transit State.

**Art.** ... The reciprocity of free transit, when this concept is embodied in the right of land-locked States to free access to the sea, is not an essential principle but may be agreed among the parties.

**Art.** ... The rights and facilities established by this Convention as inherent in the right of land-locked States to free access to the sea by reason of special geographical situation, shall be excluded from application of the most-favoured-nation clause.

*Amendment* Amend the last line of Principles 7 and 8 of the Declaration of Principles (General Assembly resolution 2749 (XXV)) to read:
"... and taking into particular consideration the interests and needs of the developing countries, especially those which are land-locked".

**Art. ...** The land-locked (developing) countries shall have the same obligations and rights as contiguous (developing) coastal States with regard to participation in the live resources of the seas adjacent to the region, the natural resources of the continental shelf and those lying in the sea-bed or the sub-soil thereof within the limits of the jurisdictional sea (Exclusive Economic Zone).

## AFGHANISTAN, BOLIVIA, CZECHOSLOVAKIA, HUNGARY, MALI, NEPAL AND ZAMBIA:
## — Draft Articles relating to Land-Locked States

> Submitted to the United Nations Seabed Committee on 2 August 1973, as UN Doc. A/AC.138/93.

*Preamble*

*Recognizing* that the right of free access to and from the sea of land-locked States is one of the essential principles of the law of the sea and forms an integral part of the established principles of international law, as the right of free access to and from the sea of land-locked States derives from the application of the fundamental principles of freedom of high seas and has further been strengthened by the principle of the Area of the sea-bed as the common heritage of mankind.

**Art. 1.** *Definitions*

For the purpose of this Convention:

(*a*) "land-locked State" means any State which has no sea coast;

(*b*) (i) the term "traffic in transit" means transit of persons, baggage, goods and means of transport across the territory of one or more transit States, when the passage across such territory, with or without trans-shipment, warehousing, breaking bulk or change in the mode of transport is only a portion of a complete journey which begins or terminates within the territory of the land-locked State;

(ii) for the purpose of traffic in transit "person in transit" means the passage of person whose movement is not prejudicial to security, law and order of the transit State;

(*c*) the term "transit State" means any State with or without a sea-coast, situated between a land-locked State and the sea, through whose territory the land-locked State shall have access to and from the sea;

(*d*) the term "means of transport" includes:

(i) any railway stock, seagoing and river vessels and road vehicles,

(ii) where the local situation so requires, porter and pack animals,

(iii) pipelines, gaslines, and storage tanks when they are used for traffic in transit and other means of transport subject to appropriate arrangements as and when necessary;

**Art. 2.** *Right of free access to and from the sea*

1. The right of land-locked States to free access to and from the sea is one of the basic principles of the law of the sea and forms an integral part of the principles of international law.

2. In order to enjoy the freedom of the seas and to participate in the exploration and exploitation of the sea-bed and its resources on equal terms with coastal States, land-locked States irrespective of the origin and characteristics of their land-locked conditions, shall have the right of free access to and from the sea in accordance with the provisions of this Convention.

3. The right of free access to and from the sea of land-locked States shall be the concern of the international community as a whole and the exercise of such right shall not depend exclusively on the transit States.

**Art. 3.** *Freedom of transit*

Transit States shall accord free and unrestricted transit for traffic in transit of land-locked States, without discrimination among them, to and from the sea by all means of transport and communication, in accordance with the provisions of this Convention.

**Art. 4.** *Right of flag and equal treatment*

1. A land-locked State shall have, equally with coastal States, the right to fly its flag on vessels which are duly registered in its territory.

2. On the high seas, vessels flying the flag of a land-locked State shall have identical rights to those enjoyed by vessels of coastal States.

3. In the territorial sea and in internal waters, vessels flying the flag of land-locked States shall have identical rights and enjoy treatment equal to that enjoyed by vessels flying the flag of coastal States.

**Art. 5.** *Right to use Maritime Ports*

1. Vessels flying the flag of a land-locked State shall have the right to use maritime ports.

2. Vessels of land-locked States are entitled to the most favoured treatment and shall under no circumstances receive a treatment less favourable than that accorded to vessels of coastal States as regards access to and exit from the maritime ports.

3. The use of these ports, facilities, installations and equipments of any kind shall be provided under the same conditions as for coastal States.

**Art. 6.** *Customs Duties and other Charges*

1. Traffic in transit shall not be subject to any customs duties, taxes or other charges except charges levied for specific services rendered in con-

bound for or coming from the land-locked State and to make arrange-nexion with such traffic.

2. If the port installations and equipments or the means of transport and communication or both existing in a transit State are primarily used by one or more land-locked States, tariffs, fees or other charges for services rendered shall be subject to agreement between the States concerned.

3. Means of transport in transit used by the land-locked State shall not be subject to taxes, tariffs or charges higher than those levied for the use of means of transport of the transit State.

**Art. 7.** *Free Zone or Other facilities*

1. For convenience of traffic in transit, free zones and/or other facilities may be provided at the ports of entry and exit in the transit States, by agreement between those States and the land-locked States.

2. Such zones shall be exempted from the customs regulations of the coastal States. They remain, however, subject to the jurisdiction of those States with regard to police and public health regulations.

**Art. 8.** *Right to Appoint Customs Officials*

Land-locked States shall have the right to appoint Customs Officials of their own in the ports of transit or free zones empowered in accordance with practice of States, to arrange the berthing of vessels whose cargo is ments for and supervise loading and unloading operations for such vessels as well as documentation and other necessary services for the speedy and smooth movement of traffic in transit.

**Art. 9.** *Transportation, Handling and Storage of goods in transit*

Transit States shall provide adequate means of transport, storage and handling facilities at the points of entry and exit, and at intermediate stages for the smooth movement of traffic in transit.

**Art. 10.** *Improvement of the Means of Transport and Communications*

When means of transport and communication in the transit States are insufficient to give effect to the rights of land-locked States of free access to and from the sea or when the aforesaid means of transport and communication or the port installations and equipment are inadequate or may be improved in any respect, the land-locked States shall have the right to construct, modify or improve them in agreement with the transit State or States concerned.

**Art. 11.** *Delays or difficulties in traffic in transit*

1. Except in cases of *force majeure* all measures shall be taken by transit States to avoid delays in or restrictions on traffic in transit.

2. Should delays or other difficulties occur in traffic in transit, the competent authorities of the transit State or States and of land-locked

States shall co-operate towards their expeditious elimination.

**Art. 12.** *Right of access to and from the sea through rivers*

A land-locked State shall have the right of access to and from the sea through navigable rivers which pass through its territory and the territory of transit States or form a common boundary between those States and the land-locked State.

**Art. 13.** *Alternative routes*

Land-locked States shall have the right to use one or more of the alternative routes or means of transport for purposes of access to and from the sea.

**Art. 14.** *Rights of Transit States*

The transit State, while maintaining full sovereignty over its territory, shall have the right to take all indispensable measures to ensure that the exercise of the right of free and unrestricted transit shall in no way infringe its legitimate interests. This provision shall not be construed as prejudicing territorial disputes of any kind.

**Art. 15.** *Temporary deviation in exceptional cases*

The measures of a general or particular character which a contracting State is obliged to take in case of an emergency affecting the security of the State or the vital interests of the country may in exceptional cases and for as short a period as possible, involve a deviation from the provisions of the above Articles, it being understood that the principle of freedom of transit must be observed to the utmost possible extent.

**Art. 16.** *Reciprocity*

Since free transit of land-locked States forms part of their right of free access to and from the sea which belongs to them in view of their special geographical position, reciprocity shall not be a condition of free transit of land-locked States required by transit States but may be agreed between the parties concerned.

**Art. 17.** *Access to and from the Sea-bed Area*

(1) Land-locked States shall have the right of free access to and from the Area of the sea-bed in order to enable them to participate in the exploration and exploitation of the Area and its resources and to derive benefits therefrom in accordance with the provisions of this Convention.

(2) For this purpose the land-locked States shall have the right to use all means and facilities provided for in this Convention with regard to traffic in transit.

**Art. 18.** *Representation of Land-locked States*

In any organ of the International Sea-bed Machinery in which not all Member States will be represented, in particular in its Council, there shall

367

be an adequate and proportionate number of land-locked States, both developing and developed.

**Art. 19.** *Decision-Making*

(1) In any organ of the Machinery, decisions on questions of substance shall be made with due regard to the special needs and problems of land-locked States.

(2) On questions of substance which affect the interests of land-locked States, decisions shall be made with their participation.

**Art. 20.** *Relation to Previous Agreements*

(1) The provisions of this Convention which govern the right of free access of land-locked States to and from the Sea shall not abrogate existing special agreements between two or more States concerning the matters which are regulated in this Convention, nor shall they raise an obstacle as regards the conclusion of such agreements in the future.

(2) In case such existing agreements provide less favourable conditions than those contained in this Convention, the States concerned undertake that they shall bring them in accord with the present provisions at the earliest occasion.

(3) The provisions contained in the preceding paragraph shall not affect existing bilateral or multi-lateral agreements relating to air transport.

**Art. 21.** *Exclusion of Application of Most-Favoured-Nation Clause*

Provisions of this Convention, as well as special agreements which regulate the exercise of the right of free access to and from the sea and the Area of the Sea-bed, establishing rights and facilities on account of special geographical position of land-locked States, are excluded from the application of the most-favoured-nation clause.

**Art. 22.** *Settlement of Disputes*

Any dispute arising from the interpretation and application of the provisions of the foregoing Articles shall be subject to the procedures for the settlement of disputes provided for in the Convention.


**URUGUAY:**

**— Draft Treaty Articles on the Territorial Sea**

> Submitted to the United Nations Seabed Committee on 3 July 1973, as UN Doc. A/AC.138/SC.II/L.24.

*Section 1-6.*
(See p. 258)

*Section 7. Regime for Countries having no Sea-Coast*

**Art. ... 1.** States having no sea-coast shall have free access to the territorial seas of coastal States which are their neighbours or which belong to the same subregion, in order to exercise the rights stipulated in such special regimes as may be instituted by bilateral or subregional agreements and to enjoy, on equal terms with coastal States, the freedoms of the high seas.

2. For the purposes specified in the preceding paragraph, States situated between the sea and a State having no sea-coast shall, in conformity with their municipal laws and such bilateral or subregional agreements as they may include on the subject, guarantee the latter State free transit through their territories, grant appropriate facilities in order to effect such transit, and accord to ships flying the flag of that State treatment equal to that accorded to their own ships as regards access to seaports and the use of such ports.

**Art. ...** Coastal States shall, through bilateral or subregional agreements, as the case may require, in which the interests of all parties are given fair consideration, accord to States having no sea-coast which are their neighbours or which belong to the same subregion preferential treatment over third States with regard to fishing rights in that area of their territorial sea which is not reserved exclusively for their nationals. Such preferential treatment shall be reserved for national enterprises of the States having no sea-coast which operate in the area exclusively with ships flying the flag of those States and whose catch is intended for domestic or industrial consumption in the said States, or for national enterprises of the States having no sea-coast which are associated with national enterprises of the coastal States.

## ECUADOR, PANAMA AND PERU:
## — Draft Articles for Inclusion in a Convention on the Law of the Sea

Submitted to the United Nations Seabed Committee on 13 July 1973, as UN Doc. A/AC.138/SC.II/L.27.

### PART I    ADJACENT SEA

*Section 1.-Section 8.*
(See p. 261)

*Section 9. Land-locked countries régime*

**Art. 15.** 1. Land-locked States shall have the right of free access to the sea for the purpose of such uses and such preferential régime as they may

369

agree upon with the neighbouring coastal States within the seas adjacent to the latter, and for enjoyment of the freedoms of the international seas.

2. Such uses and such preferential régime in the seas adjacent to the neighbouring coastal States as may be agreed upon shall be reserved to national enterprises of the land-locked State.

3. For the purposes provided for in this article, coastal States shall guarantee neighbouring land-locked States free passage through their territories, as well as equal treatment as regards entry into and use of ports, in accordance with internal legislation and any relevant agreements they may conclude.

**Art. 16.** Coastal States which are not adjacent to land-locked States in the same region or subregion shall accord uses and a preferential régime within their adjacent seas to national enterprises of such land-locked States, under regional, subregional or bilateral agreements taking the interests of the respective States into account.

... (Complementary provisions on the régime for land-locked countries)

PART II  CONTINENTAL SHELF
PART III  INTERNATIONAL SEAS
(See p. 353)


**JAMAICA:**
— **Draft Articles on Regional Facilities for Developing Geographically Disadvantaged Coastal States**

Submitted to the United Nations Seabed Committee on 13 August 1973, as UN Doc. A/AC.138/SC.II/L.55.

**Art. 1.** 1. In any region where there are geographically disadvantaged coastal States, the nationals of such States shall have the right to exploit, on a reciprocal and preferential basis, the renewable resources within maritime zones beyond 12 miles from the coasts of the States of the region for the purpose of fostering the economic development of their fishing industry and satisfying the nutritional needs of the population.

2. The procedures regulating the preferential regime referred to in paragraph 1 above shall be determined by regional, sub-regional and bilateral agreements.

**Art. 2.** Where by reason of the geography of a region or sub-region the maritime zones beyond 12 miles from the coasts of States bordering on that region or sub-region converge into each other and within the zone of convergence there are geographically disadvantaged coastal States, the nationals of such States shall have a right of equal access, to the living resources of the maritime zones in these convergent areas.

**Art. 3.** Except as provided in Article 4 nothing in Articles 1 and 2 shall apply to territories under foreign domination or forming an integral part of metropolitan powers outside the region.

**Art. 4.** In the application of Articles 1 and 2 to the Associated States, Self Governing Territories and territories under foreign domination the rights thereby conferred shall be so applied as only to confer rights on the inhabitants of such territories for the purpose of their domestic needs.

**Art. 5.** For the purposes of these Articles

(a) "geographically disadvantaged coastal States" means developing States which for geographical, biological or ecological reasons-

(i) derive no substantial advantage from the extension of their maritime jurisdiction; or

(ii) are adversely affected by the extension of maritime jurisdiction of other States

(iii) have short coastlines and cannot extend uniformly their national jurisdiction.

(b) "nationals" include enterprises substantially owned and effectively controlled by nationals.

## VIII. REGIONAL ARRANGEMENTS

## ZAIRE:
### — Draft Articles on Fishing

Submitted to the United Nations Seabed Committee on 17 August 1973, as UN Doc. A/AC.138/SC.II/L.60.

**Art. 1.** Neighbouring developing States shall grant one another preferential treatment in their respective economic zones with regard to the exploitation of living resources. The procedure for the exercise of such rights shall be settled by arrangement between the States concerned.

The benefit of the preferential treatment provided for in the first paragraph shall, however, be reserved to nationals of those States or to enterprises under the real and effective control of those States.

The conservation and management of the resources of the entire economic zone shall lie within the competence and authority of the coastal State.

**Art. 2.** Land-locked States and geographically disadvantaged States shall have the right to participate, on a footing of equality and without discrimination, in the exploitation of the living resources of the economic zones of neighbouring coastal States.

The detailed procedure for the exercise of such a right may be determined on a bilateral or regional basis in suitable arrangements.

The benefit of that right shall, however, be reserved to nationals of those States or to enterprises under the real and effective control of those States and for their sole account.

**Art. 3.** Neighbouring developing coastal States in the same region shall recognize traditional fishing rights belonging to one another and acquired before the establishment of the exclusive economic zone under this Convention, on the same terms as before the entry into force of this Convention and without prejudice to the regulations of the coastal State concerning the conservation, utilization and management of resources.

**Art. 4.** No State exercising colonial or similar domination may take advantage of the provisions of the foregoing articles to act in place of another country situated outside its national territory.


## IRAN:
### — Draft Article on Regional Arrangements

Submitted to the United Nations Seabed Committee on 16 August 1973, as UN Doc. A/AC.138/SC.II/L.62.

**Art. ...** 1. States of a region or sub-region may, in order to co-ordinate matters relating to the legal, economic and technical aspects of the Law of the Sea in their region or sub-region, conclude appropriate arrangements between themselves.

2. These arrangements will take into account:

(a) the legitimate interests of the States concerned;

(b) the orderly development of the renewable resources of the sea under their jurisdiction.

## YUGOSLAVIA:
### — Draft Article on Regional Arrangements

Submitted to the United Nations Seabed Committee on 16 August 1973, as UN Doc. A/AC.138/SC.II/L.63.

**Art. ...** 1. The States of a region or sub-region may, subject to the general provisions of this Convention, on the basis of equality and mutual respect, promote consultations and negotiate such forms of co-operation as they consider most appropriate with respect to all maritime matters, including those relating to legal, geographical, economic and ecological aspects, as well as to scientific research and the transfer of technology.

2. These arrangements should take into account (a) the legitimate interests of all States concerned, as well as (b) the orderly development and rational management of resources of the . . . . . . Zone.

## IX. PREVENTION OF MARINE POLLUTION

New Zealand, Philippines and United
Republic of Tanzania) p. 415
In addition to the proposals herein referred to, see, also, the
following texts:
A/AC.138/SC.II/L.24 (Uruguay), Sec. 5. (p. 261)
— L.27 (Ecuador, Panama and Peru), Art. 9, 22. (p. 353)
— L.35 (U.S.), Art. 2 (p. 385)
— L.37 (Argentina), Art. 11, 21. (p. 288)


## AUSTRALIA:
— **Working Paper on Preservation of the Marine Environment**

Submitted to the United Nations Seabed Committee on 6 March
1973, as UN Doc. A/AC.138/SC.III/L.27.

*Principles*

(*a*) States have, in accordance with the Charter of the United Nations
and the principles of international law, the sovereign right to exploit their
own resources pursuant to their own environmental policies. This right
shall be exercised in accordance with the duty of all States to protect and
preserve the marine environment, both in their own interests and in the
interests of mankind as a whole, and to take all practicable measures
available to prevent or minimize damage to the marine environment outside their territorial sea from all sources including land-based sources
within their national jurisdiction.

(*b*) States should co-operate with other States and competent international organizations in the further elaboration and implementation of
internationally agreed rules, standards and procedures for the prevention
of marine pollution on global, regional and national levels. In the formulation of global measures for the preservation of the marine environment,
States should take into account the special characteristics of particular
geographical and ecological regions.

(*c*) States with interests in the marine environment of a geographically
common area should co-operate in formulating common policies and
measures for the protection of such areas. States should endeavour to act
consistently with the objectives and provisions of such policies and
measures.

(*d*) States should promote, either directly or through international
bodies, programmes of scientific, technological and, where appropriate,
financial assistance, such assistance including *inter alia* the training of
scientific and technical personnel, the supply of necessary equipment and

374

facilities for research, monitoring, surveillance and the prevention or minimizing of pollution, and advice on the method of administration of pollution prevention programmes.

(e) (i) States have the responsibility to ensure that activities under their jurisdiction or control do not cause damage to other States, including the environment of other States. If activities under the jurisdiction or control of one State cause damage to areas under the jurisdiction of another State, including the environment of another State, the first-mentioned State is internationally liable to the second State and shall pay compensation accordingly;

(ii) States also have the responsibility to ensure that activities under their jurisdiction or control do not cause damage to the environment of areas beyond the limits of national jurisdiction. States shall co-operate further to develop effective procedures for the payment of compensation in respect of damage to the environment of areas beyond the limits of national jurisdiction.

(f) Coastal States have a special interest in the preservation of the marine environment adjacent to their coast. In order to protect this special interest, and to enable them to carry out their duty to protect and preserve the marine environment, coastal States shall in addition to their sovereign rights over their territorial sea, have the right to take all reasonable measures to control activities within a broad area adjacent to their coast for the purpose of preventing or minimizing damage to the marine environment. In determining the reasonableness of any measures, particular reference shall be made to international rules, standards and procedures as a primary, though not necessarily conclusive, source of evidence.

(g) The principles herein outlined shall not apply to naval vessels, military aircraft or their auxiliaries. States shall, however, ensure that to the greatest extent feasible, their naval vessels and auxiliaries act in a manner consistent with the object and purpose of these principles.

(h) Any dispute as to the interpretation of these principles shall be subject to review by an international arbitral and/or judicial tribunal at the request of any one party to that dispute.


## CANADA:
## — Draft Articles for a Comprehensive Marine Pollution Convention

Submitted to the United Nations Seabed Committee on 9 March 1973, as UN Doc. A/AC.138/SC.III/L.28. See also A/AC. 138/SC.III/L.26: Canada-Working paper on preservation of the marine environment (31 August 1972); SC.III/L.37: Canada-Prevention of Pollution from Ships (3 April 1973).

## Preamble

*States Parties to this Convention,*

*Convinced* that the marine environment and all the living organisms which it supports are of vital importance to humanity, and all people have an interest in assuring that this environment is so managed that its quality and resources are not impaired;

*Convinced* that coastal nations have a particular interest in the management of coastal area resources;

*Recognizing* that the capacity of the sea to assimilate wastes and render them harmless and its ability to regenerate natural resources are not unlimited, and that measures to prevent and control marine pollution must be regarded as an essential element in the management of the oceans and seas and their natural resources;

*Recognizing* that States have, in accordance with the Charter of the United Nations and the principles of international law, the sovereign right to exploit their own resources pursuant to their own environment policies, and the responsibility to ensure that activities within their jurisdiction or control do not cause damage to the environment of other States or of areas beyond the limits of national jurisdiction;

*Noting* that marine pollution originates from many sources, including discharges through the atmosphere or from rivers, estuaries, outfalls and pipelines and from dumping, and that it is important that States use the best practicable means to prevent such pollution;

*Being convinced* that the duty of States to protect the marine environment requires effective action, either individually or jointly, for the prevention of marine pollution through the elaboration, implementation and enforcement of appropriate control measures, taking into account existing international agreements on the protection and preservation of the marine environment, the need for elaboration of further agreements in this field at global and regional levels, and especially the need to ensure that these agreements, together with relevant national measures, comprise an effective comprehensive approach to the protection and preservation of the marine environment,

*Have agreed as follows:*

### Art. 1. *Basic obligation*

States have the obligation to protect and preserve the marine environment.

### Art. 2. *Measures for prevention of pollution*

1. States shall take measures, either individually or jointly, as appropriate, to prevent pollution of the marine environment by substances or other matter liable to create hazards to human health, to harm living

resources and marine life, to damage amenities or to interfere with other legitimate uses of the marine environment. In particular, States shall, to the best of their ability, take measures to ensure that activities under their jurisdiction or control do not cause damage to other States, including the environment of other States, by pollution of the marine environment. Such measures shall include measures (a) to control the release of the above substances or other matter from all sources within their jurisdiction, in particular land-based sources, (b) to minimize the release of toxic or dangerous substances, especially if they are persistent substances, to the fullest possible extent until it is demonstrated that their release in larger quantities or greater concentrations will not cause pollution, (c) for the prevention of accidents and the safety of operations at sea in accordance with agreed international standards including, (i) the design, equipment, operation and control of vessels, in particular those engaged in the carriage of substances whose characteristics or quantities are likely to cause pollution of the marine environment if accidentally released, (ii) the design, equipment, operation and control of installations and devices for the exploration or exploitation of the natural resources of the sea-bed or any other installations and devices operating in the marine environment.

2. In taking measures pursuant to their obligations under this Convention States shall take into account: (a) any international convention the purpose or effect of which is to protect and preserve the marine environment: (b) the relevant principles, standards, recommendations, procedures, guidelines, criteria, including water quality criteria, and action plans proposed by competent international organizations.

**Art. 3.** *Development of measures*

States should co-operate on a global basis and as appropriate on a regional basis, directly or through competent international bodies, to elaborate and implement conventions, rules, principles, standards, recommendations, procedures, guidelines, criteria, including water quality criteria, and action plans for the purpose of the prevention of pollution of the marine environment.

**Art. 4.** *Special measures*

1. Nothing in this Convention may be interpreted as preventing a State from taking such measures as may be necessary to meet the obligation under article I within the limits of its national jurisdiction, including environmental protection zones (maximum limits to be determined) (a) pending the establishment and implementation of internationally agreed measures contemplated by this Convention or, (b) following the establishment or implementation of any internationally agreed measures if such measures fail to meet the objectives of this Convention or if other

377

measures are necessary in the light of local geographical and ecological characteristics.

2. Measures taken in accordance with this article must remain within the strict limits of the objectives of this Convention and must not be discriminatory in their application.

**Art. 5.** *International programmes*

States should actively support and contribute to international programmes to acquire knowledge for the assessment of pollutant sources, pathways, exposures and risks, and those States in a position to do so should provide educational and technical and other forms of assistance to facilitate broad participation by States in such programmes regardless of their economic and technical advancement.

**Art. 6.** *Monitoring*

1. States which permit or engage in activities resulting in the release of substances or other matter into the marine environment likely to cause pollution shall take measures, consistent with the rights of other States, to determine the effects of such activities on the marine environment, having particular regard to those harmful effects referred to in article II.

2. Wide dissemination should be given to appropriate data and information respecting activities resulting in the release of substances or other matter into the marine environment, the measures taken to determine harmful effects, and measures or procedures adopted to minimize or eliminate such harmful effects.

**Art. 7.** *Compensation for damage*

1. States are liable for damage caused in or to areas under the jurisdiction of other States, including the environment of other States, by pollution of the marine environment attributable to them, and they shall co-operate in the development of international law relating to procedures for the assessment of damage, the determination of liability, the payment of compensation and the settlement of related disputes.

2. (*a*) With respect to damage caused in or to areas under the jurisdiction of a State, including the environment of that State, by pollution of the marine environment which is not attributable to another State, but which has been caused by persons under the jurisdiction of that other State, States undertake to provide recourse with a view to ensuring equitable compensation for the victims of marine pollution caused by persons under their jurisdiction, which will include procedures for the assessment of damage, the determination of liability and the payment of compensation.

(*b*) Following the exhaustion of local remedies or where no such recourse is available, the State of the damaged party may present to the

State having jurisdiction over the person or persons responsible for the damage in question, a claim for the damage caused. If no settlement of the claim is arrived at through negotiations, the States concerned shall submit, at the request of either of them, the claim to arbitration or adjudication in accordance with a procedure to be determined by agreement or by a third party nominated by them.

3. With respect to damage caused in or to areas beyond the limits of national jurisdiction by pollution of the marine environment, States undertake to co-operate in the development of international law relating to procedures for the assessment of damage, the determination of liability, the payment of compensation and the settlement of related disputes.

### Art. 8. *Abatement*

In the case of damage caused by pollution of the marine environment in areas beyond the limits of national jurisdiction, a State or group of States, in co-operation with any competent international organization or agency or otherwise, may present to the State under whose jurisdiction or control the activities causing such pollution were conducted, through diplomatic channels, a request for the termination or restriction of such activities and the restoration of the damaged environment.

### Art. 9. *Minimization*

A State which becomes aware of circumstances where the marine environment is in imminent danger of being damaged or has been damaged by pollution shall notify other States likely to be affected by such damage and these States shall co-operate in taking measures to minimize damage.

### Art. 10. *Enforcement*

1. States may enforce measures adopted pursuant to this Convention for the protection and preservation of the marine environment within the limits of their national jurisdiction, including environmental protection zones (maximum limits for the purpose of this Convention to be determined and expressed in this Convention) adjacent to their territorial sea.

2. Where vessels or aircraft registered in one State are in areas within the limits of national jurisdiction of another State, including environmental protection zones, the State of registry shall also have the duty to ensure compliance with the measures adopted pursuant to this Convention for the protection and preservation of the marine environment in such areas.

3. States shall enforce measures adopted pursuant to this Convention for the protection and preservation of the marine environment in respect of (*a*) vessels and aircraft registered in their territory operating beyond the limits of national jurisdiction, and (*b*) man-made structures or platforms operating in areas beyond the limits of national jurisdiction over the sea-bed where such structures or platforms are under the authority and con-

trol of a State (pursuant to the international sea-bed régime to be established).

**Art. 11.** *Right of intervention*
1. Any State facing grave and imminent danger from pollution or threat of pollution, following upon an incident or acts related to such an incident in areas beyond the limits of national jurisdiction, which may reasonably be expected to result in major consequences, may take such measures as may be necessary to prevent, mitigate or eliminate such danger.
2. Measures taken in accordance with this article shall be proportionate to the damage which threatens the State concerned and shall not go beyond what is reasonably necessary to achieve the objective referred to in paragraph 1.

**Art. 12.** *Sovereign immunity*
This Convention shall not apply to those vessels and aircraft entitled to sovereign immunity under international law. However, States shall ensure by the adoption of appropriate measures that such vessels and aircraft owned or operated by them act in a manner consistent with the object and purpose of this Convention.

**Art. 13.** *Settlement of disputes*
Where any dispute arises relating to the interpretation or application of this Convention, the States concerned shall, if such dispute is not resolved by negotiation, submit the claim to arbitration, at the request of any of them, in accordance with a procedure to be determined by agreement or by a third party nominated by agreement among the States concerned.


## UNION OF SOVIET SOCIALIST REPUBLICS:
— **Draft Articles for a Convention on General Principles for the Preservation of the Marine Environment**
•

> Submitted to the United Nations Seabed Committee on 15 March 1973, as UN Doc. A/AC.138/SC.III/L.32. See also A/AC.138/SC.III/L.19: U.S.S.R.-Draft Resolution on measures for preventing the pollution of the marine environment (25 July 1972).

**Art. 1.** *Scope of the Convention*
The provisions of this Convention shall apply to the areas of the world

ocean including the continental shelf but excluding States' territorial waters. States hereby assume the obligation to ensure that activities carried out under their jurisdiction to preserve the marine environment within their territorial waters do not cause damage to the environment of other States or of maritime zones beyond the limits of their territorial waters.

**Art. 2.** *Obligation to prevent pollution of the marine environment*

States undertake to adopt all necessary measures, including legislation, in order to prevent pollution of the marine environment from any source, whether marine-based, land-based or shore-based, including rivers, estuaries, water-pipes, oil pipe-lines, the atmosphere, ships, aircraft, platforms and installations, by substances which may be harmful to human health or to marine organisms or interfere with legitimate uses of the world ocean.

**Art. 3.** *Liability for pollution of the marine environment*

Each State shall be held liable for pollution causing damage to the marine environment whenever such pollution results from activities carried out by official organs of that State or by its physical and juridical persons.

**Art. 4.** *Co-operation among States*

1. Every State shall co-operate with other States and with competent international organizations for the purpose of expanding scientific programmes and research on pollution of the marine environment. They shall encourage the mutual exchange of data and scientific information relating to the prevention of marine pollution.

2. States agree to co-operate with each other, on a global or regional basis, in developing a mutually acceptable methodology of rules and standards for the prevention of marine pollution.

**Art. 5.** *Mutual assistance between States*

States agree to provide assistance to each other, when it is requested, for the elimination of the effects of major accidents, such as those involving supertankers, which may cause serious pollution of the marine environment. Such assistance will be given in the first instance to coastal developing States.

**Art. 6.** *Scientific and technical assistance for developing countries*

Scientific and technical assistance in the prevention of pollution of the marine environment will be given to developing countries at their request through the transfer of the necessary scientific and technical information, the preparation of educational programmes and the training of experts and specialists.

**Art. 7.** *States' freedom of activity at sea*

1. States agree that any rules and standards relating to the prevention

381

of pollution of the marine environment adopted at the national and international levels should take into account the need to provide for and ensure on the high seas freedom of navigation and of fisheries and the freedom to conduct research and other normal activities of States.

2. The rules and standards adopted by States for the prevention of pollution of the marine environment should not infringe upon the immunity of vessels and aircraft which enjoy such immunity under international law.

**Art. 8.** *Other conventions on preservation of the marine environment*

The provisions of this Convention shall be without prejudice to the specific obligations assumed by States under special conventions and agreements concluded previously which relate to the prevention of pollution of the marine environment nor to agreements which may be concluded in furtherance of the general principles set forth in this Convention.


**MALTA:**
**— Draft Articles on the Preservation of the Marine Environment (including, inter alia, the Prevention of Pollution)**

Submitted to the United Nations Seabed Committee on 16 March 1973, as UN Doc. A/AC.138/SC.III/L.33.

**Art. 1.** *Definitions*

1. The marine environment comprises the surface of the sea, the air space above, the water column and the sea-bed beyond the high tide mark including the biosystems therein or dependent thereon.

2. Ocean space comprises the surface of the sea, the water column and the sea-bed beyond internal waters.

3. Conservation of the marine environment means the aggregate of measures—national and international—that render possible the maintenance of the quality in all its aspects of the marine environment and the preservation of its ecological balance.

4. Pollution of the marine environment means the introduction by man, directly or indirectly, of substances or energy into the marine environment (including estuaries) resulting in such deleterious effects as harm to living resources, hazard to human health, hindrance to marine activities (inculding fishing), impairment of the quality for use of sea water and reduction of amenities.

**Art. 2.** *General*

1. Considering that the marine environment constitutes a complex of closely interlinked ecological systems vital to life and that all States have

a common interest in the maintenance of its quality, States, whether Parties to this Convention or not, have the obligation:

(*a*) Not to use their technological capability in a manner that may cause significant and extensive change in the natural state of the marine environment beyond their jurisdiction without obtaining the consent of the international community in accordance with the present Convention;

(*b*) To take effective measures to prevent the pollution of the marine environment beyond their jurisdiction caused by human activities of whatever nature in their land territory, internal waters or air space above;

(*c*) To take and to enforce all reasonable regulatory measures for the abatement of pollution within the marine environment under their jurisdiction which may be expected to cause injury to the interests of other States or to those of the international community;

(*d*) To take reasonable regulatory measures to prevent their nationals, vessels bearing their flag or activities under their sponsorship from creating in the marine environment pollution causing injury to the interests of other States or to those of the international community;

(*e*) To co-operate with the competent international institutions in the adoption and enforcement of international standards and regulations for the prevention of pollution in the marine environment beyond national jurisdiction.

2. Non-compliance with the obligations under paragraphs (a), (b), (c) and (d) shall make the offending party legally responsible when substantial injury is caused to the interests of other States or to those of the international community.

3. The appropriate organ of the International Ocean Space Institutions may bring to the attention of the International Maritime Court for adjudication and for determination of damages all events that have caused significant change in the natural state of the marine environment or significant pollution in ocean space beyond national jurisdiction.

**Art. 3.** *Ocean space under national jurisdiction*

1. Foreign vessels traversing ocean space under national jurisdiction shall comply with reasonable non-discriminatory rules and regulations enacted by the coastal State in conformity with these articles and other rules of international law; in particular, they shall comply with such rules and regulations conforming to international standards relating to transport, navigation and the prevention of pollution.

2. The coastal State shall not normally exercise its powers with regard to the abatement of pollution in a manner that hampers or obstructs the passage of vessels through ocean space under national jurisdiction.

3. Disputes on the reasonableness or otherwise of the rules and regulations enacted by the coastal State shall be arbitrated or adjudicated by the

International Maritime Court.

**Art. 4.** In the event of grave and imminent danger from serious and extensive pollution or threat of serious and extensive pollution, a coastal State may take such measures beyond its jurisdiction as may be necessary to prevent, abate or eliminate such danger after notifying the competent international institutions.

**Art. 5.** 1. A coastal State has the obligation to take and enforce in ocean space under its jurisdiction special precautions in the construction, siting and maintenance of pipelines, nuclear reactors, industrial installations and installations containing radioactive materials, petroleum or other substances which may cause serious deleterious effects to human health, to the living resources or to the quality of the marine environment. All such installations shall conform to such international standards as may be established. No such installations shall be constructed in areas subject to frequent natural destructive phenomena which could cause them serious damage.

2. Non-compliance with the obligation contained in the preceding article may be brought to the attention of the International Ocean Space Institutions by a Contracting Party. The offending party shall be legally liable for damages, to be assessed by the International Maritime Court, when omission to take the special precautions referred to in the preceding paragraph results in substantial injury to the interests of other States or to those of the international community.

**Art. 6.** *Ocean space beyond national jurisdiction*
1. The introduction of substances, whether solid or liquid or gaseous, or of energy into ocean space beyond national jurisdiction or in the air space above, whether for disposal or for other purposes, in quantities that may reasonably be expected to produce significant deleterious effects to human health, to the living resources or to the quality of marine environment shall be subject to control and regulation by the Institutions established in accordance with article . . . of this Convention.

2. Nuclear and thermonuclear explosions of whatever nature are prohibited in ocean space beyond national jurisdiction without the express authorization of the Institutions established in accordance with article . . . of this Convention.

3. The use of nuclear energy for peaceful purposes, including hydrogen fusion processes, in ocean space beyond national jurisdiction shall be subject to control and regulation by the Institutions established in accordance with article . . . of this Convention. Before adopting regulations the Institutions shall consult with the International Atomic Energy Agency.

4. The storage or disposal of radioactive wastes in ocean space beyond

national jurisdiction shall be subject to control and regulation by the Institutions established in accordance with article ... of this Convention. Before adopting regulations the Institutions shall consult with the International Atomic Energy Agency.

5. The Institutions established in accordance with article ... of this Convention, in co-operation with the International Atomic Energy Agency, shall maintain a register of the release of radioactive solids and liquids in ocean space beyond national jurisdiction. The register shall be open for inspection by any Contracting Party.

6. The Institutions, in co-operation with Contracting Parties, shall monitor ocean space for pollution and shall endeavour to ascertain the effects of potentially polluting or harmful substances in the marine environment.

**Art. 7.** *International Ocean Space Institutions* (Establishment and personality, *etc.*)

The purpose of the International Ocean Space Institutions are:

To safeguard the quality of the marine environment for all mankind so that it can be transmitted unimpaired to future generations.

**Art. 8.** *Conservation of the marine environment*

1. The Institutions may accept from any State the transfer to their administration of rocks, reefs, low-tide elevations or islands having less than 10,000 permanent inhabitants.

2. The Institutions have the obligation to take, in so far as possible, strict and effective measures for the conservation of the fauna, flora and marine environment of the rocks, reefs, low-tide elevations and islands transferred to their administration.

3. Rocks, reefs, low-tide elevations and islands transferred to the administration of the Institutions shall be used only for international community purposes, such as nature parks or preserves, marine parks, scientific stations etc.

4. The Institutions shall not accept the transfer to their administration of inhabited islands without consulting the freely expressed wishes of the inhabitants and without being satisfied that there exists among the inhabitants no significant opposition to the transfer of administration.

5. The Institutions shall not accept the transfer to their administration of inhabited islands when it might entail a substantial financial responsibility or when it might involve the Institutions in a political dispute with a member.

**Art. 9.** *Assembly*
*(Procedure, functions and powers)*

The Assembly shall approve such standards and rules of a general and

385

non-discriminating character relating to the conservation of the marine environment and the prevention of pollution as may be recommended by the Council.
*(Voting, etc.)*

**Art. 10.** *Council*
*(Composition and procedure)*
*Functions and powers*

1. In order to ensure prompt and effective action by the Institution, its members confer upon the Council primary responsibility for ... the ecological integrity of ocean space beyond national jurisdiction ....

2. The Council shall consider and submit to the Assembly with its recommendations such standards and rules of a general and non-discriminatory character, in accordance with the present Convention, relating to conservation of the marine environment and the prevention of pollution as it may consider necessary to ensure the beneficial use and ecological integrity of the marine environment beyond national jurisdiction.

3. The standards and rules referred to in the preceding paragraph shall be obligatory for all users of ocean space beyond national jurisdiction two years after their adoption by the Assembly.

4. Violation of the rules referred to in paragraph 1 entails legal responsibility when injury is caused to the rights and interests of others. Persistent violators may be excluded from the use of ocean space beyond national jurisdiction.

**Art. 11.** *Maintenance of the ecological integrity of ocean space beyond national jurisdiction*

The Council, or a body designated by the Council, may investigate any event, situation, practice or action which might cause significant and extensive change in the natural state of the marine environment or which might seriously impair the ecological integrity of ocean space beyond national jurisdiction.

**Art. 12.** 1. Should the Council determine that any event, situation, practice or action endangers the natural state of the marine environment or impairs the ecological integrity of ocean space beyond national jurisdiction, the Council, or the body designated by it, shall make and publish a report containing a statement of the facts.

2. If the event, situation, practice or action referred to in paragraph 1 has occurred in national ocean space, the Council, on reliable scientific advice, shall make such recommendations as may appear necessary to the coastal State or States concerned.

3. If the event, situation, practice or action referred to in paragraph 1 has occurred in ocean space beyond national jurisdiction, the Council shall

take such action within its powers as it deems necessary or desirable. This may include monitoring the marine environment, establishing registers of the release of harmful substances or energy, regulation of dangerous practices or technologies and the prohibition or licensing of the disposal of harmful substances in ocean space beyond national jurisdiction.

**Art. 13.** In the event of imminent danger of serious contamination of extensive areas of ocean space beyond national jurisdiction, the Council, after taking scientific advice, may proclaim a regional or a world ecological emergency.

**Art. 14.** 1. During a state of regional or world ecological emergency, States within the region or all States in the world, as the case may be, whether or not members of the Institutions, shall take promptly such action for the preservation of the ecology of ocean space as may be prescribed by the Council or by the body designated by the Council for this purpose.

2. The Council, if necessary, shall ensure compliance with its directions by taking any of the actions mentioned in articles . . . and . . . .

**Art. 15.** The International Maritime Court shall be the principal judicial organ of the International Ocean Space Institutions.

**Art. 16.** The competence of the International Maritime Court shall extend to persons, natural or juridical, other than States with respect to matters which have occurred in ocean space beyond national jurisdiction.

**Art. 17.** Any member or associate member of the Institutions may request the advisory opinion of the Court with respect to the reasonableness or non-discriminatory nature of the rules and regulations mentioned in articles 3 and 10.

. . .

**Art. 18.** *Scientific and Technological Commission*
There is established a Scientific and Technological Commission. The Scientific and Technological Commission shall be the principal scientific advisory organ of the Institutions.

**Art. 19.** (Composition, voting, relations with the United Nations and other bodies etc.)
1. The Scientific and Technological Commission shall promote through concerted action by members and associate members of the Institutions the conservation of the marine environment, its scientific investigation and the development of technologies for the exploration of ocean space and of its resources and for its peaceful use by man.

2. The Commission shall disseminate as widely as possible knowledge concerning the matters referred to in paragraph 1 and shall promote the

effective transfer of technology in respect of them.

3. The Commission shall make recommendations to the Council concerning the conservation of the marine environment and shall prepare, as appropriate, international standards, draft regulations or draft conventions thereon.

4. The Commission shall advise the Council on the proclamation of a regional or a world ecological emergency in ocean space and on requests received from States in accordance with article 2 (*a*) of this Convention.

5. The Commission may advise at their request members or associate members of the Institutions on measures required to abate pollution in ocean space under national jurisdiction.

6. The Commission shall advise the Ocean Management and Development Commission on the scientific, ecological and technological aspects of licensing the exploitation of the natural resources of international ocean space and of the exploration of its non-living resources.

7. The Commission shall be consulted on all matters within its competence by the Ocean Management and Development Commission and particularly on the scientific aspects of the matters referred to in articles ... of this Convention. The Commission shall advise the General Secretary on the administration of scientific stations and nature parks or preserves.

8. The Commission shall prepare and submit to the Council for its consideration draft technical, safety and social standards and regulations with regard to vessels, fixed installations or devices lying or floating in or traversing ocean space beyond national jurisdiction.

**Art. 20.** The Commission shall submit a biennial report on its activities to the Assembly and shall report periodically to the Council.

**Art. 21.** Regional arrangements or agreements generally conforming to such international standards and regulations as may be established, may be concluded at any time by the States directly concerned.

**MALTA:**
— **Preliminary Draft Articles on the Delimitation of Coastal State Jurisdiction in Ocean Space and on the Rights and Obligations of Coastal States in the Area under their Jurisdiction**

> Submitted to the United Nations Seabed Committee on 16 July 1973, as UN Doc. A/AC.138/SC.II/L.28. The chapter quoted hereunder should be read in conjunction with A/AC.138/SC. III/L.33.

PART I  COASTAL STATE JURISDICTION IN OCEAN SPACE
(See p. 266)

PART II  RIGHTS AND OBLIGATIONS OF THE COASTAL STATE
WITHIN NATIONAL OCEAN SPACE
*Chapter 6-13.*
(See p. 272, 307)

Chapter 14. *Waste disposal and storage*

**Art. 96.** 1. No State may utilize the national ocean space of another State for the purpose of waste disposal and for storage of petroleum or other substances without the consent of that State.

2. No State may utilize international ocean space for the purpose of waste disposal or for storage of petroleum or other substances without the consent of the international ocean space institutions.

**Art. 97.** 1. Subject to the provisions of such international conventions to which it may be a Party, every coastal State may utilize its national ocean space for the purpose of waste disposal and of storage of petroleum and other substances provided that effective measures are taken to prevent pollution of international ocean space or of ocean space subject to the jurisdiction of another State.

2. In undertaking or permitting waste disposal or storage of petroleum or other substances in its national ocean space every coastal State must comply with such international standards and rules as may be adopted by the international ocean space institutions or as are contained in widely ratified international conventions.

3. Every coastal State has the obligation to take strict precautions in the disposal and storage of radio-active wastes and of toxic organic and inorganic chemical wastes in its national ocean space.

4. Radio-active wastes and toxic chemical wastes shall be stored in special clearly delimited sites, the location of which shall be communicated to the international ocean space institutions. No such sites shall be established in areas subject to frequent natural disasters.

**Art. 98.** 1. When the failure on the part of the coastal State to take the measures and precautions indicated in the foregoing article causes significant pollution in international ocean space the international ocean space institutions may submit the matter to the International Maritime Court for binding adjudication and determination of damages.

2. When the failure on the part of the coastal State to take the measures and precautions indicated in the foregoing article causes significant pollution in the national ocean space of another State, this State may bring the

389

matter to the attention of the International Maritime Court for binding adjudication and determination of damages.

**Art. 99.** 1. Every coastal State has the obligation in so far as its capabilities permit to monitor the quality of the marine environment of its national ocean space, where desirable, in co-operation with other States in the region.

2. Every coastal State has the obligation to co-operate with the international ocean space institutions in the monitoring of the quality of the marine environment.

3. The international ocean space institutions may conduct in national ocean space beyond 12 miles from the coast investigations for the purpose of obtaining scientific data on the quality of the marine environment, giving prior notice thereof to the coastal State. The coastal State shall be offered reasonable opportunity to appoint its nationals to participate in the investigations and, in any case, shall be provided with a summary of the full data obtained and an interpretation thereof by the institutions.

*Chapter 15 - Chapter 16.*
(See p. 279)

## UNITED STATES OF AMERICA:
## — Draft Articles on the Protection of the Marine Environment and the Prevention of Marine Pollution

> Submitted to the United Nations Seabed Committee on 13 July 1973, as UN Doc. A/AC.138/SC.III/L.40. Cf. A/AC.138/ SC.III/L.36: U.S.A.—Competence to Establish Standards for Control of Vessel Source Pollution (2 April 1973).

### Section A. Obligations to Protect the Marine Environment
**Art. 1.** *General Obligation*

**Art. 2.** *Particular Obligations*
Two articles on these subjects were discussed during the March/April meeting of the Sea-Bed Committee. We take note of those drafts and the footnotes and will, of course, participate in the later consideration of them in the Working Group and the Sub-Committee.

### Section B. Competence to Etablish Standards to Protect the Marine Environment
**Art. 3.** *International Standards in General*
1. The Authority established by Chapter ———— of this Convention

shall have primary responsibility for establishing, as soon as possible and to the extent they are not in existence, international standards with respect to the sea-beds.

2. The Intergovernmental Maritime Consultative Organization shall have primary responsibility for establishing, as soon as possible and to the extent they are not in existence, international standards with respect to vessels.

3. Such standards may include special standards for special areas and problems, taking into account particular ecological circumstances.

4. These organizations shall co-operate with each other, other international organizations in the field, and the United Nations Environment Programme.

**Art. 4.** *The Right and Duty to Implement Standards*

States shall adopt laws and regulations implementing international standards in respect of marine based sources of pollution of the marine environment or may adopt and implement higher standards:

(*a*) in the exercise of their rights in the [Coastal Sea-Bed Economic Area] with respect to the activities set forth in Chapter ———, Article ——— of this Convention;

(*b*) for vessels entering their ports and offshore facilities;

(*c*) for their nationals, natural or juridical, and vessels registered in their territory or flying their flag.

### Section C. General Competence to Enforce Standards to Protect the Marine Environment

**Art. 5.** *Enforcement Instrumentalities*

For the purposes of this Chapter, a State shall act through duly authorized government vessels, aircraft, or officials. Any State may, by agreement, authorize one or more States to act for it in taking pollution enforcement measures and shall so inform other States through IMCO, or directly.

**Art. 6.** *Enforcement in the [Coastal Sea-Bed Economic Area]*

1. In the exercise of its rights in the [Coastal Sea-Bed Economic Area] pursuant to Chapter ———, the coastal State shall enforce the standards applicable in accordance with the provisions of this Chapter to the activities set forth in Chapter ———, Article ——— of this Convention.

2. The Authority established in Chapter ———, may inspect, in accordance with Article ———, the activities specified in paragraph one of this Article, in co-operation with the coastal State, to ensure that the activities are being conducted in compliance with the Standards applicable in accordance with the provisions of this Chapter.

**Art. 7.** *Ordinary Enforcement Against Vessels*

1. A State shall enforce standards applicable in accordance with the provisions of this Chapter to vessels registered in its territory or flying its flag (such State is hereinafter referred to as the "flag State").

2. A State may enforce standards applicable in accordance with the provisions of this Chapter to:

(a) vessels using its ports or offshore facilities irrespective of where the violation occurred, provided, however, that such proceedings are commenced no later than [three years] after such violation occurred (such State is hereinafter referred to as the "port State");

(b) vessels in its territorial sea for violations therein, except as otherwise provided in this Convention.

## Section D. Co-operative Enforcement Measures Against Vessels
**Art. 8.** *The Right to Monitor*

A vessel within or beyond the territorial sea shall upon request by any duly authorized government vessel, aircraft or official in the vicinity which has reason to suspect a violation of the applicable international standards, give information specifying its name, State of registry, next scheduled ports of call, and any other information required to be given by the applicable international standards.

**Art. 9.** *Denial of Port Entry*

Any State may inform a vessel at any time that it will be denied entry to its ports for non-compliance with any of its environmental requirements or its refusal to allow an immediate on-board inspection to determine the source of possible pollution. Any State may, by agreement, authorize one or more other States to act for it in this respect and shall so inform other States through IMCO, or directly.

**Art. 10.** *The Duty to Notify*

If a State has reason to suspect a violation of the applicable international standards, it shall notify the flag State or the State of one of the next ports of call or both, of the alleged violation and forward the available evidence.

**Art. 11.** *Port State Duties*

Upon receipt of such notification of the alleged violation, the port State shall undertake, upon arrival of the vessel if within six months of the alleged violation, an immediate and thorough investigation. The port State shall promptly inform the flag State and the notifying State of the results of the investigation and its actions including a statement as to whether it intends to institute proceedings and the result of any such proceedings.

**Art. 12.** *Flag State Duties*

Upon receipt of notification if within six months of an alleged violation, the flag State shall undertake an immediate and thorough investigation. If the result of its or a port State's investigation indicates that a violation has occurred, the flag State shall institute proceedings against the vessel, its operator, its master, or its owner, provided that it shall not be required to do so if proceedings have already taken place in respect of that violation. The flag State shall inform the notifying State and other State which could institute proceedings of its decisions and actions.

**Art. 13.** *Participation in Investigations*
A notifying State may participate in any investigation undertaken pursuant to its notification. A flag State may designate an observer for any investigation involving one of its flag vessels. An expert or experts designated by IMCO shall be permitted to partcipate in any investigation if so requested by a State concerned and such expert or experts may file a separate report with IMCO.

## Section E. Extraordinary Enforcement Measures and Intervention against Vessels

**Art. 14.** *Coastal State Remedy Against Flag States*
If the dispute settlement machinery established in Chapter ——— finds, upon petition by any State, that a particular flag State has unreasonably and persistently failed to enforce the applicable international standards against its flag vessels, the machinery may specify additional enforcement measures which may be taken by coastal States for violations by any vessel of that flag. Such authorization shall be interim in nature and shall be limited to those measures necessary to bring about adequate flag State enforcement. Such authorization shall be rescinded upon a showing by the flag State that it is taking adequate measures.

**Art. 15.** *Emergency Coastal State Enforcement Procedures*
Beyond the territorial sea, a coastal State may take such reasonable emergency enforcement measures as may be necessary to prevent, mitigate or eliminate imminent danger of major harmful damage to its coast or related interests from pollution arising from a particular occurrence reasonably believed to be related to a violation of the applicable international standards.

**Art. 16.** *Intervention*
(blank)

## Section F. General Articles Relating to Enforcement

**Art. 17.** *Release of Vessels*
A vessel shall be permitted to continue its voyage and shall not be detained longer than its presence is essential for investigative purposes.

It shall be promptly released if the investigation does not reveal a violation of the standards applicable in accordance with the provisions of this Chapter. Where there continues to be reason to believe a violation has occurred, vessels shall be promptly released under reasonable procedures such as bonding except where such release would present an unreasonable threat of harm to the marine environment or where other action is required or authorized by the applicable international standards.

### Art. 18. *Penalties*

All violations of the applicable international standards shall be prohibited under the law of each State. The penalties provided for such violations shall be applied so as to guarantee fair treatment, shall be adequate in severity to discourage any such violation, and shall, in any case, be at least as severe as those applied by that State for violations in its territorial sea.

### Art. 19. *Multiple Proceedings*

Whenever a State other than the flag State has instituted proceedings against a vessel, its operator, its master, or its owner, no other proceedings in respect of the same violation may be instituted except by the flag State of the vessel or by any other State in whose territorial sea or internal waters the violation has taken place. In assessing penalties, a State shall take into account any penalties assessed by other States in respect of the same violation. This shall not restrict the right of any State or person to institute a suit or claim for damages caused by pollution.

### Art. 20. *Co-operation*

States shall afford one another the greatest measure of assistance in carrying out the objectives of this Chapter and in particular in providing evidence and witnesses necessary for investigations and proceedings.

### Section G. Other Articles Relating to the Marine Environment
### Art. 21. *Liability for Unreasonable Measures*

A State shall be liable for damage resulting from investigative, enforcement or intervention measures exceeding those reasonably necessary in the light of available information.

### Art. 22. *State Responsibility*

1. A State has the responsibility to take appropriate measures to ensure, in accordance with international law, that activities under its jurisdiction or control do not cause damage to the environment of other States or to the marine environment beyond the limits of national jurisdiction.

2. States shall undertake, as soon as possible, jointly to develop international law regarding liability and compensation for pollution damage including, *inter alia*, procedures and criteria for the determination of

394

liability, the limits of liability and available defences.

3. In the absence of other adequate remedies with respect to damage to the environment of other States caused by activities under the jurisdiction or control of a State, that State has the responsibility to provide recourse for foreign states or nationals to a domestic forum empowered:

(a) to require the abatement of a continuing source of pollution of the marine environment, and

(b) to award compensation for damages.

**Art. 23.** *Sovereign Immunity*

This Chapter shall not apply to those vessels and aircraft entitled to sovereign immunity under international law. However, each State shall ensure, by the adoption of appropriate measures, that all such vessels and aircraft owned or operated by it act in a manner consistent with the object and purpose of this Chapter.

**Art. 24.** *Dispute Settlement*

Any dispute with respect to the interpretation or application of the provisions of this Chapter shall, if requested by any party to the dispute, be resolved by the compulsory dispute settlement procedures contained in Chapter ⸻

**KENYA:**
**— Draft Articles on Prevention and Control of Pollution in the Marine Environment**

> Submitted to the United Nations Seabed Committee on 16 July 1973, as UN Doc. A/AC.138/SC.III/L.41. These articles should be considered as forming a part or chapter of A/AC.138/SC.II/L.10: Kenya—Exclusive Economic Zone Draft Articles (p. . . .).

*Preamble*

(a) *States Parties to this* . . .
Recognizing the nature and the characteristics of the marine environment,

(b) *Convinced* that the marine environment and the living organisms which it supports are of vital importance to humanity;

(c) *Convinced* that coastal States have a particular interest and responsibility in the management of the marine living resources;

(d) *Aware* that modern technology has created new marine protection and conservation problems with far-reaching social, economic and biological consequences;

(*e*) *Recognizing* that the capacity of the marine environment to assimilate wastes and render them harmless and its ability to regenerate natural resources are not unlimited;

(*f*) *Realizing* that the present knowledge of the extent or intensity of marine pollution is incomplete and that marine pollution intensity vary among countries or regions and the applicability of a particular standard in one country or region may be inadequate or unsuitable in another country or region;

(*g*) *Recognizing* that States have, in accordance with the Charter of the United Nations and the principles of international law, the sovereign rights to exploit their resources pursuant to their environment policies and the responsibility to ensure that activities within their jurisdiction or control do not cause damage to the environment of other States or of areas beyond the limits of national jurisdiction.

(*h*) *Aware* that marine pollution originates from many sources, including discharges through the atmosphere, from rivers, estuaries, outfalls and pipelines and from dumping;

(*i*) *Convinced* that it is the duty of all States to protect the marine environment by promulgating and enforcing necessary laws, individually or jointly, taking into account existing international agreements on the protection and the preservation of the marine environment, the need for elaboration of further agreement aimed at ensuring an effective approach to the protection and preservation of the marine environment.

*Agree as follows:*

I. *Definitions*

For the purpose of these articles:

(*a*) "Marine control pollution zone" means the marine waters within the jurisdiction and control of a coastal State.

(*b*) "High seas" means the maritime areas beyond the limits of national jurisdiction.

(*c*) "Vessels" means the crafts of any kind, self-propelled or not, that displace themselves on the surface of the water, in the water column or in the airspace above the marine environment.

(*d*) "Marine environment" means the area comprising the surface of the sea, the airspace above, the water column and the sea-bed beyond the high tide mark, including the living and mineral resources therein.

(*e*) "Conservation of the marine environment" means the aggregate of measures taken to render possible the maintenance of the natural quality and the ecological balance of the marine environment.

(*f*) "Marine pollution" is the introduction, directly or indirectly of substances or energy into the marine environment resulting in such deleterious effects as harm to living resources, hazard to human health, hindrance to marine activities, impairment of the quality for use of marine water and reduction of marine amenities.

## II. *Rights of States*

**Art. 1.** Coastal States have a right to establish a marine pollution control zone within which they shall exercise jurisdiction to control activities for the purpose of preventing or minimizing damage to the marine environment.

**Art. 2.** The limits of the marine pollution control zone shall be fixed in nautical miles in accordance with appropriate criteria in each region and without prejudice to limits already adopted by any State within a region. The marine pollution control zone shall not in any case exceed 200 nautical miles measured from the baseline for determining the extent of the territorial sea.

**Art. 3.** The exercise of jurisdiction over the marine pollution zone shall encompass all activities carried out in the coastal State's area of jurisdiction or control.

**Art. 4.** The establishment of a marine pollution zone shall be without prejudice to other legitimate uses of the marine environment, particularly the freedom of navigation, overflight and the freedom to lay submarine cables and pipelines.

**Art. 5.** In the event of a grave or imminent danger or threat of marine pollution originating from areas beyond coastal States marine pollution zone, the coastal State has a right to take such measures as may be necessary to prevent, mitigate or eliminate such danger or threat.

**Art. 6.** Developing coastal States shall be granted preferential rights or treatment in the allocation of marine pollution funds and other technical aid facilities and in the utilization of the specialized services of international organizations set up for the purposes of the control of marine pollution.

## III. *Duties and Obligations of States*

**Art. 7.** Every State has a right to exploit its resources pursuant to its environmental policies and has a common duty and responsibility in the prevention and control of pollution of the marine environment in accordance with the provisions of these articles.

**Art. 8.** States shall take measures, individually or jointly, to prevent pollution of the marine environment. In particular, States shall take measures to ensure that activities carried out under their jurisdiction or control do not cause pollution damage to other States, including the marine environment as a whole. In formulating marine pollution control measures, States shall take into account

(*a*) provisions of the existing international pollution control conventions,

(*b*) relevant rules, standards and procedures proposed by competent international or regional organizations, (*c*) geographical, ecological and economic characteristics of States.

**Art. 9.** States shall promote research with the object of acquiring more knowledge of the possible effects of marine environment pollution and for the purposes of monitoring marine pollution activities.

**Art. 10.** States shall disseminate or exchange marine pollution research findings or information freely and timely.

**Art. 11.** States shall endeavour to adopt suitable standard systems of observation, measurement, evaluation and analysis of the effect of pollution in the marine environment.

**Art. 12.** States shall ensure that marine pollution control measures shall not discriminate in form or fact between States or persons.

IV. *Co-operation among States*

**Art. 13.** States shall co-operate in setting up international or regional programmes to acquire knowledge for the assessment of pollutant sources, pathways, exposures and risks.

**Art. 14.** States shall co-operate on global or, as appropriate, on regional basis, directly or through competent international or regional organizations to elaborate or formulate, rules, standards and procedures, and action plans for the purpose of the prevention of pollution of the marine environment.

**Art. 15.** Every State has an obligation to notify neighbouring and other States, and international or regional organizations of areas, whether within its national jurisdiction or not, it becomes aware have been polluted or are in imminent danger of being polluted.

In the case of the pollution danger being in a coastal State's marine pollution control zone, the coastal State shall terminate or minimize the danger according to its rules and regulations. For the high seas, the Authority and States concerned, in co-operation with competent international or regional organizations, shall present to the State under whose jurisdiction or control the activities causing pollution were conducted, a demand for an immediate termination or restriction of the activities.

**Art. 16.** All States, and in particular the developed States, shall bilaterally or through competent international organizations accelerate the provision of scientific and technical assistance to needy countries to enable them to effectively prevent or control pollution of the marine environment.

**Art. 17.** The United Nations Environment Programme shall centralize and co-ordinate all information regarding all aspects of the protection, preservation and control of the marine pollution. This body, with the assistance of competent organizations such as IMCO, Joint Group of Experts on the Scientific Aspects of Marine Pollution, etc., shall:—

(*a*) establish a system of monitoring, observation, measurement and evaluation of various aspects of marine pollution;

(*b*) recommend international or regional measures to be adopted to protect the marine environment;

(*c*) collect and disseminate marine pollution data, reports and other relevant information;

(*d*) distribute marine pollution funds and other scientific and technical aid facilities to needy countries;

(*e*) ...

**Art. 18.** States and international or regional organizations shall co-operate in the development of international law relating to procedures for the assessment of damage, the determination of liability, the payment of compensation and the settlement of related disputes arising from damage caused in areas under national jurisdiction as well as areas beyond the national jurisdiction.

V. *Compensation for Damage*

**Art. 19.** States and international or regional organizations shall be liable for damage caused by marine pollution attributable to them in areas under the jurisdiction of other States, including the environment of other States.

**Art. 20.** States are liable for damage by marine pollution attributable to them in areas beyond national jurisdiction or marine pollution control zone, i.e. in the high seas. The Authority to be established or competent regional or international organizations shall ensure compliance with marine pollution control measures in the high seas.

**Art. 21.** States undertake to provide recourse to ensure equitable compensation for the victims of the marine pollution caused by persons under their jurisdiction outside their marine control zone.

**Art. 22.** Following the exhaustion of local remedies or where no such are available, the State of the damaged party may present to the State having jurisdiction over the person or persons responsible for the damage in question a claim for damage caused. If no settlement of the claim is arrived at through negotiations, the States concerned shall submit the claim, at the request of either of them to arbitration or adjudication in accordance with a procedure to be determined by agreement or by a third party nominated by them.

## VI *Enforcement*

**Art. 23.** States shall institute all necessary measures to give effect to these articles for the protection and preservation of the marine environment within the limits of their national jurisdiction or their marine pollution control zone.

**Art. 24.** States shall institute all necessary measures to give effect to these articles for the protection and preservation of the marine environment in respect of the operations of: (*a*) vessels registered in their territory but operating beyond the limits of national jurisdiction (*b*) man-made structures or platforms, fixed or floating, operating in areas beyond the limits of national jurisdiction where such structures or platforms are under the control of a State.
*(other clauses may follow)*

## NORWAY:
## — Draft Articles on the Protection of the Marine Environment against Pollution

Submitted to the United Nations Seabed Committee on 19 July 1973, as UN Doc. A/AC.138/SC.III/L.43.

**Art. 1.** States have the obligation to protect and preserve the marine environment in accordance with the provisions of this convention.

**Art. 2.** *Definition of Marine Pollution*
In the present Convention pollution means the introduction by man, directly or indirectly, of substances or energy into the marine environment, which alone or together with other substances or energy, may result in such deleterious effects as harm to living resources, hazards to human health, hindrance to marine activities, including fishing, impairment of quality for use of sea water and reduction of amenities.

**Art. 3.** *General obligation of States*
1. States shall take all necessary measures to prevent pollution of the marine environment from any source, using for this purpose the best practicable means in accordance with their capabilities, individually or jointly, as appropriate. In particular, States shall take measures to ensure that activities under their jurisdiction or control, do not cause damage to other

400

States, including their environment, by pollution of the marine environment.

2. The measures taken pursuant to these articles shall deal with all sources of pollution of the marine environment, whether land, marine, or any other sources, including rivers, estuaries, the atmosphere, pipelines, outfall structures, vessels, aircraft and sea-bed installations or devices. They shall include *inter alia*:

(*a*) In respect of land-based sources of pollution of the marine environment, measures designed to minimize the release of toxic and harmful substances, especially persistent substances, into the marine environment, to the fullest possible extent;

(*b*) In respect of pollution from vessels, measures relating to the prevention of accidents, the safety of operations at sea, and intentional or other discharges, including measures relating to the design, equipment, operation and maintenance of vessels, especially of those vessels engaged in the carriage of hazardous substances whose release into the marine environment either accidentally or through normal operation of the vessel, would cause pollution of the marine environment; and

(*c*) In respect of installations or devices engaged in the exploration and exploitation of the natural resources of the sea-bed and subsoil and other installations or devices operating in the marine environment, measures for the prevention of accidents and the safety of operations at sea, and especially measures related to the design, equipment, operation and maintenance of such installations and devices.

3. The measures taken pursuant to these articles shall:

(*a*) In respect of land-based sources of pollution of the marine environment, take into account such international standards as may be elaborated.

(*b*) In respect of marine-based sources of pollution of the marine environment, conform to the generally accepted international standards.

4. In taking measures to prevent pollution of the marine environment, States shall have due regard to the legitimate uses of the marine environment and shall refrain from unjustifiable interference with such uses.

5. States shall take all reasonable measures to abate existing marine pollution.

**Art. 4.** 1. States shall enact and enforce the necessary regulations on *inter alia*:

(*a*) any industrial or other activity which may result in pollution of the marine environment;

(*b*) production, distribution or use of materials or substances which may cause such pollution;

(*c*) the disposal of waste into the marine environment;

401

(*d*) the compensation to be accorded to victims of such pollution;

(*e*) the steps to be taken in case of occurrences or accidents involving pollution of the marine environment.

2. Every State shall ensure that environmental aspects, and in particular the steps which are necessary for the prevention of marine pollution, are taken into account as a matter of the utmost importance in all planning or works done by the State or within its jurisdiction; insofar as such planning or works may affect the marine environment.

### Art. 5. *General Obligation of Co-operation*

States shall co-operate with other States and with competent international or regional organizations in order to take all possible measures to prevent, control and minimize marine pollution on global, regional and national levels, and to harmonize their efforts to this end.

### Art. 6. *Elaboration of agreed Rules, Standards and Procedures for the Prevention of Marine Pollution*

1. States shall co-operate with other States and competent international and regional organizations with regard to the elaboration and implementation of agreed rules, standards and procedures for the prevention of marine pollution on global, regional and national levels.

2. Such co-operation shall, *inter alia,* endeavour to establish international guidelines and criteria to provide the policy framework for control measures.

3. A comprehensive plan for the protection of the marine environment should be elaborated as soon as possible and be amended and revised whenever it is deemed necessary. The plan shall provide for the identification of critical pollutants and their pathways and sources, determination of exposure to these pollutants and assessment of the risks they pose. The plan shall lay down the measures which should be taken on the global, regional or national level to prevent, control and minimize the risk of marine pollution by such pollutants.

The plan may, *inter alia*, provide for standards and guidelines for the methods of production, storage, transportation, use and destruction of materials and substances that create risks of pollution of the marine environment and standards and guidelines for the prevention or reduction of discharge of harmful products or wastes into the marine environment, including measures for the destruction, storage and alteration of harmful waste to avoid the risk of pollution.

The plan shall to the extent possible establish and evaluate the regional and local variations in the effects of pollution. The plan shall take into account such variables including the ecology of the specific sea areas, economic and social conditions of the surrounding states, amenities, recreational facilities and other uses of the seas.

402

**Art. 7.** *Discharge of toxic and other harmful Substances*

1. The discharge of toxic substances or of other substances and the release of heat, in such quantities or concentrations as to exceed the capacity of the environment to render them harmless, must be halted in order to ensure that serious or irreversible damage is not inflicted upon ecosystems.

2. States shall use the best practicable means available to minimize the release to the environment of toxic or dangerous substances, especially if they are persistent substances such as heavy metals and organochloric compounds, until it has been demonstrated that their release will not give rise to unacceptable risks.

**Art. 8.** *Pollution from Land-based Sources*

1. All States are under an obligation to control, prevent and reduce such activities within their territory, which directly or indirectly may lead to or contribute to pollution of the marine environment.

2. To the extent that the territory of another State or the high seas may be affected by the discharge, deposit or emission of substances or articles in any significant quantity from the territory of a State, such discharge, deposit or emission shall be subject to registration and licensing by the State in which the activity is performed. A licence shall not be granted unless the authorities have found, with a reasonable degree of certainty, that the discharge, deposit or emission can take place without substantial damage to person, property or natural resources in the territory of another State or on the high seas.

3. The rules of paragraphs 1 and 2 of this Article shall also apply to activities which are capable of causing pollution of the air as the primary effect, if such air pollution may lead to pollution of the sea as a secondary consequence.

4. States shall exercise due diligence in the control of the types and quantities of waste which are disposed of through discharge systems, or in any other manner into inland water or into the sea; in order to prevent unjustified damage to person, property or natural resources in the territory of another State or on the high seas.

**Art. 9.** *Pollution from Vessels*

Every State shall establish and revise the necessary regulations and take all appropriate steps to ensure that all vessels flying its flag or other craft under its registry take all appropriate measures and comply with such rules which are required to avoid pollution. States shall ensure that vessels under their registration comply with internationally agreed rules and standards, *inter alia* those drawn up by the Intergovernmental Maritime Consultative Organization, relating to ship design, construction, equipment, operation, maintenance and other relevant factors.

403

**Art. 10.** *Pollution resulting from the Exploration and Exploitation of the Sea-bed and Subsoil*

1. The exploration and exploitation of the sea-bed and subsoil, within as well as beyond the limits of national jurisdiction, shall only be undertaken under the supervision of a State or the appropriate international authority, and in accordance with such safety regulations which are necessary to avoid pollution of the marine environment.

2. Coastal States shall establish and revise the necessary safety regulations and ensure that adequate and appropriate resources are available to deal with pollution incidents resulting from the exploration and exploitation of sea-bed resources within the limits of their national jurisdiction.

**Art. 11.** *Dumping*

States shall prevent the pollution of the marine environment by dumping of harmful waste into the sea within areas of jurisdiction and on the high seas. To this end they shall implement the rules and regulations laid down in regional and international conventions.

**Art. 12.** *Nuclear Material, Oil, Chemicals and other noxious or hazardous Substances*

States shall establish and enforce special regulations on the production, transportation, use and destruction of nuclear material, oil, chemicals and other noxious or hazardous substances, in order to avoid pollution of the sea and damage to person, property or natural resources. For this purpose they shall co-operate with one another and with international organizations, in particular the International Atomic Energy Agency and the Intergovernmental Maritime Consultative Organization, and take account of the guidelines and standards drawn up by such organizations.

**Art. 13.** *Transfer of Pollution*

In taking measures to prevent pollution States (as well as international organizations) shall guard against the effect of merely transferring damage or hazard (directly or indirectly) from one area to another (or from one type of pollution to another).

**Art. 14.** *Establishment of Detection and Monitoring Systems*

1. States shall, on national, regional and international levels establish detection and monitoring systems for the control of pollutants and for the prevention and punishment of infringements of existing rules and regulations.

2. States shall distribute to other States and to the interested international organizations concerned available data and information concerning activities resulting in the release of substances or other matters endangering the marine environment, the measures taken to determine harm-

404

ful effects and measures and procedures adopted to eliminate or minimize such harmful effects.

### Art. 15. *Environment Impact Statement: Consultations*

Before any State or a person within its jurisdiction undertakes an activity which may lead to significant alteration of the marine environment the State shall file an environmental impact statement with the international organization (United Nations agency) concerned. The statement shall provide all necessary information to assess the possibility of damage, and shall be communicated to competent international organizations and to other States whose interests may be affected. If such States or organizations so wish, the first-mentioned State shall consult with them before any alteration of the environment is undertaken, with a view to avoid damage to other interests and to preserve the environment against pollution.

### Art. 16. *Obligation to exercise effective Jurisdiction*

States shall, in accordance with the principles of international law, exercise effective control over areas, persons and ships under their jurisdiction in order to prevent pollution of the marine environment.

### Art. 17. *Enforcement*

1. States shall ensure that their national legislation provides adequate sanctions against infringements of existing regulations on marine pollution.

2. States shall take all appropriate steps to prevent and punish infringements of existing regulations on marine pollution.

3. Flag States shall, when receiving a report that an alleged infringement of rules or regulations to prevent pollution has been committed by a ship under its registry, take all appropriate steps to investigate the matter, to secure the necessary evidence and to prosecute violation.

The same shall apply in relation to complaints and reports received by a State in respect of marine pollution alleged to have been caused by other activities within its jurisdiction, and which is alleged to have harmful effects or which in time may affect the interests of other States or those of the international community.

### Art. 18. *Jurisdiction and Powers of Coastal States*
(blank)

### Art. 19. *Right of Intervention*
(blank)

### Art. 20. *Liability and Compensation*

1. States have the responsibility to ensure that activities under their jurisdiction or control do not cause damage to the marine environment of other States. If activities under the jurisdiction or control of one State cause damage to areas under the jurisdiction of another State, including

405

the environment of another State, the first-mentioned State shall, in accordance with the principles of international law, be internationally liable to the second State and pay compensation accordingly.

2. States have the responsibility to ensure that activities under their jurisdiction or control do not cause damage to the environment of areas beyond the limits of national jurisdiction. States shall co-operate to develop effective procedures for making reparation or paying compensation in respect of damage to the environment of areas beyond the limits of national jurisdiction.

**Art. 21.** *Violations of Obligations under the Convention*

1. When it is contended by a State that the conduct of another State is not in accordance with its obligations under the present Convention, or that serious damage may otherwise be caused to the marine environment, the States concerned shall, together with any third State whose interests may be affected, enter into negotiations. The aim of such negotiations shall be to establish the factual situation and to reach a solution in accordance with the rules of the Convention and with the need to protect and preserve the marine environment.

2. In case of violations of the obligations of the present Convention, the State responsible shall immediately take steps to put an end to such violations and, if possible, the effects thereof.

**Art. 22.** *Powers conferred upon States by the provisions of other Conventions*

Nothing in the present Article shall be deemed to prevent a State from exercising such powers with regard to protection and preservation of the marine environment which may be conferred upon it by the provisions of other conventions. Nor shall the present Articles be interpreted in such a way as to entail the effect of extending jurisdiction conferred upon States by other conventions to cover the enforcement of other rules than those which are binding according to such other conventions.

**Art. 23.**

(Nothing in this ... shall derogate from the sovereign right of a State to exploit its own resources pursuant to its environmental policies and in accordance with its duty to protect and preserve the marine environment both in its own interests and in the interests of mankind as a whole).

## FRANCE:
## — Draft Articles concerning the Rights Exercisable by Coastal States for the Purpose of Preventing Marine Pollution

Submitted to the United Nations Seabed Committee on 20 July 1973, as UN Doc. A/AC.138/SC.III/L.46.

**Art. 1.** Coastal States shall have specific rights for the purpose of suppressing acts of pollution committed by vessels or aircraft and liable to cause damage to the economic interests of coastal States or to the interests of their tourism.

**Art. 2.** The rights mentioned in article 1 shall be exercisable, in accordance with the provisions of this Convention, in a zone extending ". . . miles" from the baselines used to measure the breadth of territorial waters.

**Art. 3.** This Convention shall not apply to those vessels and aircraft entitled to sovereign immunity under international law. However, each Party shall ensure by the adoption of appropriate measures that vessels and aircraft in this category which belong to it, or are operated by it, act in a manner consistent with the object of this Convention.

**Art. 4.** Coastal States may take action in the zone defined in article 2 against acts of pollution committed in contravention of the provisions of:
    1. the London Convention of 29 December 1972 on the Prevention of Marine Pollution by Dumping of Wastes and Other Matters,
    2. the International Convention for the Prevention of Pollution of the Sea by Oil, 1954,
    3. the London Convention for the Prevention of Pollution from Ships, 1973.

**Art. 5.** In the event of acts of pollution being committed by vessels or aircraft in contravention of the provisions of regional agreements concluded between two or more States Parties to this Convention, the Contracting Governments shall accord to the coastal States concerned the particular rights deriving from the application of these agreements, provided that the said rights are consistent with the principles set forth in the Conventions listed in article 4. Such rights shall be exercisable only in the geographical area in which the agreements concerned are applicable.

**Art. 6.** In the zone defined in article 2, the Contracting Governments may investigate violations, by any vessels or aircraft, of the agreements referred to in article 4.

**Art. 7.** By virtue of such power of investigation, the competent authorities of the coastal State concerned may, if they have serious grounds for believing that a vessel or aircraft has committed a violation, exercise the following rights to the extent that it appears necessary for establishing the existence of the violation:

1. They may order the vessel to stop;

2. They may board the vessel for the purpose of preparing a report containing facts accessory to the investigation of the infringement.

Measures taken under this article must not endanger the vessel or create hazards to navigation, and must not unduly delay the vessel.

**Art. 8.** The report prepared by the competent authorities of the coastal State concerned shall be transmitted to the State under whose authority the vessel is operating. The latter State shall treat the report as though it had been prepared by its own authorities. The report shall in particular have the same value in evidence as it would have in the State whose authorities prepared it.

**Art. 9.** The rights accorded to the coastal States concerned shall not prevent the State under whose authority the vessel is operating from exercising, in the zone defined in article 2, the rights accorded to it under the provisions of the London Convention for the Prevention of Pollution from Ships, 1973.

However, proceedings shall be taken by the coastal State concerned in cases where:

(*a*) the vessel is operating under the authority of a State which is not a Party to the above-mentioned Convention,

(*b*) the flag State, although a Party to the said Convention, fails to manifest its intention to take proceedings within one month from the date on which it has been notified by the coastal State of the violations which have been committed.

**Art. 10.** The rights accorded to coastal States under this Convention shall preclude the State under whose authority the vessel or aircraft is operating from exercising, in the zone defined in article 2, the rights accorded to it under the provisions relating to violations in the London Convention of 29 December 1972 on the Prevention of Marine Pollution by Dumping of Wastes and Other Matters or in regional agreements on the matter.

**Art. 11.** Where the coastal State concerned takes proceedings under article 10, it shall apply its national legislation in dealing with vessels or aircraft which are under the jurisdiction of any one of the Contracting Governments.

**Art. 12.** For the purpose of the application of articles 10 and 11 of this Convention, in cases where dumping that requires permission is to be carried out in the zone defined in article 2, the State competent to issue the permit to dump shall give prior notification to the coastal State concerned.

**Art. 13.** The coastal State concerned shall provide the State competent to issue the permit with information on its national legislation on dumping. This information shall be supplemented by any provisions adopted or under consideration with regard to:

—the delimitation of dumping zones established within the zone defined in article 2,

—the conditions for dumping established in the light of the results of the monitoring of the marine environment by the coastal State in the zone defined in article 2 of this Convention.

**Art. 14.** 1. Any dispute between the Contracting Parties relating to the interpretation or application of the present agreement which cannot be settled by consultation shall, at the request of any one of the Contracting Parties, be referred to an arbitral tribunal consisting of three members. Each Contracting Party shall appoint one arbitrator and the third shall be designated by the first two members of the tribunal, but he may not be a national of either of the two Parties. The third arbitrator shall preside over the arbitral tribunal.

2. If either of the two Contracting Parties fails to appoint its arbitrator within 60 days, or if the third arbitrator has not been designated within 30 days, each of the Parties may request the Secretary-General of the United Nations Environment Programme to make the necessary appointment or appointments by selecting one or more arbitrators.


## ECUADOR, EL SALVADOR, PANAMA, PERU AND URUGUAY:
### — Preservation of the Marine Environment (Working paper)

Submitted to the United Nations Seabed Committee on 24 July 1973, as UN Doc. A/AC.138/SC.III/L.47.

1. All States have a legitimate interest in preventing and controlling pollution of the seas in defence of the marine environment and of the health and other interests of their inhabitants.

*Duties of States*

2. States shall include in their national laws the provisions necessary to prevent and combat marine pollution, taking into account the interests of their inhabitants and the level of development which they have attained.

3. Every State undertakes to adopt and make known in good time within the limits of its capabilities, the measures necessary to prevent pollution

of the seas through the introduction of substances, materials or energy which may constitute a danger to human health, harm living resources, create obstacles to activities carried on at sea, including fishing, be detrimental to the quality of the water and its possible use, impair the quality of marine fishing products or affect conditions for the recreation and other interests of its inhabitants.

4. States shall promote scientific research with a view to establishing the effects of pollution on the marine environment, including long-term consequences that may affect future generations.

5. States shall support the execution of international programmes for the monitoring, measurement, analysis, evaluation and control of pollution in the marine environment.

6. States shall promote the free exchange of up-to-date information and experience on pollution of the marine environment, making them available to other States, in good time and on terms which will encourage the dissemination of scientific and technical knowledge of the subject.

7. States shall be responsible for any damage caused to the marine environment of other States or to the international sea by discharges from their territory, waters subject to their sovereignty and jurisdiction and vessels flying their flag.

*Rights of the Coastal State*

8. It is for the coastal State to enact the provisions necessary for the preservation of the marine environment within the limits of its sovereignty and national jurisdiction and to adopt the most appropriate measures to protect the quality of the water and to control pollution hazards, taking into account, where relevant, the needs of co-operation with other States and the recommendations of international technical bodies.

9. Any coastal State which is confronted by a serious or imminent danger of pollution, or the threat of pollution, arising from an incident or from acts relating to an incident in areas situated beyond the limits of its sovereignty and national jurisdiction may take the measures necessary to prevent, mitigate or eliminate that danger.

*International Co-Operation*

10. States shall promote the establishment of regional machinery, in which the countries situated within a geographical area of similar characteristics and with common interests are represented, to centralize and coordinate at that level the various aspects of the protection and preservation of the marine environment.

11. States shall co-operate among themselves and with the competent international organizations in preparing and applying rules, standards and

procedures designed to protect and preserve the marine environment beyond the areas subject to their sovereignty and jurisdiction.

12. States shall assist one another in any action taken against marine pollution, irrespective of the origin of such pollution.

13. An international body shall be established to centralize and co-ordinate all information relating to the protection, preservation and control of marine pollution and to promote international co-operation.

This body shall: (a) establish a system of watchkeeping, monitoring, measurement, analysis and evaluation, at the world level, in all matters relating to the protection, prevention and control of marine pollution in areas not subject to the sovereignty and jurisdiction of coastal States; (b) recommend in good time any measures that should be adopted for the prevention, control and elimination of marine pollution; (c) publish an atlas of marine pollution containing such information as may be available on hydrobiological species existing in polluted marine areas and in those which may become polluted in the near future, and maps and charts indicating the chief oceanographic characteristics of the various areas, such as currents, winds, rocks, etc.; (d) issue annual reports announcing the results of surveys and evaluations concerning the main aspects of marine pollution and concerning systems and measures for combating it; (e) promote the conclusion of international agreements at the world and regional levels on scientific, technical and legal matters relating to pollution of the marine environment; (f) keep up to date the schedule of pollutants referred to in paragraph 14.

*Complementary Standards and Measures*

14. An international ban shall be placed on the discharge into the sea of waste containing substances, materials or energy whose harmful effects on the marine environment are duly proven and which appear in the annexed schedule No. 1.

15. The coastal State shall prohibit the discharge into waters subject to its sovereignty and jurisdiction of waste containing substances, materials or energy whose toxic effects on the marine environment are duly proven and which appear in the annexed schedule No. 2, save in special circumstances, in which the specific permission of that State shall be required.

16. States shall apply penalties for the discharge of waste by their nationals into the international sea or by any person in areas subject to their sovereignty and jurisdiction.

17. States shall supply the international body with statistics on the production and use of toxic or dangerous substances which may constitute pollutants of the marine environment, especially if they are persistent.

18. States shall for statistical purposes communicate to the international

body, in accordance with an established procedure, particulars of the nature and volume of the substances and materials for whose discharge they have given permission, together with the dates, places and the methods used.

19. Ships shall be under an obligation to transmit to the competent authority of the coastal State all possible information concerning any incident or action which arouses suspicion that the marine environment is being polluted in the waters subject to its sovereignty and jurisdiction.

20. Ships shall be under the same obligation to the international body to be established, in the case of incidents or actions occurring in the international sea.

21. States shall continuously evaluate the state of pollution in their waters with a view to determining the degree of such pollution, the pollutants that exist and the distribution and possible sources thereof.

22. States shall adopt suitable systems of monitoring, measurement, evaluation, analysis and control of the consequences of pollution in the marine environment, taking into account for that purpose the applicability, in each case, of internationally recognized provisions.

23. States shall lay down standards quality according to the uses of water and the areas where it is located, taking into account the different geographical, ecological, social and economic conditions prevailing in each region.

24. Measures taken by the coastal State to protect and preserve the marine environment from pollution shall not be such as to transfer the effects of such pollution from one area to another.


## NETHERLANDS:
## — Draft Articles on the Enforcement of International Provisions for the Prevention of Marine Pollution from Vessels

Submitted to the United Nations Seabed Committee on 10 August 1973, as UN Doc. A/AC.138/SC.III/L.48. See, also, A/AC. 138/SC.III/L.35: Netherlands-Observations in regard to Questions concerning the Preservation of the Marine Environment (23 March 1973).

**Art. 1.** 1. Violation of any of the provisions of the present convention shall be prohibited under the law of the administration of the ship concerned, wherever the violation occurs.

2. Violation of any of the provisions of the present convention, any other international convention or generally accepted international rules, with regard to discharge of harmful substances or effluent containing these

412

substances, shall, moreover, be prohibited, wherever the violation occurs, under the law of any other Contracting State, subject to the provisions of Article 2.

3. The penalties provided for under the law of a Contracting State in respect of any violation, as mentioned in paragraphs 1 and 2 above, shall be adequate in severity to discourage such violation. The penalties provided for in respect of violations outside the territorial sea of a Contracting State shall be no less severe than the penalties provided for in respect of the same infringement within its territorial sea.

**Art. 2.** 1. A Contracting State may cause proceedings to be taken when a ship to which the present Convention applies enters its ports or offshore terminals, in respect of an act prohibited under paragraph (2) of Article 1, committed by that ship, or its [owner or] master. A report of such proceedings shall be sent to the Administration of the ship.

2. For the purpose of the preceding paragraph the proceedings instituted by a Contracting State, not being the State of the Administration of the ship concerned,

(a) have to be commenced no later than [three] years after the act has been committed;

(b) shall not lead to the imposition of penalties other than fines, unless the Contracting State concerned and the State of the Administration agree otherwise.

3. Whenever a Contracting State has commenced proceedings, no other proceedings in respect of the same act may be instituted by any other Contracting State except for a Contracting State which has prosecutional priority pursuant to paragraph (4) of this Article. In case a Contracting State having prosecutional priority commences proceedings, the proceedings instituted by another Contracting State are suspended.

4. The prosecutional priorities among the Contracting States are as follows:

(a) In case a provision requires for special precautions to be observed within a certain distance from the nearest land and the alleged violation of the requirement has been committed within the distance stipulated, the coastal State of such nearest land has prosecutional priority over the Contracting States mentioned in the following sub-paragraphs.

(b) In case the alleged violation occurred within [100] nautical miles from the nearest land, the coastal State of such nearest land has prosecutional priority over the Contracting States, mentioned in the following sub-paragraphs.

(c) The State of the Administration of the ship concerned has prosecutional priority over the Contracting States mentioned in the following sub-paragraph.

(*d*) Any other Contracting State after consultation with the State of the Administration of the ship concerned.

5. A Contracting State which has commenced proceedings may transfer the prosecution to the Administration of the ship concerned. In that case the State of the Administration has, in relation to any other Contracting State, the same prosecutional priority as the Contracting State from which it has taken over the prosecution.

## JAPAN:
### — Proposal on Enforcement Measures by Coastal States for the Purpose of Preventing Marine Pollution

> Submitted to the United Nations Seabed Committee on 13 August 1973, as UN Doc. A/AC.138/SC.III/L.49.

1. A coastal State party to this Convention may investigate and prosecute natural or juridical persons under the jurisdiction of other Contracting States when such persons have discharged or dumped any harmful substances in contravention of generally accepted international rules and standards, provided that:

(*a*) there are sufficient evidences required by the law of the coastal State enacted in conformity with generally accepted international rules and standards, and

(*b*) the discharge or dumping occurred in areas adjacent to its territorial sea, the maximum limit of which areas shall be . . . . nautical miles from its coast.

2. In taking actions referred to in paragraph 1, the coastal State shall ensure that the maritime activities of the natural or juridical persons referred to in the same paragraph are not unduly interfered with.

3. The coastal State shall inform the other Contracting States referred to in paragraph 1, as well as competent international organizations, of the results of such investigation and prosecution.

## TRINIDAD AND TOBAGO:
### — Draft Articles on Responsibility and Liability

> Submitted to the United Nations Seabed Committee on 1973, as UN Doc. A/AC.138/SC.III/L.54.

**Art. 1.** Coastal States shall reserve the right to require minimum levels of insurance against pollution damage for all commercial vessels operating

414

within their territorial waters and within a broad area adjacent to its coast-line.

**Art. 2.** Liability for any damage within or beyond national jurisdiction arising from activities within the national jurisdiction of coastal States shall be borne by the entity responsible for such damage. In the case of vessel source pollution, liability shall rest directly with the polluting agent or entity. With respect to damage arising from exploration and exploitation activities on the sea bed, liability shall rest with the offshore operator.


**AUSTRALIA, CANADA, COLOMBIA, FIJI, GHANA, ICELAND, IRAN, JAMAICA, KENYA, MEXICO, NEW ZEALAND, PHILIP-PINES AND UNITED REPUBLIC OF TANZANIA:**
— **Coastal State Enforcement of Standards for Prevention of Pollution from Vessels—Basic Zonal Approach**

Submitted to the United Nations Seabed Committee on 22 August 1973, as UN Doc. A/AC.138/SC.III/L.56.

Coastal States may establish or adopt and enforce standards for the prevention of marine pollution from vessels in (areas) (zones) within their jurisdiction adjacent to their territorial sea.


## X. SCIENTIFIC RESEARCH OF OCEAN

In addition to the proposals herein referred to, see, also the following texts:

A/AC.138/SC.II/L.24 (Uruguay), Sec. 6. (p. 261)
— L.27 (Ecuador, Panama and Peru), Art. 10. (p. . . .),
    Art. 23. (p. . . .)
— L.37 (Argentina), Art. 12, 22. (p. . . .)

## CANADA:
## — Working Paper on Principles on Marine Scientific Research

Submitted to the United Nations Seabed Committee on 25 July
1972, as UN Doc. A/AC.138/SC.III/L.18.

*Preamble*

1. All mankind has an interest in the facilitation of marine scientific
research and the publication of its results.

2. Marine scientific research is any study, whether fundamental or
applied, intended to increase knowledge about the marine environment,
including all its resources and living organisms, and embraces all related
scientific activity.

3. The objectives of marine scientific research include achievement of
a level of understanding which allows accurate assessment and prediction
of oceanic processes and provide the basis for the development of a
management policy which will ensure that the quality and resources of
the marine environment are not impaired, and for the rational use of this
environment, in the service of human welfare, international equity and
economic progress and, in the interest of peace and international co-
operation among States.

*Principles*

1. Knowledge resulting from marine scientific research is part of the
common heritage of all mankind, and such knowledge and information
of a non-proprietary or non-military nature should be exchanged and made
available to the whole world.

2. Marine scientific research constitutes a legitimate activity within the
marine environment. Every State, whether coastal or not, and every
competent international organization has the right to conduct or authorize
the conduct of scientific research in the marine environment, in accordance
with the rules and recognized principles of international law and subject
to the provisions of the present principles.

3. Marine scientific research as such shall not form the legal basis for
any claims of exploitation rights or any other rights in areas beyond the
limits of national jurisdiction.

4. Marine scientific research shall be conducted in a reasonable manner, and shall not result in any unjustifiable interference with other uses of the marine environment; nor shall other uses of the marine environment result in any unjustifiable interference with marine scientific research.

5. Marine scientific research shall not entail excessive collection of specimens and samples, nor cause pollution or undue disturbance of the marine environment.

6. The availability to every State of information and knowledge resulting from marine scientific research shall be facilitated by effective international communication of proposed major programmes and their objectives, and by publication and dissemination through international channels of their results.

7. States shall take steps to further the development and growth of marine scientific research and to obviate interference with its progress, and shall co-operate in the elaboration of international rules to facilitate such research. States shall promote arrangements and agreements to advance marine scientific research and the exchange of data and information on a regional, as well as on a global basis, in co-operation with other States and with international organizations, whether governmental or non-governmental.

8. States shall, both individually and in co-operation with other States and with competent international organizations, promote the flow of scientific data and information and the transfer of experience resulting from marine scientific research to developing countries and the strengthening of the marine research capabilities of these countries to a level corresponding to their needs and resources, including programmes to provide adequate training of the technical and scientific personnel of these countries.

9. Marine scientific research in areas within the jurisdiction of a coastal State shall only be conducted with the consent of the coastal State. If such consent is granted, the coastal State shall have the right to participate or to be represented in such marine scientific research and shall have the right of utilizing samples, the right of access to data, and results, and the right to require that the results be published.

10. The coastal State prior to determining whether it will grant consent to marine scientific research in areas within its jurisdiction, may require information such as the period, location, nature and purpose of the proposed investigations, the observations to be made, the proposed disposition of all material collected, the means to be employed and, where applicable, the name of the ship with its full description, including tonnage, type and class, the name of the agency sponsoring the investigations, and the names of the Master of the vessel, the proposed scientific leaders and members of the scientific party and particulars of any proposed entry into a coastal State port. The coastal State shall be kept informed of any changes in

the above information.

11. The coastal State shall reply promptly to a request accompanied by information required by it in accordance with the provisions of Principle 10. The coastal State shall facilitate the conduct of marine scientific research to which it has consented by extending necessary facilities to ships and scientists while they are operating in areas within its jurisdiction wherever possible.

12. Marine scientific research shall comply with all the coastal State's laws and regulations when carried out in areas within the jurisdiction of the coastal State, including the resource management regulations and directions in areas where the coastal State has authority over resources appertaining to its continental shelf, the environmental protection regulations in areas where the coastal State has a primary responsibility for environmental protection, the management regulations in areas under fishery management, where in addition all information resulting from such research shall be made available to the authority managing such area, and the regulations and directions necessary to protect the security of the coastal State.

13. Marine scientific research concerning the sea-bed and ocean floor, and the subsoil thereof, beyond the limits of national jurisdiction shall comply with any regulations developed by a competent international organization to minimize disturbance and prevent pollution of the marine environment and interference with exploration and exploitation activity.

14. States shall devise means to enable responsibility to be fixed with States or international organizations that have caused damage in the course of marine scientific research or where such damage has been caused by the activities of persons under their jurisdiction, to the marine environment or to any other State or to its nationals.

**BULGARIA, POLAND, UKRAINIAN SOVIET SOCIALIST REPUBLIC, UNION OF SOVIET SOCIALIST REPUBLICS:**
— **Draft Article for a Convention on Scientific Research in the World Ocean**

Submitted to the United Nations Seabed Committee on 15 March 1973, as UN Doc. A/AC.138/SC.III/L.31. Cf. A/AC.138/SC.III/L.23 (Working paper submitted by the same sponsoring delegations on 3 August 1972).

**Art. 1.** *Definition of scientific research*
Scientific research in the world ocean means any fundamental or applied

research and related experimental work, conducted by States and their juridical and physical persons, as well as by international organizations, which does not aim directly at industrial exploitation but is designed to obtain knowledge of all aspects of the natural processes and phenomena occurring in ocean space, on the sea-bed and in the subsoil thereof, which is necessary for the peaceful activity of States for the further development of navigation and other forms of utilization of the sea and also utilization of the air space above the world ocean.

**Art. 2.** *Principle of freedom of scientific research*

All States, irrespective of their geographical location, as well as international organizations, shall enjoy on a basis of equality and without any discrimination the right of freedom to conduct scientific research in the world ocean.

The term "world ocean" as used in this Convention covers all ocean space, the sea-bed and the subsoil thereof, with the exception of internal and territorial waters and the bed and subsoil of the continental shelf.

**Art. 3.** *Means by which scientific research may be conducted*

Scientific research in the world ocean may be conducted through the use of all types of vessels, platforms, floating stations, mobile or fixed installations, aircraft and other means, both specially designed and adapted or used for such purposes, using the appropriate scientific methods and equipment.

**Art. 4.** *Co-operation among States in the conduct of scientific research*

States agree to co-operate with one another through the conclusion of bilateral and multilateral agreements in creating favourable conditions for the conduct of scientific research in the world ocean for peaceful purposes, the removal of obstacles to such research and the uniting of efforts by scientists in studying the essence of and the interrelations between the phenomena and processes occurring in the world ocean.

**Art. 5.** *Provision of assistance to developing countries and land-locked countries*

States shall co-operate in carrying out measures designed to extend the research capacity of the developing countries and the land-locked countries, including participation of scientists from such countries in scientific research, training of scientific staff from among their nationals and the transfer of expertise in the conduct of scientific research work.

**Art. 6.** *Participation of States in international scientific research programmes*

All States may participate in the conduct of international scientific research programmes in the world ocean, and shall encourage participation of their scientists in carrying out the measures provided for by such programmes. States shall co-operate in the implementation of the long-term and expanded programme of oceanic exploration conducted under the auspices of UNESCO's Intergovernmental Oceanographic Commission.

**Art. 7.** *Exchange and publication of scientific data*

States shall encourage the mutual exchange of scientific data obtained as a result of the conduct of research, and especially the provision of such data to developing countries as part of the scientific and technical assistance provided to them.

States shall also adopt and encourage measures to ensure the publication and broad dissemination of the results of scientific research in the world ocean, *inter alia* through the system of world and regional data centres.

**Art. 8.** *Simplified procedure for the entry of scientific research vessels into ports and internal maritime waters*

States shall, in the interests of international co-operation and in order to facilitate the conduct of scientific research, adopt measures, including legislation, to simplify the procedure for the entry of vessels conducting scientific research work in the world ocean into their ports and internal maritime waters.

**Art. 9.** *Legal status of installations and facilities for scientific research*

Fixed scientific research installations, whether standing on the ground or at anchor, and also floating stations or mobile installations, shall be subject to the jurisdiction of the State which installed them. However, they shall not possess the status of islands or have their own territorial waters, and their presence shall not affect the determination of the limits of the continental shelf.

**Art. 10.** *Safety of navigation and the principle of freedom of the high seas*

Safety zones may be established around fixed and temporary installations and facilities at a distance of not more than 500 metres from their outer edges. Such installations and facilities shall not be placed at points where they may obstruct international sea-lanes or air routes, or in areas of intense fishing activity.

Notice shall be given in accordance with existing maritime practice of the erection and removal of all installations and facilities.

Fixed and floating stations and installations shall bear identification markings indicating the State or international organization to which they belong, and shall carry the necessary permanent warning devices, such as signs and signals, to ensure the safety of navigation on and overflight of the high seas.

Scientific research in the world ocean shall not be subjected to unjustified interference, nor shall scientific research itself cause unjustified interference with navigation, fishing, overflight in air space or any other

420

legal activity in the world ocean.

**Art. 11.** *Prevention of pollution of the marine environment*
Existing international norms to prevent pollution of the marine environment shall be respected in the conduct of scientific research, with a view to protecting the environment from harmful effects which may interfere with its ecological balance.

**Art. 12.** *Scientific research in territorial waters and on the continental shelf*
Scientific research in territorial waters and on the continental shelf may be conducted only with the consent of the coastal State.

The coastal State shall have the right to participate or be represented in the research.

Scientific data on the results of research in the territorial waters or on the continental shelf of a coastal State shall be made available to that State on the basis of mutual agreement.

**Art. 13.** *Responsibility for possible damage caused during the conduct of scientific research*
States shall be held internationally liable for national activity in the world ocean, irrespective of whether it is carried out by government organs or by juridical or physical persons, and for ensuring that national activities are conducted in accordance with the provisions of this Convention.

States shall be held internationally liable for damage which may be caused to other States, to their juridical or physical persons, or to international organizations during the conduct of scientific research in the world ocean, on the sea-bed and in the subsoil thereof.

**Art. 14.** *Obligations under the United Nations Charter and other international agreements*
In implementing the provisions of this Convention, States shall act in accordance with the purposes and principles of the United Nations Charter and with other generally accepted norms of international law.

Nothing in this Convention shall affect the rights and obligations of States under other international treaties relating to its subject.


**MALTA:**
**— Draft Articles on Scientific Research**

> Submitted to the United Nations Seabed Committee on 23 March 1973, as UN Doc. A/AC.138/SC.III/L.34.

**Art. 1.** *Definition*
In these articles the term scientific research means any systematic in-

vestigation, whether fundamental or applied, and related experimental work the primary aim of which is to increase knowledge of the marine environment for peaceful purposes.

The marine environment comprises the surface of the sea, the air space above, the water column and the sea-bed beyond the high tide mark, including the biosystems therein or dependent thereon.

Ocean space comprises the surface of the sea, the water column and the sea-bed beyond internal waters.

Sea-bed means (a) the floor of the sea or of the ocean and (b) the subsoil or rock underlying the sea floor or ocean floor.

## General

**Art. 2.** 1. States, whether coastal or land-locked, have the right to undertake scientific research in ocean space. This right is subject to such regulation of a general and non-discriminatory character as may be prescribed by the International Ocean Space Institutions.

2. Intergovernmental organizations and physical and juridical persons have the right to undertake scientific research in ocean space. This right is subject to such regulation of a general and non-discriminatory character as may be prescribed by the International Ocean Space Institutions.

3. Scientific research shall not form a legal basis for any jurisdictional claims with regard to ocean space or its resources.

**Art. 3.** 1. The consent of the coastal State shall be obtained in respect of scientific research conducted within a belt of sea adjacent to the coast not exceeding 12 miles in breadth.

2. In the case of scientific research conducted by surface vessels, consent of the coastal State shall not be withheld:

(a) When the request together with the research programme is submitted by a person or entity registered with the International Ocean Space Institutions six weeks before the date that it is proposed to initiate the research;

(b) When the possibility is offered to the coastal State to appoint its nationals to participate in the research;

(c) When the full data and an interpretation thereof is provided to the coastal State or when the data and a report thereon will be published by the coastal State or by the International Ocean Space Institutions;

(d) When an equitable share of the samples from the research is offered to the coastal State.

3. In the case of scientific research conducted by means of unanchored floating devices the coastal State shall not withhold its consent:

(a) When the request together with precise information on the character of the proposed research is submitted four weeks before the devices are to be introduced in the sea by a person or entity registered with the International Ocean Space Institutions;

(b) When the coastal State is given the opportunity to appoint its nationals to witness the introduction of the devices in the sea;

(c) When the devices do not constitute a danger to navigation or hamper other activities in ocean space and when they are fitted with adequate means of giving warning of their presence;

(d) When the full data obtained by the devices is provided to the coastal State or to the International Ocean Space Institutions.

4. The person or entity undertaking the research is required to comply with health, customs, police, security and pollution regulations of the coastal State generally conforming to international practice or to such international standards as may be established.

5. The coastal State shall not exercise its police and other powers in such a manner as to hamper or obstruct scientific research conducted in accordance with the provisions of paragraph 4.

6. Any Contracting Party may bring to the attention of the International Ocean Space Institutions difficulties in obtaining the consent of a coastal State with regard to proposed scientific research fulfilling all the provisions of paragraph 2 or of paragraph 3 of this article, as the case may be.

*Ocean space under national jurisdiction*

**Art. 4.** 1. The coastal State may construct, maintain and operate habitats, installations, equipment and fixed or movable devices for scientific purposes on or in the sea-bed of ocean space under its jurisdiction, provided that:

(a) No habitats, installations, equipment or devices are established where interference may be caused to the use of sea lanes necessary to international navigation;

(b) Appropriate safety zones, of which prompt notice must be given to the international community through the International Ocean Space Institutions, are established around such habitats, installations, equipment or devices and adequate means for giving warning of their presence are maintained;

(c) Any habitats, installations, equipment or devices that are abandoned or disused are entirely removed.

2. Non-compliance with the obligations referred to under paragraph 1 (a), (b) and (c) shall make the coastal State legally responsible in the event of accidents of navigation.

3. Habitats, installations, equipment or devices for scientific purposes may not be established on or in the sea-bed of ocean space under the jurisdiction of a coastal State without the latter's consent. The coastal State

has the right to remove any habitats, installations, equipment or devices established without its consent on or in the sea-bed of ocean space under its jurisdiction and to keep any scientific data found.

4. The coastal State has the obligation to protect habitats, installations, equipment or devices for scientific purposes established with its consent on or in the sea-bed of ocean space under its jurisdiction and to ensure that the measures referred to under paragraph 1 (a) and (b) are taken in respect of them.

**Art. 5.** 1. The coastal State may construct, maintain and operate in ocean space under its jurisdiction floating devices or installations of whatever nature for scientific purposes joined to the sea-bed, provided that:

(*a*) Prompt notice is given to the international community through the International Ocean Space Institutions of the location of such installations;

(*b*) Permanent and adequate means for giving warning of their presence are maintained;

(*c*) No interference is caused to sea lanes necessary to international navigation;

(*d*) Devices or installations that are abandoned or disused are entirely removed.

2. Non-compliance with the obligation referred to under paragraph 1 (*a*), (*b*), (*c*) and (*d*) shall make the coastal State legally responsible in the event of accidents of navigation.

3. Floating installations of whatever nature for scientific purposes joined to the sea-bed may not be established in ocean space under the jurisdiction of a coastal State without the latter's consent. The coastal State has the right to remove such installations established without its consent in ocean space under its jurisdiction and keep any scientific data found therein.

4. The coastal State has the obligation to protect floating installations for scientific purposes joined to the sea-bed established with its consent in ocean space under its jurisdiction and to ensure that the measures referred to under paragraph 1 (*a*) and (*b*) are taken in respect of them.

**Art. 6.** 1. The coastal State may maintain unanchored floating devices for scientific purposes in ocean space under its jurisdiction provided that they are fitted with adequate means of giving warning of their presence and do not constitute a danger to navigation or hamper other activities in ocean space.

2. Non-compliance with the obligations referred to under paragraph 1 shall make the coastal State legally responsible in the event of accidents or of injury to the interests of other States or to those of the international community.

3. The coastal State has the obligation to protect unanchored floating

devices for scientific purposes installed with its consent in a belt of sea adjacent to its coast not exceeding 12 miles in breadth and may not interfere with or remove such devices found in other areas of ocean space subject to its jurisdiction.

**Art. 7.** The International Maritime Court shall be competent to adjudicate disputes arising from non-compliance with the provisions of articles 3, 4, 5 and 6.

*Ocean space beyond national jurisdiction*

*General*

**Art. 8.** 1. Contracting Parties in their conduct of scientific research shall inform as soon as reasonably possible the Institutions established in accordance with article ... of this Convention of any phenomenon which they may discover that could constitute a serious danger to the life or health of persons in ocean space.

2. The Institutions shall inform as soon as reasonably possible each Contracting Party of any phenomenon of which they have knowledge which could constitute a serious danger to the life or health of persons in ocean space.

*International Ocean Space Institutions*
*(Establishment, personality, etc.)*

**Art. 9.** The purposes of the International Ocean Space Institutions are:

...

To encourage the scientific investigation of ocean space and the dissemination of knowledge thereon, to promote international co-operation in the conduct of scientific research therein and to strengthen the research capabilities of technologically less advanced countries;

To promote the development and the practical application of advanced technologies for the penetration of ocean space and for its peaceful use by man and to disseminate knowledge thereof;

To assist Contracting Parties and their nationals in all matters relating to knowledge and development of ocean space and its resources and in particular to assist Contracting Parties to train their nationals in scientific disciplines and technologies relating to ocean space and to its peaceful uses;

...

*Organs*

**Art. 10.** 1. There are established as the principal organs of the Inter-

425

national Ocean Space Institutions: an Assembly, a Council, an International Maritime Court and a Secretariat.

2. Major subsidiary organs are an Ocean Management and Development Commission, a Scientific and Technological Commission and a Legal Commission.

## Assembly
### (Procedure, functions and powers, etc.)

**Art. 11.** The Assembly shall approve such standards and rules of a general and non-discriminatory character relating to . . . the conduct of scientific research . . . as may be recommended by the Council.
*(Voting, etc.)*

## Council

**Art. 12.** 1. The Council shall consider and submit to the Assembly with its recommendations such rules of a general and non-discriminatory character, in accordance with the present Convention, relating to . . . the conduct of scientific research . . . as it may consider necessary for an effective pursuit of the purposes of the Institutions.

2. The standards and rules referred to in the preceding paragraph shall be obligatory for all users of ocean space beyond national jurisdiction two years after their adoption by the Assembly.

3. Violation of the standards and rules referred to in paragraph 1 entails legal responsibility when injury is caused to the rights and interests of others. Persistent violators may be excluded from the use of ocean space beyond national jurisdiction.

**Art. 13.** The Council shall approve the establishment of:
(*a*) Scientific stations, nature parks or marine preserves in ocean space beyond national jurisdiction;
. . .

## International Maritime Court
### (Establishment, jurisdiction, powers etc.)
## Secretariat

**Art. 14.** The General Secretary shall:
. . .
Participate in so far as possible in scientific research conducted in ocean space beyond national jurisdiction and bring the results thereof to the attention of members and associate members of the Institutions;

Administer under rules laid down by the appropriate organs of the Institutions any islands that may be transferred to the administration of the

426

Institutions and any scientific stations, marine preserves or nature parks that may be established;

. . .

*Scientific and Technological Commission*
*(Establishment and procedure; relationship with United Nations bodies)*

**Art. 15.** The Scientific and Technological Commission shall make suitable arrangements for consultation with institutions and organizations of scientists, technicians and technologists primarily interested in questions relating to ocean space.

**Art. 16.** 1. The Scientific and Technological Commission shall promote through concerted action by members and associate members of the Institutions the conservation of the marine environment, its scientific investigation and the development of technologies for the exploration of ocean space and of its resources and for its peaceful use by man.

2. The Commission shall disseminate as widely as possible knowledge concerning the matters referred to in paragraph 1 and shall promote the effective transfer of technology in respect to these matters.

3. The Commission shall advise the Ocean Management and Development Commission on the scientific, ecological and technological aspects of licensing the exploitation of the natural resources of ocean space beyond national jurisdiction and of the investigation of its non-living resources.

4. The Commission shall be consulted on all matters within its competence by the Ocean Management and Development Commission and particularly on the scientific aspects of the matters referred to in articles . . . The Commission shall advise the General Secretary on the administration of scientific stations . . .

. . .

5. The Commission shall decide the requirements for inscription in and removal from the register referred to in article 3, paragraphs 2 (*a*) and 3 (*a*), of the present Convention. The register shall be kept in the custody of the General Secretary and shall be open for inspection by any member or associate member of the Institutions.

**Art. 17.** *Register*

1. May be inscribed in the register referred to in article 15, paragraph 5:
    (*a*) States or their organs;
    (*b*) Intergovernmental organizations;
    (*c*) Scientific institutes and scientific organizations;
    (*d*) Physical or juridical persons possessing such qualifications as may be determined by the Scientific and Technological Commission.

2. Persons or entities inscribed in the register may freely conduct

scientific research in ocean space beyond a belt of sea adjacent to the coast not exceeding 12 miles in breadth in accordance with the present Convention under such general and non-discriminatory regulations as may be prescribed by the Institutions.

3. The person or entity inscribed in the register is legally responsible for damages to the environment or for injury to the legitimate rights and interests of States or to those of the international community caused in the course of scientific research in ocean space by physical or juridical persons under its sponsorship.

4. Any member of associate member of the Institutions may bring to the attention of the Scientific and Technological Commission any instance where it believes that scientific research conducted by a person or entity inscribed in the register has caused significant damage to the marine environment or has caused injury to its legitimate rights and interests.

5. If the Scientific and Technological Commission finds that scientific research conducted by a person or entity inscribed in the register has caused significant damage to the marine environment or injury to the legitimate rights and interests of a member or associate member, it may (*a*) issue a warning to the person or entity which was responsible for the research; (*b*) suspend the person or entity from the register for a fixed period of time not exceeding two years, or (*c*) remove the person or entity from the register. The action taken by the Scientific and Technological Commission may be appealed to the International Maritime Court.

**MALTA:**
— **Preliminary Draft Articles on the Delimitation of Coastal State Jurisdiction in Ocean Space and on the Rights and Obligations of Coastal States in the Area under their Jurisdiction**

> Submitted to the United Nations Seabed Committee on 1973, as UN Doc. A/AC.138/SC.II/L.28. The chapter quoted hereunder should be read in conjunction with A/AC.138/SC.III/L.34.

PART I  COASTAL STATE JURISDICTION IN OCEAN SPACE
(See p. 266)

PART II  RIGHTS AND OBLIGATIONS OF THE COASTAL STATE
WITHIN NATIONAL OCEAN SPACE
Chapter 6 - Chapter 8.
(See p. . . . .).

428

## Chapter 9. *Scientific research*

**Art. 63.** 1. Subject to the provisions of these articles, all States, whether coastal or not, shall enjoy the right to undertake scientific research in national ocean space.

2. Scientific research means any systematic investigation, whether fundamental or applied, and related experimental work, the primary aim of which is to increase knowledge of the marine environment for peaceful purposes.

3. Scientific research activities shall not form the basis for any claims with regard to the exploitation of the natural resources of national ocean space.

**Art. 64.** The coastal State may require 30 days advance notification of the intention to conduct scientific research in its national ocean space.

**Art. 65.** 1. In view of the common interest of the international community in the acquisition of knowledge relating to ocean space, the coastal State shall not hamper or obstruct scientific research activities in national ocean space when the person or entity undertaking the research is registered with the international ocean space institutions and complies with such general and non-discriminatory standards and rules as may be adopted by the international ocean space institutions.

2. The person or entity undertaking scientific research in national ocean space is required to comply with the health, customs, police, security and pollution control regulations of the coastal State.

**Art. 66.** In the absence of relevant standards and rules adopted by the international ocean space institutions, the coastal State may enact reasonable and non-discriminatory regulations relating to the conduct of scientific research in its national ocean space.

**Art. 67.** 1. Coastal State regulations relating to the conduct of scientific research may be brought to the attention of the international ocean space institutions when these regulations are considered to be discriminatory, or to constitute an unreasonable impediment to the exercise of the right of scientific research, or to be inconsistent with such general standards and rules as may be adopted by the international ocean space institutions.

2. The international ocean space institutions may recommend that the coastal State rescind or modify regulations which are found to be discriminatory or to constitute an unreasonable impediment to the exercise of the right of scientific research or to be inconsistent with such general standards and rules as may be adopted by the international ocean space institutions.

3. In the event of continued disagreement between the international

ocean space institutions and the coastal State, the matter shall be submitted to the International Maritime Court for binding adjudication.

**Art. 68.** The coastal State may require a foreign vessel or aircraft undertaking scientific research, which does not comply with the standards and rules adopted by the international ocean space institutions or enacted by the coastal State concerning the conduct of scientific research, to leave national ocean space.

**Art. 69.** 1. Underwater habitats, installations, equipment or devices for scientific purposes may not be established on or in the sea-bed of ocean space under the jurisdiction of a coastal State without the latter's consent.

2. The coastal State has the right to inspect and the obligation to protect habitats, installations, equipment and devices for scientific purposes established with its consent on or in the sea-bed of ocean space under its jurisdiction and to ensure that they comply with the provisions of article 74 and with such relevant standards and rules as may be adopted by the international ocean space institutions.

3. The coastal State may remove underwater habitats, installations, equipment or devices established without its consent on or in the sea-bed of ocean space under its jurisdiction and to keep any scientific data found therein.

**Art. 70.** 1. Floating installations of whatever nature for scientific purposes joined to the sea-bed may not be established in ocean space under the jurisdiction of a coastal State without the latter's consent.

2. The coastal State has the right to inspect and the obligation to protect floating installations of whatever nature for scientific purposes joined to the sea-bed established with its consent in ocean space under its jurisdiction. The coastal State must ensure that such installations comply with the provisions of article 74 and with such relevant standards and rules as may be adopted by the international ocean space institutions.

3. The coastal State may remove floating installations for scientific purposes joined to the sea-bed established without its consent in ocean space under its jurisdiction and to keep any scientific data found therein.

**Art. 71.** Authorization of the coastal State shall be obtained in respect of scientific research conducted within a belt of ocean space adjacent to the coast not exceeding 12 nautical miles in breadth measured from the applicable baseline.

**Art. 72.** 1. In the case of scientific research conducted by surface vessels the authorization of the coastal State shall not be withheld:

(*a*) when the request together with the research programme is submitted by a person or entity registered with the international ocean space institutions six weeks before the date that it is proposed to initiate the research;

(b) when the person or entity conducting the research undertakes to provide the full data obtained and an interpretation thereof to the coastal State three months before publication and before release of such data to any other person or entity;

(c) when the possibility is offered to the coastal State to appoint its nationals to participate in the research;

(d) when the person or entity conducting the research undertakes to refrain from publishing or from releasing to other persons or entities for a period of time not exceeding five years, such scientific data as the coastal State may request;

(e) when the person or entity conducting the research expresses willingness reasonably to adjust the proposed research programme to accommodate research goals of the coastal State;

(f) when the person or entity conducting the research offers an equitable share of the samples from the proposed research to the coastal State.

2. The coastal State may refuse further access for scientific purposes to national ocean space within 12 nautical miles of its coast to persons or entities which do not comply with the obligations assumed by them when obtaining the authorization mentioned in article 71.

**Art. 73.** 1. In the case of scientific research conducted by means of unanchored floating devices, the consent of the coastal State shall not be withheld:

(a) when the request, together with precise information on the character of the proposed research is submitted by a person or entity registered with the international ocean space institutions six weeks before the date that it is proposed to introduce the devices in the sea;

(b) when the coastal State is given the opportunity to appoint its nationals to witness the introduction of the devices into the sea;

(c) when the devices are clearly and distinctively marked and are fitted with adequate means of giving warning of their presence and do not constitute a danger to navigation or hamper other activities in ocean space;

(d) when the person or entity conducting the research undertakes to provide the full scientific data obtained and an interpretation thereof to the coastal State before publication and before release of such data to any other person or entity;

(e) when the person or entity conducting the research undertakes to refrain from publishing or from releasing to other persons or entities, for a period of time not exceeding five years, such scientific data as a coastal State may request.

2. The coastal State may refuse further access for scientific purposes

to national ocean space within 12 nautical miles of its coast to persons or entities which do not comply with the obligations assumed by them when obtaining the authorization mentioned in article 71.

3. The coastal State has a right to inspect and an obligation to protect unanchored floating devices for scientific purposes introduced in its national ocean space with its consent. The coastal State must ensure that such devices comply with the provisions of article 75 of this Convention.

**Art. 74.** 1. The coastal State may construct, maintain and operate (*a*) underwater habitats, installations, equipment or devices for scientific purposes on or in the sea-bed of its national ocean space; (*b*) floating installations of whatever nature for scientific purposes joined to the sea-bed, provided that:

(*a*) such general and non-discriminatory standards and rules as may be adopted by the international ocean space institutions are observed;

(*b*) no interference is caused to sea lanes necessary to international navigation;

(*c*) other activities in ocean space are not unreasonably hampered;

(*d*) appropriate safety zones are established around such habitats, installations or devices;

(*e*) the international ocean space institutions are promptly notified of the location of such habitats, installations or devices and of the breadth of the safety zones which have been established around them;

(*f*) any habitats, installations, equipment or devices that are abandoned or disused are entirely removed.

2. Non-compliance with the obligations contained in the foregoing paragraph shall make the coastal State legally responsible in the event of accidents of navigation.

**Art. 75.** 1. The coastal State may maintain and operate unanchored floating devices for scientific purposes in its national ocean space provided that such devices (*a*) are clearly and distinctively marked; (*b*) are provided with adequate means of giving warning of their presence; (*c*) do not constitute a danger to navigation or unreasonably hamper other activities in ocean space; (*d*) comply with such general and non-discriminatory standards and rules as may be adopted by the international ocean space institutions.

2. Non-compliance with the obligations contained in the foregoing paragraph shall entail legal responsibility on the part of the coastal State in the event of accidents of navigation.

## CHINA:
### — Working Paper on Marine Scientific Research

Submitted to the United Nations Seabed Committee on 19 July 1973, as UN Doc. A/AC.138/SC.III/L.42.

1. To conduct marine scientific research in the sea area within the national jurisdiction of a coastal State, prior consent of the coastal State concerned must be sought, and the relevant laws and regulations of the coastal State must be observed.

A coastal State is entitled to take part in the scientific research work conducted by other States in the sea area within its own national jurisdiction and to receive data and results obtained in such work. The publication and transfer of such data and results are subject to the prior consent of the coastal State concerned.

A coastal State shall as far as possible provide necessary facilities for the marine scientific research projects to which it has given its consent.

2. The marine scientific research conducted in the international sea area must be consistent with the spirit of the Declaration of the Principles. It must be exclusively for peaceful purposes and helpful towards a better understanding of the marine environment, and effective exploitation and utilization of the said area, by the people of all States. It shall be governed by the international regime and international machinery concerned therewith.

3. All States shall, on the basis of mutual respect for sovereignty, equality and mutual benefit, promote international co-operation in marine scientific research.

4. All States and the international agencies concerned shall, on the basis of respect for sovereignty of the developing countries, actively aid these countries to enhance their capabilities in conducting marine scientific research independently.

## UNITED STATES OF AMERICA:
## — Draft Articles for a Chapter on Marine Scientific Research

Submitted to the United Nations Seabed Committee on 19 July 1973, as UN Doc. A/AC.138/SC.III/L.44.

**Art. 1.** Scientific research in the sea being essential to an understanding of the global environment, the preservation and enhancement of the sea and its rational and effective use, States shall promote and facilitate the development and conduct of all scientific research in the sea for the benefit of the international community. All States, irrespective of geographic location, as well as appropriate international organizations may engage in scientific research in the sea, recognizing the rights and interests of the international community and coastal States, particularly the interests and needs of developing countries, as provided for in this Convention.

**Art. 2.** Scientific research shall be conducted with reasonable regard to other uses of the sea, and such other uses shall be conducted with reasonable regard to the conduct of scientific research.

**Art. 3.** Scientific research shall be conducted with strict and adequate safeguards for the protection of the marine environment.

**Art. 4.** Scientific research activities shall not form the legal basis for any claim to any part of the sea or its resources.

**Art. 5.** States shall promote international co-operation in scientific research exclusively for peaceful purposes

  *a.* by participating in international programmes and by encouraging co-operation in scientific research by personnel of different countries;

  *b.* through effective publication of scientific research programmes and dissemination of the results of such research through international channels and promotion of the flow of scientific research to developing countries;

  *c.* through measures to strengthen scientific research capabilities of developing countries, including assistance in assessing the implications for their interests of scientific research data and results, the participation of their nationals in research programmes, and education and training of their personnel.

**Art. 6.** Coastal States in the exercise of their sovereignty shall co-operate in facilitating the conduct of scientific research in their territorial sea and access to their ports by research vessels.

**Art. 7.** In areas beyond the territorial sea where the coastal State exercises jurisdiction pursuant to Articles — over sea-bed resources and coastal fisheries, States and appropriate international organizations shall ensure that their vessels conducting scientific research shall respect the rights and interests of the coastal State in its exercise of such jurisdiction, and for this purpose shall

    *a.* provide the coastal State at least — days advance notification of intent to do such research, containing a description of the research project which shall be kept up to date;

    *b.* certify that the research will be conducted in accordance with this Convention by a qualified institution with a view to purely scientific research;

    *c.* ensure that the coastal State has all appropriate opportunities to participate or be represented in the research project directly or through an appropriate international institution of its choice; the coastal State shall give reasonable advance notification of its desire to participate or be represented in the research within — days after it has received notification;

    *d.* ensure that all data and samples are shared with the coastal State;

    *e.* ensure that significant research results are published as soon as possible in an open readily available scientific publication and supplied directly to the coastal State;

    *f.* assist the coastal State in assessing the implications for its interests of the data and results directly or through the procedures established pursuant to Article 5;

    *g.* ensure compliance with all applicable international environmental standards, including those established or to be established by [insert name or names of appropriate organizations].

**Art. 8.** Any dispute with respect to the interpretation or application of the provisions of this Chapter shall, if requested by either party to the dispute, be resolved by the compulsory dispute settlement procedures contained in Article —.


## BRAZIL, ECUADOR, EL SALVADOR, PERU AND URUGUAY:
## — Scientific Research Within the Zone Subject to the Sovereignty and Jurisdiction of the Coastal State

> Submitted to the United Nations Seabed Committee on 19 July 1973, as UN Doc. A/AC.138/SC.III/L.45.

    1. The coastal State shall have the right to bring under regulation scientific research activities conducted in the zone subject to its maritime sovereignty and jurisdiction.

    2. Scientific research activities in the zone subject to the maritime sovereignty and jurisdiction of the coastal State shall be conducted for peaceful purposes.

3. The coastal State shall promote, select and facilitate scientific research activities within the zone subject to its maritime sovereignty and jurisdiction with a view to promoting the development of science and technology, in order that the results may contribute to a better knowledge, and to the preservation of the marine environment and its resources and to a more efficient exploitation of those resources.

4. States, international organizations and physical or juridical persons desiring to undertake scientific research activities within the zone under the maritime sovereignty and jurisdiction of the coastal State shall apply for and obtain authorization from that State and comply with the provisions imposed by it; they shall specify: (a) the objectives and tasks of their research; (b) the means to be used; (c) the scientific staff to be employed; (d) the zones in which the activities are to be conducted; (e) the dates proposed for conducting them; and they shall undertake to transmit to the coastal State the primary data and results of the investigation and any samples obtained in the course of it.

5. The coastal State shall have the right to participate in the scientific research activities conducted within the zone subject to its maritime sovereignty and jurisdiction.

6. The scientific research activities in the zone subject to the maritime sovereignty and jurisdiction of the coastal State shall be conducted in conformity with the conditions laid down in the relevant authorization. These conditions shall not be altered by the persons conducting the investigation, except with the express consent of the coastal State.

7. Scientific research activities shall be so conducted that they do not harm the marine resources, and that they do not interfere with or obstruct the exploitation of those resources, navigation or existing services and installations.

8. The coastal State shall co-operate with other States and with the international organizations concerned in order to disseminate the results of scientific research.


## ITALY:
— **Proposal concerning Obligations of the Coastal State Regarding Scientific Marine Research**

Submitted to the United Nations Seabed Committee on 14 August 1973, as UN Doc. A/AC.138/AC.III/L.50.

Whenever, according to this Convention, the consent of the coastal State is requested, the coastal State shall give its reply promptly.

As far as marine scientific research beyond the territorial sea is concerned, the consent of the coastal State shall be presumed if there is no reply within ... months from the date of the request.

## ALGERIA, BRAZIL, CHINA, ETHIOPIA, EGYPT, IRAN, KENYA, PAKISTAN, PERU, PHILIPPINES, ROMANIA, SOMALIA, TRINIDAD AND TOBAGO, TUNISIA AND YUGOSLAVIA:
### — Draft Article on Consent to Conduct Marine Scientific Research

Submitted to the United Nations Seabed Committee on 17 August 1973, as UN Doc. A/AC.138/SC.III/L.55.

Whenever, according to this Convention, the consent of a coastal State is requested for undertaking marine scientific research in the areas under its sovereignty and national jurisdiction the explicit consent of that State shall be obtained before such activity is undertaken.

# PART VII

# FISHERY CONVENTIONS

# I. MARINE MAMMAL CONVENTIONS

## THE 1946 INTERNATIONAL CONVENTION FOR THE REGULATION OF WHALING, AS AMENDED BY THE 1956 PROTOCOL

Signed at Washington on 2 December 1946; Entered into force on 10 November 1948 between Australia, Iceland, Netherlands, Norway, Panama, South Africa, U.K., U.S., and U.S.S.R. U.N. Treaty Series, vol. 161, p. 72. Amended by the Protocol signed at Washington on 19 November 1956 and brought into force on 4 May 1959. U.N. Treaty Series, vol. 338, p. 366. The Parties to the Convention, as amended, as of 10 January 1974 are: Argentina, Australia, Brazil, Canada, Denmark, France, Iceland, Japan, Mexico, Norway, Panama, South Africa, U.K., U.S., U.S.S.R.

The Governments whose duly authorized reprensentatives have subscribed hereto,

Recognizing the interest of the nations of the world in safeguarding for future generations the great natural resources represented by the whale stocks;

Considering that the history of whaling has seen overfishing of one area after another and of one species of whale after another to such a degree that it is essential to protect all species of whales from further overfishing;

Recognizing that the whale stocks are susceptible of natural increases if whaling is properly regulated, and that increases in the size of whale stocks will permit increases in the numbers of whales which may be captured without endangering these natural resources;

Recognizing that it is in the common interest to achieve the optimum level of whale stocks as rapidly as possible without causing wide-spread economic and nutritional distress;

Recognizing that in the course of achieving these objectives, whaling operations should be confined to those species best able to sustain exploitation in order to give an interval for recovery to certain species of whales now depleted in numbers;

Desiring to establish a system of international regulation for the whale fisheries to ensure proper and effective conservation and development of whale stocks on the basis of the principles embodied in the provisions of the International Agreement for the Regulation of Whaling signed in London on June 8, 1937 and the protocols to that Agreement signed in London on June 24, 1938 and November 26, 1945; and

Having decided to conclude a convention to provide for the proper conservation of whale stocks and thus make possible the orderly development of the whaling industry;

Have agreed as follows:

**Art. I.** 1. This Convention includes the Schedule attached thereto which forms an integral part thereof. All references to "Convention" shall be understood as including the said Schedule either in its present terms or as amended in accordance with the provisions of Article V.

2. This Convention applies to factory ships, land stations, and whale catchers under the jurisdiction of the Contracting Governments, and to all waters in which whaling is prosecuted by such factory ships, land stations, and whale catchers.

**Art. II.** As used in this Convention

1. "factory ship" means a ship in which or on which whales are treated whether wholly or in part;

2. "land station" means a factory on the land at which whales are treated whether wholly or in part;

3. "whale catcher" means a helicopter, or other aircraft, or a ship, used for the purpose of hunting, taking, killing, towing, holding on to, or scouting for whales.

4. "Contracting Government" means any Government which has deposited an instrument of ratification or has given notice of adherence to this Convention.

**Art. III.** 1. The Contracting Governments agree to establish an International Whaling Commission, hereinafter referred to as the Commission, to be composed of one member from each Contracting Government. Each member shall have one vote and may be accompanied by one or more experts and advisers.

2. The Commission shall elect from its own members a Chairman and Vice Chairman and shall determine its own Rules of Procedure. Decisions of the Commission shall be taken by a simple majority of those members voting except that a three-fourths majority of those members voting shall be required for action in pursuance of Article V. The Rules of Procedure may provide for decisions otherwise than at meetings of the Commission.

3. The Commission may appoint its own Secretary and staff.

4. The Commission may set up, from among its own members and experts or advisers, such committees as it considers desirable to perform such functions as it may authorize.

5. The expenses of each member of the Commission and of his experts and advisers shall be determined and paid by his own Government.

442

6. Recognizing that specialized agencies related to the United Nations will be concerned with the conservation and development of whale fisheries and the products arising therefrom and desiring to avoid duplication of functions, the Contracting Governments will consult among themselves within two years after the coming into force of this Convention to decide whether the Commission shall be brought within the framework of a specialized agency related to the United Nations.

7. In the meantime the Government of the United Kingdom of Great Britain and Northern Ireland shall arrange, in consultation with the other Contracting Governments, to convene the first meeting of the Commission, and shall initiate the consultation referred to in paragraph 6 above.

8. Subsequent meetings of the Commission shall be convened as the Commission may determine.

**Art. IV.** 1. The Commission may either in collaboration with or through independent agencies of the Contracting Governments or other public or private agencies, establishments, or organizations, or independently

(*a*) encourage, recommend, or if necessary, organize studies and investigations relating to whales and whaling;

(*b*) collect and analyze statistical information concerning the current condition and trend of the whale stocks and the effects of whaling activities thereon;

(*c*) study, appraise, and disseminate information concerning methods of maintaining and increasing the populations of whale stocks.

2. The Commission shall arrange for the publication of reports of its activities, and it may publish independently or in collaboration with the International Bureau for Whaling Statistics at Sandefjord in Norway and other organizations and agencies such reports as it deems appropriate, as well as statistical, scientific, and other pertinent information relating to whales and whaling.

**Art. V.** 1. The Commission may amend from time to time the provisions of the Schedule by adopting regulations with respect to the conservation and utilization of whale resources, fixing (*a*) protected and unprotected species; (*b*) open and closed seasons; (*c*) open and closed waters, including the designation of sanctuary areas; (*d*) size limits for each species; (*e*) time, methods, and intenstiy of whaling (including the maximum catch of whales to be taken in any one season); (*f*) types and specifications of gear and apparatus and appliances which may be used; (*g*) methods of measurement; (*h*) catch returns and other statistical and biological records; (*i*) methods of inspection.

2. These amendments of the Schedule (*a*) shall be such as are necessary to carry out the objectives and purposes of this Convention and to provide

for the conservation, development, and optimum utilization of the whale resources; (b) shall be based on scientific findings; (c) shall not involve restrictions on the number or nationality of factory ships or land stations, nor allocate specific quotas to any factory ship or land station or to any group of factory ships or land stations; and (d) shall take into consideration the interests of the consumers of whale products and the whaling industry.

3. Each of such amendments shall become effective with respect to the Contracting Governments ninety days following notification of the amendment by the Commission to each of the Contracting Governments, except that (a) if any Government presents to the Commission objection to any amendment prior to the expiration of this ninety-day period, the amendment shall not become effective with respect to any of the Governments for an additional ninety days; (b) thereupon, any other Contracting Government may present objection to the amendment at any time prior to the expiration of the additional ninety-day period, or before the expiration of thirty days from the date of receipt of the last objection received during such additional ninety-day period, whichever date shall be the later; and (c) thereafter, the amendment shall become effective with respect to all Contracting Governments which have not presented objection but shall not become effective with respect to any Government which has so objected until such date as the objection is withdrawn. The Commission shall notify each Contracting Government immediately upon receipt of each objection and withdrawal and each Contracting Government shall acknowledge receipt of all notifications of amendments, objections, and withdrawals.

4. No amendments shall become effective before July 1, 1949.

**Art. VI.** The Commission may from time to time make recommendations to any or all Contracting Governments on any matters which relate to whales or whaling and to the objectives and purposes of this Convention.

**Art. VII.** The Contracting Governments shall ensure prompt transmission to the International Bureau for Whaling Statistics at Sandefjord in Norway, or to such other body as the Commission may designate, of notifications and statistical and other information required by this Convention in such form and manner as may be prescribed by the Commission.

**Art. VIII.** 1. Nothwithstanding anything contained in this Convention, any Contracting Government may grant to any of its nationals a special permit authorizing that national to kill, take, and treat whales for purposes of scientific research subject to such restrictions as to number and subject to such other conditions as the Contracting Government thinks fit, and the killing, taking, and treating of whales in accordance with the provisions of this Article shall be exempt from the operation of this Convention. Each Contracting Government shall report at once to the Commission all such

444

authorizations which it has granted. Each Contracting Government may at any time revoke any such special permit which it has granted.

2. Any whales taken under these special permits shall so far as practicable be processed and the proceeds shall be dealt with in accordance with directions issued by the Government by which the permit was granted.

3. Each Contracting Government shall transmit to such body as may be designated by the Commission, in so far as practicable, and at intervals of not more than one year, scientific information available to that Government with respect to whales and whaling, including the results of research conducted pursuant to paragraph 1 of this Article and to Article IV.

4. Recognizing that continuous collection and analysis of biological data in connection with the operations of factory ships and land stations are indispensable to sound and constructive management of the whale fisheries, the Contracting Governments will take all practicable measures to obtain such data.

**Art. IX.** 1. Each Contracting Government shall take appropriate measures to ensure the application of the provisions of this Convention and the punishment of infractions against the said provisions in operations carried out by persons or by vessels under its jurisdiction.

2. No bonus or other remuneration calculated with relation to the results of their work shall be paid to the gunners and crews of whale catchers in respect of any whales the taking of which is forbidden by this Convention.

3. Prosecution for infractions against or contraventions of this Convention shall be instituted by the Government having jurisdiction over the offense.

4. Each Contracting Government shall transmit to the Commission full details of each infraction of the provisions of this Convention by persons or vessels under the jurisdiction of that Government as reported by its inspectors. This information shall include a statement of measures taken for dealing with the infraction and of penalties imposed.

**Art. X.** . . . .

2. Any Government which has not signed this Convention may adhere thereto after it enters into force by a notification in writing to the Government of the United States of America.

. . . . .

**Art. XI.** Any Contracting Government may withdraw from this Convention on June thirtieth of any year by giving notice on or before January first of the same year to the depositary Government, which upon receipt of such a notice shall at once communicate it to the other Contracting Governments. Any other Contracting Government may, in like manner, within one month of the receipt of a copy of such a notice from the depositary

Government, give notice of withdrawal, so that the Convention shall cease to be in force on June thirtieth of the same year with respect to the Government giving such notice of withdrawal.

This Convention shall bear the date on which it is opened for signature and shall remain open for signature for a period of fourteen days thereafter.

**Schedule to the International Whaling Commission, revised to include the Amendments that came into operation after the twenty-fifth meeting in London, 1973**

1. (*a*) There shall be maintained on each factory ship at least two inspectors of whaling for the purpose of maintaining twenty-four hour inspection provided that at least one such inspector shall be maintained on each catcher functioning as a factory ship. These inspectors shall be appointed and paid by the Government having jurisdiction over the factory ship; provided that inspectors need not be appointed to ships which, apart from the storage of products, are used during the season solely for freezing or salting the meat and entrails of whales intended for human food or feeding animals.

(*b*) Adequate inspection shall be maintained at each land station. The inspectors serving at each land station shall be appointed and paid by the Government having jurisdiction over the land station.

(*c*) There shall be received such observers as the member countries may arrange to place on factory ships and land stations or groups of land stations of other member countries. The observers shall be appointed by the Commission acting through its Secretary and paid by the Government nominating them.

2. It is forbidden to take or kill gray whales or right whales, except by aborigines or a Contracting Government on behalf of aborigines and only when the meat and products of such whales are to be used exclusively for local consumption by the aborigines.

3. It is forbidden to take or kill calves or suckling whales or female whales which are accompanied by calves or suckling whales.

4. (1) It is forbidden to kill or attempt to kill blue whales.

(2) It is forbidden to use a factory ship or whale catcher attached thereto for the purpose of taking or treating baleen whales except minke whales in any of the following areas:

(*a*) in the waters north of 66° North Latitude except that from 150° East Longitude eastwards as far as 140° West Longitude the taking or killing of baleen whales by a factory ship or whale catcher shall be permitted between 66° North Latitude and 72° North Latitude;

(*b*) in the Atlantic Ocean and its dependent waters north of 40° South Latitude:

446

(c) in the Pacific Ocean and its dependent waters east of 150° West Longitude between 40° South Latitude and 35° North Latitude;

(d) in the Pacific Ocean and its dependent waters west of 150° West Longitude between 40° South Latitude and 20° North Latitude;

(e) in the Indian Ocean and its dependent waters north of 40° South Latitude.

5. [deleted]

6. It is forbidden to kill or attempt to kill humpback whales. Notwithstanding this prohibition the taking of 10 humpback whales not below 35 feet (10.7 metres) in length per year is permitted in Greenland waters provided that whale catchers of less than 50 gross register tonnage are used for this purpose.

7. (a) It is forbidden to use a factory ship or whale catcher attached thereto for the purpose of taking or treating baleen whales except minke whales in any waters south of 40° South Latitude, except during the period from 12th December to 7th April following, both days inclusive.

(b) It is forbidden to use a factory ship or whale catcher attached thereto for the purpose of taking or treating sperm or minke whales, except as permitted by the Contracting Governments in accordance with sub-paragraphs (c), (d) and (e) of this paragraph.

(c) Each Contracting Government shall declare for all factory ships and whale catchers attached thereto under its jursdiction, one continuous open season not to exceed eight months out of any period of twelve months during which the taking or killing of sperm whales by whale catchers may be permitted; provided that a separate open season may be declared for each factory ship and the whale catchers attached thereto.

(d) Each Contracting Government shall declare for all factory ships and whale catchers attached thereto under its jurisdiction one continuous open season not to exceed six months out of any period of twelve months during which the taking or killing of minke whales by the whale catchers may be permitted.

Provided that:

(i) a separate open season may be declared for each factory ship and the whale catchers attached thereto;

(ii) the open season need not necessarily include the whole or any part of the period declared for other baleen whales pursuant to sub-paragraph (a) of this paragraph.

(e) Each Contracting Government shall declare for all whale catchers under its jurisdiction not operating in conjunction with a factory ship or land station one continuous open season not to exceed six months out of any period of twelve months during which the taking or killing of minke whales by such whale catchers may be permitted. Nothwithstanding this

447

paragraph one continuous open season not to exceed eight months may be implemented so far as Greenland is concerned.

8. (*a*) The number of baleen whales taken during the open season in waters south of 40° South Latitude by factory ships or whale catchers attached thereto under the jurisdiction of the Contracting Governments shall not exceed 1,450 fin whales, 4,500 sei and Bryde's whales combined and 5,000 minke whales in 1973/74.[1] The taking of fin whales shall cease not later than 30 June 1976.[2]

(*b*) Notification shall be given in accordance with the provisions of Article VII of the Convention, within two days after the end of each calendar week, of data on the number of fin, sei, Bryde's and minke whales taken in any waters south of 40° South Latitude by all factory ships or whale catchers attached thereto under the jurisdiction of each Contracting Government, provided that when the number of each of these species taken is deemed by the Bureau of International Whaling Statistics to have reached 85 per cent of whatever total catch limit is imposed by the Commission notification shall be given as aforesaid at the end of each day of data on the number of each of these species taken.

(*c*) If it appears that the maximum catches of whales permitted by sub-paragraph (*a*) of this paragraph may be reached before 7th April of any year, the Bureau of Internatonal Whaling Statitics shall determine, on the basis of the data provided, the date on which the maximum catch of each of these species shall be deemed to have been reached and shall notify the master of each factory ship and each Contracting Government of that date not less than four days in advance thereof. The taking or attempting to take baleen whales, so notified, by factory ships or whale catchers attached thereto shall be illegal in any waters south of 40° South Latitude after midnight of the date so determined.

(*d*) Notification shall be given in accordance with the provisions of Article VII of the Convention of each factory ship intending to engage in whaling operations in any waters south of 40° South Latitude.

(*e*) The number of fin whales taken in the North Pacific Ocean and dependent waters excluding the catch in the East China Sea shall not exceed 550 in 1974.

(*f*) The number of sei and Bryde's whales combined taken in the North Pacific Ocean and dependent waters shall not exceed 3,000 whales in 1974.

(*g*) The number of sperm whales taken in the North Pacific Ocean and dependent waters shall not exceed 6,000 male and 4,000 female sperm whales in 1974.

(*h*) The number of sperm whales taken in the Southern Hemisphere in the 1973/74 pelagic season and the 1974 coastal season shall not exceed 8,000 males and 5,000 females.

448

The total catches in any of the Areas I to VI shall not exceed the limits shown below:[3]

|  |  | Male | Female |
|---|---|---|---|
| Areas II + III | 60° W—70° E | 1900 | 1800 |
| Areas IV + V | 70° E —170° W | 2900 | 2100 |
| Areas VI + I | 170° W—60° W | 3200 | 1100 |

9. (*a*) It is forbidden to take or kill any sei or Bryde's whales below 40 feet (12.2 metres) except that sei and Bryde's whales of not less than 35 feet (10.7 metres) in length may be taken for delivery to land stations, provided that the meat of such whales is to be used for local consumption as human or animal food.

(*b*) It is forbidden to take or kill any fin whales below 57 feet (17.4 metres) in length in the Southern Hemisphere, and it is forbidden to take or kill fin whales below 55 feet (16.8 metres) in the Northern Hemisphere; except that fin whales of not less than 55 feet (16.8 metres) may be taken for delivery to land stations in the Southern Hemisphere and fin whales of not less than 50 feet (15.2 metres) may be taken for delivery to land stations in the Northern Hemisphere, provided that in each case the meat of such whales is to be used for local consumption as human or animal food.

(*c*) It is forbidden to take or kill any sperm whales below 30 feet (9.2 metres) in length except n the North Atlantic Ocean where it is forbidden to take or kill any sperm whales below 35 feet (10.7 metres).

(*d*) Whales must be measured when at rest on deck or platform, as accurately as possible by means of a steel tape measure fitted at the zero end with a spiked handle which can be stuck into the deck planking abreast of one end of the whale. The tape measure shall be stretched in a straight line parallel with the whale's body and read abreast the other end of the whale. The ends of the whale, for measurement purposes, shall be the point of the upper jaw and the notch between the tail flukes. Measurements, after being accurately read on the tape measure, shall be logged to the nearest foot, that is to say, any whale between 75 feet 6 inches and 76 feet 6 inches shall be logged as 76 feet, and any whale between 76 feet 6 inches and 77 feet 6 inches shall be logged as 77 feet. The measurement of any whale which falls on an exact half foot shall be logged at the next half foot, *e.g.* 76 feet 6 inches precisely shall be logged as 77 feet.

10. (*a*) It is forbidden to use a whale catcher attached to a land station for the purpose of killing or attempting to kill baleen and sperm whales except as permitted by the Contracting Government in accordance with sub-paragraphs (*b*), (*c*) and (*d*) of this paragraph.

(*b*) Each Contracting Government shall declare for all land stations under its jurisdiction, and whale catchers attached to such land stations,

449

one open season during which the taking or killing of baleen except minke whales by the whale catchers shall be permitted. Such open season shall be for a period of not more than six consecutive months in any period of twelve months and shall apply to all land stations under the jurisdiction of the Contracting Government; provided that a separate open season may be declared for any land station used for the taking or treating of baleen except minke whales which is more than 1,000 miles from the nearest land station used for the taking or treating of baleen (excluding minke) whales under the jurisdiction of the same Contracting Government.

(c) Each Contracting Government shall declare for all land stations under its jurisdiction and for whale catchers attached to such land stations, one open season not to exceed eight continuous months in any one period of twelve months, during which the taking or killing of sperm whales by the whale catchers shall be permitted, such period of eight months to include the whole of the period of six months declared for baleen whales except minke whales as provided for in sub-paragraph (b) of this paragraph; provided that a separate open season may be declared for any land station used for the taking or treating of sperm whales which is more than 1,000 miles from the nearest land station used for the taking or treating of sperm whales under the jurisdiction of the same Contracting Government.[4]

(d) Each Contracting Government shall declare for all land stations under its jurisdiction and for whale catchers attached to such land stations one open season not to exceed six continuous months in any period of twelve months during which the taking or killing of minke whales by the whale catchers shall be permitted (such period not being necessarily concurrent with the period declared for other baleen whales, as provided for in sub-paragraph (b) of this paragraph); provided that a separate open season may be declared for any land station used for the taking or treating of minke whales which is more than 1,000 miles from the nearest land station used for the taking or treating of minke whales under the jurisdiction of the same Contracting Government.

Except that a separate open season may be declared for any land station used for the taking or treating of minke whales which is located in an area having oceanographic conditions clearly distinguishable from those of the area in which are located the other land stations used for the taking or treating of minke whales under the jurisdiction of the same Contracting Government; but the declaration of a separate open season by virtue of the provisions of this sub-paragraph shall not cause thereby the period of time covering the open seasons declared by the same Contracting Government to exceed nine continuous months of any twelve months.

(e) The prohibitions contained in this paragraph shall apply to all land stations as defined in Article II of the Whaling Convention of 1946 and to all factory ships which are subject to the regulations govering the operation of land stations under the provisions of paragraph 17 of this Schedule.

11. It is forbidden to use factory ship which has been used during a season in any waters south of 40° South Latitude for the purpose of treating baleen whales, apart from minke whales in any other area except the North Pacific Ocean and its dependent waters north of the Equator for the same purpose within a period of one year from the termination of that season; provided that catch limits in the North Pacific Ocean and dependent waters are established as provided in paragraph 8 (*e*) and (*f*) and provided that this paragraph shall not apply to a ship which has been used during the season solely for freezing or salting the meat and entrails of whales intended for human food or feeding animals.

12. (*a*) It is forbidden to use a factory ship or a land station for the purpose of treating any whales (whether or not killed by whale catchers under the jurisdiction of a Contracting Government) the killing of which by whale catchers under the jurisdiction of a Contracting Government is prohibited by the provisions of paragraphs 2, 4, 6, 7, 8 or 10 of this Schedule.

(*b*) All other whales (except minke whales) taken shall be delivered to the factory ship or land station and all parts of such whales shall be processed by boiling or otherwise, except the internal organs, whale bone and flippers of all whales, the meat of sperm whales and of parts of whales intended for human food or feeding animals. A Contracting Government may in less developed regions exceptionally permit treating of whales without use of land stations, provided that such whales are fully utilised in accordance with this paragraph.

(*c*) Complete treatment of the carcases of "dauhval" and of whales used as fenders will not be required in cases where the meat or bone of such whales is in bad condition.

13. (*a*) The taking of whales for treatment by a factory ship shall be so regulated or restricted by the master or person in charge of the factory ship that no whale carcase (except of a whale used as a fender, which shall be processed as soon as is reasonably practicable) shall remain in the sea for a longer period than thirty-three hours from the time of killing to the time when it is hauled up for treatment.

(*b*) Whales taken by all whale catchers, whether for factory ships or land stations, shall be clearly marked so as to identify the catcher and to indicate the order of catching.

(*c*) All whale catchers operating in conjunction with a factory ship shall report by radio to the factory ship:

(1) The time when each whale is taken

(2) Its species, and

(3) Its marking effected pursuant to sub-paragraph (*b*) of this paragraph.

451

(*d*) The information specified in sub-paragraph (*c*) of this paragraph shall be entered immediately by a factory ship in a permanent record which shall be available at all times for examination by the whaling inspectors; and in addition there shall be entered in such permanent record the following information as soon as it becomes available:

(1) Time of hauling up for treatment

(2) Length, measured pursuant to sub-paragraph (*d*) of paragraph 9

(3) Sex

(4) If female, whether milk-filled or lactating

(5) Length and sex of foetus, if present, and

(6) A full explanation of each infraction.

(*e*) A record similar to that described in sub-paragraph (*d*) of this paragraph shall be maintained by land stations, and all of the information mentioned in the said sub-paragraph shall be entered therein as soon as available.

14. Gunners and crews of factory ships, land stations, and whale catchers, shall be engaged on such terms that their remuneration shall depend to a considerable extent upon such factors as the species, size and yield of whales taken and not merely upon the number of the whales taken. No bonus or other remuneration shall be paid to the gunners or crews of whale catchers in respect of the taking of milk-filled or lactating whales.

15. A Contracting Government shall transmit to the Commission copies of all its official laws and regulations relating to whales and whaling and changes in such laws and regulations.

16. Notification shall be given in accordance with the provisions of Article VII of the Convention with regard to all factory ships and land stations of statistical information (*a*) concerning the number of whales of each species taken, the number thereof lost, and the number treated at each factory ship or land station, and (*b*) as to the aggregate amounts of oil of each grade and quantities of meal, fertiliser (guano), and other products derived from them, together with (*c*) particulars with respect to each whale treated in the factory ship or land station as to the date and approximate latitude and longitude of taking, the species and sex of the whale, its length and, if it contains a foetus, the length and sex, if ascertainable, of the foetus. The data referred to in (*a*) and (*c*) above shall be verified at the time of the tally and there shall also be notification to the Commission of any information which may be collected or obtained concerning the calving grounds and migration routes of whales.

In communicating this information there shall be specified:

(*a*) The name and gross tonnage of each factory ship

(*b*) The number of whale catchers, including separate totals for surface vessels and aircraft and specifying, in the case of surface vessels, the average length and horse power of whale catchers

(c) A list of the land stations which were in operation during the period concerned.

17. (a) A factory ship which operates solely within territorial waters in one of the areas specified in sub-paragraph (c) of this paragraph, by permission of the Government having jurisdiction over those waters, and which flies the flag of that Government shall, while so operating, be subject to the regulations governing the operation of land stations and not to the regulations governing the operation of factory ships.

(b) Such factory ship shall not, within a period of one year from the termination of the season in which she so operated, be used for the purpose of treating baleen whales in any of the other areas specified in sub-paragraph (c) of this paragraph or south of 40° South Latitude.

(c) The areas referred to in sub-paragraphs (a) and (b) are:

(1) (2) [deleted]

(3) On the coasts of Australia, namely on the whole east coast and on the west coast in the area known as Shark Bay and northward to North-west Cape and including Exmouth Gulf and King George's Sound, including the Port of Albany

(4) On the Pacific coast of the United States of America between 35° North Latitude and 49° North Latitude.

18. (1) The following expressions have the meanings respectively assigned to them, that is to say:

"baleen whale" means any whale which has baleen or whale bone in the mouth, *i.e.* any whale other than a toothed whale

"blue whale" (. . .) means any whale known by the name of blue whale, Sibbald's rorqual, or sulphur bottom

"Bryde's whale" (. . .) means any whale known by the name of "Bryde's whale"

"dauhval" means any unclaimed dead whale found floating

"fin whale" (. . .) means any whale known by the name of common finback, common rorqual, finback, finner, fin whale, herring whale, razorback, or true fin whale

"gray whale" (. . .) means any whale known by the name of gray whale, California gray, devil fish, hard head, mussel digger, gray back or rip sack

"humpback whale" (. . .) means any whale known by the name of bunch, humpback, humpback whale, humpbacked whale, hump whale or hunchbacked whale

"minke whale" (. . .) means any whale known by the name of lesser rorqual, little piked whale, minke whale, pike-headed whale or sharp headed finner

"right whale" (. . .) means any whale known by the name of Atlantic right whale, Arctic right whale, Biscayan right whale, bowhead, great polar whale, Greenland right whale, Greenland whale, Nordkaper, North Atlantic right whale, North Cape whale, Pacific right whale, pygmy right whale, Southern pygmy right whale, or Southern right whale

"sei whale" (. . .) means any whale known by the name of sei whale, Rudolphi's rorqual, pollack whale, or coalfish whale

"sperm whale" (. . .) means any whale known by the name of sperm whale, spermacet whale, cachalot or pot whale

"toothed whale" means any whale which has teeth in the jaws.

(2) "Whales taken" means whales that have been killed and either flagged or made fast to catchers.

*Note:*

1. Japan and U.S.S.R. objected with respect to "5,000 minke whales".
2. Japan objected with respect to this phrase.
3. Japan and U.S.S.R. objected with respect to this provision.
4. Australia objected with respect to the provisions of this sub-paragraph.

*Note: Total allowable catch of the Antarctic whaling*

| original | 16,000 BWU | 1962/63 | 15,000 BWU |
|----------|-----------|---------|-----------|
| 1953/54 | 15,500 | 1963/64 | 10,000 |
| 1954/55 | 15,500 | 1964/65 | — |
| 1955/56 | 15,000 | 1965/66 | 4,500 |
| 1956/57 | 15,000 | 1966/67 | 3,500 |
| 1957/58 | 15,000 | 1967/68 | 3,200 |
| 1958/59 | 15,000 | 1968/69 | 3,200 |
| 1959/60 | 15,000 | 1969/70 | 2,700 |
| 1960/61 | — | 1970/71 | 2,700 |
| 1961/62 | — | 1971/72 | 2,300 |

(BWU means blue whale unit. Since the 1972/73 seasons, national quotas are determined in terms of each species.)

## THE 1973 ARRANGEMENT FOR THE REGULATION OF ANTARCTIC PELAGIC WHALING (Japan, Norway and Union of Soviet Socialist Republics)

Signed at Tokyo on 3 August 1972; Entered into force on the same date. Replacing the 1962 Arrangement between Japan, Netherlands, Norway, U.K. and U.S.S.R., signed at London on 6 June 1962 and brought into force on 13 April 1963 (U.N. Treaty Series, Vol. 486, p. 263); the 1966, 1967, 1968, 1969, 1970, 1971 and 1972 Arrangements between Japan, Norway and U.S.S.R.

. . . . .

**Art. 1.** For the purpose of the present Arrangement, the term "season" shall mean the season during which the taking of baleen whales in the Antarctic is permitted under paragraph 7 (*a*) of the Schedule to the Convention.

**Art. 2.** The total annual catches of fin whales and sei and Bryde's whales combined, authorized under the Convention to be taken in waters south of 40° South Latitude by pelagic expeditions, shall be allocated among the countries of the signatory Governments in the following manner:

| | |
|---|---|
| Japan . . . . . . . . . . . . . | 867 fin whales |
| | 2,632 sei and Bryde's whales combined |
| Norway . . . . . . . . . . | 100 sei and Bryde's whales combined |
| Union of Soviet Socialist Republics | 583 fin whales |
| | 1,768 sei and Bryde's whales combined |

**Art. 3.** The allocations mentioned in Article 2 are not transferable as between one country and another.

**Art. 4.** If a factory ship under the jurisdiction of a Government which is not a party to the present Arrangement should engage in Antarctic pelagic whaling and that Government is or becomes a Party to the Convention, the present Arrangement shall be terminated.

**Art. 5.** . . .

**Art. 6.** The present Arrangement shall be operative until the end of the 1973/74 season.

*Note: National Quota of Antarctic pelagic Whaling*

| | Japan | Netherlands | Norway | U.S.S.R. | U.K. |
|---|---|---|---|---|---|
| original | 33% | 6% | 32% | 20% | 9% |
| 1962/63 | 41 | 6 | 28 | 20 | 5 |
| 1963/64 | 46 | 6 | 28 | 20 | — |
| 1964/65 | 52 | — | 28 | 20 | — |
| 1965/66 | 52 | — | 28 | 20 | — |
| 1966/67 | 1,633 BWU | — | 800 BWU | 1,067 BWU | — |
| 1967/68 | 1,493 | — | 731 | 976 | — |
| 1968/69 | 1,493 | — | 731 | 976 | — |
| 1969/70 | 1,493 | — | 231 | 976 | — |
| 1970/71 | 1,493 | — | 231 | 976 | — |
| 1971/72 | 1,346 | — | 50 | 904 | — |

|          | Japan |       | Norway |     | U.S.S.R. |       |
|----------|-------|-------|--------|-----|----------|-------|
| 1972/73  | F.W.  | 1,142 | S.B.   | 120 | F.W.     | 768   |
|          | S.B.  | 2,919 |        |     | S.B.     | 1,961 |
| 1973/74  | F.W.  | 867   | S.B.   | 100 | F.W.     | 583   |
|          | S.B.  | 2,632 |        |     | S.B.     | 1,768 |

(BWU = blue whale unit; F.W. = fin whale; S.B. = sei & Bryde's whale)

## THE 1973 AGREEMENT ON THE REGULATION OF NORTH PACIFIC WHALING (Japan and Union of Soviet Socialist Republics)

Signed at Tokyo on 3 August 1973; Entered into force on the same date. Replacing the 1971 Agreement between Japan, U.S. and U.S.S.R. (UN ST/LEG/SER. B/16/Add. 1, p. 59) and the 1972 Agreement between Japan and U.S.S.R.

**Art. 1.** (*a*) For the purpose of this Agreement:
  (i) The open season in 1974 for pelagic baleen whaling operations shall be the period from April 15 to October 15 both inclusive; and
  (ii) The open season in 1974 for pelagic sperm whaling operations shall be the period from March 15 to November 15 both inclusive.
(*b*) The Signatory Government having a land station or stations operating under its jurisdiction shall as soon as possible notify the other Signatory Government of the season or seasons for such station or stations.

**Art. 2.** The total catch of baleen and sperm whales authorized under the Convention to be taken in the North Pacific Ocean and dependent waters in 1974 shall be allocated between the countries of the Signatory Governments in the following manner:

  (i) Fin Whales
    Japan .................................................... 246
    Union of Soviet Socialist Republics ................. 304
  (ii) Sei and Bryde's Whales combined
    Japan .................................................... 2,017
    Union of Soviet Socialist Republics ................. 983
  (iii) Sperm Whales
    a. Male Sperm Whales
      Japan .................................................... 2,565
      Union of Soviet Socialist Republics ............... 3,435
    b. Female Sperm Whales
      Japan .................................................... 1,710
      Union of Soviet Socialist Republics ............... 2,290

**Art. 3.** . . .

**Art. 4.** The present Agreement shall be operative until December 31, 1974.

*Note: National Quota of North Pacific Whaling*

| | | | Sperm W. | |
|---|---|---|---|---|
| | Fin W. | Sei & Bryde's W. | male | female |
| 1972 Japan | 454 | 2,506 | 4,608 | |
| U.S. | 32 | 40 | 60 | |
| U.S.S.R. | 560 | 1,222 | 6,173 | |
| 1973 Japan | 291 | 2,017 | 2,565 | 1,710 |
| U.S.S.R. | 359 | 983 | 3,435 | 2,290 |
| 1974 Japan | 246 | 2,017 | 2,565 | 1,710 |
| U.S.S.R. | 304 | 983 | 3,435 | 2,290 |

## THE 1957 INTERIM CONVENTION ON CONSERVATION OF NORTH PACIFIC FUR SEALS, AS AMENDED BY THE 1963 PROTOCOL (Canada, Japan, Union of Soviet Socialist Republics and United States of America)

Signed at Washington on 9 February 1957; Entered into force on 14 October 1957. U.N. Treaty Series, vol. 314, p. 105. Amended by the Protocol signed at Washington on 8 October 1963 and brought into force on 10 April 1964. U.N. Treaty Series, vol. 494, p. 303. Letter of the U.S. Secretary of State to the Chiefs of Mission of the Governments concerned on 19 March 1969: "It is the understanding of the Government of the United States that the Parties agree, with reference to Article XIII, paragraph 4, of the amended Convention, that the Convention as amended shall continue in force for eighteen years and thereafter until the entry into force of a new or revised fur seal convention between the Parties, or until the expiration of one year after such period of eighteen years, whichever may be earlier, and, with reference to Article XI, that the Parties shall meet for the purposes set forth in that Article at a mutually acceptable time, not later than early in the eighteenth year, after further recommendations have been made by the Commission."

The Governments of Canada, Japan, the Union of Soviet Socialist Republics, and the United States of America,
Desiring to take effective measures towards achieving the maximum

457

sustainable productivity of the fur seal resources of the North Pacific Ocean so that the fur seal populations can be brought to and maintained at the levels which will provide the greatest harvest year after year, with due regard to their relation to the productivity of other living marine resources of the area,

Recognizing that in order to determine such measures it is necessary to conduct adequate scientific research on the said resources, and

Desiring to provide for international cooperation in achieving these objectives,

Agree as follows:

**Art. I.** 1. The term "pelagic sealing" is hereby defined for the purposes of this Convention as meaning the killing, taking, or hunting in any manner whatsoever of fur seals at sea.

2. The words "each year", "annual" and "annually" as used hereinafter refer to Convention year, that is, the year beginning on the date of entry into force of the Convention.

3. Nothing in this Convention shall be deemed to affect in any way the position of the Parties in regard to the limits of territorial water or to the jurisdiction over fisheries.

**Art. II.** 1. In order to realize the objectives of this Convention, the Parties agree to coordinate necessary scientific research programs and to cooperate in investigating the fur seal resources of the North Pacific Ocean to determine:

(*a*) what measures may be necessary to make possible the maximum sustainable productivity of the fur seal resources so that the fur seal populations can be brought to and maintained at the levels which will provide the greatest harvest year after year; and

(*b*) what the relationship is between fur seals and other living marine resources and whether fur seals have detrimental effects on other living marine resources substantially exploited by any of the Parties and, if so, to what extent.

2. The research referred to in the preceding paragraph shall include studies of the following subjects:

(*a*) size of each fur seal herd and its age and sex composition;

(*b*) natural mortality of the different age groups and recruitment of young to each age or size class at present and subsequent population levels;

(*c*) with regard to each of the herds, the effect upon the magnitude of recruitment of variations in the size and the age and sex composition of the annual kill;

(*d*) migration routes of fur seals and their wintering areas;

(*e*) numbers of seals from each herd found on the migration routes and in wintering areas and their ages and sexes;

458

(*f*) extent to which the food habits of fur seals affect commercial fish catches and the damage fur seals inflict on fishing gear; and

(*g*) effectiveness of each method of sealing from the viewpoint of management and rational utilization of fur seal resources for conservation purposes;

(*h*) quality of sealskins by sex, age, and time and method of sealing; and

(*i*) other subjects involved in achieving the objectives of the Convention, as determined by the Commission established under Article V, paragraph 1.

3. In furtherance of the research referred to in this Article, the Parties agree:

(*a*) to continue to mark adequate numbers of pups;

(*b*) to devote to pelagic research an effort similar in extent to that expended in recent years, provided that this shall not involve the taking of more than 2,500 seals in the Eastern and more than, 2,200 seals in the Western Pacific Ocean, unless the Commission, pursuant to Article V, paragraph 3, shall decide otherwise; and

(*c*) to carry out the determinations made by the Commission pursuant to Article V, paragraph 3.

4. Each Party agrees to provide the Commission annually with information on:

(*a*) number of black pups tagged for each breeding area;

(*b*) number of fur seals, by sex and estimated age, taken at sea and on each breeding area; and

(*c*) tagged seals recovered on land and at sea;

and, so far as is practicable, other information pertinent to scientific research which the Commission may request.

5. The Parties further agree to provide for the exchange of scientific personnel; each such exchange shall be subject to mutual consent of the Parties directly concerned.

6. The Parties agree to use for the scientific pelagic research provided for in this Article only government-owned or government-chartered vessels operating under strict control of their respective authorities. Each Party shall communicate to the other Parties the names and descriptions of vessels which are to be used for pelagic research.

**Art. III.** In order to realize the purposes of the Convention, including the carrying out of the coordinated and cooperative research, each Party agrees to prohibit pelagic sealing, except as provided in Article II, paragraph 3, in the Pacific Ocean north of the 30th parallel of north latitude including the seas of Bering, Okhotsk, and Japan by any person or vessel subject to its jurisdiction.

459

**Art. IV.** 1. Each Party shall bear the expense of its own research. Title to sealskins taken during the research shall vest in the Party conducting such research.

2. If the total number of seals of the Commander Islands breeding grounds decreases and falls below 50,000 head, according to data in official records, then commercial killing of seals and apportionment of skins may be suspended by the Union of Soviet Socialist Republics until the number of seals exceeds 50,000 head. This provision also applies to the fur seal herd of Robben Island, if the population of that herd becomes less than 50,000 head.

3. The Government of the Union of Soviet Socialist Republics upon suspending such sealing shall so inform the other Parties. In this case the Commission shall determine whether or not to reduce the level of or to suspend completely the pelagic sealing for scientific purposes in the Western Pacific Ocean during the period of the said suspension.

4. The Commission may, subsequent to the second year of operation of the Convention, modify the floor figure set forth in paragraph 2 of this Article in accordance with its findings based upon scientific data received by it; and if any such modifications are made, paragraph 2 of this Article shall be considered amended accordingly. The Commission shall notify each Party of every such amendment and of the effective date thereof.

**Art. V.** 1. The Parties agree to establish the North Pacific Fur Seal Commission to be composed of one member from each Party.

2. The duties of the Commission shall be to:

(a) formulate and coordinate research programs designed to achieve the objectives set forth in Article II, paragraph 1;

(b) recommend these coordinated research programs to the respective Parties for implementation;

(c) study the data obtained from the implementation of such co-ordinated research programs;

(d) recommend appropriate measures to the Parties on the basis of the findings obtained from the implementation of such coordinated research programs, including measures regarding the size and the sex and age composition of the seasonal commercial kill from a herd; and

(e) study whether or not pelagic sealing in conjunction with land sealing could be permitted in certain circumstances without adversely affecting achievement of the objectives of this Convention, and make recommendations thereon to the Parties at the end of the eleventh year after entry into force of this Convention and, if the Convention is continued under the provisions of Article XIII, paragraph 4, at a later year; this later year shall be fixed by the Parties at the meeting early in the twelfth year provided for in Article XI.

3. In addition to the duties specified in paragraph 2 of this Article, the Commission shall, subject to Article II, paragraph 3, determine from time to time the numbers of seals to be marked on the rookery islands, and the total number of seals which shall be taken at sea for research purposes, the times at which such seals shall be taken and the areas in which they shall be taken, as well as the number to be taken by each Party.

4. Each Party shall have one vote. Decisions and recommendations shall be made by unanimous vote. With respect to any recommendations regarding the size and the sex and age composition of the seasonal commercial kill from a herd, only those Parties sharing in the sealskins from that herd under the provisions of Article IX, paragraph 1 shall vote.

5. The Commission shall elect from its members a Chairman and other necessary officials and shall adopt rules of procedure for the conduct of its work.

6. The Commission shall hold an annual meeting at such time and place as it may decide. Additional meetings shall be held when requested by two or more members of the Commission. The time and place of the first meeting shall be determined by agreement among the Parties.

7. The expenses of each member of the Commission shall be paid by his own Government. Such joint expenses as may be incurred by the Commission shall be defrayed by the Parties by equal contributions. Each Party shall also contribute to the Commission annually an amount equivalent to the value of the sealskins it confiscates under the provisions of Article VI, paragraph 5.

8. The Commission shall submit an annual report of its activities to the Parties.

9. The Commission may from time to time make recommendations to the Parties on any matter which relates to the fur seal resources or to the administration of the Commission.

**Art. VI.** In order to implement the provisions of Article III, the Parties agree as follows:

1. When a duly authorized official of any of the Parties has reasonable cause to believe that any vessel outfitted for the harvesting of living marine resources and subject to the jurisdiction of any of the Parties is offending against the prohibition of pelagic sealing as provided for by Article III, he may, except within the territorial waters of another State, board and search such vessel. Such official shall carry a special certificate issued by the competent authorities of his Government and drawn up in the English, Japanese, and Russian languages which shall be exhibited to the master of the vessel upon request.

2. When the official after searching a vessel continues to have reasonable cause to believe that the vessel or any person on board thereof is

offending against the prohibition, he may seize or arrest such vessel or person. In that case, the Party to which the official belongs shall as soon as possible notify the Party having jurisdiction over the vessel or person of such arrest or seizure and shall deliver the vessel or person as promptly as practicable to the authorized officials of the Party having jurisdiction over the vessel or person at a place to be agreed upon by both Parties; provided, however, that when the Party receiving notification cannot immediately accept delivery of the vessel or person, the Party which gives such notification may, upon request of the other Party, keep the vessel or person under surveillance within its own territory, under the conditions agreed upon by both Parties.

3. The authorities of the Party to which such person or vessel belongs alone shall have jurisdiction to try any case arising under Article III and this Article and to impose penalties in connection therewith.

4. The witnesses or their testimony and other proofs necessary to establish the offense, so far as they are under the control of any of the Parties, shall be furnished with all reasonable promptness to the authorities of the Party having jurisdiction to try the case.

5. Sealskins discovered on seized vessels shall be subject to confiscation on the decision of the court or other authorities of the Party under whose jurisdiction the trial of a case takes place.

6. Full details of punitive measures applied to offenders against the prohibition shall be communicated to the other Parties not later than three months after the application of the penalty.

**Art. VII.** The provisions of this Convention shall not apply to Indians, Ainos, Aleuts, or Eskimos dwelling on the coast of the waters mentioned in Article III, who carry on pelagic sealing in canoes not transported by or used in connection with other vessels, and propelled entirely by oars, paddles, or sails, and manned by not more than five persons each, in the way hitherto practiced and without the use of firearms; provided that such hunters are not in the employment of other persons or under contract to deliver the skins to any person.

**Art. VIII.** 1. Each Party agrees that no person or vessel shall be permitted to use any of its ports or harbors or any part of its territory for any purpose designed to violate the prohibition set forth in Article III.

2. Each Party also agrees to prohibit the importation and delivery into and the traffic within its territories of skins of fur seals taken in the area of the North Pacific Ocean mentioned in Article III, except only those taken by the Union of Soviet Socialist Republics or the United States of America on rookeries, those taken at sea for research purposes in accordance Article II, paragraph 3, those taken under the provisions of Article VII, those confiscated under the provisions of Article VI, para-

462

graph 5, and those inadvertently captured which are taken possession of by a Party; provided, however, that all such excepted skins shall be officially marked and duly certified by the authorities of the Party concerned.

**Art. IX.** 1. The respective Parties agree that, of the total number of sealskins taken commercially each season on land, there shall at the end of the season be delivered a percentage of the gross in number and value thereof as follows:

| | | |
|---|---|---|
| By the Union of Soviet Socialist Republics | { to Canada | 15 per cent |
| | { to Canada | 15 per cent |
| By the United States of America . . . . | { to Japan | 15 per cent |
| | { to Japan | 15 per cent |

2. Each Party agrees to deliver such sealskins to an authorized agent of the recipient Party at the place of taking, or at some other place mutually agreed upon by such Parties.

3. In order more equitably to divide the direct and indirect costs of pelagic research in the Western Pacific Ocean, it is agreed that Canada and Japan for three years starting from the seventh year after entry into force of this Convention will forego the delivery of the sealskins by the Union of Soviet Socialist Republics as set forth in paragraph 1 of this Article and the Union of Soviet Socialist Republics will deliver annually to Canada and to Japan 1,500 sealskins each during these three years.

**Art. X.** 1. Each Party agrees to enact and enforce such legislation as may be necessary to guarantee the observance of this Convention and to make effective its provisions with appropriate penalties for violation thereof.

2. The Parties further agree to cooperate with each other in taking such measures as may be appropriate to carry out the purposes of this Convention, including the prohibition of pelagic sealing as provided for by Article III.

**Art. XI.** The Parties agree to meet early in the twelfth year of this Convention and, if the Convention is continued under the provisions of Article XIII, paragraph 4, to meet again at a later year, to consider the recommendations of the Commision made in accordance with Article V, paragraph 2 (e) and to determine what further agreements may be desirable in order to achieve the maximum sustainable productivity of the North Pacific fur seal herds. The above-mentioned later year shall be fixed by the Parties at the meeting early in the twelfh year.

**Art. XII.** Should any Party consider that the obligations of Article II, paragraphs 3, 4, or 5 or any other obligation undertaken by the Parties is not being carried out and notify the other Parties to that effect, all the Parties shall, within three months of the receipt of such notification, meet to consult together on the need for and nature of remedial measures. In the event that such consultation shall not lead to agreement as to the need for and nature of remedial measures, any Party may give written notice to the other Parties of intention to terminate the Convention and, nothwithstanding the provisions of Article XIII, paragraph 4, the Convention shall thereupon terminate as to all the Parties nine months from the date of such notice.

**Art. XIII.** . . .

3. This Convention shall enter into force on the date of the deposit of the fourth instrument of ratification, and upon such entry into force Article IX, paragraphs 1 and 2, shall be deemed to have been operative from June 1, 1956, provided that the Parties shall have, from the date of signing, maintained under their internal law the prohibition and effective prevention of pelagic sealing by all persons and vessels subject to their respective jurisdictions.

4. The present Convention shall continue in force for twelve years and thereafter until the entry into force of a new or revised fur seal convention between the Parties, or until the expiration of one year after such period of twelve years, whichever may be the earlier; provided, however, that it may continue in force for a further period if the Parties so decide at the meeting early in the twelfth year provided for in Article XI.

. . . . .

## THE 1972 CONVENTION FOR THE CONSERVATION OF ANTARCTIC SEALS

> Signed at London on 1 June 1972. The Signatory Parties are: Argentina, Australia, Belgium, Chile, France, Japan, New Zealand, Norway, South Africa, U.K., U.S. and U.S.S.R.

The Contracting Parties,

*Recalling* the Agreed Measures for the Conversation of Antarctic Fauna and Flora, adopted under the Antarctic Treaty signed at Washington on 1 December 1959;

*Recognizing* the general concern about the vulnerability of Antarctic seals to commercial exploitation and the consequent need for effective conservation measures;

*Recognizing* that the stocks of Antarctic seals are an important living resource in the marine environment which requires an international agreement for its effective conservation;

*Recognizing* that this resource shoul not be depleted by over-exploitation, and hence that any harvesting should be regulated so as not to exceed the levels of the optium sustainable yield;

*Recognizing* that in order to improve scientific knowledge and so place exploitation on a rational basis, every effort should be made both to encourage biological and other research on Antarctic seal populations and to gain information from such research and from the statistics of future sealing operations, so that further suitable regulations may be formulated;

*Noting* that the Scientific Committee on Antarctic Research of the International Council of Scientific Unions (SCAR) is willing to carry out the tasks requested of it in this Convention;

*Desiring* to promote and achieve the objectives of protection, scientific study and rational use of Antarctic seals, and to maintain a satisfactory balance within the ecological system,

Have agreed as follows:

**Art. 1.** *Scope*

(1) This Convention applies to the seas south of 60°. South Latitude, in respect of which the Contracting Parties affirm the provisions of Article IV of the Antarctic Treaty.

(2) This Convention may be applicable to any or all of the following species: Southern elephant seal . . . Leopard seal . . . Weddell seal . . . Crabeater seal . . . Ross seal . . . Southern fur seals . . . ,

(3) The Annex to this Convention forms an integral part thereof.

**Art. 2.** *Implementation*

(1) The Contracting Parties agree that the species of seals enumerated in Article 1 shall not be killed or captured within the Convention area by their nationals or vessels under their respective flags except in accordance with the provisions of this Convention.

(2) Each Contracting Party shall adopt for its nationals and for vessels under its flag such laws, regulations and other measures, including a permit system as appropriate, as may be necessary to implement this Convention.

**Art. 3.** *Annexed Measures*

(1) This Convention includes an Annex specifying measures which the Contracting Parties hereby adopt. Contracting Parties may from time to time in the future adopt other measures with respect to the conservation, scientific study and rational and humane use of seal resources, prescribing *inter alia*:

(a) permissible catch;

(b) protected and unprotected species;

(c) open and closed seasons;

(d) open and closed areas, including the designation of reserves;

(e) the designation of special areas where there shall be no disturbance of seals;

465

(*f*) limits relating to sex, size, or age for each species;

(*g*) restrictions relating to time of day and duration, limitations of effort and methods of sealing;

(*h*) types and specifications of gear and apparatus and appliances which may be used;

(*i*) catch returns and other statistical and biological records;

(*j*) procedures for facilitating the review and assessment of scientific information;

(*k*) other regulatory measures including an effective system of inspection.

(2) The measures adopted under paragraph (1) of this Article shall be based upon the best scientific and technical evidence available.

(3) The Annex may from time to time be amended in accordance with the procedures provided for in Article 9.

**Art. 4.** *Special Permits*

(1) Notwithstanding the provisions of this Convention, any Contracting Party may issue permits to kill or capture seals in limited quantities and in conformity with the objectives and principles of this Convention for the following purposes:

(*a*) to provide indispensable food for men or dogs;

(*b*) to provide for scientific research; or

(*c*) to provide specimens for museums, educational or cultural institutions.

(2) Each Contracting Party shall, as soon as possible, inform the other Contracting Parties and SCAR of the purpose and content of all permits issued under paragraph (1) of this Article and subsequently of the numbers of seals killed or captured under these permits.

**Art. 5.** *Exchange of Information and Scientific Advice*

(1) Each Contracting Party shall provide to the other Contracting Parties and to SCAR the information specified in the Annex within the period indicated therein.

(2) Each Contracting Party shall also provide to the oher Contracting Parties and to SCAR before 31 October each year information on any steps it has taken in accordance with Article 2 of this Convention during the preceding period 1 July to 30 June.

(3) Contracting Parties which have no information to report under the two preceding paragraphs shall indicate this formally before 31 October each year.

(4) SCAR is invited:

(*a*) to assess information received pursuant to this Article; encourage exchange of scientific data and information among the Contracting Parties; recommend programmes for scientific research; recommend statistical and

466

biological data to be collected by sealing expeditions within the Convention area; and suggest amendments to the Annex; and

(b) to report on the basis of the statistical, biological and other evidence available when the harvest of any species of seal in the Convention area is having a significantly harmful effect on the total stocks of such species or on the ecological system in any particular locality.

(5) SCAR is invited to notify the Depositary which shall report to the Contracting Parties when SCAR estimates in any sealing season that the permissible catch limits for any species are likely to be exceeded and, in that case, to provide an estimate of the date upon which the permissible catch limits will be reached. Each Contracting Party shall then take appropriate measures to prevent its nationals and vessels under its flag from killing or capturing seals of that species after the estimated date until the Contracting Parties decide otherwise.

(6) SCAR may if necessary seek the technical assistance of the Food and Agriculture Organization of the United Nations in making its assessments.

(7) Notwithstanding the provisions of paragraph (1) of Article 1 the Contracting Parties shall, in accordance with their internal law, report to each other and to SCAR, for consideration statistics relating to the Antarctic seals listed in paragraph (2) of Article 1 which have been killed or captured by their nationals and vessels under their respective flags in the area of floating sea ice north of 60° South Latitude.

**Art. 6.** *Consultations Between Contracting Parties*

(1) At any time after commercial sealing has begun a Contracting Party may propose through the Depositary that a meeting of Contracting Parties be convened with a view to:

(a) establishing by a two-thirds majority of the Contracting Parties, including the concurring votes of all States signatory to this Convention present at the meeting, an effective system of control, including inspection, over the implementation of the provisions of this Convention;

(b) establishing a commission to perform such functions under this Convention as the Contracting Parties may deem necessary; or

(c) considering other proposals, including:

(i) the provision of independent scientific advice;
(ii) the establishment, by a two-thirds majority, of a scientific advisory committee which may be assigned some or all of the functions requested of SCAR under this Convention, if commercial sealing reaches significant proportions;
(iii) the carrying out of scientific programmes with the participation of the Contracting Parties; and
(iv) the provision of further regulatory measures, including moratoria.

467

(2) If one-third of the Contracting Parties indicate agreement the Depositary shall convene such a meeting, as soon as possible.

(3) A meeting shall be held at the request of any Contracting Party, if SCAR reports that the harvest of any species of Antarctic seal in the area to which this Convention applies is having a significantly harmful effect on the total stocks or the ecological system in any particular locality.

**Art. 7.** *Review of Operations*

The Contracting Parties shall meet within five years after the entry into force of this Convention and at least every five years thereafter to review the operation of the Convention.

**Art. 8.** *Amendments to the Convention*

(1) This Convention may be amended at any time. The text of any amendment proposed by a Contracting Party shall be submitted to the Depositary, which shall transmit it to all the Contracting Parties.

(2) If one-third of the Contracting Parties request a meeting to discuss the proposed amendment the Depositary shall call such a meeting.

(3) An amendment shall enter into force when the Depositary has received instruments of ratification or acceptance thereof from all the Contracting Parties.

**Art. 9.** *Amendments to the Annex*

(1) Any Contracting Party may propose amendments to the Annex to this Convention. The text of any such proposed amendment shall be submitted to the Depositary which shall transmit it to all Contracting Parties.

(2) Each such proposed amendment shall become effective for all Contracting Parties six months after the date appearing on the notification from the Depositary to the Contracting Parties, if within 120 days of the notification date, no objection has been received and two-thirds of the Contracting Parties have notified the Depositary in writing of their approval.

(3) If an objection is received from any Contracting Party within 120 days of the notification date, the matter shall be considered by the Contracting Parties at their next meeting. If unanimity on the matter is not reached at the meeting, the Contracting Parties shall notify the Depositary within 120 days from the date of closure of the meeting of their approval or rejection of tne original amendment or of any new amendment proposed by the meeting. If, by the end of this period, two-thirds of the Contracting Parties have approved such amendment, it shall become effective six months from the date of the closure of the meeting for those Contracting Parties which have by then notified their approval.

(4) Any Contracting Party which has objected to a proposed amendment may at any time withdraw that objection, and the proposed amend-

468

ment shall become effective with respect to such Party immediately if the amendment is already in effect, or at such time as it becomes effective under the terms of this Article.

(5) The Depositary shall notify each Contracting Party immediately upon receipt of each approval or objection, of each withdrawal of objection, and of the entry into force of any amendment.

(6) Any State which becomes a party to this Convention after an amendment to the Annex has entered into force shall be bound by the Annex as so amended. Any State which becomes a Party to this Convention during the period when a proposed amendment is pending may approve or object to such an amendment within the time limits applicable to other Contracting Parties.

**Art. 10.** *Signature*

This Convention shall be open for signature at London from 1 June to 31 December 1972 by States participating in the Conference on the Conservation of Antarctic Seals held at London from 3 to 11 February 1972.

**Art. 11.** *Ratification*

This Convention is subject to ratification or acceptance. Instruments of ratification or acceptance shall be deposited with the Government of the United Kingdom of Great Britain and Northern Ireland, hereby designated as the Depositary.

**Art. 12.** *Accession*

This Convention shall be open for accession by any State which may be invited to accede to this Convention with the consent of all the Contracting Parties.

**Art. 13.** *Entry into Force*

(1) This Convention shall enter into force on the thirtieth day following the date of deposit of the seventh instrument of ratification, or acceptance.

(2) Thereafter this Convention shall enter into force for each ratifying, accepting or acceding State on the thirtieth day after deposit by such State of its instrument of ratification, acceptance or accession.

**Art. 14.** *Withdrawal*

Any Contracting Party may withdraw from this Convention on 30 June of any year by giving notice on or before 1 January of the same year to the Depositary, which upon receipt of such a notice shall at one communicate it to the other Contracting Parties. Any other Contracting Party may, in like manner, within one month of the receipt of a copy of such a notice from the Depositary, give notice of withdrawal, so that the Convention shall cease to be in force on 30 June of the same year with respect to the Contracting Party giving such notice.

**Art. 15.** *Notifications by the Depositary*

. . . . .

**Art. 16.** *Certified Copies and Règistration*

**Annex**

### 1. *Permissible Catch*

The Contracting Parties shall in any one year, which shall run from 1 July to 30 June inclusive, restrict the total number of seals of each species killed or captured to the numbers specified below. These numbers are subject to review in the light of scientific assessments.

  (*a*) in the case of Crabeater seals *Lobodon carcinophagus* 175,000;
  (*b*) in the case of Leopard seals *Hydrurga leptonyx* 12,000;
  (*c*) in the case of Weddell seals *Leptonychotes weddeli* 5,000.

### 2. *Protected Species*

  (*a*) It is forbidden to kill or capture Ross seals *Ommatophoca rossi*, Southern elephant seals *Mirounga leonina*, or fur seals of the genus *Arctocephalus*.

  (*b*) In order to protect the adult breeding stock during the period when it is most concentrated and vulnerable, it is forbidden to kill or capture any Weddell seal *Leptonychotes weddeli* one year old or older between 1 September and 31 January inclusive.

### 3. *Closed Season and Sealing Season*

The period between 1 March and 31 August inclusive is a Closed Season, during which the killing or capturing of seals is forbidden. The period 1 September to the last day in February constitutes a Sealing Season.

### 4. *Sealing Zones*

Each of the sealing zones listed in this paragraph shall be closed in numerical sequence to all sealing operations for the seal species listed in paragraph 1 of this Annex for the period 1 September to the last day of February inclusive. Such closures shall begin with the same zone as is closed under paragraph 2 of Annex B to Annex 1 of the Report of the Fifth Antarctic Treaty Consultative Meeting at the moment the Convention enters into force. Upon the expiration of each closed period, the affected zone shall reopen.

Zone 1 — between 60° and 120° West Longitude
Zone 2 — between 0° and 60° West Longitude, together with that part of the Weddell Sea lying westward of 60° West Longitude

Zone 3 — between 0° and 70° East Longitude
Zone 4 — between 70° and 130° East Longitude
Zone 5 — between 130° East Longitude and 170° West Longitude
Zone 6 — between 120° and 170° West Longitude.

## 5. Seal Reserves

It is forbidden to kill or capture seals in the following reserves, which are seal breeding areas or the site of long-term scientific research:

(a) The area around the South Orkney Islands between 60° 20′ and 60° 56′ South Latitude and 44° 05′ and 46° 25′ West Longitude.

(b) The area of the southwestern Ross Sea south of 76° South Latitude and west of 170° East Longitude.

(c) The area of Edisto Inlet south and west of a line drawn between Cape Hallet at 72° 19′ South Latitude, 170° 18′ East Longitude, and Helm Point, at 72° 11′ South Latitude, 170° 00′ East Longitude.

## 6. Exchange of Information

(a) Contracting Parties shall provide before the 31st October each year to other Contracting Parties and to SCAR a summary of statistical information on all seals killed or captured by their nationals and vessels under their respective flags in the Convention area, in respect of the preceding period 1 July to 30 June. This information shall include by zones and months:

(i) The gross and net tonnage, brake horse-power, number of crew, and number of days' operation of vessels under the flag of the Contracting Party;

(ii) The number of adult individuals and pups of each species taken. When specially requested, this information shall be provided in respect of each ship, together with its daily position at noon each operating day and the catch on that day.

(b) When an industry has started, reports of the number of seals of each species killed or captured in each zone shall be made to SCAR in the form and at the intervals (not shorter than one week) requested by that body.

(c) Contracting Parties shall provide to SCAR biological information concerning in particular

(i) Sex

(ii) Reproductive condition

(iii) Age.

SCAR may request additional information or material with the approval of the Contracting Parties.

(d) Contracting Parties shall provide to other Constructing Parties and to SCAR at least 30 days in advance of departure from their home ports, information on proposed sealing expeditions.

### 7. Sealing Methods

(*a*) SCAR is invited to report on methods of sealing and to make recommendations with a view to ensuring that the killing or capturing of seals is quick, painless and efficient. Contracting Parties, as appropriate, shall adopt rules for their nationals and vessels under their respective flags engaged in the killing and capturing of seals, giving due consideration to the views of SCAR.

(*b*) In the light of the available scientific and technical data, Contracting Parties agree to take appropriate steps to ensure that their nationals and vessels under their respective flags refrain from killing or capturing seals in the water, except in limited quantities to provide for scientific research in conformity with the objectives and principles of this Convention. Such research shall include studies as to the effectiveness of methods of sealing from the viewpoint of the management and humane and rational utilization of the Antarctic seal resources for conservation purposes. The undertaking and the results of any such scientific research programme shall be communicated to SCAR and the Depositary which shall transmit them to the Contracting Parties.

# II. TUNA CONSERVATION CONVENTIONS

## THE 1949 CONVENTION FOR THE ESTABLISHMENT OF AN INTER-AMERICAN TROPICAL TUNA COMMISSION

Signed by the Representatives of Costa Rica and United States of America at Washington on 31 May 1949; Entered into force on 3 March 1950 between the two countries. U.N. Treaty Series, vol. 80, p. 3. The Parties to the Convention as of 31 December 1973 are: Canada, Costa Rica, France, Japan, Mexico, Nicaragua, Panama and U.S.

The United States of America and the Republic of Costa Rica considering their mutual interest in maintaining the populations of yellowfin and skipjack tuna and of other kinds of fish taken by tuna fishing vessels in the eastern Pacific Ocean which by reason of continued use have come to be of common concern, and desiring to cooperate in the gathering and interpretation of factual information to facilitate maintaining the populations of these fishes at a level which will permit maximum sustained catches year after year, have agreed to conclude a Convention for these purposes . . . .

**Art. I.** 1. The High Contracting Parties agree to establish and operate a joint Commission, to be known as the Inter-American Tropical Tuna Commission, hereinafter referred to as the Commission, which shall carry out the objectives of this Convention. The Commission shall be composed of national sections, each consisting of from one to four members, appointed by the Governments of the respective High Contracting Parties.

2. The Commission shall submit annually to the Government of each High Contracting Party a report on its investigations and findings, with appropriate recommendations, and shall also inform such Governments, whenever it is deemed advisable, on any matter relating to the objectives of this Convention.

3. Each High Contracting Party shall determine and pay the expenses incurred by its section. Joint expenses incurred by the Commission shall be paid by the High Contracting Parties through contributions in the form and proportion recommended by the Commission and approved by the High Contracting Parties. The proportion of joint expenses to be paid by each High Contacting Party shall be related to the proportion of the total catch from the fisheries covered by this Convention utilized by that High Contracting Party.

4. Both the general annual program of activities and the budget of joint

expenses shall be recommended by the Commission and submitted for approval to the High Contracting Parties.

5. The Commission shall decide on the most convenient place or places for its headquarters.

6. The Commission shall meet at least once each year, and at such other times as may be requested by a national section. The date and place of the first meeting shall be determined by agreement between the High Contracting Parties.

7. At its first meeting the Commission shall select a chairman and a secretary from different national sections. The chairman and the secretary shall hold office for a period of one year. During succeeding years, selection of the chairman and the secretary from the national sections shall be in such a manner that the chairman and the secretary will be of different nationalities, and as will provide each High Contracting Party, in turn, with an opportunity to be represented in those offices.

8. Each national section shall have one vote. Decisions, resolutions, recommendations, and publications of the Commission shall be made only by a unanimous vote.

9. The Commission shall be entitled to adopt and to amend subsequently, as occasion may require, by-laws or rules for the conduct of its meetings.

10. The Commission shall be entitled to employ necessary personnel for the performance of its functions and duties.

11. Each High Contracting Party shall be entitled to establish an Advisory Committee for its section, to be composed of persons who shall be well informed concerning tuna fishery problems of common concern. Each such Advisory Committee shall be invited to attend the non-executive sessions of the Commission.

12. The Commission may hold public hearings. Each national section also may hold public hearings within its own country.

13. The Commission shall designate a Director of Investigations who shall be technically competent and who shall be responsible to the Commission and may be freely removed by it. Subject to the instruction of the Commission and with its approval, the Director of Investigations shall have charge of:

(*a*) the drafting of programs of investigations, and the preparation of budget estimates for the Commission;

(*b*) authorizing the disbursement of the funds for the joint expenses of the Commission;

(*c*) the accounting of the funds for the joint expenses of the Commission;

(*d*) the appointment and immediate direction of technical and other personnel required for the functions of the Commission;

474

(*e*) arrangements for the cooperation with other organizations or individuals in accordance with paragraph 16 of this Article;

(*f*) the coordination of the work of the Commission with that of organizations and individuals whose cooperation has been arranged for;

(*g*) the drafting of administrative, scientific and other reports for the Commission;

(*h*) the performance of such other duties as the Commission may require.

14. The official languages of the Commission shall be English and Spanish, and members of the Commission may use either language during meetings. When requested, translation shall be made to the other language. The minutes, official documents, and publications of the Commission shall be in both languages, but official correspondence of the Commission may be written, at the discretion of the secretary, in either language.

15. Each national section shall be entitled to obtain certified copies of any documents pertaining to the Commission except that the Commission will adopt and may amend subsequently rules to ensure the confidential character of records of statistics of individual catches and individual company operations.

16. In the performance of its duties and functions the Commission may request the technical and scientific services of, and information from, official agencies of the High Contracting Parties, and any international, public, or private institution or organization, or any private individual.

**Art. II.** The Commission shall perform the following functions and duties:

1. Make investigations concerning the abundance, biology, biometry, and ecology of yellowfin (*Neothunnus*) and skipjack (*Katsuwonus*) tuna in the waters of the eastern Pacific Ocean fished by the nationals of the High Contracting Parties, and the kinds of fishes commonly used as bait in the tuna fisheries, especially the anchovetta, and of other kinds of fish taken by tuna fishing vessels; and the effects of natural factors and human activities on the abundance of the populations of fishes supporting all these fisheries.

2. Collect and analyze information relating to current and past conditions and trends of the populations of fishes covered by this Convention.

3. Study and appraise information concerning methods and procedures for maintaining and increasing the populations of fishes covered by this Convention.

4. Conduct such fishing and other activities, on the high seas and in waters which are under the jurisdiction of the High Contracting Parties, as may be necessary to attain the ends referred to in subparagraphs 1, 2, and 3 of this Article.

5. Recommend from time to time, on the basis of scientific investi-

gations, proposals for joint action by the High Contracting Parties designed to keep the populations of fishes covered by this Convention at those levels of abundance which will permit the maximum sustained catch.

6. Collect statistics and all kinds of reports concerning catches and the operations of fishing boats, and other information concerning the fishing for fishes covered by this Convention, from vessels or persons engaged in these fisheries.

7. Publish or otherwise disseminate reports relative to the results of its findings and such other reports as fall within the scope of this Convention, as well as scientific, statistical, and other data relating to the fisheries maintained by the nationals of the High Contracting Parties for the fishes covered by this Convention.

**Art. III.** The High Contracting Parties agree to enact such legislation as may be necessary to carry out the purposes of this Convention.

**Art. IV.** Nothing in this Convention shall be construed to modify any existing treaty or convention with regard to the fisheries of the eastern Pacific Ocean previously concluded by a High Contracting Party, nor to preclude a High Contracting Party from entering into treaties or conventions with other States regarding these fisheries, the terms of which are not incompatible with the present Convention.

**Art. V.** . . .

3. Any government, whose nationals participate in the fisheries covered by this Convention, desiring to adhere to the present Convention, shall address a communication to that effect to each of the High Contracting Parties. Upon receiving the unanimous consent of the High Contracting Parties to adherence, such government shall deposit with the Government of the United States of America an instrument of adherence which shall stipulate the effective date thereof. The Government of the United States of America shall furnish a certified copy of the Convention to each government desiring to adhere thereto. Each adhering government shall have all the rights and obligations under the Convention as if it had been an original signatory thereof.

4. At any time after the expiration of ten years from the date of entry into force of this Convention any High Contracting Party may give notice of its intention of denouncing the Convention. Such notification shall become effective with respect to such notifying government one year after its receipt by the Government of the United States of America. After the expiration of the said one year period the Convention shall be effective only with respect to the remaining High Contracting Parties.

5. . . .

# THE 1966 INTERNATIONAL CONVENTION FOR CONSERVATION OF ATLANTIC TUNAS

Signed at Rio de Janeiro on 14 May 1966; Entered into force on 21 March 1969. U.N. Treaty Series, vol. 673, p. 63. The Parties to the Convention as of 31 December 1973 are: Brazil, Canada, France, Ghana, Ivory Coast, Japan, Korea (Rep. of), Morocco, Portugal, Senegal, South Africa, Spain and U.S.

. . . . .

**Art. I.** The area to which this Convention shall apply, hereinafter referred to as the "Convention area", shall be all waters of the Atlantic Ocean, including the adjacent Seas.

**Art. II.** Nothing in this Convention shall be considered as affecting the rights, claims or views of any Contracting Party in regard to the limits of territorial waters or the extent of jurisdiction over fisheries under international law.

**Art. III.** 1. The Contracting Parties hereby agree to establish and maintain a Commission to be known as the International Commission for the Conservation of Atlantic Tunas, hereinafter referred to as "the Commission", which shall carry out the objectives set forth in this Convention.

2. Each of the Contracting Parties shall be represented on the Commission by not more than three Delegates. Such Delegates may be assisted by experts and advisors.

3. Except as may otherwise be provided in this Convention, decisions of the Commission shall be taken by a majority of the Contracting Parties, each Contracting Party having one vote. Two-thirds of the Contracting Parties shall constitute a quorum.

4. The Commission shall hold a regular meeting once every two years. A special meeting may be called at any time at the request of a majority of the Contracting Parties or by decision of the Council as constituted in Article V.

5. At its first meeting, and thereafter at each regular meeting, the Commission shall elect from among its Members a Chairman, a first Vice-Chairman and a second Vice-Chairman who shall not be re-elected for more than one term.

6. The meetings of the Commission and its subsidiary bodies shall be public unless the Commission otherwise decides.

7. The official languages of the Commission shall be English, French and Spanish.

8. The Commission shall have authority to adopt such rules of proce-

dure and financial regulations as are necessary to carry out its functions.

9. The Commission shall submit a report to the Contracting Parties every two years on its work and findings and shall also inform any Contracting Party, whenever requested, on any matter relating to the objectives of the Convention.

**Art. IV.** 1. In order to carry out the objectives of this Convention the Commission shall be responsible for the study of the populations of tuna and tuna-like fishes (the Scombriformes with the exception of the families Trichiuridae and Gempylidae and the genus Scomber) and such other species of fishes exploited in tuna fishing in the Convention area as are not under investigation by another international fishery organization. Such study shall include research on the abundance, biometry and ecology of the fishes; the oceanography of their environment; and the effects of natural and human factors upon their abundance. The Commission, in carrying out these responsobilities shall, insofar as feasible, utilise the technical and scientific services of, and information from, official agencies of the Contracting Parties and their political sub-divisions, and may, when desirable, utilise the available services and information of any public or private institution, organization or individual, and may undertake within the limits of its budget independent research to supplement the research work being done by governments, national institutions or other international organizations.

2. The carrying out of the provisions in paragraph 1 of this Article shall include:

(*a*) collecting and analysing statistical information relating to the current conditions and trends of the tuna fishery resources of the Convention area;

(*b*) studying and appraising information concerning measures and methods to ensure maintenance of the populations of tuna and tuna-like fishes in the Convention area at levels which will permit the maximum sustainable catch and which will ensure the effective exploitation of these fishes in a manner consistent with this catch;

(*c*) recommending studies and investigations to the Contracting Parties;

(*d*) publishing and otherwise disseminating reports of its findings and statistical, biological and other scientific information relative to the tuna fisheries of the Convention area.

**Art. V.** 1. There is established within the Commission a Council which shall consist of the Chairman and the Vice-Chairmen of the Commission together with the representatives of not less than four and not more than eight Contracting Parties. The Contracting Parties represented on the Council shall be elected at each regular meeting of the Commission. How-

478

ever, if at any time the number of the Contracting Parties exceeds forty, the Commission may elect an additional two Contracting Parties to be represented on the Council. The Contracting Parties of which the Chairman and Vice-Chairmen are nationals shall not be elected to the Council. In elections to the Council the Commission shall give due consideration to the geographic, tuna fishing and tuna processing interests of the Contracting Parties, as well as to the equal right of the Contracting Parties to be represented on the Council.

2. The Council shall perform such functions as are assigned to it by this Convention or are designated by the Commission, and shall meet at least once in the interim between regular meetings of the Commission. Between meetings of the Commission the Council shall make necessary decisions on the duties to be carried out by the staff and shall issue necessary instructions to the Executive Secretary. Decisions of the Council shall be made in accordance with rules to be established by the Commission.

**Art. VI.** To carry out the objectives of this Convention the Commission may establish Panels on the basis of species, group of species, or of geographic areas. Each Panel in such case:

(*a*) shall be responsible for keeping under review the species, group of species, or geographic area under its purview, and for collecting scientific and other information relating thereto;

(*b*) may propose to the Commission, upon the basis of scientific investigations, recommendations for joint action by the Contracting Parties;

(*c*) may recommend to the Commission studies and investigations necessary for obtaining information relating to its species, group of species, or geographic area, as well as the co-ordination of programmes of investigations by the Contracting Parties.

**Art. VII.** The Commission shall appoint an Executive Secretary who shall serve at the pleasure of the Commission. The Executive Secretary, subject to such rules and procedures as may be determined by the Commission, shall have authority with respect to the selection and administration of the staff of the Commission. He shall also perform, *inter alia*, the following functions as the Commission may prescribe:

(*a*) co-ordinating the programmes of investigation by the Contracting Parties;

(*b*) preparing budget estimates for review by the Commission;

(*c*) authorizing the disbursement of funds in accordance with the Commission's budget;

(*d*) accounting for the funds of the Commission;

(*e*) arranging for co-operation with the organizations referred to in

Article XI of this Convention;

(f) preparing the collection and analysis of data necessary to accomplish the purposes of the Convention particularly those data relating to the current and maximum sustainable catch of tuna stocks;

(g) preparing for approval by the Commission scientific, administrative and other reports of the Commission and its subsidiary bodies.

**Art. VIII.** 1. (a) The Commission may, on the basis of scientific evidence make recommendations designed to maintain the populations of tuna and tuna-like fishes that may be taken in the Convention area at levels which will permit the maximum sustainable catch. These recommendations shall be applicable to the Contracting Parties under the conditions laid down in paragraphs 2 and 3 of this Article.

(b) The recommendations referred to above shall be made:
  (i) at the initiative of the Commission if an appropriate Panel has not been established or with the approval of at least two-thirds of all the Contracting Parties if an appropriate Panel has been established;
 (ii) on the proposal of an appropriate Panel if such a Panel has been established;
 (iii) on the proposal of the appropriate Panels if the recommendation in question relates to more than one geographic area, species or group of species.

2. Each recommendation made under paragraph 1 of this Article shall become effective for all Contracting Parties six months after the date of the notification from the Commission transmitting the recommendation to the Contracting Parties, except as provided in paragraph 3 of this Article.

3. (a) If any Contracting Party in the case of a recommendation made under paragraph 1 (b) (i) above, or any Contracting Party member of a Panel concerned in the case of a recommendation made under paragraph 1 (b) (ii) or (iii) above, presents to the Commission an objection to such recommendation within the six months period provided for in paragraph 2 above, the recommendation shall not become effective for an additional sixty days.

(b) Thereupon any other Contracting Party may present an objection prior to the expiration of the additional sixty days period, or within forty-five days of the date of the notification of an objection made by another Contracting Party within such additional sixty days, whichever date shall be the later.

(c) The recommendation shall become effective at the end of the extended period or periods for objection, except for those Contracting Parties that have presented an objection.

480

(*d*) However, if a recommendation has met with an objection presented by only one or less than one-fourth of the Contracting Parties, in accordance with sub-paragraphs (*a*) and (*b*) above, the Commission shall immediately notify the Contracting Party or Parties having presented such objection that it is to be considered as having no effect.

(*e*) In the case referred to in sub-paragraph (*d*) above the Contracting Party or Parties concerned shall have an additional period of sixty days from the date of said notification in which to reaffirm their objection. On the expiry of this period the recommandation shall become effective, except with respect to any Contracting Party having presented an objection and reaffirmed it within the delay provided for.

(*f*) If a recommendation has met with objection from more than one-fourth but less than the majority of the Contracting Parties, in accordance with sub-paragraphs (*a*) and (*b*) obove, the recommendation shall become effective for the Contracting Parties that have not presented an objection thereto.

(*g*) If objections have been presented by a majority of the Contracting Parties the recommendation shall not become effective.

4. Any Contracting Party objecting to a recommendation may at any time withdraw that objection, and the recommendation shall become effective with respect to such Contracting Party immediately if the recommendation is already in effect, or at such time as it may become effective under the terms of this Article.

5. The Commission shall notify each Contracting Party immediately upon receipt of each objection and of each withdrawal of an objection, and of the entry into force of any recommendation.

**Art. IX.** 1. The Contracting Parties agree to take all action necessary to ensure the enforcement of this Convention. Each Contracting Party shall transmit to the Commission, biennially or at such other times as may be required by the Commission, a statement of the action taken by it for these purposes.

2. The Contracting Parties agree:

(*a*) to furnish, on the request of the Commission, any available statistical, biological and other scientific information the Commission may need for the purposes of this Convention;

(*b*) when their official agencies are unable to obtain and furnish the said information, to allow the Commission, through the Contracting Parties, to obtain it on a voluntary basis direct from companies and individual fishermen.

3. The Contracting Parties undertake to collaborate with each other with a view to the adoption of suitable effective measures to ensure the application of the provisions of this Convention and in particular to set up

a system of international enforcement to be applied to the Convention area except the territorial sea and other waters, if any, in which a state is entitled under international law to exercise jurisdiction over fisheries.

**Art. X.** 1. The Commission shall adopt a budget for the joint expenses of the Commission for the biennium following each regular meeting.

2. Each Contracting Party shall contribute annually to the budget of the Commission an amount equal to:

(a) U.S.$1,000 (one thousand United States dollars) for Commission membership.

(b) U.S.$1,000 (one thousand United States dollars) for each Panel membership.

(c) If the proposed budget for joint expenses for any biennium should exceed the whole amount of contributions to be made by the Contracting Parties under (a) and (b) of this paragraph, one-third of the amount of such excess shall be contributed by the Contracting Parties in proportion to their contributions made under (a) and (b) of this paragraph. For the remaining two-thirds the Commission shall determine on the basis of the latest available information:

(i) the total of the round weight of catch of Atlantic tuna and tuna-like fishes and the net weight of canned products of such fishes for each Contracting Party;

(ii) the total of (i) for all Contracting Parties.

Each Contracting Party shall contribute its share of the remaining two-thirds in the same ratio that its total in (i) bears to the total in (ii). That part of the budget referred to in this sub-paragraph shall be set by agreement of all the Contracting Parties present and voting.

3. The Council shall review the second half of the biennial budget at its regular meeting between Commission meetings and, on the basis of current and anticipated developments, may authorise re-apportionment of amounts in the Commission budget for the second year within the total budget approved by the Commission.

4. The Executive Secretary of the Commission shall notify each Contracting Party of its yearly assessment. The contributions shall be payable on January first of the year for which the assessment was levied. Contributions not received before January first of the succeeding year shall be considered as in arrears.

5. Contributions to the biennial budget shall be payable in such currencies as the Commission may decide.

6. At its first meeting the Commission shall approve a budget for the balance of the first year the Commission functions and for the following biennium. It shall immediately transmit to the Contracting Parties copies of these budgets together with notices of the respective assessments for

the first annual contribution.

7. Thereafter, within a period not less than sixty days before the regular meeting of the Commission which precedes the biennium, the Executive Secretary shall submit to each Contracting Party a draft biennial budget together with a schedule of proposed assessments.

8. The Commission may suspend the voting rights of any Contracting Party when its arrears of contributions equal or exceed the amount due from it for the two preceding years.

9. The Commission shall establish a Working Capital Fund to finance operations of the Commission prior to receiving annual contributions, and for such other purposes as the Commission may determine. The Commission shall determine the level of the Fund, assess advances necessary for its establishment, and adopt regulations governing the use of the Fund.

10. The Commission shall arrange an annual independent audit of the Commission's accounts. The reports of such audits shall be reviewed and approved by the Commission, or by the Council in years when there is no regular Commission meeting.

11. The Commission may accept contributions, other than provided for in paragraph 2 of this Article, for the prosecution of its work.

**Art. XI.** 1. The Contracting Parties agree that there should be a working relationship between the Commission and the Food and Agriculture Organization of the United Nations. To this end the Commission shall enter into negotiations with the Food and Agriculture Organization of the United Nations with a view to concluding an agreement pursuant to Article XIII of the Organization's Constitution. Such agreement should provide, *inter alia*, for the Director-General of the Food and Agriculture Organization of the United Nations to appoint a Representative who would participate in all meetings of the Commission and its subsidiary bodies, but without the right to vote.

2. The Contracting Parties agree that there should be co-operation between the Commission and other international fisheries commissions and scientific organizations which might contribute to the work of the Commission. The Commission may enter into agreements with such commissions and organizations.

3. The Commission may invite any appropriate international organization and any Government which is a member of the United Nations or of any Specialized Agency of the United Nations and which is not a member of the Commission, to send observers to meetings of the Commission and its subsidiary bodies.

**Art. XII.** 1. This Convention shall remain in force for ten years and thereafter until a majority of Contracting Parties agree to terminate it.

2. At any time after ten years from the date of entry into force of this

Convention, any Contracting Party may withdraw from the Convention on December thirty-first of any year including the tenth year by written notification of withdrawal given on or before December thirty-first of the preceding year to the Director-General of the Food and Agriculture Organization of the United Nations.

3. Any other Contracting Party may thereupon withdraw from this Convention with effect from the same December thirty-first by giving written notification of withdrawal to the Director-General of the Food and Agriculture Organization of the United Nations not later than one month from the date of receipt of information from the Director-General of the Food and Agriculture Organization of the United Nations concerning any withdrawal, but not later than April first of that year.

**Art. XIII.** 1. Any Contracting Party or the Commission may propose amendments to this Convention. The Director-General of the Food and Agriculture Organization of the United Nations shall transmit a certified copy of the text of any proposed amendment to all the Contracting Parties. Any amendment not involving new obligations shall take effect for all Contracting Parties on the thirtieth day after its acceptance by three-fourths of the Contracting Parties. Any amendment involving new obligations shall take effect for each Contracting Party accepting the amendment on the ninetieth day after its acceptance by three-fourths of the Contracting Parties and thereafter for each remaining Contracting Party upon acceptance by it. Any amendment considered by one or more Contracting Parties to involve new obligations shall be deemed to involve new obligations and shall take effect accordingly. A government which becomes a Contracting Party after an amendment to this Convention has been opened for acceptance pursuant to the provisions of this Article shall be bound by the Convention as amended when the said amendment comes into force.

2. Proposed amendments shall be deposited with the Director-General of the Food and Agriculture Organization of the United Nations. Notifications of acceptance of amendments shall be deposited with the Director-General of the Food and Agriculture Organization of the United Nations.

**Art. XIV.** 1. This Convention shall be open for signature by any Government which is a member of the United Nations or of any Specialized Agency of the United Nations. Any such Government which does not sign this Convention may adhere to it at any time.

2. This Convention shall be subject to ratification or approval by signatory countries in accordance with their constitutions. Instruments of ratification, approval, or adherence shall be deposited with the Director-General of the Food and Agriculture Organization of the United Nations.

3. This Convention shall enter into force upon the deposit of instruments of ratification, approval, or adherence by seven Governments and shall

enter into force with respect to each Government which subsequently deposits an instrument of ratification, approval or adherence on the date of such deposit.

**Art. XV.** . . .

**Art. XVI.** . . .

# III. SEDENTARY FISHERY CONVENTIONS

## THE 1972 AGREEMENT RELATING TO THE KING AND TANNER CRAB FISHERIES IN THE EASTERN BERING SEA (Japan and United States of America)

> Notes constituting the Agreement were exchanged at Washington on 20 December 1972; Entered into force on the same date. Replacing the Agreement of 25 November 1964 (U.N. Treaty Series, vol. 533, p. 31), the Agreement of 29 November 1966 (U.N. Treaty Series, vol. 680, p. 382), the Agreement of 23 December 1968 (U.N. Treaty Series, vol. 714, p. 386) and the Agreement of 11 December 1970 (UN ST/LEG/SER.B/16/ Add. 1, p. 100).

1. The Government of Japan holds the view that king crabs and tanner crabs are high seas fishery resources, and that nationals and vessels of Japan are entitled to continue fishing for king crabs and tanner crabs in the eastern Bering Sea.

2. The Government of the United States of America is of the view that king crabs and tanner crabs are natural resources of the continental shelf over which the coastal state (in this case the United States of America) has exclusive jurisdiction, control, and rights of exploitation.

3. However, the two Governments, having regard to the fact that nationals and vessels of Japan have over a period of years exploited the crab resources in the eastern Bering Sea, have agreed, without prejudice to their respective positions as described above, as follows:

(1) The fisheries for king and tanner crabs by nationals and vessels of Japan in the eastern Bering Sea will continue in and near the waters which have been fished historically by Japan; that is, those waters in which migrate the crab stocks exploited in the past by Japan; provided that in order to avoid overfishing of the crab resources in the eastern Bering Sea, the Government of Japan ensures that the annual commercial catches of king and tanner crabs by nationals and vessels of Japan for the years 1973 and 1974 shall not exceed:

A. 270,000 king crabs and 6,000,000 tanner crabs in the area lying within the following designated boundaries: a line running from Cape Newenham on the Bering Sea coast of western Alaska, southwest to position 57°00′ North Latitude, 168°00′ West Longitude, thence due south to position 54°36′ North Latitude, 168°00′ West Longitude, and thence east to Cape Sarichef on the west coast of Unimak Island, Alaska.

B.  430,000 king crabs and 8,000,000 tanner crabs outside the area designated above.

(2) The two Governments shall apply such interim measures as described in the Appendix to this note to their respective nationals and vessels fishing for king and tanner crabs in the eastern Bering Sea.

(3) The International Commission under the North Pacific Fishery Convention will be asked by the two Governments to continue and intensify the study of the king and tanner crab resources in the eastern Bering Sea and to transmit to the two Governments annually by November 30 the findings of such study.

(4) For the purpose of carrying out faithfully measures under the provisions of the provisions of sub-paragraph (1) and the provisions of sub-paragraph (2) of this paragraph, the two Governments shall take appropriate and effective measures respectively, and either Government shall, if requested by the other Government, provide opportunity for observation of the conduct of enforcement.

(5) The two Governments shall meet before December 31, 1974, to review the operation of these arrangements and the conditions of the king and tanner crab fisheries of the eastern Bering Sea, and decide on future arrangements, bearing in mind paragraphs 1 and 2, and the introductory part of this paragraph, and the United States President's assurance of May 20, 1964 that full consideration would be given to Japan's long established fishery for king crab.

**Appendix** [omitted]


## THE 1973 AGREEMENT RELATING TO FISHING FOR KING AND TANNER CRAB IN THE EASTERN BERING SEA (Union of Soviet Socialist Republics and United States of America)

Signed at Moscow on 21 February 1973; Entered into force on the same date. TIAS 7571. Replacing the Agreement of 5 February 1965 (U.N. Treaty Series, vol. 541, p. 97), as amended and extended by the Agreement of 13 February 1967 (U.N. Treaty Series, vol. 688, p. 428), the Agreement of 31 January 1969 (U.N. Treaty Series, vol. 714, p. 292) and the Agreement of 12 February 1971 (U.N. Treaty Series, vol. 781), and extended by an exchange of notes of 31 December 1972.

. . . . .

1. The king crab and tanner crab are natural resources of the continental shelf over which the coastal state exercises sovereign rights for the purposes of exploration and exploitation in accordance with the provisions of Article 2 of the Convention on the Continental Shelf.

2. Nationals and vessels of the Soviet Union may continue to carry out fishing for king and tanner crab on the continental shelf of the United States for a period of two years in that area of the eastern Bering Sea described in the Appendix to this Agreement, provided that the annual commercial catch of king crab and tanner crab by Soviet nationals and vessels in such area shall not exceed 260,000 king crabs and 4.2 million tanner crabs each in 1973 and 1974.

3. Each Government will apply the measures specified in paragraphs 3 and 4 of the Appendix to this Agreement to its nationals and vessels engaged in the king and tanner crab fisheries in the eastern Bering Sea. Either Government shall, if requested by the other Government, provide opportunity for observation of the conduct of enforcement of the provisions of this Agreement and for that purpose shall permit duly authorized officers of the other Governments to board its vessels engaged in the king and tanner crab fisheries in the eastern Bering Sea. These officers will make a report on the results of their observations; the report will be forwarded to the flag Government for appropriate action, if each action should be necessary.

4. The two Governments will continue and intensify their study of the king and tanner crab resources in the eastern Bering Sea and will exchange annually by November 30 the data resulting from such study including also, to the extent possible, an estimate of the maximum sustainable yield of the resources. The data to be furnished by each Government may be prepared in accordance with its own methodology and shall include, but not be limited to, the categories of data described in the Appendix to this Agreement. The two Governments will also provide for the exchange of scientific personnel engaged in the study of the king crab and tanner crab resources.

5. This Agreement . . . shall enter in force upon signature and shall remain in force for two years. At the request of either Government, representatives of the two Governments will meet at a mutually convenient time with a view to modifying the present Agreement. In any event, representatives of the two Governments will meet at a mutually convenient time prior to the expiration of the period of validity of this Agreement to review the operation of the Agreement and to decide on future arrangements.

**Appendix**

1. The area referred to in paragraph 2 of the Agreement is that portion

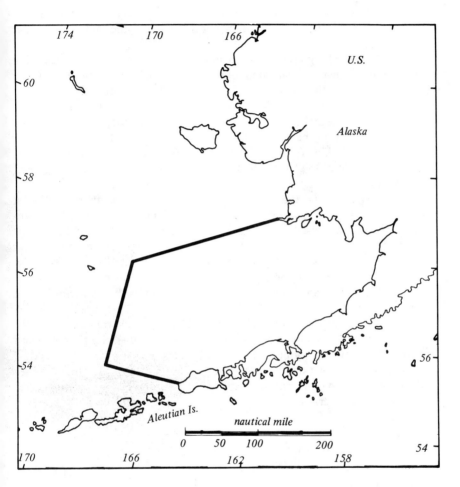

Source: Shigeru Oda

*Area of King and Tanner Crab Fishing (Agreement between Japan and U.S. and Agreement between U.S. and U.S.S.R.)*

489

of the southeastern Bering Sea lying seaward of the nine-mile zone contiguous to the territorial sea of the United States west of 160° West Longitude.

2. The annual commercial catch of king crab and tanner crab by Soviet nationals and vessels referred to in paragraph 2 of the Agreement shall not exceed:

*a.* 100,000 king crabs and 1.8 million tanner crabs in the area lying within the following designated boundaries: a line running from Cape Newenham on the Bering Sea coast of western Alaska, southwest to position 57°00′ North Latitude, 168°00′ West Longitude, thence due south to position 54°36′ North Latitude, 168°00′ West Longitude, and thence east to Cape Sarichef on the west coast of Unimak Island, Alaska.

*b.* 160,000 king crabs and 2.4 million tanner crabs in the area adjacent to the coast of the United States north and west of the area designated in subparagraph a.

3. *a.* Female king and tanner crabs, king crabs less than 15.8 cms. in maximum carapace width, and soft-shelled king and tanner crabs shall not be retained and used. Any such crabs taken incidentally, any king crabs taken in excess of the agreed quotas in each of the areas, and any tanner crabs taken in excess of the agreed quotas in each of the areas shall be returned immediately to the sea with a minimum of injury.

*b.* King crabs and tanner crabs shall not be taken by means of fishing gear other than pots.

4. Unless otherwise agreed by the two Governments, only pots may be used to capture king crabs and tanner crabs for commercial purposes and no trawling may be conducted for other species in that area lying seaward of the nine-mile zone contiguous to the territorial sea of the United States within the following boundaries: . . .

5. The data referred to in paragraph 4 of the Agreement are:

    *a.* Biological Data. . . .
    *b.* Catch Statistics. . . .
    *c.* Effort Statistics. . . .
    *d.* Production Statistics. . . .

# THE 1973 AGREEMENT RELATING TO THE CRAB FISHERIES IN THE NORTHWEST PACIFIC OCEAN (Japan and Union of Soviet Socialist Republics)

Exchange of Notes at Moscow on 11 May 1973. No English text is available; The English translation from the Japanese text of some parts of the Agreement is herewith reproduced.

1. The Government of Japan holds the view that crabs are high seas fishery resources, and that nationals and vessels of Japan are entitled to continue fishing for crabs in the Northwest Pacific Ocean.

2. The Government of the Union of Soviet Socialist Republics is of the view that crabs are natural resources of the continental shelf over which the coastal state (in this case the Union of Soviet Socialist Republics) exercises the sovereign rights for the purpose of exploring and exploiting its natural resources.

3. However, the two Governments, having regard to the fact that nationals and vessels of Japan have over a long period exploited the crab resources in the Northwest Pacific Ocean, have agreed, without prejudice to their respective positions, as follows:

(1) The fisheries for . . . crabs by nationals and vessels of Japan will continue in . . . . provided that the Government of Japan ensures that, in 1973, the following measures shall be taken with respect to the crab fisheries as mentioned above.

. . . .

# IV. REGIONAL CONSERVATION CONVENTIONS

## 1. ATLÀNTIC OCEAN

## THE 1949 INTERNATIONAL CONVENTION FOR THE NORTH-WEST ATLANTIC FISHERIES, AS AMENDED BY THE 1956, 1963, 1965 AND 1969 PROTOCOLS

> Signed at Washington on 8 February 1949; Entered into force on 3 July 1950 between Canada, Iceland, U.K. and U.S. U.N. Treaty Series, vol. 157, p. 157. Amended by the Protocol signed on 25 June 1956 and brought into force on 11 January 1959 (U.N. Treaty Series, vol. 331, p. 388), the Protocol relating to Measures of Control and the Protocol relating to Entry into Force of Proposals adopted by the Commission, signed on 29 November 1965 and brought into force on 19 December 1969, and the Protocol relating to Panel Membership and to Regulatory Measures, signed on 1 October 1969 and brought into force on 15 December 1971. See, also, the Protocol extending the Provisions of the Convention to Harp and Hood Seals, signed at Washington on 15 July 1963 and brought into force on 29 April 1966 (U.N. Treaty Series, vol. 590, p. 292) and Declaration of Understanding, signed at Washington on 24 April 1961 and brought into force on 5 June 1963 (U.N. Treaty Series, vol. 480, p. 334). The Protocol relating to Amendments to the Convention, signed on 6 October 1970, is not yet effective as of 31 December 1973. The Parties to the Convention as of 31 December 1973 are: Bulgaria, Canada, Denmark, France, Germany (Federal Rep. of), Iceland, Italy, Japan, Norway, Poland, Portugal, Romania, Spain, U.K., U.S. and U.S.S.R. France and Spain made reservations with respect to Article 1, para. 2.

The Governments ... have resolved to conclude a convention for the investigation, protection and conservation of the fisheries of the Northwest Atlantic Ocean, in order to make possible the maintenance of a maximum sustained catch from those fisheries and to that end have, through their duly authorized representatives, agreed as follows:

**Art. I.** 1. The area to which this Convention applies, hereinafter referred to as "the Convention area", shall be all waters, except territorial waters, bounded by a line ... [see the map on p. 513]

2. Nothing in this Convention shall be deemed to affect adversely (pre-

judice) the claims of any Contracting Government in regard to the limits of territorial waters or to the jurisdiction of a coastal state over fisheries.

3. The Convention area shall be divided into five sub-areas, the boundaries of which shall be those defined in the Annex to this Convention, subject to such alterations as may be made in accordance with the provisions of paragraph 2 of Article VI.

**Art. II.** 1. The Contracting Governments shall establish and maintain a Commission for the purposes of this Convention. The Commission shall be known as the International Commission for the Northwest Atlantic Fisheries, hereinafter referred to as "the Commission".

2. Each of the Contracting Governments may appoint not more than three Commissioners and one or more experts or advisers to assist its Commissioner or Commissioners.

3. The Commission shall elect from its members a Chairman and a Vice Chairman, each of whom shall serve for a term of two years and shall be eligible for re-election but not to a succeeding term. The Chairman and Vice Chairman must be Commissioners from different Contracting Governments.

4. The seat of the Commission shall be in North America at a place to be chosen by the Commission.

5. The Commission shall hold a regular annual meeting at its seat or at such other place in North America or elsewhere as may be agreed upon by the Commission.

6. Any other meeting of the Commission may be called by the Chairman at such time and place as he may determine, upon the request of the Commissioner of a Contracting Government and subject to the concurrence of the Commissioners of two other Contracting Governments, including the Commissioner of a Government in North America.

7. Each Contracting Government shall have one vote which may be cast by any Commissioner from that Government. Decisions of the Commission shall be taken by a two-thirds majority of the votes of all the Contracting Governments.

8. The Commission shall adopt, and amend as occasion may require, financial regulations and rules and by-laws for the conduct of its meetings and for the exercise of its functions and duties.

**Art. III.** 1. The Commission shall appoint an Executive Secretary according to such procedure and on such terms as it may determine.

2. The staff of the Commission shall be appointed by the Executive Secretary in accordance with such rules and procedures as may be determined and authorized by the Commission.

3. The Executive Secretary shall, subject to the general supervision of the Commission, have full power and authority over the staff and shall

perform such other functions as the Commission shall prescribe.

**Art. IV.** 1. The Contracting Governments shall establish and maintain a Panel for each of the sub-areas provided for by Article I, in order to carry out the objectives of this Convention. Each Contracting Government participating in any Panel shall be represented on such Panel by its Commissioner or Commissioners, who may be assisted by experts or advisers. Each Panel shall elect from its members a Chairman who shall serve for a period of two years and shall be eligible for re-election but not to a succeeding term.

2. Panel representation shall be reviewed annually by the Commission, which shall have the power, subject to consultation with the Panel concerned, to determine representation on each Panel on the basis of current substantial exploitation of the stocks of fish in the subarea concerned or on the basis of current substantial exploitation of harp and hood seals in the Convention Area, except that each Contracting Government with coastline adjacent to a subarea shall have the right of representation on the Panel for the subarea.

3. Each Panel may adopt, and amend as occasion may require, rules of procedure and by-laws for the conduct of its meetings and for the exercise of its functions and duties.

4. Each Government participating in a Panel shall have one vote, which shall be cast by a Commissioner representing that Government. Decisions of the Panel shall be taken by a two-thirds majority of the votes of all the Governments participating in that Panel.

5. Commissioners of Contracting Governments not participating in a particular Panel shall have the right to attend the meetings of such Panel as observers, and may be accompanied by experts and advisers.

6. The Panels shall, in the exercise of their functions and duties, use the services of the Executive Secretary and the staff of the Commission.

**Art. V.** 1. Each Contracting Government may set up an Advisory Committee composed of persons, including fishermen, vessel owners and others, well informed concerning the problems of the fisheries of the Northwest Atlantic Ocean. With the assent of the Contracting Government concerned, a representative or representatives of an Advisory Committee may attend as observers all non-executive meetings of the Commission or of any Panel in which their Government participates.

2. The Commissioners of each Contracting Government may hold public hearings within the territories they represent.

**Art. VI.** 1. The Commission shall be responsible in the field of scientific investigation for obtaining and collating the information necessary for maintaining those stocks of fish which support international fisheries in the Convention area and the Commission may, through or in collaboration with agencies of the Contracting Governments or other public or private agencies and organizations or, when necessary, independently:

(a) make such investigations as it finds necessary into the abundance, life history and ecology of any species of aquatic life in any part of the Northwest Atlantic Ocean;

(b) collect and analyze statistical information relating to the current conditions and trends of the fishery resources of the Northwest Atlantic Ocean;

(c) study and appraise information concerning the methods for maintaining and increasing stocks of fish in the Northwest Atlantic Ocean;

(d) hold or arrange such hearings as may be useful or essential in connection with the development of complete factual information necessary to carry out the provisions of this Convention;

(e) conduct fishing operations in the Convention area at any time for purposes of scientific investigation;

(f) publish and otherwise disseminate reports of its findings and statistical, scientific and other information relating to the fisheries of the Northwest Atlantic Ocean as well as such other reports as fall within the scope of this Convention.

2. Upon the unanimous recommendation of each Panel affected, the Commission may alter the boundaries of the sub-areas set out in the Annex. Any such alteration shall forthwith be reported to the Depositary Government which shall inform the Contracting Governments, and the sub-areas defined in the Annex shall be altered accordingly.

3. The Contracting Governments shall furnish to the Commission, at such time and in such form as may be required by the Commission, the statistical information referred to in paragraph 1 (b) of this Article.

**Art. VII.** 1. Each Panel established under Article IV shall be responsible for keeping under review the fisheries of its sub-area and the scientific and other information relating thereto.

2. Each Panel, upon the basis of scientific investigations, and economical and technical considerations, may make recommendations to the Commission for joint action by the Contracting Governments within the scope of paragraph 1 of Article VIII.

3. Each Panel may recommend to the Commission studies and investigations within the scope of this Convention which are deemed necessary in the development of factual information relating to its particular sub-area.

4. Any Panel may make recommendations to the Commission for the alteration of the boundaries of the sub-areas defined in the Annex.

5. Each Panel shall investigate and report to the Commission upon any

matter referred to it by the Commission.

6. A Panel shall not incur any expenditure except in accordance with directions given by the Commission.

**Art. VIII.** 1. The Commission may, on the recommendations of one or more Panels, and on the basis of scientific investigations, and economic and technical considerations, transmit to the Depositary Government appropriate proposals, for joint action by the Contracting Governments, designed to achieve the optimum utilization of the stocks of those species of fish which support international fisheries in the Convention Area.

2. Each recommendation shall be studied by the Commission and thereafter the Commission shall either

(*a*) transmit the recommendation as a proposal to the Depositary Government with such modifications or suggestions as the Commission may consider desirable, or

(*b*) refer the recommendation back to the Panel with comments for its reconsideration.

3. The Panel may, after reconsidering the recommendation returned to it by the Commission, reaffirm that recommendation, with or without modification.

4. If, after a recommendation is reaffirmed, the Commission is unable to adopt the recommendation as a proposal, it shall send a copy of the recommendation to the Depositary Government with a report of the Commission's decision. The Depositary Government shall transmit copies of the recommendation and of the Commission's report to the Contracting Governments.

5. The Commission may, after consultation with all the Panels, transmit proposals to the Depositary Government within the scope of paragraph 1 of this Article affecting the Convention area as a whole and may also, on its own initiative, make proposals for national and international measures of control on the high seas for the purposes of ensuring the application of the Convention and the measures in force thereunder.

6. The Depositary Government shall transmit any proposal received by it to the Contracting Governments for their consideration and may make such suggestions as will facilitate acceptance of the proposal.

7. (*a*) Each proposal made by the Commission under paragraphs 1 or 5 of this Article shall become effective for all Contracting Governments six months after the date on the notification from the Depositary Government transmitting the proposal to the Contracting Governments, except as otherwise provided herein.

(*b*) If any Contracting Government participating in the Panel or Panels for the sub-area or sub-areas to which a proposal applies, or any Contracting Government in the case of a proposal made under paragraph 5

496

above, presents to the Depositary Government objection to any proposal within six months of the date on the notification of the proposal by the Depositary Government, the proposal shall not become effective for any Government for an additional sixty days. Thereupon any other Contracting Government participating in the Panel or Panels concerned, or any other Contracting Government in the case of a proposal made under paragraph 5 above, may similarly object prior to the expiration of the additional sixty-day period, or within thirty days after receiving notice of an objection by another Contracting Government made within such additional sixty days, whichever date shall be the later. The proposal shall become effective for all Contracting Governments except those Governments which have presented objections, at the end of the extended period or periods for objecting. If, however, objections have been presented by a majority of Contracting Governments participating in the Panel or Panels concerned, or by a majority of all Contracting Governments in the case of a proposal made under paragraph 5, the proposal shall not become effective unless any or all of the Contracting Governments nevertheless agree as among themselves to give effect to it on an agreed date.

(c) Any Contracting Government which has objected to a proposal may at any time withdraw that objection and the proposal shall become effective with respect to such Government, immediately if the proposal is already in effect, or at such time as it becomes effective under the terms of this Article.

8. The Depositary Government shall notify each Contracting Government immediately upon receipt of each objection and of each withdrawal of objection, and of the entry into force of any proposal.

9. At any time after the expiration of one year from the date on which a proposal becomes effective, any Panel Government for the sub-area to which the proposal applies may give to the Depositary Government notice of the termination of its acceptance of the proposal and, if that notice is not withdrawn, the proposal shall cease to be effective for that Panel Government at the end of one year from the date of receipt of the notice by the Depositary Government. At any time after a proposal has ceased to be effective for a Panel Government under this paragraph, the proposal shall cease to be effective for any other Contracting Government upon the date a notice of withdrawal by such Government is received by the Depositary Government. The Depositary Government shall notify all Contracting Governments of every notice under this paragraph immediately upon the receipt thereof.

**Art. IX.** The Commission may invite the attention of any or all Contracting Governments to any matters which relate to the objectives and purposes of this Convention.

**Art. X.** 1. The Commission shall seek to establish and maintain working arrangements with other public international organizations which have related objectives, particularly the Food and Agriculture Organization of the United Nations and the International Council for the Exploration of the Sea, to ensure effective collaboration and coordination with respect to their work and, in the case of the International Council for the Exploration of the Sea, the avoidance of duplication of scientific investigations.

2. The Commission shall consider, at the expiration of two years from the date of entry into force of this Convention, whether or not it should recommend to the Contracting Governments that the Commission be brought within the framework of a specialized agency of the United Nations.

**Art. XI.** 1. Each Contracting Government shall pay the expenses of the Commissioners, experts and advisers appointed by it.

2. The Commission shall prepare an annual administrative budget of the proposed necessary administrative expenditures of the Commission and an annual special projects budget of proposed expenditures on special studies and investigations to be undertaken by or on behalf of the Commission pursuant to Article VI or by or on behalf of any Panel pursuant to Article VII.

3. The Commission shall calculate the payments due from each Contracting Government under the annual administrative budget according to the following formula:

(*a*) from the administrative budget there shall be deducted a sum of 500 United States dollars for each Contracting Government;

(*b*) the remainder shall be divided into such number of equal shares as corresponds to the total number of Panel memberships;

(*c*) the payment due from any Contracting Government shall be the equivalent of 500 United States dollars plus the number of shares equal to the number of Panels in which that Government participates.

4. The Commission shall notify each Contracting Government the sum due from that Government as calculated under paragraph 3 of this Article and as soon as possible thereafter each Contracting Government shall pay to the Commission the sum so notified.

5. The annual special projects budget shall be allocated to the Contracting Governments according to a scale to be determined by agreement among the Contracting Governments, and the sums so allocated to any Contracting Government shall be paid to the Commission by that Government.

6. Contributions shall be payable in the currency of the country in which the seat of the Commission is located, except that the Commission may accept payment in the currencies in which it may be anticipated that ex-

498

penditures of the Commission will be made from time to time, up to an amount established each year by the Commission in connection with the preparation of the annual budgets.

7. At its first meeting the Commission shall approve an administrative budget for the balance of the first financial year in which the Commission functions and shall transmit to the Contracting Governments copies of that budget together with notices of their respective allocations.

8. In subsequent financial years, the Commission shall submit to each Contracting Government drafts of the annual budgets together with a schedule of allocations, not less than six weeks before the annual meeting of the Commission at which the budgets are to be considered.

**Art. XII.** The Contracting Governments agree to take such action as may be necessary to make effective the provisions of this Convention and to implement any proposals which become effective under paragraph 8 of Article VIII. Each Contracting Government shall transmit to the Commission a statement of the action taken by it for these purposes.

**Art. XIII.** The Contracting Governments agree to invite the attention of any Government not a party to this Convention to any matter relating to the fishing activities in the Convention area of the national or vessels of that Government which appear to affect adversely the operations of the Commission or the carrying out of the objectives of this Convention.

**Art. XIV.** The Annex, as attached to this Convention and as modified from time to time, forms an integral part of this Convention.

**Art. XV.** . . .

3. Any Government which has not signed this Convention may adhere thereto by a notification in writing to the Depositary Government. Adherences received by the Depositary Government prior to the date of entry into force of this Convention shall become effective on the date this Convention enters into force. Adherences received by the Depositary Government after the date of entry into force of this Convention shall become effective on the date of receipt by the Depositary Government.

. . . . .

**Art. XVI.** 1. At any time after the expiration of ten years from the date of entry into force of this Convention, any Contracting Government may withdraw from the Convention on December thirty-first of any year by giving notice on or before the preceding June thirtieth to the Depositary Government which shall communicate copies of such notice to the other Contracting Governments.

2. Any other Contracting Government may thereupon withdraw from this Convention on the same December thirty-first by giving notice to the

Depositary Government within one month of the receipt of a copy of a notice of withdrawal given pursuant to paragraph 1 of this Article.

**Art. XVII.** . . .

**Annex**

1. The sub-areas provided for by Article I of this Convention shall be as follows: . . . (see the map on p. 513)

2. For a period of two years the date of entry into force of this Convention, Panel representation for each sub-area shall be as follows:

(*a*) *Sub-area 1*—Denmark, France, Italy, Norway, Portugal, Spain, *United Kingdom;*

(*b*) *Sub-area 2*—Denmark, France, Italy, Newfoundland;

(*c*) *Sub-area 3*—Canada, Denmark, France, Italy, Newfoundland, Portugal, Spain, United Kingdom;

(*d*) *Sub-area 4*—Canada, France, Italy, Newfoundland, Portugal, Spain, United States;

(*e*) *Sub-area 5*—Canada, United States;

. . . . .

**Protocol Extending the Provisions of the Convention to Harp and Hood Seals**

**Art. I.** The provisions of the Convention shall be applicable with respect to harp and hood seals in conformity with Articles II and III of this Protocol.

**Art. II.** 1. The Contracting Governments shall establish and maintain a Panel with jurisdiction respecting harp and hood seals in the Convention area. Initial representation on the Panel shall be determined by the International Commission for the Northwest Atlantic Fisheries on the basis of current substantial exploitation of harp and hood seals in the Convention area, except that each Contracting Government with coastline adjacent to the Convention area shall have the right to representation on the Panel.

2. Panel representation shall be reviewed annually by the Commission, which shall have the power, subject to consultation with the Panel, to determine representation on the Panel on the same basis as provided in paragraph 1 of this Article for initial representation.

**Art. III.** Proposals in accordance with Article VIII of the Convention for joint action by Contracting Governments with respect to harp and hood seals shall become effective for all Contracting Governments four months after the date on which notifications of acceptance have been received by the Depositary Government from all the Contracting Governments participating in the Panel for harp and hood seals.

500

## Declaration of Understanding

The Governments parties to the International Convention for the Northwest Atlantic Fisheries signed at Washington under date of February 8, 1949, which Convention is hereinafter referred to as the Convention, hereby declare their understanding that the words "fish", "fishes", "fishery", "fisheries", and "fishing" as they appear in the Convention include and apply to mollusks, as well as finny fish.

## Protocol Relating to Amendments to the Convention (not effective)

Article XVII of the Convention is renumbered "Article XVIII" and a new Article XVII is inserted to read as follows:

**Art. XVII.** 1. Any Contracting Government or the Commission may propose amendments to this Convention to be considered and acted upon by a regular meeting of the Commission or by a special meeting of the Commission called in accordance with the provisions of paragraph 6 of Article II of the Convention. Any such proposed amendment shall be sent to the Executive Secretary at least ninety days prior to the meeting at which it is proposed to be acted upon, and he shall immediately transmit the proposal to all Contracting Governments and to all Commissioners.

2. A proposed amendment to the Convention shall be adopted by the Commission by a three-fourths majority of the votes of all Contracting Governments. The text of any proposed amendment so adopted shall be transmitted by the Depositary Government to all Contracting Governments.

3. Any amendment shall take effect for all Contracting Governments one hundred and twenty days following the date on the notification by the Depositary Government of receipt of written notification of approval by three-fourths of all Contracting Governments unless any other Contracting Government notifies the Depositary Government that it objects to the amendment, within ninety days of the date on the notification by the Depositary Government of such receipt, in which case the amendment shall not take effect for any Contracting Government. Any Contracting Government which has objected to an amendment may at any time withdraw that objection. If all objections to an amendment are withdrawn, the amendment shall take effect for all Contracting Governments one hundred and twenty days following the date on the notification by the Depositary Government of receipt of the last withdrawal.

4. Any Government which becomes a party to the Convention after an amendment has been adopted in accordance with paragraph 2 of this Article shall be deemed to have approved the said amendment.

5. The Depositary Government shall promptly notify all Contracting

Governments of the receipts of notifications of approval of amendments, the receipt of notifications of objection or withdrawal of objections, and the entry into force of amendments.

## THE 1959 NORTH-EAST ATLANTIC FISHERIES CONVENTION

Signed at London on 24 January 1959; Entered into force on 27 June 1963 between Belgium, Denmark, France, Germany (Fed. Rep. of), Iceland, Ireland, Netherlands, Norway, Poland, Portugal, Spain, Sweden, U.K. and U.S.S.R. U.N. Treaty Series, vol. 486, p. 157. The Parties to the Convention as of 31 December 1973 are those countries as mentioned above. In depositing the instruments of ratification, the Governments of Belgium and Netherlands declared reservations with regard to Article 7, paragraph 1 (*c*) to (*f*) inclusive. *Cf*. The 1946 Convention for the Regulation of the Meshes of Fishing Nets and the Size Limits of Fish, as amended. U.N. Treaty Series, vol. 231, p. 199; vol. 354, p. 408; vol. 431, p. 304; vol. 456, p. 496; vol. 482, p. 372.

. . . . .

**Art. 1.** (1) The area to which this Convention applies (hereinafter referred to as "the Convention area") shall be all waters which are situated

(*a*) within those parts of the Atlantic and Arctic Oceans and their dependent seas which lie north of 36° north latitude and between 42° west longitude and 51° east longitude, but excluding

(i) the Baltic Sea and Belts lying to the south and east of lines drawn from Hasenore Head to Gniben Point, from Korshage to Spodsbierg and from Gilbierg Head to the Kullen, and

(ii) the Mediterranean Sea and its dependent seas as far as the point of intersection of the parallel of 36° latitude and the meridian of 5°36′ west longitude.

(*b*) within that part of the Atlantic Ocean north of 59° north latitude and between 44° west longitude and 42° west longitude.

(2) The Convention area shall be divided into regions, the boundaries of which shall be those defined in the Annex to this Convention. The regions shall be subject to such alterations as may be made in accordance with the provisions of paragraph (4) of Article 5 of this Convention.

(3) For the purposes of this Convention

(*a*) the expression "vessel" means any vessel or boat employed in fishing for sea fish or in the treatment of sea fish which is registered or owned in the territories of, or which flies the flag of, any Contracting State; and

    (*b*) the expression "territories", in relation to any Contracting State, extends to

    (i)  any territory within or adjacent to the Convention area for whose international relations the Contracting State is responsible;

    (ii)  any other territory, not situated within the Convention area or adjacent to it, for whose international relations the Contracting State is responsible and for which such State shall have made known, by written declaration to the Government of the United Kingdom of Great Britain and Northern Ireland (hereinafter referred to as the Government of the United Kingdom), either at the time of signature, of ratification, or of adherence, or subsequently, that this Convention shall apply to it;

    (iii)  the waters within the Convention area where the Contracting State has exclusive jurisdiction over fisheries.

**Art. 2.** Nothing in this Convention shall be deemed to affect the rights, claims, or views of any Contracting State in regard to the extent of jurisdiction over fisheries.

**Art. 3.** (1) A Noth-East Atlantic Fisheries Commission (hereinafter referred to as the Commission) is hereby established and shall be maintained for the purposes of this Convention.

(2) Each Contracting State may appoint as its Delegation to the Commission not more than two Commissioners and such experts and advisers to assist them as that State may determine.

(3) The Commission shall elect its own President and not more than two Vice-Presidents who need not be chosen from the Commissioners or their experts or advisers. If a member of a Delegation has been elected President he shall forthwith cease to act as a member of that Delegation, and if a Commissioner has been elected the State concerned shall have the right to appoint another person to serve in his place.

(4) The Office of the Commission shall be in London.

(5) Except where the Commission determines otherwise, it shall meet once a year in London at such time as it shall decide: provided, however, that upon the request of a Commissioner of a Contracting State and subject to the concurrence of a Commissioner of each of three other Contracting States, the President shall, as soon as practicable, summon a meeting at such time and place as he may determine.

(6) The Commission shall appoint its own Secretary and may from time to time appoint such other staff as it may require.

(7) The Commission may set up such Committees as it considers de-

sirable to perform such functions as it may determine.

(8) Each Delegation shall have one vote in the Commission which may be cast only by a Commissioner of the State concerned. Decisions shall be taken by a simple majority except where otherwise specifically provided. If there is an even division of votes on any matter which is subject to a simple majority decision, the proposal shall be regarded as rejected.

(9) Subject to the provisions of this Article, the Commission shall draw up its own Rules of Procedure, including provisions for the election of the President and Vice-Presidents and their terms of office.

(10) The Government of the United Kingdom shall call the first meeting of the Commission as soon as practicable after the coming into force of this Convention, and shall communicate the provisional agenda to each of the other Contracting States not less than two months before the date of the meeting.

(11) Reports of the proceedings of the Commission shall be transmitted and proposals and recommendations shall be notified as soon as possible to all Contracting States in English and in French.

**Art. 4.** (1) Each Contracting State shall pay the expenses of the Commissioners, experts and advisers appointed by it.

(2) The Commission shall prepare an annual budget of the proposed expenditures of the Commission.

(3) In any year in which the annual budget amounts to £200 or less for each Contracting State, the total sum shall be shared equally between Contracting States.

(4) In any year in which the annual budget exceeds £200 for each Contracting State, the Commission shall calculate the payments due from each Contracting State according to the following formula:

(*a*) from the budget there shall be deducted a sum of £200 for each Contracting State;

(*b*) the remainder shall be divided into such number of equal shares as correspond to the total number of Regional Committee memberships;

(*c*) the payment due from any Contracting State shall be the equivalent of £200 plus the number of shares equal to the number of Regional Committees in which that State participates.

(5) The Commission shall notify to each Contracting State the sum due from that State as calculated under paragraph (3) or (4) of this Article and as soon as possible thereafter each Contracting State shall pay to the Commission the sum so notified.

(6) Contributions shall be payable in the currency of the country in which the Office of the Commission is located, except that the Commission may accept payment in the currencies in which it may be expected that expenditures of the Commission will be made from time to time, up to an

504

amount established each year by the Commission when preparing the annual budget.

(7) At its first meeting the Commission shall approve a budget for the balance of the first financial year in which the Commission functions and shall transmit to the Contracting States copies of that budget together with notices of their respective contributions as assessed under paragraph (3) or (4) of this Article.

(8) In subsequent financial years, the Commission shall submit to each Contracting State drafts of annual budgets, together with a schedule of allocations, not less than six weeks before the annual meeting of the Commission at which the budgets are to be considered.

**Art. 5.** (1) The Commission shall establish a Regional Committee, with the powers and duties described in Article 6 of this Convention, for each of the regions into which the Convention area is divided.

(2) The representation on any Regional Committee so established shall be determined by the Commission, provided, however, that any Contracting State with a coastline adjacent to that region, or exploiting the fisheries of the region, has automatically the right of representation on the Regional Committee. Contracting States exploiting elsewhere a stock which is also fished in that region shall have the opportunity of being represented on the Regional Committee.

(3) Subject to the provisions of Article 6 of this Convention, the Commission shall determine the terms of reference of, and the procedure to be followed by, each Regional Committee.

(4) The Commission may at any time alter the boundaries and vary the number of the regions defined in the Annex to this Convention, provided this is by the unanimous decision of the Delegations present and voting and no objection is made within three months thereafter by any Contracting State not represented, or not voting, at the meeting.

**Art. 6.** (1) It shall be the duty of the Commission:

(*a*) to keep under review the fisheries in the Convention area;

(*b*) to consider, in the light of the technical information available, what measures may be required for the conservation of the fish stocks and for the rational exploitation of the fisheries in the area;

(*c*) to consider, at the request of any Contracting State, representations made to it by a State which is not a party to this Convention for the opening of negotiations on the conservation of fish stocks in the Convention area or any part thereof; and

(*d*) to make to Contracting States recommendations, based as far as practicable on the results of scientific research and investigation, with regard to any of the measures set out in Article 7 of this Convention.

(2) It shall be the duty of a Regional Committee to perform, in relation

to its Region, functions of review and consideration similar to those described in paragraph (1) of this Article in relation to the Commission and the Convention area. A Regional Committee may initiate proposals for measures in relation to its region and shall consider any such proposals as may be remitted to it by the Commission.

(3) A Regional Committee may prepare draft recommendations for consideration by the Commission, which may adopt any such draft recommendations, with any modifications it may consider desirable, as recommendations for the purpose of Article 7 of this Convention.

(4) A Regional Committee may at any time appoint sub-committees to study specific problems affecting parts of the Region and to report thereon to the Regional Committee.

**Art. 7.** (1) The measures relating to the objectives and purposes of this Convention which the Commission and Regional Committees may consider, and on which the Commission may make recommendations to the Contracting States, are

(a) any measures for the regulation of the size of mesh of fishing nets;

(b) any measures for the regulation of the size limits of fish that may be retained on board vessels, or landed, or exposed or offered for sale;

(c) any measures for the establishment of closed seasons;

(d) any measures for the establishment of closed areas;

(e) any measures for the regulation of fishing gear and appliances, other than regulation of the size of mesh of fishing nets;

(f) any measures for the improvement and the increase of marine resources, which may include artificial propagation, the transplantation of organisms and the transplantation of young.

(2) Measures for regulating the amount of total catch, or the amount of fishing effort in any period, or any other kinds of measures for the purpose of the conservation of the fish stocks in the Convention area, may be added to the measures listed in paragraph (1) of this Article on a proposal adopted by not less than a two-thirds majority of the Delegations present and voting and subsequently accepted by all Contracting States in accordance with their respective constitutional procedures.

(3) The measures provided for in paragraph (1) and (2) of this Article may relate to any or all species of sea fish and shell fish, but not to sea mammals; to any or all methods of fishing; and to any or all parts of the Convention area.

**Art. 8.** (1) Subject to the provisions of this Article, the Contracting States undertake to give effect to any recommendation made by the Commission under Article 7 of this Convention and adopted by not less than a two-thirds majority of the Delegations present and voting.

(2) Any Contracting State may, within ninety days of the date of notice

of a recommendation to which paragraph (1) of this Article applies, object to it and in that event shall not be under obligation to give effect to the recommendation.

(3) In the event of an objection being made within the ninety-day period, any other Contracting State may similarly object at any time within a further period of sixty days, or within thirty days after receiving notice of an objection by another Contracting State made within the further period of sixty days.

(4) If objections to a recommendation are made by three or more of the Contracting States, all the other Contracting States shall be relieved forthwith of any obligation to give effect to that recommendation but any or all of them may nevertheless agree among themselves to give effect to it.

(5) Any Contracting State which has objected to a recommendation may at any time withdraw that objection and shall then, subject to the provisions of paragraph (4) of this Article, give effect to the recommendation within ninety days, or as from the date determined by the Commission under Article 9 of this Convention, whichever is the later.

(6) The Commission shall notify each Contracting State immediately upon receipt of each objection and withdrawal.

**Art. 9.** Any recommendation to which paragraph (1) of Article 8 of this Convention applies shall, subject to the provisions of that Article, become binding on the Contracting States from the date determined by the Commission, which shall not be before the period for objection provided in Article 8 has elapsed.

**Art. 10.** (1) At any time after two years from the date on which it has been required to give effect to any recommendation to which paragraph (1) of Article 8 of this Convention applies, any Contracting State may give the Commission notice of the termination of its acceptance of the recommendation and, if that notice is not withdrawn, the recommendation shall cease to be binding on that Contracting State at the end of twelve months from the date of the notice.

(2) At any time after a recommendation has ceased to be binding on a Contracting State under paragraph (1) of this Article, the recommendation shall cease to be binding on any other Contracting State which so desires upon the date of notice to the Commission of withdrawal of acceptance of that recommendation by such other State.

(3) The Commission shall notify all Contracting States of every notice under this Article immediately upon the receipt thereof.

**Art. 11.** (1) In order that the recommendations made by the Commission for the conservation of the stocks of fish within the Convention area shall be based so far as practicable upon the results of scientific research and

507

investigation, the Commission shall when possible seek the advice of the International Council for the Exploration of the Sea and the co-operation of the Council in carrying out any necessary investigations and, for this purpose, may make such joint arrangements as may be agreed with the International Council for the Exploration of the Sea or may make such other arrangements as it may think fit.

(2) The Commission may seek to establish and maintain working arrangements with any other international organisation which has related objectives.

**Art. 12.** (1) The Contracting States undertake to furnish on the request of the Commission any available statistical and biological information the Commission may need for the purposes of this Convention.

(2) The Commission may publish or otherwise disseminate reports of its activities and such other information relating to the fisheries in the Convention area or any part of that area as it may deem appropriate.

**Art. 13.** (1) Without prejudice to the sovereign rights of States in regard to their territorial and internal waters, each Contracting State shall take in its territories and in regard to its own nationals and its own vessels appropriate measures to ensure the application of the provisions of this Convention and of the recommendations of the Commission which have become binding on that Contracting State and the punishment of infractions of the said provisions and recommendations.

(2) Each Contracting State shall transmit annually to the Commission a statement of the action taken by it for these purposes.

(3) The Commission may by a two-thirds majority make recommendations for, on the one hand, measures of national control in the territories of the Contracting States and, on the other hand, national and international measures of control on the high seas, for the purpose of ensuring the application of the Convention and the measures in force thereunder. Such recommendations shall be subject to the provisions of Articles 8, 9 and 10.

**Art. 14.** The provisions of this Convention shall not apply to fishing operations conducted solely for the purpose of scientific investigations by vessels authorised by a Contracting State for that purpose, or to fish taken in the course of such operations, but in any of the territories of any Contracting State bound by a recommendation to which paragraph (1) of Article 8 applies, fish so taken shall not be sold or exposed or offered for sale in contravention of any such recommendation.

**Art. 15.** ...

(3) Any State which has not signed this Convention may accede thereto at any time after it has come into force in accordance with paragraph (2) of this Article. Accession shall be effected by means of a notice in writing

addressed to the Government of the United Kingdom and shall take effect on the date of its receipt. Any State which accedes to this Convention shall simultaneously undertake to give effect to those recommendations which are, at the time of its accession, binding on all the other Contracting States as well as to any other recommendations which are, at that time, binding on one or more of the Contracting States and are not specifically excluded by the acceding State in its notice of accession.

(4) The Government of the United Kingdom shall inform all signatory and acceding States of all ratifications deposited and accessions received and shall notify signatory States of the date and the States in respect of which this Convention enters into force.

**Art. 16.** (1) In respect of each State Party to this Convention, the provisions of Articles 5, 6, 7, 8 and 9 and Annexes I, II and III of the Convention for the Regulation of the Meshes of Fishing Nets and the Size Limits of Fish, signed at London, on 5th April, 1946, as amended by decisions made under paragraph (10) of Article 12 of that Convention, shall remain in force but shall be deemed for the purposes of the present Convention to be a recommendation made and given effect without objection under this Convention as from the date of its entry into force in respect of that State within the area covered by the 1946 Convention; provided that in the period of two years after the coming into force of this Convention, any Contracting State may, on giving twelve month's written notice to the Government of the United Kingdom, withdraw from the whole or any part of the said recommendation. If a Contracting State has, in accordance with the provisions of this Article, given notice of its withdrawal from a part of the said recommendation, any other Contracting State may, with effect from the same date, give notice of its withdrawal from the same or any other part of the said recommendation, or from the recommendation as a whole.

(2) The provisions of the Convention for the Regulation of the Meshes of Fishing Nets and the Size Limits of Fish signed at London on 5th April, 1946, shall, save as provided in paragraph (1) of this Article, cease to apply to each Contracting State to this Convention as from the date of the entry into force of this Convention in respect of that State.

**Art. 17.** At any time after two years from the date on which this Convention has come into force with respect to a Contracting State, that State may denounce the Convention by means of a notice in writing addressed to the Government of the United Kingdom. Any such denunciation shall take effect twelve months after the date of its receipt, and shall be notified to the Contracting States by the Government of the United Kingdom.

**Annex**

The regions provided for by Article 1 of this Convention shall be as follows: ... (see the map on p. 513)

## THE 1964 CONVENTION FOR THE INTERNATIONAL COUNCIL FOR THE EXPLORATION OF THE SEA

Signed at Copenhagen on 12 September 1964; Entered into force on 22 July 1968. U.N. Treaty Series, vol. 652, p. 237. The Parties to this Agreement as of 31 December 1973 are: Belgium, Canada, Denmark, Finland, France, Germany (Federal Rep. of), Iceland, Ireland, Italy, Netherlands, Norway, Poland, Portugal, Spain, Sweden, U.K., U.S. and U.S.S.R.

The Governments of the States Parties to this Convention

Having participated in the work of the International Council for the Exploration of the Sea, which was established at Copenhagen in 1902 as a result of conferences held in Stockholm in 1899 and in Christiania in 1901 and entrusted with the task of carrying out a programme of international investigation of the sea

Desiring to provide a new constitution for the aforesaid Council with a view to facilitating the implementation of its programme

Have agreed as follows:

**Art. 1.** It shall be the duty of the International Council for the Exploration of the Sea, hereinafter referred to as the "Council",

(*a*) to promote and encourage research and investigations for the study of the sea particularly those related to the living resources thereof;

(*b*) to draw up programmes required for this purpose and to organise, in agreement with the Contracting Parties, such research and investigation as may appear necessary;

(*c*) to publish or otherwise disseminate the results of research and investigations carried out under its auspices or to encourage the publication thereof.

**Art. 2.** The Council shall be concerned with the Atlantic Ocean and its adjacent seas and primarily concerned with the North Atlantic.

**Art. 3.** (1) The Council shall be maintained in accordance with the provisions of this Convention.

(2) The seat of the Council shall remain at Copenhagen.

**Art. 4.** The Council shall seek to establish and maintain working arrange-

510

ments with other international organisations which have related objectives and cooperate, as far as possible, with them, in particular in the supply of scientific information requested.

**Art. 5.** The Contracting Parties undertake to furnish to the Council information which will contribute to the purposes of this Convention and can reasonably be made available and, wherever possible, to assist in carrying out the programmes of research coordinated by the Council.

**Art. 6.** (1) Each Contracting Party shall be represented at the Council by not more than two delegates.

(2) A delegate who is not present at a meeting of the Council may be replaced by a substitute who shall have all the powers of the delegate for that meeting.

(3) Each Contracting Party may appoint such experts and advisers as it may determine to assist in the work of the Council.

**Art. 7.** (1) The Council shall meet in ordinary session once a year. This session shall be held in Copenhagen, unless the Council decides otherwise.

(2) Extraordinary sessions of the Council may be called by the Bureau at such place and time as it may determine and shall be so called on the request of at least one-third of the Contracting Parties.

**Art. 8.** (1) Each Contracting Party shall have one vote in the Council.

(2) Decisions of the Council shall, except where otherwise in this Convention specially provided, be taken by a simple majority of the votes cast for or against. If there is an even division of votes on any matter which is subject to a simple majority decision the proposal shall be regarded as rejected.

**Art. 9.** (1) Subject to the provisions of this Convention the Council shall draw up its own Rules of Procedure which shall be adopted by a two-thirds majority of the Contracting Parties.

(2) English and French shall be the working languages of the Council.

**Art. 10.** (1) The Council shall elect from among the delegates its President, a first Vice-President and a further 5 Vice-Presidents. This last number may be augmented by a decision taken by the Council by a two-thirds majority.

(2) The President and the Vice-Presidents shall assume office on the first day of November next following their election, for a term of three years. They are eligible for re-election according to the Rules of Procedure.

(3) On assuming office the President shall cease forthwith to be a delegate.

**Art. 11.** (1) The President and Vice-Presidents shall together constitute the Bureau of the Council.

511

(2) The Bureau shall be the Executive Committee of the Council and shall carry out the decisions of the Council, draw up its agenda and convene its meetings. It shall also prepare the budget. It shall invest the reserve funds and carry out the tasks entrusted to it by the Council. It shall account to the Council for its activities.

**Art. 12.** There shall be a Consultative Committee, a Finance Committee and such other committees as the Council may deem necessary for the discharge of its functions with the duties respectively assigned to them in the Rules of Procedure.

**Art. 13.** (1) The Council shall appoint a General Secretary on such terms and to perform such duties as it may determine.

(2) Subject to any general directions of the Council the Bureau shall appoint such other staff as may be required for the purposes of the Council on such terms and to perform such duties as it may determine.

**Art. 14.** (1) Each Contracting Party shall pay the expenses of the delegates, experts and advisers appointed by it, except in so far as the Council may otherwise determine.

(2) The Council shall approve an annual budget of the proposed expenditure of the Council.

(3) In the first and second financial years after this Convention enters into force in accordance with Article 16 of this Convention the Contracting Parties shall contribute to the expenses of the Council such sums as they respectively contributed, or undertook to contribute, in respect of the year preceding the entry into force of this Convention.

(4) In respect of the third and subsequent financial years the Contracting Parties shall contribute sums calculated in accordance with a scheme to be prepared by the Council and accepted by all the Contracting Parties. This scheme may be modified by the Council with the agreement of all Contracting Parties.

(5) A Government acceding to this Convention shall contribute to the expenses of the Council such sum as may be agreed between that Government and the Council in respect of each financial year until the scheme under paragraph 4 provides for contributions from that Government.

(6) A Contracting Party which has not paid its contribution for two consecutive years shall not enjoy any rights under this Convention until it has fulfilled its financial obligations.

**Art. 15.** (1) The Council shall enjoy, in the territories of the Contracting Parties, such legal capacity as may be agreed between the Council and the Government of the Contracting Party concerned.

(2) The Council, delegates and experts, the General Secretary and other officials shall enjoy in the territories of the Contracting Parties such privi-

512

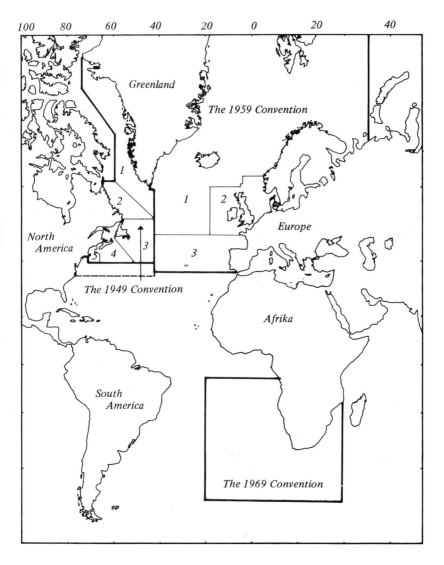

*Atlantic Ocean (The 1949 Convention, the 1959 Convention and the 1969 Convention)*

leges and immunities, necessary for the fulfilment of their functions, as may be agreed between the Council and the Government of the Contracting Party concerned.

**Art. 16.** . . .

(4) After the entry into force of this Convention in accordance with paragraph 3 of this Article, the Government of any State may apply to accede to this Convention by addressing a written application to the Government of Denmark. It shall be permitted to deposit an instrument of accession with that Government after the approval of the Governments of three quarters of the states which have already deposited their instruments of ratification, approval or accession, has been notified to the Government of Denmark. For any acceding Government this Convention shall enter into force on the date of deposit of its instrument of accession.

**Art. 17.** At any time after two years from the date on which this Convention has come into force any Contracting Party may denounce the Convention by means of a notice in writing addressed to the Government of Denmark. Any such notice shall take effect twelve months after the date of its receipt.

**Art. 18.** . . .


## THE 1969 CONVENTION ON THE CONSERVATION OF THE LIVING RESOURCES OF THE SOUTHEAST ATLANTIC

Signed at Rome on 23 October 1969; Entered into force on 24 October 1971. The Parties to the Convention as of 31 December 1973 are: Belgium, Bulgaria, France, Japan, Poland, Portugal, Spain, South Africa and U.S.S.R.

The Governments of the States parties to this Convention, considering their mutual interest in the living resources of the Southeast Atlantic and desiring to cooperate in the conservation and rational exploitation of these resources, have agreed as follows:

**Art. I.** 1. The area to which this Convention shall apply, hereinafter referred to as the "Convention Area", shall be all waters bounded by a line drawn as follows: . . . (see the map on p. 513)

2. The eastern boundary at the meridian 40° East shall be reviewed if a convention for the conservation of the living resources of the sea is established applying to an area immediately adjacent to that boundary.

**Art. II.** Nothing in this Convention shall be considered as affecting the rights, claims or views of any Contracting Party in regard to the limits of the territorial sea or to the extent of jurisdiction over fisheries under international law.

**Art. III.** This Convention shall apply to all fish and other living resources in the Convention Area, with the exception of any such resources as may be excluded pursuant to arrangements or agreements entered into by the Commission in accordance with paragraph 1 of Article XI of this Convention.

**Art. IV.** The Contracting Parties hereby agree to establish and to maintain a Commission to be known as the International Commission for the Southeast Atlantic Fisheries, hereinafter referred to as the "Commission," which shall carry out the functions set forth in this Convention.

**Art. V.** 1. The Commission shall hold a regular session at least once every two years. A special session shall be called at any time at the request of one Contracting Party provided that such request is supported by at least three other Contracting Parties.

2. Each of the Contracting Parties shall be represented on the Commission by not more than three Commissioners who may be accompanied by experts and advisers.

3. Each Contracting Party shall have one vote in the Commission. Except as may be otherwise provided in this Convention, decisions of the Commission shall be taken by a majority of two thirds of the Contracting Parties present and voting. Two thirds of the Contracting Parties shall constitute a quorum.

4. At each regular session the Commission shall elect from among the Commissioners the following officers: a Chairman, a First Vice-Chairman and a Second Vice-Chairman. These officers shall remain in office until the election of their successors at the next regular session and shall not be eligible to serve for more than two consecutive terms in the same office. A Commissioner, when acting as Chairman, shall not vote.

5. The working languages of the Commission shall be English, French and Spanish.

6. The Commission shall adopt such rules of procedure and other internal administrative regulations as are necessary to carry out its functions. The rules of procedure of subsidiary bodies established by the Commission under Article VII may be adopted by such subsidiary bodies, but shall only enter into force upon approval by the Commission.

**Art. VI.** 1. In order to achieve the objectives set out in this Convention, the Commission shall be responsible for the study of all fish and other living resources in the Convention Area. Such study shall include research on the abundance, life history, biometry and ecology of these resources;

515

and the study of their environment. In undertaking the study of these matters, the Commission shall collect, analyse, publish and disseminate, by all appropriate means, statistical, biological and other scientific information on the said resources.

2. The Commission, in carrying out its responsibilities shall, insofar as feasible, utilize the technical and scientific services of, and information from, official agencies of the Contracting Parties. The Commission may, when necessary, utilize other services and information, and may also undertake, within the limits of its supplementary budget, independent research to supplement the research being done by governments, national institutions or other international organizations.

3. The Contracting Parties shall furnish, on the request of the Commission, any available statistical and other data and information the Commission may need for the purposes of the Convention.

**Art. VII.** 1. The Commission may establish a Regional Committee for each of the regions into which the Convention Area may be divided on an ecological basis, and a Stock Committee with respect to any stock to be found in the Convention Area. The Commission may also establish a Scientific Advisory Council, hereinafter referred to as the "Council". The Commission may establish such other subsidiary bodies as are necessary for the performance of its functions, determining their composition and terms of reference in each case.

2. Regional Committees shall have the functions specified in this Article, except with respect to any stock for which a Stock Committee is competent.

3. A Regional or Stock Committee may initiate, on the basis of the results of scientific investigations, proposals regarding measures that are applicable to the region or stock for which it has been established and shall consider any proposals that may be referred to it by the Commission.

4. A Regional or Stock Committee may prepare draft recommendations for consideration by the Commission. The Commission may adopt such recommendations, with any amendments it may consider desirable, in accordance with Article VIII of this Convention.

5. The Commission shall designate the Contracting Parties that may be represented on a Regional or Stock Committee. However, when a Regional or Stock Committee is established a Contracting Party shall automatically have the right to be represented thereon if it fishes in the region; or if it exploits the stock concerned; or if it has a coastline adjacent to the region concerned or the area where the stock is to be found. If a Contracting Party exploits a stock outside the region covered by a Regional or Stock Committee, it may be eligible to be represented thereon if the Commission so decides.

6. The functions of the Council shall be to advise and assist the Commission and its Regional and Stock Committees with respect to the scientific aspects of their responsibilities.

7. Each Contracting Party may send a delegation of scientists to the Council composed of as many experts as it wishes. The Council may establish subsidiary bodies and determine their composition.

8. The Council may, with the concurrence of the Commission, invite other scientists or experts to participate in its deliberations in an advisory capacity.

9. The Council shall hold regular sessions whose timing shall be determined by the Commission in relation to its regular sessions. The Council may hold special sessions subject to the approval of the Commission.

**Art. VIII.** 1. The Commission may make, on its own initiative or on the proposal of a Regional or Stock Committee and on the basis of the results of scientific investigations, recommendations relating to the objectives of this Convention. These recommendations shall become binding on the Contracting Parties under the conditions laid down in Article IX.

2. The matters with respect to which the Commission may make recommendations shall be:

(a) the regulation of the sizes of mesh of fishing nets;

(b) the regulation of the size limits of fish that may be retained on board any fishing craft or landed, or exposed or offered for sale;

(c) the establishment of open and closed seasons;

(d) the establishment of open and closed areas;

(e) the regulation of fishing gear and appliances, other than regulation of the size of mesh of fishing nets;

(f) the improvement and the increase of living resources, which may include artificial propagation, the transplantation and acclimatization of organisms, the transplantation of young, and predator control;

(g) the regulation of the total catch by species, group of species or, if appropriate, by regions; and

(h) any other type of measure directly related to the conservation of all fish and other living resources in the Convention Area.

3. (a) If the Commission makes a recommendation under paragraph 2 (g) of this Article, it may invite the Contracting Parties concerned, as determined by the Commission, to elaborate agreements on the allocation of a total catch quota taking into account the fishing interests of all the countries and ensuring, as far as possible, that all the countries concerned abide by the Commission's recommendation for a total catch quota and by any agreed allocation.

(b) The terms of any such agreement shall be reported by the Contracting Parties concerned to the Commission as soon as possible. Without

517

prejudice to the binding force of such agreements on the parties thereto, the Commission may thereupon make recommendations, pursuant to paragraph 1 of this Article, on the subject matter of the said agreements.

4. The Commission shall notify all Contracting Parties of recommendations adopted by the Commission.

**Art. IX.** 1. Subject to the provisions of this Article, the Contracting Parties undertake to give effect to any recommendation adopted by the Commission in accordance with Article VIII.

2. Any Contracting Party may, within ninety days of notification of a recommendation, present an objection to it to the Commission and in that event shall not be under an obligation to give effect to the recommendation.

3. If an objection is presented within the ninety-day period referred to in the preceding paragraph any other Contracting Party may present an objection at any time within a further period of sixty days or within thirty days after notification of an objection presented by another Contracting Party made within the further sixty-day period.

4. If objections to a recommendation are presented by at least three Contracting Parties, all the other Contracting Parties shall be relieved forthwith of any obligation to give effect to that recommendation; nevertheless, any or all of them may agree among themselves to give effect to it.

5. Any Contracting Party which has presented an objection to a recommendation may at any time withdraw that objection and shall then, subject to the provisions of the preceding paragraph, give effect to the recommendation within ninety days.

6. The Commission shall notify all Contracting Parties of each objection or withdrawal immediately upon receipt thereof.

**Art. X.** 1. Without prejudice to the rights of States in the waters in which they are entitled under international law to exercise jurisdiction over fisheries, each Contracting Party shall take appropriate measures, in its territories and in these waters with respect to all persons and vessels, and beyond these waters with respect to its nationals and vessels, to ensure the implementation of the provisions of the present Convention and the recommendations of the Commission which have become binding on that Contracting Party, and to apply sanctions for the violation of such recommendations.

2. The Contracting Parties undertake to collaborate with each other with a view to the adoption of effective measures to ensure the implementation of this Convention and the achievement of its objectives.

3. In addition, the Contracting Parties undertake to collaborate with each other with a view to setting up, upon a recommendation by the Commission, a system of international enforcement of such recommendations as the Commission may select for inclusion under the said system, except

in the waters in which a State is entitled under international law to exercise jurisdiction over fisheries. The adoption and implementation of such a recommendation shall be governed by Articles VIII and IX of this Convention.

4. The Contracting Parties shall transmit to the Commission, biennially, or at such times as may be required by the Commission, a statement of the action that they have taken pursuant to this Article.

**Art. XI.** 1. The Commission shall seek to conclude agreements and maintain working arrangements with other international organizations which have related objectives, and in particular the Food and Agriculture Organization of the United Nations, to ensure effective collaboration and coordination and to avoid duplication with respect to their work.

2. The Commission may invite any appropriate international organization and the Government of any State eligible to become a party to this Convention under Article XVII, but which is not a member of the Commission, to be represented in an observer capacity at sessions of the Commission or its subsidiary bodies.

**Art. XII.** 1. The Commission shall appoint an Executive Secretary on such conditions as it may determine.

2. The staff of the Commission shall be appointed by the Executive Secretary in accordance with such rules and on such conditions as may be determined by the Commission.

3. The Executive Secretary shall perform such functions as the Commission may prescribe, including the following:

(*a*) receiving and transmitting the Commission's official communications;

(*b*) preparing budget estimates for review by the Commission at its regular sessions;

(*c*) preparing for submission to the Commission at its regular sessions a report on the Commission's activities and the programme of work, and arranging for the subsequent publication of this report and the proceedings of the Commission;

(*d*) arranging for the collection and analysis of statistics and other data necessary to accomplish the purposes of this Convention;

(*e*) preparing for submission to the Commission, and for possible subsequent publication, reports on statistical, biological and other matters;

(*f*) authorizing the disbursement of funds in accordance with the Commission's budget;

(*g*) accounting for the funds of the Commission; and

(*h*) arranging for cooperation with international organizations as provided for under Article XI of this Convention.

**Art. XIII.** 1. At each regular session the Commission shall adopt a budget

519

for the following fiscal period and budget estimates for the fiscal period following thereafter. The fiscal period shall be two years. However, should the Commission hold more than one regular session during a fiscal period, it may revise the current budget if required. Subject to the agreement of all Contracting Parties, the Commission may, at any session, adopt a supplementary budget.

2. The contributions to the budget and any supplementary budget to be paid by each Contracting Party shall be payable in such currency or currencies and at such time as the Commission shall decide.

3. The voting rights of any Contracting Party whose arrears of contributions equal or exceed its total contribution falling due in the preceding fiscal period shall be suspended unless the Commission decides otherwise.

4. The Commission may also accept from any private or public sources other contributions for the furtherance of its objectives. Such contributions shall be used and administered in accordance with rules to be adopted by the Commission.

5. The Commission shall arrange for an annual independent audit of its accounts to be made and submitted for review and approval by the Commission.

6. The Commission shall establish a Working Capital Fund to finance operations of the Commission prior to receiving annual contributions, and for such other purposes as the Commission may determine. The Commission shall fix the level of the Fund, assess advances necessary for its establishment, and adopt regulations governing its use.

**Art. XIV.** The Commission shall calculate the contributions to be made by the Contracting Parties to the budget including any supplementary budget according to the following formula:

(a) One third of the total amount of the budget including any supplementary budget shall be contributed by the Contracting Parties in equal parts;

(b) Each Contracting Party shall contribute in respect of each Regional or Stock Committee of which it is a member an amount equivalent to one third of its contribution under subparagraph (a) above. This proportion shall be reduced, if necessary, in order that the total amount contributed by the Contracting Parties under this subparagraph shall not exceed one third of the total budget including any supplementary budget;

(c) Any remaining portion of the budget including any supplementary budget shall be contributed by each Contracting Party in the proportion that its nominal catch in the Convention Area bears to the aggregate nominal catch of all Contracting Parties in that Area. In computing this catch the Commission shall take into account all fishes, crustaceans, molluscs and other marine invertebrates, with the exception of such species

520

as may be excluded from the application of this Convention in accordance with Article III. The catch shall be determined on the basis of the average for the last two calendar years for which statistics have been published by the Food and Agriculture Organization of the United Nations.

**Art. XV.** 1. The Commission shall determine where its seat shall be situated.

2. The Commission shall have legal personality. It shall, in particular, have capacity to contract, and to acquire and dispose of movable and immovable property.

**Art. XVI.** The provisions of this Convention shall not apply to fishing operations conducted solely for the purpose of scientific investigations, by vessels authorized by a Contracting Party for that purpose, or to fish taken in the course of such operations. However, fish so taken shall not be sold, or exposed or offered for sale in violation of a recommendation of the Commission.

**Art. XVII.** 1. This Convention shall be open for signature by the Government of any State represented at the Conference which adopted the Convention, or by the Government of any other State which is a Member of the United Nations or of any specialized agency of the United Nations.

2. Signature of this Convention shall be subject to ratification, acceptance or approval.

3. Once this Convention has entered into force, any State referred to in paragraph 1 of this Article which has not signed the Convention or any other State unanimously invited by the Commission to become a party to the Convention may adhere to it.

4. Instruments of ratification, acceptance, approval or adherence shall be deposited with the Director-General of the Food and Agriculture Organization of the United Nations. hereinafter referred to as the "Depositary."

5. Ratification, acceptance, approval or adherence may not be made subject to any reservation.

**Art. XVIII.** . . .

**Art. XIX.** 1. Any Contracting Party may propose amendments to this Convention which shall be referred to the Commission for approval at a regular or special session. Proposals for the amendment of the Convention shall be communicated to the Depositary who shall inform the Contracting Parties thereof. Any amendment shall take effect for each Contracting Party accepting the amendment on the ninetieth day after its acceptance by three fourths of the Contracting Parties and thereafter for each remaining Contracting Party on the day on which the Depositary receives the notification of such acceptance.

521

2. Any State which becomes a Contracting Party after an amendment to this Convention has been proposed for acceptance pursuant to the provisions of this Article shall be bound by the Convention as amended when the said amendment comes into force.

**Art. XX.** At any time after ten years from the date of entry into force of this Convention, any Contracting Party may withdraw from the Convention by giving written notification of withdrawal. Withdrawal shall take effect on December thirty-first of the calendar year following the year in which notification of withdrawal was communicated to the Depositary.

**Art. XXI.** . . .

## 2. EUROPE

### THE 1949 AGREEMENT FOR THE ESTABLISHMENT OF A GENERAL FISHERIES COUNCIL FOR THE MEDITERRANEAN, AS AMENDED

Signed at Rome on 24 September 1949; Entered into force on 20 February 1952. U.N. Treaty Series, vol. 126, p. 239. Amended by the Amendments adopted on 22 May 1963 by the General Fisheries Council for the Mediterranean at its 1st Special Session, Rome, 21-22 May 1963 and approved by the Conference of the FAO; Entered into force on 3 December 1963. U.N. Treaty Series, vol. 490, p. 444.

The Contracting Governments having a mutual interest in the development and proper utilization of the resources of the Mediterranean and contiguous waters, and desiring to further the attainment of their objectives through international co-operation which would be furthered by the establishment of a General Fisheries Council for the Mediterranean, agree as follows:

**Art. I.** *The Council*

1. The Contracting Governments hereby establish within the framework of the Food and Agriculture Organization of the United Nations (hereinafter referred to as "the Organization") a Council to be known as the General Fisheries Council for the Mediterranean (hereinafter referred to as "the Council"), for the purpose of exercising the functions and discharging the responsibilities set forth in Article IV below.

2. The Members of the Council shall be such Member Nations and Associate Members of the Organization and such non-member Nations

522

of the Organization that are Members of the United Nations, which accept this Agreement in accordance with the provisions of Article IX below, it being understood that these provisions shall not affect the membership status in the Council of such nations that are not Members of the United Nations as may have become parties to this Agreement prior to 22 May 1963. As regards Associate Members, this Agreement shall, in accordance with the provisions of Article XIV-5 of the Constitution and Rule XXI-3 of the General Rules of the Organization, be submitted by the Organization to the authority having responsibility for the international relations of such Associate Members.

### Art. II. *Organization*

1. Each Member shall be represented at sessions of the Council by one delegate, who may be accompanied by an alternate and by experts and advisers. Participation in meetings of the Council by alternates, experts, and advisers shall not entail the right to vote, except in the case of an alternate who is acting in the place of a delegate during his absence.

2. Each Member shall have one vote. Decisions of the Council shall be taken by a majority of the votes cast, except as otherwise provided by this Agreement. A majority of the total membership of the Council shall constitute a quorum.

3. The Council shall elect a Chairman and two Vice-Chairmen.

4. The Chairman of the Council shall normally convene a regular session of the Council at least once every two years unless otherwise directed by a majority of the Members. The site and date of all sessions shall be determined by the Council in consultation with the Director-General of the Organization.

5. The seat of the Council shall be at the Headquarters of the Organization in Rome.

6. The Organization shall provide the Secretariat for the Council and the Director-General shall appoint its Secretary, who shall be administratively responsible to him.

7. The Council may, by a two-thirds majority of its membership, adopt and amend its own Rules of Procedure which shall be consistent with the General Rules of the Organization. The Rules of the Council and any amendments thereto shall come into force as from the date of approval by the Director-General of the Organization, subject to confirmation by the Council of the Organization.

### Art. III. *Committees, Working Parties and Specialists*

1. The Council may establish temporary, special or standing committees to study and report on matters pertaining to the purposes of the Council and working parties to study and recommend on specific technical problems.

523

2. The committees and working parties referred to in paragraph 1 above shall be convened by the Chairman of the Council at such times and places as are determined by the Chairman in consultation with the Director-General of the Organization.

3. The Council may suggest to the Organization the recruitment or appointment of specialists at the expense of the Organization, for the consideration of specific questions or problems.

4. The establishment of committees and working parties referred to in paragraph 1 above and the recruitment or appointment of specialists referred to in paragraph 3 above, shall be subject to the availability of the necessary funds in the relevant chapter of the approved budget of the Organization; the determination of such availability shall be made by the Director-General of the Organization. Before taking any decision involving expenditures in connection with the establishment of committees and working parties and the recruitment or appointment of specialists, the Council shall have before it a report from the Director-General of the Organization on the administrative and financial implications thereof.

**Art. IV.** *Functions*

The Council shall have the following functions and responsibilities:

*a.* To formulate all oceanographical and technical aspects of the problems of development and proper utilization of aquatic resources;

*b.* To encourage and co-ordinate research and the application of improved methods employed in fishery and allied industries with a view to the utilization of aquatic resources;

*c.* To assemble, publish, or disseminate all oceanographical and technical information relating to aquatic resources;

*d.* To recommend to Members such national and international research and development projects as may appear necessary or desirable to fill gaps in such knowledge;

*e.* To undertake, where appropriate, co-operative research and development projects directed to this end;

*f.* To propose, and where necessary to adopt, measures to bring about the standardization of scientific equipment, techniques, and nomenclature;

*g.* To make comparative studies of fishery legislation with a view to making recommendations to its Members respecting the greatest possible co-ordination;

*h.* To encourage research into the hygiene and prevention of occupational diseases of fishermen;

*i.* To extend its good offices in assisting Member(s) to secure essential materials and equipments;

*j.* To report upon such questions relating to all oceanographical and technical problems as may be recommended to it by Members or by the

524

Organization and, if it thinks proper to do so, by other international, national, or private organizations with related interests;

*k.* To transmit, every two years, to the Director-General of the Organization, a report embodying its views, recommendations and decisions, and make such other reports to the Director-General of the Organization as may seem to it necessary or desirable. Reports of the committees and working parties of the Council provided for in Article III of this Agreement shall be transmitted to the Director-General of the Organization through the Council.

**Art. V.** *Region*

The Council shall carry out the functions and responsibilities set forth in Article IV in the region as referred to in the **Preamble**.

**Art. VI.** *Co-operation with International Organizations*

The Council shall co-operate closely with other international organizations in matters of mutual interest.

**Art. VII.** *Expenses*

1. The expenses of delegates and their alternates, experts and advisers occasioned by attendance at sessions of Council and the expenses of representatives sent to committees or working parties established in accordance with Article III of this Agreement shall be determined and paid by their respective governments.

2. The expenses of the Secretariat, including publications and communications and the expenses incurred by the Chairman and Vice-Chairmen of the Council when performing duties on behalf of the Council between Council sessions, shall be determined and paid by the Organization within the limits of the relevant appropriations provided for in the budget of the Organization.

3. The expenses of research and development projects undertaken by individual Members of the Council, whether independently or upon recommendation of the Council, shall be determined and paid by the governments concerned.

4. The expenses incurred in connection with co-operative research or development projects undertaken in accordance with the provisions of Article IV, paragraphs (*d*) and (*e*) unless otherwise available shall be determined and paid by the Members in the form and proportion to which they shall mutually agree. Co-operative projects shall be submitted to the Council of the Organization prior to implementation. Contributions for co-operative projects shall be paid into a trust fund to be established by the Organization and shall be administered by the Organization in accordance with the Financial Regulations and rules of the Organization.

5. The expenses of experts invited, with the concurrence of the Director-

General, to attend meetings of the Council, committees or working parties in their individual capacity shall be borne by the budget of the Organization.

**Art. VIII.** *Amendments*

The General Fisheries Council for the Mediterranean may amend this Agreement by a two-thirds majority of all the Members of this Council, any amendment becoming effective only after concurrence of the Council of the Organization unless the latter considers it desirable to refer the amendment to the Conference of the Organization for approval. An amendment shall become effective as from the date of the decision of the Council or Conference of the Organization as appropriate. However, any amendment involving new obligations for Members shall come into force with respect to each Member only on acceptance of it by that Member. The instruments of acceptance of amendments involving new obligations shall be deposited with the Director-General of the Organization who shall inform all the Members of the General Fisheries Council for the Mediterranean, as well as the Secretary-General of the United Nations, of the receipt of acceptance and the entry into force of such amendments. The rights and obligations of any Member of the General Fisheries Council for the Mediterranean that has not accepted an amendment involving additional obligations shall continue to be governed by the provisions of this Agreement as they stood prior to the amendment.

**Art. IX.** *Acceptance*

1. This Agreement shall be open to acceptance by Member Nations or Associate Members of the Organization.

2. The Council may, by a two-thirds majority of its membership, admit to membership such other nations that are Members of the United Nations as have submitted an application for membership and a declaration made in a formal instrument that they accept this Agreement as in force at the time of admission.

3. Participation in the activities of the Council by Members of the Council which are not Members or Associate Members of the Organization shall be contingent upon the assumption of such proportionate share in the expenses of the Secretariat as may be determined in the light of the relevant provisions of the Financial Regulations of the Organization.

4. Acceptance of this Agreement by any Member Nation or Associate Member of the Organization shall be effected by the deposit of an instrument of acceptance with the Director-General of the Organization and shall take effect on receipt of such instrument by the Director-General.

5. Acceptance of this Agreement by non-member nations of the Organization shall be effected by the deposit of an instrument of acceptance with the Director-General of the Organization. Membership shall become

effective on the date on which the Council approves the application for membership, in conformity with the provisions of paragraph 2 of this Article.

6. The Director-General of the Organization shall inform all Members of the Council, all Member Nations of the Organization and the Secretary-General of the United Nations of all acceptances that have become effective.

7. Acceptance of this Agreement may be made subject to reservations which shall become effective only upon unanimous approval by the Members of the Council. The Director-General of the Organization shall notify forthwith all Members of the Council of any reservations. Members of the Council not having replied within three months from the date of the notification shall be deemed to have accepted the reservation. Failing such approval, the Nation making the reservation shall not become a party to this Agreement.

**Art. X.** *Entry into Force*

. . . . .

**Art. XI.** *Territorial Application*

The Members of the Council shall, when accepting this Agreement, state explicitly to which territories their participation shall extend. In the absence of such a declaration, participation shall be deemed to apply to all the territories for the international relations of which the Member is responsible. Subject to the provisions of Article XII below, the scope of the territorial application may be modified by a subsequent declaration.

**Art. XII.** *Withdrawal*

1. Any Member Government may withdraw from this Agreement at any time after the expiration of two years from the date upon which the Agreement entered into force with respect to that Member, by giving written notice of its withdrawal to the Director-General of the Organization who shall immediately inform all the Members of the Council and the Member Nations of the Organization of such withdrawal. Notice of withdrawal shall become effective three months from the date of its receipt by the Director-General.

2. A Member of the Council may give notice of withdrawal with respect to one or more of the territories for the international relations of which it is responsible. When a Member gives notice of its own withdrawal from the Council it shall state to which territory or territories the withdrawal is to apply. In the absence of such a declaration, the withdrawal shall be deemed to apply to all the territories for the international relations of which the Member of the Council is responsible, with the exception of Associate Members.

3. Any Member of the Council that gives notice of withdrawal from the Organization shall be deemed to have simultaneously whithdrawn from the Council, and this withdrawal shall be deemed to apply to all the territories for the international relations of which the Member concerned is responsible, except that such withdrawal shall not be deemed to apply to an Associate Member.

**Art. XIII.** *Interpretation and Settlement of Disputes*

Any dispute regarding the interpretation or application of this Agreement, if not settled by the Council, shall be referred to a committee composed of one member appointed by each of the parties to the dispute, and in addition an independent chairman chosen by the members of the committee. The recommendations of such a committee, while not binding in character, shall become the basis for renewed consideration by the parties concerned of the matter out of which the disagreement arose. If as the result of this procedure the dispute is not settled, it shall be referred to the International Court of Justice in accordance with the Statute of the Court, unless the parties to the dispute agree to another method of settlement.

**Art. XIV.** *Termination*

This Agreement shall be automatically terminated if and when, as the result of withdrawals, the number of Members of the Council drops below five, unless the remaining Members unanimously decide otherwise.

**Art. XV.** *Certification and Registration*

. . . . .


## THE 1959 CONVENTION CONCERNING FISHING IN THE BLACK SEA (Bulgaria, Romania and Union of Soviet Socialist Republics)

Signed at Varna on 7 July 1959; Entered into force on 21 March 1960. U.N. Treaty Series, vol. 377, p. 203.


. . . . .

**Art. 1.** The Contracting Parties agree to co-operate and to assist one another, in accordance with the provisions of this Convention, in carrying on rational fishing in the Black Sea, in improving fishing technique, and in carrying out research in the field of ichthyology and hydrobiology for the purpose of maintaining and augmenting the stocks of fish in the Black Sea with a view to increasing the yield.

The provisions of this Convention shall not affect the status of the territorial and inland waters of the Contracting Parties.

**Art. 2.** Fishing vessels of the People's Republic of Bulgaria, the Romanian People's Republic and the Union of Soviet Socialist Republics engaged in fishing in the open sea may enter the following ports of refuge in order to shelter from bad weather or in case of damage:

In the People's Republic of Bulgaria: Balchik, Varna, Nesebŭr, Burgas, Sozopol and Michurin;

In the Romanian People's Republic: Constanta and Sulina;

In the Union of Soviet Socialist Republics: Odessa, Evpatoria, Yalta, Novorossysk, Sochi, Sukhum, Poti and Batum.

The list of ports of refuge may be amended by agreement among the Parties to the Convention.

**Art. 3.** In the cases referred to in article 2 of this Convention, the fishing vessels of the Contracting Parties shall where necessary be given an opportunity to repair the damage and to replenish their supplies of foodstuffs, drinking water, fuel, lubricants and other ship's stores so that the vessel may continue on its route or return to its nearest home port, and an opportunity to dispose of their catch fresh at the ports of refuge if it cannot be preserved on board the vessel.

**Art. 4.** The procedure governing the disposal of fish and payment for services rendered to fishing vessels entering ports of refuge and for fish disposed of in the cases referred to in article 3 of this Convention shall be agreed between the competent authorities of the Parties to the Convention.

**Art. 5.** The following shall be the minimum sizes at which fish may be taken:

| | |
|---|---:|
| Beluga (. . .) . | 140 cm |
| Russian sturgeon (. . .) | 80 cm |
| Sevryuga (. . .) | 75 cm |
| Turbot (. . .) . | 35 cm |
| Shad (. . .) | 16 cm |

The size of a fish shall be determined by measuring its length from the tip of the snout to the base of the tail fin.

Any fish taken which is under the prescribed size must be put back in the sea.

The taking of fish under the prescribed minimum size shall be permissible in a porportion not exceeding the following percentage by number of the total catch of each protected species:

8 per cent in the case of shad (. . .);

5 per cent in the case of turbot (. . .); and

5 per cent in the case of *Acipenseridae* (. . .).

The taking of *Acipenser nudiventris* shall be prohibited for five years from the date of entry into force of this Convention.

**Art. 6.** For the purpose of preparing forecasts for fishing in the Black Sea, the Contracting Parties agree to exchange by any suitable means operational information concerning the migration of industrial fish, indicating the time and place at which they congregate, the direction of movement, the density of the schools, and the hydrometeorological conditions in which such congregations and migrations are observed.

**Art. 7.** With a view to the rational utilization of the stocks of fish in the Black Sea, the Contracting Parties agree to exchange information annually on the results of scientific research in the fields of marine ichthyology, hydrobiology and fishing technique.

The Contracting Parties shall exchange statistical data on catches of fish.

**Art. 8.** With a view to working out and co-ordinating measures for the application of this Convention, a Mixed Commission shall be established.

Within one month after the entry into force of the Convention, each Contracting Party shall appoint one representative to the said Commission and shall communicate the name of its representative to the other Contracting Parties.

The Mixed Commission shall meet at least once a year in the territory of each of the Contracting Parties in turn.

The Mixed Commission shall function under a statute drafted by it at its first meeting and approved by the Contracting Parties.

**Art. 9.** The Mixed Commission shall have the following functions:

(1) It shall work out agreed measures to regulate fishing, with a view to the conservation and augmentation of the stocks of fish in the Black Sea, and to develop industrial fishing technique;

(2) It shall introduce amendments to article 5 of the Convention concerning the species and dimensions of fish caught in the Black Sea. Proposals for such amendments must be communicated to the representatives of the Contracting Parties on the Mixed Commission not later than three months before the opening of the Commission's regular session;

(3) It shall co-ordinate the planning of scientific research projects on matters relating to fishing in the Black Sea, to be conducted by the competent authorities of the Contracting Parties;

(4) It shall determine the nature and extent of the statistical and other data which each Contracting Party shall furnish to the Mixed Commission for the purpose of implementing this Convention;

(5) It shall exchange information concerning the application of this Convention;

(6) It shall examine such other matters as the Contracting Parties may refer to it.

**Art. 10.** The Mixed Commission shall make recommendations to the Contracting Parties on the matters referred to in article 9 with the exception of paragraph 2 of that article, on which the Commission may take decisions.

Recommendations and decisions shall be deemed to be adopted by the Mixed Commission if they receive the favourable votes of the representatives of all the Contracting Parties.

The recommendations of the Mixed Commission shall be submitted to the Contracting Parties for approval and may be given effect if none of the Parties raises objections within four months.

**Art. 11.** This Convention shall not impede the conclusion of bilateral agreements on matters relating to fishing in the Black Sea between any two Contracting Parties or between a Contracting Party and any other Black Sea State, so long as such agreements do not conflict with the terms of this Convention.

**Art. 12.** ...

**Art. 13.** This Convention is concluded for a term of five years. It shall remain in force for successive terms of five years for those Contracting Parties which do not inform the Government of the People's Republic of Bulgaria, six months before the expiry of the current five-year term, that they wish to terminate the Convention.

**Art. 14.** Other Black Sea States may accede to this Convention.

**Art. 15.** ...


# THE 1973 CONVENTION ON FISHING AND CONSERVATION OF THE LIVING RESOURCES IN THE BALTIC SEA AND THE BELTS

Signed at Gdansk on 13 September 1973; by the Representatives of Denmark, Finland, German Democratic Rep., Germany (Federal Rep. of), Poland, Sweden and U.S.S.R.

The States Parties to this Convention

bearing in mind that maximum and stable productivity of the living resources of the Baltic Sea and the Belts is of great importance to the States of the Baltic Sea basin,

recognizing their joint responsibility for the conservation of the living resources and their rational exploitation,

being convinced that the conservation of the living resources of the Baltic Sea and the Belts calls for closer and more expanded co-operation in this region, have agreed as follows:

**Art. I.** The Contracting States shall:

co-operate closely with a view to preserving and increasing the living resources of the Baltic Sea and the Belts and obtaining the optimum yield, and, in particular to expanding and co-ordinating studies towards these ends,

prepare and put into effect organizational and technical projects on conservation and growth of the living resources, including measures of artificial reproduction of valuable fish species and/or contribute financially to such measures, on a just and equitable basis, as well as take other steps towards rational and effective exploitation of the living resources.

**Art. II.** 1. The area to which this Convention applies, hereinafter referred to as "the Convention area", shall be all waters of the Baltic Sea and the Belts, excluding internal waters, bounded in the west by a line as from Hasenore Head to Gniben Point, from Korshage to Spodsbierg and from Gilbierg Head to the Kullen.

2. This Convention shall apply to all fish species and other living marine resources in the Convention Area.

**Art. III.** Nothing in this Convention shall be deemed to affect the rights, claims or views of any Contracting State in regard to the limits of territorial waters and to the extent of jurisdiction over fisheries, according to international law.

**Art. IV.** For the purpose of this Convention the term "vessel" means any vessel or boat employed in catching or treating fish or other living marine organisms and which is registered or owned in the territory of, or which flies the flag of, any Contracting State.

**Art. V.** 1. An International Baltic Sea Fishery Commission, hereinafter referred to as "the Commission", is hereby established for the purposes of this Convention.

2. Each Contracting State may appoint not more than two representatives as members of the Commission and such experts and advisers to assist them as that State may determine.

3. The Commission shall elect a Chairman and a Vice-Chairman from amongst its members who shall serve for a period of four years and who shall be eligible for re-election, but not for two consecutive terms of office.

The Chairman and the Vice-Chairman shall be elected from the representatives of different Contracting States.

4. A member of the Commission elected as its Chairman shall forthwith cease to act as a representative of a State and shall not vote. The State concerned shall have the right to appoint another representative to serve in the Chairman's place.

**Art. VI.** 1. The Office of the Commission shall be in Warsaw.

2. The Commission shall appoint its Secretary and as it may require appropriate staff to assist him.

3. The Commission shall adopt its rules of procedure and other provisions which the Commission shall consider necessary for its work.

**Art. VII.** 1. The Commission shall adopt its financial rules.

2. The Commission shall adopt a two years budget of proposed expenditures and budget estimates for the fiscal period following thereafter.

3. The total amount of the budget including any supplementary budget shall be contributed by the Contracting States in equal parts.

4. Each Contracting State shall pay the expenses related to the participation in the Commission of its representatives, experts and advisers.

**Art. VIII.** 1. Except where the Commission decides otherwise, it shall hold its sessions every two years in Warsaw at such time as it shall deem suitable. Upon the request of a representative of a Contracting State in the Commission, provided it is endorsed by a representative of another Contracting State, the Chairman of the Commission shall, as soon as possible, summon an extraordinary session at such time and place as he determines, however not later than three months from the date of the submission of the request.

2. The first session of the Commission shall be called by the Depositary Government of this Convention and shall take place within a period of ninety days from the date following the entry into force of this Convention.

3. Each Contracting State shall have one vote in the Commission. Decisions and recommendations of the Commission shall be taken by a two-thirds majority of votes of the Contracting States, present and voting at the meeting.

4. English shall be the working language of the Commission. The languages of the Signatory States are the official languages of the Commission. Only recommendations, decisions and resolutions of the Commission shall be made in these languages.

At meetings of the Commission any Contracting State has the right to have all the proceedings translated into its own language. All the costs related to such translations shall be borne by that State.

**Art. IX.** 1. It shall be the duty of the Commission:

(*a*) to keep under review the living resources and the fisheries in the Convention area by collecting, aggregating, analysing and disseminating statistical data, for example concerning catch, fishing effort, and other information,

(*b*) to work out proposals with regard to co-ordination of scientific research in the Convention area,

(*c*) to prepare and submit recommendations based as far as practicable on results of the scientific research and concerning measures referred to in Article X for consideration of the Contracting States.

2. In implementing its functions, the Commission shall, when appropriate, seek the services of the International Council for the Exploration of the Sea (ICES) and of other international technical and scientific organizations and shall make use of information provided by the official bodies of the Contracting States.

3. To perform its functions the Commission may set up working groups or other subsidiary bodies and determine their composition and terms of reference.

**Art. X.** Measures relating to the purposes of this Convention which the Commission may consider and in regard of which it may make recommendations to the Contracting States are:

*a.* any measures for the regulation of fishing gear, appliances and catching methods,

*b.* any measures regulating the size limits of fish that may be retained on board vessels or landed, exposed or offered for sale,

*c.* any measures establishing closed seasons,

*d.* any measures establishing closed areas,

*e.* any measures improving and increasing the living marine resources, including artificial reproduction and transplantation of fish and other organisms,

*i.* any measures regulating and/or allocating between the Contracting States the amount of total catch or the amount of fishing effort according to objects, kinds, regions and fishing periods,

*g.* any measures of control over the implementation of recommendations binding on the Contracting States,

*h.* any other measures related to the conservation and rational exploitation of the living marine resources.

**Art. XI.** 1. Subject to the provisions of this Article, the Contracting States undertake to give effect to any recommendation made by the Commission under Article X of this Convention from the date determined by the Commission, which shall not be before the period for objection provided for in this Article has elapsed.

2. Any Contracting State may within ninety days from the date of notification of a recommendation object to it and in that event shall not be under obligation to give effect to that recommendation.

A Contracting State may also at any time withdraw its objection and give effect to a recommendation.

In the event of an objection being made within the ninety-days period, any other Contracting State may similarly object at any time within a further period of sixty days.

534

3. If objections to a recommendation are made by three or more Contracting States, the other Contracting States shall be relieved forthwith of any obligation to give effect to that recommendation.

4. The Commission shall notify each Contracting State immediately upon receipt of each objection or withdrawal.

**Art. XII.** 1. Each Contracting State shall take in regard to its nationals and its vessels appropriate measures to ensure the application of the provisions of this Convention and of the recommendations of the Commission which have become binding for the Contracting State and in case of their infringement shall take appropriate action.

2. Without prejudice to the sovereign rights of the Contracting States in regard to their territorial sea and to the rights in their fishing zones, each Contracting State shall implement recommendations of the Commission binding on that State through its national authorities, within its territorial sea and in the waters under its fisheries jurisdiction.

3. Each Contracting State shall furnish to the Commission at such time and in such form as may be required by the Commission, the available statistical data and information referred to in Article IX paragraph 1 (a), as well as information on all actions taken by it in accordance with paragraphs 1 and 2 of this Article.

**Art. XIII.** The Commission shall draw the attention of any State which is not a party to this Convention to such fishing operations, undertaken by its nationals or vessels in the Convention area, which might affect negatively the activities of the Commission or the implementation of the purposes of this Convention.

**Art. XIV.** The provisions of this Convention shall not apply to operations conducted solely for the purpose of scientific investigations by vessels authorized by a Contracting State for that purpose, or to fish and other marine organisms taken in the course of such operations. Catch so taken shall not be sold, exposed or offered for sale.

**Art. XV.** 1. The Commission shall co-operate with other international organizations having related objectives.

2. The Commission may extend an invitation to any international organization concerned or to the Government of any State, not a party to this Convention, to participate as an observer in the sessions of the Commission or meetings of its subsidiary bodies.

**Art. XVI.** 1. Each Contracting State may propose amendments to this Convention. Any such proposed amendment shall be submitted to the Depositary Government and communicated by it to all Contracting States, which shall inform the Depositary Government about either their acceptance or rejection of the amendment as soon as possible after the receipt of the communication.

The amendment shall enter into force ninety days after the Depositary Government has received notifications of acceptance of that amendment from all Contracting States.

2. Each State which shall become a party to this Convention after the entry into force of an amendment in accordance with the provisions of paragraph 1 of this Article, is obliged to apply the Convention as amended.

**Art. XVII.** . . .

2. This Convention shall be open for accession to any State interested in preservation and rational exploitation of living resources in the Baltic Sea and the Belts, provided that this State is invited by the Contracting States. Instruments of accession shall be deposited with the Depositary Government.

**Art. XVIII.** 1. This Convention shall enter into force on the ninetieth day following the date of the deposit of the fourth instrument of ratification or approval.

2. After entry into force of this Convention in accordance with paragraph 1 of this Article, the Convention shall enter into force for any other State, the Government of which has deposited an instrument of ratification, approval or accession, on the thirtieth day following the date of deposit of such instrument with the Depositary Government.

**Art. XIX.** At any time after the expiration of five years from the date of entry into force of this Convention any Contracting State may, by giving written notice to the Depositary Government, withdraw from this Convention.

The withdrawal shall take effect for such Contracting State on the thirty-first of December of the year which follows the year in which the Depositary Government was notified of the withdrawal.

**Art. XX.** . . .


## 3. PACIFIC OCEAN

## THE 1952 INTERNATIONAL CONVENTION FOR THE HIGH SEAS FISHERIES OF THE NORTH PACIFIC OCEAN (Canada, Japan and United States of America)

> Signed at Tokyo on 9 May 1952; Entered into force on 12 June 1953. U.N. Treaty Series, vol. 205, p. 65. Annex has been amended on 24 May 1960, 2 April 1962 and 8 May 1963.

The Governments of the United States of America, Canada and Japan, . . .

Acting as sovereign nations in the light of their rights under the principles of international law and custom to exploit the fishery resources of the high seas, and

Believing that it will best serve the common interest of mankind, as well as the interests of the Contracting Parties, to ensure the maximum sustained productivity of the fishery resources of the North Pacific Ocean, and that each of the Parties should assume an obligation, on a free and equal footing, to encourage the conservation of such resources, and

Recognizing that in view of these considerations it is highly desirable (1) to establish an International Commission, representing the three Parties hereto, to promote and coordinate the scientific studies necessary to ascertain the conservation measures required to secure the maximum sustained productivity of fisheries of joint interest to the Contracting Parties and to recommend such measures to such Parties and (2) that each Party carry out such conservation recommendations, and provide for necessary restraints on its own nationals and fishing vessels.

Therefore agree as follows:

**Art. I.** 1. The area to which this Convention applies, hereinafter referred to as "the Convention area", shall be all waters, other than territorial waters, of the North Pacific Ocean which for the purposes hereof shall include the adjacent seas.

2. Nothing in this Convention shall be deemed to affect adversely (prejudice) the claims of any Contracting Party in regard to the limits of territorial waters or to the jurisdiction of a coastal state over fisheries.

3. For the purposes of this Convention the term "fishing vessel" shall mean any vessel engaged in catching fish or processing or transporting fish loaded on the high seas, or any vessel outfitted for such activities.

**Art. II.** 1. In order to realize the objectives of this Convention, the Contracting Parties shall establish and maintain the International North Pacific Fisheries Commission, hereinafter referred to as "the Commission."

2. The Commission shall be composed of three national sections, each consisting of not more than four members appointed by the governments of the respective Contracting Parties.

3. Each national section shall have one vote. All resolutions, recommendations and other decisions of the Commission shall be made only by a unanimous vote of the three national sections except when under the provisions of article III, section 1 (c) (ii) only two participate.

4. The Commission may decide upon and amend, as occasion may require, by-laws or rules for the conduct of its meetings.

5. The Commission shall meet at least once each year and at such other

times as may be requested by a majority of the national sections. The date and place of the first meeting shall be determined by agreement between the Contracting Parties.

6. At its first meeting the Commission shall select a Chairman, Vice-Chairman and Secretary from different national sections. The Chairman, Vice-Chairman and Secretary shall hold office for a period of one year. During succeeding years selection of a Chairman, Vice-Chairman and Secretary from the national sections shall be made in such a manner as will provide each Contracting Party in turn with representation in those offices.

7. The Commission shall decide on a convenient place for the establishment of the Commission's headquarters.

8. Each Contracting Party may establish an Advisory Committee for its national section to be composed of persons who shall be well informed concerning North Pacific fishery problems of common concern. Each such Advisory Committee shall be invited to attend all sessions of the Commission except those which the Commission decides to be *in camera*.

9. The Commission may hold public hearings. Each national section may also hold public hearings within its own country.

10. The official languages of the Commission shall be Japanese and English. Proposals and data may be submitted to the Commission in either language.

11. Each Contracting Party shall determine and pay the expenses incurred by its national section. Joint expenses incurred by the Commission shall be paid by the Commission through contributions made by the Contracting Parties in the form and proportion recommended by the Commission and approved by the Contracting Parties.

12. An annual budget of joint expenses shall be recommended by the Commission and submitted to the Contracting Parties for approval.

13. The Commission shall authorize the disbursement of funds for the joint expenses of the Commission and may employ personnel and acquire facilities necessary for the performance of its functions.

**Art. III.** 1. The Commission shall perform the following functions:

(*a*) In regard to any stock of fish specified in the annex, study for the purpose of determining annually whether such stock continues to qualify for abstention under the provisions of article IV. If the Commission determines that such stock no longer meets the conditions of article IV, the Commission shall recommend that it be removed from the annex. Provided, however, that with respect to the stocks of fish originally specified in the Annex, no determination or recommendation as to whether such stock continues to qualify for abstention shall be made for five years after the entry into force of this Convention.

(*b*) To permit later additions to the annex, study, on request of a Contracting Party, any stock of fish of the Convention area, the greater part of which is harvested by one or more of the Contracting Parties, for the purpose of determining whether such stock qualifies for abstention under the provisions of article IV. If the Commission decides that the particular stock fulfills the conditions of article IV it shall recommend, (1) that such stock be added to the annex, (2) that the appropriate Party or Parties abstain from fishing such stock and (3) that the Party or Parties participating in the fishing of such stock continue to carry out necessary conservation measures.

(*c*) In regard to any stock of fish in the Convention area;

(i) Study, on request of any Contracting Party concerned, any stock of fish which is under substantial exploitation by two or more of the Contracting Parties, and which is not covered by a conservation agreement between such Parties existing at the time of the conclusion of this Convention, for the purpose of determining need for joint conservation measures;

(ii) Decide and recommend necessary joint conservation measures including any relaxation thereof to be taken as a result of such study. Provided, however, that only the national sections of the Contracting Parties engaged in substantial exploitation of such stock of fish may participate in such decision and recommendation. The decisions and recommendations shall be reported regularly to all the Contracting Parties, but shall apply only to the Contracting Parties the national sections of which participated in the decisions and recommendations.

(iii) Request the Contracting Party or Parties concerned to report regularly the conservation measures adopted from time to time with regard to the stocks of fish specified in the Annex, whether or not covered by conservation agreements between the Contracting Parties, and transmit such information to the other Contracting Party or Parties.

(*d*) Consider and make recommendations to the Contracting Parties concerning the enactment of schedules of equivalent penalties for violations of this Convention.

(*e*) Compile and study the records provided by the Contracting Parties pursuant to article VIII.

(*f*) Submit annually to each Contracting Party a report on the Commission's operations, investigations and findings, with appropriate recommendations, and inform each Contracting Party, whenever it is deemed advisable, on any matter relating to the objectives of this Convention.

2. The Commission may take such steps, in agreement with the Parties concerned, as will enable it to determine the extent to which the under-

539

takings agreed to by the Parties under the provisions of article V, section 2 and the measures recommended by the Commission under the provisions of this article and accepted by the Parties concerned have been effective.

3. In the performance of its functions, the Commission shall, insofar as feasible, utilize the technical and scientific services of, and information from, official agencies of the Contracting Parties and their political subdivisions and may, when desirable and if available, utilize the services of, and information from, any public or private institution or organization or any private individual.

**Art. IV.** 1. In making its recommendations the Commission shall be guided by the spirit and intent of this Convention and by the considerations below mentioned.

(*a*) Any conservation measures for any stock of fish decided upon under the provisions of this Convention shall be recommended for equal application to all Parties engaged in substantial exploitation of such stock.

(*b*) With regard to any stock of fish which the Commission determines reasonably satisfies all the following conditions, a recommendation shall be made as provided for in article III, section 1, (*b*).

(i) Evidence based upon scientific research indicates that more intensive exploitation of the stock will not provide a substantial increase in yield which can be sustained year after year,

(ii) The exploitation of the stock is limited or otherwise regulated through legal measures by each Party which is substantially engaged in its exploitation, for the purpose of maintaining or increasing its maximum sustained productivity; such limitations and regulations being in accordance with conservation programs based upon scientific research, and

(iii) The stock is the subject of extensive scientific study designed to discover whether the stock is being fully utilized and the conditions necessary for maintaining its maximum sustained productivity.

Provided, however, that no recommendation shall be made for abstention by a Contracting Party concerned with regard to: (1) any stock of fish which at any time during the twenty-five years next preceding the entry into force of this Convention has been under substantial exploitation by that Party having regard to the conditions referred to in section 2 of this article; (2) any stock of fish which is harvested in greater part by a country or countries not party to this Convention; (3) waters in which there is historic intermingling of fishing operations of the Parties concerned, intermingling of the stocks of fish exploited by these operations, and a long-established history of joint conservation and regulation among the Parties concerned so that there is consequent impracticability of segregating the operations and administering control. It is recognized that the conditions

540

specified in subdivision (3) of this proviso apply to Canada and the United States of America in the waters off the Pacific Coasts of the United States of America and Canada from and including the waters of the Gulf of Alaska southward and, therefore, no recommendation shall be made for abstention by either the United States of America or Canada in such waters.

2. In any decision or recommendation allowances shall be made for the effect of strikes, wars, or exceptional economic or biological conditions which may have introduced temporary declines in or suspension of productivity, exploitation, or management of the stock of fish concerned.

**Art. V.** 1. The annex attached hereto forms an integral part of this Convention. All references to "Convention" shall be understood as including the said annex either in its present terms or as amended in accordance with the provisions of article VII.

2. The Contracting Parties recognize that any stock of fish originally specified in the annex to this Convention fulfills the conditions prescribed in article IV and accordingly agree that the appropriate Party or Parties shall abstain from fishing such stock and the Party or Parties participating in the fishing of such stock shall continue to carry out necessary conservation measures.

**Art. VI.** In the event that it shall come to the attention of any of the Contracting Parties that the nationals or fishing vessels of any country which is not a Party to this Convention appear to affect adversely the operations of the Commission or the carrying out of the objectives of this Convention, such Party shall call the matter to the attention of other Contracting Parties. All the Contracting Parties agree upon the request of such Party to confer upon the steps to be taken towards obviating such adverse effects or relieving any Contracting Party from such adverse effects.

**Art. VII.** 1. The annex to this Convention shall be considered amended from the date upon which the Commission receives notification from all Contracting Parties of acceptance of a recommendation to amend the annex made by the Commission in accordance with the provisions of article III, section I or of the Protocol to this Convention.

2. The Commission shall notify all the Contracting Parties of the date of receipt of each notification of acceptance of an amendment to the annex.

**Art. VIII.** The Contracting Parties agree to keep as far as practicable all records requested by the Commission and to furnish compilations of such records and other information upon request of the Commission. No Contracting Party shall be required hereunder to provide the records of individual operations.

**Art. IX.** 1. The Contracting Parties agree as follows:

(*a*) With regard to a stock of fish from the exploitation of which any Contracting Party has agreed to abstain, the nationals and fishing vessels of such Contracting Party are prohibited from engaging in the exploitation of such stock of fish in waters specified in the annex, and from loading, processing, possessing, or transporting such fish in such waters.

(*b*) With regard to a stock of fish for which a Contracting Party has agreed to continue to carry out conservation measures, the nationals and fishing vessels of such Party are prohibited from engaging in fishing activities in waters specified in the annex in violation or regulations established under such conservation measures.

2. Each Contracting Party agrees, for the purpose of rendering effective the provisions of this Convention, to enact and enforce necessary laws and regulations, with regard to its nationals and fishing vessels, with appropriate penalties against violations thereof and to transmit to the Commission a report on any action taken by it with regard thereto.

**Art. X.** 1. The Contracting Parties agree, in order to carry out faithfully the provisions of this Convention, to cooperate with each other in taking appropriate and effective measures and accordingly agree as follows:

(*a*) When a fishing vessel of a Contracting Party has been found in waters in which that Party has agreed to abstain from exploitation in accordance with the provisions of this Convention, the duly authorized officials of any Contracting Party may board such vessel to inspect its equipment, books, documents, and other articles and question the persons on board. Such officials shall present credentials issued by their respective Governments if requested by the master of the vessel.

(*b*) When any such person or fishing vessel is actually engaged in operations in violation of the provisions of this Convention, or there is reasonable ground to believe was obviously so engaged immediately prior to boarding of such vessel by any such official, the latter may arrest or seize such person or vessel. In that case, the Contracting Party to which the official belongs shall notify the Contracting Party to which such person or vessel belongs of such arrest or seizure, and shall deliver such vessel or persons as promptly as practicable to the authorized officials of the Contracting Party to which such vessel or person belongs at a place to be agreed upon by both Parties. Provided, however, that when the Contracting Party which receives such notification cannot immediately accept delivery and makes request, the Contracting Party which gives such notification may keep such person or vessel under surveillance within its own territory, under the conditions agreed upon by both of the Contracting Parties.

(*c*) Only the authorities of the Party to which the above-mentioned person or fishing vessel belongs may try the offense and impose penalties therefor. The witnesses and evidence necessary for establishing the offense, so far as they are under the control of any of the Parties to this Convention, shall be furnished as promptly as possible to the Contracting Party having jurisdiction to try the offense.

2. With regard to the nationals or fishing vessels of one or more Contracting Parties in waters with respect to which they have agreed to continue to carry out conservation measures for certain stocks of fish in accordance with the provisions of this Convention, the Contracting Parties concerned shall carry out enforcement severally or jointly. In that case, the Contracting Parties concerned agree to report periodically through the Commission to the Contracting Party which has agreed to abstain from the exploitation of such stocks of fish on the enforcement conditions, and also, if requested, to provide opportunity for observation of the conduct of enforcement.

3. The Contracting Parties agree to meet, during the sixth year of the operation of this Convention, to review the effectiveness of the enforcement provisions of this article and, if desirable, to consider means by which they may more effectively be carried out.

**Art. XI.** . . .

2. This Convention . . . shall continue in force for a period of ten years and thereafter until one year from the day on which a Contracting Party shall give notice to the other Contracting Parties of an intention of terminating the Convention, whereupon it shall terminate as to all Contracting Parties.

**Annex, as amended in 1960, 1962 and 1963**

1. With regard to the stocks of fish in the respective waters named below, Japan agrees to abstain from fishing, and Canada and the United States of America agree to continue to carry out necessary conservation measures, in accordance with the provisions of Article V, Section 2 of this Convention:

(*a*) Halibut (. . .) The Convention area off the coasts of Canada and the United States of America, exclusive of the Bering Sea, in which commercial fishing for halibut is being or can be prosecuted. Halibut referred to herein shall be those originating along the coast of North America.

(*b*) Herring (. . .) The Convention area off the coasts of Canada in which commercial fishing for herring of Canadian origin is being or can be prosecuted, exclusive of the waters of the high seas north of 51°56′ North Latitude and west of the Queen Charlotte Islands and west of a line drawn between Langara Point on Langara Island, Queen Charlotte Islands, and Cape Muzon on Dall Island in Southeast Alaska.

(c) Salmon (. . .) The Convention area off the coasts of Canada and the United States of America, exclusive of the Bering Sea and of the waters of the North Pacific Ocean west of a provisional line following the meridian passing through the western extremity of Atka Island; in which commercial fishing for salmon originating in the rivers of Canada and the United States of America is being or can be prosecuted.

2. With regard to the stocks of fish in the waters named below, Canada and Japan agree to abstain from fishing, and the United States of America agreed to continue to carry out necessary conservation measures, in accordance with the provisions of Article V, Section 2 of the Convention:

Salmon (. . .)

The Convention area of the Bering Sea east of the line starting from Cape Prince of Wales on the west coast of Alaska, running westward to 168°58′22.59″ West Longitude; thence due south to a point 65°15′00″ North Latitude; thence along the great circle course which passes through 51° North Latitude and 167° East Longitude, to its intersection with meridian 175° West Longitude; thence south along a provisional line which follows this meridian to the territorial waters limit of Atka Island; in which commercial fishing for salmon originating in the rivers of the United States of America is being or can be prosecuted.

### Protocol to the International Convention for the High Seas Fisheries of the North Pacific Ocean

. . . . .

The Governments of the United States of America, Canada and Japan agree that the line of meridian 175° West Longitude and the line following the meridian passing through the western extremity of Atka Island, which have been adopted for determining the areas in which the exploitation of salmon is abstained or the conservation measures for salmon continue to be enforced in accordance with the provisions of the annex to this Convention, shall be considered as provisional lines which shall continue in effect subject to confirmation or readjustment in accordance with the procedure mentioned below.

The Commission to be established under the Convention shall, as expeditiously as practicable, investigate the waters of the Convention area to determine if there are areas in which salmon originating in the rivers of Canada and of the United States of America intermingle with salmon originating in the rivers of Asia. If such areas are found the Commission shall conduct suitable studies to determine a line or lines which best divide salmon of Asiatic origin and salmon of Canadian and United States of America origin, from which certain Contracting Parties have agreed to abstain in accordance with the provisions of article V, section 2, and

544

whether it can be shown beyond a reasonable doubt that this line or lines more equitably divide such salmon than the provisional lines specified in sections 1 (c) and 2 of the annex. In accordance with these determinations the Commission shall recommend that such provisional lines be confirmed or that they be changed in accordance with these results, giving due consideration to adjustments required to simplify administration.

In the event, however, the Commission fails within a reasonable period of time to recommend unanimously such line or lines, it is agreed that the matter shall be referred to a special committee of scientists consisting of three competent and disinterested persons, no one of whom shall be a national of a Contracting Party, selected by mutual agreement of all Parties for the determination of this matter.

It is further agreed that when a determination has been made by a majority of such special committee, the Commission shall make a recommendation in accordance therewith.

The Governments of the United States of America, Canada and Japan, in signing this Protocol, desire to make it clear that the procedure set forth herein is designed to cover a special situation. It is not, therefore, to be considered a precedent for the final resolution of any matters which may, in the future, come before the Commission.

## THE 1953 CONVENTION FOR THE PRESERVATION OF THE HALIBUT FISHERY OF THE NORTHERN PACIFIC OCEAN AND BERING SEA (Canada and United States of America)

> Signed at Ottawa on 2 March 1953; Entered into force on 28 October 1953. U.N. Treaty Series, vol. 222, p. 77. Replacing the Convention signed at Ottawa on 29 January 1937 (U.N. Treaty Series, vol. 181, p. 209).

. . . . .

**Art. I.** 1. The nationals and inhabitants and fishing vessels and boats of the United States of America and of Canada, respectively, are hereby prohibited from fishing for halibut (*Hippoglossus*) in Convention waters as herein defined, except as provided by the International Pacific Halibut Commission in regulations designed to develop the stocks of halibut in the Convention waters to those levels which will permit the maximum sustained yield and to maintain the stocks at those levels pursuant to Article III of this Convention.

2. "Convention waters" means the territorial waters and the high seas

of the western coasts of the United States of America and of Canada, including the southern as well as the western coasts of Alaska.

3. It is understood that nothing contained in this Convention shall prohibit the nationals or inhabitants or the fishing vessels or boats of the United States of America or of Canada from fishing in the Convention waters for other species of fish during any season when fishing for halibut in the Convention waters is prohibited by this Convention or any regulations adopted pursuant to this Convention. It is further understood that nothing contained in this Convention shall prohibit the International Pacific Halibut Commission from conducting or authorizing fishing operations for investigation purposes at any time.

**Art. II.** 1. Every national or inhabitant, vessel or boat of the United States of America or of Canada engaged in fishing on the high seas in violation of this Convention or of any regulation adopted pursuant thereto may be seized by duly authorized officers of either Contracting Party and detained by the officers making such seizure and delivered as soon as practicable to an authorized official of the country to which such person, vessel or boat belongs, at the nearest point to the place of seizure or elsewhere as may be agreed upon. The authorities of the country to which such person, vessel or boat belongs alone shall have jurisdiction to conduct prosecutions for the violation of the provisions of this Convention or any regulations which may be adopted in pursuance thereof and to impose penalties for such violation, and the witnesses and proof necessary for such prosecutions, so far as any witnesses or proofs are under the control of the other Contracting Party, shall be furnished with all reasonable promptitude to the authorities having jurisdiction to conduct the prosecutions.

2. Each Contracting Party shall be responsible for the proper observance of this Convention and of any regulations adopted under the provisions thereof in the portion of its waters covered thereby.

**Art. III.** 1. The Contracting Parties agree to continue under this Convention the Commission known as the International Fisheries Commission established by the Convention for the preservation of the halibut fishery, signed at Washington, March 2, 1923, continued by the Convention signed at Ottawa, May 9, 1930 and further continued by the Convention, signed at Ottawa, January 29, 1937, except that after the date of entry into force of this Convention it shall consist of six members, three appointed by each Contracting Party, and shall be known as the International Pacific Halibut Commission. This Commission shall make such investigations as are necessary into the life history of the halibut in the Convention waters and shall publish a report of its activities and investigations from time to time. Each Contracting Party shall have power to fill, and shall fill from time to time, vacancies which may occur in its representation on the Com-

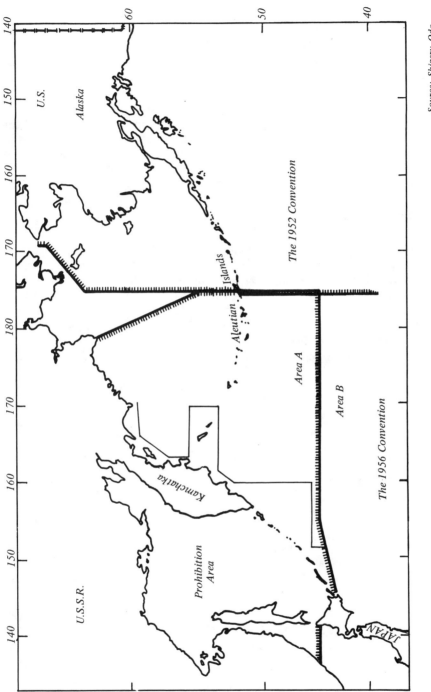

*North Pacific Ocean (The 1952 Convention and the 1956 Convention)*

Source: Shigeru Oda

mission. Each Contracting Party shall pay the salaries and expenses of its own members. Joint expenses incurred by the Commission shall be paid by the two Contracting Parties in equal moieties. All decisions of the Commission shall be made by a concurring vote of at least two of the Commissioners of each Contracting Party.

2. The Contracting Parties agree that for the purpose of developing the stocks of halibut of the Northern Pacific Ocean and Bering Sea to levels which will permit the maximum sustained yield from that fishery and for maintaining the stocks at those levels, the International Pacific Halibut Commission, with the approval of the President of the United States of America and of the Governor General in Council of Canada, may, after investigation has indicated such action to be necessary, in respect of the nationals and inhabitants and fishing vessels and boats of the United States of America and of Canada, and in respect of halibut:

(*a*) divide the Convention waters into areas;

(*b*) establish one or more open or closed seasons, as to each area;

(*c*) limit the size of the fish and the quantity of the catch to be taken from each area within any season during which fishing is allowed;

(*d*) during both open and closed seasons, permit, limit, regulate or prohibit, the incidental catch of halibut that may be taken, retained, possessed, or landed from each area or portion of an area, by vessels fishing for other species of fish;

(*e*) prohibit departure of vessels from any port or place, or from any receiving vessel or station, to any area for halibut fishing, after any date when in the judgment of the International Pacific Halibut Commission the vessels which have departed for that area prior to that date or which are known to be fishing in that area shall suffice to catch the limit which shall have been set for that area under section (*c*) for this paragraph;

(*f*) fix the size and character of halibut fishing appliances to be used in any area;

(*g*) make such regulations for the licencing and departure of vessels and for the collection of statistics of the catch of halibut as it shall find necessary to determine the condition and trend of the halibut fishery and to carry out the other provisions of this Convention;

(*h*) close to all taking of halibut such portion or portions of an area or areas as the International Pacific Halibut Commission finds to be populated by small, immature halibut and designates as nursery grounds.

**Art. IV.** The Contracting Parties agree to enact and enforce such legislation as may be necessary to make effective the provisions of this Convention and any regulation adopted thereunder, with appropriate penalties for violations thereof.

**Art. V.** . . .

548

2. This Convention ... shall remain in force for a period of five years and thereafter until two years from the date on which either Contracting Party shall have given notice to the other of its desire to terminate it.

3. This Convention shall, from the date of the exchange of ratifications, replace and terminate the Convention for the preservation of the halibut fishery signed at Ottawa, January 29, 1937.


## THE 1956 CONVENTION CONCERNING THE HIGH SEAS FISHERIES OF THE NORTHWEST PACIFIC OCEAN, AS AMENDED
(Japan and Union of Soviet Socialist Republics)

> Signed at Moscow on 14 May 1956; Entered into force on 12 December 1956. Unofficial English translation of the original text is printed at The Japanese Annual of International Law, vol. 1, p. 119. The Annex has been extensively revised, but its English version is not available.

The Governments of Japan and the Union of Soviet Socialist Republics,

Considering the common interest of the Contracting Parties with respect to the development, on a rational basis, of the fisheries in the Northwest Pacific Ocean, and their mutual responsibility with respect to the condition of the fish and other marine living resources, as well as to the effective utilization of those resources,

Recognizing that it will serve the common interest of mankind, as well as the interests of the Contracting Parties to maintain the maximum sustained productivity of fisheries in the Northwest Pacific Ocean,

Considering that each of the Contracting Parties should assume an obligation, on a free and equal footing, to conserve and increase the above mentioned resources,

Recognizing that it is highly desirable to promote and coordinate the scientific studies of the Contracting Parties, the purpose of which is to maintain the maximum sustained productivity of fisheries of interest to the two Contracting Parties,

Have, therefore, decided to conclude this Convention, and for this purpose have appointed their respective representatives who have agreed as follows:

**Art. I.** 1. The area to which this Convention applies, hereinafter referred to as "the Convention area," shall be all waters, other than territorial waters, of the Northwest Pacific Ocean, including the Japan Sea, the Okhotsk Sea and the Bering Sea.

2. Nothing in this Convention shall be deemed to affect in any way the position of the Contracting Parties in regard to the limits of territorial sea or to the jurisdiction over fisheries.

**Art. II.** 1. The Contracting Parties in order to conserve and develop the fish and other marine living resources, hereinafter referred to as the "fishery resources," agree to carry out in the Convention area, the co-ordinated measures specified in the Annex to this Convention.

2. The Annex attached hereto shall form an integral part of this Convention. All references to the "Convention" shall be understood as including the said Annex either in its present terms or as revised in accordance with the provisions of paragraph (*a*) of Article IV.

**Art. III.** 1. In order to realize the objectives of this Convention, the Contracting Parties shall establish the Japan-Soviet Northwest Pacific Fisheries Commission, hereinafter referred to as "the Commission."

2. The Commission shall be composed of two national sections, each consisting of three members appointed by the governments of the respective Contracting Parties.

3. All resolutions, recommendations and other decisions of the Commission shall be made only by agreement between the national sections.

4. The Commission may decide upon and revise, as occasion may require, the rules for the conduct of its meetings.

5. The Commission shall meet at least once each year and at such other times as may be requested by one of the national sections. The date and place of the first meeting shall be determined by agreement between the Contracting Parties.

6. At its first meeting the Commission shall select a Chairman and Vice-Chairman from different national sections. The Chairman and Vice-Chairman shall hold office for a period of one year. The selection of a Chairman and Vice-Chairman from the national sections shall be made in such a manner as will yearly provide each Contracting Party in turn with representation in those offices.

7. The official languages of the Commission shall be Japanese and Russian.

8. The expenses incurred by a member of the Commission in connection with participation in the meetings of the Commission shall be paid by the appointing government. Joint expenses incurred by the Commission shall be paid by the Commission through contributions made by the Contracting Parties in the form and proportion recommended by the Commission and approved by the Contracting Parties.

**Art. IV.** The Commission shall perform the following functions:

(*a*) At the regular annual meeting, consider the appropriateness of coordinated measure being enforced at the time, and if necessary revise the Annex to this Convention. Such revision shall be determined on the basis of scientific findings.

(b) When it is required by the Annex to fix the total annual catch of a stock of fish, determine the total annual catch of such stock by the Contracting Parties and notify the said Parties.

(c) Determine the kind and scope of statistics and other reports to be submitted to the Commission by each of the Contracting Parties for carrying out the provisions of this Convention.

(d) For the purpose of studying the fishery resources, prepare and adjust co-ordinated scientific research programs and recommend them to the Contracting Parties.

(e) Submit annually to the Contracting Parties a report on the operations of the Commission.

(f) In addition to the functions stipulated above, make recommendations to the Contracting Parties with respect to the matter of conservation and increase of fishery resources in the Convention area.

**Art. V.** The Contracting Parties agree, for the purpose of mutually exchanging experiences concerning the study and conservation of fishery resources and regulation of fisheries, to exchange men of learning and experience in fisheries. The exchange of such men shall be conducted by agreement from time to time between the two Parties.

**Art. VI.** 1. The Contracting Parties shall take appropriate and effective measures in order to carry out the provisions of this Convention.

2. When in receipt of the notification from the Commission concerning the total annual catch fixed for each of the Contracting Parties in accordance with paragraph (b) of Article IV, the Contracting Parties shall issue license or certificate to their fishing vessels and inform each other of all such licenses and certificates issued.

3. The licenses and certificates issued by the Contracting Parties shall be in both Japanese and Russian languages, and the fishing vessels, when engaged in fishing operations, shall have on board their license or certificate without fail.

4. The Contracting Parties agree, for the purpose of rendering effective the provisions of this Convention, to enact and enforce necessary laws and regulations, with regard to their nationals, organizations and fishing vessels, with appropriate penalties against violations thereof and to sumbit to the Commission a report on any action taken by them with regard thereto.

**Art. VII.** 1. When authorized officials of the either of the Contracting Parties have reasonable ground to believe that a fishing vessel of other Party is actually violating the provisions of this Convention, such officials may board and search the vessel to ascertain whether the said provisions are being observed.

Such officials shall present credentials issued by their Government and written in both Japanese and Russian languages, if requested by the master of the vessel.

2. If it becomes clear as a result of the search conducted by such officials that there is evidence that the fishing vessel or any person on board such vessel is violating the Convention, the said officials may seize such vessel or arrest such person.

In that case, the Contracting Party to which the officials belong shall notify as soon as possible the other Contracting Party to which such fishing vessel or person belongs of the arrest or seizure, and shall deliver such vessel or person as promptly as practicable to the authorized officials of the Contracting Party to which the vessel or person belongs at the place of arrest or seizure unless another place is agreed upon by the Contracting Parties. Provided, however, that when the Contracting Party which receives such notification cannot immediately accept delivery and requests of the other Contracting Party, the latter Party receiving the request may keep such vessel or person under surveillance within its own territory, under the conditions agreed upon by the Contracting Parties.

3. Only the authorities of the Party to which the above mentioned fishing vessel or person belongs have jurisdiction to try cases arising in connection with this Article and impose penalties therefor. Written evidence and proof establishing the offense shall be furnished as promptly as possible to the Contracting Party having jurisdiction to try the case.

**Art. VIII.** 1. This Convention shall become effective from the date of entry into force of the Peace Treaty between Japan and the Union of Soviet Socialist Republics or from the date of restoration of diplomatic relations between the said countries.

2. After this Convention has remained in force for a period of ten years, either Contracting Party may give notice to the other Contracting Party of an intention to abrogate the said Convention, and it shall terminate one year after the date of receipt of the said notification by the latter Party.

**Annex, as amended up to 1973**

The Contracting Parties agree to regulate, within the Convention area, the fishing of the stocks of fish named below:
1. Salmon
   Chun Salmon (Oncorhynchus keta)
   Pink Salmon (Oncorhynchus gorbuscha)
   Silver Salmon (Oncorhynchus kisutch)

Sockeye Salmon (Oncorhynchus nerka)
King Salmon (Oncorhynchus tschawytscha)

(a) The Convention area is divided into two areas:
    Area A—the Northwest Pacific Ocean (including the Okhotsk Sea and Bering Sea) bounded on the east and south by a line running from Cape Navarin to intersection of 55° North Latitude and 000° West Longitude; thence south to intersection of 45° North Latitude and 175° West Longitude; thence west to intersection of 45° North Latitude and 155° East Longitude; thence southwest to Akiyuri XXXXXXX and the Japan Sea north of 45° North Latitude.
    Area B—The Convention area except Area A.

(b) Sea-fishery with movable fishing gear shall be prohibited in the following areas: .... (see the chart)

(c) The total amount of catch for the year of 1973, as an odd year, shall be 101,000 metric tons, 91,000 metric tons for Japan and 10,000 metric tons for the Union of Soviet Socialist Republics respectively.

(d) With respect to mothership-type fishing operations, the catch per year (in raw fish weight) by each fishing vessel and investigation ship shall not exceed three hundred metric tons and one hundred and fifty metric tons respectively.
    The total amount of catch by all the fishing vessels and investigation ships belonging to a mothership shall not exceed the total catch by each fishing vessel and investigation vessel may exceed to some degree the above amounts fixed for each fishing vessel and investigation vessel respectively.

(e) The fishing season shall start, as follows: ...
    The fishing season shall end, as follows: ...

(f) The length of drifting nets set in the sea by a fishing vessel shall be, as follows: ...

(g) The diameter of a twig-line of long-line used for long-line fishery in the Area B (except the Japan Sea) ...
    Long-line fishery shall not be allowed in Area A.

2. Herring (Clupea Pallasii)

Fishing of small inmature herring of less than twenty-one centimetres in length (from tip of snout to the end of vertabral column at the caudal fin) shall be prohibited.

Incidental catch of such small herrings, if not in large quantity, shall be allowed. The allowable extent of such catch shall be determined by the Commission.

# THE 1965 AGREEMENT ON FISHERIES
## (Japan and Republic of Korea)

Signed at Tokyo on 22 June 1965; Entered into force on 18 December 1965. U.N. Treaty Series, vol. 583, p. 129.

Japan and the Republic of Korea,

Desiring that the maximum sustained productivity of the fishery resources in waters of their common interest be maintained;

Being convinced that the conservation of the said resources and their rational exploitation and development will serve the interest of both countries;

Confirming that the principle of the freedom of the high seas shall be respected unless otherwise specifically provided in the present Agreement;

Recognizing the desirability of eliminating causes of disputes which may arise from their geographical proximity and the intermingling of their fisheries; and

Desiring to cooperate mutually for the development of their fisheries;
Have agreed as follows:

**Art. I.** 1. The Contracting Parties mutually recognize that each Contracting Party has the right to establish within twelve nautical miles measured from its coastal baseline a sea zone over which it exercises exclusive jurisdiction with respect to fisheries (hereinafter referred to as "fishery zone"). However, in case where either Contracting Party uses a straight baseline in establishing its fishery zone, it shall determine such straight baseline upon consultation with the other Contracting Party.

2. The Contracting Parties shall not raise against each other any objection to the exclusion by either Contracting Party of the fishing vessels of the other Contracting Party from engaging in fishing operation in the fishery zone of that either Contracting Party.

3. The overlapping part of the fishery zones of the Contracting Parties shall be divided into two by the straight lines joining the two end-points of the part with the mid-point of the straight line drawn across that area at its widest point.

**Art. II.** The Contracting Parties shall establish a joint regulation zone enclosed by the lines described below (excluding any territorial seas and the fishery zone of the Republic of Korea). . . . [see the map on p. 559]

**Art. III.** The Contracting Parties shall implement in the joint regulation zone, until such time as conservation measures necessary for the maintenance of the maximum sustained productivity of fishery resources are implemented on the basis of sufficient scientific surveys, the provisional

554

regulation measures for fisheries described in the Annex, which constitutes an integral part of the present Agreement, with respect to drag-net fishing and seine fishing and to mackerel-angling fishing by fishing vessels of not less than 60 tons. (Tonnage is in gross tonnage and is indicated by deducting the tonnage allowed for improving living quarters of the vessel.)

**Art. IV.** 1. Policing (including halting and inspecting of vessel) and court jurisdiction in the waters outside the fishery zone shall be carried out and exercised only by the Contracting Party to which the fishing vessel belongs.

2. Each Contracting Party shall give and exercise pertinent guidance and supervision in order to ensure that its nationals and fishing vessels observe faithfully the provisional regulation measures for fisheries, and shall enforce domestic measures, including appropriate penalties against violations thereof.

**Art. V.** Joint resources survey zones shall be established outside the joint regulation zone. The extent of the said survey zones and the survey to be conducted within these zones shall be determined upon consultation between the two Contracting Parties on the basis of recommendation to be made by the Joint Fisheries Commission provided for in Article VI of the present Agreement.

**Art. VI.** 1. The Contracting Parties shall establish and maintain the Japan-Republic of Korea Joint Fisheries Commission (hereinafter referred to as "the Commission") in order to realize the objectives of the present Agreement.

2. The Commission shall be composed of two national sections, each consisting of three members appointed by the Governments of the respective Contracting Parties.

3. All resolutions, recommendations, and other decisions of the Commission shall be made only by agreement between the national sections.

4. The Commission may decide upon and amend, as occasion may require, rules for the conduct of its meetings.

5. The Commission shall meet at least once each year and at such other times as may be requested by either of the national sections. The date and place of the first meeting shall be determined by agreement between the Contracting Parties.

6. At its first meeting, the Commission shall select a Chairman and a Vice-Chairman from different national sections. The Chairman and the Vice-Chairman shall hold office for a period of one year. Selection of the Chairman and the Vice-Chairman from the national sections shall be made in such a manner as will provide in turn each Contracting Party with representation in these offices.

7. A permanent secretariat shall be established under the Commission

555

to carry out the business of the Commission.

8. The official languages of the Commission shall be Japanese and Korean. Proposals and data may be submitted in either official language, or, if necessary, in English.

9. In case the Commission concludes that joint expenses are necessary, such expenses shall be paid by the Commission through contributions made by the Contracting Parties in the form and proportion recommended by the Commission and approved by the Contracting Parties.

10. The Commission may delegate the disbursement of funds for the joint expenses.

**Art. VII.** 1. The Commission shall perform the following functions:

(*a*) Recommend to the Contracting Parties with respect to scientific survey to be conducted for the purpose of studying the fishery resources in waters of their common interest and to the regulation measures to be taken within the joint regulation zone on the basis of the results of such survey and study;

(*b*) Recommend to the Contracting Parties with respect to the extent of the joint resources survey zones;

(*c*) Review, when necessary, matters concerning the provisional regulation measures for fisheries and recommend to the Contracting Parties with respect to measures, including the revision of the provisional regulation measures, to be taken on the basis of the results of such review;

(*d*) Deliberate on necessary matters concerning the safety and order of operation between the fishing vessels of the Contracting Parties and on general principles of measures for handling accidents at sea between the fishing vessels of the Contracting Parties, and recommend to the Contracting Parties with respect to measures to be taken on the basis of the results of such deliberation;

(*e*) Compile and study data, statistics and records to be provided by the Contracting Parties at the request of the Commission;

(*f*) Consider and recommend to the Contracting Parties with respect to the enactment of schedules of equivalent penalties for violations of the present Agreement;

(*g*) Submit annually to the Contracting Parties a report on the operations of the Commission; and

(*h*) In addition to the foregoing, deliberate on various technical questions arising from the implementation of the present Agreement, and recommend, when deemed necessary, to the Contracting Parties with respect to measures to be taken.

2. The Commission, in order to perform its functions, may, when necessary, establish subordinate organs composed of experts.

3. The Governments of the Contracting Parties shall respect to the

556

extent possible the recommendations made by the Commission under the provisions of paragraph 1.

**Art. VIII.** 1. The Contracting Parties shall take measures deemed pertinent toward their respective nationals and fishing vessels in order to have them observe international practices concerning navigation, to ensure safety and maintain proper order in operation between the fishing vessels of the Contracting Parties and to seek smooth and speedy settlements of accidents at sea between the fishing vessels of the Contracting Parties.

2. For the purposes set forth in paragraph 1, the authorities concerned of the Contracting Parties shall, to the extent possible, maintain close contact and cooperate with each other.

**Art. IX.** 1. Any dispute between the Contracting Parties concerning the interpretation and implementation of the present Agreement shall be settled, first of all, through diplomatic channels.

2. Any dispute which fails to be settled under the provisions of paragraph 1 shall be referred for decision to an arbitration board composed of three arbitrators, one each to be appointed by the Government of each Contracting Party within a period of thirty days from the date of receipt by the Government of either Contracting Party from the Government of the other of a note requesting arbitration of the dispute, and the third arbitrator to be agreed upon by the two arbitrators so chosen within a further period of thirty days or the third arbitrator to be appointed by the government of a third country agreed upon within such further period by the two arbitrators, provided that the third arbitrator shall not be a national of either Contracting Party.

3. If, within the periods respectively referred to, the Government of either Contracting Party fails to appoint an arbitrator, or the third arbitrator or a third country is not agreed upon, the arbitration board shall be composed of the two arbitrators to be designated by each of the governments of the two countries respectively chosen by the Governments of the Contracting Parties within a period of thirty days and the third arbitrator to be designated by the governments of a third country to be determined upon consultation between the governments so chosen.

4. The Governments of the Contracting Parties shall abide by any award made by the arbitration board under the provisions of the present Article.

**Art. X.** . . .
2. The present Agreement shall remain in force for a period of five years and thereafter until one year from the day on which either Contracting Party shall give notice to the other of its intention to terminate the present Agreement.

557

## Annex

The provisional regulation measures for fisheries provided for in Article 3 of the present Agreement shall apply to each of the two Contracting Parties and shall be as follows:

1. The maximum number of fishing vessels or fishing units in operation (that is, the maximum number of fishing vessels or units operating at a given time within the joint regulation zone, holding licences and bearing identification markings for fishing operation within the said zone):

(a) For drag-net fishing by fishing vessels of less than 50 tons, 115 vessels.

(b) For drag-net fishing by fishing vessels of not less than 50 tons

(i) 270 vessels during the period November 1 to April 30 of the following year,

(ii) 100 vessels during the period May 1 to October 31.

(c) For seine fishing

(i) 60 fishing units during the period January 16 to May 15,

(ii) 120 fishing units during the period May 16 to January 15 of the following year.

(d) For mackerel-angling fishing by fishing vessels of not less than 60 tons, 15 vessels; provided that the period for fishing operation shall be from June 1 to December 31, and that the fishing operation zone shall be . . .

(e) While there exists a difference in fish-catching capability between fishing vessels of Japan and of the Republic of Korea, the number of fishing vessels of units in operation of the Republic of Korea shall be adjusted through consultation between the Governments of the two Contracting Parties, with the maximum number of fishing vessels or units in operation provided for in the present Agreement as a standard and paying regard to such difference.

2. Size of fishing vessels:

(a) For drag-net fishing . . .

(b) For seine fishing . . .

(c) For mackerel-angling fishing . . .

3. Mesh size (inner diameter when in sea water):

(a) For drag-net fishing by fishing vessels of less than 50 tons, . . .

(b) For drag-net fishing by fishing vessels of not less than 50 tons, . . .

(c) For the main net for horse mackerel or mackerel of seine fishing, . . .

4. Power of fish-luring lights (total installation capacity of generators):

(a) For seine fishing

(b) For mackerel-angling fishing by fishing vessels of not less than 60 tons, . . .

558

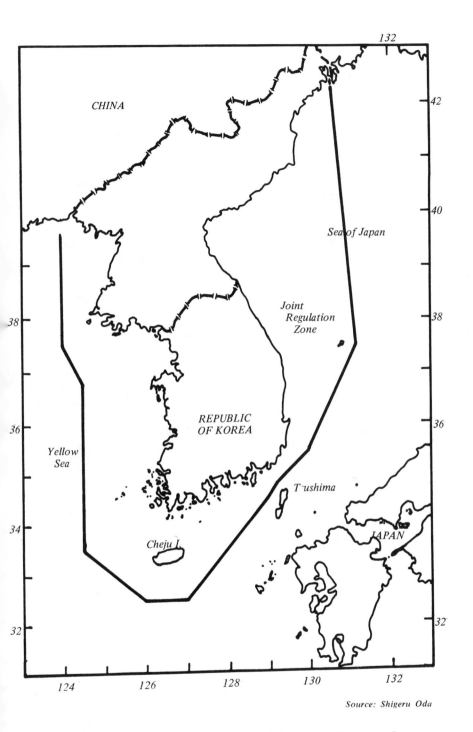

CHINA

Sea of Japan

Joint
Regulation
Zone

REPUBLIC
OF KOREA

Yellow
Sea

T·ushima

JAPAN

Cheju I.

*Joint Regulation Zone around Korea (Agreement between Japan
and Republic of Korea)*

5. Licences and identification markings:

(*a*) Fishing vessels operating in the joint regulation zone shall hold licences and shall bear identification markings, issued by the respective Governments. However, with respect to fishing vessels engaging in seine fishing, fishing vessels other than seine vessels are not required to hold licences, and seine vessels shall display principal markings while vessels other than seine vessels shall bear submarkings which correspond with principal markings.

(*b*) The total number of licences and of identification markings (with respect to fishing vessels engaging in drag-net fishing and mackerel-angling fishing, two markings borne by each fishing vessel shall be counted as one, and with respect to fishing vessels engaging in seine fishing, two principal markings borne by each seine vessel shall be counted as one) shall be, for each fishery subject to the provisional regulation measures for fisheries, the same as the maximum number of fishing vessels and units in operation for such fishery. However, in view of the realities of fisheries, the number of issuance may be increased over the maximum number of fishing vessels in operation by 15 percent with respect to drag-net fishing by fishing vessels of not less than 50 tons and by 20 percent with respect to drag-net fishing by fishing vessels of less than 50 tons.

(*c*) The form of identification markings and the place where they shall be borne shall be determined upon consultations between the Governments of the two Contracting Parties.

**Exchange of notes concerning the straight baselines in connection with the establishment of the fishery zone of the Republic of Korea:** [omitted]

**Exchange of notes concerning the fishery zone of the Republic of Korea**

As a provisional measure, the waters enclosed by the lines delimiting the fishery zone to be established by the Republic of Korea and the following lines shall for the time being be treated as being included in the fishery zone of the Republic of Korea. . . .

**Agreed Minutes:** [omitted]

# THE 1972 AGREEMENT ON FISHERIES (Republic of Korea and United States of America)

Signed at Washington on 24 November 1972; Entered into force on 12 December 1972. TIAS 7517.

The Government of the United States of America and the Government of the Republic of Korea,

Desiring to continue and to expand their cooperation in the conservation and rational exploitation of fishery resources and in the acquisition of scientific knowledge necessary thereto, and

Being mutually concerned to have the fisheries in the Northeastern Pacific Ocean and Bering Sea conducted with due regard to their respective interests,

Have agreed as follows:

**Art. I.** The Government of the United States of America and the Government of the Republic of Korea consider it desirable to expand research concerning species of fish of mutual interest to both parties through both national and joint or coordinated programs. The specialized agencies of both Governments will exchange scientific and statistical data, published studies and other results of fishery research.

**Art. II.** The Government of the United States of America will:

*a.* continue to provide technical advice, as may be needed, regarding the propagation under sanitary conditions of shellfish in the Republic of Korea and, subject to its domestic laws and regulations, assist in other ways in the further development of the shellfish industry in Korea;

*b.* continue to provide technical assistance toward the establishment and development of salmon resources in waters of the Republic of Korea, including the continued provision of salmon eggs as available.

**Art. III.** Fishing vessels of the Republic of Korea may conduct loading operations in the following areas within the nine-mile zone contiguous to the territorial sea of the United States:

*a.* On the north side of Unalaska Island, Alaska, between 167°30′ and 167°35′ west longitude.

*b.* On the north side of St. Matthew Island, Alaska, between 172°29′ and 172°46′ west longitude and on the south side of St. Matthew Island between 172°17′ and 172°35′ west longitude and between 172°54′ and 173°04′ west longitude.

*c.* Off St. George Island in the Pribilofs.

**Art. IV.** Both Governments will encourage and assist by appropriate means the establishment and development of commercial fisheries ventures with the joint participation of nationals of the two countries, bearing in mind the conservation requirements of the stocks of fish to be harvested.

**Art. V.** Both Governments will ensure that fishing operations by their nationals and vessels in the Northeastern Pacific Ocean and Bering Sea are conducted with a view to the maintenance of the maximum sustainable yield of the living resources. In view of the cooperative programs for the development of fisheries of the Republic of Korea as set forth in preceding articles, the Government of the Republic of Korea will take the measures necessary to ensure that nationals and vessels of Korea will refrain from fishing for salmon and halibut in the Northeastern Pacific Ocean and Bering Sea east of 175° west longitude.

**Art. VI.** With respect to areas of concentration of fishing operations of both countries, each Government will take appropriate measures aimed at prevention of damage to fishing gear, including measures for improvement of the means of marking fixed gear, measures to ensure that fixed gear is set with due regard for the operation of mobile gear and measures to ensure that vessels operating with mobile gear will operate with due regard for fixed gear. In the event that gear conflicts should arise between the fisheries of the two countries, prompt consultations will be held between the two Governments as may be appropriate in each case.

**Art. VII.** Both Governments will seek to ensure that their nationals and vessels engaged in the fisheries refrain from practices which would result in pollution of the seas and consequent deleterious effects on living marine resources.

**Art. VIII.** Nothing in this Agreement shall be interpreted as prejudicing the views of either Government with regard to freedom of fishing on the high seas, nor will be construed as limiting the rights of either Government under international law.

**Art. IX.** At the request of either Government, representatives of the two Governments will meet at a mutually convenient time with a view to modifying the present Agreement. In any event, representatives of the two Governments will meet at a mutually convenient time prior to the expiration of the period of validity of this Agreement to review its operation and to decide on future arrangements.

**Art. X.** The Agreement shall remain in force for a period of five years.

**Agreed Minutes:** [omitted]

## 4. INDO-PACIFIC

## THE 1948 AGREEMENT FOR THE ESTABLISHMENT OF INDO-PACIFIC FISHERIES COUNCIL, AS AMENDED

Formulated at Baguio on 26 February 1948 and approved by the Conference of the FAO in Washington, November 1948; Entered into force on 9 November 1948. U.N. Treaty Series, vol. 120, p. 59. Amended by the 1952, 1955, 1958 and 1961 Amendments. U.N. Treaty Series, vol. 190, p. 383; vol. 227, p. 322; vol. 343, p. 343; vol. 418, p. 348. The Parties to this Agreement as of 31 December 1973 are: Australia, Burma, France, India, Indonesia, Japan, Khmer, Korea (Rep. of), Malaysia, Netherlands, New Zealand, Pakistan, Philippines, Sri Lanka, Thailand, U.K., U.S. and Vietnam.

The Governments of Burma, China, France, India, the Netherlands, the Republic of the Philippines, the United Kingdom and the United States of America, Members of the Food and Agriculture Organization of the United Nations, having a mutual interest in the development and proper utilization of the living aquatic resources of the Indo-Pacific Areas, and desiring to further the attainment of these ends through international cooperation by the establishment of an Indo-Pacific Fisheries Council agree as follows:

**Art. I.** *The Council*

1. The contracting Governments agree to establish, within the framework of the Food and Agriculture Organization of the United Nations (hereinafter referred to as "the Organization") a Council, to be known as the Indo-Pacific Fisheries Counci[1], for the purpose of carrying out the functions and duties hereinafter set forth in Article IV.

2. The Members of the Council shall be such Member Nations and Associate Members of the Organization and such non-member nations of the Organization which are Members of the United Nations that accept this Agreement in accordance with the provisions of Article IX thereof. As regards Associate Members, this Agreement shall, in accordance with the provisions of Article XIV-5 of the Constitution and Rule XXXI-3 of the General Rules of the Organization, be submitted by the Organization to the authority having responsibility for the international relations of such Associate Members.

**Art. II.** *Organization*

1. Each Member shall be represented at sessions of the Council by a single delegate, who may be accompanied by an alternate and by experts

and advisers. Participation in sessions of the Council by alternates, experts and advisers shall not entail the right to vote, except in the case of an alternate who is acting in the place of a delegate during his absence.

2. Each Member shall have one vote. Decisions of the Council shall be taken by a majority of the votes cast, except when a greater majority is required by this Agreement or by the Rules governing the procedure of the Council. A majority of the total membership of the Council shall constitute a quorum.

3. The Council shall at each regular session elect a Chairman and a Vice-Chairman who shall serve until the end of the next regular session.

4. The Chairman of the Council in consultation with the Director-General of the Organization shall convene a regular session of the Council at least once in every two years unless otherwise directed by a majority of the Members. The site and date of all sessions shall be determined by the Council in consultation with the Director-General of the Organization.

5. The seat of the Council shall be at the seat of the Regional Office of the Organization most conveniently situated within the area defined in Article V. Pending the establishment of such a Regional Office, the Council shall select a temporary seat within that area.

6. The Organization shall provide the Secretariat for the Council and the Director-General shall appoint its Secretary, who shall be administratively responsible to him.

7. The Council may, by a two-thirds majority of its membership, adopt and amend its own Rules of Procedure which shall be consistent with the General Rules of the Organization. The Rules of the Council and any amendments thereto shall come into force as from the date of approval by the Director-General of the Organization, subject to confirmation by the Council of the Organization.

**Art. III.** *Committees and Working Parties*

1. There shall be an Executive Committee consisting of the Chairman, the Vice-Chairman and the immediately retiring Chairman. In the unavoidable absence of one or two members of the Executive Committee from a Committee session, the Chairman shall have the power to co-opt the chairman of one or two of the Technical Committees which may from time to time be established in accordance with the Rules governing the procedure of the Council, at his discretion, to substitute the absent Committee member or members for that Committee session only, provided that one permanent member of the Executive Committee shall always be present and that the number of voting members attending the Committee session shall in no case exceed three.

2. The Council may in addition establish temporary, special or standing

committees to study and report on matters pertaining to the purpose of the Council.

3. The Council may establish working parties to study and recommend on specific technical problems. These working parties shall be convened by the Director-General of the Organization at such times and places as are in accordance with the objectives for which they were established.

4. The establishment of committees and working parties referred to in paragraphs 2 and 3 above shall be subject to the availability of the necessary funds in the relevant chapter of the approved budget of the Organization; the determination of such availability shall be made by the Director-General. Before taking any decision involving expenditures in connection with the establishment of committees and working parties the Council shall have before it a report from the Director-General on the administrative and financial implications thereof.

**Art. IV.** *Functions*

The Council shall have the following functions and duties:

*a.* To formulate the oceanographical, biological and other technical aspects of the problems of development and proper utilization of living aquatic resources;

*b.* To encourage and co-ordinate research and application of improved methods in every day practice;

*c.* To assemble, publish or otherwise disseminate oceanographical, biological and other technical information relating to living aquatic resources;

*d.* To recommend to Members such national or co-operative research and development projects as may appear necessary or desirable to fill gaps in such knowledge;

*e.* To undertake, where appropriate, co-operative research and development projects directed to this end;

*f.* To propose, and where necessary to adopt, measures to bring about the standardization of scientific equipment, techniques and nomenclature;

*g.* To extend its good offices in assisting its Members to secure essential material and equipment;

*h.* To report upon such questions relating to oceanographical, biological and other technical problems as may be recommended to it by Members or by the Organization and other international, national or private organizations with related interests;

*i.* To transmit biennially to the Director-General of the Organizations a report embodying its views, recommendations and decisions, and make such other reports to the Director-General of the Organization as may seem to it necessary or desirable. Reports of the committees and working parties of the Council provided for in Article III of this Agreement shall be transmitted to the Director-General through the Council.

### Art. V. *Area*

The Council shall carry out the functions and duties set forth in Article IV in the Indo-Pacific area.

### Art. VI. *Cooperation with International Bodies*

The Council shall co-operate closely with other international bodies in matters of mutual interest.

### Art. VII. *Expenses*

1. The expenses of delegates and their alternates, experts and advisers occasioned by attendance at sessions of the Council and the expenses of representatives on committees or working parties established in accordance with Article III of this Agreement shall be determined and paid by their respective governments.

2. The expenses of the Secretariat, including publications and communications, and of the Chairman, the Vice-Chairman and the immediately retired Chairman of the Council, when performing duties connected with its work during intervals between its sessions, shall be determined and paid by the Organization within the limits of a biennial budget prepared and approved in accordance with the Constitution, the General Rules and Financial Regulations of the Organization.

3. The expenses of research or development projects undertaken by individual members of the Council, whether independently or upon the recommendation of the Council, shall be determined and paid by their respective Governments.

4. The expenses incurred in connection with co-operative research or development projects undertaken in accordance with the provisions of Article IV, paragraphs (*d*) and (*e*) unless otherwise available shall be determined and paid by the Members in the form and proportion to which they shall mutually agree. Co-operative projects shall be submitted to the Council of the Organization prior to implementation. Contributions for co-operative projects shall be paid into a trust fund to be established by the Organization and shall be administered by the Organization in accordance with the Financial regulations and Rules of the Organization.

5. The expenses of experts invited, with the concurrence of the Director-General, to attend meetings of the Council, committees or working parties in their individual capacity shall be borne by the budget of the Organization.

### Art. VIII. *Amendments*

The Indo-Pacific Fisheries Council may amend this Agreement by a two-thirds majority of all the Members of this Council, any amendment becoming effective only after concurrence of the Council of the Organization unless the latter considers it desirable to refer the amendment to the Conference of the Organization for approval. An amendment shall become effective as from the date of the decision of the Council or Conference of the Organization as appropriate. However, any amendment involving new obligations for Members shall come into force with respect to each Member only on acceptance of it by that Member. The instruments of acceptance of amendments involving new obligations shall be deposited with the Director-General of the Organization who shall inform all the Members of the Indo-Pacific Fisheries Council as well as the Secretary-General of the United Nations of the receipt of acceptances and the entry into force of such amendments. The rights and obligations of any Member of the Indo-Pacific Fisheries Council that has not accepted an amendment involving additional obligations shall continue to be governed by the provisions of this Agreement as they stood prior to the amendment.

**Art. IX.** *Acceptance*

1. This Agreement shall be open to acceptance by Member Nations or Associate Members of the Organization.

2. The Council may, by a two-thirds majority of its membership, admit to membership such other nations that are Members of the United Nations as have submitted an application for membership and a declaration made in a formal instrument that they accept this Agreement as in force at the time of admission. Participation by such Nations in the activities of the Council shall be contingent upon the assumption of a proportionate share in the expenses of the Secretariat, as determined by the Organization.

3. Acceptance of this Agreement by any Member Nation or Associate Member of the Organization shall be effected by the deposit of an instrument of acceptance with the Director-General of the Organization and shall take effect on receipt of such instrument by the Director-General.

4. Acceptance of this Agreement by non-member nations of the Organization shall be effected by the deposit of an instrument of acceptance with the Director-General of the Organization. Membership shall become effective on the date on which the Council approves the application for membership, in conformity with the provisions of paragraph 2 of this Article.

5. The Director-General of the Organization shall inform all Members of the Council, all Member Nations of the Organization and the Secretary-General of the United Nations of all acceptances that have become effective.

6. Acceptance of this Agreement may be made subject to reservations which shall become effective only upon unanimous approval by the Members of the Council. The Director-General of the Organization shall notify forthwith all Members of the Council of any reservations. Members of

the Council not having replied within three months from the date of the notification shall be deemed to have accepted the reservation. Failing such approval the Nation making the reservation shall not become a party to this Agreement.

**Art. X.** *Entry into Force*

This Agreement shall enter into force upon the date of receipt of the fifth instrument of acceptance.

**Art. XI.** *Territorial Application*

The Members of the Council shall, when accepting this Agreement, state explicitly to which territories their participation shall extend. In the absence of such a declaration, participation shall be deemed to apply to all the territories for the international relations of which the Member is responsible. Subject to the provisions of Article XII below, the scope of the territorial application may be modified by a subsequent declaration.

**Art. XII.** *Withdrawal*

1. Any Member may withdraw from this Agreement at any time after the expiration of two years from the date upon which the Agreement entered into force with respect to that Member by giving written notice of such withdrawal to the Director-General of the Organization who shall immediately inform of such withdrawal all the Members of the Council and the Member Nations of the Organization as well as the Secretary-General of the United Nations. Notice of withdrawal shall become effective three months from the date of its receipt by the Director-General.

2. A Member of the Council may give notice of withdrawal with respect to one or more of the territories for the international relations of which it is responsible. When a Member gives notice of its own withdrawal from the Council it shall state to which territory or territories the withdrawal is to apply. In the absence of such a declaration, the withdrawal shall be deemed to apply to all the territories for the international relations of which the Member of the Council is responsible, except that such withdrawal shall not be deemed to apply to an Associate Member. Any Member of the Council that gives notice of withdrawal from the Organization shall be deemed to have simultaneously withdrawn from the Council, and this withdrawal shall be deemed to apply to all the territories for the international relations of which the Member concerned is responsible, except that such withdrawal shall not be deemed to apply to an Associate Member.

**Art. XIII.** *Interpretation and Settlement of Disputes*

Any dispute regarding the interpretation or application of this Agreement if not settled by the Council shall be referred to a committee composed of one member appointed by each of the parties to the dispute, and in addition an independent chairman chosen by the members of the com-

568

mittee. The recommendations of such a committee, while not binding in character, shall become the basis for renewed consideration by the parties concerned of the matter out of which the disagreement arose. If as the result of this procedure the dispute is not settled, it shall be referred to the International Court of Justice in accordance with the Statute of the Court, unless the parties to the dispute agree to another method of settlement.

**Art. XIV.** *Termination*

This Agreement shall be considered terminated if and when the number of Members of the Council drops below five unless the remaining Members of the Council unanimously decide otherwise.

**Art. XV.** *Certification and Registration*

. . . . .

# V. FISHING OPERATIONS AGREEMENTS

## THE 1967 CONVENTION ON CONDUCT OF FISHING OPERATIONS IN THE NORTH ATLANTIC

Signed at London on 1 June 1967 by the representatives of Belgium, Canada, Denmark, France, Germany (Fed. Rep. of), Iceland, Ireland, Italy, Luxembourg, Netherlands, Norway, Poland, Portugal, Spain, Sweden, U.K., U.S. and U.S.S.R.

. . . . .

Desiring to ensure good order and conduct on the fishing grounds in the North Atlantic area;

Have agreed as follows:

**Art. 1.** (1) The present Convention applies to the waters of the Atlantic and Arctic Oceans and their dependent seas which are more specifically defined in Annex I to this Convention.

(2) In this Convention

"fishing vessel" means any vessel engaged in the business of catching fish;

"vessel" means any fishing vessel and any vessel engaged in the business of processing fish or providing supplies or services to fishing vessels.

**Art. 2.** Nothing in this Convention shall be deemed to affect the rights, claims or views of any Contracting Party in regard to the limits of territorial waters or national fishery limits, or of the jurisdiction of a coastal State over fisheries.

**Art. 3.** (1) The fishing vessels of each Contracting Party shall be registered and marked in accordance with the regulations of that Party in order to ensure their identification at sea.

(2) The competent authority of each Contracting Party shall specify one or more letters and a series of numbers for each port or district.

(3) Each Contracting Party shall draw up a list showing these letters.

(4) This list, and all modifications which may subsequenty be made in it, shall be notified to the other Contracting Parties.

(5) The provisions of Annex II to this Convention shall apply to fishing vessels and their small boats and fishing implements.

**Art. 4.** (1) In addition to complying with the rules relating to signals as prescribed in the International Regulations for Preventing Collisions at Sea, the fishing vessels of each Contracting Party shall comply with the

570

provisions of Annex III to this Convention.

(2) No other additional light and sound signals than those provided in the Annex shall be used.

**Art. 5.** Nets, lines and other gear anchored in the sea and nets or lines which drift in the sea shall be marked in order to indicate their position and extent. The marking shall be in accordance with the provisions of Annex IV to this Convention.

**Art. 6.** (1) Subject to compliance with the International Regulations for Preventing Collisions at Sea all vessels shall conduct their operations so as not to interfere with the operations of fishing vessels or fishing gear and shall conform to the provisions of Annex V to this Convention.

(2) For the better implementation of these provisions the competent authorities of Contracting Parties may at their discretion notify the competent authorities of other Contracting Parties likely to be concerned of concentrations or probable concentrations known to them of fishing vessels or fishing gear, and Contracting Paries receiving such notification shall take such steps as are practicable to inform their vessels thereof. The authorised officers appointed in accordance with Article 9 of this Convention may also draw the attention of vessels to fishing gear placed in the sea.

**Art. 7.** (1) In any dispute that arises between the nationals of different Contracting Parties concerning damaged gear or damage to vessels resulting from entanglement of gear, the following procedure will apply in the absence of agreement among the Contracting Parties concerning the resolution of such disputes:

At the request of the Contracting Party of a complainant each Contracting Party concerned will appoint a review board or other appropriate authority for handling the claim. These boards or other authorities will examine the facts and endeavour to bring about a settlement.

(2) These arrangements are without prejudice to the rights of complainants to prosecute their claims by way of ordinary legal procedure.

**Art. 8.** (1) Each Contracting Party undertakes to take such measures as may be appropriate to implement and enforce the provisions of this Convention with respect to its vessels and gear.

(2) Within the area where a coastal State has jurisdiction over fisheries, the implementation and enforcement of the provisions of this Convention shall be the responsibility of the coastal State.

(3) Within that area the coastal State may make special rules and exemptions from any of the Rules in Annexes II to V to this Convention for vessels or gear which by reason of their size or type operate or are set only in coastal waters, provided that there shall be no discrimination in

571

form or in fact against vessels of other Contracting Parties entitled to fish in those waters. Before making special rules and exemptions under this paragraph in respect of areas in which foreign fishing vessels operate a Contracting Party shall inform the Contracting Parties concerned of their intentions and consult them if they so wish.

**Art. 9.** (1) To facilitate the implementation of the provisions of the Convention the arrangements set out in this Article and in Annex VI to this Convention shall apply outside national fishery limits.

(2) Authorised officers means officers who may be appointed by the Conracting Parties for the purpose of these arrangements.

(3) Any Contracting Party shall, upon the request of another Contracting Party, notify the latter of the names of the authorised officers who have been appointed or of the ships in which such officers are carried.

(4) Authorised officers shall observe whether the provisions of the Convention are being carried out, enquire and report on infringements of the provisions of the Convention, seek information in cases of damage, where desirable draw the attention of vessels of Contracting Parties to the provisions of the Convention, and shall co-operate for these purposes with the authorised officers of other Contracting Parties.

(5) If an authorised officer has reason to believe that a vessel of any Contracting Party is not complying with the provisions of the Convention, he may identify the vessel, seek to obtain the necessary information from the vessel and report. If the matter is sufficiently serious, he may order the vessel to stop and, if it is necessary in order to verify the facts of the case, he may board the vessel for enquiry and report.

(6) If an authorised officer has reason to believe that a vessel or its gear has caused damage to a vessel or fishing gear and that this may be due to a breach of the Convention, he may, under the same conditions as in the preceding paragraph, order any vessel concerned to stop and board it for enquiry and report.

(7) An authorised officer shall not order a fishing vessel to stop while it is actually fishing or engaged in shooting or hauling gear except in an emergency to avoid damage to vessels or gear.

(8) An authorised officer shall not pursue his enquiries further than is necessary to satisfy him either that there has been no breach of the Convention, or, where it appears to him that a breach has occurred, to secure information about the relevant facts, always acting in such a manner that vessels suffer the minimum interference and inconvenience.

(9) An authorised officer may, in case of damage to a vessel or fishing gear, offer to conciliate at sea, and if the parties concerned agree to this, assist them in reaching a settlement. At the request of the parties concerned the authorised officer shall draw up a protocol recording the settlement

reached.

(10) Resistance by a vessel to the directions of an authorised officer shall be deemed as resistance to the authority of the flag State of that vessel.

(11) The Contracting Parties shall consider and act on reports of foreign authorised officers under these arrangements on the same basis as reports of national officers. The provisions of this paragraph shall not impose any obligation on a Contracting Party to give the report of a foreign authorised officer a higher evidential value than it would possess in the authorised officer's own country. Contracting Parties shall collaborate in order to facilitate judicial or other proceedings arising from a report of an authorised officer under this Convention.

(12) An authorised officer shall not exercise his powers to board a vessel of another Contracting Party if an authorised officer of that Contracting Party is available and in a position to do so himself.

**Art. 10.** (1) Any Contracting Party may propose amendments to the Articles of this Convention. The text of any proposed amendment shall be sent to the depositary Government, which shall transmit copies thereof to all Contracting Parties and signatory Governments. Any amendment shall take effect on the thirtieth day after its acceptance by all Contracting Parties.

(2) When requested by one-fourth of the Contracting Parties, the depositary Government shall convene a meeting of Contracting Parties to consider the need for amending the Articles of this Convention. Amendments shall be adopted unanimously at such a meeting and shall be notified by the depositary Government to all Contracting Parties and shall take effect on the thirtieth day after they have been accepted by all Contracting Parties.

(3) Notifications of acceptance of amendments shall be sent to the depositary Government.

**Art. 11.** (1) Any Contracting Party may propose amendments to the Annexes to this Convention. The text of any proposed amendment shall be sent to the depositary Government, which shall transmit copies thereof to all Contracting Parties and signatory Governments. The depositary Government shall inform all Contracting Parties of the date on which notices of acceptance of an amendment by two-thirds of the Contracting Parties have been received. The amendment shall take effect with respect to all Contracting Parties on the one hundred and fiftieth day after that date, unless within a period of one hundred and twenty days from the same date any Contracting Party notifies the depositary Government of its objection to the amendment, in which case the amendment will have no effect.

(2) When requested by three Contracting Parties the depositary Gov-

ernment shall convene a meeting of Contracting Parties to consider the need for amending the Annexes to this Convention. An amendment adopted at such a meeting by a two-thirds majority of the Contracting Parties represented shall be notified by the depositary Government to all Contracting Parties and shall take effect with respect to all Contracting Parties on the two hundred and tenth day after the date of notification, unless within one hundred and eighty days from the date of notification any Contracting Party notifies the depositary Government of its objection to the amendment, in which case the amendment will have no effect.

**Art. 12.** The Contracting Parties shall notify the depositary Government of the competent authorities they have designated for the purposes of each of the relevant provisions of this Convention. The depositary Government shall inform the Contracting Parties of any such notification.

**Art. 13.** (1) Any dispute between two or more Contracting Parties concerning the interpretation or application of this Convention which cannot be settled through negotiation shall, at the request of one of them, be submitted to arbitration.

(2) The request for arbitration shall include a description of the claim to be submitted and a summary statement of the grounds on which the claim is based.

(3) Unless the parties agree otherwise, the arbitration commission shall be composed of one member appointed by each party to the dispute and an additional member, who shall be the chairman, chosen in common agreement between the parties. The arbitration commission shall decide on the matters placed before it by simple majority and its decisions shall be binding on the parties. Other details of procedure shall be determined by special agreement between the parties.

(4) Notwithstanding the provisions of paragraph (3), the parties may agree to submit the dispute to arbitration in accordance with another arrangement operating between the parties.

(5) If within six months from the date of the request for arbitration the parties are unable to agree on the organisation of the arbitration, any one of those parties may refer the dispute (as referred to in paragraph (1)) to the International Court of Justice by request in conformity with the Statute of the Court.

(6) Notwithstanding the provision of paragraph (1), the parties may agree to submit the dispute to the International Court of Justice.

**Art. 14.** (1) Except as provided in paragraphs (2) and (3) below and paragraph (3) of Article 17, no reservations may be made to the present Convention without the agreement of the Contracting Parties and signatory Governments. When one year has elapsed after the entry into force of the

574

Convention, the agreement of the Contracting Parties only shall be required.

(2) At the time of signature, ratification, approval or accession any State may make a reservation to Article 13 of the present Convention.

(3) Any State may, at the time of signature, ratification, approval or accession, make a reservation to paragraphs (5) and (6) of Article 9 with respect to one or more of the other Contracting Parties or signatory Governments.

(4) Any State which has made a reservation in accordance with the preceding paragraphs or paragraph (3) of Article 17 may at any time withdraw the reservation by a communication to that effect addressed to the depositary Government.

**Art. 15.** . . .

**Art. 16.** (1) The present Convention shall enter into force on the ninetieth day following the date of deposit of the tenth instrument of ratification or approval.

(2) Thereafter the Convention shall enter into force for each State on the ninetieth day after deposit of its instrument of ratification or approval.

**Art. 17.** (1) Any State which has not signed the Convention may accede thereto at any time after the Convention has entered into force, provided that three-fourths of the Contracting Parties and signatory Governments agree to the proposed accession. When one year has elapsed after the entry into force of the Convention, the agreement of three-fourths of the Contracting Parties only shall be required.

(2) Accession shall be effected by the deposit of an instrument of accession with the Government of the United Kingdom of Great Britain and Northern Ireland. The Convention shall enter into force for each acceding State on the ninetieth day after the deposit of its instrument of accession.

(3) At any time up to the entry into force of the Convention for a State which accedes under this Article, a Contracting Party may make a reservation to paragraphs (5) and (6) of Article 9 with respect to that State.

**Art. 18.** (1) Any Contracting Party may, when depositing its instrument of ratification, approval or accession, or at any later date, by declaration addressed to the depositary Government, extend this Convention to any territory or territories for whose international relations it is responsible. The provisions of this Convention shall enter into force for such territory or territories on the ninetieth day after receipt of such declaration, or on the date on which the Convention enters into force in accordance with paragraph (1) of Article 16, whichever is the later.

(2) Any declaration made in pursuance of the preceding paragraph may,

in respect of any territory mentioned in such declaration, be withdrawn according to the procedure laid down in Article 19.

**Art. 19.** At any time after four years from the date on which this Convention has entered into force in accordance with paragraph (1) of Article 16, any Contracting Party may denounce the Convention by means of a notice in writing addressed to the depositary Government. Any such notice shall take effect twelve months after the date of its receipt. The Convention shall remain in force as between the other Parties.

**Art. 20.** . . .

**Annex I—Area of Application of Convention:** [omitted]
**Annex II—Identification and Marking of Fishing Vessels and Gear:** [omitted]
**Annex III—Additional Signals to be Used by Fishing Vessels:** [omitted]
**Annex IV—Marking of Nets, Lines and Other Gear:** [omitted]

**Annex V—Rules Governing the Operations of Vessels**

**Rule 1.** Subject to compliance with the International Regulations for Preventing Collisions at Sea all vessels shall conduct their operations so as not to interfere with the operations of fishing vessels, or fishing gear.

**Rule 2.** Vessels arriving on fishing grounds where fishing vessels are already fishing or have set their gear for that purpose shall inform themselves of the position and extent of gear already placed in the sea and shall not place themselves or their fishing gear so as to interfere with or obstruct fishing operations already in progress.

**Rule 3.** No vessel shall anchor or remain on a fishing ground where fishing is in progress if it would interfere with such fishing unless required for the purpose of its own fishing operations or in consequence of accident or other circumstances beyond its control.

**Rule 4.** Except in cases of *force majeure* no vessel shall dump in the sea any article or substance which may interfere with fishing or obstruct or cause damage to fish, fishing gear or fishing vessels.

**Rule 5.** No vessel shall use or have on board explosives intended for the catching of fish.

**Rule 6.** In order to prevent damage, fishing vessels engaged in trawling and other fishing vessels with gear in motion shall take all practicable steps to avoid nets and lines or other gear which is not being towed.

**Rule 7.** (1) When nets belonging to different fishing vessels get foul of

576

each other, they shall not be severed without the consent of the parties concerned unless it is impossible to disengage them by other means.

(2) When fishing vessels fishing with lines entangle their lines, the fishing vessel which hauls up the lines shall not sever them unless they cannot be disengaged in any other way, in which case any lines which may be severed shall where possible be immediately joined together again.

(3) Except in cases of salvage and the cases to which the two preceding paragraphs relate, nets, lines or other gear shall not under any pretext whatever, be cut, hooked, held on to or lifted up except by the fishing vessel to which they belong.

(4) When a vessel fouls or otherwise interferes with gear not belonging to it, it shall take all necessary measures for reducing to a minimum the injury which may result to such gear. The fishing vessel to which the gear belongs shall, at the same time, avoid any action tending to aggravate such damage.

**Annex VI—Rules applying to Authorised Officers:** [omitted]

## THE 1973 AGREEMENT RELATING TO FISHING OPERATIONS IN THE NORTHEASTERN PACIFIC OCEAN (Union of Soviet Socialist Republics and United States of America)

> Signed at Moscow on 21 February 1973. International Legal Materials, vol. 12, p. 550. Replacing the Agreement of 14 December 1964 (U.N. Treaty Series, vol. 531, p. 212), as amended by the Agreements of 31 January 1969 (TIAS 6637) and of 12 February 1971, the latter having been extended by an exchange of notes of 31 December 1972.

The Government of the United States of America and the Government of the Union of Soviet Socialist Republics,

Being mutually concerned that fishing operations in the northeastern Pacific Ocean carried on by the fishermen of the two countries be conducted with due consideration for the interests of both Parties,

Considering it desirable to take measures for the prevention of damage to the fishing gear used by the fishermen of both countries,

Considering it desirable also to provide for appropriate contacts between representatives of both Parties on questions related to the conduct of the fisheries,

Have agreed on the following measures:

1. The Parties will take measures to emphasize to their officials, fishing

industry organizations and fishermen the importance of special efforts to protect fishing gear belonging to each side from damage by vessels and fishing gear of the other side, when conducting fishing operations in the northeastern Pacific Ocean. Each Party will encourage the use by its officials, fishing industry organizations and fishermen of devices, detectable both day and night, to mark the location of fixed fishing gear. The Parties will inform each other of the devices and the manner in which they are used. Each Party will promote the exercise of necessary caution on the part of persons responsible for the operation of vessels and gear so as to aid to the maximum extent practicable in timely detection of the vessels and gear of the other Party and prevention of damage thereto.

2. In the waters seaward of the nine-mile zone contiguous to the territorial sea of the United States fishing operations using mobile fishing gear will not be conducted during the periods specified below in the six areas off Kodiak Island bounded respectively by straight lines connecting in each of the following groups the coordinates in the order listed:

    *a.* From August 15 to April 30 inclusive: . . .

    *b.* From August 15 to January 15 inclusive: . . .

3. The provisions of paragraph 2 shall not apply to small shrimp craft conducting trawling operations in such a way as not to interfere with fixed gear in the above areas, or to United States vessels engaged—in scallop fishing operations.

4. It is understood that the right of fishermen of the Soviet Union to fish does not extend to waters within 12 nautical miles seaward from the baseline from which the territorial sea of the United States is measured.

5. It is understood that some vessels are likely to operate fixed gear outside the areas described in paragraph 2. Each Party will take special measures to promote the use by persons operating such vessels of means of marking such gear in addition to those ordinarily used. In order to inform the trawling fleet of the locations of such fixed gear, officials of the Alaska Department of Fish and Game, or of the United States National Marine Fisheries Service, and the Chief of the Joint Expedition of the Main Administration of DALRYBA will, if the necessity arises, transmit timely information to each other on the location of such vessels and fishing gear. Arrangements for such transmissions, including the designation of working frequencies and times of transmission, will be agreed upon between the above-mentioned officials. The persons responsible for the operation of trawlers will be given specific instructions regarding extraordinary precautionary measures to be taken when operating in the vicinity of fixed gear the positions of which have been reported, or other fixed gear which is detected.

6. The United States will cary out further research designed to develop a more effective and practical method for marking the location of fixed

gear. Soviet technicians will cooperate with those of the United States in this effort, particularly in connection with the testing of the effectiveness of new gear markers.

7. This Agreement is without prejudice to the views and rights of either Party with respect to the conduct of fishing operations on the high seas.

8. The Parties consider it desirable to expand contacts between government officials, representatives of the fishing industry, and fishery scientific workers of both countries for the discussion of questions of mutual interest and the achievement of greater mutual understanding.

9. ... This Agreement shall remain in effect for a period of two years. At the request of either Government, representatives of the two Governments will meet at a mutually convenient time with a view to modifying the present Agreement. In any event, representatives of the two Governments will meet at a mutually convenient time prior to the expiration of the period of validity of this Agreement to review its operation and to decide on future arrangements.

**INTERNATIONAL CONVENTION FOR THE PREVENTION OF POLLUTION FROM SHIPS, 1973**
(printed in pp. 182-193)

**Appendix I-III** [omitted]

**Appendix I-V** [omitted]

**Appendix** [omitted]

## PROTOCOL I

### PROVISIONS CONCERNING REPORTS ON INCIDENTS INVOLVING HARMFUL SUBSTANCES
(in accordance with Article 8 of the Convention)

### Article I

### *Duty to Report*

(1)    The Master of a ship involved in an incident referred to in Article III of this Protocol, or other person having charge of the ship, shall report the particulars of such incident without delay and to the fullest extent possible in accordance with the provisions of this Protocol.

(2)    In the event of the ship referred to in paragraph (1) of the present Article being abandoned, or in the event of a report from such ship being incomplete or unobtainable, the owner, charterer, manager or operator of the ship, or their agents shall, to the fullest extent possible assume the obligations placed upon the Master under the provisions of this Protocol.

### Article II

### *Methods of Reporting*

(1)    Each report shall be made by radio whenever possible, but in any case by the fastest channels available at the time the report is made. Reports made by radio shall be given the highest possible priority.

(2)    Reports shall be directed to the appropriate officer or agency specified in paragraph (2)(a) of Article 8 of the Convention.

### Article III

### *When to make Reports*

The report shall be made whenever an incident involves:

(a)    a discharge other than as permitted under the present Convention; or

(b) a discharge permitted under the present Convention by virtue of the fact that:

    (i) it is for the purpose of securing the safety of a ship or saving life at sea; or

    (ii) it results from damage to the ship or its equipment; or

(c) a discharge of a harmful substance for the purpose of combating a specific pollution incident or for purposes of legitimate scientific research into pollution abatement or control; or

(d) the probability of a discharge referred to in sub-paragraphs (a), (b) or (c) of the present Article.

### Article IV

#### Contents of Report

(1) Each report shall contain in general:

    (a) the identity of the ship;

    (b) the time and date of the occurrence of the incident;

    (c) the geographic position of the ship when the incident occurred;

    (d) the wind and sea conditions prevailing at the time of the incident; and

    (e) relevant details respecting the condition of the ship.

(2) Each report shall contain, in particular:

    (a) a clear indication or description of the harmful substances involved, including, if possible, the correct technical names of such substances (trade names should not be used in place of the correct technical names);

    (b) a statement or estimate of the quantities, concentrations and likely conditions of harmful substances discharged or likely to be discharged into the sea; and

    (c) where relevant, a description of the packaging and identifying marks; and

    (d) if possible, the names of the consignor, consignee or manufacturer.

(3) Each report shall clearly indicate whether the harmful substance discharged, or likely to be discharged is oil, a noxious liquid substance, a noxious solid substance or a noxious gaseous substance and whether such substance was or is carried in bulk or contained in packaged form, freight containers, portable tanks, or road and rail tank wagons.

(4) Each report shall be supplemented as necessary by any other relevant information requested by a recipient of the report or which the person sending the report deems appropriate.

581

## Article V

### *Supplementary Report*

Any person who is obliged under the provisions of this Protocol to send a report shall, when possible:

(a) supplement the initial report, as necessary, with information concerning further developments; and

(b) comply as fully as possible with requests from affected States for additional information concerning the incident.

## PROTOCOL II

### ARBITRATION
(in accordance with Article 10 of the Convention)

### Article I

Arbitration procedure, unless the Parties to the dispute decide otherwise, shall be in accordance with the rules set out in this Protocol.

### Article II

(1) An Arbitration Tribunal shall be established upon the request of one Party to the Convention addressed to another in application of Article 10 of the present Convention. The request for arbitration shall consist of a statement of the case together with any supporting documents.

(2) The requesting Party shall inform the Secretary-General of the Organization of the fact that it has applied for the establishment of a Tribunal, of the names of the Parties to the dispute, and of the Articles of the Convention or Regulations over which there is in its opinion disagreement concerning their interpretation or application. The Secretary-General shall transmit this information to all Parties.

### Article III

The Tribunal shall consist of three members: one Arbitrator nominated by each Party to the dispute and a third Arbitrator who shall be nominated by agreement between the two first named, and shall act as its Chairman.

### Article IV

(1) If, at the end of a period of sixty days from the nomination of the second Arbitrator, the Chairman of the Tribunal shall not have been nominated, the Secretary-General of the Organization upon request of either Party shall within a further period of sixty days proceed to such nomination, selecting him from a list of qualified persons previously drawn up by the Council of the Organization.

582

(2) If, within a period of sixty days from the date of the receipt of the request, one of the Parties shall not have nominated the member of the Tribunal for whose designation it is responsible, the other Party may directly inform the Secretary-General of the Organization who shall nominate the Chairman of the Tribunal within a period of sixty days, selecting him from the list prescribed in paragraph (1) of the present Article.

(3) The Chairman of the Tribunal shall, upon nomination, request the Party which has not provided an Arbitrator, to do so in the same manner and under the same conditions. If the Party does not make the required nomination, the Chairman of the Tribunal shall request the Secretary-General of the Organization to make the nomination in the form and conditions prescribed in the preceding paragraph.

(4) The Chairman of the Tribunal, if nominated under the provisions of the present Article, shall not be or have been a national of one of the Parties concerned, except with the consent of the other Party.

(5) In the case of the decease or default of an Arbitrator for whose nomination one of the Parties is responsible, the said Party shall nominate a replacement within a period of sixty days from the date of decease or default. Should the said Party not make the nomination, the arbitration shall proceed under the remaining Arbitrators. In case of the decease or default of the Chairman of the Tribunal, a replacement shall be nominated in accordance with the provisions of Article III above, or in the absence of agreement between the members of the Tribunal within a period of sixty days of the decease or default, according to the provisions of the present Article.

### Article V

The Tribunal may hear and determine counter-claims arising directly out of the subject matter of the dispute.

### Article VI

Each Party shall be responsible for the remuneration of its Arbitrator and connected costs and for the costs entailed by the preparation of its own case. The remuneration of the Chairman of the Tribunal and of all general expenses incurred by the Arbitration shall be borne equally by the Parties. The Tribunal shall keep a record of all its expenses and shall furnish a final statement thereof.

### Article VII

Any Party to the Convention which has an interest of a legal nature and which may be affected by the decision in the case may, after giving written notice to the Parties which have originally initiated the procedure, join in the arbitration procedure with the consent of the Tribunal.

583

## Article VIII

Any Arbitration Tribunal established under the provisions of the present Protocol shall decide its own rules of procedure.

## Article IX

(1) Decisions of the Tribunal both as to its procedure and its place of meeting and as to any question laid before it, shall be taken by majority votes of its members; the absence or abstention of one of the members of the Tribunal for whose nomination the Parties were responsible, shall not constitute an impediment to the Tribunal reaching a decision. In cases of equal voting, the vote of the Chairman shall be decisive.

(2) The Parties shall facilitate the work of the Tribunal and in particular, in accordance with their legislation, and using all means at their disposal:

    (a)   provide the Tribunal with the necessary documents and information;

    (b)   enable the Tribunal to enter their territory, to hear witnesses or experts, and to visit the scene.

(3) Absence or default of one Party shall not constitute an impediment to the procedure.

## Article X

(1) The Tribunal shall render its award within a period of five months from the time it is established unless it decides, in the case of necessity, to extend the time limit for a further period not exceeding three months. The award of the Tribunal shall be accompanied by a statement of reasons. It shall be final and without appeal and shall be communicated to the Secretary-General of the Organization. The Parties shall immediately comply with the award.

(2) Any controversy which may arise between the Parties as regards interpretation or execution of the award may be submitted by either Party for judgment to the Tribunal which made the award, or, if it is not available to another Tribunal constituted for this purpose, in the same manner as the original Tribunal.

# ANNEX I

## REGULATIONS FOR THE PREVENTION OF POLLUTION BY OIL

### CHAPTER I – GENERAL

### Regulation 1

*Definitions*

For the purposes of this Annex:

(1)  "Oil" means petroleum in any form including crude oil, fuel oil, sludge, oil refuse and refined products (other than petrochemicals which are subject to the provisions of Annex II of the present Convention) and, without limiting the generality of the foregoing, includes the substances listed in Appendix I to this Annex.

(2)  "Oily mixture" means a mixture with any oil content.

(3)  "Oil fuel" means any oil used as fuel in connexion with the propulsion and auxiliary machinery of the ship in which such oil is carried.

(4)  "Oil tanker" means a ship constructed or adapted primarily to carry oil in bulk in its cargo spaces and includes combination carriers and any "chemical tanker" as defined in Annex II of the present Convention when it is carrying a cargo or part cargo of oil in bulk.

(5)  "Combination carrier" means a ship designed to carry either oil or solid cargoes in bulk.

(6)  "New ship" means a ship:

(a)  for which the building contract is placed after 31 December 1975; or

(b)  in the absence of a building contract, the keel of which is laid or which is at a similar stage of construction after 30 June 1976; or

(c)  the delivery of which is after 31 December 1979; or

(d)  which has undergone a major conversion:

(i)  for which the contract is placed after 31 December 1975; or

(ii)  in the absence of a contract, the construction work of which is begun after 30 June 1976; or

(iii)  which is completed after 31 December 1979.

(7)  "Existing ship" means a ship which is not a new ship.

(8) "Major conversion" means a conversion of an existing ship:

(a) which substantially alters the dimensions or carrying capacity of the ship; or

(b) which changes the type of the ship; or

(c) the intent of which in the opinion of the Administration is substantially to prolong its life; or

(d) which otherwise so alters the ship that if it were a new ship, it would become subject to relevant provisions of the present Convention not applicable to it as an existing ship.

(9) "Nearest land". The term "from the nearest land" means from the baseline from which the territorial sea of the territory in question is established in accordance with international law, except that, for the purposes of the present Convention "from the nearest land" off the north eastern coast of Australia shall mean from a line drawn from a point on the coast of Australia in

latitude 11°00′ South, longitude 142°08′ East to a point in
latitude 10°35′ South,
longitude 141°55′ East — thence to a point latitude 10°00′ South,
longitude 142°00′ East, thence to a point latitude 9°10′ South,
longitude 143°52′ East, thence to a point latitude 9°00′ South,
longitude 144°30′ East, thence to a point latitude 13°00′ South,
longitude 144°00′ East, thence to a point latitude 15°00′ South,
longitude 146°00′ East, thence to a point latitude 18°00′ South,
longitude 147°00′ East, thence to a point latitude 21°00′ South,
longitude 153°00′ East, thence to a point on the coast of Australia
in latitude 24°42′ South, longitude 153°15′ East.

(10) "Special area" means a sea area where for recognized technical reasons in relation to its oceanographical and ecological condition and to the particular character of its traffic the adoption of special mandatory methods for the prevention of sea pollution by oil is required. Special areas shall include those listed in Regulation 10 of this Annex.

(11) "Instantaneous rate of discharge of oil content" means the rate of discharge of oil in litres per hour at any instant divided by the speed of the ship in knots at the same instant.

(12) "Tank" means an enclosed space which is formed by the permanent structure of a ship and which is designed for the carriage of liquid in bulk.

(13) "Wing tank" means any tank adjacent to the side shell plating.

(14) "Centre tank" means any tank inboard of a longitudinal bulkhead.

(15) "Slop tank" means a tank specifically designated for the collection of tank drainings, tank washings and other oily mixtures.

(16) "Clean ballast" means the ballast in a tank which since oil was last carried therein, has been so cleaned that effluent therefrom if it were discharged from a ship which is stationary into clean calm water on a clear day would not produce visible traces of oil on the surface of the water or on adjoining shorelines or cause

586

a sludge or emulsion to be deposited beneath the surface of the water or upon adjoining shorelines. If the ballast is discharged through an oil discharge monitoring and control system approved by the Administration, evidence based on such a system to the effect that the oil content of the effluent did not exceed 15 parts per million shall be determinative that the ballast was clean, notwithstanding the presence of visible traces.

(17) "Segregated ballast" means the ballast water introduced into a tank which is completely separated from the cargo oil and oil fuel system and which is permanently allocated to the carriage of ballast or to the carriage of ballast or cargoes other than oil or noxious substances as variously defined in the Annexes of the present Convention.

(18) "Length" (L) means 96 per cent of the total length on a waterline at 85 per cent of the least moulded depth measured from the top of the keel, or the length from the foreside of the stem to the axis of the rudder stock on that waterline, if that be greater. In ships designed with a rake of keel the waterline on which this length is measured shall be parallel to the designed waterline. The length (L) shall be measured in metres.

(19) "Forward and after perpendiculars" shall be taken at the forward and after ends of the length (L). The forward perpendicular shall coincide with the foreside of the stem on the waterline on which the length is measured.

(20) "Amidships" is at the middle of the length (L).

(21) "Breadth" (B) means the maximum breadth of the ship, measured amidships to the moulded line of the frame in a ship with a metal shell and to the outer surface of the hull in a ship with a shell of any other material. The breadth (B) shall be measured in metres.

(22) "Deadweight" (DW) means the difference in metric tons between the displacement of a ship in water of a specific gravity of 1.025 at the load waterline corresponding to the assigned summer freeboard and the lightweight of the ship.

(23) "Lightweight" means the displacement of a ship in metric tons without cargo, oil fuel, lubricating oil, ballast water, fresh water and feedwater in tanks, consumable stores, passengers and their effects.

(24) "Permeability" of a space means the ratio of the volume within that space which is assumed to be occupied by water to the total volume of that space.

(25) "Volumes" and "areas" in a ship shall be calculated in all cases to moulded lines.


## Regulation 2

### Application

(1)   Unless expressly provided otherwise, the provisions of this Annex shall apply to all ships.

(2)　In ships other than oil tankers fitted with cargo spaces which are constructed and utilized to carry oil in bulk of an aggregate capacity of 200 cubic metres or more, the requirements of Regulations 9, 10, 14, 15(1), (2) and (3), 18, 20 and 24(4) of this Annex for oil tankers shall also apply to the construction and operation of those spaces, except that where such aggregate capacity is less than 1,000 cubic metres the requirements of Regulation 15(4) of this Annex may apply in lieu of Regulation 15(1), (2) and (3).

(3)　Where a cargo subject to the provisions of Annex II of the present Convention is carried in a cargo space of an oil tanker, the appropriate requirements of Annex II of the present Convention shall also apply.

(4)　(a)　Any hydrofoil, air-cushion vehicle and other new type of vessel (near-surface craft, submarine craft, etc.) whose constructional features are such as to render the application of any of the provisions of Chapters II and III of this Annex relating to construction and equipment unreasonable or impracticable may be exempted by the Administration from such provisions, provided that the construction and equipment of that ship provides equivalent protection against pollution by oil, having regard to the service for which it is intended.

(b)　Particulars of any such exemption granted by the Administration shall be indicated in the Certificate referred to in Regulation 5 of this Annex.

(c)　The Administration which allows any such exemption shall, as soon as possible, but not more than ninety days thereafter, communicate to the Organization particulars of same and the reasons therefor, which the Organization shall circulate to the Parties to the Convention for their information and appropriate action, if any.

## Regulation 3

### Equivalents

(1)　The Administration may allow any fitting, material, appliance or apparatus to be fitted in a ship as an alternative to that required by this Annex if such fitting, material, appliance or apparatus is at least as effective as that required by this Annex. This authority of the Administration shall not extend to substitution of operational methods to effect the control of discharge of oil as equivalent to those design and construction features which are prescribed by Regulations in this Annex.

(2)　The Administration which allows a fitting, material, appliance or apparatus, as an alternative to that required by this Annex shall communicate to the Organization for circulation to the Parties to the Convention particulars thereof, for their information and appropriate action, if any.

## Regulation 4

### Surveys

(1)　Every oil tanker of 150 tons gross tonnage and above, and every other ship of 400 tons gross tonnage and above shall be subject to the surveys specified below:

588

(a) An initial survey before the ship is put in service or before the Certificate required under Regulation 5 of this Annex is issued for the first time, which shall include a complete survey of its structure, equipment, fittings, arrangements and material in so far as the ship is covered by this Annex. This survey shall be such as to ensure that the structure, equipment, fittings, arrangements and material fully comply with the applicable requirements of this Annex.

(b) Periodical surveys at intervals specified by the Administration, but not exceeding five years, which shall be such as to ensure that the structure, equipment, fittings, arrangements and material fully comply with the applicable requirements of this Annex. However, where the duration of the International Oil Pollution Prevention Certificate (1973) is extended as specified in Regulation 8(3) or (4) of this Annex, the interval of the periodical survey may be extended correspondingly.

(c) Intermediate surveys at intervals specified by the Administration but not exceeding thirty months, which shall be such as to ensure that the equipment and associated pump and piping systems, including oil discharge monitoring and control systems, oily-water separating equipment and oil filtering systems, fully comply with the applicable requirements of this Annex and are in good working order. Such intermediate surveys shall be endorsed on the International Oil Pollution Prevention Certificate (1973) issued under Regulation 5 of this Annex.

(2) The Administration shall establish appropriate measures for ships which are not subject to the provisions of paragraph (1) of this Regulation in order to ensure that the applicable provisions of this Annex are complied with.

(3) Surveys of the ship as regards enforcement of the provisions of this Annex shall be carried out by officers of the Administration. The Administration may, however, entrust the surveys either to surveyors nominated for the purpose or to organizations recognized by it. In every case the Administration concerned fully guarantees the completeness and efficiency of the surveys.

(4) After any survey of the ship under this Regulation has been completed, no significant change shall be made in the structure, equipment, fittings, arrangements or material covered by the survey without the sanction of the Administration, except the direct replacement of such equipment or fittings.

### Regulation 5

#### Issue of Certificate

(1) An International Oil Pollution Prevention Certificate (1973) shall be issued, after survey in accordance with the provisions of Regulation 4 of this Annex, to any oil tanker of 150 tons gross tonnage and above and any other ships of 400 tons gross tonnage and above which are engaged in voyages to ports or off-shore terminals under the jurisdiction of other Parties to the Convention. In the case of existing ships this requirement shall apply twelve months after the date of entry into force of the present Convention.

(2) Such Certificate shall be issued either by the Administration or by any persons or organization duly authorized by it. In every case the Administration assumes full responsibility for the Certificate.

### Regulation 6

*Issue of a Certificate by another Government*

(1)   The Government of a Party to the Convention may, at the request of the Administration, cause a ship to be surveyed and, if satisfied that the provisions of this Annex are complied with, shall issue or authorize the issue of an International Oil Pollution Prevention Certificate (1973) to the ship in accordance with this Annex.

(2)   A copy of the Certificate and a copy of the survey report shall be transmitted as soon as possible to the requesting Administration.

(3)   A Certificate so issued shall contain a statement to the effect that it has been issued at the request of the Administration and it shall have the same force and receive the same recognition as the Certificate issued under Regulation 5 of this Annex.

(4)   No International Oil Pollution Prevention Certificate (1973) shall be issued to a ship which is entitled to fly the flag of a State which is not a Party.

### Regulation 7

*Form of Certificate*

The International Oil Pollution Prevention Certificate (1973) shall be drawn up in an official language of the issuing country in the form corresponding to the model given in Appendix II to this Annex. If the language used is neither English nor French, the text shall include a translation into one of these languages.

### Regulation 8

*Duration of Certificate*

(1)   An International Oil Pollution Prevention Certificate (1973) shall be issued for a period specified by the Administration, which shall not exceed five years from the date of issue, except as provided in paragraphs (2), (3) and (4) of this Regulation.

(2)   If a ship at the time when the Certificate expires is not in a port or off-shore terminal under the jurisdiction of the Party to the Convention whose flag the ship is entitled to fly, the Certificate may be extended by the Administration, but such extension shall be granted only for the purpose of allowing the ship to complete its voyage to the State whose flag the ship is entitled to fly or in which it is to be surveyed and then only in cases where it appears proper and reasonable to do so.

(3)   No Certificate shall be thus extended for a period longer than five months and a ship to which such extension is granted shall not on its arrival in the State whose flag it is entitled to fly or the port in which it is to be surveyed, be entitled by virtue of such extension to leave that port or State without having obtained a new Certificate.

(4)    A Certificate which has not been extended under the provisions of paragraph (2) of this Regulation may be extended by the Administration for a period of grace of up to one month from the date of expiry stated on it.

(5)    A Certificate shall cease to be valid if significant alterations have taken place in the construction, equipment, fittings, arrangements, or material required without the sanction of the Administration, except the direct replacement of such equipment or fittings, or if intermediate surveys as specified by the Administration under Regulation 4(1)(c) of this Annex are not carried out.

(6)    A Certificate issued to a ship shall cease to be valid upon transfer of such a ship to the flag of another State, except as provided in paragraph (7) of this Regulation.

(7)    Upon transfer of a ship to the flag of another Party, the Certificate shall remain in force for a period not exceeding five months provided that it would not have expired before the end of that period, or until the Administration issues a replacement Certificate, whichever is earlier. As soon as possible after the transfer has taken place the Government of the Party whose flag the ship was formerly entitled to fly shall transmit to the Administration a copy of the Certificate carried by the ship before the transfer and, if available, a copy of the relevant survey report.

CHAPTER II  –  REQUIREMENTS FOR CONTROL OF
OPERATIONAL POLLUTION

### Regulation 9

*Control of Discharge of Oil*

(1)    Subject to the provisions of Regulations 10 and 11 of this Annex and paragraph (2) of this Regulation, any discharge into the sea of oil or oily mixtures from ships to which this Annex applies shall be prohibited except when all the following conditions are satisfied:

(a)    for an oil tanker, except as provided for in sub-paragraph (b) of this paragraph:

   (i)    the tanker is not within a special area;

   (ii)    the tanker is more than 50 nautical miles from the nearest land;

   (iii)    the tanker is proceeding en route;

   (iv)    the instantaneous rate of discharge of oil content does not exceed 60 litres per nautical mile;

   (v)    the total quantity of oil discharged into the sea does not exceed for existing tankers 1/15,000 of the total quantity of the particular cargo of which the residue formed a part, and for new tankers 1/30,000 of the total quantity of the particular cargo of which the residue formed a part; and

(vi)  the tanker has in operation, except as provided for in Regulation 15(3) of this Annex, an oil discharge monitoring and control system and a slop tank arrangement as required by Regulation 15 of this Annex;

(b)  from a ship of 400 tons gross tonnage and above other than an oil tanker and from machinery space bilges excluding cargo pump room bilges of an oil tanker unless mixed with oil cargo residue:

  (i)  the ship is not within a special area;

  (ii)  the ship is more than 12 nautical miles from the nearest land;

  (iii)  the ship is proceeding en route;

  (iv)  the oil content of the effluent is less than 100 parts per million; and

  (v)  the ship has in operation an oil discharge monitoring and control system, oily-water separating equipment, oil filtering system or other installation as required by Regulation 16 of this Annex.

(2)  In the case of a ship of less than 400 tons gross tonnage other than an oil tanker whilst outside the special area, the Administration shall ensure that it is equipped as far as practicable and reasonable with installations to ensure the storage of oil residues on board and their discharge to reception facilities or into the sea in compliance with the requirements of paragraph (1)(b) of this Regulation.

(3)  Whenever visible traces of oil are observed on or below the surface of the water in the immediate vicinity of a ship or its wake, Governments of Parties to the Convention should, to the extent they are reasonably able to do so, promptly investigate the facts bearing on the issue of whether there has been a violation of the provisions of this Regulation or Regulation 10 of this Annex. The investigation should include, in particular, the wind and sea conditions, the track and speed of the ship, other possible sources of the visible traces in the vicinity, and any relevant oil discharge records.

(4)  The provisions of paragraph (1) of this Regulation shall not apply to the discharge of clean or segregated ballast. The provisions of sub-paragraph (1)(b) of this Regulation shall not apply to the discharge of oily mixture which without dilution has an oil content not exceeding 15 parts per million.

(5)  No discharge into the sea shall contain chemicals or other substances in quantities or concentrations which are hazardous to the marine environment or chemicals or other substances introduced for the purpose of circumventing the conditions of discharge specified in this Regulation.

(6)  The oil residues which cannot be discharged into the sea in compliance with paragraphs (1), (2) and (4) of this Regulation shall be retained on board or discharged to reception facilities.

**Regulation 10**

*Methods for the Prevention of Oil Pollution from Ships while operating in Special Areas*

(1)  For the purposes of this Annex the special areas are the Mediterranean Sea area, the Baltic Sea area, the Black Sea area, the Red Sea area and the Gulfs area which are defined as follows:

(a) The Mediterranean Sea area means the Mediterranean Sea proper including the gulfs and seas therein with the boundary between the Mediterranean and the Black Sea constituted by the 41°N parallel and bounded to the west by the Straits of Gibraltar at the meridian of 5° 36′W.

(b) The Baltic Sea area means the Baltic Sea proper with the Gulf of Bothnia, the Gulf of Finland and the entrance to the Baltic Sea bounded by the parallel of the Skaw in the Skagerrak at 57° 44.8′N.

(c) The Black Sea area means the Black Sea proper with the boundary between the Mediterranean and the Black Sea constituted by the parallel 41°N.

(d) The Red Sea area means the Red Sea proper including the Gulfs of Suez and Aqaba bounded at the south by the rhumb line between Ras si Ane (12° 8.5′N, 43° 19.6′E) and Husn Murad (12° 40.4′N, 43° 30.2′E).

(e) The Gulfs area means the sea area located north west of the rhumb line between Ras al Hadd (22° 30′N, 59° 48′E) and Ras Al Fasteh (25° 04′N, 61° 25′E).

(2) (a) Subject to the provisions of Regulation 11 of this Annex, any discharge into the sea of oil or oily mixture from any oil tanker and any ship of 400 tons gross tonnage and above other than an oil tanker shall be prohibited, while in a special area.

(b) Such ships while in a special area shall retain on board all oil drainage and sludge, dirty ballast and tank washing waters and discharge them only to reception facilities.

(3) (a) Subject to the provisions of Regulation 11 of this Annex, any discharge into the sea of oil or oily mixture from a ship of less than 400 tons gross tonnage, other than an oil tanker, shall be prohibited while in a special area, except when the oil content of the effluent without dilution does not exceed 15 parts per million or alternatively when all of the following conditions are satisfied:

    (i) the ship is proceeding en route;

    (ii) the oil content of the effluent is less than 100 parts per million; and

    (iii) the discharge is made as far as practicable from the land, but in no case less than 12 nautical miles from the nearest land.

(b) No discharge into the sea shall contain chemicals or other substances in quantities or concentrations which are hazardous to the marine environment or chemicals or other substances introduced for the purpose of circumventing the conditions of discharge specified in this Regulation.

(c) The oil residues which cannot be discharged into the sea in compliance with sub-paragraph (a) of this paragraph shall be retained on board or discharged to reception facilities.

(4) The provisions of this Regulation shall not apply to the discharge of clean or segregated ballast.

(5)   Nothing in this Regulation shall prohibit a ship on a voyage only part of which is in a special area from discharging outside the special area in accordance with Regulation 9 of this Annex.

(6)   Whenever visible traces of oil are observed on or below the surface of the water in the immediate vicinity of a ship or its wake, the Governments of Parties to the Convention should, to the extent they are reasonably able to do so, promptly investigate the facts bearing on the issue of whether there has been a violation of the provisions of this Regulation or Regulation 9 of this Annex. The investigation should include, in particular, the wind and sea conditions, the track and speed of the ship, other possible sources of the visible traces in the vicinity, and any relevant oil discharge records.

(7)   Reception facilities within special areas:

   (a)   Mediterranean Sea, Black Sea and Baltic Sea areas:

      (i)   The Government of each Party to the Convention, the coastline of which borders on any given special area, undertakes to ensure that not later than 1 January 1977 all oil loading terminals and repair ports within the special area are provided with facilities adequate for the reception and treatment of all the dirty ballast and tank washing water from oil tankers. In addition all ports within the special area shall be provided with adequate reception facilities for other residues and oily mixtures from all ships. Such facilities shall have adequate capacity to meet the needs of the ships using them without causing undue delay.

      (ii)   The Government of each Party having under its jurisdiction entrances to seawater courses with low depth contour which might require a reduction of draught by the discharge of ballast undertakes to ensure the provision of the facilities referred to in sub-paragraph (a)(i) of this paragraph but with the proviso that ships required to discharge slops or dirty ballast could be subject to some delay.

      (iii)   During the period between the entry into force of the present Convention (if earlier than 1 January 1977) and 1 January 1977 ships while navigating in the special areas shall comply with the requirements of Regulation 9 of this Annex. However, the Governments of Parties the coastlines of which border on any of the special areas under this sub-paragraph may establish a date earlier than 1 January 1977 but after the date of entry into force of the present Convention, from which the requirements of this Regulation in respect of the special areas in question shall take effect:

        (1)   if all the reception facilities required have been provided by the date so established; and

        (2)   provided that the Parties concerned notify the Organization of the date so established at least six months in advance, for circulation to other Parties.

      (iv)   After 1 January 1977, or the date established in accordance with sub-paragraph (a)(iii) of this paragraph if earlier, each Party shall notify the Organization for transmission to the Contracting Governments concerned of all cases where the facilities are alleged to be inadequate.

(b)    Red Sea area and Gulfs area:

(i)    The Government of each Party the coastline of which borders on the special areas undertakes to ensure that as soon as possible all oil loading terminals and repair ports within these special areas are provided with facilities adequate for the reception and treatment of all the dirty ballast and tank washing water from tankers. In addition all ports within the special area shall be provided with adequate reception facilities for other residues and oily mixtures from all ships. Such facilities shall have adequate capacity to meet the needs of the ships using them without causing undue delay.

(ii)    The Government of each Party having under its jurisdiction entrances to seawater courses with low depth contour which might require a reduction of draught by the discharge of ballast shall undertake to ensure the provision of the facilities referred to in sub-paragraph (b)(i) of this paragraph but with the proviso that ships required to discharge slops or dirty ballast could be subject to some delay.

(iii)    Each Party concerned shall notify the Organization of the measures taken pursuant to provisions of sub-paragraph (b)(i) and (ii) of this paragraph. Upon receipt of sufficient notifications the Organization shall establish a date from which the requirements of this Regulation in respect of the area in question shall take effect. The Organization shall notify all Parties of the date so established no less than twelve months in advance of that date.

(iv)    During the period between the entry into force of the present Convention and the date so established, ships while navigating in the special area shall comply with the requirements of Regulation 9 of this Annex.

(v)    After such date oil tankers loading in ports in these special areas where such facilities are not yet available shall also fully comply with the requirements of this Regulation. However, oil tankers entering these special areas for the purpose of loading shall make every effort to enter the area with only clean ballast on board.

(vi)    After the date on which the requirements for the special area in question take effect, each Party shall notify the Organization for transmission to the Parties concerned of all cases where the facilities are alleged to be inadequate.

(vii)    At least the reception facilities as prescribed in Regulation 12 of this Annex shall be provided by 1 January 1977 or one year after the date of entry into force of the present Convention, whichever occurs later.

595

### Regulation 11

*Exceptions*

Regulations 9 and 10 of this Annex shall not apply to:

(a) the discharge into the sea of oil or oily mixture necessary for the purpose of securing the safety of a ship or saving life at sea; or

(b) the discharge into the sea of oil or oily mixture resulting from damage to a ship or its equipment:

    (i) provided that all reasonable precautions have been taken after the occurrence of the damage or discovery of the discharge for the purpose of preventing or minimizing the discharge; and

    (ii) except if the owner or the Master acted either with intent to cause damage, or recklessly and with knowledge that damage would probably result; or

(c) the discharge into the sea of substances containing oil, approved by the Administration, when being used for the purpose of combating specific pollution incidents in order to minimize the damage from pollution. Any such discharge shall be subject to the approval of any Government in whose jurisdiction it is contemplated the discharge will occur.

### Regulation 12

*Reception Facilities*

(1) Subject to the provisions of Regulation 10 of this Annex, the Government of each Party undertakes to ensure the provision at oil loading terminals, repair ports, and in other ports in which ships have oily residues to discharge, of facilities for the reception of such residues and oily mixtures as remain from oil tankers and other ships adequate to meet the needs of the ships using them without causing undue delay to ships.

(2) Reception facilities in accordance with paragraph (1) of this Regulation shall be provided in:

(a) all ports and terminals in which crude oil is loaded into oil tankers where such tankers have immediately prior to arrival completed a ballast voyage of not more than 72 hours or not more than 1,200 nautical miles;

(b) all ports and terminals in which oil other than crude oil in bulk is loaded at an average quantity of more than 1,000 metric tons per day;

(c) all ports having ship repair yards or tank cleaning facilities;

(d) all ports and terminals which handle ships provided with the sludge tank(s) required by Regulation 17 of this Annex;

(e) all ports in respect of oily bilge waters and other residues, which cannot be discharged in accordance with Regulation 9 of this Annex; and

(f) all loading ports for bulk cargoes in respect of oil residues from combination carriers which cannot be discharged in accordance with Regulation 9 of this Annex.

(3) The capacity for the reception facilities shall be as follows:

(a) Crude oil loading terminals shall have sufficient reception facilities to receive oil and oily mixtures which cannot be discharged in accordance with the provisions of Regulation 9(1)(a) of this Annex from all oil tankers on voyages as described in paragraph (2)(a) of this Regulation.

(b) Loading ports and terminals referred to in paragraph (2)(b) of this Regulation shall have sufficient reception facilities to receive oil and oily mixtures which cannot be discharged in accordance with the provisions of Regulation 9(1)(a) of this Annex from oil tankers which load oil other than crude oil in bulk.

(c) All ports having ship repair yards or tank cleaning facilities shall have sufficient reception facilities to receive all residues and oily mixtures which remain on board for disposal from ships prior to entering such yards or facilities.

(d) All facilities provided in ports and terminals under paragraph (2)(d) of this Regulation shall be sufficient to receive all residues retained according to Regulation 17 of this Annex from all ships that may reasonably be expected to call at such ports and terminals.

(e) All facilities provided in ports and terminals under this Regulation shall be sufficient to receive oily bilge waters and other residues which cannot be discharged in accordance with Regulation 9 of this Annex.

(f) The facilities provided in loading ports for bulk cargoes shall take into account the special problems of combination carriers as appropriate.

(4) The reception facilities prescribed in paragraphs (2) and (3) of this Regulation shall be made available no later than one year from the date of entry into force of the present Convention or by 1 January 1977, whichever occurs later.

(5) Each Party shall notify the Organization for transmission to the Parties concerned of all cases where the facilities provided under this Regulation are alleged to be inadequate.

## Regulation 13

### Segregated Ballast Oil Tankers

(1) Every new oil tanker of 70,000 tons deadweight and above shall be provided with segregated ballast tanks and shall comply with the requirements of this Regulation.

(2) The capacity of the segregated ballast tanks shall be so determined that the ship may operate safely on ballast voyages without recourse to the use of oil tanks for water ballast except as provided for in paragraph (3) of this Regulation. In all cases, however, the capacity of segregated ballast tanks shall be at least such that in

any ballast condition at any part of the voyage, including the conditions consisting of lightweight plus segregated ballast only, the ship's draughts and trim can meet each of the following requirements:

(a)  the moulded draught amidships (dm) in metres (without taking into account any ship's deformation) shall not be less than:

dm = 2.0 + 0.02L;

(b)  the draughts at the forward and after perpendiculars shall correspond to those determined by the draught amidships (dm), as specified in sub-paragraph (a) of this paragraph, in association with the trim by the stern of not greater than 0.015L; and

(c)  in any case the draught at the after perpendicular shall not be less than that which is necessary to obtain full immersion of the propeller(s).

(3)  In no case shall ballast water be carried in oil tanks except in weather conditions so severe that, in the opinion of the Master, it is necessary to carry additional ballast water in oil tanks for the safety of the ship. Such additional ballast water shall be processed and discharged in compliance with Regulation 9 and in accordance with the requirements of Regulation 15 of this Annex, and entry shall be made in the Oil Record Book referred to in Regulation 20 of this Annex.

(4)  Any oil tanker which is not required to be provided with segregated ballast tanks in accordance with paragraph (1) of this Regulation may, however, be qualified as a segregated ballast tanker, provided that in the case of an oil tanker of 150 metres in length and above it fully complies with the requirements of paragraphs (2) and (3) of this Regulation and in the case of an oil tanker of less than 150 metres in length the segregated ballast conditions shall be to the satisfaction of the Administration.

### Regulation 14

#### Segregation of Oil and Water Ballast

(1)  Except as provided in paragraph (2) of this Regulation, in new ships of 4,000 tons gross tonnage and above other than oil tankers, and in new oil tankers of 150 tons gross tonnage and above, no ballast water shall be carried in any oil fuel tank.

(2)  Where abnormal conditions or the need to carry large quantities of oil fuel render it necessary to carry ballast water which is not a clean ballast in any oil fuel tank, such ballast water shall be discharged to reception facilities or into the sea in compliance with Regulation 9 using the equipment specified in Regulation 16(2) of this Annex, and an entry shall be made in the Oil Record Book to this effect.

(3)  All other ships shall comply with the requirements of paragraph (1) of this Regulation as far as reasonable and practicable.

598

## Regulation 15

*Retention of Oil on Board*

(1)   Subject to the provisions of paragraphs (5) and (6) of this Regulation, oil tankers of 150 tons gross tonnage and above shall be provided with arrangements in accordance with the requirements of paragraphs (2) and (3) of this Regulation, provided that in the case of existing tankers the requirements for oil discharge monitoring and control systems and slop tank arrangements shall apply three years after the date of entry into force of the present Convention.

(2)   (a)   Adequate means shall be provided for cleaning the cargo tanks and transferring the dirty ballast residue and tank washings from the cargo tanks into a slop tank approved by the Administration. In existing oil tankers, any cargo tank may be designated as a slop tank.

(b)   In this system arrangements shall be provided to transfer the oily waste into a slop tank or combination of slop tanks in such a way that any effluent discharged into the sea will be such as to comply with the provisions of Regulation 9 of this Annex.

(c)   The arrangements of the slop tank or combination of slop tanks shall have a capacity necessary to retain the slops generated by tank washing, oil residues and dirty ballast residues but the total shall be not less than 3 per cent of the oil carrying capacity of the ship, except that, where segregated ballast tanks are provided in accordance with Regulation 13 of this Annex, or where arrangements such as eductors involving the use of water additional to the washing water are not fitted, the Administration may accept 2 per cent. New oil tankers over 70,000 tons dead-weight shall be provided with at least two slop tanks.

(d)   Slop tanks shall be so designed particularly in respect of the position of inlets, outlets, baffles or weirs where fitted, so as to avoid excessive turbulence and entrainment of oil or emulsion with the water.

(3)   (a)   An oil discharge monitoring and control system approved by the Administration shall be fitted. In considering the design of the oil content meter to be incorporated in the system, the Administration shall have regard to the specification recommended by the Organization.* The system shall be fitted with a recording device to provide a continuous record of the discharge in litres per nautical mile and total quantity discharged, or the oil content and rate of discharge. This record shall be identifiable as to time and date and shall be kept for at least three years. The oil discharge monitor and control system shall come into operation when there is any discharge of effluent into the sea and shall be such as will ensure that any discharge of oily mixture is automatically stopped when the instantaneous rate of discharge of oil exceeds that permitted by Regulation 9(1)(a) of this Annex. Any failure of this monitoring and control system shall stop the discharge

---

* Reference is made to the Recommendation on International Performance Specifications for Oily-Water Separating Equipment and Oil Content Meters adopted by the Organization by Resolution A.233(VII).

and be noted in the Oil Record Book. A manually operated alternative method shall be provided and may be used in the event of such failure, but the defective unit shall be made operable before the oil tanker commences its next ballast voyage unless it is proceeding to a repair port. Existing oil tankers shall comply with all of the provisions specified above except that the stopping of the discharge may be performed manually and the rate of discharge may be estimated from the pump characteristic.

(b)   Effective oil/water interface detectors approved by the Administration shall be provided for a rapid and accurate determination of the oil/water interface in slop tanks and shall be available for use in other tanks where the separation of oil and water is effected and from which it is intended to discharge effluent direct to the sea.

(c)   Instructions as to the operation of the system shall be in accordance with an operational manual approved by the Administration. They shall cover manual as well as automatic operations and shall be intended to ensure that at no time shall oil be discharged except in compliance with the conditions specified in Regulation 9 of this Annex.*

(4)   The requirements of paragraphs (1), (2) and (3) of this Regulation shall not apply to oil tankers of less than 150 tons gross tonnage, for which the control of discharge of oil under Regulation 9 of this Annex shall be effected by the retention of oil on board with subsequent discharge of all contaminated washings to reception facilities. The total quantity of oil and water used for washing and returned to a storage tank shall be recorded in the Oil Record Book. This total quantity shall be discharged to reception facilities unless adequate arrangements are made to ensure that any effluent which is allowed to be discharged into the sea is effectively monitored to ensure that the provisions of Regulation 9 of this Annex are complied with.

(5)   The Administration may waive the requirements of paragraphs (1), (2) and (3) of this Regulation for any oil tanker which engages exclusively on voyages both of 72 hours or less in duration and within 50 miles from the nearest land, provided that the oil tanker is not required to hold and does not hold an International Oil Pollution Prevention Certificate (1973). Any such waiver shall be subject to the requirement that the oil tanker shall retain on board all oily mixtures for subsequent discharge to reception facilities and to the determination by the Administration that facilities available to receive such oily mixtures are adequate.

(6)   Where in the view of the Organization equipment required by Regulation 9(1)(a)(vi) of this Annex and specified in sub-paragraph (3)(a) of this Regulation is not obtainable for the monitoring of discharge of light refined products (white oils), the Administration may waive compliance with such requirement, provided that discharge shall be permitted only in compliance with procedures established by the Organization which shall satisfy the conditions of Regulation 9(1)(a) of this Annex except the obligation to have an oil discharge monitoring and control system in operation. The Organization shall review the availability of equipment at intervals not exceeding twelve months.

---

* Reference is made to "Clean Seas Guide for Oil Tankers", published by the International Chamber of Shipping and the Oil Companies International Marine Forum.

(7)   The requirements of paragraphs (1), (2) and (3) of this Regulation shall not apply to oil tankers carrying asphalt, for which the control of discharge of asphalt under Regulation 9 of this Annex shall be effected by the retention of asphalt residues on board with discharge of all contaminated washings to reception facilities.

## Regulation 16

### *Oil Discharge Monitoring and Control System and Oily-Water Separating Equipment*

(1)   Any ship of 400 tons gross tonnage and above shall be fitted with an oily-water separating equipment or filtering system complying with the provisions of paragraph (6) of this Regulation. Any such ship which carries large quantities of oil fuel shall comply with paragraph (2) of this Regulation or paragraph (1) of Regulation 14.

(2)   Any ship of 10,000 tons gross tonnage and above shall be fitted:

(a)   in addition to the requirements of paragraph (1) of this Regulation with an oil discharge monitoring and control system complying with paragraph (5) of this Regulation; or

(b)   as an alternative to the requirements of paragraph (1) and sub-paragraph (2)(a) of this Regulation, with an oily-water separating equipment complying with paragraph (6) of this Regulation and an effective filtering system, complying with paragraph (7) of this Regulation.

(3)   The Administration shall ensure that ships of less than 400 tons gross tonnage are equipped, as far as practicable, to retain on board oil or oily mixtures or discharge them in accordance with the requirements of Regulation 9(1)(b) of this Annex.

(4)   For existing ships the requirements of paragraphs (1), (2) and (3) of this Regulation shall apply three years after the date of entry into force of the present Convention.

(5)   An oil discharge monitoring and control system shall be of a design approved by the Administration. In considering the design of the oil content meter to be incorporated into the system, the Administration shall have regard to the specification recommended by the Organization.* The system shall be fitted with a recording device to provide a continuous record of the oil content in parts per million. This record shall be identifiable as to time and date and shall be kept for at least three years. The monitoring and control system shall come into operation when there is any discharge of effluent into the sea and shall be such as will ensure that any discharge of oily mixture is automatically stopped when the oil content of effluent exceeds that permitted by Regulation 9(1)(b) of this Annex. Any failure of this monitoring and control system shall stop the discharge and be noted in the

---

*   Reference is made to the Recommendation on International Performance Specifications for Oily-Water Separating Equipment and Oil Content Meters adopted by the Organization by Resolution A.233(VII).

Oil Record Book. The defective unit shall be made operable before the ship commences its next voyage unless it is proceeding to a repair port. Existing ships shall comply with all of the provisions specified above except that the stopping of the discharge may be performed manually.

(6)  Oily-water separating equipment or an oil filtering system shall be of a design approved by the Administration and shall be such as will ensure that any oily mixture discharged into the sea after passing through the separator or filtering systems shall have an oil content of not more than 100 parts per million. In considering the design of such equipment, the Administration shall have regard to the specification recommended by the Organization.*

(7)  The oil filtering system referred to in paragraph (2)(b) of this Regulation shall be of a design approved by the Administration and shall be such that it will accept the discharge from the separating system and produce an effluent the oil content of which does not exceed 15 parts per million. It shall be provided with alarm arrangements to indicate when this level cannot be maintained.

## Regulation 17

### Tanks for Oil Residues (Sludge)

(1)  Every ship of 400 tons gross tonnage and above shall be provided with a tank or tanks of adequate capacity, having regard to the type of machinery and length of voyage, to receive the oily residues (sludges) which cannot be dealt with otherwise in accordance with the requirements of this Annex, such as those resulting from the purification of fuel and lubricating oils and oil leakages in the machinery spaces.

(2)  In new ships, such tanks shall be designed and constructed so as to facilitate their cleaning and the discharge of residues to reception facilities. Existing ships shall comply with this requirement as far as is reasonable and practicable.

## Regulation 18

### Pumping, Piping and Discharge Arrangements of Oil Tankers

(1)  In every oil tanker, a discharge manifold for connexion to reception facilities for the discharge of dirty ballast water or oil contaminated water shall be located on the open deck on both sides of the ship.

(2)  In every oil tanker, pipelines for the discharge to the sea of effluent which may be permitted under Regulation 9 of this Annex shall be led to the open deck or to the ship's side above the waterline in the deepest ballast condition. Different piping arrangements to permit operation in the manner permitted in sub-paragraphs (4)(a) and (b) of this Regulation may be accepted.

---

*  Reference is made to the Recommendation on International Performance Specifications for Oily-Water Separating Equipment and Oil Content Meters adopted by the Organization by Resolution A.233(VII).

(3)   In new oil tankers means shall be provided for stopping the discharge of effluent into the sea from a position on upper deck or above located so that the manifold in use referred to in paragraph (1) of this Regulation and the effluent from the pipelines referred to in paragraph (2) of this Regulation may be visually observed. Means for stopping the discharge need not be provided at the observation position if a positive communication system such as telephone or radio system is provided between the observation position and the discharge control position.

(4)   All discharges shall take place above the waterline except as follows:

(a)   Segregated ballast and clean ballast may be discharged below the waterline in ports or at off-shore terminals.

(b)   Existing ships which, without modification, are not capable of discharging segregated ballast above the waterline may discharge segregated ballast below the waterline provided that an examination of the tank immediately before the discharge has established that no contamination with oil has taken place.

## Regulation 19

### Standard Discharge Connection

To enable pipes of reception facilities to be connected with the ship's discharge pipeline for residues from machinery bilges, both lines shall be fitted with a standard discharge connection in accordance with the following table:

STANDARD DIMENSIONS OF FLANGES FOR DISCHARGE CONNECTIONS

| Description | Dimension |
|---|---|
| Outside diameter | 215 mm |
| Inner diameter | According to pipe outside diameter |
| Bolt circle diameter | 183 mm |
| Slots in flange | 6 holes 22 mm in diameter equidistantly placed on a bolt circle of the above diameter, slotted to the flange periphery. The slot width to be 22 mm |
| Flange thickness | 20 mm |
| Bolts and nuts: quantity, diameter | 6, each of 20 mm in diameter and of suitable length |

The flange is designed to accept pipes up to a maximum internal diameter of 125 mm and shall be of steel or other equivalent material having a flat face. This flange, together with a gasket of oilproof material, shall be suitable for a service pressure of 6 kg/cm$^2$.

### Regulation 20

*Oil Record Book*

(1)    Every oil tanker of 150 tons gross tonnage and above and every ship of 400 tons gross tonnage and above other than an oil tanker shall be provided with an Oil Record Book, whether as part of the ship's official log book or otherwise, in the form specified in Appendix III to this Annex.

(2)    The Oil Record Book shall be completed on each occasion, on a tank-to-tank basis, whenever any of the following operations take place in the ship:

    (a)    For oil tankers

        (i)    loading of oil cargo;

        (ii)    internal transfer of oil cargo during voyage;

        (iii)    opening or closing before and after loading and unloading operations of valves or similar devices which inter-connect cargo tanks;

        (iv)    opening or closing of means of communication between cargo piping and seawater ballast piping;

        (v)    opening or closing of ships' side valves before, during and after loading and unloading operations;

        (vi)    loading of oil cargo;

        (vii)    ballasting of cargo tanks;

       (viii)    cleaning of cargo tanks;

        (ix)    discharge of ballast except from segregated ballast tanks;

        (x)    discharge of water from slop tanks;

        (xi)    disposal of residues;

        (xii)    discharge overboard of bilge water which has accumulated in machinery spaces whilst in port, and the routine discharge at sea of bilge water which has accumulated in machinery spaces.

    (b)    For ships other than oil tankers

        (i)    ballasting or cleaning of fuel oil tanks or oil cargo spaces;

        (ii)    discharge of ballast or cleaning water from tanks referred to under (i) of this sub-paragraph;

        (iii)    disposal of residues;

        (iv)    discharge overboard of bilge water which has accumulated in machinery spaces whilst in port, and the routine discharge at sea of bilge water which has accumulated in machinery spaces.

(3)    In the event of such discharge of oil or oily mixture as is referred to in Regulation 11 of this Annex or in the event of accidental or other exceptional discharge of oil not excepted by that Regulation, a statement shall be made in the Oil Record Book of the circumstances of, and the reasons for, the discharge.

(4)    Each operation described in paragraph (2) of this Regulation shall be fully recorded without delay in the Oil Record Book so that all the entries in the book appropriate to that operation are completed. Each section of the book shall be signed by the officer or officers in charge of the operations concerned and shall be countersigned by the Master of the ship. The entries in the Oil Record Book shall be in an official language of the State whose flag the ship is entitled to fly, and, for ships holding an International Oil Pollution Prevention Certificate (1973),in English or French. The entries in an official national language of the State whose flag the ship is entitled to fly shall prevail in case of a dispute or discrepancy.

(5)    The Oil Record Book shall be kept in such a place as to be readily available for inspection at all reasonable times and, except in the case of unmanned ships under tow, shall be kept on board the ship. It shall be preserved for a period of three years after the last entry has been made.

(6)    The competent authority of the Government of a Party to the Convention may inspect the Oil Record Book on board any ship to which this Annex applies while the ship is in its port or off-shore terminals and may make a copy of any entry in that book and may require the Master of the ship to certify that the copy is a true copy of such entry. Any copy so made which has been certified by the Master of the ship as a true copy of an entry in the ship's Oil Record Book shall be made admissible in any judicial proceedings as evidence of the facts stated in the entry. The inspection of an Oil Record Book and the taking of a certified copy by the competent authority under this paragraph shall be performed as expeditiously as possible without causing the ship to be unduly delayed.

## Regulation 21

### *Special Requirements for Drilling Rigs and other Platforms*

Fixed and floating drilling rigs when engaged in the exploration, exploitation and associated off-shore processing of sea-bed mineral resources and other platforms shall comply with the requirements of this Annex applicable to ships of 400 tons gross tonnage and above other than oil tankers, except that:

(a)    they shall be equipped as far as practicable with the installations required in Regulations 16 and 17 of this Annex;

(b)    they shall keep a record of all operations involving oil or oily mixture discharges, in a form approved by the Administration; and

(c)    in any special area and subject to the provisions of Regulation 11 of this Annex, the discharge into the sea of oil or oily mixture shall be prohibited except when the oil content of the discharge without dilution does not exceed 15 parts per million.

## Regulation 22

*Damage Assumptions*

(1)  For the purpose of calculating hypothetical oil outflow from oil tankers, three dimensions of the extent of damage of a parallelepiped on the side and bottom of the ship are assumed as follows. In the case of bottom damages two conditions are set forth to be applied individually to the stated portions of the oil tanker.

(a)  *Side damage*

(i)  Longitudinal extent ($\ell_c$):  $\frac{1}{3}L^{\frac{2}{3}}$ or 14.5 metres, whichever is less

(ii)  Transverse extent ($t_s$): (inboard from the ship's side at right angles to the centre-line at the level corresponding to the assigned summer freeboard)  $\frac{B}{5}$ or 11.5 metres, whichever is less

(iii)  Vertical extent ($v_c$):  from the base line upwards without limit

(b)  *Bottom damage*

|  |  | For 0.3L from the forward perpendicular of the ship | Any other part of the ship |
|---|---|---|---|
| (i) | Longitudinal extent ($\ell_s$): | $\frac{L}{10}$ | $\frac{L}{10}$ or 5 metres, whichever is less |
| (ii) | Transverse extent ($t_s$): | $\frac{B}{6}$ or 10 metres, whichever is less but not less than 5 metres | 5 metres |
| (iii) | Vertical extent from the base line ($v_s$): | $\frac{B}{15}$ or 6 metres, whichever is less | |

(2)  Wherever the symbols given in this Regulation appear in this Chapter, they have the meaning as defined in this Regulation.

606

**Regulation 23**

*Hypothetical Outflow of Oil*

(1)   The hypothetical outflow of oil in the case of side damage $(O_c)$ and bottom damage $(O_s)$ shall be calculated by the following formulae with respect to compartments breached by damage to all conceivable locations along the length of the ship to the extent as defined in Regulation 22 of this Annex.

(a)   for side damages:

$$O_c = \Sigma W_i + \Sigma K_i C_i \qquad\qquad (I)$$

(b)   for bottom damages:

$$O_s = \tfrac{1}{3}(\Sigma Z_i W_i + \Sigma Z_i C_i) \qquad\qquad (II)$$

where:   $W_i$ = volume of a wing tank in cubic metres assumed to be breached by the damage as specified in Regulation 22 of this Annex; $W_i$ for a segregated ballast tank may be taken equal to zero,

$C_i$ = volume of a centre tank in cubic metres assumed to be breached by the damage as specified in Regulation 22 of this Annex; $C_i$ for a segregated ballast tank may be taken equal to zero,

$K_i = 1 - \dfrac{b_i}{t_c}$   when $b_i$ is equal to or greater than $t_c$, $K_i$ shall be taken equal to zero,

$Z_i = 1 - \dfrac{h_i}{v_s}$   when $h_i$ is equal to or greater than $v_s$, $Z_i$ shall be taken equal to zero,

$b_i$ = width of wing tank in metres under consideration measured inboard from the ship's side at right angles to the centreline at the level corresponding to the assigned summer freeboard,

$h_i$ = minimum depth of the double bottom in metres under consideration; where no double bottom is fitted $h_i$ shall be taken equal to zero.

Whenever symbols given in this paragraph appear in this Chapter, they have the meaning as defined in this Regulation.

(2)   If a void space or segregated ballast tank of a length less than $\ell_c$ as defined in Regulation 22 of this Annex is located between wing oil tanks, $O_c$ in formula (I) may be calculated on the basis of volume $W_i$ being the actual volume of one such tank (where they are of equal capacity) or the smaller of the two tanks (if they differ in capacity), adjacent to such space, multiplied by $S_i$ as defined below and taking for all other wing tanks involved in such a collision the value of the actual full volume.

$$S_i = 1 - \dfrac{\ell_i}{\ell_c}$$

where $\ell_i$ = length in metres of void space or segregated ballast tank under consideration.

(3) (a) Credit shall only be given in respect of double bottom tanks which are either empty or carrying clean water when cargo is carried in the tanks above.

(b) Where the double bottom does not extend for the full length and width of the tank involved, the double bottom is considered non-existent and the volume of the tanks above the area of the bottom damage shall be included in formula (II) even if the tank is not considered breached because of the installation of such a partial double bottom.

(c) Suction wells may be neglected in the determination of the value $h_i$ provided such wells are not excessive in area and extend below the tank for a minimum distance and in no case more than half the height of the double bottom. If the depth of such a well exceeds half the height of the double bottom, $h_i$ shall be taken equal to the double bottom height minus the well height.

Piping serving such wells if installed within the double bottom shall be fitted with valves or other closing arrangements located at the point of connexion to the tank served to prevent oil outflow in the event of damage to the piping. Such piping shall be installed as high from the bottom shell as possible. These valves shall be kept closed at sea at any time when the tank contains oil cargo, except that they may be opened only for cargo transfer needed for the purpose of trimming of the ship.

(4) In the case where bottom damage simultaneously involves four centre tanks, the value of $O_s$ may be calculated according to the formula

$$O_s = \tfrac{1}{4}(\Sigma Z_i W_i + \Sigma Z_i C_i) \qquad\qquad \text{(III)}$$

(5) An Administration may credit as reducing oil outflow in case of bottom damage, an installed cargo transfer system having an emergency high suction in each cargo oil tank, capable of transferring from a breached tank or tanks to segregated ballast tanks or to available cargo tankage if it can be assured that such tanks will have sufficient ullage. Credit for such a system would be governed by ability to transfer in two hours of operation oil equal to one half of the largest of the breached tanks involved and by availability of equivalent receiving capacity in ballast or cargo tanks. The credit shall be confined to permitting calculation of $O_s$ according to formula (III). The pipes for such suctions shall be installed at least at a height not less than the vertical extent of the bottom damage $v_s$. The Administration shall supply the Organization with the information concerning the arrangements accepted by it, for circulation to other Parties to the Convention.

### Regulation 24

*Limitation of Size and Arrangement of Cargo Tanks*

(1) Every new oil tanker shall comply with the provisions of this Regulation. Every existing oil tanker shall be required, within two years after the date of entry into force of the present Convention, to comply with the provisions of this Regulation if such a tanker falls into either of the following categories:

608

(a)   a tanker, the delivery of which is after 1 January 1977; or

(b)   a tanker to which both the following conditions apply:

    (i)   delivery is not later than 1 January 1977; and

    (ii)  the building contract is placed after 1 January 1974, or in cases where no building contract has previously been placed, the keel is laid or the tanker is at a similar stage of construction after 30 June 1974.

(2)   Cargo tanks of oil tankers shall be of such size and arrangements that the hypothetical outflow $O_c$ or $O_s$ calculated in accordance with the provisions of Regulation 23 of this Annex anywhere in the length of the ship does not exceed 30,000 cubic metres or $400 \sqrt[3]{DW}$, whichever is the greater, but subject to a maximum of 40,000 cubic metres.

(3)   The volume of any one wing cargo oil tank of an oil tanker shall not exceed seventy-five per cent of the limits of the hypothetical oil outflow referred to in paragraph (2) of this Regulation. The volume of any one centre cargo oil tank shall not exceed 50,000 cubic metres. However, in segregated ballast oil tankers as defined in Regulation 13 of this Annex, the permitted volume of a wing cargo oil tank situated between two segregated ballast tanks, each exceeding $\ell_c$ in length, may be increased to the maximum limit of hypothetical oil outflow provided that the width of the wing tanks exceeds $t_c$.

(4)   The length of each cargo tank shall not exceed 10 metres or one of the following values, whichever is the greater:

(a)   where no longitudinal bulkhead is provided:

    0.1L

(b)   where a longitudinal bulkhead is provided at the centreline only:

    0.15L

(c)   where two or more longitudinal bulkheads are provided:

    (i)   for wing tanks:

        0.2L

    (ii)  for centre tanks:

        (1)   if $\dfrac{b_i}{B}$ is equal to or greater than $\frac{1}{5}$:

            0.2L

        (2)   if $\dfrac{b_i}{B}$ is less than $\frac{1}{5}$:

            — where no centreline longitudinal bulkhead is provided:

$$(0.5\,\frac{b_i}{B} + 0.1)L$$

            — where a centreline longitudinal bulkhead is provided:

$$(0.25\,\frac{b_i}{B} + 0.15)L$$

(5)   In order not to exceed the volume limits established by paragraphs (2), (3) and (4) of this Regulation and irrespective of the accepted type of cargo transfer system installed, when such system inter-connects two or more cargo tanks, valves or other similar closing devices shall be provided for separating the tanks from each other. These valves or devices shall be closed when the tanker is at sea.

(6)   Lines of piping which run through cargo tanks in a position less than $t_c$ from the ship's side or less than $v_c$ from the ship's bottom shall be fitted with valves or similar closing devices at the point at which they open into any cargo tank. These valves shall be kept closed at sea at any time when the tanks contain cargo oil, except that they may be opened only for cargo transfer needed for the purpose of trimming of the ship.

### Regulation 25

*Subdivision and Stability*

(1)   Every new oil tanker shall comply with the subdivision and damage stability criteria as specified in paragraph (3) of this Regulation, after the assumed side or bottom damage as specified in paragraph (2) of this Regulation, for any operating draught reflecting actual partial or full load conditions consistent with trim and strength of the ship as well as specific gravities of the cargo. Such damage shall be applied to all conceivable locations along the length of the ship as follows:

(a)   in tankers of more than 225 metres in length, anywhere in the ship's length;

(b)   in tankers of more than 150 metres, but not exceeding 225 metres in length, anywhere in the ship's length except involving either after or forward bulkhead bounding the machinery space located aft. The machinery space shall be treated as a single floodable compartment;

(c)   in tankers not exceeding 150 metres in length, anywhere in the ship's length between adjacent transverse bulkheads with the exception of the machinery space. For tankers of 100 metres or less in length where all requirements of paragraph (3) of this Regulation cannot be fulfilled without materially impairing the operational qualities of the ship, Administrations may allow relaxations from these requirements.

Ballast conditions where the tanker is not carrying oil in cargo tanks excluding any oil residues, shall not be considered.

(2)   The following provisions regarding the extent and the character of the assumed damage shall apply:

(a)   The extent of side or bottom damage shall be as specified in Regulation 22 of this Annex, except that the longitudinal extent of bottom damage within 0.3L from the forward perpendicular shall be the same as for side damage, as specified in Regulation 22(1)(a)(i) of this Annex. If any damage of lesser extent results in a more severe condition such damage shall be assumed.

610

(b)   Where the damage involving transverse bulkheads is envisaged as specified in sub-paragraphs (1)(a) and (b) of this Regulation, transverse watertight bulkheads shall be spaced at least at a distance equal to the longitudinal extent of assumed damage specified in sub-paragraph (a) of this paragraph in order to be considered effective. Where transverse bulkheads are spaced at a lesser distance, one or more of these bulkheads within such extent of damage shall be assumed as non-existent for the purpose of determining flooded compartments.

(c)   Where the damage between adjacent transverse watertight bulkheads is envisaged as specified in sub-paragraph (1)(c) of this Regulation, no main transverse bulkhead or a transverse bulkhead bounding side tanks or double bottom tanks shall be assumed damaged, unless:

   (i)    the spacing of the adjacent bulkheads is less than the longitudinal extent of assumed damage specified in sub-paragraph (a) of this paragraph; or

   (ii)   there is a step or a recess in a transverse bulkhead of more than 3.05 metres in length, located within the extent of penetration of assumed damage. The step formed by the after peak bulkhead and after peak tank top shall not be regarded as a step for the purpose of this Regulation.

(d)   If pipes, ducts or tunnels are situated within the assumed extent of damage, arrangements shall be made so that progressive flooding cannot thereby extend to compartments other than those assumed to be floodable for each case of damage.

(3)   Oil tankers shall be regarded as complying with the damage stability criteria if the following requirements are met:

(a)   The final waterline, taking into account sinkage, heel and trim, shall be below the lower edge of any opening through which progressive flooding may take place. Such openings shall include air pipes and those which are closed by means of weathertight doors or hatch covers and may exclude those openings closed by means of watertight manhole covers and flush scuttles, small watertight cargo tank hatch covers which maintain the high integrity of the deck, remotely operated watertight sliding doors, and side scuttles of the non-opening type.

(b)   In the final stage of flooding, the angle of heel due to unsymmetrical flooding shall not exceed 25 degrees, provided that this angle may be increased up to 30 degrees if no deck edge immersion occurs.

(c)   The stability in the final stage of flooding shall be investigated and may be regarded as sufficient if the righting lever curve has at least a range of 20 degrees beyond the position of equilibrium in association with a maximum residual righting lever of at least 0.1 metre. The Administration shall give consideration to the potential hazard presented by protected or unprotected openings which may become temporarily immersed within the range of residual stability.

(d)   The Administration shall be satisfied that the stability is sufficient during intermediate stages of flooding.

611

(4)    The requirements of paragraph (1) of this Regulation shall be confirmed by calculations which take into consideration the design characteristics of the ship, the arrangements, configuration and contents of the damaged compartments; and the distribution, specific gravities and the free surface effect of liquids. The calculations shall be based on the following:

(a)    Account shall be taken of any empty or partially filled tank, the specific gravity of cargoes carried, as well as any outflow of liquids from damaged compartments.

(b)    The permeabilities are assumed as follows:

| Spaces | Permeability |
|---|---|
| Appropriated to stores | 0.60 |
| Occupied by accommodation | 0.95 |
| Occupied by machinery | 0.85 |
| Voids | 0.95 |
| Intended for consumable liquids | 0 or 0.95* |
| Intended for other liquids | 0 to 0.95** |

* Whichever results in the more severe requirements.

** The permeability of partially filled compartments shall be consistent with the amount of liquid carried.

(c)    The buoyancy of any superstructure directly above the side damage shall be disregarded. The unflooded parts of superstructures beyond the extent of damage, however, may be taken into consideration provided that they are separated from the damaged space by watertight bulkheads and the requirements of sub-paragraph (3)(a) of this Regulation in respect of these intact spaces are complied with. Hinged watertight doors may be acceptable in watertight bulkheads in the superstructure.

(d)    The free surface effect shall be calculated at an angle of heel of 5 degrees for each individual compartment. The Administration may require or allow the free surface corrections to be calculated at an angle of heel greater than 5 degrees for partially filled tanks.

(e)    In calculating the effect of free surfaces of consumable liquids it shall be assumed that, for each type of liquid at least one transverse pair or a single centreline tank has a free surface and the tank or combination of tanks to be taken into account shall be those where the effect of free surfaces is the greatest.

(5)    The Master of every oil tanker and the person in charge of a non-self-propelled oil tanker to which this Annex applies shall be supplied in an approved form with:

(a)    information relative to loading and distribution of cargo necessary to ensure compliance with the provisions of this Regulation; and

(b)    date on the ability of the ship to comply with damage stability criteria as determined by this Regulation, including the effect of relaxations that may have been allowed under sub-paragraph (1)(c) of this Regulation.

## ANNEX II

### REGULATIONS FOR THE CONTROL OF POLLUTION BY NOXIOUS LIQUID SUBSTANCES IN BULK

### Regulation 1

#### *Definitions*

For the purposes of this Annex:

(1)   "Chemical tanker" means a ship constructed or adapted primarily to carry a cargo of noxious liquid substances in bulk and includes an "oil tanker" as defined in Annex I of the present Convention when carrying a cargo or part cargo of noxious liquid substances in bulk.

(2)   "Clean ballast" means ballast carried in a tank which, since it was last used to carry a cargo containing a substance in Category A, B, C or D has been thoroughly cleaned and the residues resulting therefrom have been discharged and the tank emptied in accordance with the appropriate requirements of this Annex.

(3)   "Segregated ballast" means ballast water introduced into a tank permanently allocated to the carriage of ballast or to the carriage of ballast or cargoes other than oil or noxious liquid substances as variously defined in the Annexes of the present Convention, and which is completely separated from the cargo and oil fuel system.

(4)   "Nearest land" is as defined in Regulation 1(9) of Annex I of the present Convention.

(5)   "Liquid substances" are those having a vapour pressure not exceeding 2.8 kp/cm$^2$ at a temperature of 37.8°C.

(6)   "Noxious liquid substance" means any substance designated in Appendix II to this Annex or provisionally assessed under the provisions of Regulation 3(4) as falling into Category A, B, C or D.

(7)   "Special area" means a sea area where for recognized technical reasons in relation to its oceanographic and ecological condition and to its peculiar transportation traffic the adoption of special mandatory methods for the prevention of sea pollution by noxious liquid substances is required.

Special areas shall be:

(a)   The Baltic Sea Area, and

(b)   The Black Sea Area.

(8)   "Baltic Sea Area" is as defined in Regulation 10(1)(b) of Annex I of the present Convention.

(9)   "Black Sea Area" is as defined in Regulation 10(1)(c) of Annex I of the present Convention.

## Regulation 2

### *Application*

(1)   Unless expressly provided otherwise the provisions of this Annex shall apply to all ships carrying noxious liquid substances in bulk.

(2)   Where a cargo subject to the provisions of Annex I of the present Convention is carried in a cargo space of a chemical tanker, the appropriate requirements of Annex I of the present Convention shall also apply.

(3)   Regulation 13 of this Annex shall apply only to ships carrying substances which are categorized for discharge control purposes in Category A, B or C.

## Regulation 3

### *Categorization and Listing of Noxious Liquid Substances*

(1)   For the purpose of the Regulations of this Annex, except Regulation 13, noxious liquid substances shall be divided into four categories as follows:

(a)   Category A – Noxious liquid substances which if discharged into the sea from tank cleaning or deballasting operations would present a major hazard to either marine resources or human health or cause serious harm to amenities or other legitimate uses of the sea and therefore justify the application of stringent anti-pollution measures.

(b)   Category B – Noxious liquid substances which if discharged into the sea from tank cleaning or deballasting operations would present a hazard to either marine resources or human health or cause harm to amenities or other legitimate uses of the sea and therefore justify the application of special anti-pollution measures.

(c)   Category C – Noxious liquid substances which if discharged into the sea from tank cleaning or deballasting operations would present a minor hazard to either marine resources or human health or cause minor harm to amenities or other legitimate uses of the sea and therefore require special operational conditions.

(d)   Category D – Noxious liquid substances which if discharged into the sea from tank cleaning or deballasting operations would present a recognizable hazard to either marine resources or human health or cause minimal harm to amenities or other legitimate uses of the sea and therefore require some attention in operational conditions.

(2)   Guidelines for use in the categorization of noxious liquid substances are given in Appendix I to this Annex.

(3)   The list of noxious liquid substances carried in bulk and presently categorized which are subject to the provisions of this Annex is set out in Appendix II to this Annex.

614

(4)   Where it is proposed to carry a liquid substance in bulk which has not been categorized under paragraph (1) of this Regulation or evaluated as referred to in Regulation 4(1) of this Annex, the Governments of Parties to the Convention involved in the proposed operation shall establish and agree on a provisional assessment for the proposed operation on the basis of the guidelines referred to in paragraph (2) of this Regulation. Until full agreement between the Governments involved has been reached, the substance shall be carried under the most severe conditions proposed. As soon as possible, but not later than ninety days after its first carriage, the Administration concerned shall notify the Organization and provide details of the substance and the provisional assessment for prompt circulation to all Parties for their information and consideration. The Government of each Party shall have a period of ninety days in which to forward its comments to the Organization, with a view to the assessment of the substance.

## Regulation 4

### *Other Liquid Substances*

(1)   The substances listed in Appendix III to this Annex have been evaluated and found to fall outside the Categories A, B, C and D, as defined in Regulation 3(1) of this Annex because they are presently considered to present no harm to human health, marine resources, amenities or other legitimate uses of the sea, when discharged into the sea from tank cleaning or deballasting operations.

(2)   The discharge of bilge or ballast water or other residues or mixtures containing only substances listed in Appendix III to this Annex shall not be subject to any requirement of this Annex.

(3)   The discharge into the sea of clean ballast or segregated ballast shall not be subject to any requirement of this Annex.

## Regulation 5

### *Discharge of Noxious Liquid Substances*

**Categories A, B and C Substances outside Special Areas and Category D Substances in all Areas**

Subject to the provisions of Regulation 6 of this Annex,

(1)   The discharge into the sea of substances in Category A as defined in Regulation 3(1)(a) of this Annex or of those provisionally assessed as such or ballast water, tank washings, or other residues or mixtures containing such substances shall be prohibited. If tanks containing such substances or mixtures are to be washed, the resulting residues shall be discharged to a reception facility until the concentration of the substance in the effluent to such facility is at or below the residual concentration prescribed for that substance in column III of Appendix II to this Annex and until the tank is empty. Provided that the residue then remaining in the tank is subsequently diluted by the addition of a volume of water of not less than 5 per cent of the total volume of the tank, it may be discharged into the sea when all the following conditions are also satisfied:

615

(a)   the ship is proceeding en route at a speed of at least 7 knots in the case of self-propelled ships or at least 4 knots in the case of ships which are not self-propelled;

(b)   the discharge is made below the waterline, taking into account the location of the seawater intakes; and

(c.   the discharge is made at a distance of not less than 12 nautical miles from the nearest land and in a depth of water of not less than 25 metres.

(2)   The discharge into the sea of substances in Category B as defined in Regulation 3(1)(b) of this Annex or of those provisionally assessed as such, or ballast water, tank washings, or other residues or mixtures containing such substances shall be prohibited except when all the following conditions are satisfied:

(a)   the ship is proceeding en route at a speed of at least 7 knots in the case of self-propelled ships or at least 4 knots in the case of ships which are not self-propelled;

(b)   the procedures and arrangements for discharge are approved by the Administration. Such procedures and arrangements shall be based upon standards developed by the Organization and shall ensure that the concentration and rate of discharge of the effluent is such that the concentration of the substance in the wake astern of the ship does not exceed 1 part per million;

(c)   the maximum quantity of cargo discharged from each tank and its associated piping system does not exceed the maximum quantity approved in accordance with the procedures referred to in subparagraph (b) of this paragraph, which shall in no case exceed the greater of 1 cubic metre or 1/3,000 of the tank capacity in cubic metres;

(d)   the discharge is made below the waterline, taking into account the location of the seawater intakes; and

(e)   the discharge is made at a distance of not less than 12 nautical miles from the nearest land and in a depth of water of not less than 25 metres.

(3)   The discharge into the sea of substances in Category C as defined in Regulation 3(1)(c) of this Annex or of those provisionally assessed as such, or ballast water, tank washings, or other residues or mixtures containing such substances shall be prohibited except when all the following conditions are satisfied:

(a)   the ship is proceeding en route at a speed of at least 7 knots in the case of self-propelled ships or at least 4 knots in the case of ships which are not self-propelled;

(b)   the procedures and arrangements for discharge are approved by the Administration. Such procedures and arrangements shall be based upon standards developed by the Organization and shall ensure that the concentration and rate of discharge of the effluent is such that the concentration of the substance in the wake astern of the ship does not exceed 10 parts per million;

(c)    the maximum quantity of cargo discharged from each tank and its associated piping system does not exceed the maximum quantity approved in accordance with the procedures referred to in sub-paragraph (b) of this paragraph, which shall in no case exceed the greater of 3 cubic metres or 1/1,000 of the tank capacity in cubic metres;

(d)    the discharge is made below the waterline, taking into account the location of the seawater intakes; and

(e)    the discharge is made at a distance of not less than 12 nautical miles from the nearest land and in a depth of water of not less than 25 metres.

(4)    The discharge into the sea of substances in Category D as defined in Regulation 3(1)(d) of this Annex, or of those provisionally assessed as such, or ballast water, tank washings, or other residues or mixtures containing such substances shall be prohibited except when all the following conditions are satisfied:

(a)    the ship is proceeding en route at a speed of at least 7 knots in the case of self-propelled ships or at least 4 knots in the case of ships which are not self-propelled;

(b)    such mixtures are of a concentration not greater than one part of the substance in ten parts of water; and

(c)    the discharge is made at a distance of not less than 12 nautical miles from the nearest land.

(5)    Ventilation procedures approved by the Administration may be used to remove cargo residues from a tank. Such procedures shall be based upon standards developed by the Organization. If subsequent washing of the tank is necessary, the discharge into the sea of the resulting tank washings shall be made in accordance with paragraph (1), (2), (3) or (4) of this Regulation, whichever is applicable.

(6)    The discharge into the sea of substances which have not been categorized, provisionally assessed, or evaluated as referred to in Regulation 4(1) of this Annex, or of ballast water, tank washings, or other residues or mixtures containing such substances shall be prohibited.

### Categories A, B and C Substances within Special Areas

Subject to the provisions of Regulation 6 of this Annex,

(7)    The discharge into the sea of substances in Category A as defined in Regulation 3(1)(a) of this Annex, or of those provisionally assessed as such, or ballast water, tank washings, or other residues or mixtures containing such substances shall be prohibited. If tanks containing such substances or mixtures are to be washed the resulting residues shall be discharged to a reception facility which the States bordering the special area shall provide in accordance with Regulation 7 of this Annex, until the concentration of the substance in the effluent to such facility is at or below the residual concentration prescribed for that substance in column IV of Appendix II to this Annex and until the tank is empty. Provided that the residue then remaining in the tank is subsequently diluted by the addition of a volume of water of not less than 5 per cent of the total volume of the tank, it may be discharged into the sea when all the following conditions are also satisfied:

617

(a)　the ship is proceeding en route at a speed of at least 7 knots in the case of self-propelled ships or at least 4 knots in the case of ships which are not self-propelled;

(b)　the discharge is made below the waterline, taking into account the location of the seawater intakes; and

(c)　the discharge is made at a distance of not less than 12 nautical miles from the nearest land and in a depth of water of not less than 25 metres.

(8)　The discharge into the sea of substances in Category B as defined in Regulation 3(1)(b) of this Annex or of those provisionally assessed as such, or ballast water, tank washings, or other residues or mixtures containing such substances shall be prohibited except when all the following conditions are satisfied:

(a)　the tank has been washed after unloading with a volume of water of not less than 0.5 per cent of the total volume of the tank, and the resulting residues have been discharged to a reception facility until the tank is empty;

(b)　the ship is proceeding en route at a speed of at least 7 knots in the case of self-propelled ships or at least 4 knots in the case of ships which are not self-propelled;

(c)　the procedures and arrangements for discharge and washings are approved by the Administration. Such procedures and arrangements shall be based upon standards developed by the Organization and shall ensure that the concentration and rate of discharge of the effluent is such that the concentration of the substance in the wake astern of the ship does not exceed 1 part per million;

(d)　the discharge is made below the waterline, taking into account the location of the seawater intakes; and

(e)　the discharge is made at a distance of not less than 12 nautical miles from the nearest land and in a depth of water of not less than 25 metres.

(9)　The discharge into the sea of substances in Category C as defined in Regulation 3(1)(c) of this Annex or of those provisionally assessed as such, ·or ballast water, tank washings, or other residues or mixtures containing such substances shall be prohibited except when all the following conditions are satisfied:

(a)　the ship is proceeding en route at a speed of at least 7 knots in the case of self-propelled ships or at least 4 knots in the case of ships which are not self-propelled;

(b)　the procedures and arrangements for discharge are approved by the Administration. Such procedures and arrangements shall be based upon standards developed by the Organization and shall ensure that the concentration and rate of discharge of the effluent is such that the concentration of the substance in the wake astern of the ship does not exceed 1 part per million;

618

(c)    the maximum quantity of cargo discharged from each tank and its associated piping system does not exceed the maximum quantity approved in accordance with the procedures referred to in sub-paragraph (b) of this paragraph which shall in no case exceed the greater of 1 cubic metre or 1/3,000 of the tank capacity in cubic metres;

(d)    the discharge is made below the waterline, taking into account the location of the seawater intakes; and

(e)    the discharge is made at a distance of not less than 12 nautical miles from the nearest land and in a depth of water of not less than 25 metres.

(10) Ventilation procedures approved by the Administration may be used to remove cargo residues from a tank. Such procedures shall be based upon standards developed by the Organization. If subsequent washing of the tank is necessary, the discharge into the sea of the resulting tank washings shall be made in accordance with paragraph (7), (8), or (9) of this Regulation, whichever is applicable.

(11) The discharge into the sea of substances which have not been categorized, provisionally assessed or evaluated as referred to in Regulation 4(1) of this Annex, or of ballast water, tank washings, or other residues or mixtures containing such substances shall be prohibited.

(12) Nothing in this Regulation shall prohibit a ship from retaining on board the residues from a Category B or C cargo and discharging such residues into the sea outside a special area in accordance with paragraph (2) or (3) of this Regulation, respectively.

(13) (a)    The Governments of Parties to the Convention, the coastlines of which border on any given special area, shall collectively agree and establish a date by which time the requirement of Regulation 7(1) of this Annex will be fulfilled and from which the requirements of paragraphs (7), (8), (9) and (10) of this Regulation in respect of that area shall take effect and notify the Organization of the date so established at least six months in advance of that date. The Organization shall then promptly notify all Parties of that date.

(b)    If the date of entry into force of the present Convention is earlier than the date established in accordance with sub-paragraph (a) of this paragraph, the requirements of paragraphs (1), (2) and (3) of this Regulation shall apply during the interim period.

### Regulation 6

*Exceptions*

Regulation 5 of this Annex shall not apply to:

(a)    the discharge into the sea of noxious liquid substances or mixtures containing such substances necessary for the purpose of securing the safety of a ship or saving life at sea; or

619

(b) the discharge into the sea of noxious liquid substances or mixtures containing such substances resulting from damage to a ship or its equipment:

    (i) provided that all reasonable precautions have been taken after the occurrence of the damage or discovery of the discharge for the purpose of preventing or minimizing the discharge; and

    (ii) except if the owner or the Master acted either with intent to cause damage, or recklessly and with knowledge that damage would probably result; or

(c) the discharge into the sea of noxious liquid substances or mixtures containing such substances, approved by the Administration, when being used for the purpose of combating specific pollution incidents in order to minimize the damage from pollution. Any such discharge shall be subject to the approval of any Government in whose jurisdiction it is contemplated the discharge will occur.

## Regulation 7

### Reception Facilities

(1) The Government of each Party to the Convention undertakes to ensure the provision of reception facilities according to the needs of ships using its ports, terminals or repair ports as follows:

(a) cargo loading and unloading ports and terminals shall have facilities adequate for reception without undue delay to ships of such residues and mixtures containing noxious liquid substances as would remain for disposal from ships carrying them as a consequence of the application of this Annex; and

(b) ship repair ports undertaking repairs to chemical tankers shall have facilities adequate for the reception of residues and mixtures containing noxious liquid substances.

(2) The Government of each Party shall determine the types of facilities provided for the purpose of paragraph (1) of this Regulation at each cargo loading and unloading port, terminal and ship repair port in its territories and notify the Organization thereof.

(3) Each Party shall notify the Organization, for transmission to the Parties concerned, of any case where facilities required under paragraph (1) of this Regulation are alleged to be inadequate.

## Regulation 8

### Measures of Control

(1) The Government of each Party to the Convention shall appoint or authorize surveyors for the purpose of implementing this Regulation.

620

## Category A Substances in all Areas

(2) (a) If a tank is partially unloaded or unloaded but not cleaned, an appropriate entry shall be made in the Cargo Record Book.

(b) Until that tank is cleaned every subsequent pumping or transfer operation carried out in connexion with that tank shall also be entered in the Cargo Record Book.

(3) If the tank is to be washed:

(a) the effluent from the tank washing operation shall be discharged from the ship to a reception facility at least until the concentration of the substance in the discharge, as indicated by analyses of samples of the effluent taken by the surveyor, has fallen to the residual concentration specified for that substance in Appendix II to this Annex. When the required residual concentration has been achieved, remaining tank washings shall continue to be discharged to the reception facility until the tank is empty. Appropriate entries of these operations shall be made in the Cargo Record Book and certified by the surveyor; and

(b) after diluting the residue then remaining in the tank with at least 5 per cent of the tank capacity of water, this mixture may be discharged into the sea in accordance with the provisions of sub-paragraphs (1)(a), (b) and (c) or 7(a), (b) and (c), whichever is applicable, of Regulation 5 of this Annex. Appropriate entries of these operations shall be made in the Cargo Record Book.

(4) Where the Government of the receiving Party is satisfied that it is impracticable to measure the concentration of the substance in the effluent without causing undue delay to the ship, that Party may accept an alternative procedure as being equivalent to sub-paragraph (3)(a) provided that:

(a) a precleaning procedure for that tank and that substance, based on standards developed by the Organization, is approved by the Administration and that Party is satisfied that such procedure will fulfil the requirements of paragraph (1) or (7), whichever is applicable, of Regulation 5 of this Annex with respect to the attainment of the prescribed residual concentrations;

(b) a surveyor duly authorized by that Party shall certify in the Cargo Record Book that:

(i) the tank, its pump and piping system have been emptied, and that the quantity of cargo remaining in the tank is at or below the quantity on which the approved precleaning procedure referred to in sub-paragraph (ii) of this paragraph has been based;

(ii) precleaning has been carried out in accordance with the precleaning procedure approved by the Administration for that tank and that substance; and

(iii) the tank washings resulting from such precleaning have been discharged to a reception facility and the tank is empty;

621

(c) the discharge into the sea of any remaining residues shall be in accordance with the provisions of paragraph (3)(b) of this Regulation and an appropriate entry is made in the Cargo Record Book.

## Category B Substances outside Special Areas and Category C Substances in all Areas

(5) Subject to such surveillance and approval by the authorized or appointed surveyor as may be deemed necessary by the Government of the Party, the Master of a ship shall, with respect to a Category B substance outside special areas or a Category C substance in all areas, ensure compliance with the following:

(a) If a tank is partially unloaded or unloaded but not cleaned, an appropriate entry shall be made in the Cargo Record Book.

(b) If the tank is to be cleaned at sea:

  (i) the cargo piping system serving that tank shall be drained and an appropriate entry made in the Cargo Record Book;

  (ii) the quantity of substance remaining in the tank shall not exceed the maximum quantity which may be discharged into the sea for that substance under Regulation 5(2)(c) of this Annex outside special areas in the case of Category B substances, or under Regulations 5(3)(c) and 5(9)(c) outside and within special areas respectively in the case of Category C substances. An appropriate entry shall be made in the Cargo Record Book;

  (iii) where it is intended to discharge the quantity of substance remaining into the sea the approved procedures shall be complied with, and the necessary dilution of the substance satisfactory for such a discharge shall be achieved. An appropriate entry shall be made in the Cargo Record Book; or

  (iv) where the tank washings are not discharged into the sea, if any internal transfer of tank washings takes place from that tank an appropriate entry shall be made in the Cargo Record Book; and

  (v) any subsequent discharge into the sea of such tank washings shall be made in accordance with the requirements of Regulation 5 of this Annex for the appropriate area and Category of substance involved.

(c) If the tank is to be cleaned in port:

  (i) the tank washings shall be discharged to a reception facility and an appropriate entry shall be made in the Cargo Record Book; or

  (ii) the tank washings shall be retained on board the ship and an appropriate entry shall be made in the Cargo Record Book indicating the location and disposition of the tank washings.

(d) If after unloading a Category C substance within a special area, any residues or tank washings are to be retained on board until the ship is outside the special area, the Master shall so indicate by an appropriate entry in the Cargo Record Book and in this case the procedures set out in Regulation 5(3) of this Annex shall be applicable.

## Category B Substances within Special Areas

(6)   Subject to such surveillance and approval by the authorized or appointed surveyor as may be deemed necessary by the Government of the Party, the Master of a ship shall, with respect to a Category B substance within a special area, ensure compliance with the following:

(a)   If a tank is partially unloaded or unloaded but not cleaned, an appropriate entry shall be made in the Cargo Record Book.

(b)   Until that tank is cleaned every subsequent pumping or transfer operation carried out in connexion with that tank shall also be entered in the Cargo Record Book.

(c)   If the tank is to be washed, the effluent from the tank washing operation, which shall contain a volume of water not less than 0.5 per cent of the total volume of the tank, shall be discharged from the ship to a reception facility until the tank, its pump and piping system are empty. An appropriate entry shall be made in the Cargo Record Book.

(d)   If the tank is to be further cleaned and emptied at sea, the Master shall:

  (i)   ensure that the approved procedures referred to in Regulation 5(8)(c) of this Annex are complied with and that the appropriate entries are made in the Cargo Record Book; and

  (ii)   ensure that any discharge into the sea is made in accordance with the requirements of Regulation 5(8) of this Annex and an appropriate entry is made in the Cargo Record Book.

(e)   If after unloading a Category B substance within a special area, any residues or tank washings are to be retained on board until the ship is outside the special area, the Master shall so indicate by an appropriate entry in the Cargo Record Book and in this case the procedures set out in Regulation 5(2) of this Annex shall be applicable.

## Category D Substances in all Areas

(7)   The Master of a ship shall, with respect to a Category D substance, ensure compliance with the following:

(a)   If a tank is partially unloaded or unloaded but not cleaned, an appropriate entry shall be made in the Cargo Record Book.

(b)   If the tank is to be cleaned at sea:

  (i)   the cargo piping system serving that tank shall be drained and an appropriate entry made in the Cargo Record Book;

  (ii)   where it is intended to discharge the quantity of substance remaining into the sea, the necessary dilution of the substance satisfactory for such a discharge shall be achieved. An appropriate entry shall be made in the Cargo Record Book; or

  (iii)   where the tank washings are not discharged into the sea, if any internal transfer of tank washings takes place from that tank an appropriate entry shall be made in the Cargo Record Book; and

623

     (iv)   any subsequent discharge into the sea of such tank washings shall be made in accordance with the requirements of Regulation 5(4) of this Annex.

(c)   If the tank is to be cleaned in port:

     (i)   the tank washings shall be discharged to a reception facility and an appropriate entry shall be made in the Cargo Record Book; or

     (ii)   the tank washings shall be retained on board the ship and an appropriate entry shall be made in the Cargo Record Book indicating the location and disposition of the tank washings.

### Discharge from a Slop Tank

(8)   Any residues retained on board in a slop tank, including those from pump room bilges, which contain a Category A substance, or within a special area either a Category A or a Category B substance, shall be discharged to a reception facility in accordance with the provisions of Regulation 5(1), (7) or (8) of this Annex, whichever is applicable. An appropriate entry shall be made in the Cargo Record Book.

(9)   Any residues retained on board in a slop tank, including those from pump room bilges, which contain a quantity of a Category B substance outside a special area or a Category C substance in all areas in excess of the aggregate of the maximum quantities specified in Regulation 5(2)(c), (3)(c), or (9)(c) of this Annex, whichever is applicable, shall be discharged to a reception facility. An appropriate entry shall be made in the Cargo Record Book.

**Regulation 9**

*Cargo Record Book*

(1)   Every ship to which this Annex applies shall be provided with a Cargo Record Book, whether as part of the ship's official log book or otherwise, in the form specified in Appendix IV to this Annex.

(2)   The Cargo Record Book shall be completed, on a tank-to-tank basis, whenever any of the following operations with respect to a noxious liquid substance take place in the ship:

     (i)   loading of cargo;

     (ii)   unloading of cargo;

     (iii)   transfer of cargo;

     (iv)   transfer of cargo, cargo residues or mixtures containing cargo to a slop tank;

     (v)   cleaning of cargo tanks;

     (vi)   transfer from slop tanks;

     (vii)   ballasting of cargo tanks;

     (viii)   transfer of dirty ballast water;

     (ix)   discharge into the sea in accordance with Regulation 5 of this Annex.

(3)   In the event of any discharge of the kind referred to in Article 7 of the present Convention and Regulation 6 of this Annex of any noxious liquid substance or mixture containing such substance, whether intentional or accidental, an entry shall be made in the Cargo Record Book stating the circumstances of, and the reason for, the discharge.

(4)   When a surveyor appointed or authorized by the Government of the Party to the Convention to supervise any operations under this Annex has inspected a ship, then that surveyor shall make an appropriate entry in the Cargo Record Book.

(5)   Each operation referred to in paragraphs (2) and (3) of this Regulation shall be fully recorded without delay in the Cargo Record Book so that all the entries in the Book appropriate to that operation are completed. Each entry shall be signed by the officer or officers in charge of the operation concerned and, when the ship is manned, each page shall be signed by the Master of the ship. The entries in the Cargo Record Book shall be in an official language of the State whose flag the ship is entitled to fly, and, for ships holding an International Pollution Prevention Certificate for the Carriage of Noxious Liquid Substances in Bulk (1973), in English or French. The entries in an official national language of the State whose flag the ship is entitled to fly shall prevail in case of a dispute or discrepancy.

(6)   The Cargo Record Book shall be kept in such a place as to be readily available for inspection and, except in the case of unmanned ships under tow, shall be kept on board the ship. It shall be retained for a period of two years after the last entry has been made.

(7)   The competent authority of the Government of a Party may inspect the Cargo Record Book on board any ship to which this Annex applies while the ship is in its port, and may make a copy of any entry in that book and may require the Master of the ship to certify that the copy is a true copy of such entry. Any copy so made which has been certified by the Master of the ship as a true copy of an entry in the ship's Cargo Record Book shall be made admissible in any judicial proceedings as evidence of the facts stated in the entry. The inspection of a Cargo Record Book and the taking of a certified copy by the competent authority under this paragraph shall be performed as expeditiously as possible without causing the ship to be unduly delayed.

## Regulation 10

### Surveys

(1)   Ships which are subject to the provisions of this Annex and which carry noxious liquid substances in bulk shall be surveyed as follows:

   (a)   An initial survey before a ship is put into service or before the certificate required by Regulation 11 of this Annex is issued for the first time, which shall include a complete inspection of its structure, equipment, fittings, arrangements and material in so far as the ship is covered by this Annex. The survey shall be such as to ensure full compliance with the applicable requirements of this Annex.

625

(b) Periodical surveys at intervals specified by the Administration which shall not exceed five years and which shall be such as to ensure that the structure, equipment, fittings, arrangements and material fully comply with the applicable requirements of this Annex. However, where the duration of the International Pollution Prevention Certificate for the Carriage of Noxious Liquid Substances in Bulk (1973) is extended as specified in Regulation 12(2) or (4) of this Annex, the interval of the periodical survey may be extended correspondingly.

(c) Intermediate surveys at intervals specified by the Administration which shall not exceed thirty months and which shall be such as to ensure that the equipment and associated pumps and piping systems, fully comply with the applicable requirements of this Annex and are in good working order. The survey shall be endorsed on the International Pollution Prevention Certificate for the Carriage of Noxious Liquid Substances in Bulk (1973) issued under Regulation 11 of this Annex.

(2) Surveys of a ship with respect to the enforcement of the provisions of this Annex shall be carried out by officers of the Administration. The Administration may, however, entrust the surveys either to surveyors nominated for the purpose or to organizations recognized by it. In every case the Administration concerned shall fully guarantee the completeness and efficiency of the surveys.

(3) After any survey of a ship under this Regulation has been completed, no significant change shall be made in the structure, equipment, fittings, arrangements or material, covered by the survey without the sanction of the Administration, except the direct replacement of such equipment and fittings for the purpose of repair or maintenance.

## Regulation 11

### Issue of Certificate

(1) An International Pollution Prevention Certificate for the Carriage of Noxious Liquid Substances in Bulk (1973) shall be issued to any ship carrying noxious liquid substances which is engaged in voyages to ports or off-shore terminals under the jurisdiction of other Parties to the Convention after survey of such ship in accordance with the provisions of Regulation 10 of this Annex.

(2) Such Certificate shall be issued either by the Administration or by a person or organization duly authorized by it. In every case the Administration shall assume full responsibility for the Certificate.

(3) (a) The Government of a Party may, at the request of the Administration, cause a ship to be surveyed and if satisfied that the provisions of this Annex are complied with shall issue or authorize the issue of a Certificate to the ship in accordance with this Annex.

(b) A copy of the Certificate and a copy of the survey report shall be transmitted as soon as possible to the requesting Administration.

(c) A Certificate so issued shall contain a statement to the effect that it has been issued at the request of the Administration and shall have the same force and receive the same recognition as a certificate issued under paragraph (1) of this Regulation.

626

(d)     No International Pollution Prevention Certificate for the Carriage of Noxious Liquid Substances in Bulk (1973) shall be issued to any ship which is entitled to fly the flag of a State which is not a Party.

(4)     The Certificate shall be drawn up in an official language of the issuing country in a form corresponding to the model given in Appendix V to this Annex. If the language used is neither English nor French, the text shall include a translation into one of these languages.

### Regulation 12

*Duration of Certificate*

(1)     An International Pollution Prevention Certificate for the Carriage of Noxious Liquid Substances in Bulk (1973) shall be issued for a period specified by the Administration, which shall not exceed five years from the date of issue, except as provided in paragraphs (2) and (4) of this Regulation.

(2)     If a ship at the time when the Certificate expires is not in a port or off-shore terminal under the jurisdiction of the Party to the Convention whose flag the ship is entitled to fly, the Certificate may be extended by the Administration, but such extension shall be granted only for the purpose of allowing the ship to complete its voyage to the State whose flag the ship is entitled to fly or in which it is to be surveyed and then only in cases where it appears proper and reasonable to do so.

(3)     No Certificate shall be thus extended for a period longer than five months and a ship to which such extension is granted shall not on its arrival in the State whose flag it is entitled to fly or the port in which it is to be surveyed, be entitled by virtue of such extension to leave that port or State without having obtained a new Certificate.

(4)     A Certificate which has not been extended under the provisions of paragraph (2) of this Regulation may be extended by the Administration for a period of grace of up to one month from the date of expiry stated on it.

(5)     A Certificate shall cease to be valid if significant alterations have taken place in the structure, equipment, fittings, arrangements and material required by this Annex without the sanction of the Administration, except the direct replacement of such equipment or fitting for the purpose of repair or maintenance or if intermediate surveys as specified by the Administration under Regulation 10(1)(c) of this Annex are not carried out.

(6)     A Certificate issued to a ship shall cease to be valid upon transfer of such a ship to the flag of another State, except as provided in paragraph (7) of this Regulation.

(7)     Upon transfer of a ship to the flag of another Party, the Certificate shall remain in force for a period not exceeding five months provided that it would not have expired before the end of that period, or until the Administration issues a replacement Certificate, whichever is earlier. As soon as possible after the transfer has taken place the Government of the Party whose flag the ship was formerly entitled to fly shall transmit to the Administration a copy of the Certificate carried by the ship before the transfer and, if available, a copy of the relevant survey report.

## Regulation 13

*Requirements for Minimizing accidental Pollution*

(1)    The design, construction, equipment and operation of ships carrying noxious liquid substances in bulk which are subject to the provisions of this Annex shall be such as to minimize the uncontrolled discharge into the sea of such substances.

(2)    Pursuant to the provisions of paragraph (1) of this Regulation, the Government of each Party shall issue, or cause to be issued, detailed requirements on the design, construction, equipment and operation of such ships.

(3)    In respect of chemical tankers, the requirements referred to in paragraph (2) of this Regulation shall contain at least all the provisions given in the Code for the Construction and Equipment of Ships carrying Dangerous Chemicals in Bulk adopted by the Assembly of the Organization in Resolution A.212(VII) and as may be amended by the Organization, provided that the amendments to that Code are adopted and brought into force in accordance with the provisions of Article 16 of the present Convention for amendment procedures to an Appendix to an Annex.

# SELECTED LIST OF UNITED NATIONS DOCUMENTS RELATING TO OCEAN DEVELOPMENT

## I. RELEVANT VOLUMES OF THE UNITED NATIONS LEGISLATIVE SERIES

| | |
|---|---|
| ST/LEG/SER.B/16 | National Legislation and Treaties relating to the Law of the Sea (Sales No. E/F/74.V.2) |
| ST/LEG/SER.B/18 & Add. 1 | National Legislation and Treaties relating to the Law of the Sea (Preliminary issue) |

## II. REPORTS OF THE UNITED NATIONS SEA-BED COMMITTEE

| | |
|---|---|
| A/8721 | Report of the Committee on the Peaceful Uses of the Sea-bed and the Ocean Floor beyond the Limits of National Jurisdiction (1972) (GAOR, 27th Session, Supplement No. 21) |
| A/9021 | Report of the Committee on the Peaceful Uses of the Sea-bed and the Ocean Floor beyond the Limits of National Jurisdiction (1973), Vol. I—Vol. VI (GAOR, 28th Session, Supplement, No. 21) |

## III. DOCUMENTS SUBMITTED TO THE UNITED NATIONS SEA-BED COMMITTEE

| | |
|---|---|
| A/AC.138/73 | Additional notes on the possible economic implications of mineral production from the international sea-bed area—Report of the Secretary-General (12 May 1972) |
| A/AC.138/87 | Economic significance, in terms of sea-bed mineral resources, of the various limits proposed for national jurisdiction—Report of the Secretary-General (4 June 1973) |
| A/AC.138/88 | Examples of precedents of provisional application, pending their entry into force, of multilateral treaties, especially treaties which have established international organizations and/or regimes—Report of the Secretary-General (12 June 1973) |
| A/AC.138/90 | Sea-bed mineral resources: recent developments—Progress report by the Secretary-General (3 July 1973) |
| A/AC.138/94/Add.1 | Texts illustrating areas of agreement and disagreement on items 1 and 2 of the (First) Sub-Committee's programme of work (A/9021, Vol. II, pp. 39-165) |

A/AC.138/L.10    Comparative table of draft treaties, working papers and draft articles (28 January 1972)

A/AC.138/SC.III/L.30    Work of the Inter-Governmental Maritime Consultative Organization in relation to the preservation of the marine environment (1972/73), submitted by the Secretariat of IMCO

## IV. DOCUMENTS SUBMITTED TO THE THIRD UNITED NATIONS CONFERENCE ON THE LAW OF THE SEA

A/CONF.62/25    Economic implications of sea-bed mineral development in the international area: report of the Secretary-General (22 May 1974)

A/CONF.62/26    Reports submitted by the United Nations Conference on Trade and Development (6 June 1974)

A/CONF.62/27    The activities of the Inter-Governmental Maritime Consultative Organization in relation to shipping and related matters (13 June 1974)

A/CONF.62/C.1/L.5    United States: working paper on the economic effects of deep sea-bed exploitation (8 August 1974)

A/CONF.62/C.1/L.11    Chile: working paper on the economic implications for the developing countries of the exploration of the sea-bed beyond the limits of jurisdiction (26 August 1974)

A/CONF.62/C.2/L.1    United States: Comparative table of proposals related directly to living resources (21 February 1974)

A/CONF.62/C.3/L.3    Problems of acquisition and transfer of marine technology, prepared by the Secretariat of the Third United Nations Conference on the Law of the Sea (25 July 1974)

## V. OTHER DOCUMENTS RELEVANT TO OCEAN DEVELOPMENT

E/5120    Use of the Sea—study prepared by the Secretary-General (28 April 1972)

TD/113/Supp. 4    Mineral production from the area of the sea-bed beyond national jurisdiction: issues of international commodity policy

TD/B/449    Exploitation of the mineral resources of the sea-bed beyond national jurisdiction: issues of international commodity policy. Note by the UNCTAD Secretariat

| | |
|---|---|
| TD/B/449/Add. 1 | Exploitation of the mineral resources of the sea-bed beyond national jurisdiction: case study of cobalt |
| TD/B/483 | The effects of production of manganese from the sea-bed, with particular reference to effects on developing countries producers of manganese ore |
| TD/B/484 | The effects of possible exploitation of the sea-bed on the earnings of developing countries from copper exports: Report of the UNCTAD Secretariat |

# INDEX OF STATE PARTIES TO TREATIES

**Eastern Europe**

| | | | |
|---|---|---|---|
| Bulgaria | 492, 514, 528 | U.S.S.R. | 127, 130, 134, 137, |
| German Demo- | 531 | | 441, 454, 457, 464, |
| cratic Rep. | | | 487, 491, 492, 502, |
| Poland | 128, 131, 492, 502, | | 510, 514, 528, 531, |
| | 510, 514, 531, 570 | | 549, 570, 577 |
| Romania | 492, 528 | | |

# INDEX OF PROPOSALS AT THE UNITED NATIONS SEABED COMMITTEE

635

| L.56 | Australia, Canada, Colombia, Fiji, Ghana, Iceland, Iran, Jamaica, Kenya, Mexico, New Zealand, Philippines, Tanzania | basic zonal approach | 415 |

**Asia** — *document*

| | |
|---|---|
| Afghanistan | 55, 93, II/L.39 |
| China | II/L.34, II/L.45, III/L.42, III/L.55 |
| Cyprus | II/L.18, II/L.19 |
| Fiji | II/L.15, II/L.42, II/L.48, III/L.56 |
| India | **II/L.38** |
| Indonesia | II/L.15, II/L.18, II/L.48 |
| Iran | II/L.62, III/L.55, III/L.56 |
| Japan | 63, II/L.12, II/L.56, III/L.49 |
| Malaysia | II/L.18 |
| Nepal | 55, 93, II/L.39 |
| Pakistan | II/L.52, III/L.55 |
| Philippines | II/L.15, II/L.18, II/L.46, II/L.47/Rev.1, II/L.48, II/L.55, III/L.56 |
| Singapore | 55, II/L.39 |
| Sri Lanka | II/L.38 |
| Turkey | I/L.21, II/L.16/Rev.1, II/L.22/Rev.1, II/L.31, II/L.32, II/L.33, II/L.43 |
| Yemen | II/L.18 |

**Africa**

| | |
|---|---|
| Algeria | II/L.40, III/L.55 |
| Cameroon | II/L.40, II/L.43 |
| Egypt | III/L.55 |
| Ethiopia | III/L.55 |
| Ghana | II/L.40, III/L.56 |
| Ivory Coast | II/L.40 |
| Kenya | II/L.10, II/L.38, II/L.40, II/L.43, III/L.41, III/L.55, III/L.56 |
| Liberia | II/L.40 |
| Madagascar | II/L.40, II/L.43 |
| Mali | 93 |
| Mauritius | II/L.15, II/L.40, II/L.48 |
| Morocco | II/L.18 |
| Senegal | II/L.40 |
| Sierra Leone | II/L.40 |
| Somalia | II/L.40, III/L.55 |
| Sudan | II/L.40 |
| Tanzania | 33, II/L.40, III/L.56 |
| Tunisia | II/L.31, II/L.32, II/L.33, II/L.40, II/L.43, III/L.55 |
| Uganda | II/L.41 |

| | |
|---|---|
| Zaire | II/L.60 |
| Zambia | 93, II/L.41 |

**Latin America**

| | |
|---|---|
| Argentina | II/L.37 |
| Bolivia | 92, 93, II/L.39 |
| Brazil | II/L.25, III/L.45, III/L.55 |
| Chile | 49 |
| Colombia | 49, II/L.21, III/L.56 |
| Ecuador | 49, II/L.27, II/L.54, III/L.45, III/L.47 |
| El Salvador | **49, III/L.45, III/L.47** |
| Guatemala | 49 |
| Guyana | 49 |
| Jamaica | 49, II/L.55, II/L.56 |
| Mexico | 49, II/L.21, III/L.56 |
| Panama | 49, II/L.27, II/L.54 |
| Peru | 49, II/L.27, II/L.54, III/L.45, III/L.47, III/L.55 |
| Trinidad and Tobago | 49, III/L.54, III/L.55 |
| Uruguay | 49, II/L.24, III/L.45, III/L.47 |
| Venezuela | 49, II/L.21 |

**Western Europe and others**

| | |
|---|---|
| Australia | II/L.11, II/L.36, III/L.27, III/L.56 |
| Austria | 55, II/L.39 |
| Belgium | 55, 91, II/L.39 |
| Canada | 59, II/L.38, III/L.18, IV/L.18, III/L.28, III/L.56 |
| France | 27, III/L.46 |
| Greece | I/L.16, I/L.25, II/L.17, II/L.18, II/L.29 |
| Iceland | II/L.23, III/L.56 |
| Italy | I/L.24, I/L.26, I/L.30, III/L.50 |
| Malta | 53, II/L.28, III/L.33, III/L.34 |
| Netherlands | 55, II/L.59, III/L.48 |
| New Zealand | II/L.11, III/L.56 |
| Norway | II/L.36, III/L.43 |
| Spain | II/L.18 |
| U.K. | 26, 46, II/L.44 |
| U.S. | 25, II/L.4, II/L.9, II/L.35, III/L.40, III/L.44 |

**Eastern Europe**

| | |
|---|---|
| Bulgaria | II/L.51, III/L.31 |
| Czechoslovakia | 93 |
| Hungary | 55, 93 |
| Poland | 44, II/L.49, III/L.31 |
| Romania | II/L.53, III/L.55 |
| Ukrainian SSR | III/L.31 |
| U.S.S.R. | 43, I/L.28, II/L.6, II/L.7, II/L.7/Add.1, II/L.26, III/L.31, III/L.32 |
| Yugoslavia | II/L.63, III/L.55 |